Information Sources of
Political Science,
Fifth Edition

Information Sources of Political Science, Fifth Edition

Stephen W. Green and
Douglas J. Ernest, Editors

A B C  C L I O

Santa Barbara, California   Denver, Colorado   Oxford, England

Library of Congress Cataloging-in-Publication Data
Information sources of political science / Stephen W. Green and Douglas J. Ernest, editors.— 5th ed.
    p.   cm.
  Rev. ed. of: Information sources of political science / Frederick L. Holler. 4th ed. c1986.
  Also available online.
  Includes bibliographical references and indexes.
  ISBN 1-57607-104-9 (hardback : alk. paper) — ISBN 1-57607-557-5 (ebook)   1. Political
science—Bibliography.   I. Green, Stephen W. II. Ernest, Douglas, 1947–   III. Holler, Frederick L.
Information sources of political science.

  Z7161.I543 2005
  [JA71]
  016.32—dc22

                                                                              2005014121

07 06 05   10 9 8 7 6 5 4 3 2 1

This book is also available on the World Wide Web as an e-book. Visit
http://www.abc-clio.com for details.

ABC-CLIO, Inc.
130 Cremona Drive, P.O. Box 1911
Santa Barbara, California 93116–1911

This book is printed on acid-free paper ∞ .
Manufactured in the United States of America

This book is dedicated to my mother and father.
Stephen W. Green
This book is dedicated to my mother, Ruth Ernest.
Douglas J. Ernest

Contents

Contents

Contents

6 International Relations and International Organization Reference Sources, 253

8 Public Administration and Policy Studies Reference Sources, 405

9 Biographical Reference Sources for Political Figures, 509

Preface

This fifth edition comes out almost twenty years after the publication of the fourth edition, written by Frederick L. Holler. The world has changed dramatically over the last two decades on a number of levels, especially the international political landscape and the technology that is a driving force behind so many of the new services and initiatives put forth by academic, public, and special libraries in this postmillennial era.

On the political side of the ledger, the bipolar world has ended with the relatively sudden collapse of the Berlin Wall and the opening of borders in Eastern European countries and much of the former Soviet Union itself. China is quickly becoming an economic giant, while Japan's economic miracle has stagnated for years. The AIDS epidemic is devastating the lives of many African peoples, while tribal conflicts largely traced to the drawing of the continent's political boundaries by the former colonial powers operating in Africa continue unabated. A number of the European countries are currently subject to strong demographic currents that are impairing their ability to maintain a relatively high caliber of social services to their respective citizens. With unemployment quite high and social unrest in the eastern sector on the rise, Germany has had a difficult time in digesting what had been East Germany into its vision for a united Germany. Some things have a more timeless ring, such as the seemingly intractable battles and conflicts that rage in the Middle East among the Israelis, the Palestinians, and many in the Arab world. In the United States itself, the major event over the past twenty years was undoubtedly the hijacked jetliners that killed thousands of people when they plowed into the twin towers of the World Trade Center in New York City, the Pentagon, and a field in rural Pennsylvania. This event has had a tremendous effect on how the United States and its leaders see the world today and in the decision to undertake a military incursion into Iraq using primarily U.S. troops. Tony Blair's Labour government in the United Kingdom has been America's most vocal international proponent in this effort and has committed the second-largest number of ground troops to the Iraqi conflict. Other issues are bigger than any one nation on earth, and these include global warming and its effects on the polar ice floes and the issue of the overall quality of the air we all breathe.

While changes in libraries cannot match the dramatic events that have unfolded over the last two decades in the world at large, libraries are certainly not the same institutions they were in the early to mid-1980s. Digital technology and telecommunications are by far the leading change agents today and probably will continue to be so for years to come. While some technologies, such as CD-ROMs and computer networking, were fairly short-lived blips on the radar screen, the Internet appears to have a longer future. Electronic books are on the verge of breaking through the popularity threshold, and electronic journals are proving themselves highly successful with certain segments of academe and the population in general. Chat rooms and e-mail continue to be major functions of personal-computer use in a number of public and academic libraries. Journal articles in electronic format have taken off with the rise of the so-called aggregator databases that allow full-text access to many of these journals formerly available only in print. The "Open Source" software movement continues to advance with more and more proponents. Libraries have taken on some attributes of the microcomputer lab, with full Internet access, Microsoft, and other productivity software such as word processing and spread-sheet applications, PowerPoint presentation software, scanning software and image management, and more.

The fifth edition of *Information Sources of Political Science* shares many similarities with the previous edition but also has incorporated some fundamental changes into its scope and characteristic elements. Generally, print reference works or electronic resources covering either the field of law or government publications are no longer included. From the beginning of this effort, the authors felt that there were already sufficient and high-quality published guides to the legal literature and to government documents. The decision was made to refrain from competing with or simply reiterating what appears elsewhere. The discerning reader will indeed come across a couple of legal or government documents references as representative samples only. Foreign-language materials have also been omitted from consideration unless those works include an English translation as part of the work. (Some Chinese materials are examples of this category.) The work continues to include materials published in the English language from all over the world. Since the bulk of English-language materials have been and continue to be published in the United States and the United Kingdom, some relatively older materials that might not normally have been included were indeed kept if they were published in a developing country.

The work itself is divided into nine separate chapters, a format fairly similar to the previous edition. The major chapters are the ones on U.S. politics and government, international relations and international organization, comparative politics and government, and the general social science sources. Most chapters are arranged by reference format, such as dictionary, bibliography, and encyclopedia, and then alphabetically by title. The previous edition was a rigorous analysis of political science from an information science and documentation perspective. Its intent, in general, was to formulate a new political science reference theory in a most scholarly manner. The fifth edition lacks Frederick L. Holler's intellectual commitment to redefining the discipline from the sheer taxonomy of its reference materials. This new edition, while still highly critical and often comparative in the annotations, is a more straightforward production that is designed to help students and others at point of use while doing their research in political science. Naturally, electronic resources are interwoven through this edition in a way inconceivable during the era of the fourth edition.

The scope of this work is similar to the previous edition. It is intended to be as broad as possible at the expense of depth of coverage. The goal was to uncover reference and information resources helpful to the widest possible number of political science researchers at levels ranging from the beginning student to the more serious researcher. The resources listed in the fifth edition are those that are typically found in larger public libraries and medium-to-

large academic libraries. No attempt has been made to find that one unique source that may reside on the shelves at some great research library or the Library of Congress. The sheer number of published print and electronic resources prohibits a truly comprehensive compilation. Many of the titles or electronic resources so listed may not be available at a student's home public or academic library. Needless to say, the larger libraries will tend to have a higher percentage of the items listed throughout this resource guide. Failure to include a source should not be regarded necessarily as a statement about its overall quality or value to the discipline. The fact is the authors probably just missed some, perhaps one of your very favorites.

Over the last twenty years since publication of the fourth edition, some reference works have seen two or more editions published. Only the most recent edition is listed. Major shifts in the scope or content of a reference item will be noted when this occurs. Over 98 percent of the print and electronic resources listed in this edition have received full annotations that are often critical and comparative in nature. Works are often compared to other similar titles, and their relative strengths and weaknesses are noted along with a description of the structure, organization, content, and reading level of the work. A few titles were included without annotations because they were not available for inspection by the authors for one reason or another. They may have been lost items, shelved improperly, in use, or not purchased by the ten or so libraries visited for the purposes of writing this book. The libraries used most heavily by the two authors include those at the University of Illinois at Urbana–Champaign, the University of Colorado at Boulder, Colorado State University, the University of North Carolina at Chapel Hill, the University of North Carolina at Charlotte, Duke University, and the Auraria Library in Denver.

The inclusion dates for materials range from the mid-1980s, the date of the fourth edition's publication, up to 2003. A few scattered 2004 imprints have been included if they more or less fell into our laps. Generally, items already listed in the fourth edition have not been listed again in the fifth edition, especially the political science materials. Researchers requiring the full set of political science reference materials must use the fifth edition along with the previous edition.

The Internet sites listed may be available either from your home, your local public library, or perhaps the nearest large university library that welcomes people who are not affiliated with that institution as student, faculty, or staff member. Some Web sites are free, while others are accessible only through payment of a licensing fee, which is often considerable or not available directly to individuals. Other Web sites require a researcher to register as an individual but no fee is required. URLs are given for some Web sites but not others for a number of reasons too complicated to explain in this modest introduction. Needless to say, URLs are notorious for changing and changing frequently, so if

the URL given does not access the Web site being sought, try going to one of the search engines, such as Google or Yahoo, and key in the name of the Web site being sought. Internet site listings, while ample, are highly selective given the sheer number of those out there in cyberspace. The decision was made to select stable Internet sites that have stood the test of time for at least a couple of years.

Every item listed in this fifth edition was checked in various standard sources, such as Worldcat, to determine if any print items were also available as Internet resources, CD-ROMs, or e-books. This has been noted in each instance so students and researchers will have the option of using the print or electronic version depending on the resources available in the library that person is using. Larger libraries will have more in the way of print and electronic resources. Most of these resources should be available to anyone walking through the doors of the institution. Those institutions will not, however, generally provide you with off-site access to their reference works, again because of licensing restrictions. To date, the print and electronic versions tend to be quite similar if not exactly the same.

In addition to all the electronic materials appearing in the fifth edition, the section on the policy sciences was increased to include a number of major public policy issues that are essential to modern political scientists' and students' studies. These include such topics as AIDS, health care, environmental matters, immigration, economic development, and many more. The policy sciences and public administration are two of the faster growing components of political science.

A chapter that consolidates most of the biographical reference works has also been added as a new feature. Formerly, these works had been scattered throughout the work.

Using this guide to print and online reference sources is relatively simple, and it was designed to be useful to all levels of students, faculty, and researchers in the study of politics, government institutions, public administration, international organization, and the policy sciences. Most people using this book will be looking for a reference source that will provide them with the information they are seeking. If someone is doing work in U.S. politics, that person should turn immediately to that chapter and look through the items arranged by format and then by title. If one requires a list of periodical articles on a particular topic, then he or she should go to the appropriate chapter and then to the section on "abstracts and indexing services." If that fails, then try the general chapter on political science. Those individuals needing definitions of terms or background information should be directed at once to the sections on "dictionaries" and/or "encyclopedias" within the appropriate chapter for the subject area being researched. Those approaching this work with a topic may want to consult the indexes that have been made available at the back of this book, especially the general index, to determine whether or not any works or electronic resources have been published in that specific area of interest. One may also consult the title in the index to determine where a particular work may have been placed in the overall scheme of the book in order to find similar or related works. In any case, the authors strongly advise the user to browse through the area or areas of interest to get a better understanding of what is available and where it may be located within the organizational scheme of this book. Cross-references have been built into many of the relevant entries for purposes of comparative analysis, contrast, or publication history. If there is no cross-reference available, then try the indexes.

The authors would also like to point out that this edition could be envisioned as a momentary snapshot in the great migration from a print-based society to one that is tied more decisively to digital resources in old and new formats. There is a strong element of fin de siècle in this effort to serve as a bridge between the print and digital worlds. In the not-too-distant future, this fifth edition may provide the added value of demonstrating to the next generation the way research was conducted and the types of resources that were available during this transitional era.

—*Stephen W. Green*
Research/Special Projects Librarian
Atkins Library
University of North Carolina at Charlotte
Charlotte, NC

—*Douglas J. Ernest*
Government Publications Specialist
Morgan Library
Colorado State University
Fort Collins, CO

Acknowledgments

I would like to acknowledge the assistance rendered by Mady G. Kassanoff in helping with several aspects of the work that went into completing this book. Her patience over the last six years is also duly noted. The staff members of all the libraries I listed in the preface were quite helpful to me, and I sincerely appreciate their assistance.

—*Stephen W. Green*

I wish to acknowledge assistance rendered by the following individuals: Mady G. Kassanoff, for assistance during a visit to the University of Denver; Sarah Robida, for a yeoman effort in tracking bibliographic errors; and my supervisor, Allison Cowgill, for finding student work-study labor when it was very much needed.

—*Douglas J. Ernest*

1

General Reference Sources

The literature of reference books is so voluminous that no attempt has been made here to reproduce a comprehensive listing of individual items. Rather, the reader will find annotations for standard sources that compile annotations and information relating to reference works. Some are overarching in nature, while others concentrate upon either subject encyclopedias, bibliographic resources, countries other than the United States, or disciplines in the humanities. Reference works pertaining to the social science disciplines appear in the next chapter. Finally, this section includes a brief grouping of dictionaries that apply to numerous disciplines, including both those in the social sciences and those extraneous to that realm.

Literature Guides

1-1. Wynar, Bohdan S., ed. *American Reference Books Annual.* Annual. Englewood, CO: Libraries Unlimited, 1970–. 732 pp. Indexes. ISSN: 0065-9959.

A standard for over thirty years, this publication reviews reference books appearing in the English language in the United States and Canada during the course of a single year. In addition to newly published items, this source also includes new editions and periodically reviews ongoing publications such as almanacs and indexing and abstracting services. The 1990 volume, for example, included reviews of over 1,500 items. Each annual issue is arranged into several broad categories corresponding to general reference works, the social sciences, science and technology, and the humanities. Within each of these major categories, one finds additional subdivisions, including a section for political science. Compact disc products are reviewed as well as books. Reviews are signed by the contributors, many from the library field. Annotations are both descriptive and critical, and are usually a couple of paragraphs long. There are indexes by author/title and by subject. This work is the most thorough listing of English-language reference sources that appears on a continuing basis.

1-2. Bell, Barbara L. *Annotated Guide to Current National Bibliographies.* (UBCIM Publications, New Series Vol. 18.) 2nd rev. ed. Munchen: K. G. Saur, 1998. 487 pp. ISBN: 3-598-11376-5.

Ideally, a national bibliography comprehensively compiles and updates a listing of publications that appear in a particular nation. This guide provides an annotated listing, arranged by country, of such national bibliographies. Among the pieces of information included are title, compiler, contents, arrangement, and availability. The back of the volume also contains a section on regional bibliographies as well as a bibliography on the subject of national bibliographies themselves. Although aimed at a library audience, this book will be helpful to scholars attempting to identify major bibliographic resources in individual nations of the world.

1-3. Awe, Susan C., ed. *ARBA Guide to Subject Encyclopedias and Dictionaries.* 2nd ed. Englewood, CO: Libraries Unlimited, 1997. 482 pp. Indexes. ISBN: 1-563-08467-8.

The subject dictionaries and encyclopedias included in this volume were selected from *American Reference Books Annual* [entry 1-1] over the ten years prior to 1997. Certain other works of lasting value that predate 1986 were also included. Reviews were rewritten as necessary to update them. Altogether, there are 1,061 entries, all in the format familiar to users of *American Reference Books Annual.* Each item is accorded complete bibliographic information as

well as a detailed annotation that is evaluative as well as descriptive in nature. The arrangement of entries is by subject area, with "Social Sciences," "Humanities," and "Science and Technology" making up the three major portions of the volume. Each is further subdivided by discipline. There are indexes by author/title and by subject. This relatively recent source can be consulted by both librarians and library users who wish to identify some of the core sources represented in larger reference collections and encompassing nearly the full range of subject areas.

1-4. Ryan, Joe, ed. *First Stop: The Master Index to Subject Encyclopedias.* Phoenix: Oryx Press, 1989. 1582 pp. ISBN: 0-897-74397-0.

Joe Ryan, then a reference librarian at the University of Vermont, compiled this unique reference work. The heart of the volume is a keyword index to almost 40,000 topics that are contained in 430 English-language subject encyclopedias, handbooks, dictionaries, comprehensive textbooks, and similar reference sources. These sources were in print in 1989 and included articles that were analytical in nature, at least 250 words in length, and included a bibliography. The keyword index is alphabetical. Examples of keywords include "Federal," "Hospitality," "History," "Systems," and "Thought." As one can ascertain from this list, the subject approach of the keywords is quite broad in nature, although biographical sources, plot summaries, and arts criticism represent areas not included. Each keyword includes a listing of sources containing information; each of these listings includes the title of the article, abbreviations for the source, and appropriate page references. The introductory matter includes a list of all sources by their abbreviations (with bibliographic information) and a "Broad Subject Index" that provides the reader with a listing of subject-oriented reference works by topics such as "Education," "History," and "Religion." This compilation, an amazingly detailed work, is unfortunately many years old but may still be useful to reference librarians seeking brief information on out-of-the-way topics.

1-5. American Library Association. Government Documents Round Table. *Guide to Official Publications of Foreign Countries.* 2nd ed. Bethesda, MD: CIS, 1997. 494 pp. Index.

This second edition updates the first, published in 1990, in several respects. It reflects political changes by adding listings for a number of new countries, most of them in the former Soviet Union. Information on constitutions is a new offering, as is a listing for "Electronic Sources" that appears in the front matter. Also new are additional categories of publications dealing with the environment and with the rights and status of women. Otherwise, the format is similar to the first edition. Countries are listed alphabetically, with each listing encompassing up to nineteen categories of official publications. Some examples include "Government Directories and Organization Manuals," "Statistical Yearbooks,"

"Legislative Proceedings," "Census," and "Court Reports." In order to keep the volume a manageable size, only principal publications are included. Individual entries include bibliographic information and often a set of notes that act as a descriptive annotation. There is an index of titles arranged by country, and the front matter provides helpful information for libraries that wish to acquire these publications. Foreign-government publications will be a mystery for many library users and librarians themselves, and this guide is an excellent starting point for identifying these publications.

1-6. Balay, Robert, ed. *Guide to Reference Books.* 11th ed. Chicago: American Library Association, 1996. 2020 pp. Index. ISBN: 0-838-90669-9.

The first edition of this famous work appeared in 1907. This eleventh edition presents a total of 15,875 entries, approximately 400 more than its immediate predecessor. The aim of the volume is "to assist information workers by selecting and describing the reference sources that have been found most useful in libraries in North America, and the desire to continue the tradition of excellence set by the compilers of earlier editions" (Balay 1996, foreword). Some outdated items have been dropped, while titles that are new or that were omitted in earlier editions have been added. The arrangement is by subject category and includes the following broad divisions: "General Reference Works," "Humanities," "Social and Behavioral Sciences," "History and Area Studies," and "Science, Technology, and Medicine." Individual entries represent those titles most likely to be found in the collection of a larger research library. Each receives an annotation ranging in length from a single sentence to several paragraphs, depending on both the importance and complexity of the work under discussion. Bullets indicate those items available in electronic format. Those who use this work will notice its emphasis upon the social sciences and humanities, and its emphasis upon publications found in North American libraries; those researchers wishing a British emphasis should consult *Walford's Guide* [entry 1-10]. Nevertheless, this book is a standard starting point for information on reference works in all disciplines.

1-7. Blazek, Ronald, and Elizabeth Aversa. *Humanities: A Selective Guide to Information Sources.* 5th ed. Englewood, CO: Libraries Unlimited, 2000. 603 pp. Indexes. ISBN: 0-563-08602-6.

Although the humanities are extraneous to a compilation of information sources regarding political science, this book is a useful resource for those researchers unfamiliar with the major disciplines in the humanities and who require an initiation into reference works in those fields. There are twelve chapters in this book; in general, odd-numbered chapters describe access to resources in a particular discipline, while even-numbered chapters provide annotations to specific works. The chapters on access are relatively brief and address themselves to computers, definitions, and directory information.

The chapters dealing with annotations include categories for such standard formats as bibliographies, dictionaries, encyclopedias, and biographies. Annotations are fairly detailed and provide some analysis as well as descriptions. The first two chapters discuss the humanities in general, while remaining chapters are devoted to philosophy; religion, mythology, and folklore; the visual arts; the performing arts; and language and literature. There are indexes by author/title and by subject.

1-8. *Reference Books Bulletin.* Annual. Chicago: American Library Association, 1984–. 142 pp. Indexes. ISSN: 8755-0962.

The reviews that appear in this annual publication are compiled from the periodical *Booklist.* While less thorough in its coverage than *American Reference Books Annual* [entry 1-1], this work does provide "Omnibus Reviews" that discuss recent publications in particular categories for comparative purposes. Otherwise, the arrangement is by subject area, with political science works appearing primarily in the section for the social sciences. Reviews are quite detailed and are both descriptive and critical; however, they are unsigned. There are indexes by subject, title, and type of material. The reference works reviewed here are those most likely to be found across the library spectrum, including libraries in schools and public and academic institutions.

1-9. Mirwis, Allan N. *Subject Encyclopedias: User Guide, Review Citations, and*

Keyword Index. 2 vols. Phoenix: Oryx Press, 1999. 726 pp. Indexes. ISBN: 1-573-56199-1.

The first volume of this set is a user guide that lists over 1,100 subject encyclopedias published between 1990 and 1997. The arrangement is by Library of Congress call number classification; for example, subject encyclopedias relating to political science are found in the "J" section. The listings include bibliographic information and citations to reviews. Also provided are listings of awards received by individual titles as well as an elaborate rating system intended to assist librarians in book selection. This volume includes indexes by title, subject heading, Dewey Decimal call number, publisher, and rating. The second volume is a keyword index to ninety-eight of the subject encyclopedias listed in the first volume. These were selected as those being most appropriate for library patrons beginning their research and include representative items from the social sciences. The references in this second volume refer the reader to the appropriate subject encyclopedia (listed by call number) as found in the first volume and also provide page references. This second volume serves as a welcome update to *First Stop* [entry 1-4] and is perhaps the more valuable of this two-volume set.

1-10. Day, Alan, and Michael Walsh. *Walford's Guide to Reference Material.* Vol. 2, *Social and Historical Sciences, Philosophy and Religion.* 8th ed. London: Library Association Publishing,

2000. 808 pp. Indexes. ISBN: 1-856-04369-X.

Part of a three-volume set (the other two volumes deal with the humanities and the sciences), this volume is a long-time standard. Published in the United Kingdom, it attempts to be comprehensive in its coverage of English-language reference works, but naturally has a more British emphasis than the *Guide to Reference Books* [entry 1-6], which is published in the United States. The two complement one another nicely. All types of materials are included here, among them electronic databases and compact disc products. The arrangement is by Universal Decimal Classification, with which many readers will not be familiar. However, this is not a handicap to use of the volume. It is easy enough to find areas of relevance by scanning the table of contents and then skimming through the section or sections in question. Annotations are brief and descriptive in nature. There are indexes by author and title, subject, and electronic product. The sections in the volume most relevant to political scientists are those on "Politics" and "Public Administration."

Annuals and Yearbooks
1-11. *Whitaker's Almanack.* Annual. London: Stationery Office, 1869–. ISBN: 0-117-02179-2.

Like most almanacs, this contains a miscellany of statistics and brief information. In the late 1990s, this venerable publication fell under the auspices of

Her Majesty's Stationery Office after having been published by Whitaker and Sons for more than a century. It provides the usual brief survey of current topics, for example, countries of the world, events of the year, weights and measures, sports results, awards, and an overview of the activities of various governmental agencies throughout the United Kingdom. The format is considerably more sober-minded than that found in American almanacs; time will tell whether the Stationery Office will institute any major changes. Found in almost all sizable libraries, *Whitaker's* will likely continue to be a standard source for introductory information about the United Kingdom.

Directories

1-12. *Associations Unlimited.* Database. Farmington Hills, MI: Thomson Gale, 1989—. Index.

This database provides directory information on national, international, state, regional, and local organizations, as well as 501(c) nonprofit groups. There are nearly a half-million listings. One can search by organization name or acronym, or by keyword. It is also possible to restrict the search to national, international, or regional, state, and local organizations. Such restrictions are usually necessary to assist in pinpointing the more significant groups. The database includes paragraph-length information on most organizations, contact information, and a hyperlink to the organization's Web site, if one exists. *Associations Unlimited* is a continuation of the print *Encyclopedia of Associations* and is an invaluable resource for finding specific organizations or organizations pertaining to a particular area of interest. 💻

1-13. Brooker, Peter. *Concise Glossary of Cultural Theory.* London: Oxford University Press, 1999. 256 pp. ISBN: 0-340-69147-6.

Those researchers interested in cultural studies will wish to consult this dictionary, which provides extended definitions of terminology particular to that field. Among the topic areas covered are feminism, Marxism, the sociology of culture, and psychoanalysis. Definitions are arranged alphabetically and include entries such as "Cultural Politics," "Elite," "Multiculturalism," "Patriarchy," and "Representation." Most definitions are a page or more in length, with cross-references indicated in uppercase. References to the relevant literature also appear in the text of the definition; full bibliographic listings can be found at the back of the volume. The author is a British literature professor. The audience for this work will consist of scholars new to the field of cultural theory or those who require a refresher and referral to the appropriate literature.

1-14. Payne, Michael, ed. *Dictionary of Cultural and Critical Theory.* Oxford: Blackwell Publishers, 1996. 644 pp. Index. ISBN: 0-631-17197-5.

This reference work describes itself as a "reference guide to modern ideas in the broad interdisciplinary fields of cultural and critical theory, which have developed from interactions among modern linguistic, literary, anthropological, philosophical, political, and historical traditions of thought" (Payne 1996, preface). Major emphasis is upon ideas and theories that might collectively be described as postmodern; structuralism, poststructuralism, feminism, and hermeneutics are among the concepts discussed. The basic arrangement is alphabetical, with entries ranging from a paragraph to three or four pages long. Reading lists are provided at the end of each entry, while cross-references are indicated through the use of uppercase. Entries are signed by the contributor; all are academicians drawn from institutions throughout the English-speaking world, although a significant number are from Bucknell University in the United States. A lengthy bibliography at the end of the volume compiles the references found in the reading lists throughout the dictionary. Although the contributors have attempted to write for a general audience, the general complexity of many of the concepts makes this a volume of greater use to advanced students and scholars than to beginners.

1-15. Appiah, Kwame Anthony, and Henry Louis Gates, Jr, eds. *The Dictionary of Global Culture.* New York: Alfred A. Knopf, 1996. 717 pp. ISBN: 0-394-58581-X.

The editors, believing that Westerners dealing with an expanding global society need a greater acquaintance with achievements of cultures other than their own, compiled this dictionary as a sampler of cultural contributions from around the globe. The style is bland and nonjudgmental, and the approach is to avoid controversy. The selection of entries was suggested by scholars from other cultures and Western scholars of those societies to eliminate Western bias. As a self-described sampler, this volume suffers from space limitation that allows inclusion of only the most obvious cultural references. However, this handy desktop volume does provide researchers brief introductions to non-Western figures and ideas.

1-16. Bothamley, Jennifer. *Dictionary of Theories.* London: Gale Research International, 1993. 637 pp. Indexes. ISBN: 1-873-47705-8.

Bothamley's work provides brief definitions of theories from a wide variety of fields in the humanities, social sciences, and sciences. Each definition includes the time when the theory was promulgated, the field where it originated, the name of the originator, and a short definition, usually a paragraph or two in length. Most entries have cross-references and a bibliographic citation to a book or monograph for further discussion of the topic. The volume concludes with indexes of theorists and of theories arranged by subject. Those seeking beginning information on such topics as Maoism, Marbe's Law, and marginal-utility theory or attempting to identify theories by discipline will find this dictionary useful. Published initially in the United Kingdom, this work might have a slight British bias; Americans might be bemused, for example, by the cock-up theory of history.

1-17. Rohmann, Chris. *World of Ideas: A Dictionary of Important Theories, Concepts, Beliefs, and Thinkers.* New York: Ballantine Books, 1999. 496 pp. Index. ISBN: 0-345-39059-8.

The author took on this project in order to create a dictionary of ideas written for the nonspecialist and incorporating contemporary as well as historic thinkers. Among the fields covered are psychology, politics, history, economics, and sociology. Altogether, there are 444 entries, of which one-fourth are profiles of individuals, emphasizing their financial ideas rather than biographical background. Entries are arranged alphabetically and generally are a half page to a page in length, although some topics of core significance to the contemporary world, such as democracy and feminism, receive additional sidebar coverage. Cross-references to other relevant entries are included, but there are no bibliographic references other than a short bibliography at the back of the book. This work has a twofold value: it can be readily understood by undergraduates and other nonacademic readers, and it can be consulted for contemporary as well as past ideas.

2

Social Sciences
Reference Sources

This chapter compiles annotations for those items that pertain to the social sciences in general. The book by Herron is a particularly useful overview of the literature thanks to its relatively recent publication date. Among the indexes, the *Social Sciences Index* (now with an electronic version entitled *Social Sciences Abstracts*) has been a standby for decades. Another standard has been *International Encyclopedia of the Social Sciences;* however, the recently published *International Encyclopedia of the Social and Behavioral Sciences* serves as a welcome update.

General Social Sciences
Literature Guides
2-1. Fisher, David, Sandra P. Price, and Terry Hanstock, eds. *Information Sources in the Social Sciences.* Munich: K. G. Saur, 2002. 511 pp. Index. ISBN: 3-598-24439-8.

This guide includes anthropology, sociology, psychology, criminology, education, political science, economics, human ser-

vices, and human geography, but it excludes history. There is also a chapter on general social science information sources. Entries are arranged by type of material, including such standard classifications as annuals, dictionaries, encyclopedias, and statistics. Material types also include Web sites, indexes, and databases. Each chapter was prepared by a separate author, so there may be some overlap between chapters. Almost all the contributors are associated with higher education institutions in the United Kingdom, so this volume has something of a British emphasis but nevertheless is worth consulting by American researchers.

2-2. Li, Tze-chung. *Social Science Reference Sources: A Practical Guide.* 3rd ed. Westport, CT: Greenwood Press, 2000. 495 pp. Indexes. ISBN: 0-313-30483-1.

This edition excludes most imprints before 1980 and most after December 1998. An extensive introductory section covers general social science sources, including statistical sources, periodicals, and government publications. The remainder of the volume describes sources in the various social science disciplines. These include cultural anthropology, business, economics, education, geography, history, law, political science, psychology, and sociology. There are indexes by name and title and by subject. Electronic resources have been included, but these will of course have experienced some change in the years since publication. The usefulness of this work will be enhanced if it is consulted in conjunction with other guidebooks described in this section.

2-3. Herron, Nancy L., ed. *Social Sciences: A Cross-Disciplinary Guide to Selected Sources.* 3rd ed. Englewood, CO: Teacher Press, 2002. 494 pp. Indexes. ISBN: 1-563-08985-8.

This second edition presents over 1,000 annotated citations arranged into four parts. In order, these parts are "General Literature of the Social Sciences," "Literature of the Established Disciplines of the Social Sciences," "Literature of the Emerging Disciplines of the Social Sciences—Those with a Social Origin or Those Having Acquired a Social Aspect," and "Literature of the Disciplines Related to the Social Sciences—Those With Recognized Social Implications." Disciplines encompassed in the second part include political science, economics, business, history, law, anthropology, and sociology. The third part includes education and psychology, while the fields of geography and communication appear in

the final part. Each discipline is accorded a chapter of its own, written by a librarian who is a specialist in that field. Within each chapter, the reader finds an introductory essay assessing the field and its literature; this is followed by sections on such standard formats as abstracting and indexing services, bibliographies, dictionaries, encyclopedias, and the like. Annotations are comparatively brief and provide some analysis along with description. There are separate indexes by author, title, and subject. This is a useful overview of the literature of the social sciences and has the advantage of having been published fairly recently.

2-4. Wepsiec, Jan. *Social Sciences: An International Bibliography of Serial Literature, 1830–1985.* London: Continuum Instructional Publishing Group, 1992. 486 pp. Index. ISBN: 0-720-12109-4.

Listings for 5,254 serial publications appear in this reference work. The year 1830 marked the publication of the first journal in a social sciences discipline and hence was selected as the starting date for inclusion. Six disciplines were identified as core social sciences: economics, political science, cultural anthropology, sociology, international public law, and comparative law. Four other disciplines, education, psychology, history, and geography, were included on a peripheral basis. Publications by international organizations were also included on a comprehensive basis. Each entry provides a bibliographic description, a history of title changes, and a listing of services that index that particular journal. There are no annotations. The entries are arranged alphabetically, but the index provides access by subject. This is a specialized resource of interest primarily to advanced researchers, who will welcome its international, multilanguage approach.

2-5. Webb, William H., ed. *Sources of Information in the Social Sciences: A Guide to the Literature.* 3rd ed. Chicago: American Library Association, 1986. 777 pp. Index. ISBN: 0-838-90405-X.

Earlier editions of this work were edited by Carl M. White. This edition is similar in approach to its immediate predecessor. There are nine major sections: "Social Science Literature," "History," "Geography," "Economics and Business Administration," "Sociology," "Anthropology," "Psychology," "Education," and "Political Science." Each is written by a specialist in that particular field. The format differs from the usual guide to reference sources by providing a selection of core monographs appropriate to the disciplines. The discussion of monographs begins each of the disciplinary sections; descriptions and annotations of standard reference sources then follow. In some cases, each item receives its own annotations, but in other instances group annotations describe a number of entries. A single, detailed index provides access by author, title, and subject. Although this publication is now some years old, it is still useful for its summary of both key monographic and reference literature for the social science disciplines through the mid-1980s.

Abstracting and Indexing Services

2-6. *Alternative Press Index: Access to Movements, News, Policy, and Theory.* Quarterly. Baltimore, MD: Alternative Press Center, 1969–. Indexes. ISSN: 0002-662X.

Among the subjects covered in this indexing service are African Americans, gay/lesbian studies, community organization, prisons, labor studies, feminism, and ecology. As of 1999, approximately 300 periodical titles were indexed here. The first three quarterly issues of the year include citations to the actual articles themselves, citations to reviews of books and performances, citations to "Autobiographies, Biographies, Obituaries," and an author index. The citations provide bibliographic information but no abstracts. The final quarterly issue of the year provides a detailed subject index as well as various other indexes. *Alternative Press Index* is also available electronically. 🖥

2-7. *Combined Retrospective Index to Book Reviews in Scholarly Journals, 1886–1974.* 15 vols. Arlington, VA: Gale Group, 1979–1982. Index. ISBN: 0-840-80172-6 (Varies).

With the advent of electronic technology, it has become much simpler to identify book reviews, but this set still serves a useful purpose thanks to its access to reviews of books that predate computer databases. Altogether, this index includes more than one million book reviews appearing in 459 scholarly journals in the fields of political science, history, and sociology. The bulk of the set is an arrangement by the author of the book under review, but the final three volumes provide a title index that identifies author names. Citations are to name of journal, volume, year, issue (when applicable), and page. The journals represented are standards in their disciplines and will be found in most larger academic libraries.

2-8. *Social Sciences Index.* Quarterly. Bronx, NY: H. W. Wilson. 1974–. ISSN: 0094-4920.

This index, under other names, has been a staple in American academic libraries for many decades. As of 1999, it indexed approximately 400 titles in the social sciences. Among the areas of interest to political scientists and their students are international relations, law, planning and public administration, policy sciences, political science itself, and urban studies. All the titles indexed are in English; most are professional journals. The arrangement is alphabetical by subject, with numerous cross-references provided. A bound cumulative volume appears annually. Many libraries now have this index available electronically under the title *Social Sciences Abstracts*; abstracting was added to the citations in 1994. Although there are more comprehensive and more specialized indexing and abstracting services available today, this source retains its value for those researchers requiring access to the core journal literature in political science and related social science disciplines. ⌨

Dictionaries
2-9. Vogt, W. Paul. *Dictionary of Statistics and Methodology: A Nontechnical Guide for the Social Sciences.* 2nd ed. Thousand Oaks, CA: Sage Publications, 1998. 318 pp. ISBN: 0-761-91273-8.

As the subtitle indicates, this work is aimed at readers whose knowledge of statistical methods and mathematics is fairly elementary. For that reason, the definitions found here attempt verbal explanations rather than using mathematical symbols and formulas, and use examples that attempt to explain the definition or concept in question. Definitions are arranged alphabetically and are usually only a sentence or two in length; examples tend to be longer than the definitions themselves. The numerous cross-references are indicated with asterisks. Examples of the definitions include "Dependent Event," "Fan Spread," "Model," "Partial Relations," and "Standard Error." A bibliography will lead readers to other relevant sources. The audience for this work will consist of serious researchers rather than casual readers.

2-10. Trahair, Richard C. S. *From Aristotelian to Reaganomics: A Dictionary of Eponyms with Biographies in the Social Sciences.* Westport, CT: Greenwood Press, 1994. 721 pp. Index. ISBN: 0-313-27961-6.

This reference work "provides information about individuals whose names have been given to the language used by social scientists and those in related occupations and professions" (Trahair 1994, introduction). Some examples include "Arnoldists," "Hamiltonian Circuit," "Moonies," "Packwood Case," and "Ullman's Bases for Interaction." The social sciences are defined broadly to include not just the usual disciplines but also fields such as education, journalism, management, and popular culture. Approximately one thousand entries are included and are arranged alphabetically. Each entry includes a definition of the term itself, a brief biography of the individual (or individuals) after whom the eponym was named, and a list of sources for additional reading. The index refers the reader to main entries as well as to names of individuals discussed within entries. This is a useful source, but is limited by the fact that all possible eponyms cannot realistically appear in a work such as this; inevitably, the choice for inclusion will be somewhat idiosyncratic. If, however, one does find a particular eponym here, the listing of sources provides a handy shortcut for tracking down more information.

Encyclopedias

2-11. Seligman, Edwin R. A., ed. *Encyclopaedia of the Social Sciences.* 15 vols. New York: Macmillan, 1937. Index. ISBN: 0-026-09130-5.

Believing that the time had come for the individual social sciences to begin an assessment of what the several disciplines have in common, as opposed to what makes them distinct, the editors emphasized that their encyclopedia would indicate relationships among disciplines. Those disciplines considered most central to the social sciences, at least for the purposes of this work, are politics, economics, law, anthropology, sociology, penology, and social work. Contributors came from both Europe and North America, although the latter predominate due to the limitations of communication overseas at the time. The first volume contains a 350-page introductory section that describes the historical development of social thought and institutions, and provides capsule histories of the development of the individual social sciences in countries and regions throughout the world, with particular emphasis upon Europe and the United States. The articles that follow are arranged alphabetically and range in length from a paragraph up to 20,000 words. Each is signed by the contributor; affiliations appear at the beginning of each volume. If there are cross-references, they appear at the end of the article, and the reader is also provided with a list of references for additional research. There are no illustrations other than occasional tables. Approximately one-fifth of all the articles are biographies, all of individuals who were deceased at the time of publication. The final volume includes a relatively brief index to the entire set. Obviously, this set represents the thinking of scholars in the first third of the twentieth century, and readers will want to consult newer encyclopedias described in this section.

2-12. Smelser, Neil J., and Paul B. Baltes, eds. *International Encyclopedia of the Social and Behavioral Sciences.* 26 vols. Amsterdam: Elsevier, 2001. Indexes. ISBN: 0-080-43076-7.

An updated comprehensive encyclopedia of the social sciences has been needed for some time; the earlier encyclopedias discussed in this section are now decades old. In their introduction, the editors of this new set comment on the need for a new work. They also mention the need to incorporate new and more scientific information available for the various social science disciplines. The first volume of the set provides an alphabetical listing of the articles throughout. These range from "Aboriginal Rights" to "Zooarchaeology." The articles are usually several pages long and are written by specialists in the field. Each article concludes with a bibliography of relevant books and periodical articles. Occasional illustrations and graphic displays accompany the text. The final two volumes are comprehensive name and subject indexes. The writing style is accessible to undergraduates, but this encyclopedia can be consulted profitably by advanced researchers as well.

2-13. Sills, David L., ed. *International Encyclopedia of the Social Sciences.* 17 vols. New York: Macmillan and Free Press, 1968. Index. ISBN: 0-318-75259-X.

Coming more than thirty years after the publication of the *Encyclopaedia of the Social Sciences* [entry 2-11], this set aims to complement rather than replace its predecessor. It was felt that the growth of the social sciences, and their use in many different arenas of life, made it necessary "to reflect and encourage the rapid development of the social sciences throughout the world" (Sills 1968, introduction) by producing a new encyclopedia on the subject. This set expanded the disciplines covered to include anthropology, economics, geography, history, law, political science, psychiatry, psychology, sociology, and statistics. The basic arrangement of articles is alphabetical, but to meet the needs of a multidisciplinary approach, many longer articles are subdivided to reflect theory from different disciplines. For example, the article on aging includes entries by three different contributors describing respectively the psychological, social, and economic aspects of that topic. Altogether, the entries for aging are approximately twenty-five pages in length, which is typical for those subjects treated in depth. Headers and outlines help the reader to navigate these longer entries. Cross-references lead to other relevant articles, and bibliographies list sources for additional information. Approximately 600 biographies are among the entries. All are of individuals born after 1890, and treatment is in greater detail than in the earlier encyclopedia. The final volume includes a directory of contributors, with their affiliation and the article or articles to their credit, a classified list of articles, and a detailed index to the entire set. Like the earlier encyclopedia, this one is now many years old but will repay those researchers who wish to delve into past thought on social science ideas still under discussion in the contemporary world. For a recent multivolume examination of the social sciences, researchers should consult the *International Encyclopedia of the Social and Behavioral Sciences* [entry 2-12].

2-14. Sills, David L., ed. *International Encyclopedia of the Social Sciences: Biographical Supplement.* New York: Free Press, 1979. 820 pp. ISBN: 0-028-95510-2.

As one would guess from the title, this work, which serves as the eighteenth volume of the *International Encyclopedia of the Social Sciences* [entry 2-13], adds 215 biographies to the 600 in the original set. Entries are similar to those in the original, with each biographee receiving two to four pages of discussion, with emphasis upon contributions to the discipline for which the individual is noted. Each article concludes with a listing of works written by the biographee and, when appropriate, additional bibliographic entries critiquing his or her work. The biographees are classified by discipline in the front matter, which also includes a directory of contributors and their affiliations.

2-15. Sills, David L., and Robert K. Merton, eds. *International Encyclopedia of the Social Sciences: Social Science Quotations.* New York: Free Press, 1991. 437 pp. Index. ISBN: 0-029-28751-0.

Presented as the nineteenth volume of the *International Encyclopedia of the Social Sciences* [entry 2-13], this work compiles quotations from the works of noteworthy social scientists. Those included need not have been scholars or researchers active only in this century; the scope is broad enough to include politicians such as Abraham Lincoln and figures from the past such as Machi-avelli. In general, quotations must contain "memorable ideas memorably expressed" (Sills and Merton 1991, introduction) and must have substantial bearing upon social thought or the social sciences. Quotations tend to be longer than in ordinary quotation dictionaries in order to include the context in which the original thought was expressed. The basic arrangement is alphabetical by name of quoted authority. Each quotation includes a citation to the original source. These give only incomplete information, but full bibliographic citations can be found in a bibliography at the end of the volume. The index allows access to the quotations by author and keyword. This work has obvious use for those wishing to track down a quotation that might not appear in the standard sources or for a researcher looking for key quotes that represent core thinking of noteworthy social scientists; on the other hand, it may be easily overlooked given the fact that most libraries will shelve it with its parent set rather than with the standard quotation dictionaries.

2-16. Kuper, Adam, and Jessica Kuper. *Social Science Encyclopedia.* 2nd ed. London: Routledge, 1999. 952 pp. ISBN: 0-415-20794-0.

The first edition of this work appeared in 1995; the second updates the first to reflect new approaches and ideas in the social sciences. "Post-Modernism" is an example of one of the newer theoretical concepts described here. The scope of the encyclopedia includes major articles on social science disciplines and articles on the specialties, theories, methods, philosophies, key individuals, and schools of thought in this arena. Utilitarian applications of the social sciences to the larger society are also examined. Articles are arranged alphabetically and generally range from one to three pages in length, concluding with listings of references to core sources. Cross-references are also indicated at the end of each entry. Not only are the entries signed with the complete name of the contributor, but the contributor's affiliation is also indicated at that point. Graphic displays appear as necessary. Included in the front matter is a listing of entries by discipline and subject; this is an important feature of this work, for there is no index. Those researchers needing relatively brief information on social science topics can be referred to this volume, which is suitable for both undergraduates and advanced scholars.

Anthropology

In addition to the "General Reference" and "Social Sciences Reference" works found in those chapters of this guide, the newcomer to the field of anthropology can consult a number of dictionaries and encyclopedias annotated in this section. Those wishing a scholarly overview of many world cultures can consult the work by O'Leary. Conversely, the beginning student requiring descriptions of customs found in 500 world societies will profit by consulting Gall.

Literature Guides
2-17. Dutton, Lee S., ed. *Anthropological Resources: A Guide to Archival, Library and Museum Collections.* New York: Garland Publishing, 1999. 517 pp. Indexes. ISBN: 0-815-31188-5.

Dutton is associated with the Library-Anthropology Resource Group, which has compiled a number of resource books for that discipline. This volume includes almost 250 entries pertaining to repositories of anthropological resources. These are defined as "original scholars' fieldnotes, site reports, papers, manuscripts, archives, oral history collections, sound recordings, photographs, films and videos" (Dutton 1999, preface). The compilation is reasonably complete for the United States and Canada, with some attention also paid to Western Europe; other parts of the world are covered only selectively. Collections in Canada and the United States appear first and are arranged by province or state. Throughout, each entry includes important access information, and some entries also provide detailed descriptions of the collections. There are two indexes: one provides access to personal names, while the other provides access to names of ethnic groups. Most of the groups can be described as small-scale societies rather than those in urban areas. This guide is for serious researchers rather than beginning students.

Abstracting and Indexing Services
2-18. *Abstracts in Anthropology.* Annual. Amityville, NY: Baywood Publishing, 1970–. Indexes. ISSN: 0001-3455.

A standard print index in the field of anthropology, this serial publication "covers a broad spectrum of significant, current anthropological topics from several hundred periodicals" (*Abstracts in Anthropology* 1970, front matter). Eight issues appear annually and are divided into two volume-numbering sequences. Each issue includes indexes by author and subject as well as a listing of periodicals abstracted, which may be considerably fewer than the total abstracted during the course of the year. Several abstractors, who are listed inside the front cover by name but without credentials, are responsible for each issue. Individual issues include as many as 750 abstracts. The contents are arranged very broadly by linguistic and cultural anthropology, with further subdivisions within each of these two major areas. Thus, the reader with a specific subject interest can browse through the pages devoted to that particular aspect of the discipline, although many will wish to consult the subject index as well. The last issue of each volume includes cumulative indexes by entry number; entry numbers are sequential from the first issue of the current year through the final, eighth issue of the year. This is one of several indexing sources, either print or electronic, of which anthropology researchers need to be aware.

Directories

2-19. American Anthropological Association. *Guide to Programs; Directory of Members.* Annual. Arlington, VA: American Anthropological Association, 1962–. 578 pp. Indexes. ISBN: 0-913-16789-4.

Those seeking timely directory information for the field of anthropology can consult this directory published by the American Anthropological Association (AAA). As one might expect, the contents are oriented heavily toward academic programs; of the four types of program listings, 434 represent academic departments, and the approximately 100 additional entries are listings of programs offered through museums, research firms, and government agencies. The basic arrangement is alphabetical by name of institution. Listings generally include information on faculty members and their research interests, addresses (including e-mail), numbers of students and degrees granted, academic requirements, and other information of interest to prospective students. Those interested in individuals can turn to the directory portion of this volume, which includes an alphabetical list of AAA members with their postal and e-mail addresses. The final portion of the guide provides statistical information on enrollment of anthropology students, degrees granted, and listings of dissertations. One can also find indexes for individuals by program and academic departments by state. This is an obvious source for students interested in an anthropology major or degree.

Dictionaries

2-20. Barfield, Thomas, ed. *Dictionary of Anthropology.* Oxford: Blackwell Publishers, 1997. 626 pp. ISBN: 1-557-86282-6.

The parameters of this reference work are thoroughly explained in its preface.

Responding to the idea that anthropology literature falls between two extremes, textbook approaches on one hand and narrow professional treatises on the other, this dictionary seeks to occupy a middle ground providing "clear and concise statements laying out the important issues, significant concepts, methodologies, and theories in anthropology along with a guide to the key literature on these topics." In addition to addressing the nonspecialist, this work also treats the complex disciplines within the field, encompassing cultural and social anthropology, with some emphasis also on archeology, biological anthropology, and linguistics. Along with these topics, there are also biographies for prominent anthropologists, particularly those now deceased. Specific cultures are deliberately not included. Entries range in length from a paragraph to several pages. Cross-references are indicated in uppercase, and entries are initialed by the contributors, who are listed with their affiliation in the front matter. Brief references for further reading conclude most entries. Complete references are then found in a bibliography at the back of the volume. There are almost no illustrations. This work should succeed in its mission to introduce nonspecialist readers to the field of anthropology. 🖳

2-21. Winthrop, Robert H. *Dictionary of Concepts in Cultural Anthropology.* Reference Sources for the Social Sciences and Humanities Series. New York: Greenwood Press, 1991. 360 pp. Indexes. ISBN: 0-313-24280-1.

Like other "dictionary of concepts" volumes published by Greenwood, this work attempts to describe a particular discipline through its major concepts using a format whereby each concept receives a page or two of discussion followed by a list of annotated references to which the text refers. This in turn is followed by "Sources of Additional Information," which provides a brief overview of the concept through the means of a bibliographic essay. Cross-references to other articles are indicated in uppercase. This particular entry in the series includes approximately eighty concepts; among them are "chiefdom," "marriage," and "taboo." In the preface, the author defines cultural anthropology as describing and interpreting "the culturally patterned thought and behavior of contemporary and near-contemporary societies." He also indicates that his point of view "is that of the English-speaking world," particularly American and British anthropologists. The volume concludes with two indexes, one of names and the other of subjects. Advanced students and specialists alike will find this work of value as a guide to concepts in cultural anthropology and, in particular, as a starting point for the literature pertaining to those concepts.

2-22. Stevenson, Joan C. *Dictionary of Concepts in Physical Anthropology.* Reference Sources for the Social Sciences and Humanities Series. New York: Greenwood Press, 1991. 448 pp. Indexes. ISBN: 0-313-24756-0.

As is the case with other "dictionary of concepts" volumes published by Greenwood, this work seeks to explain concepts in the field of physical (or biological) anthropology through articles that trace the development of the concept from its origins to the present. Typical entries in this work include "altruism," "inbreeding," and "primates." The entries themselves are up to three pages in length, and each includes an extensive list of references to which the text refers. The references are annotated, and the author also provides brief bibliographic essays for "Sources of Additional Information." Cross-references are indicated in uppercase. There are indexes by both name and subject. Like its companions in this series, this is a useful work for those researchers who wish to identify the development of major concepts within a particular discipline. The text is accessible to more advanced undergraduates as well as to a specialist audience, and the bibliographic references are a particularly valuable component of this volume.

Encyclopedias

2-23. Ingold, Tim, ed. *Companion Encyclopedia of Anthropology.* 2nd ed. London: Routledge, 2002. 1127 pp. Index. ISBN: 0-415-28604-2.

Going beyond the traditional disciplinary boundaries of anthropology, this work attempts to describe the human race in thirty-eight articles divided among three different parts: humanity, culture, and social life. The first part, "Humanity," deals with the evolutionary history of humans and their cultural artifacts; the other two parts are more self-explana-

tory. In the "General Introduction," the editor outlines three goals for the work. The first is to counteract overspecialization, the second to provide a state-of-the-art examination of anthropological concerns and their possible future direction, and the final goal is to demonstrate the relevance of anthropology to other disciplines. The articles average about twenty-eight pages in length. Each ends with a bibliography for reference or for further reading. Credentials for each of the contributors can be found in some detail in the front matter. Most contributors are American or British. There are a number of graphic displays, and a detailed index provides additional access to the text itself. The writing style is accessible to serious undergraduates and to specialists outside the field of anthropology, so this work can be recommended to an audience other than anthropologists.

2-24. Levinson, David, and Melvin Ember, eds. *Encyclopedia of Cultural Anthropology.* 4 vols. New York: Henry Holt, 1996. 1486 pp. Index. ISBN: 0-805-02877-3.

The editors assert that articles in this encyclopedia exemplify three core concepts in the field of cultural anthropology. These include a cross-cultural perspective, the "intensive study of particular cultures, and the reliance on ethnographic fieldwork to produce the basic knowledge of the discipline" (Levinson and Ember 1996, introduction). The 340 articles attempt to discuss the field in a comprehensive fashion, examining both historic and contemporary trends and theories, and touching upon topics that are controversial in nature. While emphasis is upon cultural anthropology, information from the other fields of anthropology (linguistics, biological anthropology, and archeology) is included on a selective basis. In general, articles range in length from one to four pages, with a short bibliography included. Cross-references are indicated at the end of each article. Articles are signed by the contributors, whose affiliations appear at the beginning of the first volume. The articles are arranged alphabetically. The final volume includes a comprehensive index and an appendix listing anthropology periodicals, although this latter does not include complete addresses. The text is accessible to both student and specialist audiences, and this will be a useful starting point for many library users interested in anthropology.

2-25. Barnard, Alan, and Jonathan Spencer, eds. *Encyclopedia of Social and Cultural Anthropology.* London: Routledge, 2002. 658 pp. Indexes. ISBN: 0-415-28558-5.

One among a number of recently published anthropology encyclopedias, this work uses a somewhat different format than its competitors. The main portion of the text consists of 231 articles, arranged alphabetically and ranging in length from one to six pages. Acting as adjuncts to the main text are three separate listings. The first is an "analytical table of contents" that shows the reader articles that pertain to a particular broad subject. Examples include "ethnographic surveys" and "his-

tory of anthropology." The second is an appendix that provides very brief biographies of noted figures in the field of anthropology; these biographies are no more than a paragraph in length, but they do note the major publications of these individuals. The third component is a glossary nearly forty pages in length. Within the articles themselves, cross-references are indicated with asterisks as well as with "see also" listings. Contributors are identified, and each article ends with listings of items for additional reading. There are indexes to names, people and places, and subjects. In the introduction, the editors indicate that the "social and cultural" portion of their title is intended to indicate an incorporation of both American and European practice, and that they have aimed to provide as many points of view as possible in the selection of their contributors. Their audience is intended to be students and professionals within anthropology and other disciplines, as well as the interested reader. The general arrangement of this volume is a bit more complicated than some other similar works, but most readers will not be seriously handicapped by this added complication.

2-26. Gonen, Amiram, ed. *Encyclopedia of the Peoples of the World.* New York: Henry Holt, 1993. 703 pp. Index. ISBN: 0-805-02256-2.

Like other reference works that focus upon ethnic or national groups, this work attempts to describe for the general reader those groups active today that may be involved in political or military disputes with larger entities. The arrangement is alphabetical by name of group. Entries are also provided for nation-states composed of important ethnic constituencies. Some entries are relatively short, no more than a couple of paragraphs, while others, such as the article on Croats, take up a couple of pages. There are numerous cross-references, indicated in uppercase. Approximately 250 black-and-white maps supplement the text. This work would have been more useful had bibliographic references been included. On the other hand, the text is suitable for both high-school and undergraduate students requiring brief information on many peoples extant in the world today.

2-27. O'Leary, Timothy J., and David Levinson, eds. *Encyclopedia of World Cultures.* 10 vols. Boston: G. K. Hall, 1991–1996. Indexes. ISBN: 0-816-88840-X.

The preface found in the first volume of this encyclopedia outlines the scope of the work. The intention is to assemble "a basic reference source that provides accurate, clear, and concise descriptions of the cultures of the world." Contributors take into consideration not only the past history of each culture but also trends, often dramatic, that have affected most cultures in this century. Most of the contributors are experts on the culture to which they address themselves; other entries are written using the resources of the Human Relations Area Files. In general, six criteria were applied in the selection of cultural groups: (1) geographical

localization; (2) identification in the social science literature as a distinct group; (3) distinct language; (4) shared traditions, religion, folklore, or values; (5) maintenance of identity in the face of strong assimilative pressures; and (6) previous listing in an inventory of the world's cultures. Extinct and immigrant cultures are generally excluded. Each of the first nine volumes of this set is devoted to a particular geographic region, usually a continent or subcontinent. These volumes each include their own set of maps and relevant appendixes, including a filmography. Individual cultural descriptions range up to six pages in length and summarize a number of facets pertaining to that community, including economy, kinship, marriage and family, and religion, among others. A bibliography for each culture indicates core sources, including both books and articles. The final volume includes comprehensive indexes to subjects, ethnonyms, and cultures by country. The intended audience consists of specialists and students alike, as well as interested lay readers. This is an invaluable resource, one that reference librarians will consult again and again. It is a splendid starting point for an overview of numerous cultural groups for which information can otherwise be difficult to locate readily, and it provides easy reference to other key sources.

2-28. Green, Thomas A., ed. *Folklore: An Encyclopedia of Beliefs, Customs, Tales, Music, and Art.* 2 vols. Santa Barbara, CA: ABC-CLIO, 1997. 892 pp. Index. ISBN: 0-874-36986-X.

Most folklore dictionaries and encyclopedias tend to be compilations of motifs and tales from world folk literature. This reference work instead treats the subject as a theoretical discipline, presented in approximately 200 entries. Both current and historical theories are addressed. Entries are usually several pages in length, are signed by the contributor, and conclude with cross-references and a list of sources for additional reading. Typical topics include "artifact," "gossip," "night hag," "postmodernism," and "structuralism." The article on postmodernism is indicative of an attempt to stay abreast of contemporary concerns. Occasional illustrations supplement the text. Contributors and their affiliations appear at the beginning of the first volume, which also includes a listing of entries. Access to the text is enhanced by a detailed index. This work represents a useful starting point for students new to the subject but will be of value to specialists as well.

2-29. Gall, Timothy L., ed. *Worldmark Encyclopedia of Cultures and Daily Life.* 4 vols. Detroit: Gale Research, 1997. 2422 pp. Indexes. ISBN: 0-787-60552-2.

Compilations of information regarding countries of the world are commonplace, but this set can be distinguished from many others by the fact that it provides information pertaining to social life and customs around the world. There are articles for approximately 500 groups, including not merely entries for individual countries but also entries for individual groups within many countries. For example, there is a general article in regard to Americans, but there also articles describing a number of ethnic groups in this country. All articles are arranged into twenty numbered segments, each dealing with a particular aspect of that nationality or ethnic group. Typical sections describe folklore, holidays, rites of passage, interpersonal relations, clothing, family life, and food. The final numbered section is a brief bibliography. The numbering system allows for easy comparison among the various groups. The four volumes are each devoted to a particular region of the world: Africa, the Americas, Asia and Oceania, and Europe. Each volume includes an index by country (which lists entries for each nationality or ethnic group within that nation) and a general index; thus the reader can use any one of the four volumes to determine what entries can be found in other volumes. The style of writing is relatively basic, making this a set to be consulted by high-school and college students more than by specialists. However, questions regarding social life around the world are relatively frequent, and this is an excellent set to which such inquiries can be directed.

Guides and Handbooks
2-30. Price, David H. *Atlas of World Cultures: A Geographical Guide to Ethnographic Literature.* Newbury Park, CA: Sage Publications, 1989. 155 pp. Index. ISBN: 0-803-93240-5.

In his introduction, Price (1989) states "this atlas is designed to direct cross-cultural researchers to key ethnographic works regarding a geographical region of interest, and to help locate groups commonly discussed in the ethnographic literature." Forty outline maps show cultural groups in various parts of the world at the time the author considers them to have received their "classic" description in the literature of anthropology. Numbered identifiers appear for each group on the appropriate map, and identifiers are listed numerically on the opposite page. The user can refer to these maps or may choose to start with the "Culture Index" located at the back of the volume. This index lists all cultures alphabetically and includes one or two citations to core literature, a reference to the map on which the group appears, a listing for the Human Relations Area File code, and a listing for the identification codes used in Murdock's *Ethnographic Atlas*. The citations, 1,237 in number, are arranged by accession number in the bibliography section of the volume. The format of this work is simple enough once it is understood, but most users will have to consult Price's introductory materials to understand how best to use this volume.

Economics

For the nonspecialist, the discipline of economics is perhaps one of the more formidable in the social sciences. Fortunately, there are a number of dictionaries and encyclopedias that assist in gaining knowledge of this field. Those with a more advanced background will benefit by consulting the Palgrave reference works, while the beginner will opt for Henderson or Magill. The *Gale Encyclo-*

pedia of U.S. Economic History is a helpful starting point for topics dealing with the American economy.

This section also includes a number of volumes dealing either with labor or with miscellaneous statistical compilations. Among those of note are *Value of a Dollar* and the three volumes dealing with *International Historical Statistics*. Each provides an easy entry to statistical questions that are relatively common and otherwise can be time-consuming to answer properly. Finally, Lavin's guide to the census is of great assistance to the researcher attempting to determine what data has been gathered by the U.S. Census and where it can be found.

Literature Guides

2-31. Sichel, Beatrice, and Werner Sichel, comps. *Economics Journals and Serials: An Analytical Guide.* Annotated Bibliographies of Serials: A Subject Approach, No. 5. New York: Greenwood Press, 1986. 285 pp. Indexes. ISBN: 0-313-23810-3.

The authors examined approximately 700 titles for a final selection of 450 that appear in this volume. Those publications whose primary focus was upon disciplines other than economics were excluded. The arrangement is alphabetical by title. Each listing provides up to twenty-one pieces of information as well as an abstract. Along with the usual bibliographic detail, the reader will also find information pertinent to advertising, circulation, selection of manuscripts, reprints, book reviews, indexing and abstracting, and the target audience. Annotations are analytical as well as descriptive and also include a description of a "typical issue." The scope is international, encompassing periodicals published in English in countries other than the United States. There are indexes by geographical locale and by publisher, as well as a classification of titles by subject. The value of this work is obviously limited by its mid-1980s publication date, but it still may be useful for descriptions of economics periodicals through that time frame.

Abstracting and Indexing Services

2-32. *Journal of Economic Literature.* Quarterly. Nashville, TN: American Economic Association, 1963–. ISSN: 0022-0515.

This is a core journal in the field of economics, but its value for most researchers lies in the fact that it also provides indexing and abstracting for the discipline. In addition to the usual scholarly articles and book reviews, each issue of the journal provides listings for both new books and current periodicals. Both books and periodical articles are arranged through the use of an elaborate classification scheme. Books receive an annotation that is descriptive of the contents, rather than a critique. The arrangement for periodical articles is more complicated. Both a table-of-contents approach and a classification scheme are utilized; thus, the reader can browse by journal title or use the classification approach. The latter includes annotations that again are descriptive rather than critical. Access is also provided through an index of authors for those articles that appear in the classification scheme. Also appearing in the quarterly issues are listings of recent doctoral dissertations. The final issue for the volume year includes a cumulative index of authors of new books but no other cumulative indexing. In general, the indexing scheme found here is so complex and tedious that most users will gladly turn to the computerized version of this publication rather than struggle with the print version. 💻

Annuals and Yearbooks

2-33. American Chamber of Commerce Research Association. *ACCRA Cost of Living Index.* Quarterly. Alexandria, VA: American Chamber of Commerce Research Association, 1968–. ISSN: 0740-9169.

Cost-of-living figures are available through the federal government, and one can calculate differences from one metropolitan area to another using devices on the Internet. Nevertheless, this printed publication continues to be a rich source of data in regard to this subject. Each quarterly issue provides data and comparisons for over 300 urban areas; the number varies from issue to issue, depending upon reporting from individual chambers of commerce. Only those chambers that collect data and cooperate in the project are included by ACCRA. Each issue is arranged first by state, then by community. The first portion of the issue is devoted to cost-of-living indexes that use percentage figures. Composite, grocery items, housing, utilities, transportation, health care, and miscellaneous goods and services are the categories reported. The second half of the issue consists of price reports for each of the communities. This provides dollar figures for almost forty separate consumer items, housing components, and services. For example, one can compare the price of ground beef or cigarettes from one urban area to another. The compilers caution that variations from one issue to another invalidate inflation measures, but many users will consult this publication for just that information unless libraries discard past issues. To fully master the data requires some study, but even casual researchers will find this an important resource.

2-34. BRIDGE Commodity Research Bureau. *CRB Commodity Yearbook.* Annual. New York: John Wiley and Sons, 1939–. ISSN: 1076-2906.

Known formerly as the *Commodity Yearbook*, this annual volume keeps the reader up to date in regard to commodity statistics. Introductory material informs the user about commodity trends and provides help in understanding the commodities market. The bulk of the volume, however, is devoted to individual commodities, arrayed alphabetically, from aluminum to zinc, not excluding coffee, corn, rice, pork bellies, and the like. Each commodity receives from one to several pages of discussion. This includes text describing the current status of the commodity as well as tables of relevant statistics. Data is displayed for as much as ten years prior to the current volume. Brief reference is made to

sources for statistical data. In addition, graphs display futures performances for each commodity, often for many decades past. This standard source has a twofold value: researchers familiar with commodities can consult it for reasonably indepth information pertinent to this economic arena, while students can use it for basic information applicable to the major commodities.

2-35. *Employment and Training Reporter: The Journal of Record in Job Training since 1969.* Weekly. Washington, DC: Manpower Information, 1969–. Index. ISSN: 0146–9673.

This loose-leaf service is aimed at those practitioners and academicians who wish to stay abreast of developments in the field of employment and employment training. Each weekly issue includes three sections. The first, "WashingtonGram," reports on recent developments within the federal government in regard to employment. A second section, "Current National Developments," summarizes events and trends from locales around the United States. The final section, "Text," reprints information published by the federal government. Sometimes, this consists of text of announcements, while in other cases, statistics or data maps are reprinted. Access to the weekly issues is provided by a cumulative index. This is a publication aimed at a fairly specialized audience, for whom it is beneficial; students, on the other hand, are less likely to find it of value unless they are patient enough to master the vocabulary or background required for optimum use of this source.

2-36. *Prices and Earnings around the Globe.* Irregular. Zurich, Switzerland: Union Bank of Switzerland, 1971–.

Produced by the Economic Research Department of the Union Bank of Switzerland, this little publication is a handy source for both data and background on comparative prices and earnings in major cities around the world. According to the foreword, data is gathered by two teams working independently in each of the cities. The number of cities involved is fifty-six; all represent locales frequented by members of the international business community. The initial portion of the text provides overview information highlighting the most expensive cities, comparative working hours, and other illuminating tidbits. The bulk of the text then provides comparative data in regard to food prices, clothing prices, public transport, hotels, and the like. The third section discusses comparisons of wages. Finally, comparative data is provided for all fifty-six cities in terms of income and working hours for a number of white-collar and blue-collar occupations. In many instances, index figures are used for comparative purposes rather than dollar amounts. For that reason, the reader will have to put in a bit of thought to determine an everyday figure for costs. The Internet now has available calculators that allow easy calculation for cost of living from one city to another, but this booklet retains its value, for it allows comparisons that provide a better overall picture of cost-of-living differences in major markets worldwide.

2-37. *World Cost of Living Survey.* 2nd ed. Detroit: Gale Group, 1999. 619 pp. ISBN: 0-787-62470-5.

This compilation provides approximately 30,000 prices for nearly 4,000 goods and services found in 741 locales in the world. The arrangement is alphabetical by country. In many instances, there are multiple entries representing the nation as a whole and/or individual major cities within a given nation. Among the items generally covered are "Clothing and Accessories," "Groceries," "Household Goods and Services," and "Recreation and Entertainment." Standard items provided for each category include value (in U.S. dollars) per number or size, the date of the data, and a reference number that corresponds to a bibliography of sources at the back. Some of the data is drawn from standard U.S. government sources, but some is derived from magazine articles and Web sites. Published in monograph form as it is, this work can only provide a snapshot of prices rather than up-to-date listings; however, it is useful for comparison purposes if the reader finds the time in reporting to be acceptable.

2-38. International Labour Office. *Yearbook of Labour Statistics.* Annual. Geneva: International Labour Office, 1935–. Index. ISSN: 0084-3857.

One of a number of standard statistical yearbooks published by international agencies, this publication provides detailed information in regard to labor markets. The statistical tables are arranged into a number of broad categories, such as employment, wages, and consumer prices. Within each of these major categories, there are a number of tables devoted to more specific subjects and that provide data on a country-by-country basis. Rather than an alphabetical arrangement, the nations are grouped by continent or region. Whenever possible, data is provided for each of the most recent ten years. A somewhat complicated index allows the reader to determine page references for each table in which an individual nation is represented. Informational text appears in English, French, and Spanish. Since 1992, the *Yearbook* has appeared with a second volume entitled *Sources and Methods*. Each is focused upon a single topic, such as consumer price indexes; collectively, they provide in-depth explanations of the methodologies behind the compilation of the data for the *Yearbook*. During intervals between publications of the yearbooks, the reader can find updated information in the *Bulletin of Labor Statistics*.

Directories

2-39. Gifford, Courtney D., ed. *Directory of U.S. Labor Organizations.* Annual. Washington, DC: Bureau of National Affairs, 1982–. Indexes. ISSN: 0734-6786.

Foremost a directory of the AFL-CIO, this reference source provides information on labor unions external to the AFL-CIO in a somewhat incidental fashion.

Well over half the text provides information on the AFL-CIO and its component bodies, including regional and state units, and Central Labor Councils within the states. These listings are relatively brief, including the name of the unit, its address and phone number, and a contact person, often the president of the unit. These entries are followed by a list of national labor organizations arranged alphabetically by keyword. Here, the detail is somewhat greater; in addition to the usual contact information, one can find listings of officers, titles of publications (if any), brief information on conventions, and membership numbers. Three indexes provide access to the various directories. The first is a listing by abbreviations, the second a listing of unions by common name, and the third a listing of officers. The last two indexes are somewhat awkward. For example, in the common-name index, labor organizations are listed by keyword. Thus, one must look under "Education Association, National" rather than "National Education Association" to find the page reference for this group. The listing of officers gives only a page reference without indication of affiliation, forcing the reader to scan through the entire page to find the officer in question. These caveats aside, this is an inexpensive resource for basic directory information on labor unions.

2-40. Craft, Donna, and Terrance W. Peck, eds. *Profiles of American Labor Unions.* 2nd ed. Detroit: Gale Research, 1998. 1650 pp. Indexes. ISBN: 0-810-39059-0.

Formerly known as the *American Directory of Organized Labor,* this reference volume provides basic information on American labor unions. The bulk of the work describes "Parent Unions." Here, the reader finds contact information, listings of important officials, financial data, and a description of that union's activities and history. The depth of this information varies from union to union. Also included is a listing of that union's bargaining agreements and contact information for state and local affiliates. This lengthy section is followed by briefer components that deal with independent unions, bargaining agreements arranged by employer, biographies of approximately 170 past and present labor officials, and several indexes. Among the latter are listings by industry, by geography, of officials, and a master index. Altogether, this work describes about 300 major unions and represents a good starting point for those researchers requiring contact information or basic background in regard to particular unions.

Dictionaries

2-41. Shim, Jae K., and Joel G. Siegel. *Dictionary of Economics.* Business Dictionary Series. New York: John Wiley and Sons, 1995. 373 pp. ISBN: 0-471-01317-X.

The goal of this reference volume, as stated in the preface, is to address an audience of "businesspeople and students wishing to understand the use of economic terminology in their work or study." Its intent is to approach economics from the viewpoint of everyday situations rather than theory. Entries are generally brief, usually one or two sentences. More important or more complex topics, however, receive up to a column. Cross-references are shown in italics. There are a number of diagrams and other graphic displays. An appendix includes nine tables of statistical values, such as "The Future Value of $1.00" and "Standard Normal Distribution." Compared to other economics dictionaries and encyclopedias, this is probably a better starting point for beginning students, given its emphasis upon business economics and definitions easily understood by the layperson. Inevitably, some concepts are so business-centered that full understanding by the reader presupposes a working knowledge of basic statistics and business mathematics.

2-42. Murray, R. Emmett. *Lexicon of Labor.* New York: New Press, 1998. 208 pp. ISBN: 1-565-84456-4.

As the subtitle states, this work contains "more than 500 key terms, biographical sketches, and historical insights concerning labor in America." It is Murray's contention that fewer and fewer Americans understand the language of labor; his compilation intends to assist those who need to acquaint themselves with it. The arrangement is alphabetical and includes entries for legislation, legal terminology, major unions, important individuals, and labor history. Some entries are short, no more than a sentence, but more significant topics receive a couple of pages of explanation. Cross-references are indicated in boldface. Occasional small illustrations, often of individuals, supplement the text. Among the appendixes are a listing of major unions and an annotated bibliography arranged by title. Although brief in nature, this reference work is a useful starting point for those lacking knowledge of the U.S. labor movement.

2-43. Eatwell, John, Murray Milgate, and Peter Newman, eds. *The New Palgrave: A Dictionary of Economics*. 4 vols. London: Macmillan, 2002. Indexes. ISBN: 0-935-85910-1.

The interaction of economics and the law holds interest for political scientists and government employees dealing with regulation, so this specialized encyclopedia will be of help to those groups. The set is arranged alphabetically and includes almost 400 essays averaging about 5,000 words in length. Typical essay topics include "Adoption," "Antitrust Policy," "Immigration Policy," "Privacy," and "Sexual Harassment." Cross-references and bibliographies conclude each essay, along with citations to relevant statutes and cases as necessary. There is no index, but each volume includes an alphabetical listing of entries and cross-references, as well as a subject-classification scheme divided into seven categories, with relevant articles further classified within each of the seven categories. The final volume also includes page references to statutes, treaties, directives, and cases. The contributors are drawn from the international academic community; many are affiliated with law schools. Although this work does attempt to avoid too much emphasis upon theory, the text

is definitely more suitable for knowledgeable researchers than it is for novice students.

2-44. Newman, Peter, Murray Milgate, and John Eatwell, eds. *New Palgrave Dictionary of Money and Finance*. 3 vols. New York: Palgrave Macmillan, 1992. ISBN: 1-561-59 041-X.

A companion to *The New Palgrave: A Dictionary of Economics* [entry 2-43], this set concentrates upon money and finance, two separate disciplines despite their obvious overlap. One of the aims of the set is to indicate both the similarities and differences between the two topics; another is to present articles that demonstrate both theoretical and applied work, with the latter including policy analysis and descriptions of institutions. The major difference between this and the companion set is the fact that *Money and Finance* presents no biographies among its 1,000 essays. The basic arrangement of the set is alphabetical, although a list of all entries, including cross-references, appears at the beginning of each volume. Articles range in length from a single page to several. Cross-references are listed at the end of each, along with a bibliography. Articles are signed by the contributors, who, with their affiliation, appear at the end of the third volume, which also has a subject-classification scheme, grouping all the essays into twelve categories. Graphic displays appear as necessary. There is no general index, so the reader must rely upon the cross-references, listing of entries, and the classification scheme in order to find his or her way about the set. In general, the articles are technical to the extent that this set will be of value to specialists and scholars more than to laypeople and beginning students.

2-45. Rutherford, Donald. *Routledge Dictionary of Economics.* 2nd ed. London: Routledge, 2002. 671 pp. Index. ISBN: 0-415-25091-9.

This truly is a dictionary rather than a miniature encyclopedia; most entries are brief, perhaps no more than a sentence or a short paragraph. The longer entries range up to a column in length. The author compiled his terminology by consulting economics textbooks, specialist studies, journals, and newspapers. For that reason, entries include some topics peculiar to economics itself and others more familiar to the general layperson. Cross-references are shown in boldface, and many entries include one or more bibliographic references. Each entry is also assigned a classification number derived from a scheme used by the British *Economic Journal.* This classification scheme serves as a kind of index; by consulting the subject-classification index at the back of the volume, the reader can see what entries have been assigned to each number. For example, "Agriculture" is assigned the number 710 and has almost fifty articles in the dictionary. There are no illustrations other than the usual economics diagrams. Although the author is British, there does not seem to be an undue emphasis upon circumstances in the United Kingdom. Economics students and professionals are the most likely beneficiaries

of this reference work, but the general writing style is such that nonspecialists can also consult it with profit.

Encyclopedias

2-46. Northrup, Cynthia Clark, ed. *The American Economy: A Historical Encyclopedia.* 2 vols. Santa Barbara, CA: ABC-CLIO, 2003. 709 pp. Index. ISBN: 1-576-07866-3.

This set emphasizes the "formation and development of economic policy throughout American history" (Northrup 2003, introduction). The first volume is an alphabetical array of short articles, usually about half a page, on subjects such as "Bank Failures," "Forty Acres and a Mule," and "Oil Embargos." There are also biographies of noteworthy individuals and descriptions of particular depressions and "panics." The second volume provides essays of several pages in length on topics such as "Antitrust Legislation," "Big Business and Government Relationships," "Labor," and "Taxation." In addition, the second volume provides texts of primary sources ranging from the Ordinance of the Northwest Territory (1787) to remarks by Ronald Reagan during the air traffic controllers' strike in 1981. The writing style is suitable for undergraduates. This set is somewhat similar to the *Gale Encyclopedia of U.S. Economic History* [entry 2-50], but is preferable as a starting point when researchers need a thematic overview as provided by the essays found in this encyclopedia. 💻

2-47. Kurz, Heinz D., and Neri Salvadori, eds. *Elgar Companion to Classi-*

cal Economics. 2 vols. Northampton, MA: Edward Elgar, 1998. 1056 pp. Index. ISBN: 1-858-98282-0.

As interpreted in this volume, "classical economics" refers to theories prevalent before the twentieth century. Entries are arranged alphabetically and can be categorized into five areas. There are entries on classical economic authors, analytical issues raised by them, past interpreters of classical authors, recent interpretations, and classical economics as exemplified in major countries. Typical articles include "Circular Flow," "Competition," "Corn Model," "Falling Rate of Profit," and "Invisible Hand." Articles average about five pages in length. Each of the volumes has a name index, and bibliographies are provided at the end of the articles. Contributors are drawn from the international academic community and include scholars from Canada, France, the United States, and many from Italy. The audience for this work will be advanced students and academicians with a working knowledge of economics.

2-48. Porter, Glenn. *Encyclopedia of American Economic History: Studies of the Principal Movements and Ideas.* 3 vols. New York: Macmillan Reference, 1980. 1285 pp. Index. ISBN: 0-684-16271-7.

Economics, like the law, is often a puzzle for both laypersons and students. Nevertheless, economic history is an important component of the American scene, with its emphasis upon material goods. This encyclopedia approaches the subject from a topical framework rather than an alphabetical arrangement of entries. There are five major parts to the encyclopedia: "The Historiography of American Economic History," "The Chronology of American Economic History," "The Framework of American Economic Growth," "The Institutional Framework," and "The Social Framework." Each of these major parts includes a number of separate articles. For example, articles on technology, transportation, and agriculture, among others, appear in the part dealing with the framework of economic growth, while articles on the family, women, and blacks appear in the part dealing with the social framework. Cross-references are provided at the end of each article, and there is a comprehensive index in the final volume to help guide the reader to the appropriate article. The contributors are U.S. academicians in the economics and history fields; each has provided the reader with a useful annotated bibliography at the end of his or her article. There are no illustrations other than tables and graphs. In general, the level of writing will be accessible to undergraduates as well as to scholars. Given the date this set was published, many users may wish to look for new material to supplement information found here.

2-49. Henderson, David R. *Fortune Encyclopedia of Economics.* New York: Warner Books, 1993. 876 pp. Index. ISBN: 0-446-51637-6.

In his preface, Henderson states that economists agree among themselves more frequently than is commonly perceived. This work sets out to indicate those areas of agreement as well as topics on which they disagree. The arrangement is topical rather than alphabetical. Fourteen chapters cover basic concepts, macroeconomics, taxes, money and banking, and the marketplace, among others. Each chapter includes a number of sections written by a specialist in the field. These contributors include journalists as well as economists. Each of the contributor sections includes a bibliography. There are no illustrations other than tables. A separate section at the back of the volume includes biographies of well-known economists as well as listings such as winners of the Nobel Prize in economics. Users of the volume will benefit by consulting both the table of contents and the index to find topics of interest. In general, the writing style is quite accessible to the nonspecialist; this is probably one of the better reference works on economics in terms of usability for beginning students.

2-50. Carson, Thomas, ed. *Gale Encyclopedia of U.S. Economic History.* 2 vols. Farmington Hills, MI: Gale Group, 1999. 1250 pp. Index. ISBN: 0-787-63888-9.

Slightly over 1,000 articles appear in this set, arranged alphabetically. About half the entries are definitions of economic, historical, and geographic terms. The rest of the articles deal with "overviews, issues, biographies, state economic histories, historical events, and company and industry histories" (Carson 1999, preface). These types of articles are usually a page or more in length and conclude with

a bibliography for additional reading. Chronologically, this set begins with the precolonial era and encompasses the emergence of the Internet in the 1990s. Examples of articles include "Corn," "Steamboats," "Brooklyn Bridge," "Transcontinental Railroad," and "United Farm Workers." In addition, there are ten articles that describe U.S. history during its different eras; the placement of these is awkward, for they are arranged alphabetically by entry rather than being sequestered in a separate section. There are numerous illustrations and cross-references. The writing style is suitable for both undergraduate and high-school students. This is a valuable work, discussing as it does topics that are often excluded from history reference works. Researchers should also consult *The American Economy: A Historical Encyclopedia* [entry 2-46].

2-51. Greenwald, Douglas, ed. *McGraw-Hill Encyclopedia of Economics.* 2nd ed. New York: McGraw-Hill, 1994. 1093 pp. Indexes. ISBN: 0-070-24410-3.

The first edition of this reference work appeared in 1981; this second edition incorporates changes in events and scholarship that occurred in the intervening years. The approximately 300 articles each receive several pages of treatment. Typical entries include "Cost of Living," "Factors of Production," and "Marginal Revenue." Cross-references to other articles appear at the end of each entry, as does a listing of bibliographic references. Articles are signed by the contributor, with a list of the contributors and their affiliations appearing at the front of the volume. There are indexes of both names and subjects. There are no illustrations other than occasional charts, graphs, and tables. The preface states that the goal of this single-volume work is to provide "meaningful and useful articles, written by the experts, on the most important subjects in economics and related fields." Contributors were encouraged to write for a graduate-student level or above, so this is not a resource to be recommended to beginning students. Practitioners and informed students and laypeople will find it of value, and one does not necessarily need to be an economics expert to understand most of the content.

2-52. Magill, Frank N., ed. *Survey of Social Science: Economics Series.* 5 vols. Pasadena, CA: Salem Press, 1991. 2494 pp. Index. ISBN: 0-893-56725-6.

This was the first set published in the Survey of Social Science series. Like the others, this set follows a standard format. The arrangement is alphabetical, with entries on subjects such as "Credit," "Exports and Imports," "Housing Economics," "Inventory," and "Leisure Class." Altogether, there are 393 articles dealing with issues in economic theory, economic systems, microeconomics, macroeconomics, and the like. Each article begins with summaries and definitions, followed by an overview, information on applications of the topic in practice, and contextual information. A bibliography and cross-references conclude the article. Each of the five volumes also includes two listings of all the articles, with one listing arranged by category and the other alphabetically. The final volume includes a glossary and a comprehensive index. Despite the potential complexity of this discipline, the writing style is accessible to general readers, including high-school and college students. Indeed, any researcher requiring basic and nontechnical explanations of economic matters can consult this work.

Guides and Handbooks

2-53. Darnay, Arsen J., ed. *Economic Indicators Handbook: Time Series, Conversions, Documentation.* 6th ed. Detroit: Gale Research, 2002. 1154 pp. Index. ISBN: 0-787-63557-X.

As stated in the introduction, the intent of this volume is to present "a wide range of statistical series commonly used for measuring the economy of the United States." Major statistical categories include gross national product, gross domestic product, business cycle indicators, cyclic indicators, economic series, consumer price index, producer price index, and stock market price indexes. Within the category for consumer prices, data is presented for U.S. city averages as well as for twenty-seven important metropolitan areas around the country, from Anchorage, Alaska, to Washington, D.C. The producer price index is also a category with much detail, as it presents statistics dealing with a number of agricultural and manufactured commodities. Most times series extend back to the 1940s; in some cases, data is available almost to the beginning of the twentieth century. Access to the statistics is provided by a very detailed table of contents as well as by a brief keyword index. Statistical tables are derived from federal government sources, and, in fact, most appear to be reproduced verbatim from those sources. Nevertheless, this is a useful quick source for historical data that might not otherwise be available without searching through a number of publications.

2-54. Plocek, Joseph E. *Economic Indicators: How America Reads Its Financial Health.* New York: New York Institute of Finance, 1991. 396 pp. Index. ISBN: 0-136-26896-X.

The federal government publishes a multitude of economic indicators on almost a daily basis, yet these measures are no doubt mysterious to many outside the spheres of business and economics. This volume takes a textbook approach to the topic, describing major indicators in a style that is both serious but accessible to the layperson. For example, the reader interested in the producer price index can turn to that name in the index to find the appropriate page references that include a discussion of the measurement complete with graphic displays to further elucidate the subject. Some of the major categories for indicators include employment, personal income, consumption, the industrial sector, construction, exports, monetary policy, and prices. Some indicators come from sources other than the federal government. One of the strengths of this volume is the fact that it discusses the uses and significance of the measures as well as describing them. A

final chapter shows the reader the "big picture" by indicating the role played by the Federal Reserve and the gross national product in the economy. A glossary and a ten-page list of references round out the text. This is a handy source for all levels of researchers, but of course it does not take into account happenings in the 1990s, including the dissemination of economic indicators through electronic resources such as the Internet.

2-55. Kurian, George Thomas. *Global Data Locator.* Lanham, MD: Bernan Press, 1997. 375 pp. Index. ISBN: 0-890-59039-7.

This extraordinarily useful reference book describes major world statistical sources appearing in both print and electronic formats. Descriptions are provided for "240 statistical publications published by both official and commercial organizations" (Kurian 1997, introduction). Information for print sources includes publisher, purpose, scope, data organization, methodology, and a listing of contents. The latter is often quite detailed. Information for electronic sources is somewhat similar in nature, providing the reader with publisher contact information and a description of content, coverage, time span, and updating. Descriptions of statistical sources are arranged into print and electronic categories, with a breakdown by subject within each. Consultation of the lengthy table of contents will assist the reader in finding sources by subject. Appendixes provide information on publishers and their products. The reader can also consult the index to find page references for individual entries for each of the 240 publications described; there is no subject access through the index, however. If this volume is updated on a regular basis, it will continue to be a handy guide to statistical publications; otherwise, it will date quickly.

2-56. Frumkin, Norman. *Guide to Economic Indicators.* rev. and exp. 3rd ed. Armonk, NY: M. E. Sharpe, 2000. 328 pp. Index. ISBN: 0-765-60436-1.

Frumkin, an economic consultant, here describes approximately "60 statistical measures of the performance of the American economy" (2000, preface). Most are gathered by federal government sources, but there are also descriptions of measures from other entities, such as the University of Michigan, Dun and Bradstreet, and the Conference Board. Each receives a description up to several pages in length; tables often accompany the text. References are given to the original source for the data, including the time of its issuance. There is a detailed table of contents, a listing of illustrations, and a reasonably detailed index, all of which assist the reader in locating the desired indicator. The author indicates that his work is aimed at both economists and those without an economics background. Compared to the volume by Plocek [entry 2-54], this publication is perhaps more readily understood by the layperson. The contents would have been strengthened had a separate listing of all the indicators been provided, and of course it does not reflect changes

wrought by the recent use of electronic means to distribute this type of data.

2-57. Rogers, R. Mark. *Handbook of Key Economic Indicators.* 2nd ed. New York: McGraw-Hill, 1998. 303 pp. Index. ISBN: 0-070-54045-4.

This second edition takes into consideration changes that have occurred in the issuance of economic indicators since the first edition was published in 1994. Among other happenings, the U.S. Commerce Department has handed over composite indicators to the Conference Board. The audience of this volume is intended to be "market analysts and investors who want to improve their expertise and ability to correctly gauge the strength and direction of the economy" (Rogers 1998, preface). Each major indicator receives a chapter-length discussion. Among the indicators are the familiar consumer price index, producer price index, and indicators relating to construction, industrial production, and gross domestic product. Numerous graphs and statistical tables accompany the text, and each chapter ends with footnotes and a bibliography. Those readers not wishing or needing the thorough technical analysis provided within each chapter can probably obtain the basic information they desire by simply reading the introductory paragraphs for the appropriate chapter. Thanks to its timeliness, this is the preferred source for information pertaining to economic indicators.

2-58. Dodd, Donald B., comp. *Historical Statistics of the States of the United States:*

Two Centuries of the Census, 1790–1990. Westport, CT: Greenwood Press, 1993. 578 pp. ISBN: 0-313-28309-5.

As stated in the preface, this volume is a "census-focused compilation of state-level population, agriculture, and manufacturing data for the fifty states and the District of Columbia." The statistics are compiled from standard government sources, so the real value of this work is the fact that it presents two centuries of historical data in a single place, eliminating the need to consult a number of separate works when certain basic time series are needed. For each census of population, eighteen pieces of data are provided for each state, including total population. Time series for agriculture number twenty-seven, while statistics presented for manufacturing are eighteen in number. Tables are arranged by state rather than by statistical category. A table at the back of the volume provides populations for cities that numbered over 100,000 inhabitants in 1990; for older cities, this data extends as far back as 1790. The preface explains problems inherent in earlier censuses and describes the relation of this work to the federal government publications from which it was compiled. Those researchers seeking historical statistics for the individual states will find this to be a valuable resource.

2-59. Lerner, William, ed. U.S. Department of Commerce. Bureau of the Census. *Historical Statistics of the United States, Colonial Times to 1970.* 2 vols. Washington, DC: Diane Pub., 2001. 1263 pp. Index. ISBN: 0-756-71571-7.

Published as part of the nation's bicentennial, this two-volume set presents more than 12,500 time series. The introduction states that *Historical Statistics* has two objectives: "assembling, selecting, and arranging data from hundreds of sources and making them available within a single source" and the use of annotations to refer the reader to "sources of greater detail." The two volumes include twenty-four chapters arranged by subject. Examples include population, labor, agriculture, transportation, energy, and government. Each group of statistical tables within the chapters is supplemented with text material that explains the data and refers the reader to the sources from which it was compiled. The index assists the user in locating subjects of interest. Most of the data pertains to more traditional topics, such as politics, economics, and business measurements, rather than to cultural and social measures. Still, this is an invaluable resource, one that can be used by both beginning students and advanced researchers.

2-60. National Safety Council. *International Accident Facts.* Annual. 2nd ed. Itasca, IL: National Safety Council. 106 pp. ISBN: 0-879-12205-6.

The National Safety Council for many years has published *Accident Facts*, an annual compilation of statistical data pertaining to accidents in the United States. Now it has moved into the field of international comparisons. *Interna-*

tional *Accident Facts* has three components. The first is a section entitled "International Comparisons," which uses a combination of text and colorful graphics to demonstrate accident trends internationally. The second component is a series of tables that shows statistics themselves for the countries in question. Typical categories include deaths from various causes (such as fire, drowning, or motor vehicles), injuries and deaths in the workplace, and work time lost to accidents. The final component is an arrangement of text and graphics on a country-by-country basis. The three sections are color coded so that the user can easily flip from one to the other, and text is presented in three languages: English, French, and Spanish. Sources are noted, and mention is made of the difficulty in gathering and comparing data on an international basis. About eighty countries are included in the comparisons; third world nations are somewhat underrepresented, probably due to a lack of data. For those needing accident statistics for nations other than the United States, this is an excellent starting point.

2-61. Mitchell, B. R. *International Historical Statistics: Africa, Asia and Oceania, 1750–2001.* 4th ed. New York: Palgrave Macmillan, 2003. 1144 pp. ISBN: 0-333-99412-4.

This compilation of historical data will be of value to those researchers needing basic statistics on subjects such as population, labor force, industry, finance, and others. Format and intent are very similar to that of other volumes in this series

covering the Americas and Europe (described below). Data for Russia appears in the volume for Europe rather than in this one.

2-62. Mitchell, B. R. *International Historical Statistics: Europe, 1750–2000.* 5th ed. New York: Palgrave Macmillan, 2003. 942 pp. ISBN: 0-333-99411-6.

Similar to other volumes in the International Historical Statistics series described previously, this work presents statistics for the countries of Europe beginning with the year 1750. Mitchell explains that this date was chosen because data for earlier time periods is too incomplete to be satisfactory. The introduction explains methodology for the gathering of the data and the problems involved in statistical comparisons over a period of years and a number of different political entities. The statistical tables are arranged into ten major categories, including topics such as population, agriculture, industry, prices, and education. Reference is made to the sources of the data in explanatory text and footnotes. There is no index, so the reader must rely upon the table of contents to find the data in question. Like the other volumes in this series, this can be recommended to those researchers requiring a handy compilation of basic historical statistics for the nations of Europe.

2-63. Mitchell, B. R. *International Historical Statistics: The Americas, 1750–2000.* 5th ed. New York: Palgrave

Macmillan, 2003. 856 pp. ISBN: 0-333-99410-8.

Reference books that compile and reformat statistics are numerous; this is one of the better entries in the field. One of a series of volumes that collects historical statistics on a continental basis, this work presents statistics regarding the nation-states of North and South America. The introduction explains the complexities that accompany the gathering of statistics from a number of different national sources over a period of time measured in centuries. The various nations seldom use the same parameters in the compilation of statistics, complicating comparison among them. Changes in boundaries and in currencies add to the complexity. Still, this is a source to which researchers can turn for a good deal of basic historical data. Major statistical categories include population and vital statistics, labor force, agriculture, industry, external trade, transport and communications, finance, prices, education, and national accounts. Hence, coverage concentrates on demographics and business and economic measures rather than on social and cultural comparisons. Explanatory text and footnotes accompany each table. Sources are indicated; in general, they are major official statistical abstracts, not the more detailed publications produced by many government agencies. There is no index, so the user must rely upon the table of contents to find the statistical information of interest to him or her. This fifth edition omits climate tables found in earlier editions.

2-64. Lavin, Michael R. *Understanding the Census: A Guide for Marketers, Planners, Grant Writers and Other Data Users.* Kenmore, NY: Epoch Books, 1996. 545 pp. Index. ISBN: 0-962-95861-1.

The 1990 census represents a formidable and confusing body of statistics, but this volume is an excellent resource for those seeking to understand both the data itself and the publications in which it appears. Lavin has a threefold purpose: "to explain Census concepts, methods, terminology, and data sources in an understandable manner; to assist Census users in locating needed Census data; and to impress upon readers how easy it is to use inappropriate figures, or to interpret appropriate numbers incorrectly" (1996, preface). The various chapters introduce the U.S. Census, explain its terminology, discuss its print and electronic publications, and describe methods for locating data. Many graphics and sidebars accompany the text, which is reasonably understandable to general readers given the complexity of the subject. Any researcher struggling with the 1990 census should consult this reference work as a likely source for answers.

2-65. Derks, Scott, ed. *Value of a Dollar: Millennium Edition.* 3rd ed. Millerton, NY: Grey House Publishing, 2004. 664 pp. ISBN: 1-592-37074-8.

Inquiries regarding purchasing power at different times during the history of the United States are fairly common; this volume provides a wealth of information to answer that question for both the specialist and the beginning student. The basic format of the volume is chronological, with separate sections for two or more decades from 1860 through 1989. Each section includes an introductory essay; a chronological listing of events; prices and values for investments, income, wages, and food; "Selected Prices," a compilation of prices for individual items advertised during the epoch in question; and "Standard Prices," a tracking of prices for individual consumer items over a range of several years. The cautious researcher will check the prices for a particular era against the hourly and weekly wages for annual incomes that are displayed for typical occupations, thus getting a better notion of the actual cost to contemporaries. For example, the fact that a new automobile cost as little as $1,500 in 1954 must be measured against the fact that the average annual income was approximately $4,000 at that same time period. It is now possible to find calculators on the Internet that will display the value of a dollar for many past years against current values. Nevertheless, this volume continues to be of use for the detail it provides on the income earned by the average American and the prices once paid for consumer goods.

Education

For reference purposes, the strength in this field for decades has been the ERIC reporting system, funded by the federal government. ERIC is currently undergoing dramatic restructuring. Also of interest are the numerous encyclopedias, both single volume and multivolume, that pertain to this field. Some provide an overview, while others address themselves to particular subject areas; coverage is available for both the United States and for other nations.

Literature Guides

2-66. Berry, Dorothea M. *A Bibliographic Guide to Educational Research.* 3rd ed. Metuchen, NJ: Scarecrow Press, 1990. 500 pp. Indexes. ISBN: 0-810-82343-8.

Berry, formerly a librarian at the University of California, Riverside, includes 1,050 entries in this edition of a work first published in 1980. The contents are divided into seven major categories: books, periodicals, research studies, government publications, special materials (such as children's literature and textbooks), other reference materials, and information on writing research papers. For some reason, about 30 items are relegated to sections for addenda or appendixes. Most entries receive descriptive annotations. There are three indexes, by subject, title, and author/editor/compiler. This guide is suitable for students as well as for more advanced scholars, but it is now severely outdated thanks to advances in electronic resources, so the user is advised to seek out newer bibliographic guides to supplement information found here.

Abstracting and Indexing Services

2-67. *ERIC.* Monthly. Rockville, MD: U.S. Department of Education, ERIC

Processing and Reference Facility, 1966–. Indexes.

For decades, the *ERIC* indexing system has been a standby for professionals in the field of education as a search aid for finding literature both published and unpublished. It includes two components, each appearing monthly. The first, *Resources in Education* (RIE), provides annotated references to full-text documents submitted to the ERIC central office. Historically, these have been placed on microfiche cards that can be found in many libraries. This component provides national access to lesson plans and other documents produced locally. The second component, *Current Index to Journals in Education* (CIJE), is an index to approximately 2,000 journals in the discipline. Almost one million items are now represented in the system. *ERIC* was one of the first major indexing services to become available in a CD-ROM format in the 1980s and now is available online through several vendors. *ERIC* is undergoing a number of changes during the course of the George W. Bush administrations, and its future is unclear. For example, as of the autumn of 2004, the intent was to exclude lesson plans from the database. Nevertheless, no researcher in the field of education can afford to ignore this resource.

2-68. *Higher Education Abstracts.* Quarterly. Claremont, CA: Claremont Graduate University, 1965–. Indexes. ISSN: 0748-4364.

This service presents well over a thousand abstracts annually in regard to higher education. Major topic areas include students, faculty, administration, and general issues pertaining to the field, such as enrollment, external relations, learning and teaching, and instructional programs. Most of the sources abstracted are relevant journals, but there is also coverage of association papers and monographs. Each of the quarterly issues includes separate indexes by author and subject; these cumulate in the final issue of the year. Also included in each issue is a listing of the journals that are regularly reviewed. Abstracts are descriptive, not evaluative. This service, formerly known as *College Student Personnel Abstracts,* will be of interest to those researchers who desire a greater focus upon higher education than that found in *ERIC* [entry 2-67].

2-69. *Special Educational Needs Abstracts.* Quarterly. Abingdon, Oxfordshire, UK: Carfax Publishing, 1989–. Indexes. ISSN: 0954-0822.

"Special needs education" is defined rather broadly in this abstracting service to include physical, intellectual, emotional, and social problems and handicaps of both children and adults. Between 400 and 500 abstracts are published annually. Most are drawn from journals published in the English-speaking world. Abstracts are descriptive rather than evaluative. Each of the quarterly issues includes indexes by both author and subject, and a listing of the journals abstracted, including their addresses. The final issue of the year includes cumulative indexing. This specialized service will be of interest primarily to specialists in the field of education working with those who have special needs.

Directories

2-70. Cabell, David W. E., ed. *Cabell's Directory of Publishing Opportunities in Education.* 5th ed. 2 vols. Beaumont, TX: Cabell Publishing, 1998. 1319 pp. Index. ISBN: 0-911-75312-5.

Published periodically, this reference acquaints readers with journals in education and related fields, including librarianship. There are listings for approximately 440 journals, arranged alphabetically through the two volumes. Each listing includes extensive information that assists the prospective author with submission information. Each of the periodicals is also assigned one or more of twenty-seven subject headings. The index in the second volume is arranged by these headings, allowing the user to select those periodicals that fall within a particular area of interest.

2-71. Klebba, Caryn E., ed. *Directory of American Scholars.* 10th ed. 5 vols. Detroit: Gale Group, 2002. Indexes. ISBN: 0-787-65013-7.

First published in 1942 by the American Council of Learned Societies, this directory is a welcome replacement for the previous edition, published in 1982. The five volumes are arranged as follows: history; English, speech, and drama; foreign languages, linguistics, and philology; philosophy, religion, and law; and indexes. Approximately 24,000 scholars are included from both the United States

and Canada. Those listed were nominated by a variety of means and asked to fill out a questionnaire, with final inclusion based upon a number of achievements. Listings in each volume are arranged alphabetically and include personal information, specific discipline, education background, career information, honors and awards, memberships, research interests, selected publications, and address (including e-mail). Each volume includes a geographic index arranged by state or province and community. The final volume includes indexes by institution, geographic locale, and discipline, as well as a comprehensive alphabetical index. Those researchers needing brief biographical background on scholars in the humanities will turn to this set with appreciation.

2-72. *National Faculty Directory.* Annual. 3 vols. Detroit: Gale Research, 1971–. 4184 pp. ISSN: 0077-4472.

Long a standard directory, this publication continues to be a reasonably comprehensive listing of faculty members at higher education institutions in the United States and Canada. Approximately 3,600 American colleges and universities, and another 240 Canadian institutions are included; as of 1998, there were 670,000 individuals listed. All are teaching faculty who use instructional materials such as textbooks. In general, nonteaching faculty and librarians are excluded. The alphabetical listings include name, unit, institution, and street address. There are no phone numbers or e-mail listings. Each of the three volumes includes at the front a list of abbreviations as well as a roster of institutions that are encompassed in the directory. These are arranged by state and by province. Junior colleges and a number of vocational institutions are included along with the usual four-year colleges and universities. Individual listings for many faculty members can be obtained through the Internet, but this publication is still useful for its comprehensive approach.

Encyclopedias

2-73. Dejnozka, Edward L., and David E. Kapel. *American Educators Encyclopedia.* rev. ed. New York: Greenwood Press, 1991. 716 pp. Index. ISBN: 0-313-25269-6.

Unlike most encyclopedias, this work was written by the two authors with input from a panel of experts rather than relying upon contributors. Those involved are all associated with the higher education community. Articles are generally brief and are arranged alphabetically. Most are one or two paragraphs. Cross-references are provided to related topics, and each entry includes a list of references. There are about 2,000 entries "based on the names and terms frequently found in the literature of professional education" (Dejnozka and Kapel 1991, preface). There are only a handful of black-and-white illustrations, relating mostly to statistical terms. The intent of this work is to provide educators in the United States with a handy single-volume reference to topics of general concern or to needed background. For those requiring information current as of the early

1990s or that has not changed, this will be a useful source; other users may wish to consult more up-to-date volumes.

2-74. Unger, Harlow G. *Encyclopedia of American Education.* 2nd ed. 3 vols. New York: Facts on File, 2001. 1350 pp. Index. ISBN: 0-816-04344-2.

This encyclopedia is essentially the work of Unger, assisted by an editorial board of seven individuals in the field of education. The arrangement is alphabetical, and most entries are relatively short, from a paragraph to a page in length. Some, such as those dealing with athletics or at-risk students, are somewhat longer. The author has attempted to cover the broad range of education, including "administration, pedagogy, history, reform, and such complex problems as child labor, church-state conflicts, civil rights, minority education and women's education" (Unger 2001, preface). There are numerous short biographies of individuals influential in the American education establishment from colonial times to the present. Occasional illustrations and photographs supplement the text. All articles, even those that are quite brief, conclude with one or more references to the source for the information. In addition, a forty-page bibliography appears in the final volume, along with a chronology and a listing of federal education enactments from 1787 through 1993. This final volume also includes an appendix of significant Supreme Court decisions. While the information in this set tends to be brief rather than comprehensive, this encyclopedia is more up to date than some of the competition and is also suitable for both high-school and college students.

2-75. Williams, Leslie R., and Doris Pronin Fromberg, eds. *Encyclopedia of Early Childhood Education.* Garland Reference Library of the Social Sciences, Vol. 504. Hamden, CT: Garland, 1992. 518 pp. Index. ISBN: 0-824-04626-9.

The field of early childhood education, as defined here, includes the education and care of children through the age of eight, the training of the adults who work with them, relevant policy issues, and material resources. Rather than an alphabetical array of articles, the arrangement of this volume is by topic. The six chapters provide a general introduction; an examination of the history and philosophy; social, cultural, political, and economic contexts; curricula; and perspectives on children and educators alike. Each chapter begins with an outline of its contents, allowing the reader to determine those entries of immediate interest. Many entries are relatively brief, perhaps a page or two. Bibliographic references are included with each; some are fairly extensive. There are no illustrations. The writing style is suitable for undergraduate students and other researchers in higher education. This work will be a useful introduction for those new to the subject and will be of assistance to professional educators as well.

2-76. Guthrie, James W., ed. *Encyclopedia of Education.* 2nd ed. 8 vols. New York: Macmillan Reference, 2003. 3557 pp. Index. ISBN: 0-028-65594-X.

The first edition of this encyclopedia appeared in 1971 and obviously needed updating, so this new edition will be welcomed by educational researchers. The arrangement is alphabetical. Articles range in length from about a page to several pages. Some examples of topics include "Bilingual Education," "Catholic Schools," and "College and Its Effect on Students." There are also biographies of individuals influential in the field. The emphasis is upon the contemporary scene, but some historical background is also provided. Articles conclude with bibliographies. There are no illustrations other than occasional graphics. The final volume provides not only an index but also various appendixes. Court cases, Internet resources, and a listing of assessment and achievement tests are among the appendixes. The content and writing style of this encyclopedia is suitable for both undergraduate researchers and those with more advanced interests.

2-77. Alkin, Marvin C., ed. *Encyclopedia of Educational Research.* 7th ed. 4 vols. New York: Macmillan, 2001. 1606 pp. Index. ISBN: 0-028-64945-1.

As the title indicates, this encyclopedia aims to summarize the results of research in education rather than merely to describe the topic. The entries were selected based on their relevance and the extent to which research has actually been done. "Research" is defined broadly to include a variety of research methodologies, not just those based on experimental studies. Articles are arranged alphabetically and generally are at least several pages long. Typical subjects include elementary education, health services, job training programs, statistical methods, teaching effectiveness, and vocational education. Each article includes an extensive listing of references that in effect represent research on that topic. Articles are signed by the contributor and also include cross-references to other relevant articles. The only illustrations consist of statistical tables and graphic displays. A comprehensive index in the final volume provides additional access to the text. The writing style is scholarly in nature, so this is a source that will be of greater value to more advanced students than to beginners; nevertheless, this latest edition of a standard source is an excellent starting point for those delving into educational topics for in-depth research.

2-78. Clark, Burton R., and Guy R. Neave, eds. *Encyclopedia of Higher Education.* 4 vols. Oxford: Pergamon Press, 1992. 2530 pp. Indexes. ISBN: 0-080-37251-1.

Higher education as exemplified by universities has been in existence for eight centuries and has spread around the world. This set attempts a multilevel approach to the topic. Rather than an alphabetical arrangement, each volume has its own thematic approach. The first volume includes articles on higher education in each of the countries of the world. The second and third volumes are devoted to groupings of articles into five

"Analytical Perspectives." These include: "Higher Education and Society," "Institutional Fabric of the Higher Education System," "Governance, Administration, and Finance," "Faculty and Students: Teaching, Learning, and Research," and "Disciplinary Perspectives on Higher Education." Each of these categories is examined through a number of separate articles. The final volume is composed of articles that describe the major academic disciplines. In general, articles throughout the set are about ten to fifteen pages in length and include bibliographies. The final volume includes indexes to contributors, personal names, and subjects. As much as possible, contributors were drawn from the global education community. The writing style is scholarly in tone and is more suitable for college students and scholars than it is for high-school readers.

2-79. Reynolds, Cecil R., and Elaine Fletcher-Janzen, eds. *Encyclopedia of Special Education.* 2nd ed. 3 vols. New York: John Wiley and Sons, 2000. 1998 pp. Indexes. ISBN: 0-471-25309-X.

The first edition of this encyclopedia appeared in 1987; the second edition is generally similar, but reflects changes in multiculturalism, delivery of special-education services, expansion of those services, accountability, and the Internet. Of the 2,000 entries in the second edition, approximately 200 are completely new, and another 700 are updated or rewritten. The arrangement is alphabetical. Many entries are relatively short, perhaps a column in length, but more substantive subjects receive up to three pages of treatment. Many articles include a list of references for additional research. Cross-references to other entries are relatively scarce, and there are few illustrations. Most of the contributors are drawn from the U.S. academic community, but there is occasional representation from abroad as well. The final volume includes indexes by author and subject. The main audience for this work will be individuals in the special-education field, but the text is also accessible to undergraduate researchers as well.

2-80. Fagan, Thomas K., and Paul G. Warden. *Historical Encyclopedia of School Psychology.* Westport, CT: Greenwood Press, 1996. 464 pp. Index. ISBN: 0-313-29015-6.

School psychology is a relatively recent field, dating back to about 1930. This volume attempts to provide a source for school psychologists and other readers to find brief information on both historical and contemporary aspects of the field. School psychology is defined here as a field that "studies the individual learner's adjustments to ... processes" that deal with learning and instruction (Fagan and Warden 1996, introduction). It is therefore distinct from educational psychology, which deals with more general processes of learning and instruction. The volume contains about 400 entries, each normally one-half to one page long and concluding with cross-references and citations to other relevant literature. Each entry is signed by its contributor,

and all the contributors are professionals in this field. Some entries are biographies, some describe organizations, and others explain topics particular to psychology, such as assessment, intervention, and consultation. An appendix suggests additional sources for study. This reference work will be of more use to scholars and graduate students than to beginning researchers.

2-81. Husen, Torsten, and T. Neville Postlethwaite, eds. *International Encyclopedia of Education.* 2nd ed. 12 vols. Tarrytown, NY: Pergamon Press/Elsevier Science, 1994. 7740 pp. Indexes. ISBN: 0-080-41046-4.

This second edition is a substantial revision of the first edition, published in 1985. As stated in the preface, this work "represents the first major attempt to present an up-to-date overview of the international scholarship being conducted on educational problems, theories, practices, and institutions." The *Encyclopedia* contains 1,266 entries written by contributors drawn from approximately ninety-five countries. Among the many fields covered are "Adult Education," "Comparative and International Education," "Curriculum," "Human Development," "National Systems of Education," and "Teacher Education." Articles are generally several pages in length and conclude with cross-references and bibliographic listings. There are articles for most nations of the world. There are no illustrations other than occasional graphic displays. The final volume of the set includes a classified listing of the entries as well as indexes by name and subject. Although not particularly heavy on jargon in most instances, the articles in this reference work are more suitable for researchers in higher education than they are for neophytes. Particularly useful is the information provided in regard to educational systems in the various countries of the world.

2-82. Anderson, Lorin W., ed. *International Encyclopedia of Teaching and Teacher Education.* 2nd ed. Tarrytown, NY: Pergamon Press, 1995. 684 pp. Indexes. ISBN: 0-080-42304-3.

The first edition of this volume appeared in 1985. The second edition includes a somewhat greater number of contributors from North America and fewer from Australia and New Zealand; about one-third of them come from Europe and Asia. This new edition also takes into account theoretical changes taking place in the field of teaching during the interval. The arrangement is topical rather than alphabetical. For example, the first part of the volume is devoted to teaching and includes numerous separate articles prepared by individual contributors. A further breakdown by sections examines topics such as classroom management and learning environments. The final portion of the volume discusses teacher education. Individual articles are normally from three to eight pages in length. Each includes cross-references to other relevant articles and a listing of citations to other sources. The table of contents is quite detailed, and most readers will profit by looking through it first. Indexes

by subject and by name provide additional access to the text. The contributors are all professionals in this discipline, so this work is primarily of interest to teaching professionals but can also be of value to scholars from outside that field.

2-83. Altbach, Philip G., ed. *International Higher Education: An Encyclopedia.* 2 vols. New York: Garland, 1991. 1165 pp. Index. ISBN: 0-824-04847-4.

The intent of this reference volume is not to cover all aspects of international higher education but rather to "provide comprehensive and in depth coverage of a more limited number of countries, regions, and themes" (Altbach 1991, introduction). A significant portion of the first volume of the set is devoted to articles on fifteen topics in higher education. Some examples include academic freedom, accountability, costs, graduate education, history, and women in higher education. These articles range in length from fifteen to about twenty-five pages. The rest of the encyclopedia is devoted to articles on higher education in regions and significant countries; the latter includes approximately fifty-two nations. These articles are somewhat shorter, ranging in length from ten to twenty pages. Endnotes provide the reader with references to additional sources, and a bibliography at the end of the second volume provides a lengthy listing of relevant items arranged topically and by country. There are no illustrations other than a number of statistical tables and graphic displays. The individual contributors are from academe and are drawn from around the world. Although the writing style is aimed at a learned audience, the text is suitable for college students, particularly those seeking information on higher education in major nations internationally.

2-84. Chambliss, J. J., ed. *Philosophy of Education: An Encyclopedia.* New York: Garland, 1996. 720 pp. Index. ISBN: 0-815-31177-X.

The philosophy of education draws from many aspects of Western culture, including politics, religion, and the social sciences. This volume includes 228 articles designed to demonstrate the diversity of the subject. Entries range in time from ancient Greece to the present. There are articles for individuals, such as Aristotle and Charles Darwin, and articles on general subjects, such as democracy, discipline, feminism, and justice. Most of the entries are from 600 to 5,000 words in length, and each ends with cross-references and a short bibliography. The contributors are for the most part professors at colleges and universities in the United States. There are no illustrations. The introduction indicates that this work is "addressed to general readers, university students, and scholars." The writing style of the contributors is designed for such an audience, making this work less useful for high-school students. The reader should also know that the emphasis is truly upon philosophy rather than the specific practice of education.

2-85. Marlow-Ferguson, Rebecca, ed. *World Education Encyclopedia: A Survey of Educational Systems Worldwide.* 2nd ed. 3 vols. Detroit: Gale Group, 2002. 1747 pp. Index. ISBN: 0-787-65577-5.

This encyclopedia is a welcome update to the 1980 edition. The nations of the world are arranged alphabetically throughout. Articles vary in length, depending upon the history and complexity of education in a particular country. The article for France, for example, is about fifteen pages long, whereas Equatorial Guinea receives about three pages. Information includes historical background, legal considerations, and descriptions of educational basics from primary school through higher education. A concluding summary provides an assessment of the present situation. Occasional graphics help explicate the text, and a short bibliography at the end of the article will lead interested researchers to additional resources. One of the appendixes compiles statistical comparisons. Altogether, this encyclopedia takes precedence over all others pertaining to worldwide educational systems thanks to its timeliness.

Guides and Handbooks

2-86. Fonseca, James W., and Alice C. Andrews. *Atlas of American Higher Education.* New York: New York University Press, 1993. 257 pp. Index. ISBN: 0-814-72610-0.

The two authors, both geographers, assert in their introduction that U.S. higher education needs to be seen spatially due to the fact that there are fifty different states, each with its own approach to the arena. There are almost 100 maps or graphic displays, all presented in a black-and-white format that is easy to read. Each map is accompanied by a page of explanatory text. The volume includes ten chapters dealing with subjects such as enrollment, faculty, diversity, outcomes, student costs, financing, and the like. A number of statistical tables conclude the volume. Sources are listed at the back of the volume as well. Some are derived from private-sector sources, while others are publications of the federal government. Unfortunately, sources are not noted with the individual maps and their accompanying text. Nevertheless, this is a handy source for students requiring information on higher education among the fifty states.

2-87. Freed, Melvyn N., Robert K. Hess, and Joseph M. Ryan. *Educator's Desk Reference (EDR): A Sourcebook of Educational Information and Research.* 2nd ed. Westport, CT: Praeger, 2002. 584 pp. Index. ISBN: 1-573-56359-5.

The scope of this volume is somewhat broader than the typical literature guide that accompanies most disciplines. The initial section of the work describes the usual reference sources, but later sections are devoted to other topics. These include an author's guide to education publications (including journals); a guide to microcomputer software; and background on standardized tests, educational research purposes, and major organizations in the field. The intended audience is professional in nature although not necessarily limited to the educational field. This was a useful publica-

tion at the time it first appeared, but advances in electronic resources have made a good deal of the information contained herein obsolete, so readers must turn to newer resources.

2-88. Collins, John W., III, and Catherine Snow, eds. *Greenwood Dictionary of Education.* Westport, CT: Greenwood Press, 2003. 431 pp. ISBN: 0-897-74860-3.

Approximately 2,600 terms are briefly defined and described in this volume. The array is alphabetical. A large number of specialists assisted in providing definitions; their initials are appended to each definition, with full names appearing in a listing at the back. A useful bibliography about twenty-five pages in length appears at the back of the volume also. There is no index, but occasional cross-references are provided. This work is valuable for its timely definitions, which collectively provide a window into educational thinking in the early twenty-first century.

Geography

A number of items pertaining to environmental research appear in this section along with the more traditional geography sources. The books by Eagle and Lees provide the reader with useful jumping off points for resources on the environment, albeit with a British emphasis. (The volumes described in the section for general social science reference books should also be consulted; several include sections on geography.) Finally, the presence of a number of dictionaries and encyclopedias, most of fairly recent vintage, assists newcomers to this discipline. They are described here.

This section also includes annotations for a number of works that provide comparative information on geographical entities, either nations or states of the United States; some include rankings. Finally, the reader will find here annotations for several atlases that help to address either environmental issues or comparisons among locales.

Literature Guides
2-89. Lees, Nigel, and Helen Woolston. *Environmental Information: A Guide to Sources.* 2nd ed. London: British Library, 1997. 271 pp. Index. ISBN: 0-712-30825-3.

The first edition of this book appeared in 1992; the second edition updates information appearing in the initial volume and adds four new chapters: "Environmental Information on the Internet," "Chemicals and the Environment," "Contaminated Land and Liability," and "Noise Pollution." Altogether, there are fourteen chapters covering such topics as air pollution, water pollution, solid waste, energy, recycling, and agriculture, in addition to the four new topics. In general, chapters first discuss databases and data banks, then go on to describe printed resources, with emphasis upon journals and handbooks. A final section describes key organizations. Annotations accompany each listing. Introductory chapters describe environmental information in general, business, and environmental law. The emphasis throughout is on resources relevant to the United Kingdom and the European Union. However, serious researchers in the United States will also wish to consult this volume for potential leads.

2-90. Eagle, Selwyn, and Judith Deschamps, eds. *Information Sources in Environmental Protection.* London: Bowker-Saur, 1997. 280 pp. Index. ISBN: 1-857-39062-8.

Those researchers desiring a British approach to environmental protection issues will want to peruse this volume. Almost all the contributors are Britons, and examples of issues are those pertinent to the United Kingdom. The approach of the editors is to "provide a narrative introduction to the principal sources of information on the subject of environmental protection and such relevant information about the natural environment as is necessary for understanding the problems raised" (Eagle and Deschamps 1997, introduction). Each of the seventeen chapters is written by one or more of the contributors. Chapters cover such topics as government policies, water pollution, waste management, land use, and environmental law. The chapters each provide a narrative on their chosen subject, with like resources appearing in subdivisions within each chapter. Complete references appear at the end of the chapter. The contributors endeavor to cover both print and electronic resources; the latter include Web sites. An appendix provides directory information on selected organizations and associations. The index provides access to the text but not to the list of references, which must be consulted individually because no comprehensive listing is included. The primary clientele for this work will be British, but American researchers may wish to consult it for comparative purposes.

2-91. Scarrott, Martin. *Sport, Leisure and Tourism Information Sources: A Guide for Researchers.* Oxford: Butterworth-Heinemann, 1999. 267 pp. Index. ISBN: 0-750-63864-8.

The editor of this work indicates that it is intended as "a starting point in the search for information which offers advice and indicates some of the main sources which are available" (Scarrott 1999, introduction). There are nine chapters, each the work of a different contributor or contributors. The initial chapter discusses the state-of-the-art research in sport, leisure, and tourism. Ensuing chapters describe Internet sources, library resources, journals, indexing and abstracting services, statistics, information from the European Union, organizations, and videos. Some chapters provide annotations to individual sources, while others are compilations of directory information. Although the contributors are mostly British and this title has a United Kingdom emphasis, it also should be of value to researchers in the United States.

Abstracting and Indexing Services

2-92. *Energy Information Abstracts.* Monthly. New Providence, NJ: Bowker A and I Publishing, 1975–1993. Indexes. ISSN: 0739-3679.

Although many of the items abstracted in this service are technical in nature, there are enough entries dealing with policy issues for *Energy Information Abstracts* to be of interest for political science researchers. Abstracts are arranged into a number of categories; some examples include "U.S. Policy and Planning," "Research and Development," "Consumption and Conservation," and "Environmental Impact." Monthly issues include a listing of journals abstracted as well as indexes by subject, author, industry, and source. Annual volumes provide not only cumulative indexing but also reprint all the abstracts that appeared during the course of the year. The annual volumes also include several articles summarizing the year's activities in the energy field, as well as a number of statistical tables and charts reprinted from both governmental and private-sector sources. Complete texts of many of the abstracted items are available from the publisher on microfiche. As is the case with almost all printed abstracting services, this one is available electronically (not described here) and will be the one preferred by most users. 💻

2-93. *Leisure, Recreation and Tourism Abstracts.* Quarterly. Wallingford, Oxon, UK: Cab International, 1976–. Indexes. ISSN: 0261-1392.

Published quarterly, this abstracting service covers economic, environmental, and social aspects pertaining to the planning and management of leisure, recreation, and tourism. As of 1996, approximately 2,500 abstracts were appearing per year. Sources include books, journals, bulletins, reports, and proceedings. Each issue is divided into a number of standard categories; those dealing with leisure, recreation, natural resources and the environment, tourism, and travel all have application for the policy aspects of political science. The bibliographic citations accompanying each abstract are reasonably complete and avoid the use of abbreviations. Language of origin is indicated. Each issue also includes tables of contents for recent issues of selected journals in the field. In addition to the four quarterly issues, a separate annual index volume provides name and subject access to the abstracts. One of the strengths of this abstracting service is its international approach that includes citations to literature from around the world; conversely, some of the cited references almost certainly will not be found except through interlibrary loan facilities. Most researchers, of course, will wish to access the electronic version of this service (not described here). 💻

Dictionaries

2-94. Smith, Stephen L. J. *Dictionary of Concepts in Recreation and Leisure Studies.* New York: Greenwood Press, 1990. 372 pp. Indexes. ISBN: 0-313-25262-9.

As is the case with other volumes in Greenwood's Dictionary of Concepts series, this one seeks to identify key concepts in its field, describing them with an emphasis on both historical and contemporary contexts. Typical entries are up to several pages in length and conclude with an annotated bibliography to literature cited in the entry itself. The reader thereby can obtain an easy overview of the theoretical history of the concept. Cross-references to other relevant entries are indicated in uppercase. There are many entries of interest to political scientists; some examples include "Community Development," "Conservation," "Region," and "Wilderness." There are two indexes. The first is a name index to bibliographic references throughout the text, while the second is an index to subjects. The latter indicates main entries in boldface. The major drawback to this reference work is that it is now a decade old and therefore does not cite or discuss developments in the 1990s. With this caveat in mind, this work can be referred to both specialists and serious students requiring basic information for this discipline.

2-95. Art, Henry W., ed. *Dictionary of Ecology and Environmental Science.* New York: Henry Holt, 1993. 632 pp. ISBN: 0-805-02079-9.

Those researchers seeking brief definitions dealing with environmental topics can turn to this volume. Definitions are relatively brief, generally no more than a sentence or two. However, cross-references to other entries assist in leading the reader to additional information; especially helpful are cross-references that advise the reader to compare or contrast other entries with the one at hand. The emphasis of this volume is on science rather than political, economic, or social impacts of environmental situations. A series of appendixes provide additional information, including ecological models, SI (International System of Units) units, chemical elements, geological nomenclature, a "Table of Minerals and Diagnostic Properties," and the like. There are no bibliographic references. This, plus the publication date, somewhat limits the value of this publication to current researchers. Nevertheless, it is a handy source for basic definitions for those students and laypersons new to the environmental field.

2-96. Porteous, Andrew. *Dictionary of Environmental Science.* 3rd ed. New York: John Wiley, 1996. 704 pp. ISBN: 0-471-63376-3.

The author states that "this book is written in the hope that it may contribute to environmental literature by providing basic definitions and data plus demonstrate the nature of the issues" (Porteous 1996, introduction). For that reason, the definitions found here are accessible to the informed layperson as well as to specialists. Definitions range in length from a sentence to more than a page in length. Longer entries often include a short listing of sources. Cross-references are indicated in uppercase. There are a number of black-and-white illustrations, tables, and graphic displays. The volume concludes with several appendixes: a listing of organizations, the periodic table, chemical elements, and information on SI units. The listing of organizations has a heavy British emphasis, as indeed does the entire text. Nevertheless, American researchers will also find this a useful information source, one less technical in nature than that by Henry Art [entry 2-95].

2-97. Johnston, R. J., Derek Gregory, and David M. Smith, eds. *Dictionary of Human Geography.* 3rd rev. ed. Oxford: Basil Blackwell, 1994. 724 pp. Index. ISBN: 0-631-18141-5.

In their preface, the editors state their purpose is "to provide students and others with a general series of philosophical and theoretical frameworks for situating, understanding, and interrogating the modern lexicon" of human geography. They also enumerate three major changes from earlier editions. First, this edition has 700 entries, 200 more than the first edition. Second, there has been effort to include more contributors from countries outside England; approximately one-third of the contributors to this edition are American or Canadian. This broadening of the contributor base has also taken into account issues of ethnocentrism and feminism. Finally, this edition incorporates disciplinary trends and changes that have taken place since the first edition was published in 1981. The entries themselves range from a paragraph to several pages in length. Regardless of the length of discussion, each entry concludes with a list of additional reading and/or references. Cross-references to other articles are indicated in uppercase. Occasional graphic displays supplement the text. Access to this dictionary is enhanced by the inclusion of a detailed index, which helpfully indicates main discussion pages in boldface. The audience for this work will consist mostly of professionals and advanced researchers; beginning students probably should be directed to more basic sources.

2-98. Goudie, Andrew, ed. *Encyclopedic Dictionary of Physical Geography.* 2nd ed. Oxford: Basil Blackwell, 1994. 611 pp. Index. ISBN: 0-631-13292-9.

This dictionary concentrates upon brief definitions but also includes more lengthy discussion when necessary. These latter entries are normally about a paragraph in length, but a few topics receive a page or more of text. Many entries are accompanied by a list of references for additional reading, and all are initialed by the contributor. A listing of contributors appears at the front of the volume; most are from the United Kingdom. Illustrations, both photographs and graphic displays, are abundant. A listing of physical geography abbreviations appears at the front of the text, while the index provides an additional access point to subject matter. Cross-references are indicated with uppercase type. The intended audience of this work consists of professional geographers, researchers in associated fields, students, and secondary-school teachers. Though this is a specialized discipline, those outside the field can derive some benefit from consultation of this volume.

2-99. McDowell, Linda, and Joanne P. Sharp, eds. *A Feminist Glossary of Human Geography.* London: Oxford University Press, 1999. 372 pp. ISBN: 0-340-70659-7.

According to the editors, the discipline of geography in recent years has "found itself right in the middle of many of the debates that have dominated not only the social sciences but also the humanities" (McDowell and Sharp 1999, introduction). This glossary incorporates feminist ideas in regard to these debates. The arrangement is alphabetical, with entries ranging in length from a single paragraph to a couple of pages. Some of the entries are terms that one would expect to find in a traditional geography dictionary: "Environment," "Homeland," "Land," and "Migrant/Migration." Others, however, are fairly new to this arena: "Abortion," "Homosexual/Homosexuality," "Pornography," and "Witch/Crone." Cross-references are indicated in uppercase. Each entry includes references to relevant scholarly literature; complete citations can be found in a bibliography of nearly seventy pages that appears at the back of the volume. Contributors are drawn heavily from the British academic community, but North America is also represented. The audience for this work will consist of more advanced scholars.

2-100. Clark, Audrey N. *Longman Dictionary of Geography: Human and Physical.* Burnt Mill, Harlow, Essex, UK: Longman Group, 1985. 724 pp. ISBN: 0-582-35261-4.

The objective of this reference work "is to provide, in text and maps, essential information on spelling, pronunciation, type of feature, location, and depending on the nature of the entry, population, size (as area, height, depth, or length), economy, history, and other matters of importance" (Clark 1985, preface). Surprisingly for a British publisher, there is a good deal of concentration on places in the United States and Canada. However, coverage is worldwide in scope, though of course limited by the single-volume format. Over 200 black-and-white maps accompany the text; most are of individual nations, states, and Canadian provinces, and all can be found through a listing at the front of the text. The edition published prior to this appeared in 1972, so this third edition incorporates a quarter-century of new information and change. This reference source provides quick information that will resolve many questions relating to geographical places around the world.

2-101. *Merriam-Webster's Geographical Dictionary.* 3rd ed. Springfield, MA: Merriam-Webster, 1997. 1361 pp. ISBN: 0-877-79546-0.

According to the preface, this volume "covers the terms commonly used in geographical writing over the past 100 years," a time that saw the field progress from a fairly uncomplicated area of knowledge to one that is complex and multidisciplinary in scope. Aimed at an audience that includes professional geographers as well as students, this dictionary includes terms that are strictly geographical, those from other fields of knowledge that are of application, and terms from foreign languages. Numerous cross-references, which appear in uppercase, lead the user from one definition to those that are of related interest. The arrangement is alphabetical, with most entries ranging in length from a sentence to a short paragraph. The author has attempted to include Americanisms as well as British usage. There are appendixes for Greek and Latin roots, conversion tables, a time-zone map, and a table of random numbers. This volume is a beginning point for the specialized vocabulary of this discipline.

Encyclopedias

2-102. Douglas, Ian, Richard Huggett, and Mike Robinson, eds. *Companion Encyclopedia of Geography: The Environment and Humankind.* London: Routledge, 1996. 1021 pp. Index. ISBN: 0-415-07417-7.

As the title suggests, this volume takes the view that geography is "about the interdependence of people and their environment" (Douglas, Huggett, and Robinson 1996, preface). The editors selected a number of contributors to represent this viewpoint in a series of separately authored chapters. Chapters are grouped into six major categories that collectively examine the geological evolution of the earth and its human inhabitants, with heavy emphasis on the latter part of the twentieth century, and concluding with a survey of the response of the geographic discipline now and potentially in the future. Detailed background on the contributors appears in the front matter; most are from academic institutions in the United Kingdom. Chapters average about twenty-one pages in length and conclude with listings of references and items for further reading. There are occasional illustrations in the form of graphs, tables, and maps. In general, the text is more suitable for specialized researchers than for beginning students. To call this volume an encyclopedia is something of a misnomer, because the contents are not arranged in the usual alphabetical and topical array. However, the user can gain access to subject matter not only through the table of contents, but also through the index, a detailed listing almost fifty pages long.

2-103. Kurian, George Thomas, ed. *Encyclopedia of the Third World.* 4th ed. 3 vols. New York: Facts on File, 1992. 2363 pp. Index. ISBN: 0-816-02261-5.

This well-known reference set encompasses the world's less industrialized nations. In general, these are the nations on the continents of South America, Africa, and Asia, although the editor has excluded both China and Taiwan. The arrangement is alphabetical by name of country, and each country receives the same format of coverage. This includes approximately thirty-six categories of information, including standard topics such as defense, education, health, and governmental background. Most entries range from ten to twenty pages in length. A black-and-white map is provided for each nation, as is a list of additional reading. The first volume also includes basic information on a number of international organizations, while the final volume provides several statistical appendixes as well as a comprehensive index. The writing

style is suitable for both high-school and college students. While much of this information might be found in encyclopedias or other annual reference works dealing with the countries of the world, it is handy to have information on third world nations compiled in a single set; however, the 1992 publication date will be of concern for some researchers.

2-104. *Worldmark Encyclopedia of the States.* 3rd ed. Detroit: Gale Research, 1995. 758 pp. ISBN: 0-810-39877-X.

Background on states of the United States is not difficult to find, but this work is useful because it provides reasonably comprehensive information in a single volume. The text for each state is divided into numbered categories. Some categories, such as climate, population, education, and economy are similar to those found in a general encyclopedia; others, however, are more unique, including environmental protection, armed forces, consumer protection, and economic policy. Occasional statistical tables complement the text. There are no illustrations other than a map of each state showing the counties, major cities and towns, major highways, and parks and reserves. In addition to entries for the fifty states, the book has entries for the District of Columbia, Puerto Rico, and U.S. dependencies, and a summary section for the nation itself. Each entry concludes with a brief bibliography of general sources likely to be found in larger libraries. This is a valuable source for students and might be consulted by specialists for quick information.

Guides and Handbooks

2-105. Law, Gwillim. *Administrative Subdivisions of Countries: A Comprehensive World Reference, 1900 through 1998.* Jefferson, NC: McFarland, 1999. 457 pp. Index. ISBN: 0-786-40729-8.

Most countries of the world are subdivided into "Major Administrative Divisions" or "Primary Symbol Divisions," as the introduction to this volume indicates. States and provinces are among the possibilities. The arrangement is alphabetical by nation. Each entry begins with a listing of the major divisions, including specific pieces of information: codes (such as postal and time zone), a recent census figure, area (in both square kilometers and square miles), and name of capital. This is followed by narratives describing anomalies, origins of names, and history of boundary changes. In those instances in which statistical information is available, there are census figures for each division extending as far back as 1900. The index provides access by name of division. Although some of the contents of this work can be found in standard annual publications, much of it can be difficult to find in the usual sources, and the information on boundary changes and census figures is especially useful to those researchers seeking a handy source for this subject.

2-106. Hornor, Edith R., ed. *Almanac of the Fifty States: Basic Data Profiles with Comparative Tables.* Annual. Burlington, VT: Information Publications, 1986–. ISSN: 0887-0519.

There are a number of reference books that compile information on the states; this one is oriented toward statistical data rather than text. Each state is accorded eight pages of text, divided into a number of categories. These include statistics in regard to geography, demographics, vital statistics, education, welfare, housing and construction, government and elections, governmental finance, crime, labor, economy, communication, transportation, and energy. For the most part, statistics are gathered from standard federal government publications and represent data collected within the last several years. At the conclusion of the volume are more than fifty tables that rank the states, allowing for easy comparison in most of the same categories represented in the individual state sections. One caveat is the fact that only incomplete bibliographic citations are given for the original sources from which the data was gathered. Otherwise, this annual volume serves as a good, quick guide to basic statistical information on the fifty states.

2-107. Kane, Joseph Nathan. *The American Counties: Origins of County Names, Dates of Creation and Organization, Area, Population Including 1980 Census Figures, Historical Data, and Published Sources.* 4th ed. Metuchen, NJ: Scarecrow Press, 1983. 546 pp. ISBN: 0-810-81558-3.

As its lengthy subtitle suggests, this volume provides the user with a good deal of information regarding counties and their origin. The main part of the text is an alphabetical listing of county names that includes the state to which they belong, date of establishment, square miles, population figures from 1950 through 1980, county seat, and origins of the county name. If the county was named for an individual, brief biographical information is appended, and often there is a reference to a county history. Other portions of the text list counties by state and by date of establishment, including statutory authority, if such exists. There are also listings for independent cities and Alaska boroughs. At present, the era of county and state creation appears to have ended, so the fact that this edition appeared in 1983 is perhaps not a concern. Kane's book may be consulted more by historians than by political scientists, but it remains a handy, quick resource for basic information on the counties.

2-108. Hobson, Archie. *Cambridge Gazetteer of the United States and Canada.* Cambridge: Cambridge University Press, 1995. 743 pp. ISBN: 0-521-41579-9.

Intended to resemble an encyclopedia rather than a dictionary, this gazetteer presents an alphabetical array of place names for both the United States and Canada. Certain categories were automatically included: states, provinces, and territories; their capitals; and all incorporated municipalities with a population of more than 10,000 in the United States or 8,000 in Canada. Other entries, such as neighborhoods, defunct municipalities, military sites, and national forests, were chosen for the likelihood that readers need the information. Entries are up to a paragraph in length and include information pertaining to population, history, acreage, and geography. The volume concludes with an eclectic collection of maps. This is not an indispensable source but is useful for those seeking brief information on localities in the United States and Canada but not wishing to consult a gazetteer of worldwide scope.

2-109. Cohen, Saul B., ed. *Columbia Gazetteer of the World.* 3 vols. New York: Columbia University Press, 1998. 3578 pp. ISBN: 0-231-11040-5.

This bulky reference work is a successor to the *Columbia-Lippincott Gazetteer of the World,* published in 1952. It is an attempt to be a comprehensive resource for both geographical places and features, and it takes into account changes that have occurred since 1952, including the quadrupling in number of nation-states. It also attempts to reflect a viewpoint that is more global in nature than was the case in the past. Nevertheless, there is still a notable orientation toward the English-speaking world; the United States is accorded 40,000 entries, including all incorporated places and all counties, far more than the 6,000 entries for Russia. Still, this is an impressive resource. Entries for individual countries are similar to brief encyclopedia articles, and in addition to components that describe places in terms of the usual geographic factors (such as population, elevation, and local products and industries), there is also an emphasis upon history found in entries for locales such as Burgundy. Also welcome is the fact that pronunciation is shown for most places, including those in the English-speaking nations. In all, this is a core source that should be found in most libraries.

2-110. Kane, Joseph Nathan, Janet Podell, and Steven Anzovin. *Facts about the States.* 2nd ed. New York: H. W. Wilson, 1994. 624 pp. ISBN: 0-824-20849-8.

Although brief information about the states can be found in many sources, including encyclopedias, this volume compiles a number of quick facts in a single resource. The following categories are included for each state: geography and climate, national sites (such as parks), a chronology of historical events, demographic data, government and politics, finances, economy, environment, culture and education, "unusual state facts," and a bibliography of additional sources, both fiction and nonfiction. The latter category is particularly useful for suggesting core titles for additional research and reading. The listing for each state averages about twelve pages in length, and there are articles also for the District of Columbia and Puerto Rico. The volume concludes with a set of "Comparative Tables" that allow for easy comparison of statistics among all the states. Most data is drawn from federal government sources. Each state article includes a black-and-white reproduction of the state seal and a map of the United States indicating the location of the state; otherwise, there are no illustrations. This volume, of special use to student researchers, will be found in most library reference collections.

2-111. DeMers, Michael N. *Fundamentals of Geographic Information Systems.* New York: John Wiley, 1997. 486 pp. Index. ISBN: 0-471-14284-0.

This volume is a textbook rather than a reference book, but it has value in a reference setting. The author's purpose "is to serve two educational missions, both reflecting the current growth of GIS technology and its intellectual content" (DeMers 1997, preface). One mission was to assist technicians to understand geographic information systems (GIS) to enable them to work more effectively with GIS software; the other mission was to inform academicians of basic technical needs to enhance communication between them and the technicians. The volume itself is a standard textbook, complete with review questions and a listing of references following each chapter. The author also provides a glossary of almost twenty pages in length. There are numerous illustrations that assist in the explanation of concepts discussed in the accompanying text. Until standard reference sources pertaining to GIS are developed and published, textbooks such as this may be the best starting point for researchers seeking information on this fast-moving field.

2-112. Kurian, George Thomas. *Illustrated Book of World Rankings.* 5th ed. Armonk, NY: Sharpe Reference, 2001. 471 pp. Index. ISBN: 0-765-68026-2.

As the preface explains, this volume "is designed as an international scorecard that compares and ranks over 190 nations of the world according to their performance in more than 300 key areas." Data is selected according to five concepts: availability, comparability, usability, reliability, and rankability. Problems with data collection in the comparison are explained in the front matter. The 300 key areas are divided into 25 sections, each of which deals with a general topic. Examples include environment, consumption, crime and law enforcement, culture, and women. Each table displays a ranking that generally includes the top ten countries, various middle groupings, and the bottom ten. Statistics as well as rankings are included for each country. Each table also includes a source reference; however, no additional bibliographic information is provided beyond a listing of the organization responsible for producing each statistical source. Text introduces each section and table, and a number of graphic displays also help the reader to interpret the data. Although this volume includes relatively basic data, it is extremely valuable for many researchers, from high-school students to academic faculty members, who need comparative information for the nations of the world.

2-113. Frome, Michael. *National Park Guide.* New York: McMillan Travel, 1966–. 20 pp. Index. ISSN: 0734-7960.

A standard source for many years, this guide is aimed at the general reader but can be useful to researchers needing basic historical and location information on U.S. national parks. Major parks, approximately fifty in number, receive a listing of several pages each, with a color photo and sometimes a map. The smaller or lesser known sites receive much-briefer coverage, but each park or site includes an address and phone number. The index is valuable chiefly for its listing of each site. National parks are an important tourist destination, and this volume will be found in most libraries.

2-114. Meltzer, Ellen, ed. *New Book of American Rankings.* rev. ed. New York: Facts on File, 1998. 272 pp. Index. ISBN: 0-816-02878-8.

This reference work ranks the fifty states and the District of Columbia in a number of statistical parameters. Altogether, approximately 400 different categories are presented. Tables are gathered into broad groupings, such as geography, labor, population, housing, and transportation. Each table is supplemented with brief explanatory text, including the date and source of the data. Most sources are federal government publications. In most cases, the bibliographic information is brief, consisting of name of agency and name of publication. The tables themselves show the states in rank order along with statistical figures and sometimes accompanying percentages. This publication also includes statistical measurements pertaining to social and cultural topics, such as numbers of adherents to the larger religious denominations and funding for the arts. The concluding portion of the volume gives listings for each state, showing its rank in approximately forty categories. Here, only the ranking is given; the reader must turn to the tables themselves to obtain statistical figures. Access to the tables is provided through an index and a detailed table of contents. Like its competitors, this volume can be consulted profitably by both beginning students and more advanced researchers.

2-115. Arlinghaus, Sandra Lach. *Practical Handbook of Digital Mapping: Concepts and Terminology.* Boca Raton, FL: CRC Press, 1994. 335 pp. Indexes. ISBN: 0-849-30131-9.

Digital maps are produced and stored in computers. Essentially, this is a dictionary of terms in the field. Many definitions are quite brief, no more than a sentence, but up to a paragraph of information is presented when necessary. All illustrations are examples of digital mapping. Also included are a case study, a list of acronyms and abbreviations, a listing of nearly 300 references, and three indexes, by case study, colored plates, and references. Terminology is related to a number of fields including geography, natural resources, public health, computer science, and remote sensing, among others. The primary audience for this volume will be professionals in these fields and other researchers with specialized mapping needs. Of course, newer texts must be consulted as well.

2-116. Shearer, Benjamin F., and Barbara S. Shearer. *State Names, Seals, Flags, and Symbols: A Historical Guide.* rev. ed. Westport, CT: Greenwood Press, 1994. 440 pp. Index. ISBN: 0-313-28862-3.

Seeking mottoes or flags, flowers or trees, songs or postage stamps? Look no further than this book, which includes these categories and others for the states of the United States. Arrangement is by category. For example, a chapter on birds describes songsters state by state. Chapters conclude with endnotes that cite the official sources. Among the categories for which information might otherwise be difficult to find are license plates and state fairs. The volume ends with a bibliography of state and territory histories and an index. Readers at all levels will find this a useful source.

Atlases

2-117. Doyle, Rodger P. *Atlas of Contemporary America: A Portrait of the Nation's Politics, Economy, Environment, Ethnic and Religious Diversity.* New York: Facts on File, 1994. 256 pp. Index. ISBN: 0-816-02545-2.

The preface to this volume states that "emphasis in this book is upon the domestic American scene." The author also attempts to indicate background to common news topics through the use of maps and graphs. There are major subdivisions for demography, ethnicity, language, religion, environment, politics, the economy, health, and "Contentious Issues." Most maps are in color and display the entire United States with boundaries by state and county. This allows for easy comparison; for example, one can readily identify those geographical regions where Baptists or Mormons predominate. Several paragraphs of text accompany each map. The section on contentious issues includes topics such as capital punishment, hate groups, gay rights, and privacy. Most of the data was based on results from the 1990 census. A five-page bibliography indicates other sources of information. This fascinating volume is one of the more effective atlases that portray social, economic, and political information, and it will be of value to researchers at all levels.

2-118. Lean, Geoffrey. *Atlas of the Environment* 3rd ed. Santa Barbara, CA: ABC-CLIO, 1994. 192 pp. Index. ISBN: 0-874-36768-9.

World heads of state met for the Earth Summit in Brazil in June 1992, affirming the need to address global environmental problems. This atlas follows upon that meeting by presenting for the general reader maps and basic text that attempt to demonstrate how humanity is affecting nature. Topics are wide-ranging, including such subjects as demographics, drinking water, education, development, deserts, forest destruction, hazardous wastes, and nuclear energy. A detailed table of contents outlines the structure of the atlas and is the best means to access the maps and text. Maps are multicolored and should be easily understood by all users. A bibliography of several pages concludes the volume. As is the case with several other environmental atlases, this work will be most useful for the beginning researcher or others requiring a nontechnical approach to global environmental issues through the use of maps.

2-119. Kurian, George, ed. *Atlas of the Third World.* 2nd ed. New York: Facts on File, 1992. 384 pp. Index. ISBN: 0-816-01930-4.

The introduction to the first edition of this work, published in 1984, states that it "presents a comprehensive selection of maps and statistical information in graphic form organized under topical headings to depict important aspects of the current economic and social conditions in the Third World and in their underlying historical dynamics." The 1992 edition updates the earlier edition and provides a picture of the third world shortly before the end of the twentieth century. The first portion of the volume is taken up by "Thematic Profiles," which depict the entire third world in maps and graphs that demonstrate the following points: development, political instability, population, finance, trade, food, education, health, energy, employment, and interdependence. The second portion of the text consists of reports on eighty-one individual nations. Each receives several pages of maps, pie charts, and graphs, as well as brief textual information. The country reports include information pertaining to population growth, gross national product, educational enrollment, budget expenditures, agriculture, vegetation, and a number of other parameters. The usefulness of this source is limited by its publication date, although it does provide a valuable snapshot of the third world in the early 1990s.

2-120. Mason, Robert J., and Mark T. Mattson. *Atlas of United States Environmental Issues.* New York: Macmillan,

1990. 252 pp. Index. ISBN: 0-028-97261-9.

The foreword to this volume states that "we need to understand the state of the American environment today and especially the ways that we are altering it." Reflecting that concern, the atlas presents text, maps, and graphics pertaining to a great variety of environmental circumstances. These include agriculture, rangelands, wetlands, forests, coastal zones, air quality, water use, noise pollution, solid waste, hazardous waste, energy, nonfuel minerals, parks, natural hazards, politics, and the environmental future. Text materials are extensive, more than complementing the maps. Color is used effectively throughout. One of the appendixes lists important environmental legislation chronologically (although no actual text is included), and there is an extensive glossary and bibliography. Provided that users bear in mind that this volume reflects the environmental situation as of the late 1980s, researchers at both the basic and advanced levels will find it of value as a beginning point.

2-121. Mattson, Catherine M., and Mark T. Mattson. *Contemporary Atlas of the United States.* New York: Macmillan, 1990. 119 pp. Index. ISBN: 0-028-97281-3.

The authors state that this volume "makes connections between the geography of the United States and the issues and events which shape the daily lives of every American" (Mattson and Mattson 1990, preface). Major map categories include land, history, people, the economy, transportation and communication, government, and environment. Each major category includes a number of maps further broken down into more specific topic areas. For example, under "Health," we find maps with data on infant mortality, hospital beds, life expectancy, and similar subjects. Several paragraphs of text accompany the maps and graphs and aid in interpretation. This reference work is similar in approach to the *Atlas of Contemporary America* [entry 2-117], which will probably be the preferred choice of most users. Not only is it more up to date, including data from the 1990 census, but it also provides greater detail than the Mattsons' book. The maps in Mattson and Mattson show only state boundaries, while its competitor includes both state and county boundaries. However, each atlas includes some information not found in the other, so both are worthy of consultation.

2-122. Seager, Joni. *New State of the Earth Atlas: A Concise Survey of the Environment through Full-Color International Maps.* New York: Simon and Schuster, 1990. 128 pp. Index. ISBN: 0-671-89103-0.

The introduction to this volume states that "our purpose in undertaking this atlas is to translate specialist information into a form that can be more widely appreciated." To that end, a combination of maps and graphs convey information on thirty-seven environmental topics grouped under general headings pertaining to such topics as food and water, industry, and consumption. Categories generally feature global maps accompanied by statistical data and graphs. Textual information appears at the back along with a separate multipage table comparing individual nations in eleven categories. The textual commentaries also include brief listings of sources. A decade has passed since this volume was published, so it is more useful for a summary of environmental thinking at the time of publication than for other purposes. Users wanting contemporary information and data will have to look elsewhere.

2-123. Henwood, Doug. *The State of the U.S.A. Atlas: The Changing Face of American Life in Maps and Graphics.* New York: Simon and Schuster/Touchstone, 1994. 127 pp. ISBN: 0-671-79696-8.

The format of this volume is similar to that of other *State of . . .* works: a combination of colorful maps, graphics, and text conveys social statistics pertaining to American life at the beginning of the 1990s. The thirty-five map categories are arranged into four major subdivisions; these include demographics, the economy, society, and government. Accompanying text information, including references to sources, appears at the back of the volume, which also includes a "State Table" that allows easy comparison among the states in a number of arenas. There is no index, so the user must rely upon the table of contents, which contains enough detail to provide easy access to subjects of interest. The view-

point of the author is left of center, but this bias is easily detected and does not distract from the contents. The value of this volume lies in the fact that it compiles a good deal of comparative data that would be tedious or time-consuming to find otherwise.

2-124. Thomas, Alan, and Ben Crow, eds. *Third World Atlas.* 2nd ed. Bristol, PA: Taylor and Francis, 1994. 80 pp. ISBN: 1-560-32322-1.

Like its competitor the *State of the World Atlas*, this volume portrays the contemporary world with a combination of full-color maps and graphics that allow for comparison among nations. Here, obviously, emphasis is upon the third world, which is loosely defined as those nations that are still developing economically. The author and his colleagues are especially at pains to demonstrate inequalities among nations. Reasonably extensive text helps to interpret the data presented graphically and through maps. Topics include colonization, hunger and famine, disease, environmental degradation, and the like. Tables at the end of the volume provide comparative data, in a nation-by-nation format, in regard to human development and economic indicators. There is no bibliography, but a listing of sources does suggest additional reading for those so inclined. This source will particularly appeal to students needing introductory information on current global issues. Its major drawback is the fact that some of the data will become outdated unless newer editions are forthcoming.

2-125. Lean, Geoffrey, Don Hinrichsen, and Adam Markham. *World Wildlife Fund Atlas of the Environment.* New York: Prentice Hall, 1990. 192 pp. ISBN: 0-130-50469-6.

Alarm for the global environment was the inspiration for this volume. It contains the usual combination of text, colored maps, graphs, and tables. Forty-two subject areas are examined; they range from population to deserts to conservation efforts. Each receives a couple of pages of text along with the graphics, allowing for greater depth of treatment than is sometimes the case with atlas formats. There is no index, so the reader must depend upon the table of contents to locate information. A six-page bibliography concludes the volume. The authors state they have attempted to avoid polemics, and, indeed, treatment does seem to be reasonably balanced. Of course, given the publication date, coverage does not extend into the 1990s, so readers will have to consult other sources for newer information.

History

The reference literature for the discipline of history is more extensive than in many other subject areas, hence the length of this section. Fortunately, there are several general guidebooks that introduce both beginners and practitioners to research in the field. These include volumes by Benjamin, Fritze, Prucha, and Slavens, all published in the early 1990s. Another major category is that of historical biography. Americans are well represented, but library researchers should also have success when seeking information on noteworthy individuals from elsewhere. Other history reference works deal with chronology or with collections of selected documents. By far the largest groupings, however, are those for dictionaries and encyclopedias. These represent many specific topics and geographical locations in the United States. For other countries and continents, the reader can often find a reference work devoted to a particular topic. Several publishers, especially Macmillan, Oxford University Press, and Scribner's, have published excellent multivolume encyclopedias that assist the student in bridging the gap between historical information found in general encyclopedias and that found in monographs.

Finally, this section also describes some of the basic resources for research in archaeology.

Literature Guides

2-126. Bentley, Michael, ed. *Companion to Historiography.* London: Routledge, 2003. 1024 pp. Index. ISBN: 0-415-28557-7.

This reference volume provides a useful introduction to historiography, an important component of the discipline. Forty scholars, most of them British, have contributed lengthy essays that explore in detail historiographical practices in many eras and places, from ancient times to the present. The final ten essays compare historiography with philosophy, anthropology, archaeology, and Western art, and discuss various contextual approaches to the writing of history. An essay approach does provide greater readability than a dictionary approach but also has its weaknesses. For example, Frederick Jackson Turner is discussed in the context of his own time, but the index contains no reference to the frontier thesis or the controversies that have recently swirled around it. Nevertheless, most scholars and readers can profit from this volume, whose value is enhanced by the lengthy list of references that follow each essay.

2-127. Prucha, Paul Francis. *Handbook for Research in American History: A Guide to Bibliographies and Other Reference Works.* 2nd rev. ed. Lincoln: University of Nebraska Press, 1994. 214 pp. Index. ISBN: 0-803-23701-4.

This second edition differs from the first, published in 1987, in two respects. First, greater attention is given to electronic resources, reflecting the changes that have taken place. Second, a listing of bibliographies that had occupied a substantial portion of the first edition is omitted from the second on the grounds that researchers who learn how to use the resources included in this volume will have the skills to compile bibliographies of their own. Otherwise, the intent of the volume remains the same: to acquaint graduate students in American history with intelligent use of resources in libraries. Each chapter is devoted to a particular category of materials, including, for example, library catalogs, book-review indexes, oral histories, and dictionaries and encyclopedias. Much of the author's work is encapsulated in essay form,

with occasional listings by entry number supplementing the essay texts. The index includes reference to subjects as well as to specific entries. Despite the advent of computerized information, the author admits that most of the resources are print-based rather than electronic. Given the nature of the field, this is not a major drawback, and this work will continue to be of value to history researchers.

2-128. Steiner, Dale R., and Casey R. Phillips. *Historical Journals: A Handbook for Writers and Reviewers.* 2nd ed. Jefferson, NC: McFarland, 1993. 274 pp. Index. ISBN: 0-899-50801-4.

In the preface, the authors state that this edition is necessary because the first edition, published in 1981, is out of date. The new edition lists nearly 700 journals published in the United States, Canada, and Great Britain. Each entry includes the editor's name, address, manuscript-submission guidelines, and book-review guidelines. A brief subject index allows searching for journals by subject (e.g., there are three listings for Quakers). The authors also provide helpful ideas on writing and submitting an article or a book review. This volume is obviously aimed at professional historians in the United States but is of value to anyone who wants to identify major journals in this field.

2-129. Fritze, Ronald H. *Reference Sources in History: An Introductory Guide.* Santa Barbara, CA: ABC-CLIO, 1990. 319 pp. Index. ISBN: 0-874-36164-8.

One of several competing guides to the historical sciences, this volume is aimed at undergraduate and graduate students in English-speaking countries and, accordingly, emphasizes works in that language. Each of the nearly 700 items includes a paragraph-length annotation with cross-references to related entries. Arrangement is by type of publication (e.g., bibliographies, periodical indexes and abstracts, dissertations and theses, dictionaries and encyclopedias, and historical statistical resources). A single index cites entries for authors, titles, and subjects but is confusing because it refers to page numbers rather than to the entry number assigned to each annotation. This book omits electronic resources, generated after its 1990 publication date, but is a valuable reference for historical works categorized by publication type. (Note: The 2004 edition was not seen.) 🖳

2-130. Slavens, Thomas P. *Sources of Information for Historical Research.* New York: Neal-Schuman Publishers, 1994. 577 pp. Indexes. ISBN: 1-555-70093-4.

The newest and lengthiest of several guides to historical research, this volume is arranged by Library of Congress (LC) call numbers, including C, D, E, F, HQ, JX, and Z. The value of this arrangement is that similar reference works are grouped together. For example, historical dictionaries on Great Britain are found at DA34. Those not familiar with the LC system, however, will have to rely on the study index. In addition, the lengthy Z section, which includes bibli-

ographies, separates that type of publication from other types relating to the same topic. Paragraph-length annotations, more descriptive than critical, are provided for each of the entries; and both a subject index and an author-title index are provided. This reference work is probably more useful to librarians than to other researchers, but it is relatively recent and does provide access to standard resources for parts of the world other than North America and Europe.

2-131. Benjamin, Jules R. *A Student's Guide to History.* 8th ed. New York: St. Martin's Press, 2001. 233 pp. ISBN: 0-312-24765-6.

As the title indicates, this reference work is aimed at the undergraduate student and is written at a level suitable for that audience. Most of the volume deals with basic study habits, but the final fifty pages are useful to the more advanced researcher, for those pages provide a handy listing of basic reference sources. Most are unannotated, but this volume does provide a recent overview of reference sources in history.

2-132. Blazek, Ron, and Anna H. Perrault. *United States History: A Multicultural, Interdisciplinary Guide to Information Sources.* 2nd ed. Westport, CT: Libraries Unlimited, 2003. 661 pp. Indexes. ISBN: 1-563-08874-6.

A total of 947 items are described in this annotated bibliography. The arrangement is thematic in nature, with the first part of the volume devoted to those items dealing with U.S. history in general. The rest of the work is divided into several chapters having the following titles: "Politics and Government," "Diplomatic History and Foreign Affairs," "Military History," "Social, Cultural, and Intellectual History," "Regional History," and "Economic History." As the chapter titles indicate, both traditional and newer topics of research receive attention; for example, there are sections on ethnic groups, gays, and entertainment, all subjects that might have been neglected in similar compilations published in earlier years. Topical coverage extends through the end of the Vietnam War in the mid-1970s. Annotations are usually quite detailed and provide some analysis as well as description. There are indexes by author and title, and by subject. This compilation will be especially useful for college students, both graduate and undergraduate. 🖥

Abstracting and Indexing Services

2-133. *America: History and Life.* Monthly. Santa Barbara, CA: ABC-CLIO, 1954–. Indexes.

This database is the electronic version of the print index by the same name. It covers U.S. and Canadian history from prehistory to the present. Coverage of historical journals is very thorough. At present, most of the citations retrieved are only bibliographic, but there are increasing instances of linkage to full-text versions elsewhere. All the usual search functions are present. The print version was always somewhat tedious to search, so students and historical professionals will naturally gravitate to the electronic version of this resource. The companion database cover-

ing other parts of the world is *Historical Abstracts* [entry 2-134]. 🖥

2-134. *Historical Abstracts.* Monthly. Santa Barbara, CA: ABC-CLIO, 1954–. Indexes.

This database is the companion to *America: History and Life,* covering the entire world other than the United States and Canada. Together, the two represent the premier resource for journal-literature searches in the field of history. It is important to note that the time frame covered begins with the year 1450; ancient and medieval times are excluded. Otherwise, this database is very similar to *America: History and Life,* described previously [entry 2-133]. 🖥

2-135. *Index Islamicus: A Bibliography of Publications on Islam and the Moslem World since 1906.* Triannual and cumulative. East Grinstead, West Sussex, UK: Brill Academic Publishers, 1958–. Indexes. ISSN: 1360-0982.

This indexing service has a rather complicated publishing history. It began with a single volume, edited by J. D. Pearson, covering the years 1908 through 1955. Additional volumes were issued through 1986, when the name of the publication was changed to *Quarterly Index Islamicus.* The current name was resumed in 1992, and publication became quarterly, culminating in an annual bound volume. Arrangement and focus of coverage has, of course, varied through the years. The initial emphasis by Pearson on the theology, law, art, philosophy, and history of Islam has continued; but geographical coverage has expanded from the initial focus on North Africa and the Middle East to include other regions where Islam is practiced. The literature cited is in English and other European languages. Currently, each issue or volume includes an outline of the contents, a listing of reviews, and indexes of subjects and names. This is a complex work of more value to advanced researchers than to undergraduates.

Annuals and Yearbooks
2-136. *Chase's Calendar of Events.* Annual. Chicago: McGraw-Hill Trade/Contemporary Publishing, 1958–. Index. ISSN 0740-5286.

A familiar source found in most library reference collections, *Chase's* annually provides a listing of events that have taken place on every day of the year. Many are birth dates of well-known individuals; for example, we learn that Cesar Chavez, Descartes, and Mozart were all born March 1. A brief biography is provided for each individual; and holidays, such as Valentine's Day, are given a short history. Each annual volume also lists upcoming events, ranging from the Florida Manatee Festival to the California Prune Festival. Some listings are amusing or frivolous; it comes as no surprise to discover that readers are invited to submit their own entries. A detailed index includes events and birthdays by date; each date lists not only the distinguished deceased but also contemporaries. Both the front matter and the back matter provide a hodgepodge of additional information, such as the naming of hurricanes. *Chase's* has always been a good source for day-by-day historical events, but it also provides a good deal of entertainment. 🖥

2-137. *Current Biography Yearbook.* Annual. New York: H. W. Wilson, 1940–. Index. ISSN: 0084-9499.

A standard for several decades, *Current Biography* continues to provide lengthy biographies of public individuals in the United States. The *Yearbook* is the accumulation of all entries in the monthly issues. Biographies are generally several pages in length and eschew controversy; both criticism and encomiums are provided. Although the scope is broad— politicians to educators to celebrities— the large number of entries for athletes and motion picture and television celebrities in the 1997 *Yearbook* is, perhaps, indicative of our times. Each entry concludes with references to newspaper and magazine articles, and each volume includes an index and short obituaries of biographees from previous years who died during the current year.

2-138. *Editorials on File.* Semimonthly. New York: Facts on File, 1970–. Index. ISSN: 0013-0966.

Each issue of this loose-leaf service focuses on nine or ten issues that have made headlines in the United States in recent weeks. Each topic is preceded by a column-length introduction, outlining the facts pertaining to the event, followed by reprints of editorials about the topic from approximately 150 daily newspapers from all regions in the

United States and Canada. Indexes cumulate throughout the year. A service such as this one naturally covers events that prove to be ephemeral but does provide a pro-and-con review of the news as seen by U.S. and Canadian newspaper editors.

2-139. *Facts on File: World News Digest with Index.* Weekly. New York: Facts on File, 1940–. Index. ISSN: 0014-6641.

This well-known news service provides a historical record of events around the world, though the United States is the major focus. Coverage mimics that of major newspapers, with emphasis on political events but including natural disasters, sports, and brief obituaries of noteworthy individuals. The stories are factual and vary greatly in length. Cumulative indexes are published throughout the year, with an annual index supplemented with multiyear indexes for quick searches. This is a good source for events in the United States, but coverage of the rest of the world is less detailed. *Keesing's Record of World Events* [entry 2-141] is a better resource for the latter.

2-140. *Historic Documents of [Year].* Annual. Washington, DC: Congressional Quarterly, 1972–. Index. ISSN: 0892-080X.

Having begun in 1972, this annual publication has become a standard found in many American libraries. It includes complete texts or lengthy excerpts of documents pertaining to a wide variety of topics under discussion during the year in question. Documents are arranged in chronological order and receive introductory comments that help place them in context and provide necessary background. Among the documents provided are "official statements, news conferences, speeches, special studies, and court decisions" (*Historic Documents* 1997, preface). A detailed table of contents precedes the documents, and there is a lengthy index as well. Indexes cumulate from time to time, and the index to all the annuals from 1972 through 1995 has been published as a separate volume. Though the editors of course have to be selective in their choice of documents that are reproduced, this publication nevertheless is a good starting point for major primary sources dealing with current topics of political and social import.

2-141. *Keesing's Record of World Events.* Monthly. Cambridge, UK: Keesing's Worldwide, 1931–. Indexes. ISSN: 0950-6128.

A staple for many years, this publication continues to record world events, mainly political, and includes very little celebrity or sports news. Each monthly issue is arranged first by continent, then by nation, with a final section for international agencies. Although this service is published in Great Britain, that country is not given substantially more space than other major nations. Indexes of names and subjects, including individual countries, cumulate throughout the year. Monthly publication means that coverage lags well behind real-time events, though it remains an excellent source for happenings in nations around the globe and provides details not always found in its American competitor *Facts on File* [entry 2-139]. (Note: *Keesing's* is now available electronically; the electronic version was not seen.) 💻

Directories

2-142. Jamail, Milton H., and Margo Gutierrez. *The Border Guide: Institutions and Organizations of the United States-Mexico Borderlands.* 2nd ed. Austin: University of Texas Center for Mexican American Studies, 1992. 193 pp. ISBN: 0-292-70778-9.

The border between the United States and Mexico is of concern not only to scholars and residents in that region, but also to policy makers in both countries. This guidebook provides a directory to numerous organizations concerned with the topic. Among them are border communities; the U.S., Mexican, and state governments; Maquiladora-related organizations; news media; and educational institutions. Also included are a lengthy bibliography, suggestions for library research, and a number of appendixes with particular emphasis upon demographic issues. This directory must be used with some caution, for many of the addresses and names of personnel will obviously have changed since 1992. On the other hand, this guide does provide overview information that is still of value and, if nothing else, provides a starting point for those interested in this subject.

2-143. Foster, Janet, and Julia Sheppard. *British Archives: A Guide to Archive Resources in the United King-*

dom. 3rd rev. and enlarged ed. New York: Groves Dictionaries, 1995. 627 pp. Indexes. ISBN: 1-561-59172-6.

The purpose of this volume is to provide a starting point for the first-time user of archival resources in the United Kingdom. Information was gathered from questionnaires mailed to archival agencies and includes address, telephone, access, major collections, search aids, and facilities. Arrangement is first by town and then by archival location. Three appendixes list institutions with archives housed elsewhere, institutions without archives, and institutions that did not respond to the questionnaires. A detailed index lists specific topics and is particularly useful for personal names. A separate index lists items by subject, from addition to zoology. The authors recognize that this volume is a beginning point, not a comprehensive resource. Some of the information (e.g., names of personnel and hours) is subject to rapid obsolescence. With these limitations in mind, readers can use this volume to locate specific archival collections.

2-144. National Historical Publications and Records Commission. *Directory of Archives and Manuscript Repositories in the United States.* Phoenix: Oryx Press, 1988. 852 pp. Indexes. ISBN: 0-897-74475-6.

This guide lists more than 4,000 institutions that maintain archival collections and is arranged by state and city, with entry numbers assigned to each institution or collection. Most are public or academic libraries, historical societies, or government entities in the fifty states, Puerto Rico, and the Virgin Islands. "Information" includes address, phone number, hours, facilities for copying, holdings, and cross-references to other bibliographic resources that cite the same collection and might provide additional detail. "Holdings" includes volumes in linear feet, dates of the collection, and a paragraph-length description of the subjects cited. The two indexes provide listings by name of repository and by subject. This volume has been a standard starting point for quick information about U.S. archives and their holdings. The future of print updates is uncertain, however, because of a planned electronic version, which was not seen. This 1988 edition, then, is of limited value.

2-145. Wheeler, Mary Bray, ed. *Directory of Historical Organizations in the United States and Canada.* Irregular. Nashville, TN: Alta Mira Press, 1936–. Indexes. ISSN: 1045-465X.

Long a standard resource, this directory, by the fifteenth edition, published in 2001, had grown to a listing of over 13,000 entries. Arrangement is by state or province, then by town or city. The more detailed listings include brief descriptions of museums, programs, and collections. Even the briefest listings include an address and, in most instances, the name of a contact person. Inclusion of libraries and academic history departments is somewhat sporadic. A separate section provides state-by-state information on agencies dealing with historical topics. Yet another section is a listing of

product and service vendors of interest to the historical community. There are two indexes: a standard alphabetical index and a program index. For local-history researchers, this is a core resource.

2-146. American Historical Association. *Directory of History Departments and Organizations in the United States and Canada.* Annual. Washington, DC: American Historical Association, 1975–. Index. ISSN: 1077-8500.

This directory is the standard source for basic information about history departments in the United States and Canada. The listing is alphabetical by name of institution and includes information on programs and admissions and a list of faculty, with specialization, in each department. Information on major historical organizations is also included, as well as an alphabetical listing of historians with their contact information and areas of specialty. (Note: The 2001 edition was the newest seen.)

Bibliographies

2-147. Norton, Mary Beth, ed. *American Historical Association's Guide to Historical Literature.* 3rd ed. 2 vols. New York: Oxford University Press, 1995. 2064 pp. Indexes. ISBN: 0-195-05727-9.

The publication of the third edition of the set in 1995 was welcome because the second edition had been published more than thirty years before, in 1961, and was seriously outdated. This edition is divided into forty-two subject areas covering all time periods and geographical locales. An essay by a specialist in the field precedes each section, identifies recent trends in scholarship, and often mentions core titles. The essays are followed by an extended bibliography divided into sections that group entries by time period or subject matter. Each entry includes a sentence-length annotation. The essayists and compilers are keenly aware of late twentieth-century historical trends and controversies, including multicultural and gender issues. Although coverage is global, the historical literature for Europe and the Americas receives greater emphasis than that for other parts of the world. Most of the second volume is devoted to two lengthy indexes, one by author and the other by subject. This is an excellent resource, though the reader would benefit had a table of contents been provided at the beginning of both volumes rather than just the first.

2-148. Valk, Barbara G., ed. *Borderline: A Bibliography of the United States-Mexico Borderlands.* Los Angeles: University of California–Los Angeles, Latin American Center Publications, 1988. 711 pp. Index. ISBN: 0-879-03112-3.

According to the introduction, this bibliography "cites materials in the sciences, social sciences, and the humanities treating the four U.S. and six Mexican states that form the border region—Arizona, California, New Mexico, Texas, Baja California, Chihuahua, Coahuila, Nuevo Leon, Sonora, and Tamaulipas." There are entries for 8,692 items, all arranged by accession number. A detailed contents listing and an index by author provide access to the listings. Among the subjects covered are history, physical characteristics, environmental characteristics, demography, economics, social characteristics, and education, among others. There are entries for Spanish-language materials as well as for those in English. The citations include only bibliographic information; there are no annotations. Despite its age, this bibliography, which covers the literature on the subject that appeared from 1960 through 1985, continues to be of use to researchers in this field.

2-149. Parish, Peter J., ed. *Reader's Guide to American History.* Chicago: Fitzroy Dearborn Publishers, 1997. 880 pp. Indexes. ISBN: 1-884-96422-2.

Reflecting a historiographic approach to research, this reference work provides the reader with an alphabetical list of essays, each of which describes an event, individual, or topic in American history. Each essay begins with a bibliography of key sources, then goes on to describe each source in relation to the topic at hand. The reader thus learns how historical thinking has been modified through the years and can turn to the literature most relevant to his or her purpose. Cross-references lead to additional essays. There are two indexes, one a listing of books to which the essays refer and the other a general index. Reference to the latter is sometimes necessary; for example, there is no essay for "frontier," so the reader must turn to the index to find page references pertaining to the frontier. The volume deliberately concentrates upon political, social, and economic history to the exclusion of literature, art and architecture, and science and medicine. In addition, more bibliographic references are to books rather than journal or periodical articles. This work also reflects recent scholarship in regard to the expansion of historiographic inquiry into gender and minority issues. Any reader seeking core literature on American historical issues will probably want to consult Parish.

Dictionaries

2-150. Barker, Graeme, ed. *Companion Encyclopedia of Archaeology.* 2 vols. London: Routledge, 1999. 1219 pp. Index. ISBN: 0-415-06448-1.

Rather than utilize an alphabetical approach, this archeology encyclopedia is arranged by topic. There are three major parts to this set: "Origins, Aims and Methods," "Themes and Approaches," and "Writing Archaeological History." Each of these three major parts includes about ten separate chapters on specific subjects. Examples include "Reconstructing the Environment and Natural Landscape," "Food and Farming," and "Europe in the Middle Ages." Altogether, there are twenty-nine of these chapters, averaging about forty pages apiece. Each is written by a separate contributor or contributors, most of whom are academicians in the United Kingdom, although there is also representation from the United States and Western Europe. Each chapter concludes with an extensive list of references. Graphs, graphical displays, and photographs supplement the text. The index provides additional access by subject. Although the contributors have written for a nonspecialized audience, this work will have its greatest value for undergraduates and other academic researchers.

2-151. Ritter, Harry. *Dictionary of Concepts in History.* New York: Greenwood Press, 1986. 490 pp. Index. ISBN: 0-313-22700-4.

This volume provides a conceptual context for a particular discipline through essays that describe those key concepts. Ritter explains that historians often are reluctant to describe their discipline in theoretical terms but that such a theoretical underpinning does exist. The essays cover such topics as alienation, imperialism, and zeitgeist and also include cross-references to related topics and bibliographic references to other sources. The topic index provides yet another approach to the contents. This volume is useful to those seeking detailed information on the theoretical aspects of history but, because it was published in 1986, does not consider the more recent trends in historiography.

2-152. Townson, Duncan. *Dictionary of Contemporary History: 1945 to the Present.* Malden, MA: Blackwell Publishers, 1999. 447 pp. ISBN: 0-631-20937-9.

Coverage of this book extends from the end of the Second World War to early 1998 and focuses upon politics, economic history, and international relations to the exclusion of science, art, music, and literature. Although the entries are short, the author has attempted to provide some analysis. The arrangement is alphabetical. Entries range in length from a single paragraph to a couple of pages. More substantive entries include one or two bibliographic references. Cross-references are indicated in uppercase. There are no illustrations. Many of the entries are for individuals, and this will probably prove to be the most useful entry point for most users, who can than follow the cross-references to other relevant subjects. There is some emphasis upon events in the United Kingdom. Otherwise, this will be a handy starting point for those novice researchers who require only brief background on the late twentieth century and its central figures and events. ⌨

2-153. Kohn, George Childs. *Dictionary of Wars.* rev. ed. New York: Facts on File, 1999. 614 pp. Indexes. ISBN: 0-816-04157-1.

This revised edition adds 70 new articles, bringing the total to approximately 1,800 entries. The wars included range among a number of types of conflicts: international wars, civil wars, rebellions, and revolutions, among others. Entries are arranged alphabetically by name of episode, with cross-references from alternative headings. Cross-references lead the reader to other relevant entries. Many entries are relatively short; more significant conflicts, such as the Second World War, receive up to four pages of coverage. Warfare in Africa, Asia, and South America receives rather more attention than is usually the case. There

are no illustrations, maps, or bibliographic references. There are separate indexes of geographical regions and subjects. This work will be suitable for those high-school students and undergraduates requiring only a brief explanation of noteworthy conflicts throughout history.

2-154. Lenman, Bruce P. *Larousse Dictionary of World History.* New York: Larousse, 1994. 996 pp. ISBN: 0-752-35001-3.

No single-volume dictionary of world history can be comprehensive, but this one, at least, is relatively recent and includes information through the early 1990s. Entries are arranged alphabetically and include individuals, organizations, episodes, and events. Most entries are only a sentence or two, but some, such as descriptions of wars, are much longer and usually include a map. Otherwise, the only other illustrations are occasional listings of members of royal houses. Cross-references are in boldface. The introduction explains that space limitations restricted coverage to political, military, and diplomatic history, the traditional approach to historical events. Although emphasis is on European and North American societies, an attempt has been made to provide at least basic coverage of other parts of the world. This competent volume supplies very basic information on historical events relating to political and military events.

2-155. Hornblower, Simon, and Antony Spawforth, eds. *Oxford Classical Dictio-*

nary. 3rd rev. ed. Oxford: Oxford University Press, 2003. 1640 pp. ISBN: 0-198-60641-9.

Earlier editions of this standard reference work have been a basic source for information on ancient Greece and Rome. This edition not only updates the earlier works but also improves on them in several ways. It is interdisciplinary in character; for example, it incorporates archeological methods previously absent and includes topics of recent concern, particularly the history of women. Thematic entries include topics such as disease, ecology, and motherhood. Untranslated Greek and Latin have been minimized to make the text more accessible to those not familiar with those languages. As before, entries are arranged alphabetically and initialed by the contributor; a list of contributors appears at the front. Entries range in length from a sentence or two to two or three pages, and cross-references are indicated by an asterisk. Major entries include a listing of both ancient and modern references. Although the text might prove formidable to many undergraduates, this source continues to be a major starting point for researchers needing brief information on topics in this field of history.

Encyclopedias
2-156. Stearns, Peter N., ed. *Encyclopedia of Social History.* New York: Garland, 1994. 856 pp. Index. ISBN: 0-815-30342-4.

The introduction to this single-volume work describes the differences between social history and more traditional modes of historical inquiry, then goes on to state the intent of the work: "this *Encyclopedia* emphasizes extensive coverage of the major social history topics and methods, thus defining the most characteristic features and issues in the field." Unlike the *Encyclopedia of American Social History* [entry 2-184], this publication is worldwide in scope, although, of necessity, coverage is brief. For example, the article on "African Regions" discusses geography, peoples, societies, and external historical factors in about two pages. Separate articles deal with the slave trade, slavery, and organization in Africa. Examples of topical articles include "Frontier Societies," "Juvenile Delinquency," and "Punishment and Prisons." Most articles conclude with a listing of cross-references to other topics in the volume. A short list of references to significant books and articles is also appended to each. Articles are signed, and the front matter includes descriptions of the affiliations of the contributors, including at times a listing of their significant works. The index provides additional access to the text. There are no illustrations. In general, the style of writing is accessible to students and laypersons as well as specialists. While one might quibble with some of the opinions expressed by the editor and contributors, this volume nevertheless is a useful source for all library patrons seeking introductory information on aspects of social history. 💻

2-157. Dupuy, R. Ernest, and Trevor N. Dupuy. *The Harper Encyclopedia of Military History: From 3500 BC to the*

Present. 4th ed. New York: Harper Information Publishers, 1993. 1654 pp. Indexes. ISBN: 0-062-70058-1.

This encyclopedia provides a chronological overview of military events, campaigns, and battles. The authors, both military historians, briefly describe military and naval engagements worldwide from ancient times to about 1990. Each chapter covers a specific period of time and includes a discussion of trends in military technology and thinking, and often a map. The volume concludes with three indexes—a general index, an index of wars, and an index of battles and sieges—and a bibliography of additional sources, generally popular rather than scholarly. Recent epochs and events in Europe and North America receive more attention than other times and places, but most readers will likely be searching for those topics in any case.

2-158. Langer, William L., ed. *The New Illustrated Encyclopedia of World History.* 2 vols. New York: Harry N. Abrams, 1975. 1368 pp. Index. ISBN: 0-810-90117-X.

This illustrated edition of William Langer's standard work is both informative and handsomely produced. Langer, a distinguished historian, takes the reader on a chronological journey from prehistoric times to the late twentieth century. Emphasis is on political, diplomatic, and military events, but other facets of life, including the arts and philosophy, are covered. The entries end with World War II; the last 200 pages are devoted to a country-by-country survey, concluding

with an overview of space exploration and science and technology. A lengthy index leads the reader to individuals, events, and subjects. This edition attempts to cover regions of the world other than Europe and North America in greater detail than earlier editions, but it does not, of course, reflect recent multicultural concerns. This work has been a standard in libraries for decades and will continue to attract those in need of brief information on Western historical events.

2-159. Fagan, Brian M., ed. *The Oxford Companion to Archaeology.* New York: Oxford University Press, 1996. 844 pp. Index. ISBN: 0-195-07618-4.

This volume, in typical encyclopedia format, lists entries alphabetically. Entries range in length from several paragraphs to several pages; each includes cross-references and concludes with a list of references and the contributor's name. A list of the contributors and their affiliations appears at the front. The volume concludes with a section of maps, chronological tables, and an index. The editor's aim is to be comprehensive yet accessible to general audiences. The volume discusses how archeology began and developed, how it works, how it explains the past, and how it explains human evolution and changes in behavior over time. Typical entries include "Field Systems," "Frontier Sites of the American West," "Funan Culture," and "General Systems Theory." Coverage is global and incorporates recent theory and research findings. This handy volume provides basic information on archeology and is a delight to use because of its literate approach to the topic.

American History
Guides and Handbooks

2-160. *America in the Twentieth Century.* 11 vols. New York: Marshall Cavendish, 1995. 1536 pp. Indexes. ISBN: 1-854-35736-0.

Each of the first ten volumes of this set is devoted to a particular decade in U.S. history during the twentieth century, including the first half of the 1990s. The general format is similar from one volume to the next. Each includes an introductory chapter and concludes with a summary and analysis of the decade. In between, there are chapters that discuss topics such as social policy, popular culture, politics, foreign relations, literature, sports, the environment, and a number of others. Sidebars provide biographies of and quotations from leading individuals, including women and minorities, of that decade. There are numerous illustrations, many in color. A chronology and a short list of readings appear at the end of each of the "decade" volumes. Each volume also includes a table of contents for the entire set as well as its own index. The final volume includes a comprehensive chronology through 1994, a glossary, a comprehensive bibliography that includes listings found in the individual volumes, and a number of separate indexes. This is a set that will be attractive to both high-school and undergraduate students; the volumes dealing with recent decades will probably be those of most interest.

2-161. Tompkins, Vincent, ed. *American Decades, 1900–1909.* Detroit: Gale Research, 1996. 589 pp. Index. ISBN: 0-810-35722-4.

Chronologically, this is the first in a series of volumes that describes the American decades of the twentieth century through the 1980s. The format is much the same for each. A brief introduction sets the stage and is followed by chapters devoted to subjects such as the arts, government and politics, media, religion, and sports. Each chapter is accorded an outline of contents that includes a chronology, an overview, "Topics in the News," "Headline Makers," "People in the News," deaths, and contemporary publications. The "Headline Makers" section provides background information on key figures of the decade for each subject. There are numerous illustrations and occasional sidebars. The volume concludes with a multipage listing of references. Volumes in this series are obviously targeted to beginning students, either high-school or college level, rather than to specialists or advanced students. The set can be recommended to this group, as can this publisher's American Eras series [entry 2-171 and passim]; together, the two provide comprehensive coverage of American history from the sixteenth century to almost the end of the twentieth century. Individual volumes appear below.

2-162. Tompkins, Vincent, ed. *American Decades, 1910–1919.* Detroit: Gale Research, 1996. 632 pp. Index. ISBN: 0-810-35723-2.

2-163. Baughman, Judith S., ed. *American Decades, 1920–1929*. Detroit: Gale Research, 1995. 554 pp. Index. ISBN: 0-810-35724-0.

2-164. Bondi, Victor, ed. *American Decades, 1930–1939*. Detroit: Gale Research, 1995. 612 pp. Index. ISBN: 0-810-35725-9.

2-165. Bondi, Victor, ed. *American Decades, 1940–1949*. Detroit: Gale Research, 1995. 641 pp. Index. ISBN: 0-810-35726-7.

2-166. Tompkins, Vincent, and Victor Bondi, eds. *American Decades, 1950–1959*. 6th ed. Detroit: Gale Research, 1994. 521 pp. Index. ISBN: 0-810-35727-5.

2-167. Layman, Richard, and Matthew J. Bruccoli, eds. *American Decades, 1960–1969*. 7th ed. Detroit: Gale Research, 1994. 595 pp. Index. ISBN: 0-810-38883-9.

2-168. Bruccoli, Matthew, and Richard Layman, eds. *American Decades, 1970–1979*. 8th ed. Detroit: Gale Research, 1995. 623 pp. Index. ISBN: 0-810-38882-0.

2-169. Bruccoli, Matthew, and Richard Layman, eds. *American Decades, 1980–1989*. 9th ed. Detroit: Gale Research, 1996. 774 pp. Index. ISBN: 0-810-38881-2.

2-170. McConnell, Tandy, ed. *American Decades, 1990–1999*. Detroit: Gale Group, 2001. 673 pp. Index. ISBN: 0-787-64030-1.

2-171. Kross, Jessica. *American Eras: The Colonial Era, 1600–1754*. Detroit: Gale Research, 1998. 455 pp. Index. ISBN: 0-787-61479-3.

This reference work is representative of the format of this series. A brief introduction sets the stage for a dozen chapters, each on a specific subject, such as education, law and justice, religion, and sports and recreation. Each chapter begins with an outline of the contents divided into the following categories: chronology, overview, "Topics in the News," "Headline Makers," and publications. The last three categories describe significant events and circumstances, and provide brief biographies of important individuals and a listing of noteworthy contemporary publications. There are numerous illustrations and sidebars. Each volume concludes with a bibliography, information on contributors, and an index. This series is aimed at high-school and undergraduate researchers who require a somewhat undemanding introduction to the past. Although of little value to specialists and advanced students, it is useful to librarians and instructors needing introductory information for the beginning researcher. Individual volumes are listed below.

2-172. Allison, Robert J., ed. *American Eras: The Revolutionary Era, 1754–1783*. Detroit: Gale Research, 1998. 394 pp. Index. ISBN: 0-787-61480-7.

2-173. Allison, Robert J., ed. *American Eras: Development of a Nation, 1783–1815.* Detroit: Gale Research, 1997. 423 pp. Index. ISBN: 0-787-61481-5.

2-174. Prokopowicz, Gerald J., ed. *American Eras: The Reform Era and Eastern U.S. Development, 1815–1850.* Detroit: Gale Research, 1998. 379 pp. Index. ISBN: 0-787-61482-3.

2-175. Brown, Thomas J., ed. *American Eras: Civil War and Reconstruction, 1850–1877.* Detroit: Gale Research, 1997. 433 pp. Index. ISBN: 0-787-61484-X.

2-176. Tompkins, Vincent, ed. *American Eras: Development of the Industrial United States, 1878–1899.* Detroit: Gale Research, 1997. 455 pp. Index. ISBN: 0-787-61485-8.

2-177. Gross, Ernie. *American Years: A Chronology of United States History.* New York: Charles Scribner's Sons, 1999. 655 pp. Index. ISBN: 0-684-80590-1.

The chronology in this volume accords a separate listing for each year from 1776 through 1997. Within each yearly listing, the following categories are possible: "International," "National," "Business/Industry/Inventions," "Transportation," "Science/Medicine," "Education," "Religion," "Arts/Music," "Literature/Journalism," "Entertainment," "Sports," and "Miscellaneous." Not every category is represented each year. Within each cate-gory, a sentence or paragraph is devoted to each event or circumstance worthy of notice. Detail for the second century of American history tends to be somewhat greater than that prior to the Civil War. Numerous illustrations accompany the text. Although there are a number of chronologies of American history, this volume is useful for its emphasis on happenings outside the sphere of politics and for its attractive and accessible format. It can be used by both high-school and undergraduate students.

2-178. Fox, Richard Wightman, and James T. Kloppenberg, eds. *A Companion to American Thought.* Cambridge, MA: Blackwell Publishers, 1995. 804 pp. Index. ISBN: 1-557-86268-0.

An alphabetical arrangement of ideas, concepts, and key individuals, this reference work strives to present a picture of U.S. intellectual thinking without digressing into the cultural wars of the 1990s. In the introduction, the editors stress that they try to take a moderate position between those on the right, who defend the canon, and those on the left, who attack it. Entries range in length from 100 to 2,500 words, depending on significance. Each ends with a listing of sources for additional reading and cross-references to related topics in the volume. Topic entries include "Academic Freedom," "Citizenship," and "Social Science"; individuals include Gompers, Holmes, Henry James, and Rorty. Although it is impossible for the contributors to eliminate their viewpoints from their essays, this work is, in general, reasonably unbiased and can serve as an introduction to the U.S. intellectual tradition for both students and specialists. 🖳

2-179. Kutler, Stanley I., ed. *Dictionary of American History.* 10 vols. New York: Charles Scribner's Sons, 2003. Index. ISBN: 0-684-80533-2.

The original edition of the *Dictionary of American History* appeared in 1940, with the publication of the second edition taking place in 1976. This new third edition reflects new interpretations and new emphases in historical study in recent decades. Greater attention to ethnic diversity is one of the themes of this edition. The alphabetical arrangement has been retained, but illustrations have been added for the first time. Articles generally range in length from a single paragraph to several pages. Regardless of length, the articles conclude with a bibliography and often include cross-references to other relevant articles. Each article is signed by the historian or authority responsible for its content. The ninth volume provides reproductions of archival maps and a large number of representative excerpts from primary sources from 1550 to 2001. The final volume provides an index to the entire set. This is an essential resource for researchers at all levels.

2-180. *Dictionary of Twentieth-Century Culture: American Culture after World War II.* Detroit: Gale Research, 1994. 393 pp. Index. ISBN: 0-810-38481-7.

One of a series of Gale publications that discuss twentieth-century culture in a number of countries and regions, this work concentrates upon happenings in the humanities and associated arenas. These include art, music, literature, drama, radio and television, motion pictures, and dance. The arrangement is alphabetical. Entries are relatively brief; few are over 1,000 words. Many of the entries are biographies, but there are also articles on subjects such as feminism, Native Americans, punk rock, and game shows. Photographs are included with the text. Particularly useful is a table of contents arranged by topic, allowing the reader to see a listing of all entries that deal with art or literature, for example. Individual entries include listings for additional reading. The reading level is suitable for both high-school and undergraduate students. Because of the strong emphasis upon biographies, most users will benefit by consulting the list of topics to get an overview of a particular area of interest.

2-181. Commager, Henry Steele, ed. *Documents of American History.* 10th ed. 2 vols. Englewood Cliffs, NJ: Prentice-Hall, 1988. Index. ISBN: 0-132-17274-7; 0-132-17282-8.

This well-known compilation of the texts of important American documents extends from 1492 through 1987 and includes 727 entries. Each includes a brief introduction by the editor, often with a reference or references to other sources of information, and a citation back to the original source. In the preface, Commager delineates his criteria for inclusion; these are too lengthy to list here but, in essence, consist of "documents of an official and quasi-official character." As he, himself, admits, most such publications do not illuminate social life. Nevertheless, this is a valuable resource for texts pertaining to political, diplomatic, and military events. The two volumes break at 1898, and each has its own index. Some of the documents included in this set are now available on various Web sites, but this reference work includes many that might not appear readily elsewhere and also provides useful commentary, bibliographies, and citations to expedite additional research.

2-182. Carruth, Gordon. *Encyclopedia of American Facts and Dates*. 10th ed. New York: HarperCollins Publishers, 1997. 1096 pp. Index. ISBN: 0-062-70192-4.

Among the many single-volume encyclopedias and dictionaries of American history, this is perhaps the best of those with a chronological approach. Entries extend from the tenth century through 1992 and range in length from a single sentence to a lengthy paragraph. The format lends particular value to the information: entries are arranged in four columns on facing pages. The first column deals with standard political, military, and diplomatic events; the second pertains to the arts; the third covers labor, economics, education, religion, and the like; and the fourth discusses folkways. Thus, the reader can review a particular year and, by reading across columns, learn what was taking place in various arenas simultaneously. A detailed index provides an-

other access point to the contents. This volume is especially useful for students but has value for specialized researchers as well.

2-183. Nash, Gary B., ed. *Encyclopedia of American History*. 11 vols. New York: Facts on File, 2003. Index. ISBN: 0-816-04371-X

The *Encyclopedia of American History* has a somewhat different format than most encyclopedias. Aside from the index, each of the volumes represents a particular historical era, with the first volume concentrating on events up to 1607 and the final volume covering events from 1946 to 1968. Each volume contains an alphabetical array of articles ranging in length from a few paragraphs to several pages. A brief listing for further reading concludes each article. There are numerous cross-references within the same volume. Maps and illustrations accompany the text. There is particular emphasis on issues of ethnic diversity, and articles are included that might not be found in a more traditional encyclopedia, for example, a brief biography of Bob Dylan. Each volume concludes with a chronology, several primary-source documents, a bibliography, and an index. The final volume provides an index to the entire set. The writing style is suitable for undergraduates, but more advanced researchers will consult this set also. The only caveats are that some entries are not signed and credentials of the contributors are not given. Nevertheless, most library reference collections should include both this encyclopedia and the

Dictionary of American History [entry 2-179].

2-184. Cayton, Mary Kupiec, Elliott J. Gorn, and Peter W. Williams, eds. *Encyclopedia of American Social History.* 3 vols. New York: Charles Scribner's Sons, 1993. 2653 pp. Index. ISBN: 0-684-19246-2.

Social history, which has burgeoned in recent decades, is of interest to historians, sociologists, and political scientists alike. The editors explain that this encyclopedia attempts "to capture the results of the generation long paradigm shift that has led to a radical rethinking of the historian's craft" (Cayton, Gorn, and Williams 1993, preface). Articles in the encyclopedia are up to twenty pages in length. Arrangement is topical rather than alphabetical. Essays in the first volume describe periods in American history, methodology, social identity, and social-change processes. The second volume is devoted to ethnic cultures, regionalism, geographical influences, everyday life, and "Work and Labor." The third volume deals with popular culture, family history, social problems, science, and education. Each of the three volumes includes a complete table of contents, facilitating access; the index in the final volume is quite detailed and will probably be consulted by most users. Each essay concludes with an extensive bibliography. Essays are signed, and brief biographical information on contributors appears in the third volume. Most are academicians. There are no illustrations other than a few graphic displays. Cross-references are also somewhat limited in number and appear only at the very end of the essay, after the bibliography. This is a minor inconvenience, however. This is an excellent resource, one that will provide both advanced researchers and beginners with in-depth and lucid treatment of many topics in the arena of social history.

2-185. Wilson, Charles Reagan, and William Ferris, eds. *Encyclopedia of Southern Culture.* Chapel Hill: University of North Carolina Press, 1989. 1634 pp. Index. ISBN: 0-807-81823-2.

Defining culture as a "way of life," the editors assert that this reference work is particularly concerned to "identify distinctive regional characteristics" and to address the issue of "continuity and change in southern culture" (Wilson and Ferris 1989, introduction). Toward this end, they have chosen a topical approach to the subject as opposed to an alphabetical array. There are major entries on subjects such as agriculture, folk life, and violence. Each of these major categories is introduced with a general essay that is then followed by articles on specific topics. Each article is signed by the contributor. Most contributors are academicians at Southern institutions. Articles include bibliographic listings and, when necessary, cross-references to other sections of the volume. The arrangement of articles by topic area has its strengths, but it is also somewhat idiosyncratic and does force the reader to consult the index more than might be the case if the arrangement were strictly alphabetical.

Nevertheless, this is a handy source for a great deal of information on the South.

2-186. Phillips, Charles, and Alan Axelrod, eds. *Encyclopedia of the American West.* 4 vols. New York: Macmillan Reference, 1996. 1935 pp. Index. ISBN: 0-028-97495-6.

The American West has been the subject of contentious debate between the "new West" historians of the late twentieth century and those who take a more traditional approach to the history of the region. This new encyclopedia attempts to synthesize viewpoints on the West and to address issues and topics both old and new. Arrangement is alphabetical, with articles ranging in length from a paragraph or two to those entries that are several pages in length. There are entries for individuals and for the western states (defined here as those states west of the Mississippi, including Alaska and Hawaii) as well as more general topics, such as "grazing," "intermarriage," and "oil and gas industry." Articles are signed by the contributors, most of whom are academicians. Brief bibliographies are included for each article, and there are numerous illustrations and maps. There is somewhat greater emphasis on periods before the twentieth century, although earlier decades of this century do receive attention. The writing style makes this set appropriate for use by undergraduates, while scholars will appreciate the even-handed treatment of controversial topics.

2-187. Cooke, Jacob Ernest, ed. *Encyclopedia of the North American Colonies.*

3 vols. New York: Charles Scribner's Sons, 1993. 2397 pp. Index. ISBN: 0-684-19269-1.

Like a number of other recent subject encyclopedias, this set capitalizes on new thinking and new research in presenting information about North American colonies. While traditional works concentrated on the English-speaking colonies, this one includes colonies of other European nations and provides background information on Native Americans and their society. Emphasis is on demographic, cultural, economic, and social features of the colonies arranged by topic; for example, "Landholding" is discussed by four different contributors, each responsible for a different national group (British, Dutch, French, or Spanish). Each article is signed and has a bibliography. There are maps but no other illustrations. Information on contributors and an index complete the third volume. The text is accessible and useful for both undergraduates and more specialized researchers.

2-188. Kutler, Stanley I., ed. *Encyclopedia of the United States in the Twentieth Century.* 4 vols. New York: Charles Scribner's Sons, 1996. 1941 pp. Index. ISBN: 0-132-10535-7.

Organized thematically, this encyclopedia provides an in-depth introduction to the history of the twentieth-century United States, incorporating recent historical perspectives. The four volumes of this set are organized into six major categories, focusing upon the American people; politics; the foreign scene; science, technology, and medicine; the economy;

and culture. Each of these major subdivisions includes a number of encyclopedia-length articles pertaining to aspects of that category and written by individual scholars. The articles conclude with detailed annotated bibliographies. Cross-references are provided to other relevant articles in the encyclopedia. There are no illustrations other than occasional graphs, tables, and maps. The final volume describes the credentials of the contributors and provides a comprehensive index. This encyclopedia is accessible to undergraduate students, but also provides enough detail and bibliographic references to be of value to graduate students and advanced researchers requiring introductory information to a topic. With its emphasis upon economic, social, and cultural history as well as the more traditional area of politics, this is a welcome addition to reference works dealing with the recent history of the United States.

World History
Encyclopedias
2-189. Hook, Brian, and Denis Twitchett, eds. *Cambridge Encyclopedia of China.* 2nd ed. New York: Cambridge University Press, 1991. 502 pp. Index. ISBN: 0-521-35594-X.

This second edition of the *Cambridge Encyclopedia of China* updates the first by taking into account those changes that took place in the 1970s and 1980s. The arrangement is topical rather than alphabetical. There are major sections for "Land and Resources," "Peoples," "Society," history, "the Mind and Senses of China," "Arts and Architecture," and sci-

ence and technology. Most articles are relatively short, from a page to about three pages. Numerous illustrations, some in color, and maps supplement the text. There are several appendixes, most of them displaying information on language transliteration or directories. A glossary and a short bibliography conclude the work. Similar in approach to the "regional" encyclopedias also published by Cambridge, this work presents the reader with a reasonably comprehensive overview of China and its history and culture in a format that is attractive to general readers, including undergraduates, as well as to scholars who are not Chinese specialists. The only caveat is that this work is now ten years old, so many users may wish to supplement its text with more recent sources.

2-190. Robinson, Francis, ed. *Cambridge Encyclopedia of India, Pakistan, Bangladesh, Sri Lanka, Nepal, Bhutan and the Maldives.* Cambridge, UK: Cambridge University Press, 520 pp. Index. ISBN: 0-521-33451-9.

Like other Cambridge regional encyclopedias, this work hopes to be of value to the general public and the specialist alike. The countries covered in the volume are indicated in the title. The arrangement is not alphabetical, but rather topical. Major chapters deal with the land, its inhabitants, history, politics, foreign relations, economy, religion, society, and culture. There are many illustrations, graphic displays, and maps; some are in color. Some information is provided in sidebars. Each of the major chapters is divided into articles, each of which includes a short bibliography. Although this is an attractive volume, the format does remind the reader of an encyclopedia, with its emphasis on facts and figures. Nevertheless, this work provides a useful single-volume resource for information on South Asia, and it will be of greatest value to undergraduates and other academic researchers. Of course, with a publication date of 1989, it will not be helpful to those individuals seeking contemporary information on these countries.

2-191. Collier, Simon, Thomas E. Skidmore, and Harold Blakemore, eds. *Cambridge Encyclopedia of Latin America and the Caribbean.* 2nd ed. Cambridge, UK: Cambridge University Press, 1992. 479 pp. Index. ISBN: 0-521-41322-2.

This volume is similar in nature to other Cambridge regional encyclopedias. The nations included here are those from Mexico through Central and South America, and the Caribbean. The text is divided into six major units: "Physical Environment," "Economy," "Peoples," "History," "Politics and Society," and "Culture." Each of these major units is further subdivided into distinct components. For example, the unit on the economy includes sections on agriculture, mining, energy, and several others. For the most part, discussion deals with Latin America as a whole; only in the history unit are there subdivisions for individual nations or regions. Many entries include brief listings for additional reading. There are numerous maps, graphic displays, and illustrations, many in color. The text has a heavy emphasis on facts and figures, so is somewhat dry. Still, this will be a useful work for both high-school and college students seeking general information on Latin America in a single source.

2-192. Mostyn, Trevor, ed. *Cambridge Encyclopedia of the Middle East and North Africa.* Cambridge, UK: Cambridge University Press, 1988. 504 pp. Index. ISBN: 0-521-32190-5.

This attractive reference work presents an overview in some detail of the Middle East and its history. The arrangement is topical, not alphabetical. The six major parts of the contents deal with "Lands and Peoples," "History," "Societies and Economies," "Culture," "the Countries," and "Inter-state Relations." Each of the major parts is further subdivided by subject; thus, the section on culture provides lengthy discussions of religion, literature, arts, music, and science. Geographically, the countries discussed range from Morocco to Iran. There are numerous illustrations, maps, and graphic displays, many in color. Bibliographies for additional reading are provided with each major entry. The writing style is more suitable for researchers in higher education than it will be for many general readers. Although this work is now over a decade old, it remains suitable for readers requiring detailed introductory information on the Middle East exclusive of contemporary events.

2-193. *The Canadian Encyclopedia.* 2nd ed. 4 vols. Toronto: McClelland and

Stewart, 2000. 2573 pp. Index. ISBN: 0-771-02099-6.

The introduction to the first edition states that this encyclopedia seeks "to provide coverage of all aspects of life in Canada, of all regions, over a vast time scale from the geological formation of the ancient rocks of the Shield to the most recent political events." The second edition provided updated material as well as an expanded index and additional tables, cross-references, and chronologies. The basic format is similar to that found in most general encyclopedias: an alphabetical array of articles of varying lengths is accompanied by illustrations where appropriate. Longer articles include a brief list of additional reading, and all articles are signed by the contributor. Many of the illustrations are in color. The use of three columns per page, a relatively small typeface, and illustrations that usually are themselves small leads to a format that seems rather cramped in appearance. However, those readers needing information on Canada in greater depth than can be found in encyclopedias published in the United States will turn to this set for assistance. It will be of use to undergraduate students and scholars alike.

2-194. Grant, Michael, and Rachel Kitzinger, eds. *Civilization of the Ancient Mediterranean: Greece and Rome.* 3 vols. New York: Charles Scribner's Sons, 1988. 1980 pp. Index. ISBN: 0-684-17594-0.

The editors of this encyclopedia chose a topical approach to their subject matter. Approximately 100 essays describe particular aspects of Greek and Roman civilization. The first volume includes historical summaries for each of the two civilizations and then provides essays on ecology, population, agriculture and food, technology, and government and society. The second volume describes economics, religion, and private and social life. The final volume discusses women and family life, literary and performing arts, philosophy, and the visual arts. Essays are up to thirty pages in length, and each concludes with a bibliography delineating both ancient sources and modern studies. Illustrations appear as needed. The final volume concludes with a set of maps, a list of contributors, and an index for the entire set. This reference work intends to be of service to both specialists and nonspecialists and generally succeeds, though some readers might prefer a source providing the more traditional alphabetical approach.

2-195. Sasson, Jack M., ed. *Civilizations of the Ancient Near East.* 4 vols. New York: Charles Scribner's Sons, 1995. 2966 pp. Index. ISBN: 0-684-19279-9.

As the introduction to this encyclopedia states, the ancient Near East was home to a number of highly diverse societies and civilizations and, therefore, holds special interest to the present. The arrangement of this set is topical, and each volume presents essays concerning a common theme. Volume one describes the ancient Near East as it is depicted by Western thought, the environment, population, and social institutions. The second volume deals with history and culture, and the third, with economy, trade, technology, and artistic production. The final volume covers language, writing, literature, and visual and performing arts and includes descriptions of contributors and an extensive index. Coverage extends from the third millennium BCE through the reign of Alexander the Great, from Egypt and Turkey on the west through Iran on the east. The set contains nearly 200 thematic essays, ranging from ten to twenty pages in length, with illustrations, and each concludes with a bibliography emphasizing scholarly resources. The text is accessible to most levels of readership, and the intelligently constructed index provides easy referral to the contents.

2-196. Strayer, Joseph R., ed. *Dictionary of the Middle Ages.* 13 vols. New York: Charles Scribner's Sons, 1989. 8725 pp. Index. ISBN: 0-684-19073-7.

This reference set was created in response to the proliferation of topics and scholars in medieval studies. The editors also expanded the subject matter to include not only the Latin West but also eastern Europe and lands bordering the Mediterranean as well as including contributions from Byzantine and Muslim societies, often neglected in older scholarship. Entries, arranged alphabetically, cover the period from AD 500 to 1500 and range in length up to 10,000 words, concluding with a bibliography and the name of the contributor. All aspects of medieval society, including economics and science, are discussed. The final volume contains an index to the entire set

and a comprehensive list of contributors and their affiliations. Most come from U.S. and Canadian institutions, reflecting the editor's intent to target a North American audience. The text is accessible to both undergraduates and specialists, while the bibliographic listings point to scholarly resources elsewhere. Supplement one was published in 2003 and is approximately 600 pages long.

2-197. Standish, Peter, ed. *Dictionary of Twentieth-Century Culture: Hispanic Culture of South America.* Detroit: Gale Research, 1995. 340 pp. Indexes. ISBN: 0-810-38483-3.

One of a series of dictionaries dealing with twentieth-century culture, this volume, as the title indicates, has the Spanish-speaking countries of South America as its subject. The scope of the volume incorporates "people, places, terms, art forms, and organizations associated with creative expression in the humanities, those forms of creativity that seek to describe and interpret the human condition" (Standish 1995, "Editorial Plan"). The articles are arranged in an alphabetical array and range in length from a paragraph to three pages. There are references to additional reading. There are numerous illustrations; these are indexed separately. The cultural manifestations described here often have political overtones, so this volume will be of use to undergraduates seeking basic information on both. Scholars and other advanced researchers will want to turn to more detailed sources.

2-198. Middleton, John, ed. *Encyclopedia of Africa South of the Sahara.* 4 vols. New York: Charles Scribner's Sons, 1997. 2466 pp. Index. ISBN: 0-684-80466-2.

This encyclopedia is the result of a conscious effort to describe and discuss Africa in light of new thinking and research. In addition to the usual articles on individual countries and topics, including religion, economy, and medicine, this work provides background on such matters as nationalism, ideology, and historical interpretation. Approximately 40 percent of the contributors are African, and the viewpoint is decidedly Afrocentric. Entries range in length from two or three paragraphs to many pages, are signed, and include brief bibliographies. There are many maps, but other illustrations are infrequent. The final volume includes an index and three appendixes. The first describes African studies; the second provides a chronology of African history; and the third is a lengthy listing of ethnic groups, with a brief discussion of each. In all, this is a valuable resource for students and specialists alike.

2-199. Embree, Ainslie T., ed. *Encyclopedia of Asian History.* 4 vols. New York: Charles Scribner's Sons, 1988. 2060 pp. Index. ISBN: 0-684-18619-5.

Prepared under the auspices of the Asian Society, this encyclopedia aims to present scholarly information in a manner accessible to the nonspecialist. "Asia" is defined here as excluding portions of the Middle East nearest Europe and part of the former Soviet Union so as to concentrate on East, South, and Central Asia. Articles are arranged alphabetically and range from a paragraph to several pages in length. Cross-references are noted in brackets at the end of the entry, and many articles are accompanied by a bibliography of additional sources. Articles are signed by the author. The final volume includes a "Directory of Contributors," an index, a "Synoptic Outline," an alphabetical list of entries, a list of maps, and a Wade-Giles/pinyin conversion table. Some of this information might more appropriately have been found in the first volume, but it is convenient to have all this material in one spot. This encyclopedia will be of value to those unfamiliar with Asian history but seeking information about its political history, religion, individuals, or culture.

2-200. Magocsi, Paul Robert, ed. *Encyclopedia of Canada's Peoples.* Toronto: University of Toronto Press, 1999. 1334 pp. ISBN: 0-802-02938-8.

Canada, like the United States, is a nation of immigrants. This volume has 119 articles on such groups, chosen for characteristics such as place of birth, language or dialect, religion, and self-identification as a distinctive group. The arrangement is alphabetical, with an initial article dealing with "Aboriginal Peoples," which is further divided into eleven linguistic groups. Elsewhere in the volume, entries are as much as fifty pages in length. They are divided into topics such as "Origins," "Migration," "Arrival and Settlement," "Economic Life," "Family and Kinship,"

"Culture and Community Life," "Education and Religion," "Politics," "Intergroup Relations," and "Group Maintenance and Ethnic Commitment." Articles conclude with a bibliography that emphasizes the Canadian experience of the immigrant groups. There are also a number of thematic entries for subjects such as "Canadian Identity," "Multiculturalism," and "Themes in Immigration History." The authors of the individual articles are generally drawn from the ranks of Canadian academicians. The writing style is suitable for an audience at the collegiate level.

2-201. Childs, Peter, and Mike Storry, eds. *Encyclopedia of Contemporary British Culture.* London: Routledge, 1999. 628 pp. Index. ISBN: 0-415-14726-3.

Although this reference book discusses British culture since the 1960s, emphasis is on the final decade of the twentieth century in many instances. The arrangement is alphabetical, with entries ranging in length from a single paragraph to a couple of pages. Most entries include cross-references and a short bibliography. The front matter includes a "Classified Entry List," which arranges entries by subject matter, beginning with "Architecture" and concluding with "Youth and Alternative Culture." A glance through this listing indicates that most of the articles do indeed deal with aspects of culture rather than political and economic matters. There are no illustrations. The audience for this volume will consist of undergraduates and other aca-

demic researchers interested in the contemporary British scene.

2-202. Hughes, Alex, and Keith Reader, eds. *Encyclopedia of Contemporary French Culture.* London: Routledge, 1998. 618 pp. Index. ISBN: 0-415-13186-3.

Asserting that a vibrant French culture continues to influence British and American culture and society in many ways, this reference work attempts to sum up for the reader the major aspects of the French cultural scene. Topics covered go beyond language and literature to include the cinema, political institutions, social institutions, gender studies, critical theory, and popular culture. The arrangement is alphabetical. Some entries, especially biographies, are quite short, no more than a couple of sentences. Institutions, concepts, and broad subject areas receive more detailed treatment, however. For example, an article on "Concert Music" is about three pages long, while an article on existentialism is about a page and a half. Cross-references are indicated in boldface, and the index provides additional access to the text. Many articles include a short annotated list for further reading. There are no illustrations. Entries are signed by the contributors, most of whom are British academicians. This work will be of use to undergraduates and scholars seeking brief information on contemporary France.

2-203. Sandford, John, ed. *Encyclopedia of Contemporary German Culture.* New

York: Routledge, 2002. 696 pp. Index. ISBN: 0-415-12448-4.

This volume is similar to other works on contemporary European cultures from this same publisher. Short articles are arranged alphabetically. Most are a couple of paragraphs in length, with longer articles extending up to three pages. Cross-references are numerous, and many entries include a short list for additional reading. Many of the entries are for individuals significant in postwar Germany, but there also articles on subjects such as "Beer," "Fashion," and "Satire." A "Thematic Entry List" at the beginning of the volume will assist readers in locating groupings of articles relevant to one another. Although the emphasis is upon West Germany, at least up to 1990, there are also entries pertinent to East Germany, Austria, and German-speaking Switzerland. Most readers approaching this work as novices in recent German culture will consult those entries dealing with the general aspects of culture, while those with a bit more knowledge may turn first to those articles discussing prominent individuals in the various arenas of both high and popular culture. ⌨

2-204. Rodgers, Eamonn, ed. *Encyclopedia of Contemporary Spanish Culture.* London: Routledge, 1999. 591 pp. Index. ISBN: 0-415-13187-1.

In the final decades of the twentieth century, Spain made a remarkable transition from an autocratic government to a democratic political system. This work helps to chronicle that transition. Entries discuss both high and popular culture as well as relevant political and social subjects. Entries range in length from a single paragraph to almost three pages. Most entries include a short list of items for additional reading. Many of the entries are for individuals, but there are also subject entries for items such as "Censorship," "Class," and "Religion." Cross-references are indicated in boldface. A "Thematic Entry List" precedes the main alphabetical array and arranges entries by subject areas such as "Intellectual Life" and "Sport and Leisure." Attention is given to regional cultures such as Basque and Catalan. The audience for this volume will consist of those students requiring basic background on contemporary Spanish society and culture, as well as those scholars needing a quick reference.

2-205. *Encyclopedia of Islam.* rev. ed. 11 vols.. Leiden: Brill Academic Publishers, 1960–2002. Indexes. ISBN: varies.

Formidable in both its scholarship and presentation, this ongoing encyclopedia had, by 2002, finally been completed through the letter "Z." Articles range in length from a brief paragraph to many pages and are usually accompanied by a bibliography of references in a number of languages. The writing style is more accessible than one might anticipate, though the reader is expected to deal with a multitude of unfamiliar terms and spellings. Articles are signed, and the affiliations of the authors are listed separately. This is a multinational project, and many of the contributors come from the Islamic world. The text includes maps as needed but no other illustrations. A subject index and an index and glossary of technical terms appear separately. This work is aimed at a fairly specialized audience but is also useful to diligent researchers and those seeking detailed information about Islamic matters.

2-206. Perkins, Dorothy. *Encyclopedia of Japan: Japanese History and Culture, from Abacus to Zori.* New York: Facts on File, 1991. 410 pp. Index. ISBN: 0-816-01934-7.

This single-volume work provides an overview of Japan that touches upon many subjects of general interest: cities, geography, government and politics, business, religion, language, literature, and family life, among others. The arrangement is alphabetical. Most entries are brief, less than a page. However, cross-references are provided to other relevant entries. Individual entries lack bibliographies, but there is a general bibliography at the end of the volume. There are occasional photographs and other illustrations, but the single map at the front of the volume is not very detailed. The writing style is suitable for both high-school and undergraduate students despite the complexities of having to describe a society quite different from that of North America or Europe. For that reason, this work is a useful beginning point for students who require only brief information on Japan and Japanese topics and who do not need information pertaining to the 1990s.

2-207. Tenenbaum, Barbara A., ed. *Encyclopedia of Latin American History and Culture.* 5 vols. New York: Charles Scribner's Sons, 1995. 3137 pp. Index. ISBN: 0-684-19253-5.

According to the preface, this encyclopedia "strives to organize current knowledge of Latin America for the literate and curious public." As is usually the case with recent subject encyclopedias, the editorial staff also includes recent theoretical and methodological concepts that have broadened historical and cultural research. In addition to those articles on individuals, countries, and events that one expects in such an encyclopedia, there are entries for popular culture and subjects such as "banana industry" and "banditry." Coverage includes not only all of Central and South America, but also those areas to the north that were once part of the Spanish Empire. There are over 5,000 articles, mostly a page or less in length. However, there are cross-references to other relevant articles, and short bibliographies suggest additional reading. Illustrations are relatively few in number. The final volume includes an appendix listing biographees by occupation, a listing of contributors and their affiliations, and an index. This encyclopedia is an excellent starting point for researchers at all levels.

2-208. Werner, Michael S., ed. *Encyclopedia of Mexico: History, Society and Culture.* 2 vols. Chicago: Fitzroy Dearborn Publishers, 1997. 1749 pp. Index. ISBN: 1-884-96431-1.

Mexico has had a lasting impact on the history and culture of the United States, so this reference work should prove of value to many researchers dealing with the U.S. neighbor to the south. The arrangement is alphabetical, with a decided emphasis upon longer articles that synthesize aspects of Mexico. Examples include the conquest, the Catholic Church, and gender. There are also shorter articles that deal with historical events, individuals, and institutions. Cross-references and bibliographies appear at the end of each article; bibliographic entries include both English- and Spanish-language items. Illustrations are relatively few and usually appear with articles such as those dealing with architecture and the visual arts. There are also a number of maps. Most of the contributors are academicians from the United States and Mexico. Each of the volumes includes an alphabetical list of entries in the entire set, and the index provides additional access to the text. The writing style is suitable for the nonspecialist. This work will be of special value to the undergraduate researcher and those students knowledgeable in Spanish, who will benefit from the bibliographies.

2-209. Simon, Reeva S., Philip Mattar, and Richard W. Bulliet, eds. *Encyclopedia of the Modern Middle East.* 4 vols. New York: Macmillan Reference, 1996. 2182 pp. Index. ISBN: 0-028-96011-4.

This encyclopedia is somewhat different in scope than other works dealing with this region of the world. Instead of focusing on Islam, the editors also include material on other religious groups in the region from Morocco to Afghanistan and

ethnic groups regardless of religious affiliation. It covers the last two centuries and concentrates on Egypt, Israel, and Turkey on the assumption that English-speaking readers have a greater interest in those countries and their conflicts than in other parts of the Middle East. Recent events in Iraq and Afghanistan no doubt change these priorities. Arrangement is alphabetical, and most articles are only a few paragraphs in length. Topics include individuals, political and economic agencies and events, countries, and cities. Thematic articles are fewer in number than one might expect. Articles are signed and often include a short bibliography. The final volume includes a directory of contributors, genealogies, a categorization of biographies, and a comprehensive index. The text is accessible to general readers and undergraduates as well as to scholars.

2-210. Buse, Dieter K., and Juergen C. Doerr, eds. *Modern Germany: An Encyclopedia of History, People, and Culture, 1871–1990.* 2 vols. New York: Garland, 1998. 1158 pp. Index. ISBN: 0-815-30503-6.

Germany has been a major player on the world stage for over a century; this reference work helps a researcher to obtain an overview of the nation and controversies in which it has been involved. As well as the usual emphasis on political affairs, this work also delineates subjects dealing with the arts, religion, philosophy, technology, society, and other aspects of German history and culture. Typical articles include "Air Forces," "Country Life,"

"Social Mobility," and "Urbanization." There are also biographies of individuals in many lines of endeavor. Most articles are one to two pages in length and include cross-references to other relevant entries. Bibliographies are included and cite literature in both English and German languages. A chronology is provided as well as a subject listing of entries. Illustrations supplement the text. The contributors are scholars with appropriate expertise, and the writing style is suitable for an academic audience, including undergraduates.

2-211. Mackerras, Colin, and Amanda Yorke. *The New Cambridge Handbook of Contemporary China.* New York: Cambridge University Press, 2001. 313 pp. Index. ISBN: 0-521-78143-4.

The authors, who are academicians in Australia, have as their intent the presentation of "useful and accurate information, dates and statistics concerning contemporary China in a manageable and accessible form" (Mackerras and Yorke 2001, preface). They have selected a format that is topical rather than alphabetical. Following a chronology, there are chapters on politics, contemporary figures, foreign relations, the Chinese economy, population, minority nationalities, education, and culture and society; a bibliography and gazetteer are also included. A number of graphic displays, including maps, accompany the text, but there are no other illustrations. Taiwan and Hong Kong are not examined in detail. In many ways, this reference work resembles a very lengthy encyclopedia article on the People's Republic of China. The style is heavy on facts and figures, and accompanied by unexciting prose. This work will be of use to those researchers who need reasonably in-depth text about China in a single volume and who do not require up-to-date information.

2-212. Meyers, Eric M., ed. *Oxford Encyclopedia of Archeology in the Near East.* 5 vols. New York: Oxford University Press, 1997. 2608 pp. Index. ISBN: 0-195-06512-3.

The central role of the Middle East in contemporary events and as the birthplace of three major religions makes archeology in that region especially interesting. This encyclopedia defines the Near East roughly as the region extending from North Africa through Iran and covers the time from prehistory through the era of the Crusades. Emphasis is on individual site descriptions, but the contributors endeavor to place the sites in the economic, political, and social milieu of the times and civilizations. Photographs, diagrams, and maps accompany many of the entries, which are generally several pages in length. Articles are signed and include a bibliography; cross-references lead to other related entries. The final volume includes several appendixes, including maps, a listing of contributors and their affiliations, a synoptic outline, and an index. This encyclopedia provides students and scholars alike with a useful overview of topics that might otherwise reside only in specialized publications.

2-213. Esposito, John L., ed. *Oxford Encyclopedia of the Modern Islamic World.* 4 vols. New York: Oxford University Press, 1995. Index. ISBN: 0-195-06613-8.

Intending to complement the *Encyclopedia of Islam* [entry 2-205], this recent encyclopedia focuses on recent centuries, relies on social science methodologies, and deals with both the practice and theory of Islam. Equally important, it deals with Islam throughout the world, not just in the Middle East or the Arab nations. It is arranged alphabetically, and most articles are two to four pages in length; all articles are signed by the contributor. Besides the usual articles on important individuals and countries, it includes thematic subjects such as "astronomy" and "birth rites." Bibliographies that highlight important sources, both primary and secondary, follow each article, and each bibliographic entry has a brief annotation, enhancing its value. The final volume includes a list of contributor affiliations, a synoptic outline, and an index to the entire set. This encyclopedia will be useful to all levels of researchers, as well as to the general public.

Guides and Handbooks

2-214. *Chronology of World History.* 4 vols. Santa Barbara, CA: ABC-CLIO, 1999. 3109 pp. Indexes. ISBN: 1-576-07155-3.

Altogether, this four-volume set includes approximately 70,000 entries. The first volume covers the time frame from prehistory through 1491 AD, while the final three volumes encompass 1492–1775, 1776–1900, and 1901–1998, respectively. The chronological listings are grouped into four major categories: "Politics, Government, and Economics," "Science, Technology, and Medicine," "Arts and Ideas," and "Society." Individual entries include the date and one to two sentences of description. Occasional sidebars provide separate chronologies for specific topics, with particular emphasis on major wars. Each volume has its own indexes by subject matter and by title of literary works. Europe and the Americas naturally receive the greatest attention, but there is also some coverage of other parts of the globe. The fact that this set provides more than the usual detail found in many chronologies, combined with its emphasis on events beyond the usual political and military framework, will make it of use to those researchers requiring a more comprehensive approach to world chronology.

2-215. Grun, Bernard. *The Timetables of History: A Horizontal Linkage of People and Events.* 3rd rev. ed. New York: Simon and Schuster, 1991. 724 pp. Index. ISBN: 0-671-74919-6.

Most of the larger library reference collections include several chronologies of history; this is one of the better ones. Based on a work first published in Germany in 1946, this English-language edition begins with 5000 BC and finished with 1990. Some chronologies emphasize political and military events, but this work includes not only those subject areas but also others, such as literature, religion, philosophy, science, music, and daily life. Time periods before AD 501 are grouped in fifty-year or century-long divisions, but each year after that date has an entry of its own, even if little or nothing of significance is known to have occurred. Information is, of course, much more complete for recent centuries. The year 1776, for example, lists not only the events relating to the American Revolution but also the activities of Adam Smith, Mozart, and Captain Cook. The index allows the reader to search by name or subject and find the year with which it is associated. The most glaring weakness of this work is its strongly Western orientation; little of the viewpoints of other societies appears, not surprising, perhaps, given the midcentury German origin of this publication.

Biography: Contemporary

2-216. *International Who's Who of Women.* 2nd ed. London: Europa Publications Limited, 1992–. Index. ISSN: 0965-3775.

A new entrant in the Who's Who field, this reference book compiles more than 5,000 biographies of women based on the observation that the gender is underrepresented in other publications. Most biographees were selected for their professional importance and reputation. Entries include nationality, profession, birth date, education, career history, and the like. A useful "Index by Career" identifies biographees by occupation, including art, diplomacy, fashion, medicine, and religion. Although the editors claim a worldwide scope, the great majority of individuals are European or North American.

2-217. *Wer Ist Wer? Das Deutsche Who's Who.* Irregular. Lubeck: International Publications Service, 1905–. 1616 pp. ISBN: 3-795-02005-0.

Published irregularly but similar in scope and contents to Who's Who publications in other countries, this volume provides brief biographical information on the careers of 40,000 noteworthy individuals in Germany. By the early 1990s, coverage had been expanded to include the former East Germany. Along with the biographies are sections that list those who have died since the last edition was published and a list of biographees by date of birth. Introductory information is in English and French as well as German, but the biographies themselves are in German, and approximately 2,000 include photographs. The format is standard for this type of reference book.

2-218. *Who's Who.* Annual. New York: St. Martin's Press, 1849–. ISBN: 0-312-29475-1.

The inspiration for an entire category of reference books of Who's Who compilations, this volume is now beyond its 150th year of publication. Although claiming to cover the entire globe, this volume emphasizes Britons because the publisher is from the United Kingdom. Foreigners do appear, but their biographies are briefer than those for many Britons of much less noteworthiness. Biographical information, typical of this type of reference book, concentrates on a chronological sequence of career activities but concludes with an address for the subject; some are e-mail addresses.

Abbreviations are used heavily to save space, with a list of abbreviations at the front of the volume. Information comes from the subjects, contacted annually for revisions. This famous source is indispensable for short biographies of those considered noteworthy in contemporary Britain.

2-219. *Who's Who among African Americans*. Irregular. Detroit: Gale Research, 1976–. Indexes. ISSN: 1081-1400.

The fifteenth edition of this work, published in 2002, includes biographies for more than 20,000 individuals. According to the introduction, inclusion was based upon several criteria: "by virtue of positions held through election or appointment to office, notable career achievements, or outstanding community service." Data was gathered from the biographee and includes name, occupation, personal data, education, career information, affiliations, honors, special achievements, military service, and address and telephone number. Listings are alphabetical, and the general format is typical of the Who's Who category of publication. Two indexes provide listings by state and community, and by occupation. This last index will be especially useful to those wishing to find listings of notable African Americans in particular career fields. No doubt, a number of these individuals can be found in other Who's Who books, but this volume serves as a useful supplement to those seeking an ethnic approach to current biographical materials.

2-220. *Who's Who in France*. Annual. Paris: Editions Jacques Lafitte, 1953–. ISSN: 0083-9531.

Similar in scope to other Who's Who publications, this volume provides information on citizens of France, concentrating on chronological career achievements and concluding with a postal address for the individual. In addition to the biographies, the volume includes listings of members of major institutions and government officials throughout France. Although the text is in French, the format is similar to that of other publications of this type.

2-221. *Who's Who in the Arab World*. Biennial. Beirut: Publitec Publications, 1965–. Index. ISSN: 0083-9752.

Like most publications of this type, this volume presents biographies of noteworthy individuals, mostly politicians, military figures, civil servants, or members of the professions from nineteen Arab countries. As usual, the biographies concentrate on career achievements and end with an address. The 1997–1998 edition includes 6,000 biographies but, unlike similar reference works, also includes background information on the countries and an "Outline of the Arab World," which surveys history and current problems. The index categorizes biographees by country and profession, and a brief bibliography concludes the volume. This book presents many fewer biographies than most such works but is a handy source of information on the Arab world, even though it excludes Lebanon, the subject of a separate Who's

Who volume from this publisher.

2-222. *Who's Who in the World.* Annual. New Providence, NJ: Marquis Who's Who, 2003. ISSN: 0083-9825.

Using the familiar Marquis Who's Who format, this volume presents brief biographies of 40,000 individuals of contemporary interest. Some are included for their political, military, or diplomatic position; others, including scholars, scientists, physicians, artists, and athletes, are included for their achievements in the professions. As usual for this type of publication, the publisher gathered information directly from the biographee, presumably to ensure its accuracy. Entries are usually about a paragraph in length with information ranging from name through office address. Variation in length might reflect either variation in actual achievements or the amount of detail provided. Most individuals are Western European or North American and sometimes East Asian. This volume is a standard source and can be found in most American libraries.

2-223. *Who's Who of American Women.* Biennial. New Providence, NJ: Marquis Who's Who, 1958–. ISSN: 0083-9841.

This is one of the many useful Who's Who books produced by this publisher. The editors ask biographees, selected through standard criteria, to provide information about themselves. The first edition drew heavily from volunteer workers in civic, religious, and club activities, but the 29,000 entries in the latest edition represent a much broader range of endeavors, including positions in government and other agencies. Up to nineteen pieces of information are reported for each individual. This volume provides brief information on contemporary women and should be found in most libraries.

Biography: Past

2-224. American Council of Learned Societies. *American National Biography.* 24 vols. New York: Oxford University Press, 1999. 22,968 pp. Indexes. ISBN: 0-195-20635-5.

Conceived as a replacement for the *Dictionary of American Biography* [entry 2-225], published between 1926 and 1937, this set expands coverage beyond the original. Criteria for inclusion are now defined "as someone whose significant actions occurred during his or her residence within what is now the United States or whose life or career directly influenced the course of American history" (ACLS 1999, preface). This broadened criteria allow for inclusion of more women and minority figures than was the case with the previous set. All subjects, however, had to have died before 1996. The set is arranged alphabetically. The individual entries range in length from 750 to 7,500 words and conclude with a bibliography that usually includes both primary and secondary sources. There are no illustrations. The writing style is erudite but accessible to the general reader, including undergraduates. The final volume includes indexes of subjects, contributors, places of birth, and occupations. This set is an excellent starting point for any researcher requiring comparatively brief biographical information on American figures and incorporating the latest historical thinking.

2-225. American Council of Learned Societies. *Dictionary of American Biography.* 21 vols. New York: Charles Scribner's Sons, 1928–1937. Indexes ISBN 0-684-17323-9.

One of those reference works that scarcely needs an introduction (or annotation), this set originated early in the twentieth century. Inspired by the example of the *Dictionary of National Biography* [entry 2-227], the editorial board set out to create a similar work for Americans. Three groups were excluded: persons still living, those who had never lived in the United States, and British officers serving in America after independence was declared. In addition to the soldiers, statesmen, and clergymen who had figured in earlier biographical compilations, this set attempts to include scientists, social scientists, and those in the arts and industry. More than 13,000 biographies are included; a few are more than 5,000 words in length, but most are much shorter. Each article is initialed by the contributor and includes a bibliography of sources, both primary and secondary. The index volume includes listings by birthplace, attendance at an educational institution, and occupation, among others. Although this set inevitably reflects the thinking of the time of its publication, it will remain the standard source until an updated version appears. For a discussion of supplementary volumes, see entry 2-226.

2-226. *Dictionary of American Biography. Supplement.* New York: Charles Scribner's Sons, 1944–. Index. ISBN: 0-684-80482-4.

Occasional supplementary volumes to the *Dictionary of American Biography* continue to appear, though they are no longer under the auspices of the American Council of Learned Societies. As of 1998, ten supplements and an index volume had appeared, covering biographees through December 31, 1980. Criteria continue to be the same, and the index volume is similar to that of the original set [entry 2-225].

2-227. *Dictionary of National Biography.* 32 vols. Oxford: Oxford University Press, 1885–. Indexes. ISBN: 9-198-65101-5.

This venerable set compiles biographies of deceased British subjects. Begun in the nineteenth century, the set now runs to many volumes and editors. Biographies vary in length according to the perceived importance of the subject and sometimes the availability of source material. Each biography is signed or initialed by the author. The style of writing is both informative and pleasurable to read. Given that publication has taken place over an entire century, concerns and attitudes expressed by the authors reflect the thinking of the time. This is minor compared with the achievement of compiling biographies of noteworthy figures in British history, culture, and society. Occasional supplementary volumes bring the set up to date with biographies of persons who have died in the last few years. There are indexes for both individual volumes and the set as a whole. (Note that a new edition, entitled *Oxford Dictionary of National Biography*, was published in late 2004. It incorporated rewriting of the original text with additional emphasis upon inclusion of women, business and labor leaders, and figures from the twentieth century.)

2-228. Byers, Paula Kay, and Suzanne Michele Bourgoin, eds. *Encyclopedia of World Biography.* 2nd ed. 23 vols. Detroit: Gale Research, 1998. Index. ISBN: 0-787-62221-4.

In the introduction, the editors state that the 7,000 biographees "have reputations that stand the test of time." Each entry includes birth and death dates, an essay ranging in length from a column to two or three pages, and a listing of further readings. This work attempts to be more global and multicultural in content than traditional reference works of this type. For example, Volume 1 includes Yassir Arafat, Elizabeth Arden, and Joan Baez but also Klaus Barbie. Volume 17 is an alphabetical and subject index to the entire set, with cross-references. Entries are not signed by the contributor, nor is there a list of contributors other than the editorial staff provided. The twentieth century is heavily represented, but this set is nevertheless a useful starting point for essay-length biographical information on a wide range of reasonably well-known individuals. The latest supplemental volume is dated 2004.

2-229. Egan, Edward W., Constance B. Hintz, and L. F. Wise, eds. *Kings, Rulers and Statesmen.* rev. ed. New York: Sterling Publishing, 1976. 512 pp. ISBN: 0-806-90050-4.

This well-known reference book provides listings of rulers of political entities worldwide, both current and long defunct, such as Carthage or the Vandal Empire. Entries are chronological, and each includes the individual's name, term of office, and title. Numerous illustrations, some with a thumbnail sketch or anecdote about the subject of the illustration, appear throughout the text. The volume is arranged by name of nation or political entity, but no index is provided. This edition is now more than twenty years old but is nevertheless useful for the vast number of obscure individuals and dynasties from both major and minor states, ancient and modern, and sometimes their subdivisions. For example, the entry for "France" includes Anjou, Brittany, Normandy, and several other provinces.

2-230. *National Cyclopedia of American Biography.* 77 vols. New York: James T. White, 1891–1986. Index. ISBN: 0-883-71029-3.

Initiated several decades before the *Dictionary of American Biography* [entry 2-225], this set differs from its later competitor in a couple of respects. First, biographies of living individuals are included. Second, the publishers place a greater emphasis on including people associated with business and the professions. The format is somewhat complicated. For several years, a current series appeared concurrently with a permanent series, which included biographies of deceased individuals who had originally appeared in the current series. In addition, arrangement is by occupation rather than alphabetical, with an overall index volume published in 1984. Biographical entries, a half-page or page in length, are usually accompanied by a photograph or portrait of the subject. No bibliographic references or sources are listed. Some might object that this is primarily a listing of living and dead white males, many of whom have sunk into obscurity; but this work does provide a massive number of biographies for individuals who might otherwise have escaped attention.

2-231. Jackson, Kenneth T., ed. *Scribner Encyclopedia of American Lives.* 2 vols. New York: Charles Scribner's Sons, 1998–. Indexes. ISBN: 0-684-80492-1 (Vol. 1); 0-684-80491-3 (Vol. 2).

Scribner's published the *Dictionary of American Biography* [entry 2-225] and intends this set to be something of an update to the earlier work. The first volume includes those notable Americans whose deaths occurred between 1981 and 1985, while the second volume covers deaths between 1986 and 1990. Altogether, 1,000 biographies are included, and it is the intention of the publisher to issue new volumes every five years. Those selected for inclusion must have made their major professional or artistic contributions while in the United States, though they need not have been born

there. Some of the fields represented include politics, the military, science, the performing arts, sports, and popular culture. The lengths of the biographies vary by subject, with most entries receiving at least a couple of pages. Each entry includes a photograph of the individual and concludes with a brief annotated bibliography. Many of the contributors are academicians, but other fields are represented as well. The second volume includes cumulative indexes for occupations and for biographees. The writing style is suitable for both high-school and undergraduate students.

2-232. *Who Was Who.* 8 vols. New York: St. Martin's Press, 1897–. Index. ISBN: 0-312-87746-3.

A companion to *Who's Who* [entry 2-218], this set provides biographies of those in the initial volumes who have since died. A new volume appears every ten years; a separate volume cumulates indexing.

2-233. Jackson, Guida M. *Women Rulers throughout the Ages: An Illustrated Guide.* Santa Barbara, CA: ABC-CLIO, 1999. 471 pp. Index. ISBN: 1-576-07091-3.

Based upon a previous book entitled *Women Who Ruled*, this work is half again the size of the original. Those included had to meet the criteria "of any woman who held the reins of power, regardless of the extent to which she exercised that power and regardless of her official sanction to do so" (Jackson 1999, preface). Such a definition allows for the inclusion of those women who were tribal leaders as well as those presiding from a seat of government. Both written records and oral traditions were considered in selecting individuals for inclusion, and a few are legendary in nature. The biographies are arranged alphabetically by name, and they range in length from a single paragraph to a couple of pages. Each includes a list of references for additional reading, and occasional portraits accompany the text. The listing of alphabetical entries is preceded by a chronological listing of ruler names arranged by geographical entity, allowing the reader to find those women rulers associated with France, for example. Information here is quite brief, but will serve as a starting point for those high-school and undergraduate students needing to find examples of women in positions of political power. 🖥

Psychology

PsycINFO (formerly *Psychological Abstracts* in its print version) is, of course, a major resource for this discipline. However, the field is also blessed with a number of recent dictionaries and encyclopedias that assist both beginning and advanced researchers. Some describe the discipline as a whole, while others concentrate upon specific subjects: creativity, emotions, intelligence, and phobias. Among the other reference books described here are those that deal with mental-health and psychiatric issues. Finally, psychological and intelligence tests are a topic of perennial interest; several standard volumes that assess many such tests are included in this chapter.

Literature Guides

2-234. American Psychological Association. *Journals in Psychology: A Resource Listing for Authors.* 5th ed. Washington, DC: American Psychological Association, 1997. 257 pp. ISBN: 1-557-98438-7.

Intended as an aid for psychologists seeking a publishing venue, this guide lists 355 English-language periodicals that publish articles on psychology. Each entry includes publisher, editor, editorial policy, selective notes on submissions, journal frequency, articles/pages published per year, total subscribers, whether book reviews are accepted, and rejection rates. This information should be sufficient to assess the scope of each journal and its applicability for a reader manuscript. Listing is alphabetical, with an alphabetical index of titles and an index by specialty. The major drawback of this type of listing is that it can date rapidly. Furthermore, this information is becoming readily available on the Internet, as publishers and journals create Web sites for themselves. Nevertheless, this volume remains useful as an overview of major journals in psychology and their areas of specialty.

2-235. Baxter, Pam M. *Psychology: A Guide to Reference and Information Sources.* Englewood, CO: Libraries Unlimited, 1993. 219 pp. Index. ISBN: 0-872-87708-6.

This volume, intended for undergraduate and graduate students, describes approximately 500 sources in psychology and related disciplines published mostly between 1970 and 1992. The author first describes general social science reference sources, then individual disciplines, including education, economics, sociology, social work, anthropology, history, political science, and criminal justice. The third and fourth parts are devoted to general psychology reference sources and special topics in psychology, respectively. Arrangement within topics is by guides, bibliographies, handbooks, and so forth. Annotations are usually one or two paragraphs in length and are both critical and descriptive. The largest section is devoted to special psychology topics. The indexes are by author/title and subject. Although online databases are annotated, the book predates the Internet and the explosion of electronic access to information. This volume provides a basic introduction to printed sources in psychology.

2-236. Murphy, Linda L., ed. *Tests in Print VI: An Index to Tests, Test Reviews, and the Literature on Specific Tests.* Lincoln, NE: Buros Institute of Mental Measurements, 2002. 1130 pp. Indexes. ISBN: 0-910-67456-6.

A companion to the well-known *Mental Measurements Yearbook* [entry 2-259], this work differs from its sister set in that it lacks critical essays and is cumulative in nature. In other words, all tests in print at the date of publication appear in this set; there is no need to consult earlier editions. Each includes bibliographic and publisher information as well as a brief description of the purpose of the test, its population, scores, and other pertinent information. Some tests also include references to appropriate articles. There are indexes of titles, acronyms, subjects, publishers, personal names, and scores. For those individuals seeking only brief information on tests currently available, this is a better starting point than the *Mental Measurements Yearbook*.

Abstracting and Indexing Services

2-237. *PsycINFO.* Weekly updates. Washington, DC: American Psychological Association, 1887–. Indexes.

In the era of print indexes, *Psychological Abstracts* became the premier resource for scholarly literature in the field of psychology. Under the database name *PsycINFO*, this publication has retained its central position in the online age. As of October 2004, the database included almost two million records, accessing literature from 1887 to the present. Coverage includes close to 2,000 journal titles as well as doctoral dissertations, books, and chapters from edited books. The usual entry points by keyword, subject heading, author, title, and journal are all present. It is also possible to limit a search to human subjects. This database is available through library vendors, with additional subscription information available at the American Psychological Association Web site (http://www.apa.org). Any researcher requiring a comprehensive approach to the field of psychology will need to consult *PsycINFO*.

Directories

2-238. American Psychological Association (APA). *Directory of the American Psychological Association.* Irregular.

Washington, DC: American Psychological Association, 1978–. ISSN: 0196-6545.

All members of the APA are listed in this irregularly published volume. Information for each member includes name, address, phone and fax numbers, e-mail address, birth data, highest degree, major field, professional background, and current employment. Members are also listed by state and by APA division. The volume includes membership statistics, APA officers, the association's by-laws and ethical codes, and state licensing information. A separate listing for international affiliates limits information to the address of the affiliate.

2-239. American Psychological Association. *Graduate Study in Psychology.* Biennial. Washington, DC: American Psychological Association, 1992–. 865 pp. ISSN: 0742-7220.

The popularity of psychology as a field of study is demonstrated by this thick volume, which lists information on more than 600 programs, all accredited by one of six standard regional accrediting agencies. The format is complicated by the arrangement of departments within four categories. One category lists departments of psychology and schools of psychology that offer the doctoral degree. The second category lists other departments that offer that degree. The other two categories list departments that offer degrees below the doctoral level. Entries include application information, types of programs offered, degree requirements, admission requirements, financial assistance, and other information of value to the prospective student. Introductory information explains the format and discusses the procedures for selecting programs and submitting an application. A standard for more than thirty years, this publication appears every second year, with an addendum that provides additional annual information.

Dictionaries

2-240. Sheehy, Noel, Antony J. Chapman, and Wendy A. Conroy, eds. *Biographical Dictionary of Psychology.* London: Routledge, 1997. 675 pp. Indexes. ISBN: 0-415-09997-9.

This volume compiles biographies of some 500 individuals of significance in psychology who were selected by a rather complex combination of citation analysis and editorial review. Each entry includes birth and death (where applicable) dates, nationality, education, appointments, and awards, followed by a listing of principal publications and a biography of about one column in length. The biographies emphasize the individual's contributions to psychology rather than life events. Emphasis seems to be on contemporary researchers from English-speaking countries, though some are deceased or from other parts of the world. A few individuals from disciplines other than psychology, such as Noam Chomsky, are included because of their effect on the field. The volume concludes with indexes of interests, institutions, and key terms.

2-241. Popplestone, John A., and Marion White McPherson. *Dictionary of*

Concepts in General Psychology. New York: Greenwood Press, 1988. 391 pp. ISBN: 0-313-23190-7.

Like other volumes in this series, this one attempts to describe concepts in some detail and to place them in context as they have evolved. In particular, this work explains behavior in behavioral rather than biological terms and, rather than the hundreds or thousands of entries common in competing works, includes only about twenty entries. All entries are written by the two authors; each entry is several pages in length and concludes with a list of references. This allows the user to trace the historical development of each concept and the state of the art at time of publication, in 1988. Concepts discussed include aggression, cognition, dogmatism, and hostility. A short subject index concludes the volume. Given the publication date, this volume is of greater use for historical examination than for current information.

2-242. Stuart-Hamilton, Ian. *Dictionary of Developmental Psychology.* rev. ed. London: Jessica Kingsley Publishers, 1996. 168 pp. ISBN: 1-853-02146-6.

This brief volume provides definitions of terms that appear frequently in textbooks and journal articles, except for terms that are rare or esoteric. Definitions range in length from a short sentence to several-hundred words. The aim is to provide information to the general public and undergraduates rather than trained psychologists, and it avoids detailed descriptions of tests. References were omitted because they would have made the dictionary "too long." The brevity and lack of references limits the usefulness of this volume.

2-243. Cardwell, Mike. *Dictionary of Psychology.* London: Fitzroy Dearborn Publishers, 1996. 249 pp. ISBN: 1-579-58064-5.

Published originally in the United Kingdom in 1996, this volume was published again in the United States in 1999. It will be of greatest use to those readers needing brief introductory information in language suitable to the layperson. Definitions are arranged alphabetically and range in length from a single sentence to several paragraphs. There are numerous cross-references, some appearing within the text of the definition, and others appearing at the end. All are indicated through the use of italics. The layout is attractive, featuring the use of bullets and numerous diagrams. One drawback to this work is the fact that it lacks bibliographic references. On the other hand, it is written at a level that will make it suitable for high-school and college students alike.

2-244. Corsini, Raymond J. *Dictionary of Psychology.* Philadelphia: Brunner-Mazel, 2002. 1156 pp. ISBN: 1-583-91028-X.

For the compilation of this dictionary, Corsini consulted with about one hundred psychologists, asking their wishes for a psychology dictionary. In general, they wanted as many definitions as possible, a minimum of movement from page to page in order to find definitions, and definitions that did not require another definition to understand. This dictionary attempts to fill those needs. It is arranged alphabetically in a single sequence. Definitions are short, averaging thirty-one words. Cross-references and equivalent definitions are included. Occasional diagrams supplement the text. There are ten appendixes at the conclusion of the alphabetical sequence: "Prefixes, Suffixes, Affixes," "DSM-IV Terms," "The Greek Alphabet," "Medical Prescription Terms," "Systems of Treatment," "Measuring Instruments," "Symbols," "Learning Theory Symbols," "Rorschach Descriptors," and "Biographies." There are no bibliographic references. Although the definitions found here are brief, this source will recommend itself to those researchers requiring a reasonably comprehensive volume for psychology terminology.

2-245. Stratton, Peter, and Nicky Hayes. *A Student's Dictionary of Psychology.* 3rd ed. London: Oxford University Press, 1999. 322 pp. ISBN: 0-340-70583-3.

This handy volume provides psychology definitions accessible to beginning students. Entries are short, no more than a single paragraph, with italicized cross-references. Numerous illustrations, including some amusing sketches to define concepts such as "personal space," would appeal to the undergraduate researcher. A short bibliography concludes the volume. This work is of value for brief and comparatively recent definitions in this discipline; but because the definitions include references to other definitions, the reader must page to and fro to acquire a complete understanding of a given concept.

Encyclopedias

2-246. Benner, David G., and Peter C. Hill, eds. *Baker Encyclopedia of Psychology and Counseling.* 2nd ed. Grand Rapids, MI: Baker Books, 1999. 1276 pp. ISBN: 0-801-02100-6.

Both the first and second editions of this work differ from other psychology handbooks in the fact that they treat the field of psychology from a Christian viewpoint. The first edition appeared in 1985; its successor incorporates changes in psychology that occurred in the intervening years, as well as according more attention to pastoral care and counseling. The volume includes over 1,000 articles ranging in length from a single paragraph to several pages. The arrangement is alphabetical and includes cross-references to other relevant entries. Many articles also include brief lists of references and readings that encompass both books and periodical articles. Some typical articles include "Body Image," "Classification of Mental Disorders," "Divorce," and "Sexuality." Some articles reflect the specific viewpoint of this volume: "Christian Psychology" and "Clinical Pastoral Education" are examples of this latter category. Entries are signed by the authors, most of whom are professionals in the field of psychology. A "Category Index" at the beginning of the volume provides a subject arrangement to titles of entries. This work is of obvious value to those practitioners with a Christian background, but it can also be of use to students and other researchers exploring the role of psychology within a particular religion.

2-247. Colman, Andrew M., ed. *Companion Encyclopedia of Psychology.* 2 vols. London: Routledge, 1994. 1356 pp. Index. ISBN: 0-415-06446-5.

This two-volume set attempts to inform specialists and nonspecialists alike of basic information and recent developments in all fields of psychology. The discipline is divided into thirteen categories in this work with several separate contributions by different authors in each category. Most authors are from the United Kingdom; almost all of the rest are Americans. Each category includes introductory remarks as well as the individual contributions. Among the categories are biological aspects of behavior, sensation and perception, cognition, developmental psychology, social psychology, and abnormal psychology. Each contribution includes an outline of its contents as well as a listing of references and further reading materials. Graphics and illustrations are found frequently. In general, the writing style does appear accessible to the lay reader without being condescending or overly simplistic. An index at the end of the second volume helps to provide access to the contents. The second volume also includes a glossary of frequently used psychological terms. Social science researchers from fields other than psychology should find this work to be of assistance in explaining the more fundamental concepts.

2-248. Kastenbaum, Robert, ed. *Encyclopedia of Adult Development.* Phoenix: Oryx Press, 1993. 574 pp. Index. ISBN: 0-897-74669-4.

The editor invited researchers to contribute to this volume essays that would represent the current status of their field, with an emphasis on the middle years of life. Entries are arranged alphabetically and are usually several pages in length. Each ends with a list of cross-references and a list of references to books and articles. At the front of the volume is a list of contributors, an alphabetical list of the articles, and a list of articles by subject matter. An index further enhances access to the contents of this one-volume encyclopedia. This work has a most relaxed and engaging writing style, and readers will find themselves hard-pressed not to read more than they intended to, thereby enlarging their knowledge of adult psychological development.

2-249. Nadel, Lynn, ed. *Encyclopedia of Cognitive Science.* 4 vols. London: Nature Publishing Group, 2003. Index. ISBN: 0-333-79261-0.

The intent of this encyclopedia is to capture "current thinking about the workings of the mind and brain" (Nadel 2003, preface). The intent is also to describe what is new in the field since the 1980s. The arrangement is alphabetical, with several pages devoted to most articles. Some typical examples from the first volume include "Amnesia," "Binding Theory," and "Down Syndrome." Contributors and their affiliations appear at the beginning of each article. The contributors are drawn from the professional community throughout the world, although those from English-speaking countries predominate. There are numerous illustrations. Given the often-technical nature of the subject matter, this encyclopedia is more approachable for students with some background already in place. The final volume includes a glossary and a subject index that should assist those less well versed in cognitive science.

2-250. Ramachandran, V. S., ed. *Encyclopedia of Human Behavior.* 4 vols. San Diego: Academic Press, 1994. 2765 pp. Index. ISBN: 0-122-26920-9.

This four-volume set presents about 240 review essays on all aspects of human behavior. Arrangement is alphabetical by topic; most essays range from five to ten pages in length. Each topic includes a brief outline, a glossary of terms specific to the subject, cross-references, a short bibliography, and illustrations as necessary. The first volume includes the tables of contents for the entire set. The final volume includes the index for the entire set and a listing of contributors with name, institutional address, and area of expertise. Most are associated with academic institutions in the United States. Written in a reasonably accessible style, this will be a good starting point for specialists and students seeking background in various concepts in behavioral psychology.

2-251. Levinson, David, James J. Ponzetti Jr, and Peter F. Jorgensen, eds.

Encyclopedia of Human Emotions. 2 vols. New York: Macmillan Reference, 1999. 768 pp. Indexes. ISBN: 0-028-64766-1.

According to the preface of this set, there are five models for the study of emotions: psychoanalytic, psychological, behavioral, cognitive, and biological. The articles that appear in the encyclopedia encompass all these models and address the four major topics of specific emotions and their expression, conceptual and theoretical issues, "emotions in society and in the human experience," and individual biographies. Altogether, there are 146 entries addressing not only individual emotions but also such subjects as "Color," "Drama and Theater," "Personality," and "Sports." Articles are generally several pages in length and include cross-references and a short bibliography. Most of the authors are U.S. academicians. There are indexes of subject and bibliographic entries. Occasional illustrations supplement the text, which is written at a level that will be accessible to undergraduate researchers while retaining value for those with more advanced interests. This is an excellent starting point for the gamut of human emotions—anger, desire, prejudice, shame, and many others—which can be difficult to find in other reference books.

2-252. Sternberg, Robert J., ed. *Encyclopedia of Human Intelligence.* 2 vols. New York: Macmillan, 1994. 1235 pp. Index. ISBN: 0-028-97407-7.

A welcome addition to the often-controversial subject of intelligence, this encyclopedia provides evenhanded treatment of issues such as ethnicity and intelligence quotient. Less obvious topics, such as musical intelligence, are also discussed, along with significant individuals, such as Edward Thorndike. Of the nearly 300 entries, most range in length from a single column to several pages, with illustrations, graphs, and tables as appropriate. Each entry includes cross-references, a bibliography, and the name of the contributor. A list of contributors at the front of the first volume includes affiliation and the articles for which the person is responsible. This is a model subject encyclopedia that provides sufficient detail in a readily understandable fashion for students.

2-253. Friedman, Howard S., ed. *Encyclopedia of Mental Health.* 3 vols. San Diego: Academic Press, 1998. 2398 pp. Index. ISBN: 0-122-26675-7.

This encyclopedia attempts broad coverage of the subject of mental health; as the preface explains, it "encompasses all levels of analysis, from the molecular and biological, through the social and family, to the cultural." Titles of articles indicate some of the scope: "Alcohol Problems," "Body Image," "Divorce," "Managed Care," "Rape," and "Television Viewing." A complete table of contents appears at the beginning of each volume. Articles are arranged alphabetically and average about ten pages in length. Each includes an outline, a glossary, cross-references, and a bibliography. The contributors are specialists and academicians in appropriate fields. There are no illustrations

other than occasional tables or graphic displays. Although some of the articles dealing with the scientific aspects of mental health may be challenging to the nonspecialist, there are many entries that will be of value to undergraduate students researching the social and cultural aspects of the subject. The index to the final volume will assist these researchers in locating information specific to their needs.

2-254. Kahn, Ada P., and Jan Fawcett, eds. *Encyclopedia of Mental Health.* 2nd ed. New York: Facts on File, 2001. 468 pp. Index. ISBN: 0-816-04062-1.

For those researchers seeking a less comprehensive approach to mental-health topics than that found in multiple-volume sets, this single-volume work is a helpful starting point. The editors indicate that they intend their book for lay readers and "have worked to provide the most factual and accurate definitions of terms relating to many emotional, mental and behavioral situations existing today" (Kahn and Fawcett 2001, preface). The arrangement is alphabetical and most entries are brief, no more than a paragraph or two. More substantive or complex topics receive several pages of treatment. Some examples of the latter include "Abortion," "Anxiety Disorders," "Headaches," and "Suicide." There are numerous cross-references, and many entries include a short listing of bibliographic references. A comprehensive bibliography, arranged by topic, also appears at the end of the volume. Many of the entries deal with clinical subjects, but others have social and economic implications, hence the usefulness of this volume for social science research.

2-255. Corsini, Raymond J., ed. *Encyclopedia of Psychology*. 2nd ed. 4 vols. New York: John Wiley, 1994. Indexes. ISBN: 0-471-55819-2.

Unlike its competitors, this set concentrates on breadth of scope (about 2,500 entries), rather than depth of discussion (each entry is no more than one or two columns). Each entry is signed, and many include brief bibliographies. At the beginning of the first volume is a listing of contributors, their institutional affiliations, and the entries they wrote. Most are academicians. The final volume includes a complete bibliography, name and subject indexes, an appendix containing psychology ethical codes, and biographical entries for psychologists past and present. Placement of these biographies in the last volume is unfortunate because many readers will not realize that they exist. This work will be of most value to researchers and students who prefer relatively brief descriptions.

2-256. Strickland, Bonnie B. *Gale Encyclopedia of Psychology*. 2nd ed. Detroit: Gale Research, 2001. 701 pp. Indexes. ISBN: 0-787-64786-1.

Many high schools now teach psychology courses that are similar in format to those in higher education. This encyclopedia is designed to assist high-school students who may need to upgrade their knowledge of psychology in order to better cope with demands at the collegiate level.

The volume includes approximately 450 articles that range in length from a paragraph to a couple of pages. In general, the entries discuss major psychological concepts (including both cognitive and biological psychology), major theories, and biographies of important figures in the history of the field. Cross-references are indicated in boldface, and many articles also include "see also" references. Short listings for additional reading conclude the entries, while a general bibliography also appears at the back of the volume. There are two indexes, one for subfields and the other for subjects. The volume includes numerous photographs intended to pique the interest of the reader. Although intended for a high-school audience, this work is also suitable for undergraduate students who may not need more in-depth information.

2-257. De Corte, Erik, and Franz E. Weinert, eds. *International Encyclopedia of Developmental and Instructional Psychology*. Tarrytown, NY: Pergamon, 1996. 882 pp. Indexes. ISBN: 0-080-42980-7.

This volume is mainly a compilation of articles that originally appeared in the 1994 edition of the *International Encyclopedia of Education* with about ten new entries. The editors explain that they have done this because the distinction between developmental and educational psychology is rapidly disappearing and to provide organization for the remainder of the articles. The arrangement is by section (e.g., "Classroom Learning Environments" with several specific entries within each section). Each entry includes references and the name of the author. A list of contributors and their credentials, and both a name and subject index are at the back of the book. Although a handy source, this volume seems aimed at the layperson rather than advanced researchers.

2-258. Piotrowski, Nancy A., ed. *Magill's Encyclopedia of Social Science: Psychology.* 4 vols. Pasadena, CA: Salem Press, 2003. 1810 pp. Index. ISBN: 1-587-65130-0.

This encyclopedia is a revision of the *Survey of Social Science: Psychology Series* [entry 2-261] and includes some material that appeared originally in the earlier set. However, the new revision more closely resembles the standard encyclopedia format than its predecessor. The arrangement is alphabetical; some typical articles include "Aggression," "Bipolar Disorder," and "Teenage Suicide." Articles are generally several pages in length and conclude with an annotated bibliography. There are occasional illustrations. Articles are signed, with most of the contributors drawn from the U.S. academic community. The final volume includes an index to the entire set. This encyclopedia is aimed at high-school and college students as well as the general public and can be recommended as a starting point for those researchers lacking professional expertise in psychology.

2-259. Impara, James C., Barbara S. Plake, and Robert A. Spies, eds. *Mental*

Measurements Yearbook. Lincoln: University of Nebraska–Lincoln/Buros Institute of Mental Measurements, 1938–. Indexes. ISSN: 0076-6461.

As of 2003, this standard reference work was in its fifteenth edition. Entries for the individual tests include complete bibliographic information, information on scores, a listing of references (sometimes quite lengthy), and one or more critiques. Included in the bibliographic information are cross-references to reviews in earlier editions of this set as well as its companion volumes *Tests in Print* [entry 2-236]. There are numerous indexes, allowing for access by various entry points. Although this work and its predecessors and companions are obviously aimed at a professional audience, the critical reviews can generally be understood by the student and the informed layperson; the latter may be surprised or disappointed by the lack of inclusion of the tests themselves. Searching through earlier volumes for older tests can obviously be tedious, so most users will prefer the electronic version of this publication (not described here). 💻

2-260. Wilson, Robert A., ed. *MIT Encyclopedia of the Cognitive Sciences.* Cambridge, MA: MIT Press, 1999. 964 pp. Indexes. ISBN: 0-262-73124-X.

Altogether, this volume contains 471 articles of a length from 1,000 to 1,500 words on subjects pertaining to the cognitive sciences. These are defined to include "psychology, neuroscience, linguistics, philosophy, anthropology and the social sciences more generally, evolutionary biology, education, computer science, artificial intelligence, and ethology" (Wilson 1999, preface). The articles are arranged alphabetically and include references and readings that are quite extensive given the relatively short nature of the entries themselves. Cross-references are provided to other relevant entries, and the articles are signed by the authors, who represent an international body of scholars from noteworthy institutions. To assist in a multidisciplinary approach, there are six introductory essays preceding the alphabetical array of entries. These essays, describing various related disciplines, are titled: "Philosophy," "Psychology," "Neurosciences," "Computational Intelligence," "Linguistics and Language," and "Culture, Cognition, and Evolution." As well as providing an overview, these essays also reference relevant articles in the alphabetical sequence. This is an erudite work, one that will appeal to an audience of advanced undergraduates, graduate students, and scholars seeking guidance to the disciplines of the cognitive sciences.

2-261. Magill, Frank N., ed. *Survey of Social Science: Psychology Series.* 6 vols. Pasadena, CA: Salem Press, 1993. 2698 pp. Indexes. ISBN: 0-893-56732-9.

This work presents approximately 410 articles of about six pages each and arranged alphabetically. Among the major areas discussed are developmental psychology, the physiology of behavior, personality, psychotherapy, and social psychology. Each article is assigned a position under the categories of "Type of Psychology" and "Fields of Study"; in the final volume, these category lists appear, allowing the reader to find related articles. Each article also defines principal terms, provides an overview, discusses applications and context, and concludes with a bibliography and additional cross-references. In addition to the listing by category, the final volume also includes a glossary, an alphabetical list of articles, and a general index. Contributors are drawn from the U.S. academic community. There are no illustrations. Like its sister sets, this work is suitable for both high-school and undergraduate students. Note that this set has been superseded by *Magill's Encyclopedia of Social Science: Psychology* [entry 2-258].

Guides and Handbooks
2-262. Gregory, Richard L., ed. *The Oxford Companion to the Mind.* 2nd ed. Oxford: Oxford University Press, 2004. 1004 pp. Index. ISBN: 0-198-66224-6.

This one-volume work is broader in scope than the usual psychology dictionary or encyclopedia. Subjects well outside the physiological are defined and described in entries including, for example, education theory, evolution, ghost, and military mind. Entries range in length from a couple of paragraphs to as many as ten pages and include biographies of important individuals identified with the study of the mind. Some entries include bibliographies. Arrangement is alphabetical, and an excellent detailed index concludes the volume. At the front of the volume is a listing of contributors and their affiliation; most are British academicians or medical researchers. This second edition incorporates new knowledge not available when the first edition appeared in 1987.

2-263. Keyser, Daniel J., and Richard C. Sweetland, eds. *Test Critiques.* Austin, TX: Pro-Ed, 1984–. Indexes. ISBN: 0-890-79521-5.

This series, now in its tenth volume (1994), began publication under the auspices of the Test Corporation of America, although the editors have been with the project since its inception. The purpose of this project is to update and add depth to *Tests: A Comprehensive Reference for Assessments in Psychology, Education, and Business* [entry 2-264] by providing information about the reliability, validity, and normative development of the tests. Tests, selected through a survey of interested professionals, are those considered most frequently in use and are arranged alphabetically in each volume, with the name and affiliation of the individual responsible for the critique. Most entries are several pages in length and each includes an introductory statement, practical applications, technical aspects, a summary critique, and a list of references. Several indexes are provided; most important is a cumulative index of test titles that appears in every volume since the third. Although not as comprehensive as the *Mental Measurements Yearbook* [entry 2-259], this series does provide a quick source for reason-

ably detailed information about important tests published prior to 1994.

2-264. Maddox, Taddy, ed. *Tests: A Comprehensive Reference for Assessments in Psychology, Education, and Business.* 5th ed. Austin, TX: Pro-Ed, 2003. 581 pp. Indexes. ISBN: 0-890-79897-4.

This standard work, now in its fifth edition, aims to provide concise descriptions of thousands of tests used by psychologists, educators, and human-resources personnel. Information is brief and usually includes copyright, population, purpose, description, format, scoring, cost, and publisher. Most entries are about one-half a column in length. The volume is divided into three sections: psychology, education, and business instruments. Several indexes, including an alphabetical list of test titles, provide access to the contents; perhaps the most useful is the index of cross-references, which lists test titles by subject regardless of classification in the volume itself. Readers needing in-depth critiques of specific tests will turn to *Test Critiques* [entry 2-263], the companion series to this work.

Sociology and Social Work
Reference works for both sociology and social work are described in this section. Researchers requiring more information on resources for sociology can turn to the excellent work by Aby. Both disciplines are well served by dictionaries and encyclopedias, and each has a major abstracting service that the student can consult: *Sociological Abstracts* and *Social Work Abstracts.*

This section also describes some of the basic resources for population studies.

Literature Guides

2-265. Mendelsohn, Henry N. *Author's Guide to Social Work Journals.* 4th ed. Washington, DC: NASW Press, 1997. 377 pp. ISBN: 0-871-01271-5.

Information on almost 200 journals of interest to social work researchers is provided in this publication. A table of contents lists all the periodicals alphabetically by title. Information on each is quite complete, providing the usual contact information as well as guidelines on submissions, manuscript formats, the review process, and reprints. E-mail addresses are also included. An appendix includes a bibliographic listing of style and usage guides. The description of each journal includes an "Editorial Focus," which is of value not only to social work professionals but also to other researchers trying to familiarize themselves with the periodical literature in this field. However, an updated edition would be welcome.

2-266. Aby, Stephen H. *Sociology: A Guide to Reference and Information Sources.* 2nd ed. Englewood, CO: Libraries Unlimited, 1997. 227 pp. Indexes. ISBN: 1-563-08422-8.

In a brief but well-written introduction, Aby (1997) describes the purpose of his book: "to provide undergraduate and graduate students, faculty, librarians, and researchers with descriptions of 576 of the major reference sources in sociology, its subdisciplines, and related social sciences." The volume has four parts. The first two describe general social science reference sources and sources peculiar to social science disciplines other than sociology. These include anthropology, economics, education, history, political science, psychology, and social work. These two parts are relatively brief, occupying only about one-fourth of the entire text. The final two parts are devoted to reference sources for the entire field of sociology and to sources pertaining to fields within the discipline. Sources are divided into categories that will be familiar to reference librarians: guides, bibliographies, indexes and abstracts, handbooks, dictionaries, encyclopedias, and directories. Internet sites and databases are also included. Each entry receives an annotation that is descriptive in nature, with critical analysis included when necessary. The volume concludes with two indexes, one of authors and titles, and the other of subjects. The table of contents and the general format are a model for clarity.

Abstracting and Indexing Services

2-267. National Council on the Aging, Inc. *Abstracts in Social Gerontology: Current Literature on Aging.* Quarterly. Thousand Oaks, CA: Sage Publications, 1957–. Indexes. ISSN: 1047-4862.

Each issue of this abstracting service contains about 250 abstracts and an additional 250 "Related Citations." Most of the abstracts describe appropriate journal literature, but there are occasional entries for other types of publications as well. Abstracts within each issue are grouped into a number of basic subject areas. Some examples include "Medical Disorders and Diagnoses," "Psychology of Aging," "Economic Issues," and "Community Services." An author index is included. The final issue of the year also includes cumulative author and subject indexes, as well as a listing of the sources for the abstracts. The "Related Citations" that appear in each issue are strictly bibliographic in nature, with no abstract or entry number assigned. Users must therefore peruse this section on an issue-by-issue basis. No specific criteria are provided for the selection of these bibliographic citations, but most appear to be from collateral journal and periodical literature. This abstracting service is somewhat more approachable than many others aimed at a professional audience but nevertheless will be of greater interest to advanced researchers than to undergraduates.

2-268. *Human Resources Abstracts.* Quarterly. Newbury Park, CA: Sage Publications, 1966–. Indexes. ISSN: 1099-2453.

Human Resources Abstracts follows the same format as other abstracting services published by Sage. Each quarterly issue includes about 250 abstracts with accompanying descriptors. Most abstracts are drawn from relevant books and journal articles. Each issue is arranged into approximately fifteen subject areas, grouping like abstracts together. Author and subject indexes appear in each issue and are accumulated at the end of the year. The final annual issue also includes a listing of journal sources; almost all are English-language publications drawn from the United States and elsewhere. Despite its name, this publication is not really devoted to personnel issues. Instead, it focuses upon human, social, and manpower problems relating to cities and will be of interest to scholars and professionals dealing with urban issues.

2-269. *Population Index.* Quarterly. Princeton, NJ: Office of Population Research, Princeton University, 1935–1999. Indexes. ISSN: 0032-4701.

Demographics and population are the subjects included in this bibliography, which encompasses monographs, serial publications, journals, working papers, dissertations, and databases. Approximately 400 journal titles are surveyed regularly, as are certain abstracting and indexing services. Although English is the language used in this indexing service, there are citations to and abstracts of publications originating in other languages; in these cases, the language of origin is noted. Each quarterly issue is arranged into five broad topic areas: "General Population Studies and Theories," "Regional Population Studies," "Spatial Distribution," "Trends in Population Growth and Size," and "Mortality." Within each of these major categories, there are further subdivisions. Entries include complete bibliographic information as well as descriptive annotations. Quarterly issues include separate author and geographical indexes, and cumulative indexes of both appear at the end of the year.

2-270. *Social Planning/Policy and Development Abstracts.* Biannual. San Diego: Sociological Abstracts, 1979–1996. Indexes. ISSN: 0195-7988.

Formerly known as *Social Welfare, Social Planning/Policy and Social Development* (the title changed in 1985), this abstracting service appears twice annually in its print version. As of 1996, three major subject areas are represented in each issue: social welfare, social planning/policy, and social development. Each of these broad categories is further subdivided into more specific topic areas. Some examples include "addiction," "problems of minorities," "community development," and "urban development." Each entry includes the usual bibliographic information as well as a paragraph-length abstract. Three formats of publication are also represented. These include abstracts of journal articles, dissertation citations, and book-review citations. In 1996, the last category appeared in a separate section of the service entitled "International Review of Publications in Social Planning/Policy and Development." Each issue includes indexes by author, source, and subject. Coverage of this indexing service includes several-hundred journals worldwide, although most are English-language. This publication is of obvious value to political scientists, but the print format is tedious to use, so most researchers will prefer an electronic approach.

2-271. *Social Work Abstracts.* Quarterly. Washington, DC: National Association of Social Workers, 1965–. Indexes. ISSN: 1070-5317.

Each issue of this publication presents about 450 abstracts drawn from approximately the same number of journals reviewed during the course of the entire year. A listing of the journals reviewed appears at the beginning of each issue; core journals are indicated in italics. The core journals are reviewed completely, while the others are reviewed selectively. Abstracts are categorized into four major areas: "Social Work Profession," "Theory and Practice," "Areas of Service," and "Social Issues/Social Problems." Each of these four category areas is further subdivided by subject, allowing the reader to peruse abstracts dealing with the same topic. Cross-references to other relevant entries also are included. The abstracts include the author's address as well as the usual bibliographic information. Subject and author indexes appear at the end of each issue. Unfortunately, the final issue of the year is not cumulative in its indexing. Almost all users will prefer the electronic version of this service, not described here. 💻

2-272. International Sociological Association. *Sociological Abstracts.* Seven issues per year. Bethesda, MD: Cambridge Scientific Abstracts, 1953–. Indexes. ISSN: 0038-0202.

This extraordinarily complex abstracting service defies brief explanation. Six of the seven issues appearing annually abstract journal articles, books, and book chapters, and provide listings of relevant dissertations. These issues also include book reviews, which are grouped together under the rubric of "International Review of Publications in Sociology." (Formerly, the "International Review" included book and book-chapter abstracts, but beginning in 1997 these were integrated with journal-article abstracts and dissertation listings.) The seventh issue each year is devoted to abstracts of conference papers. Author, source, and subject indexes provide access to the abstracts; the indexes cumulate in two separate volumes appearing at the end of the year. The abstracts are arranged by a classification scheme, although entry by way of the indexes is through accession numbers. The inclusion of conference-paper abstracts can be confusing to beginning users, as many of these papers may be available only from the author. Fortunately, advances in technology have eased this problem, for e-mail addresses now allow authors to be more readily contacted than might have been the case in the past. Those researchers who might be using this abstracting service on an ongoing basis would be well advised to read through the instructions that appear at the front of each issue; alternatively, users can turn instead to the electronic version of *Sociological Abstracts*, not described here. 🖳

Directories

2-273. American Sociological Association (ASA). *Directory of Members.* Biennial. Washington, DC: American Sociological Association, 1970–. Indexes. ISSN: 1052-7148.

As the title indicates, this publication is a directory of the approximately 13,000 members of the American Sociological Association (ASA), both here and abroad. When available, information for each member includes his or her name, membership category, mailing address, work phone, membership in one or more of the specialized sections of the ASA, and an e-mail address. As of 1995–1996, e-mail addresses were listed in a separate index of members; presumably this information will be more conveniently located in the main listing in future editions. Also included is a geographic index that lists members by state, territory, or nation. (Note: Editions after 1996 were not seen.)

2-274. American Sociological Association (ASA). *Guide to Graduate Departments of Sociology.* Washington, DC: American Sociological Association, 1965–. Indexes. ISSN: 0091-7052.

The 2003 edition of this publication included listings for 250 graduate departments of sociology. Of these, 211 were in the United States, with most of the remainder in either Canada or Great Britain. The basic arrangement is alphabetical by name of institution. Institutions in the United States appear first, while there are separate listings for each of the other seven countries included. Complete information for institutions includes address, telephone, fax, e-mail address, URL, name of chair and other administrative officers, listings of degrees offered, information pertaining to financial aid, deadlines, numbers of graduate students and undergraduate majors, and other pieces of information of interest to prospective applicants. Program specialties are listed, as are names of faculty members, their academic background, and their areas of expertise. There are indexes of faculty, special programs, and PhD recipients. Although information on most individual institutions can be found on the Internet, this is still a handy source that allows for easy comparison among the programs.

Dictionaries

2-275. Johnson, Allan G. *Blackwell Dictionary of Sociology: A User's Guide to Sociological Language.* 2nd ed. Malden, MA: Blackwell Publishers, 2000. 413 pp. Index. ISBN: 0-631-21680-4.

All the entries in this work were written by Allan Johnson himself in the hope of lending a coherence not perhaps found in a dictionary that represents the work of many collaborators. He also states, "I have tried to represent the classical conceptual core of the discipline along with a representative sampling of diverse areas within sociology and a few fundamentally important concepts from related disciplines such as philosophy" (Johnson 2000, "About This Book"). There are also entries for those individuals who influenced the field. Entries range in length from a paragraph to as much as a page and are written in jargon-free language accessible to undergraduate students. Cross-references are indicated in uppercase. One or more bibliographic references conclude most entries; in general, these lead the reader to core works in the discipline. The index

provides additional access to the text. The biographical sketches are placed in a separate section at the end of the main dictionary, an awkward arrangement that may cause some readers to miss these entries. Otherwise, this is a useful resource for all levels of readers needing a quick guide to sociology. 💻

2-276. Boudon, Raymond, and Francois Bourricauld. *A Critical Dictionary of Sociology.* Chicago: University of Chicago Press, 1989. 438 pp. Index. ISBN: 0-226-06728-9.

This work originally appeared in France in the mid-1980s. The American edition has been translated by Peter Hamilton, who also did some editing of the original by eliminating a number of the entries. The two French authors prepared their work as an answer to a perceived decline in sociology after 1970. Their approach to sociological topics and questions reflects their own viewpoint, which Hamilton describes as somewhat right of center. Those articles omitted by Hamilton represent those that he felt would be of little interest to an American audience or else failed to reflect current scholarship. Typical remaining entries include "Capitalism," "Dialectic," "Function," and "Social Mobility." The general style resembles that of an essay rather than the usual encyclopedia article. Most are several pages in length and conclude with a listing of cross-references and a bibliography. The latter has been edited by Hamilton to include those works most of interest to an English-speaking audience. A short "Thematic Index" provides additional access to the text. Due to its somewhat idiosyncratic approach, this dictionary is more appropriate for users already conversant with the discipline than to those new to sociology. ▄

2-277. Marshall, Gordon, ed. *Dictionary of Sociology.* 2nd ed. Oxford: Oxford University Press, 1998. 710 pp. ISBN: 0-192-80081-7.

Compiled by a British academician and his associates, this dictionary is "intended primarily for those who are relatively new to the discipline" (Marshall 1998, preface to the first edition). Arrangement is alphabetical. Some entries are relatively brief, but many resemble short essays rather than dictionary definitions. Cross-references are indicated by an asterisk within the text of each entry, as well as by "see also" references that appear at the end of the entry. Brief bibliographic references are also included. In addition to sociological terms, there also entries for several of the cognate disciplines, such as economics, psychology, and anthropology. Biographies have been excluded for all but a number of deceased individuals whose work has had a major impact on the field. No doubt there is some British bias to be detected in this work, but most readers will find it useful for its pithy approach, readily understood by the student or nonspecialist.

2-278. Jary, David, and Julia Jary. *Harper-Collins Dictionary of Sociology.* New York: HarperCollins Perennial Publishers, 1991. 601 pp. ISBN: 0-062-71543-7.

This dictionary hopes to present the terminology of sociology and the other disciplines with which it overlaps. Most entries are relatively short, about a paragraph, but a few range up to a couple of pages in length. Cross-references, indicated in uppercase, are abundant. Each entry begins with a basic definition, allowing the reader whose interest extends no further to obtain a quick answer. There are a number of entries for individuals whose work is important to the field. The work ends with a bibliography of approximately forty pages; essentially, it includes those works discussed within the dictionary entries. Definitions are presented with a minimum of jargon or specialized language, so this is a useful source to which nonspecialists can be directed for brief information on sociological topics.

2-279. Barker, Robert L. *Social Work Dictionary.* 4th ed. Washington, DC: National Association of Social Workers, 1999. 584 pp. ISBN: 0-871-01290-7.

Believing that social work students and practitioners need a guide to the increasingly complex vocabulary of the profession, Barker has compiled several editions of this dictionary. This fourth edition includes 8,000 definitions. The terms chosen for definition were selected from the indexes of relevant journals and textbooks over the last several decades; in addition, suggestions were accepted from the author's colleagues. Definitions are arranged alphabetically and are no more than a paragraph in length. Cross-references are indicated in italics. There is no bibliography, but Barker does provide a detailed chronology of happenings important to the social work field. Other end matter includes the social work code of ethics, addresses of state social work agencies, and addresses of National Association of Social Workers chapter offices. Although this dictionary is intended for a professional group, the definitions are written in a style accessible to students and others who are not social workers.

Encyclopedias

2-280. Outhwaite, William, and Tom Bottomore, eds. *Blackwell Dictionary of Twentieth-Century Social Thought.* Cambridge, MA: Blackwell, 1993. 864 pp. Index. ISBN: 0-631-15262-8.

This reference work incorporates three themes: "first, the major concepts which figure in social thought; second, the principal schools and movements of thought; and third, those institutions and organizations which have either been important objects of social analysis, or have themselves engendered significant doctrines and ideas" (Outhwaite and Bottomore 1993, preface). Typical topics include Communism, conservatism, consumer society, participation, unemployment, and the women's movement. Biographical entries are relegated to an appendix rather than being included in the main alphabetical array. Entries are usually about two pages in length. Cross-references are included, as are listings of readings for each entry. A general bibliography can be found at the back to the volume as well. There are no illustrations.

Contributors generally are academicians from British institutions, although there is representation from the United States and other countries as well. The writing style of the contributors is erudite in nature, and this work will be of greater value to advanced undergraduates and other scholarly researchers than it will be to beginners or general readers. 💻

2-281. Manstead, Antony S. R., and Miles Hewstone. *Blackwell Encyclopedia of Social Psychology.* Oxford: Basil Blackwell, 1995. 694 pp. Index. ISBN: 0-631-18146-6.

In the preface, the editors express the hope that this will be "a volume to which students, instructors, researchers, and practitioners can turn when they want to discover more about a particular phenomenon, concept, or theory" in social psychology. Entries are arranged alphabetically and are signed by the contributors, who hail from academic institutions in North America and western Europe. Cross-references are indicated in uppercase. Of the approximately 300 entries, 93 are "feature items" receiving treatment of about 3,000 words. The rest of the entries are shorter in length, including 90 items that fall into the category of "glossary" and receive no more than 50 words. All entries except those in the glossary category include bibliographies of two, five, or ten items. Typical entries include "Depression," "Group Processes," "Intergroup Relations," and "Risk." There are no illustrations other than a handful of graphic displays. For the most part, contributors have succeeded in writing at a level that is accessible to undergraduates as well as to more advanced researchers, so this volume can be recommended to most library users who require basic information in regard to the field of social psychology. ⌨

2-282. Birren, James E., ed. *Encyclopedia of Gerontology: Age, Aging, and the Aged.* 2 vols. San Diego: Academic Press, 1996. 1474 pp. Index. ISBN: 0-122-26860-1.

As the preface to this work indicates, persons over sixty-five years of age made up the smallest portion of developed societies only a century ago, whereas today they are on their way to becoming the largest. Therefore, there is an obvious need for information about the subject of aging in all its aspects. This set describes the biology and psychology of aging as well as its relation to the social sciences, health sciences, and the humanities. Articles are arranged alphabetically and are written by scholars and specialists in the field. Articles average about ten pages in length and include an initial outline and glossary as well as a bibliography of references to both secondary and research literature. Cross-references to other relevant articles are indicated in uppercase within the text, and there is a subject index in the second volume. Reference to the latter is important, particularly for the nonspecialist. For example, information on Alzheimer's disease appears in the article on "Dementia" rather than having a separate entry of its own. Some of the articles on the biological and psychological aspects

of aging may go beyond the needs of general readers and beginning students, but those on nontechnical subjects are accessible to undergraduate researchers and others within higher education.

2-283. Ness, Immanuel, and James Ciment. *Encyclopedia of Global Population and Demographics.* 2 vols. Armonk, NY: M. E. Sharpe Reference, 1999. 967 pp. Index. ISBN: 1-563-24710-0.

About 90 percent of this set consists of tables pertaining to individual nations of the world, arranged alphabetically by name of country. The individual sets of tables are usually about six pages in length and provide statistics on subjects such as geography, population, ethnicity, vital statistics, health, and education. Whenever figures are available, data is provided for 1965, 1980, and 1995. This allows the reader to determine at a glance changes over the final decades of the twentieth century. Brief introductory information provides background on the nation in question. In some instances, the tables are supplemented by graphic displays. The first volume of this set provides about 100 pages of essays discussing demography in relation to subjects such as the environment, vital statistics, the economy, migration, and health care. Each of the essays concludes with a reading list; these references are repeated in a bibliography that appears at the end of the second volume. While much of the data can be found in other standard sources, this encyclopedia is useful for its straightforward approach, suitable for high-school and undergraduate students alike, and for its comparisons from 1965 through 1995. CD-ROM.

2-284. *Encyclopedia of Social Work.* 19th ed. 3 vols. Washington, DC: National Association of Social Workers, 1995. 4644 pp. Index. ISBN: 0-871-01255-3.

Although one might assume that this long-standing reference work would be of value primarily to social work students and professionals, in truth it is also a valuable source for the laypeople and college students as well. While some of the articles deal with professional issues, many discuss topics of general societal interest. Some examples include children's rights, cults, gang violence, AIDS, and sexual harassment. There are many useful articles relating to ethnic groups as well. Most articles are several pages in length at the minimum. Longer articles or topics are further subdivided into their component parts. There are many user aids, including cross-references and references to keywords. Articles conclude with listings of references and readings. These include works from outside the social work profession as well as from within. Those articles that deal with legal questions provide references to legal cases and legislation. Each of the three volumes includes a comprehensive index to the entire set, with references to entire entries marked in boldface. There are no illustrations other than statistical tables and graphic displays. This encyclopedia can be highly recommended to both students and advanced researchers

who need solid information on issues of current interest in American society. This work has a 1997 supplemental volume.

2-285. Borgatta, Edgar F., and Rhonda J. V. Montgomery, eds. *Encyclopedia of Sociology.* 2nd ed. 5 vols. New York: Macmillan Reference, 2000. Index. ISBN: 0-028-64853-6.

The preface outlines the incentives to publication of this set, citing the rise of rival disciplines such as social work, criticism of sociology for its apparent inability to remedy social problems, the rise of statistical applications to the field, and the broadening of sociology into a number of subfields. Articles are arranged alphabetically, with several pages devoted to most topics. Cross-references appear at the end of each entry along with a list of references to which the text refers. Articles are signed, and a list of the contributors, with their affiliation, appears at the beginning of the first volume. The great majority of contributors are academicians at U.S. and Canadian institutions. There are no illustrations other than occasional mathematical tables and figures. The index provides additional access to the text. The preface states that this work is intended for sociologists, scholars in other fields, and students. Contributors were asked to write at a level suitable for all these audiences; only technical articles were exempted from this stipulation. As is often the case with subject encyclopedias, this set serves as an excellent starting point for those readers needing a reasonably detailed but nonspecialized introduction to the topics that concern a specific discipline, sociology in this instance. 🖥

2-286. Hogg, Michael A., ed. *Social Psychology.* 4 vols. Sage Benchmarks in Psychology. London: Sage Publications, 2003. ISBN: 0-761-94044-8.

This set is a compilation of seventy-one classic articles pertaining to social psychology. Most were written within the last two decades, but there are also a few from the 1950s and one originally written in 1935. The articles are arranged by major subject matter, such as "Social Interaction" and "People in Groups." Additional subdivision occurs within each of these major categories. The articles are of course written for the professional reader, but a lengthy introduction to social psychology that appears in the first volume will assist the beginning researcher to some extent. Bibliographies lead to additional resources.

2-287. Magill, Frank N., ed. *Survey of Social Science: Sociology Series.* 5 vols. Pasadena, CA: Salem Press, 1994. Index. ISBN: 0-893-56739-6.

Like others in the Survey of Social Science series, this set follows a standard format. Articles are arranged alphabetically. Each article begins with summary information, including definitions. This is followed by an overview introducing and explaining the topic. A section on "Applications" then explains how the subject is put into practice. Next, a section on context explains the subject within the entire field of sociology. Arti-

cles conclude with a bibliography and a listing of cross-references. Each of the volumes also includes an alphabetical listing of all articles as well as a listing of all articles arranged by subject. In total, there are 338 articles averaging about six pages in length. Typical entries include "Measures of Variability," "Political Machines and Bosses," "Pornography," "Religious Miracles and Visions," and "Social Groups." The final volume includes a glossary and a comprehensive index. As is the case with other Survey of Social Science sets, this reference work provides a useful nontechnical introduction to a potentially difficult discipline for those high-school and undergraduate students new to the field.

2-288. Palmisano, Joseph M., ed. *World of Sociology.* 2 vols. Detroit: Gale Group, 2001. 803 pp. Indexes. ISBN: 0-787-64965-1.

The student researcher new to the field of sociology will be well served by this set, which includes about 1,000 entries pertaining to sociology topics. Theories, concepts, organizations, and biographies are among the categories of topics. Arrangement is alphabetical, with articles generally ranging in length from a few paragraphs to about a page. The second volume includes a chronology and indexes. Cross-references and illustrations accompany the articles. Contributors are not indicated, and there are no individual bibliographic listings, although the second volume does include a lengthy list of "Sources Consulted."

Beginning students may prefer to start with this set rather than the *Encyclopedia of Sociology* [entry 2-285].

Guides and Handbooks

2-289. American Sociological Association (ASA). *ASA Style Guide.* 2nd ed. Washington, DC: American Sociological Association, 1997. 39 pp. ISBN: 0-912-76429-5.

As stated in the preface, this brief style manual "is based on what editors, managing editors, and copy editors for ASA journals have observed to be the most common style and format problems in manuscripts accepted for publication." This guide, therefore, will be used primarily by academicians and other researchers submitting manuscripts to sociology journals that do not require some other standard format in regard to style.

2-290. Ginsberg, Leon H. *Social Work Almanac.* 2nd ed. Washington, DC: National Association of Social Workers, 1995. 391 pp. Index. ISBN: 0-871-01248-0.

Unlike its companion works, the *Encyclopedia of Social Work* [entry 2-284] and the *Social Work Dictionary* [entry 2-279], this publication is primarily devoted to the compilation of statistical data that support the information in the other sets.

Most of the data pertains to the United States and is drawn from federal government sources. Major categories include demographics, children, crime, education, health and mortality, mental illness, "Older Adults," and statistics pertaining to social welfare issues. Explanatory text accompanies the tables, which also include references to the original sources. This is a useful source for those wishing to focus upon statistical measures of relevance to social issues, at least through the early 1990s; otherwise, more recent statistics must be sought out.

2-291. Roberts, Albert R., and Gilbert J. Greene, eds. *Social Workers' Desk Reference.* Oxford: Oxford University Press, 2002. 910 pp. Indexes. ISBN: 0-195-14211-X.

A compilation of 146 chapters written by social work professionals in the United States and Canada, this volume intends to serve social workers needing a quick overview of topics of concern. The chapters are grouped into fourteen parts; among them, for example, are "Social Work Ethics and Values," "Working with Couples and Families," and "Community Practices." The volume concludes with a glossary and name and subject indexes. Students with a grounding in social work will find this a valuable resource.

3

General Political Science
Reference Sources

Works listed in this chapter have relevance to the entire discipline of political science or at least to several or more of its standard components. This chapter includes national and international sources, news and directories of political science associations, general political science dictionaries, political-quotation books, and Web sites that tend to treat the entire range of political science issues, topics, and fundamental concepts. More specialized materials have been placed into their proper major segment of political science, such as international relations, American politics, and the others.

General Political Science Sources
Literature Guides
3-1. Polsby, Nelson W., ed. *Annual Review of Political Science.* Palo Alto, CA: Annual Reviews, 1998–. ISSN: 1094-2939. http://polisci.annualreviews.org.

This review appears in both print and Web versions for every year of publication beginning with 1998. Approximately twenty articles per issue appear that

were written by international scholars who are faculty in a number of political science departments. The articles provide a concise overview of the topic and then go on to recount the most recent scholarship that pertains to the discipline and subdisciplines covered. A few articles tend to be highly theoretical, while others will be more relevant to nonspecialists and undergraduate students. The majority of articles published are situated somewhere in between these two levels. Topics of articles range from "Reinventing Government" to "Decline of Parties" and "Government Formation." The section on cited literature offers an excellent bibliographic introduction to a topic's more recently published books, journal articles, research reports, and other publications of value. The editor, Nelson W. Polsby, is an eminent and widely published author on topics related to American government and politics. ⌨

3-2. York, Henry E. *Political Science: A Guide to Reference and Information*

Sources. Englewood, CO: Libraries Unlimited, 1990. 249 pp. ISBN: 0-872-87794-9.

This is another resource guide to the literature of the social sciences and political science for monographs published between 1980 and 1987. Serials are included regardless of the original date of publication. Most works listed are in English and published either in the United States or in the United Kingdom. The main body of the book is in six distinct parts and has a total of over 800 entries. Some of these six parts are: "Social Science Disciplines," "Political Science—General Reference Sources," and "Public Policy." Each entry has a brief yet descriptive annotation and is subdivided further into such form headings as atlases, bibliographies, handbooks, and others. Many documents and legal publications are excluded. Online resources are included but are relatively few in number.

3-3. Magill, Frank N., ed. *Survey of Social Science: Government and Politics Series.* 5 vols. Pasadena, CA: Salem Press, 1995. Index. ISBN: 0-893-56745-0.

The goal of this multivolume set is to provide the more general reader with an organized introduction to the fields of government and politics. There are a grand total of 342 articles, averaging about six pages long. The preponderance of articles is about the institutions, governments, and politics of North America, particularly the United States. Each article is divided into three similar parts: an overview (introductions and discussion topics), applications (case studies), and context (situates the term within its historical, geographic, and/or philosophical frameworks). These articles are followed by a brief annotated bibliography and list of cross-references. Individual entries include political philosophers (Aristotle), terms (anarchism), topics (class conflict), and international organizations (United Nations). A "category list" places all 342 main entries into one of thirteen broad areas, such as "Civil Rights and Liberties," "Economic Issues," "Types of Government," and others. The index is fairly scant for a five-volume set.

Abstracting and Indexing Services

3-4. *CSA Political Science and Government.* 6 issues per year. Bethesda, MD: Cambridge Scientific Abstracts, 2001–. Indexes. ISSN: 0001-0456.

Previously titled ABC Political Science, this standard publication indexes political science citations drawn from the academic-journal literature. Each issue contains a table of contents, an author index, a source index, and a subject index. Every citation included falls into a classified scheme using fourteen standard political science headings, some with additional subdivisions. The citations are assigned a control number and arranged alphabetically by author. All entries are annotated except for those indexed in non-English-language works. The subject index is the real key to successful access to relevant materials. The last volume published for the year has a set of cumulative indexes. ⌨

3-5. *International Bibliography of Political Science.* Annual. London: British Library of Political and Economic Science, 1954–. ISSN: 0085-2058.

This annual publication has been a mainstay of political science research for about fifty years. It usually is published a year or so behind the current year because of the work involved in its massive compilation of materials that make up the bibliography. The bibliography covers journal articles and books that have been published around the world in a number of different languages. Each entry has an English-language title translation if necessary. There appears to be a growing use of international resources from developing and East European nations. Until 1989, the publisher was UNESCO; since then, it has been published by the British Library of Political and Economic Science at the London School of Economics. The works on political science materials are part of a four-volume annual package that also includes economics, sociology, and social and cultural anthropology. Over the course of the latest year, over 100,000 articles were indexed from over 2,500 journal titles and 20,000 monographs. The indexing system used in the main body of the work is by a broad and hierarchical classification scheme in both English and French. There are no abstracts. Users of this work may want to consult the *Thematic List of Descriptors—Political Science* [London; New York: Routledge, 1989]. One section is alphabetical, and another thematic, pegged to terms used in the *Bibliography*. 🖥

3-6. *International Political Science Abstracts [Documentation Politique Internationale].* Bimonthly. Oxford: Basil Blackwell; Paris: Presses Universitaires de France, 1951–. Indexes. ISSN: 0020-8345.

This authoritative bimonthly has been a standard political science bibliographic abstracting service for over one-half a century. It indexes and abstracts the more respected political science journals and yearbooks published from around the world. Because of this, coverage is especially good for information on the developing world and those other countries that are not economic, political, or military powers. Entries are arranged by using a classification system associated with the entire *International Bibliography of the Social Sciences* series. The exceptionally well-crafted abstracts of the articles in English are written in English, while those articles published in any language other than English are written in French. Every title, however, is translated into French and/or English. The major political science journals receive comprehensive indexing/abstracting, while the less important ones get more selective treatment. The final issue of each volume includes cumulative author and subject indexes. A Web version is available. 🖥

3-7. *PAIS International in Print.* New York: Public Affairs Information Service, 1991–. ISSN: 1051-4015.

For over a century, *PAIS* has been doing indexing of selected books, journals, government publications at all levels, international publications, and non-governmental agency reports with heavy emphasis on domestic and foreign-policy issues. This is truly a standard in the field of accessing the literature of politics and the policy sciences. Foreign-language materials constitute a regular percentage of each issue's indexed items. A thesaurus of subject terminology is published separately to be used in conjunction with the *PAIS* database or print index. This publication may also have value as a more general social sciences index depending on the topic chosen. Most researchers should look for the Web version available at many libraries. *PAIS International in Print* was formed by the merger of *PAIS Bulletin* and *PAIS Foreign Language Index*. 💻

Directories

3-8. *Directory of Members of the American Political Science Association, 1997–1999.* Washington, DC: American Political Science Association, 1997. 496 pp. Indexes. ISBN: 1-878-14725-0. http://www.apsanet.org.

Published since 1980, this triennial publication now lists 14,000 members of the American Political Science Association (APSA) from the United States and seventy other nations as of November 15, 1996. This alphabetical directory adopts a standardized style that gives the individual's title, address, telephone number, fax number, e-mail address, degrees earned along with year and conferring institution, fields of specialization, and membership in any of APSA's organized sections. There are a number of useful indexes, such as one by minority status and fields of specialization. This directory is great for finding speakers, setting up mailing lists, and so on. 💻

3-9. *Directory of Political Science Faculty, 2002–2004.* Washington, DC: American Political Science Association, 2002–.

This new directory is the result of a merger of *Graduate Faculty and Programs in Political Science* [entry 3-10] and the *Directory of Undergraduate Political Science Faculty*. It is a guide to political science faculty and those in related areas of U.S. and international affairs. Its scope of coverage includes faculty at academic institutions in the United States, Canada, the United Kingdom, and Ireland that offer one or more degrees in the discipline of political science or related areas. All institutions included offer a major in political science. The main body offers standard directory-type information including department, address, telephone number, fax, e-mail, and Web site. It also provides the individual faculty member's fields of specialization. Overall, the main arrangement is alphabetical by school. Many of the entries give the administration of each department, such as chair, graduate director, and undergraduate director.

3-10. Engel, Elizabeth Weaver, ed. *Graduate Faculty and Programs in Political Science, 1998–2000.* 14th ed. Washington, DC: American Political Science Association, 1998. Index. ISSN 1065-6049.

This work is a triennial directory, and continues the former title of *Guide to*

Graduate Study in Political Science. It lists the faculty members and various graduate-degree programs within the United States, the United Kingdom, and Canada. There is a college-by-college description of the political science departments. These entries provide information on degree requirements, program descriptions, and a roster of faculty members with their PhD dates and conferring institutions, current professorial rank, and specialty areas of both teaching and research. An index of faculty members named throughout the directory is included. Most programs now have their own institutional Web sites, so interested students can compile much of this information in an updated fashion from the Internet.

Bibliographies

3-11. Johansen, Elaine R. *Political Corruption: Scope and Resources: An Annotated Bibliography.* Garland Reference Library of Social Science, Vol. 616. New York: Garland, 1990. 241 pp. Index. ISBN: 0-824-03529-1.

This bibliography includes approximately 900 references, most drawn from the twenty years prior to publication and reflecting such varied sources as journal articles, dissertations, books, legal cases, hearings, and government documents. Although emphasis is on the latter part of the twentieth century, a couple of chapters also include items from the Progressive movement and urban corruption early in the century. Annotations are descriptive rather than analytic and are divided into ten chapters, each ad-

dressing itself to a particular subject area. Some of the chapter titles are "Legal Writings," "Public Opinion and Corruption," and "Historical and Comparative Studies." All the literature cited is in the English language. The chapter on federal government documents lacks annotations on the theory that the titles adequately represent the contents. The arrangement is a bit confusing because each chapter has its own set of entry numbers; however, the index will lead readers to specific authors through the use of page references. A mix of scholarly sources and popular books and articles of a substantive nature, this bibliography will be consulted by specialists rather than beginning students.

3-12. Brunk, Gregory G., comp. *Theories of Political Processes: A Bibliographic Guide to the Journal Literature, 1965–1995.* Westport, CT: Greenwood Press, 1997. 251 pp. Indexes. ISBN: 0-313-30259-6.

This is a bibliography of unannotated journal articles drawn from a number of standard international and U.S. journals. There are approximately 10,000 such entries, all of which have been divided into broad chapters and then arranged into various useful subdivisions. The journal articles are then arranged alphabetically by the author. Typical main chapters are those on citizen participation, economic policy, political parties, and social choice. Subdivisions under the social choice chapter include median voter, risk and uncertainty, and coalitions. There is both an author index and a separate subject index, the latter being an especially important addition.

Dictionaries

3-13. Bealey, Frank. *Blackwell Dictionary of Political Science: A User's Guide to Its Terms.* Malden, MA: Blackwell Publishers, 1999. 384 pp. ISBN: 0-631-20694-9.

This dictionary is concerned exclusively with the terminology of political science as a discipline. Neither political parties nor politicians are included as entries. Instead, the reader will find included those terms more closely related to policies and political movements that possess a more general significance to political science scholars and the interested general public alike. Several terms culled from this dictionary are: "Privatization," "Socialism," and "Nationalization." Cross-references are built in via the use of uppercase within the text. Short reading lists are appended to most entries. Entries can be as short as a sentence or two, or can spread over several long paragraphs. A British audience will be more at home with the terms chosen, spellings, and style of writing employed here than will American readers. A modest section on biography is included. ⌨

3-14. Comfort, Nicholas. *Brewer's Politics: A Phrase and Fable Dictionary.* London: Cassell, 1993. 693 pp. ISBN: 0-304-34085-5.

This is not just another political dictionary that dutifully defines a particular term; rather, it features a large streak of irreverence, much like the tone set in *Brewer's Dictionary of Phrase and Fable* (not covered). The 5,000 entries, in alphabetical order, express well the political jargon and terms and the rich folklore of politics. It is a work that is meant to entertain as well as educate. Entries on particular individuals are written with a wry sense of humor. Some entries you may not find in other, more staid, political science dictionaries are "Kennedy Dynasty," "Remember the Maine," and "Plum Book."

3-15. *Cassell Dictionary of Modern Politics.* London: Cassell, 1994. 340 pp. Index. ISBN: 0-304-34432-X.

This dictionary covers the period from 1945 to the middle of 1994 and includes one-paragraph definitions of terms that readers would be likely to encounter in their daily dose of newspaper, television, or radio stories of the era, such as "arms for hostages" or "ethnic cleansing." Other terms are selected based on their relatively colorful use thirty years ago, such as the "Gang of Four." Other terms may seem obscure to today's reader, such as "Nkomati Accord." Overall, a nice selection of terms has been included. A biographical index rounds out the work.

3-16. Robertson, David. *A Dictionary of Modern Politics.* 2nd ed. London: Europa Publications, 1993. 495 pp. ISBN: 0-946-65375-5.

Each entry appearing in this second edition was either slightly or comprehensively rewritten. There is also a significant amount of new material to make it roughly 50 percent longer than the first edition. Terms and individuals chosen as entries tend to be core ones, especially for the last century or so. The one-page entries are alphabetically arranged and contain cross-references in boldface. A few typical entries include "Class," "Liberty," "Reaganomics," "Terrorism," and "Containments." A third edition was published in 2002, but was unseen.

3-17. Raymond, Walter John. *The Dictionary of Politics: Selected American and Foreign Political and Legal Terms.* 7th ed. Lawrenceville, VA: Brunswick Publishing, 1992. 760 pp. ISBN: 1-556-18008-X.

This dictionary of politics starts off with a terrific introduction to political terminology. While the entries themselves may be generally on the short side, they are authoritative. It gives comparable state tables of the governor's powers, information on the state courts, and the like. Some of the appendix materials may already be quite out of date since they include U.S. legislative-process charts, load works, and Supreme Court opinions on the legislative and executive powers, state authority, federal authority, freedom of religion, and due process. Individuals selected for inclusion have deeper historical perspective and range, from St. Thomas Aquinas to David Hume.

3-18. Hadjor, Kofi Buenor. *Dictionary of Third World Terms.* New York: Penguin Books, 1993. 305 pp. ISBN: 0-140-51293-4.

Examining a number of different terms from a third world perspective, the core of the work is an alphabetically arranged dictionary of terms. The work is highly selective, and terms were ostensibly chosen for their relative importance to the developing nations of the world. However, why some terms were selected and by what criteria any such term is included are two questions a reader might ponder. Sample longer entries include: "African Socialism," "Development," and "New International Economic Order (NIEO)." Some individuals warranting brief coverage are Antonio A. Neto and Patrice Lumumba. Looking up the term "International Monetary Fund (IMF)" will give the reader a good example of how this book's intended perspective plays out. The IMF entry is not shrill or extreme in its exploration of issues and answers surrounding the IMF's work in the third world, as controversial as that may be. It does give the pluses and minuses associated with IMF intervention in third world monetary and economic policies. Even third world–based organizations such as the Organization of African Unity (OAU) come in for close scrutiny. This work is on very acidic paper and may not last much longer on library shelves in usable condition.

3-19. Hawkesworth, Mary, ed. *Encyclopedia of Government and Politics.* 2nd ed. 2 vols. New York: Routledge, 2004. ISBN: 0-415-27622-5.

An international roster of scholars and subject specialists write lengthy overviews of broad topics and offer criticism of the methodological approaches taken by others in research on each topic. The central theme is the focus on political studies of the latter part of the twentieth century. The main body of this two-volume work is dedicated to publishing a fairly general introduction and nine chapters on a broad array of topics, such as political theory, political institutions, and international relations, all of which have between five and nineteen subchapters, each written by one individual and signed. Entries frequently take up about fifteen to twenty printed pages. There are references and further reading lists that lean toward the academic. The tone of this set is decidedly scholarly, which makes it perfect for political science specialists or students who require more than a cursory definition of a topic. There is an adequate index, which is important because entries lack cross-referencing. The first edition of this encyclopedia was published in 1992 as the *Routledge Encyclopedia of Government and Politics.*

3-20. Stempel, Guido H., ed. *Historical Dictionary of Political Communication in the United States.* Westport, CT: Greenwood Press, 1999. 171 pp. Index. ISBN: 0-313-29545-X.

This specialized dictionary includes listings of people, organizations, events, and ideas that have been regarded as important in political communication in the United States since 1800. The definition of political communication used here touches upon politics and government, all aspects of political campaigns, and individual politicians. It includes political speeches, debates, newspaper editorials, media exposés, photo opportunities, and publicity churned out by the staff of various politicians. Entries are alphabetic in order and include such items as "Kennedy-Nixon Debates," "CNN," "Fairness Doctrine (FCC)," and "Political Cartoons." The source of each definition or entry is given, and these sources cited are often of a more popular bent, such as *Current Biography Yearbook, Contemporary Authors,* or other published works. Each entry is signed. There are a relatively large number of biographical entries. An index is included.

3-21. Roberts, Geoffrey K. *A New Dictionary of Political Analysis.* New York: E. Arnold, 1991. 153 pp. ISBN: 0-340-52860-5.

This is a work aimed at high-school students or college undergraduates who require definitions of basic terms most likely found in political science textbooks. There are no entries for individuals except where their names are inexorably linked to a political or philosophical idea, such as Marx, or where a name is associated closely with a particular term, such as D'Hondt's method of calculating seats in a legislative body. Definitions of many core political science terms are found here. There is no index.

3-22. Robertson, David. *The Routledge Dictionary of Politics.* 3rd ed. London: Routledge, 2003. 528 pp. ISBN: 0-415-32377-0.

This dictionary utilizes expository techniques that emphasize short, topical essays over short definitions, which are standard fare for most general-subject lexicons. The 500 single-authored essays of political terminology, ideologies, institutions, and ideas contain a significant number of new entries over the second edition of this work. Only a few entries have been dropped from the previous edition. The strength of this particular dictionary of politics is its copious entries about the ideas shaping modern politics over the last century. A few of the typical entries are "Legislative Veto," "Interest Groups," "Coalition Theory," and "Game Theory."

3-23. Safire, William. *Safire's New Political Dictionary: The Definitive Guide to the New Language of Politics.* New York: Random House, 1993. 930 pp. ISBN: 0-679-42068-1.

William Safire has a long affiliation with the *New York Times* as a conservative journalist, and he has compiled a marvelously humorous, literate, and irreverent dictionary devoted mainly to the U.S. political scene from about the late 1960s to the date of publication. It is decidedly not a dictionary of government. Look to the more standard political dictionaries for that. The definitions and usage included in his book are uniformly colorful yet authoritative. Onc could easily use this dictionary to look up a term, but one could be equally happy simply reading it cover to cover because of its strong literary value. This work has undergone several revisions, and hopefully will continue to undergo more.

Guides and Handbooks

3-24. Axelrod-Contrada, Joan. *Career Opportunities in Politics, Government, and Activism.* New York: Ferguson, 2003. 274 pp. ISBN: 0-816-04317-5.

Not seen.

3-25. *Careers and the Study of Political Science: A Guide for Undergraduates.* 5th rev. and exp. ed. Washington, DC: American Political Science Association, 2001. 84 pp. ISBN: 1-878-14730-7.

This handy little booklet explains a wide set of career options available to those undergraduate students who decide to major or minor in the discipline of political science. A range of prominent and most likely career opportunities, including teaching, are given and discussed. This work is divided into a number of career areas, such as the federal government, nonprofit agencies, law, business, international careers, public service, and others. It offers a number of good, sound questions to ask in terms of your present personality qualities and professional interests.

3-26. Shively, W. Phillips. *The Craft of Political Research.* 5th ed. Upper Saddle River, NJ: Prentice Hall, 2002. 162 pp. ISBN: 0-130-92232-3.

This political science research guide is aimed at undergraduates in a manner they may find attractive and useful. It includes many fundamental arguments and investigations. For the purposes of this book, the author breaks political science up into two distinct parts: part one is providing answers to a specific problem, while part two is serving as a means to focus on discovering new facts or looking at old ones in a different perspective. Other chapters touch upon identifying good theoretical constructs, deciding whether or not to quantify data, dealing with how to measure a concept, and working with internal data. This book was designed with undergraduates in mind, but graduate students may find this somewhat helpful as well.

3-27. DMZ Open Directory Project. Society: Politics. http://dmoz.org/society/politics.

This is a directory for over forty political science topics. In terms of format, the directory is not dissimilar to the directories appearing on other major Web search engines, such as the ones on Yahoo. There are links into every nook and corner of political science, its major subdisciplines, and topics of interest to political science students and researchers. This "Open Directory" project is founded in the same spirit as the "Open Source" movement. It is available to anyone free of charge. It is aimed at good Netizens who are willing to assist in editing their favorite Web categories, whether in political science or elsewhere. Ample links are provided to policy institutions, international relations, democracy, alternative political systems, and other topics. One of the particular strengths of this Web site is the sheer number of links established to materials in languages other than English. This includes Indonesian,

Danish, and Turkish, among seventy such language links. 💻

3-28. Schmidt, Diane E. *Expository Writing in Political Science: A Practical Guide*. New York: HarperCollins College Publishers, 1993. 283 pp. ISBN: 0-065-00816-2.

This writing guide is divided into twelve chapters to help undergraduate students in putting together research papers exclusively in the discipline of political science. It warns students not to consider this as a basic manual for learning general basic writing skills. Chapters explore such topics as examining formats, researching a particular topic, and common writing problems. A chapter may offer terminology, fundamental indexing and abstracting services, and core academic journals in political science, as well as examining the role of the campus writing center and the like.

3-29. Greenstein, Fred I., and Nelson W. Polsby, eds. *Handbook of Political Science*. 8 vols. Reading, MA: Addison-Wesley Publishing, 1975. Indexes. ISBN: 0-201-02611-2.

First conceived in 1965 and finally published a decade later, this set attempted to provide a state-of-the-art look at political science. Various organizational schemes were the final results indicated by the titles of the separate volumes. The editors considered it of greater importance to enlist significant scholars as contributors rather than to limit the contributors to narrowly defined subjects. Each volume includes from four to eight separate chapters. The multivolume format allows for each chapter (and each contributor) to treat its subject matter at some length. Each chapter also includes an extensive list of references. Individual volumes possess their own index, and the final volume cumulates indexing for the entire set. While the field has undergone obvious changes in the past quarter century, this set is still valuable for its historical overview of the discipline.

3-30. *Handbook of the International Political Science Association.* Dublin, Ireland: International Political Science Association, 2000. 305 pp. ISBN: 1-902-27727-9.

The primary purpose for this handbook is to serve as a guide to current members of the International Political Science Association (IPSA). A secondary role is to inform the larger community of political scientists located around the world so that they too may become members of the association. Based in Paris, the IPSA's objectives are aimed at promoting overall advancement of political science by means of scholarly collaboration around the globe. Chapters 2 through 5 center on the IPSA itself, including membership, governing bodies, the scope of academic activities, its constitution and procedural rules, and networks of research communications. The remaining chapters list various national political science associations, IPSA associate members, an international roster of political scientists, and political science departments in higher education.

3-31. Internet Resources for Political Science and Public Administration Students. http://sciences.aum.edu/popa/links.htm.

This site is noteworthy for both political science and for public administration topics. The home page is graphically divided into ten categories, including "Interest Groups," "Foreign Governments," "State and Local Government," and seven additional ones. The section on current political news provides browsers with a decent listing of foreign and domestic newspapers, newswire services, political opinion pieces, magazines, and television and radio stations. The segment on "Foreign Government and International Organizations" should be singled out for greater thoroughness. There is also a surprisingly good set of links for career-planning and job-seeking resources. 🖳

3-32. Librarians Index to the Internet (LII). http://lii.org.

This is a site dedicated to librarian-selected and librarian-organized Internet resources for all topics, including political science. The user can navigate this site successfully by entering the Web site via the category of "Society and Social Issues." The politics page itself is divided into four categories. They are: "Popular Topics," such as elections, media and politics, and voting machines; "Parties and Positions," including conservatism, Democratic Party, and Socialism; "People," which contains women in politics, politicians, and several other subjects; and "Places," where the user will find links to international governments and the state of California politics and government matters. This latter strength is not surprising given that funding for this project was started up through the Library of California. The last section for "Places" has a terrific set of links regarding the ongoing war in Iraq. Basic and advanced search modes are available to customize searches beyond the established categories. ⌨

3-33. LSU Libraries Political Science/ Law. http://www.lib.lsu.edu/soc/polisci.

This Web site will find itself relevant to the great majority of political science students and researchers. The home page is organized into headings around such major terms as "American Politics," "General Resources," "International Resources," "Political Theory," "Public Policy/Administration," and others of equal importance. These lead to links relevant to the category selected. Sites are fully annotated. It is a solid, worthwhile listing and a relatively stable Web site. The site is currently maintained by the staff at the LSU University Library system. ⌨

3-34. Goodin, Robert E., ed. *A New Handbook of Political Science*. New York: Oxford University Press, 1996. 845 pp. ISBN: 0-198-28015-7.

This handbook attempts to take a snapshot of the discipline of political science and analyze its recent past and future prospects. It is especially good in bringing to light the growing interest in the politics of religion, ethnicity, and different aspects of pluralism. Changes in the methodologies and theoretical frameworks within the discipline have been tracked and scrutinized for new approaches. This is a scholarly product with well-documented articles on various facets of the "Political Economy," "Political Theory," "Comparative Politics," "Political Behavior," and so on. There are several subtopical articles appearing under each section. The contributors are all experts in their respective fields, and their work as a whole lends support to the notion that there is a growing diversity of thought and ideas at the international level for the discipline of political science and its practitioners. The articles appearing in this handbook are bibliographic essays citing the more important research in the fields and subfields of political science.

3-35. Political Resources on the Net. http://www.politicalresources.net.

This is a particularly good resource for undertaking Web research on the developing nations of the global community. Links are provided for rulers and leaders, a wide array of political parties, government information, current events, culture, education, politics, the media, and much more. Also, students may find information on upcoming or recent elections, interest groups, constitutional issues, and general news commentary about the political agendas. The coverage is decidedly international, with Web links provided for most countries on earth. Even the smaller Caribbean islands such as Grenada and Antigua get attention. ⌨

3-36. Political Science: A Net Station. http://www.library.ubc.ca/poli.

While this Web site highlights a superb source of electronic resources on Canadian domestic and foreign affairs, it should not be overlooked for its more extensive links beyond this specialty area. The Canadian links to its election results, foreign policy, and foreign relations are truly top-notch in quantity and quality. Another relatively lengthy section is the one on international relations and international organization. Also quite good is the list of Web sources appearing under the "Methodology/Survey Research/Public Opinion" heading. The "Law, Civil/Human Rights" section is broken down into more general links on human rights, war crimes, and genocide, then into separate cases of genocide such as "Armenian Genocide," "Genocide in Rwanda," or a number of other atrocities. The scope and overall extent of the genocide section may indicate a special interest of the person maintaining this Web site. It has been maintained by Iza Laponce at the University of British Columbia Library. 💻

3-37. Lowery, Roger C. *Political Science: Illustrated Search Strategy and Sources.* Ann Arbor, MI: Pierian Press, 1993. 204 pp. ISBN: 0-876-50290-7.

This work offers undergraduates a reasonable strategy in how to approach an individual political science term paper. Some legal research is included here as well. The purpose of this work is to link a student's term paper to a library-research strategy and to recommend a highly select number of reference works. While the overall research strategy may still be of value, the reference works mentioned as well as the illustrations and concrete examples chosen are all woefully out of date.

3-38. Martin, Fenton S. *Political Science Journal Information.* 3rd ed. Washington, DC: American Political Science Association, 1990. 111 pp. ISBN: 1-878-14701-3.

The aim of this specialized work is to advise political scientists on where and how to present their research for publication and also how to satisfy the review and manuscript-preparation procedures used by the seventy-five journals included here. Stylistic requirements are given for each journal listed. It also provides the scope and purpose of the political science journals listed here. There is a standardized format followed for each entry. This format includes the year publication started, circulation totals, where the journal is indexed and abstracted, subject areas the journal tends to publish, and length of manuscript. The seventy-five journals chosen are all mainstream political science titles, many of which have been publishing for decades. Some journals now provide some or all of this information through their Web site, but a single-volume listing such as this is still useful.

3-39. Crotty, William, ed. *Political Science: Looking to the Future.* 4 vols. Evanston, IL: Northwestern University Press, 1991. ISBN varies.

Issued at a time when the discipline of political science was thought to be at a crossroads due to the retirement of many prominent practitioners, this set hopes to indicate "where the discipline is to go, who are to be its intellectual patrons, and what concepts, theories, problem areas, or approaches are likely to dominate its collective consciousness" (Crotty 1991, introduction). Each volume receives a separate title and can stand alone. The four volumes have these titles: *The Theory and Practice of Political Science; Comparative Politics, Policy, and International Relations; Political Behavior;* and *American Institutions.* Half-a-dozen or more essays appear in each volume, with individual essays addressing themselves to a topic of interest within the bounds of that volume. For example, the first volume includes essays on the history of the discipline, political theory, and gender, while the final volume presents essays on such topics as interest groups, political parties, and urban politics. The essays, contributed by political scientists throughout the United States, range in length from about twenty pages to as many as fifty. Although contributors were not asked to provide balanced accounts for a comprehensive review of the literature, each essay does include a list of references for those readers who wish to pursue the matter. This set will be of obvious interest to graduate students and political science faculty members wishing a state-of-the-art approach to the discipline as of the early 1990s.

3-40. Jones, Lawrence F. *Political Science Research: A Handbook of Scope and Methods.* New York: HarperCollins College Publishers, 1996. 433 pp. ISBN: 0-065-01637-8.

This handbook is "an introductory text to be used by those schools requiring scope and methods courses of second- or third-year political science majors" (Jones 1996, introduction). There are three major objectives in this work: (1) teaching about the scope of political science as a discipline; (2) familiarizing the student with the methods of political science research, including statistics; and (3) guiding the student through each stage of the research process of topic selection, literature review, data collection, writing, and so on. The target audience for this handbook is upper-division undergraduate students.

3-41. Political Science Research Resources. http://www.vanderbilt.edu/~rtucker/polisci.

This Web site is a bit different from some of the others in that it specializes in political science links to game theory, artificial intelligence, and econometrics Web resources. This is the place to begin for those interested in the more quantitative aspects of the study of politics. The main section on "Internet guides" points to the traditional types of political science materials in areas such as international relations, comparative politics, methodology, and political theory/thought. This is a very good jumping-off spot for some of the major Web sites in the field that are listed here. 🖥

3-42. Political Science Resources. http://sun3.lib.uci.edu/~dtsang/pol.htm.

All traditional subdisciplines of the field of political science are covered here with the apparent exception of political theory/thought. The sections on Canadian and California government, law, and politics are particularly strong. Overall, this Web site is a very good option for virtually all aspects of political science research done on the Internet to be used in conjunction with more comprehensive and/or specialized sites. This site is maintained by Dan Tsang, a social sciences bibliographer at the University of California, Irvine's Main Library. ⌨

3-43. Political Science Resources on the Web. http://www.lib.umich.edu/govdocs/frames/polscifr.html.

This Web site is an excellent source for a wide range of political science materials. There are numerous and credible links to area studies; political theory; foreign politics; international relations; local, state, and federal U.S. politics; and other related Web resources. An accompanying broad subject index has links to more customized Web sites. This is a well-organized site that identifies many of the standard Web products of interest to various political science students and researchers. The site was organized and is maintained by the Documents Center at the University of Michigan and, as such, contains a number of Web sites that, because of standard licensing restrictions, may not be available to those unaffiliated with the university who desire remote access to them. ⌨

3-44. Poly-Cy: Internet Resources for Political Science. http://www.polsci.wvu.edu/PolyCy.

This site will appeal to political science researchers in the fields of international relations, public policy, public affairs, U.S. politics and government, and comparative politics. Links have been established to academic research institutions, a political science teaching clearinghouse of course reading lists, Web texts, syllabi, and the like. Research resources linked include libraries, data sites, statistics, software programs, and grant information, all appearing on the Web. The major subfields within the discipline of political science are broken into topical components, including animal rights, religion and politics, health and medicine, consumer issues, and others. In addition, there are links to foreign governments, counties, local governments, international organizations, foreign embassies, and so forth. West Virginia materials receive comprehensive coverage, not surprising given that this Web site is maintained by Bob Duval for the West Virginia University Department of Political Science and the West Virginia Institute of Public Affairs. ⌨

3-45. Resources for Political Science. http://www.library.vanderbilt.edu/romans/polsci.

A very good midlevel political science general-purpose Web site that includes comparative politics, political thought, U.S. politics, international relations and organization, and public policy issues. Links captured tend to be standard and relatively stable ones. The "Yahoo Directory" is cited frequently as a source. The most comprehensive and detailed section appears to be the one on U.S. politics. This is a lengthy category with numerous subcategories. It is terrific for U.S. government agencies. This site is maintained by the Jean and Alexander Heard Library at Vanderbilt University. 🖳

3-46. Richard Kimber's Political Science Resources. http://www.psr.keele.ac.uk.

While this is a very good site for all aspects of political science research as a whole, it appears to be quite strong in European comparative politics and British politics in particular. The area-studies section covers virtually the entire globe on a nation-by-nation basis. Also, nations awaiting official state status, such as Kurdistan, are also listed here. The section on data sets pertinent to political science research is another featured component of the Web site. The ones on voting and election results exemplify this. The section on international relations is best suited for European and Commonwealth nations, but it is indeed international in overall scope. The Web links under political parties should get special attention for their breadth and depth, and for the fact many are in their native language. Local and regional resources are mostly but not exclusively devoted to U.S. and U.K. links. The political thought portion is quite diverse in political orientation and range, listing as it does Cyber-leninism, http://www.leninism.org, and the Free Market Net Directory, http://www.free-market.net/find. 🖳

3-47. The American Political Science Association (APSA). Committee on Publications. *Style Manual for Political Science*. rev. ed. Washington, DC: APSA, 1993. 22 pp. ISBN: 1-878-14709-9.

This is a cogent style manual for political science students and for those planning on submitting a manuscript to the American Political Science Association (APSA) for publication. It gives instruction in how to handle acronyms; explains the preferred use of gender-neutral language; provides guidance for the use of numbers; and provides examples of references from books, edited works, multi-volume sets, and the like. This is no substitute for the more comprehensive, standard style manuals available in all academic libraries or excerpted over the Internet today. It follows quite closely the *Chicago Manual of Style*.

3-48. Ultimate Political Science Links. http://www.rvc.cc.il.us/faclinks/pruckman/pslinks.htm.

This is a selective list of Web resources that has been in existence since 1995. The main political science page begins by listing major associations in the field. After this is a section of about thirty different "areas of study," such as "Latin American Studies," "Political Thought," and "International Political Economy." Underneath this section is one on "resource links," which is an eclectic array of indexes, directory resources, political newsgroups, sundry teaching aids, statistical sources, atlases, and more. The "Political Philosophy" section has a larger percentage of full-text links from articles, research reports, news/media sites, and other information resources. Last but not least is a rather diverting section on political humor from the living and the dearly departed. 🖳

Quotations
Dictionaries
3-49. Weeks, Albert L., ed. *Brassey's Soviet and Communist Quotations.* McLean, VA: Pergamon Brassey's International Defense Publishers, 1987. 387 pp. ISBN: 0-080-34488-7.

Over 2,100 quotations from the movers and shakers of Soviet politics, government, or Marxist origins are displayed in this work. There are seventeen chapters broken down into broad topics, such as "Revolution," "Capitalism and Socialism," "Communist Party," and others of this ilk, all further broken down into various subdivisions. Some quotes are repeated in several sections because they were deemed relevant in more than one category. Most quotes were taken from Soviet luminaries or those of some influence in the Soviet government or Communist Party. Lenin, Marx, and Engels are quoted, too. Most of the quotes included in this work were drawn from certain key publications of the Soviet press, like *Pravda.* More recent Soviet leaders, such as Brezhnev and Gorbachev, are quoted liberally. Most original-source documents are in the Russian language, but sufficient bibliographic information is given in order to find the original quotes. This work provides a superb insight into Soviet political perspectives and is terrific for tracking attitudes over time.

3-50. O'Clery, Conor. *The Dictionary of Political Quotations on Ireland 1886–1987: Phrases Make History Here.* Boston: G. K. Hall, 1987. 232 pp. ISBN: 0-816-18939-0.

Not seen, but title appears fairly descriptive.

3-51. Hill, Kathleen Thompson. *The Facts on File Dictionary of American Politics.* New York: Checkmark Books, 2001. 436 pp. ISBN: 0-816-04520-8.

This political dictionary covers the politics of Canada as well as the United States. Its primary purpose is to get behind the "politbabble" of both countries when discussing political terms and concepts, and to get at the real meaning of the terms when used. The historical context of some terms is provided within the entries. Entries are relatively brief, about one paragraph long. Many of the terms selected relate to the structure of government in the two countries. There are some colorful terms included, such as "stalking horse," "photo op," and "feminazi." Subjectivity sometimes creeps into some of the definitions, especially around liberal and conservative perspectives of issues.

3-52. Eigen, Lewis D. *The MacMillan Dictionary of Political Quotations.* New York: Macmillan, 1993. 785 pp. Indexes. ISBN: 0-026-10650-7.

This quotation dictionary contains roughly 11,000 different entries arranged around 100 broad content categories, such as abortion, United Nations, foreign policy, and gun control. Within each chapter, the authors of the quotes are arranged alphabetically. There is a clear albeit admitted bias toward quotations from males, and this "reflects the political gender discrimination of many centuries" (Eigen 1993, introduction). Also, the great majority of quotations originated in an English-speaking country, so quotations rooted in the developing nations of the world are scarce. There was no attempt made to create a more balanced approach on controversial issues. Quotations tend to be drawn from relatively contemporary figures. Each quote has a source, but an occasional tendency to provide only partial bibliographic information makes finding the original-source document a more challenging effort than is necessary. There are author and concept (i.e., subject) indexes. The overall design layout is quite visually appealing.

3-53. Jay, Antony, ed. *The Oxford Dictionary of Political Quotations.* 2nd ed. Oxford: Oxford University Press, 2001. 497 pp. Index. ISBN: 0-198-63167-7.

Familiarity within the English-speaking world is the key criterion for inclusion for quotations in this standard work. Other quotations are given space at the sole discretion of the editor. This quotation dictionary goes after two kinds of users. They are people who remember a quote or part of it and intend to verify the actual quote or its author, or those who are looking for quotes on a particular topic or from a specific author. There is a definite attempt to balance contemporary with

more vintage political quotes. Readers will find quotes by George F. Kennan nestled next to those of Benjamin Disraeli. The main body is in alphabetical order by author. Many of the quotations listed have dates attached. The source of the quotation is always given, if known. The index is by keyword and refers back to the page and numbered quote, but it can be hit or miss for words actually in a quote. Look up several words within a known quote before concluding that one has been omitted.

3-54. Baker, Daniel B., ed. *Political Quotations: A Collection of Notable Sayings on Politics from Antiquity through 1989.* Detroit: Gale, 1990. 509 pp. ISBN: 0-810-34920-5.

This dictionary is a treasure trove of over 5,000 quotations on all types of political topics, especially quotes pertaining to the modern world. Entries are arranged by broad general heading and then by date under each subject. The quotations included here are derived mainly from fifteen standard quote books, such as *Bartlett's Familiar Quotations, Oxford Dictionary of Quotations,* and others, including one in French and another in German. This particular collected work of quotations is best for the more conventional or well-established quotes by men and women in positions of authority. A reader seeking quotes from more offbeat or alternative political views would do best to look elsewhere. Each entry has a source citation for proper attribution purposes.

3-55. Thomsett, Michael C., comp. *Political Quotations: A Worldwide Dictionary of Thoughts and Pronouncements from Politicians, Literary Figures, Humorists, and Others.* Jefferson, NC: McFarland, 1994. 344 pp. Indexes. ISBN: 0-899-50951-7.

This quotation book has its main body divided into approximately 100 categories of several pages each. This is not an alphabetically arranged work, but instead uses categories. Typical headings used in the work include "Power," "Tyranny," and "Justice." The purpose of these categories is to place complementary and/or contradictory quotes next to one another of the same general topic. Citations provide the person to whom the quote is attributed, the year first uttered, and where originally cited. There are a total of 4,009 such entries. There is a person index for quotes and a lengthier subject index by keyword in context.

3-56. Wilcox, Laird M. *Selected Quotations for the Ideological Skeptic.* Olathe, KS: L. Wilcox, 1988. 104 pp. ISBN: 0-933-59246-9.

A patently idiosyncratic political dictionary with no table of contents and a quality of typography best described as primitive. The quotations are located in the main body by using broad topics and appropriate subheadings. Within these topics are found the author of the quote, and the general source of the quote is provided. People quoted range from H. L. Mencken to Napoléon Bonaparte to Eric Hoffer. The topics under which the quotes are found can be quite precise. Two such examples are "Fanatics/Ideologues/Crusaders" and "Civil Liberties/Due Process." This is the place to look for relatively offbeat political quotations. There are neither indexes nor cross-references provided, a real drawback for more serious use.

3-57. Henning, Charles. *The Wit and Wisdom of Politics.* rev. and exp. ed. Golden, CO: Fulcrum, 1996. 266 pp. Index. ISBN: 1-555-91333-4.

This dictionary of politics rather than political science quotations is arranged in one alphabetical sequence by term, such as "apathy," "leadership," "liberals," or "corruption." Brief quotes, arranged in no particular order, are listed beneath each term. A person's name is assigned as the source of every quotation. There is a single index that is organized by the individual coining the quotation printed up in the main body of this work. This quotation dictionary is best suited for people requiring such information on current events, day-to-day politics, or general social science terms. A number of the quotations selected are outside the realm of politics and government.

4

Political Theory and Political Theorists Reference Sources

This chapter attempts to identify the standard reference sources used when undertaking research on political theory and the great political thinkers from the classical Greek and Roman periods up to more modern times. The discipline of political science carries with it some eminent names as major political theorists and political philosophers. Such people as Aristotle, Locke, Rousseau, and Foucault have written about the fundamental concepts and issues that make up many of the building blocks of political science as coherent discipline. Many of these political philosophers are also regarded as philosophers in general and are taught simultaneously in many philosophy classes.

Abstracting and Indexing Services

4-1. *The Left Index.* Santa Cruz, CA: Left Index, 1982–. ISSN: 0733-2998.

This was a quarterly publication up through 1999, and then it became an Internet-only resource beginning in 2000. It is one of the few sources available through which to find leftist journals with a radical, Marxist, or leftist political perspective. No newsletters or newspapers are indexed. The subject headings used are based on standard Library of Congress (LC) headings. The index consists of four main parts. Part 1 is an alphabetical author list section. Part 2 is a subject index, with issue 4 serving as a cumulative subject index. Part 3 is for book reviews, and the last section is a journal index. It is a complete list of periodicals indexed, about ninety titles in all. There are numerous "see" and "see also" references. Entries are not annotated. 💻

Directories

4-2. O Maolain, Ciaran. *The Radical Right: A World Directory.* Burnt Mill, Harlow, Essex, UK: Longman, 1987. 500 pp. Index. ISBN: 0-874-36514-7.

This directory is a global listing of radical right-wing groups that is arranged alphabetically by individual country. Each country entry kicks off with a short introduction of a specific nation's right-wing movement, then in alphabetical order lists those far-right groups active during the compiling of this book from 1985 through 1987. The more prominent defunct groups are also listed, as well as lesser known groups and individual right-wing activists not affiliated with any specific organized group or movement. Main entries provide history, contact information, general policy, and publications issued. Two U.S. entries are "Soldier of Fortune" and "Posse Comitatus." The work is geared toward political activists, students, journalists, security specialists, and others concerned with the activities of the radical right wing around the world. The high level of secrecy often surrounding many rightist groups may have been the source of some errors throughout this work, according to the editor. Some of the material published in this work has been published previously under the title *Latin American Political Movements*, published in 1986. An index is available.

Bibliographies

4-3. Nursey-Bray, Paul. *Anarchist Thinkers and Thought: An Annotated Bibliography*. Westport, CT: Greenwood Press, 1992. 284 pp. ISBN: 0-313-27592-0.

The purpose of this book is to show the broad diversity of anarchist thought, thinking, and movements that have come into existence. This bibliography is limited to works written in English, except for those instances where a thinker's works are available in another language. Works cited include books, journal articles, library catalogs, and dissertations. Every entry is annotated. There are two principal chapters and several minor ones. The first substantive chapter is entitled "Anarchist Philosophers and Thinkers." This is an alphabetical listing by individual. The entry for each anarchist includes a bibliography of works by that person and another list of works on that person. The second-largest chapter, "The Anarchist Experience," is arranged by country, providing an overview of anarchist thinking and movements in that part of the world. There is also a list of both current and defunct journals with frequent writings on anarchism.

4-4. Kahan, Vilem, ed. *Bibliography of the Communist International (1919–1979)*. Vol. 1. Kinder Hook, NY: E. J. Brill, 1990. 400 pp. ISBN: 9-004-09320-6.

This will eventually comprise a three-volume set when completed. It will list publications by and about the Comintern published in more than twenty languages. Volume 1 has 3,200 nonannotated citations referring to the works from the seven congresses from 1919 to 1935 and to the Executive Committee sessions as well as the studies concerning the Communist International appearing in print from 1919 to 1979. Volume 2 will treat publications of organizations affiliated with the Communist International. Volume 1 is based largely on a card-file index set up by Kahan. The bibliography includes mainly books and pamphlets. It does contain some journal articles (1943–1979) published since the dissolution of the Communist International.

There are no works in any Asian language. Books are ordered by Congress, or by plenum or Executive Committee dates. Elected members to the highest bodies of the Communist International are listed from 1919 to 1943.

4-5. Haynes, John Earl. *Communism and Anti-Communism in the United States: An Annotated Guide to Historical Writings.* New York: Garland, 1987. 321 pp. Index. ISBN: 0-824-08520-5.

This is a bibliography that picks up books, essays, articles, and unpublished dissertations and theses. The 2,086 entries chosen tend toward scholarly, rather than journalistic or popular, accounts. The emphasis is the history of the mainstream Communist movement in the United States, but there is also information of some of the larger splinter groups. There are very few articles chosen on the theoretical aspects of Marxism-Leninism. The bibliography has chapters that are both chronological and thematic in approach. This guide is very good for bringing to light research materials for the study of Communism or anti-Communism in the individual states within the United States. About 50 percent of the entries are annotated. There is an author index only.

4-6. Kinnell, Susan K. *Communism in the World since 1945: An Annotated Bibliography.* Santa Barbara, CA: ABC-CLIO, 1987. 415 pp. Indexes. ISBN: 0-874-36169-9.

This bibliography's geographic scope is global. Most entries deal with the political history of the larger Communist and Socialist nations of the world. It is especially strong in journal-literature citations. There are a total of 415 entries drawn largely from the standard indexing/abstracting services, *America: History and Life* and *Historical Abstracts.* Coverage of cited works span the period from 1974 to 1985. There are also books and dissertations included, but they are much more selectively chosen and are clearly secondary in importance. English-language abstracts accompany each entry. Citations are arranged into eight broad categories, and within them are several subcategories. The largest chapter is "Communism in Europe," which is subdivided again into "Eurocommunism," "Eastern Europe," "Western Europe," and the like. This chapter alone is over 150 pages. There are two indexes. One is by subject and the other is by author.

4-7. Van Wyk, J. J. *Contemporary Democracy: A Bibliography of Periodical Literature, 1974–1994.* Washington, DC: Congressional Quarterly, 1997. 449 pp. Index. ISBN: 1-568-02244-1.

Here is a large bibliography including roughly 8,000 entries in two alphabets. Of the 8,000 entries, 7,842 are arranged by author's name, while 114 others are arranged as a collection of articles. The intent of this bibliography is to present a multidisciplinary approach to the topic of democracy as related to the literature in the fields of political science, law, business, education, sociology, and public administration, as well as other areas. While most entries are in English, a fair number of them are in other languages. This work is not annotated. The standard political science journals are especially well represented in this bibliography. The index is exceptionally deep and thorough.

4-8. Skidmore, Gail. *From Radical Left to Extreme Right: A Bibliography of Current Periodicals of Protest, Controversy, Advocacy or Dissent.* 3rd rev. ed. Metuchen, NJ: Scarecrow, 1987. 491 pp. ISBN: 0-810-81967-8.

This relatively unique if somewhat dated directory features a bibliography of left- and right-wing periodicals that are arranged into broad subject categories. Some of these sample categories include "Labor and Unions," "Rights for the Disabled," "Libertarian," and "Anti-Communist." Each periodical title listed receives a lengthy "unbiased" review. Opinions are usually labeled as such. Many of these periodicals are the type that come and go fairly quickly, so a large percentage of the periodicals listed are no longer actively publishing, but may still be of value for researchers. Periodicals covered tend to be smaller publications and therefore may not find their way into the standard periodical directories, such as *Ulrich's International Periodicals Directory.* This directory is not to be confused with a subject bibliography of articles drawn from leftist or right-wing publications.

4-9. Lubitz, Wolfgang, ed. *Trotsky Bibliography: A Classified List of Published Items about Leon Trotsky and Trotskyism.* 2nd ed. Munich; New York: K.G.

Saur, 1988. 581 pp. Indexes. ISBN: 3-598-10754-4.

This is an extensive, yet unannotated, bibliography on all aspects of Leon Trotsky or Trotskyism. Many of the publications listed are in languages other than English. There is an extensive section on Russian-language materials, but Greek and Turkish materials are specifically excluded, along with audio-visual sources, manuscripts, and archival materials. The period from 1960 to 1979 accounts for 45 percent of all materials cited. English materials add up to only 33 percent of the total works. The main body's format is structured in a complex and detailed classification scheme. Several indexes are attached.

4-10. Eccleshall, Robert. *Western Political Thought: A Bibliographic Guide to Post-War Research.* Manchester, UK: Manchester University Press, 1995. 342 pp. Index. ISBN: 0-719-03569-4.

This select bibliography is directed at undergraduates, graduate students, and faculty who require quick and ready access to books and journal articles that are deemed "most important and useful." The bibliography begins with citations of more general works with a methodological or historiographical nature. After this, it proceeds to broad chronological divisions arranged thematically. Most entries in this bibliography are annotated and include books and articles on political thought published from 1945 up to the mid-1990s. The materials cited are limited to the political thought of the United Kingdom, Europe, and North

America. Works on political ideologies are excluded. There are eight chapters more or less in broad chronological order. The smallest breakdown is by topic (Utilitarianism) and thinker. A key to journal-article abbreviations is included. Annotations, while pithy, are both evaluative and informative. The items chosen for this bibliography tend to be quality works. There is one index by personal name only.

Dictionaries
4-11. Miller, David, ed. *Blackwell Encyclopaedia of Political Thought.* Oxford, UK: Blackwell, 1991. 570 pp. ISBN: 0-631-17944-5.

Each of the 350 entries in this alphabetically arranged subject dictionary pertains to purely Western historical perspectives of political thought or philosophy in the contemporary world. Each entry, of a full page or so, relates to a particular political philosopher and is replete with cross-references. There are also some broad survey articles on "Industrial Society," "Renaissance Political Thought," "Freedom," and others. Reading lists attached to each entry include mostly English-language sources. This work is appropriate for high-school students and undergraduates. See also *Encyclopedia of Political Thought* [entry 4-25] by Garrett Ward Sheldon in the section on encyclopedias.

4-12. Filler, Louis. *Dictionary of American Conservatism.* New York: Philosophical Library, 1987. 380 pp. ISBN: 0-802-22506-3.

This alphabetical dictionary includes terms and subjects with a conservative position and individuals who tend to hold this political orientation and social philosophy close to their hearts. It is decidedly selective in overall scope, and it is especially strong in including American and British conservatives. This work can be considered an early attempt to define past and present concepts of conservatism. Definitions are written with a lively tempo, and one may find it difficult not to question one's previous perception of what or who is a conservative or a liberal. Impartiality may be seen as slipping at times in the adjectives used to describe nonconservative positions or tenets. Definitions can be up to one page long and recount the history of a colorful term, who used it, and for what purpose. About 50 percent of the entries are for individuals. Citations range from the Equal Rights Amendment to Phyllis Schlafly.

4-13. Ashford, Nigel, and Stephen Davies, eds. *Dictionary of Conservative and Libertarian Thought.* New York: Routledge/Chapman and Hall, 1991. 288 pp. ISBN: 0-415-00302-4.

Serious reference works on the subject of conservatism are not always easy to find. This book treats the subject from a theoretical and philosophical viewpoint, emphasizing an intellectual tradition rather than daily applications of conservative thought in regard to public policy. The authors also examined libertarian thought, believing it to be associated with conservatism because both take similar stances in regard to intervention of the state in economic matters. The volume includes approximately ninety entries arranged alphabetically, beginning with "American Conservatism," and concluding with "Welfare." Examples of other topics include "Capitalism," "Environment," "Invisible Hand," and "Tradition." Entries average about three or four pages in length and are initialed by one of eleven contributors. Despite an emphasis on ideas, the writing style is accessible to undergraduate researchers as well as more advanced scholars. Brief reading lists included with the entries will lead readers to other sources. Particularly useful is the examination of conservative thought in Great Britain, France, and Germany, as well as the United States.

4-14. Riff, M. A., ed. *Dictionary of Modern Political Ideologies.* New York: St. Martin's Press, 1987. 226 pp. ISBN: 0-312-00928-3.

The contributors to this dictionary are overwhelmingly British scholars and faculty members. This book is based in part on another book entitled *The Encyclopedia of Modern History* and its chapter on ideological movements. Each entry gives that person's or term's contribution and discusses the origins of movements in their political and/or social contexts. The editor admits to a Eurocentric bias in coverage by beginning with the era of the Enlightenment. Concentration is centered on ideologies within certain political movements. The main assumption here is that this has been a very ideolog-

ical age. About thirty-six articles on the many "isms" that help constitute the core of political science as a separate discipline, including American nationalism, anti-Semitism, conservatism, isolationism, Socialism, and so on. These and other entries are tightly written yet highly informative. There are listings of additional readings, but the quality of the citations is questionable at best.

4-15. Evans, Graham. *The Dictionary of World Politics: Ideas and Institutions.* rev. ed. New York: Harvester Wheatsheaf, 1992. 364 pp. ISBN: 0-745-01223-X.

Inclusion in this political dictionary is based on either an idea or institution deemed essential to the fundamental comprehension of global politics. Others, while important, are considered relevant for more specialized books or journal articles. Individuals are generally omitted except where their names are associated with a term or policy in an eponymic way, such as "Truman Doctrine." The overall arrangement is standard alphabetical with heavy use of cross-references within the articles in lieu of an index. The work itself is stronger for Western politics and weaker for terms or individuals of greater interest to third world nations or the former Soviet state. Terms chosen are hit or miss; for instance, there is no entry for "Democracy." The terms that are included are quite well explained and offer a valuable historical dimension to them.

4-16. Carber, Terrell. *A Marx Dictionary.* Totowa, NJ: Barnes and Noble

Books, 1987. 164 pp. Index. ISBN: 0-389-20684-9.

This work is aimed squarely at undergraduate students and others facing the social and economic theories of Karl Marx for the first time. The book opens with a thirty-page essay on the life and work of Karl Marx. This essay is followed by sixteen chapters that have headings representing the more essential concepts of Marxian philosophy. Sample chapters are those on dialectical materialism, the state, and exploitation. A bibliographical essay appears prior to the index and lists basic works by Marx and secondary works about him and his ideas. While highly selective, these references are very often still the standard or key works in the study of Marx or on the various aspects of Marx's theories. All in all, this is perhaps more of a study guide than a special dictionary.

4-17. Benewick, Robert, ed. *The Routledge Dictionary of Twentieth-Century Political Thinkers*. 2nd ed. New York: Routledge, 1998. 277 pp. Index. ISBN: 0-415-15881-8.

This biographical dictionary includes both political theorists as well as practitioners in the political realm. The editors have made a conscious effort to inject non-Western dimensions into their selection criteria for political thinkers over the last century or so. Individuals like Frantz Fanon and Fidel Castro are two such non-Western political theorists chosen, many of whom were influenced by new political movements around such issues as gender, ethnicity, environmental-

ism, and other sociopolitical concerns. Each of the well-written main entries contains biographical information as well as the person's political ideas and/or political involvement. A list of works both by and about the individual follows each entry. The index is arranged around such broad concepts as "Black Nationalism," "Anarchism," "Feminism," and "Religion and Politics." Every one of the 174 individuals included in this dictionary is placed under one or more of these broad headings.

Encyclopedias

4-18. Miner, Brad. *The Concise Conservative Encyclopedia: Two Hundred of the Most Important Ideas, Individuals, Incitements, and Institutions That Have Shaped the Movement: A Personal View*. New York: Free Press, 1996. 318 pp. ISBN: 0-684-80043-8.

This work is aimed squarely at more general readers. The main body of the work is organized into five short essays including "Greco-Roman Influence," "Jewish Tradition," "Christian Tradition," "Reformation and Revolution," and "American Centuries." Each chapter is written by a different person. The chapters trace the history of conservatism mainly from the year 1790, when Edmund Burke wrote *Reflections on the Revolution in France*. The selection of people chosen reflects a bias in favor of the deceased rather than the living. The five essays are inserted at odd places and make the arrangement of the overall book somewhat confusing. There are numerous cross-references that are boldly underlined. The biographical entries themselves are short and to the point. Some cite the more important published works or quotations of the person. A decent basic bibliography is included. The viewpoint of the author is decidedly favorable toward conservatism and reflects his own conservative pedigree and activism. The book is published on highly acidic paper.

4-19. Lipset, Seymour Martin, ed. *The Encyclopedia of Democracy.* 4 vols. Washington, DC: Congressional Quarterly, 1995. Index. ISBN: 0-871-87675-2.

What exactly is meant by "democracy"? Where is it thriving in today's world? What are its characteristics? These are some of the questions posed and answered by this standard reference source, edited by the eminent social scientist Seymour Martin Lipset. There are about 420 separate articles contained within this four-volume set on individual countries, regions of the world, historical eras, people, philosophies, and ideas as related to the notion of democracy. The articles range in length from 300 to 8,500 words. Brief bibliographies are appended to the longer entries. Articles are all signed by the international collection of scholars who served as contributors. Features of a democratic system of government are seen as one that has fair elections, citizen's participation in electing their leaders, and the existence of civil and political liberties. There are four distinct types of articles in this encyclopedia: biographical sketches, country studies, area overviews, and topical analyses. Ample pictures and maps help the reader. The entries are

consistently well written yet concise. There is one major appendix which gives the twenty "seminal" documents pertaining to democracy, arranged by date. They range from the constitution of Japan to the African Charter on Human and People's Rights. The superb index should facilitate research and efficient use of this set. See also *Democracy in Asia and Africa* and *Democracy in Europe and the Americas* [entries 7-24 and 7-25] in the encyclopedia section of Chapter 7 on applied aspects of democracy in regional settings.

4-20. Clarke, Paul Barry, ed. *Encyclopedia of Democratic Thought.* New York: Routledge, 2001. 748 pp. Indexes. ISBN: 0-415-19396-6.

The past, present, and even the future aspects of democracy are explored through a set of coordinated essays rather than relying on individual entries. This work examines democratic ideas, practice, and quality of democratic governance. There is a global perspective here, with most of the contributors either U.S. or British scholars. A number of them are faculty at the University of Essex. Entries are alphabetically arranged and average about two to three pages each. The scope and content are aimed primarily at undergraduate students, but graduate students and other researchers will find this a useful and authoritative work on democracy. Further-reading lists are dutifully appended to every article. There is a name index and a subject index. This appears to be an Internet resource as well as in print format. 💻

4-21. Atkins, Stephen E. *Encyclopedia of Modern American Extremists and Extremist Groups.* Westport, CT: Greenwood, 2002. 375 pp. ISBN: 0-313-31502-7.

Individuals or groups have been chosen for this book as examples of extremism because they deviate significantly from normal economic, political, religious, or social standards as currently practiced. They also tend to pursue practices or ideas that are far outside normal personal behavior. Criminals are excluded, as are foreign terrorists active in the United States. Political extremists appear to constitute the largest group of extremists in this work. Since the mid-1970s, the most radical groups have been drawn from the Far Right. About 75 percent of the entries discuss groups and individuals around since 1980. A chronology of major activities carried out either by or against extremist groups is listed for the time period 1866–2001. The work is in standard alphabetical format and contains black-and-white photographs and numerous cross-references. Some of the entries include "Turner Diaries," "Ruby Ridge Incident," and "Skinheads." Some of the groups selected as extremist might challenge one's idea of extremism, such as "Gay Liberation Movement," "Russell Means," and "Greenpeace." 💻

4-22. Hewitt, Christopher. *Encyclopedia of Modern Separatist Movements.* Santa Barbara, CA: ABC-CLIO, 2000. 366 pp. ISBN: 1-576-07007-7.

This work defines separatist movements as groups using violence in pursuit of separatist goals or instances in which a separatist political party contests elections. Irredentist territorial claims by a particular government are included as well if they have resulted in some kind of military confrontation. The amount of space devoted to entries is linked to the overall importance of the movement. Most entries concern disputed territories and geographic areas of conflict. Countries with numerous separatist groups earn their own entries. There are also over 100 other entries of important separatist leaders, political parties and organizations, and the like. Some pictures and maps are included. Entries are alphabetical throughout the book. Typical entries are between one-half and two pages long. They include "Parti Quebecois," "Abdullah Ocalan," "Armenia," and "Turkish Kurds." A chronology from 1945 to the late 1990s is included. High-school students and undergraduates will benefit most from this work.

4-23. Gay, Kathlyn. *Encyclopedia of Political Anarchy.* Santa Barbara, CA: ABC-CLIO, 1999. 242 pp. ISBN: 0-874-36982-7.

This book is not simply a list of famous anarchists; it also has entries on relevant political movements, historical precursors to anarchism and significant events in the annals of anarchy, and expositions on the differences in content and style of the differing national brands of anarchy and the people who played a role in its history. An introduction presents the reader with an opening survey of anarchism and the manner in which anarchists have been perceived by society over time. Entries are about one-and-a-half pages long, and each one has a short reading list attached. Many of the people entered probably would not label themselves as anarchists, such as I. F. Stone and E. Zapata. These and other of their ilk have been linked to anarchism apparently for their general anti-big-government fervor. The style of this work would appeal mostly to general readers and undergraduate or high-school students.

4-24. Goldstone, Jack A., ed. *The Encyclopedia of Political Revolutions.* Washington, DC: Congressional Quarterly, 1998. 580 pp. Index. ISBN: 1-568-02206-9.

This work provides a global view of politically inspired revolutions since the year 1500 AD to the date of publication. It includes coup d'etats, civil wars, mass protests, guerilla warfare, and so on that had a lasting impact on a political system. These events must have actually altered the political order of the day. There are three types of essays included in this encyclopedia. One is on revolutionary events, the second is on revolutionary leaders, and the third relates to revolutionary ideas and concepts. The contributors are scholars drawn from around the world. About 350 articles constitute the main body of this work, and they average several pages each. The style is clearly at a very basic level, which makes it most valuable for high-school students or lower-division undergraduates. There are numerous photographs and pictures available throughout the book. Typical

entries include the "Chinese Boxer Uprising," the "French Revolution," and the "Nigerian Civil War of 1967–1970." A good index is helpful.

4-25. Sheldon, Garrett Ward, ed. *Encyclopedia of Political Thought.* New York: Facts on File, 2001. 342 pp. Index. ISBN: 0-816-04351-5.

This ambitious work covers the entire span of human political activity, from the ancients up to contemporary society. Specific coverage focuses on abstract and ideal issues, major thinkers, contemporary political movements from around the world, and much more. The main body is strictly alphabetical, and articles can easily be several pages long. There are numerous cross-references within each entry. There is an occasional photograph or picture scattered throughout the pages. About 50 percent of the entries are for people. There is a chronology of political thoughts and events that put ideas into a historical perspective. An index is included. See also David Miller's *Blackwell Encyclopaedia of Political Thought* [entry 4-11] in the dictionary section.

4-26. Buhle, Mary Jo, ed. *Encyclopedia of the American Left.* 2nd ed. New York: Oxford University Press, 1998. 988 pp. Index. ISBN: 0-195-12088-4.

The emphasis in this encyclopedia is on the anarchists, Socialists, and Communists from the more radical end of the American Left. The reformist wing is not included in this work. The emphasis in this work on the American Left is from

1870 to date. Included as entries are biographies, mass political movements, labor organizations, unions, civil rights and women's issues, environmental concerns, and more. Ethnic and racial groups also receive considerable attention. The contributors to this encyclopedia are overwhelmingly academic, and each article is signed. Entries end with a short bibliography of additional readings. The entries themselves are especially well written and have such topics as "Attica," "International Socialist Review," the "Workmen's Circle" (in New York City), and so on. Numerous cross-references and an excellent index make this a great first choice for background material on topics touching upon the political Left in America over the last 125 years or so. An indication of the comprehensive nature of this work is the inclusion of such entries as "Phil Ochs" and the "*Realist*." The article on folk music of the 1970s through the 1990s is, by itself, worth the shelf space.

4-27. Docherty, James C. *Historical Dictionary of Socialism*. Lanham, MD: Scarecrow, 1997. 395 pp. ISBN: 0-810-83358-1.

This work is designed to track the evolution of Socialism from 1800 to the mid-1990s. Within these pages are 327 main entries that provide information on the main political figures, including those with a full membership in the Socialist International or in a party-leadership position. This work is not comprehensive in its treatment of the topic but was intended to present as broad a view as possible of the topic to its general and undergraduate readers. An introductory essay on the history of Socialism and its potential for the future is followed by a chronology of events, statistical data on Socialism and Socialist political parties, membership figures, and more. A lengthy bibliography arranged by format, topic, and specific countries with Socialist movements is included. Books in the English language make up the bulk of this bibliography. The main body of the work is in alphabetical dictionary format and includes one-half-page entries. This work is relatively strong in providing information on Socialist personalities, especially those who lived or were born in Europe. There are no indexes, but cross-references are placed within each entry.

4-28. Lipset, Seymour Martin, ed. *Political Philosophy: Theories, Thinkers, Concepts*. Washington, DC: CQ Press, 2001. 510 pp. Index. ISBN: 1-568-02688-9.

This encyclopedic venture, turned out by an established scholar in the social sciences, is a compilation of 100 substantive essays penned by a number of international researchers. Overall, the work provides a good introduction of the ancient, modern, and contemporary philosophies and political philosophers. The work is divided into three separate sections. The first part examines the major Western and the non-Western philosophies and concentrates on the isms of political philosophy, such as Socialism, republicanism, populism, and so forth. Part two provides basic intellectual and biographical information about twenty-six eminent political philosophers, such as Gandhi, Locke, and Rousseau. The third part of the book contains thirty-four essays that explore those philosophical ideas that influenced political systems, such as bureaucracy, class, civil society, and others. There are numerous "see also" references and an index. All essays have been signed.

Guides and Handbooks

4-29. Lunardini, Christine A., *The ABC-CLIO Companion to the American Peace Movement in the Twentieth Century*. Denver, CO: ABC-CLIO, 1994. 269 pp. ISBN: 0-874-36714-X.

This work's purpose is to demonstrate to readers the very wide range of philosophies underlying the American peace movement and the individuals associated with it. People and organizations that have been especially prominent in the U.S. peace movement from the late 1800s to the present constitute the bulk of the entries in this book. A concise introduction to the first 100 years of the peace movement offers the reader a chance to understand the context of the social and political milieu in which these people and groups operated. Entries are strictly alphabetical and average about one-half to one page long and are done in a style that may appeal more strongly to the general reader. Entries for individuals provide information on their education, work experience, and peace-advocacy activities and conclude with a short list of additional readings. A number of black-and-white pictures are in-

terspersed throughout. The work appears to be especially strong in Vietnam-era organizations, events, and terminology. Women are well represented as entries. Some typical terms are "Port Huron Statement" and "Jane Fonda."

4-30. Bell, David, and Charles Hobday. *Communist and Marxist Parties of the World*. 2nd ed. Chicago: St. James Press, 1990. 596 pp. ISBN: 0-582-06038-9.

The world's myriad Marxist political parties are examined in this work in as objective a manner as possible. Included are Marxist parties of all stripes. Chapter 1 is a historical overview of Communist movements that puts ensuing sections of individual parties into the appropriate international perspective. Chapter 2 constitutes the main body of the book. It is broken down into nine subsections using broad geographical areas as headings, then it lists states alphabetically within. These entries for the individual Marxist parties are fairly standardized in arrangement. They all have history, leadership structure, membership, electoral influence, orientation (such as Stalinist or Trotskyite), party program, publications, and international affiliations. The three appendixes cover Marxist parties clustered around orientation; a selective but growing (from the first edition) number of Marxist/Communist document extracts, such as passages from Khrushchev, Che Guevara, and Santiago Carrillo; and finally a highly selective bibliography of English-language books for additional reading.

4-31. Alexander, Robert J. *International Trotskyism, 1929–1985: A Documented Analysis of the Movement.* Durham, NC: Duke University Press, 1991. 1124 pp. ISBN: 0-822-30975-0.

This work reputes to be the first major published monograph on the topic of "International Trotskyism." The purpose of this handbook is to produce a general survey of the entire international Trotskyite movement. The main body concentrates exclusively on the world movement that Trotsky helped put together after his exile from the Soviet Union in 1929. It excludes any discussion of the Trotskyite movement within the borders of the USSR after then because it was fairly well eliminated during the purge years. The work starts off with a short essay or two on the origins of international Trotskyism. After this, the reader is taken around the globe on a country-by-country analysis and history of how Trotskyism has fared in that particular nation. Larger countries often contain several chapters broken down into chronological periods. Some active countries contain entries that are more than twenty-five pages in length. Numerous sources are listed within these entries. A large number of the works cited are in non-English-language materials. This work is a major achievement and serves as a superb source for tracking the successes and failures of the international Trotskyism movement and learning about the people and organizations tied to its political coattails and vision of revolutionary theory.

4-32. Wilcox, Derek Arned, ed. *The Left Guide: A Guide to Left-of-Center Organizations.* Ann Arbor, MI: Economics America, 1996. 516 pp. ISBN: 0-914-16903-3.

This directory serves as an aid to finding various U.S. organizations that tend to take a leftist political stance on a majority of public policy issues. Terms used to define which types of groups are listed include such concepts as civil libertarians, progressives, leftists, Socialists, and radicals. These organizations all rely significantly on coalition-building strategies with their grassroots constituencies and on exercising political power when necessary. The main body of the text is organized around a number of major categories that capture a specific organization's primary leftist orientation and activities. These categories are: "Abortion and Reproductive Rights," "Education," "Feminists," "Gun Control," and others. Under these headings, there is an alphabetically arranged directory listing of organizations fitting into these categories. Each entry has a standard format that includes mission, officers, tax status, accomplishments, net revenues, and the like.

4-33. Hamilton, Neil A. *Militias in America: A Reference Handbook.* Santa Barbara, CA: ABC-CLIO, 1996. 235 pp. ISBN: 0-874-36859-6.

This book examines the world of militia movements in contemporary society at a time when they may have reached their high-water mark in popularity and public interest. This handbook delves into the roots, viewpoints, and many controversies surrounding the militia movements' activities and existence in the United States in recent history. The book is arranged into seven main chapters that include chronologies, biographical sketches, directory listings of organizations, primary and secondary documents, and others. Much of the paranoia and anger against the government and other institutions that characterize the majority of these groups permeates this work. There is a large chapter on the people and organizations that monitor the propaganda and military-like tactics of the militia movement adherents. A bibliography of books and journal articles on militia groups is included, along with a listing of right-wing militia resources on the Web. 💻

4-34. Button, John. *The Radicalism Handbook: Radical Activists, Groups, and Movements of the Twentieth Century.* Santa Barbara, CA: ABC-CLIO, 1995. 460 pp. Index. ISBN: 0-874-36838-3.

Previously published as *Cassell Handbook of Radicalism*, this handbook attempts to list all the twentieth-century individuals and groups who have worked for a peaceful, just, safe, and sustainable world order. These people could have been drawn from all aspects of movements or activities associated with the arts, civil and human rights, gay and lesbian rights, peace movements, women's rights, radical education or economics,

and other causes. Over time, "Doers" are favored over "Thinkers" with regard to inclusion. Chapters are divided into broad chronological and/or topical headings. A dozen or so "radical forerunners," such as William Goodwin and John Stuart Mill, are listed. The bulk of the book is the listing of twentieth-century radicals. Some typical individual entries are Chinua Achebe, Rita Mae Brown, Germaine Greer, and Herbert Marcuse. Their respective publications are selectively listed. Some typical organizational entries are Greenpeace and Die Gruenen. An index is available for use.

Atlases

4-35. Stern, Geoffrey, ed. *Atlas of Communism.* New York: Macmillan, 1991. 256 pp. ISBN: 0-028-972651.

This historical and political atlas covers the period from 1848 to 1990 in five main chapters, each of which covers a meaningful span of time. For instance, Chapter 1 is "The Roots of Communism, 1848–1917," Chapter 2 is "The Soviet Experience, 1917–1945," and Chapter 3 is "The Cold War Communism, 1945–1962." The running text is secondary in importance to the full-color and clear maps contained within. These maps range from Lenin's October Revolution in Petrograd in 1917 to the Cuban Missile Crisis and the Vietnam conflict. The many black-and-white or color pictures bring history alive in an informative manner that is great for high-school and lower-division undergraduate students. The overall tone is more journalistic than scholarly.

5

U.S. Politics and U.S. Government Reference Sources

This chapter is devoted to the study of the U.S. political system and its local, state, and national governments. Government publications have been largely excluded from this chapter because so many good guides to document sources have already been published and are fairly current. The previous editions of *Information Sources of Political Science* also contain entries for selected government publications. The works presented here tend to be issued by a number of standard commercial publishers over the years. A growing segment of these works will end up as electronic resources in the near future, even though print editions will probably remain in existence for a number of these titles. This is one of the longer chapters in this book, which is probably an accurate indicator of the popularity and relatively large number of reference materials, either print or digital, published in any one year.

Federal Government Publications

The world of federal government publications can be a most intimidating place to the beginning researcher. If anything, the advent of electronic resources has at times complicated rather than simplified the picture. While access and indexing is often easier through the use of electronic means, there is sometimes uncertainty whether information will more likely be found in print or electronic format. Also, current display and navigation options often are not overly user friendly to the student or researcher. The reference works in this section should at a minimum assist the researcher in identifying the most likely sources, including those on the Internet and other electronic devices. There are a number of approaches to the compilation of bibliographies and search aids for federal documents. Some are arranged by subject, while at least one other uses an approach by popular name. The most recent guide, and one of the best, is that by Morehead; those exploring government publications in depth will benefit by perusing his work.

Literature Guides

5-1. Schwarzkopf, LeRoy C., comp. *Government Reference Books: A Biennial Guide to U.S. Government Publications.* Biennial. Englewood, CO: Libraries Unlimited, 1969–1993. Index. ISSN: 0072-5188.

The federal government is a prolific publisher; this volume provides a guide to reference materials issued in the most recent two years. The arrangement is by topic and begins with those materials relevant to general library reference. Three major sections follow, devoted to social sciences, science and technology, and arts and humanities. The latter part is far smaller than those encompassing the social sciences and science and technology. Within these broad sections, there is further breakdown into headings such as "Armed Forces and Military Affairs," "Housing and Urban Development," "Health Sciences," and "Transportation." The extensive bibliographic information includes Superintendent of Documents call numbers, which are in standard use in most libraries with extensive federal government collections. Descriptive annotations accompany the bibliographic citations, and there is a single index of authors, titles, and subjects. Only those items that can be generally described as books appear in this work; a companion volume, *Government Reference Serials* [entry 5-2], describes those publications that appear on an ongoing basis.

5-2. Schwarzkopf, LeRoy C. *Government Reference Serials.* Englewood, CO: Libraries Unlimited, 1988. 344 pp. Indexes. ISBN: 0-872-87451-6.

Compiled as a companion to *Government Reference Books* [entry 5-1], this volume includes ongoing publications of the federal government omitted from its sister work as of the 1984–1985 edition of the latter. The format is very similar. A section devoted to "General Library Reference" begins the volume and is followed by separate sections for the social sciences, science and technology, and the humanities. Each of the major sections is further subdivided by topic; for example, within the section for science and technology, the reader finds a subsection for "Biological Sciences," which is further subdivided into biology and zoology. Detailed bibliography information, including Superintendent of Documents call numbers, is included for each entry, along with a descriptive annotation. There are indexes by title, author, subject, and Superintendent of Documents number. Used in conjunction with its companion publications, this work can be a useful introduction to the federal documents labyrinth as it existed before the digital era.

5-3. Bailey, William G., comp. *Guide to Popular U.S. Government Publications.* 5th ed. Englewood, CO: Libraries Unlimited, 1998. 300 pp. Indexes. ISBN: 1-563-08607-7.

Approximately 2,500 federal government publications are described in this compilation; most date from the 1980s. Each item selected for inclusion had to be a "carefully prepared publication that was absorbing and exhibited wide appeal" (Bailey 1998, introduction). In other words, these publications are of value to the layperson rather than to the specialist specifically. The book is arranged alphabetically by topic area. Some example topics include "Alcohol and Drug Abuse," "Cities and Urban Affairs," "Elections," "Handicapped," and "Social and Ethical Issues." Annotations are brief and descriptive in nature, while the bibliographic information includes Superintendent of Documents call numbers, used in most federal document library collections. There are separate indexes by title and subject. 🖳

5-4. Morehead, Joe. *Introduction to United States Government Information Sources.* 6th ed. Englewood, CO: Libraries Unlimited, 1999. 491 pp. Index. ISBN: 1-563-08734-0.

Morehead has become one of the better known authors engaged in the task of explaining government publications. His is a reasonably thorough treatise that provides librarians and serious researchers with both a general overview and enough specifics to delve into the mysteries of congressional publications, for example. All the major branches and agencies of the federal government are covered. As this edition appeared, the Government Printing Office was just beginning a gradual conversion from print to electronic dissemination, so Morehead's work does not encompass important new components of digital-information retrieval.

Nevertheless, this book is indispensable for understanding the basics of federal print publications; such an understanding is necessary for serious researchers. 🖳

5-5. Williams, Wiley J. *Subject Guide to Major United States Government Publications.* 2nd ed. Chicago: American Library Association, 1987. 257 pp. Index. ISBN: 0-838-90475-0.

Those government publications considered to be of enduring significance are indexed by subject here. Some typical subjects include "Climate," "Historic Buildings," "Photographs," and "Transportation." Annotations are provided along with bibliographic information, usually including a Superintendent of Documents call number that will allow for retrieval in those libraries that use that system. This publication targets an audience of librarians, but it can be of use to specialized researchers as well. Electronic access, including the Internet, has lessened the value of compilations such as this one, but it still can be used for access to older materials or to determine if the federal government has published on a particular topic of general interest. Most readers will also wish to consult a newer volume, *Subject Guide to U.S. Government Reference Sources* [entry 5-6].

5-6. Hardy, Gayle J., and Judith Schiek Robinson. *Subject Guide to U.S. Government Reference Sources.* 2nd ed. Englewood, CO: Libraries Unlimited, 1996. 358 pp. Index. ISBN: 1-563-08189-X.

Both print and electronic federal government sources are described in this volume; Internet sites are among the entries. The format is very similar to *Government Reference Books* [entry 5-1] and *Government Reference Serials* [entry 5-2], both products of this same publisher. There are major sections devoted to "General Reference Sources," social sciences, science and technology, and the humanities. Each is further subdivided by topic. Bibliographic information includes Superintendent of Documents call numbers, which can be used to access print publications in libraries using that system. Descriptive annotations are provided for each entry. Although government document librarians will be an obvious audience for this work, it can be consulted profitably by undergraduates, advanced researchers, and the general public as well when an entry point is needed to help sort out the complexities of government publications.

5-7. Sears, Jean L., and Marilyn K. Moody. *Using Government Information Sources, Print and Electronic.* 2nd ed. Phoenix: Oryx Press, 1994. 539 pp. Index. ISBN: 0-897-74670-8.

The first edition of this book, *Using Government Publications*, appeared in 1985; this second edition provides an update through the early 1990s. There are four major categories of information here. One group of chapters is devoted to subject searches and includes subjects such as taxes, travel, copyright, climate, agriculture, and education. A second grouping describes agency searches and encompasses regulations, administrative actions and decisions, and presidential documents. A third category provides a number of chapters dealing with statistical searches on topics such as population, employment, crime, and defense. A final category, "Special Techniques," introduces the reader to legislative histories, budget analysis, technical reports, patents and trademarks, and similar complex government publication groupings. Some electronic publications appear here, but most reflect the use of compact disc technology prevalent at the time of publication rather than Internet sources. Nevertheless, the structure and chronological sequence of government publications series is as important as the format in which they appear, so this volume retains its value for those exploring the world of federal government sources.

Abstracting and Indexing Services

5-8. *Index to U.S. Government Periodicals.* Quarterly and Annual Cumulation. Chicago: Infodata International, 1993–. ISSN: 1076-3163.

The federal government produces many periodicals; some are well known and are represented in standard indexing and extracting services, while others are considerably more obscure. This indexing service provides access to about 170 titles deemed among the more important. Indexing is provided by both subject and author. With the advance of electronic indexing and the Internet, this set is of importance largely to government documents librarians and those researchers requiring access to government periodicals perhaps not represented electronically during the time that this index was published. 🖳

Directories

5-9. American Library Association. Government Documents Round Table. *Directory of Government Document Collections and Librarians.* 8th ed. Washington DC: Congressional Information Service, 2003. ISSN: 0276-959X.

Government publications, whether international, national, state, or local, are often housed separately in extensive collections in libraries. Even in the early twenty-first century, when more and more government publications are being delivered electronically, print collections remain valuable for their retrospective materials and for those items not yet delivered in a digital format. The major portion of this directory, a standard in the field, provides listings of document collections in public, academic, and special libraries. The listings include contact information and other relevant specifics. Although information for individual institutions in many instances may now be available through the Internet, this directory is valuable for a global picture of document collections, particularly for researchers interested in learning about collections in their geographic region.

Dictionaries

5-10. Garwood, Alfred N., and Louise L. Hornor, eds. *Dictionary of U.S. Government Statistical Terms.* Palo Alto, CA: Information Publications, 1991. 247 pp. ISBN: 0-931-84525-4.

The federal government has many specialized definitions for terms used by its agencies. This dictionary presupposes that the user has met with such a term in a federal publication and is seeking an explanation. Entries are arranged alphabetically and include not only a definition but also an indication of the agency originating the term and cross-references to other relevant definitions. Definitions range from a single sentence in length to a couple of paragraphs. Enough information is provided to describe appropriate context, but detailed methodology is excluded. Some examples of terms defined are "Disposable Personal Income," "Earnings," "Household Crimes," and "Occupational Injury." Many of the definitions are those promulgated by either the Census Bureau or the Bureau of Labor Statistics, and those researchers making use of the publications and statistical series of those agencies will welcome this dictionary.

Congress and the Legislative Branch

Like the material for the presidency, the reference information on the federal legislative branch of the government is voluminous. Several indexes provide access to current and past congressional publications, but access to recent laws, bills, reports, and hearings is much more readily available now than in the past, thanks to electronic databases. Two standard print sources, *CQ Weekly* and *National Journal*, continue to provide up-to-date information on congressional actions in both print and electronic formats. Congressional Quarterly is also responsible for a number of retrospective volumes that allow the researcher ready access to a narrative in regard to major legislation from 1945 to the present. A number of dictionaries and encyclopedias assist the reader who requires beginning information on the U.S. Congress. Directories, both current and retrospective, are also readily available, as are biographical resources. Information on the makeup of both Congress and its committees over the past two centuries is another category of information found in this section. In short, almost any important topic of interest relating to the legislative branch has one or more reference works to which researchers can turn for enlightenment.

Abstracting and Indexing Services

5-11. Commerce Clearing House, Inc. *Congressional Index.* Loose leaf. Chicago: Commerce Clearing House, 1938–. Indexes. ISSN: 0162-1203.

Long a reference standard, this publication provides the reader with ongoing indexes and information pertaining to congressional actions. There are two loose-leaf volumes per year. They each include information on House and Senate bills and resolutions, including their current status and voting records. Also provided are listings of enactments, listings for treaties and nominations, committee memberships, hearing information, committee assignments, and biographies of legislators. There are indexes of subjects and authors of bills. As is often the case with loose-leaf services, the arrangement of subject matter and indexes is complicated, and researchers

using this publication will benefit by familiarizing themselves with the format beforehand. Some of this information is now available through one or more electronic services, including some that are available free on the Internet, so this publication is perhaps less useful and necessary than in past years. Its greatest use may be for the retention of a historical record of congressional activities.

5-12. *Congressional Information Service Annual.* Annual. 3 vols. Washington, DC: Congressional Information Service, 1970–. Indexes. ISSN 0091-5319.

Much of the work of Congress takes place within committees, and the results are reflected in publications originating with those committees. This abstracting service represents the most thorough indexing that was long available for congressional publications, including hearings, committee prints, House and Senate reports, and documents. The topics of the three volumes are "Abstracts," "Indexes," and "Legislative Histories." The format is too complex to be thoroughly described in a brief annotation such as this, but suffice it to say that entries for publications of Congress include very complete bibliographic citations (with Superintendent of Documents call numbers) and listings of witnesses at hearings. The annotations allow the reader to determine whether the publication will be of relevance to his or her research. There are numerous indexes, including those to titles, bill numbers, report numbers, and the like, as well as an index to chairs of committees and subcommittees. This service is now available electronically through *LEXIS-NEXIS Congressional* (not described here), including links to full text from about 1989, so almost all researchers will gladly avoid the complicated print version. 💻

5-13. Law Librarians' Society of Washington, D.C. Legislative Source Book. http://www.llsdc.org/sourcebook/. E-mail contact: management@llsdc.org.

This Web site compiles a number of PDF documents that collectively are invaluable for librarians and serious researchers into Congress, legislation, and congressional publications. Among the recommended files are "Federal Legislative History Documents: Listings of Electronic Sources with Years/Congresses Available," "Federal Legislative History Research: A Practitioner's Guide to Compiling the Documents and Sifting for Legislative Intent," "An Overview of the Congressional Record and Its Predecessor Publications," "Schedule of Volumes of the U.S. Congressional Serial Set: 1970 to Current," "Sessions of Congress with Corresponding Debate Record Volume Numbers," and "Table of Congressional Publication Volumes and Presidential Issuances." Other files provide research information on the executive branch of the federal government and state-level resources. 💻

5-14. *LEXIS-NEXIS Congressional Historical Indexes, 1789–1969.* Bethesda, MD: LEXIS-NEXIS, 1998-. Indexes.

At present a component of *LEXIS-NEXIS Congressional,* this database rep-resents a number of print indexes published about 1970 by the Congressional Information Service Company. Collectively, they provide indexing for congressional reports and documents (essentially the U.S. Congressional Serial Set), hearings, and committee prints. Searching the database is a vast improvement over the tedious and time-consuming searches required when consulting the print indexes. The researcher must still bear in mind that access points and bibliographic control for congressional publications before the twentieth century left much to be desired, so search techniques must be thorough and informed to retrieve all potential results of interest. 💻

Annuals and Yearbooks

5-15. *Congress and the Nation: A Review of Government and Politics.* Quadrennial. Washington, DC: Congressional Quarterly, 1965-. Index. ISSN: 1047-1324.

Now in its ninth volume, *Congress and the Nation* provides a detailed review of politics and public policy from 1945 through 1996. Each volume is massive, often over 1,000 pages. The first volume in the series covered the years from 1945 through 1964, while each of the succeeding volumes is devoted to a four-year time frame. Each volume is divided into a number of chapters representing major subject areas, such as foreign policy, defense, environment, education, and labor. Other chapters address more general subjects, including politics within both the Congress and the presidency. Most of the information appears in narrative format, but there also numerous sidebars, several charts, occasional graphic displays, and a lengthy appendix devoted to such subjects as key votes, the members of Congress, and presidential documents. To a certain extent, this series summarizes information that initially appeared in *CQ Weekly* [entry 5-20] and *Congressional Quarterly Almanac* [entry 5-16]. However, *Congress and the Nation* is highly useful because it provides a detailed look at policy issues and federal government politics over the second half of the twentieth century without the need to consult individual volumes and issues of the companion publications. Among them, these three publications of Congressional Quarterly are a stock source found in many libraries. The writing style is suitable for high-school and undergraduate researchers while remaining valuable for more advanced scholars as well.

5-16. *Congressional Quarterly Almanac.* Annual. Washington, DC: Congressional Quarterly, 1948–. Index. ISSN: 0095-6007.

A reference standard for half a century, this work provides detailed discussion on the activities of Congress as well as salient information on the executive and judiciary branches as well. As of 1998, the format differs somewhat from earlier years. Whereas previous editions provided lengthy summaries of important pieces of legislation and the actions taken on them, the new edition provides brief summaries followed by pertinent articles reprinted from *CQ Weekly*

[entry 5-20]. The 1998 edition included twenty-four chapters, each representing a particular subject area, such as abortion, defense, environment, and taxes. In addition to the reprinted articles, each major piece of legislation under discussion receives a "Box Score" that highlights actions taken. Some text appears in sidebars. Voluminous appendixes provide further information, some of it tabular, in regard to members of Congress, voting results, significant texts, and a listing of public laws approved. *Congressional Quarterly Almanac* has been a mainstay for those researchers tracking past legislation and political activities.

5-17. *Congressional Roll Call.* Annual. Washington, DC: Congressional Quarterly, 1972–. Indexes. ISSN: 0191-1473.

This publication provides a number of services to the user. A short introductory section briefly summarizes the year's legislation. Several studies of votes then follow. These describe such topics as support of the president's position, votes that reflect majority-party stands, and votes that indicate alliances. Statistics and graphic displays accompany the studies. The bulk of the volume, however, reports on votes by members of Congress for individual bills. There are separate sections for the Senate and for the House. Each includes an index by number and another by subject. Each bill is also briefly described as are vote totals and totals by party, with a distinction as well between Northern and Southern Democrats. This publication has been in existence for a number of years and therefore is valuable not only for the information it provides on recent legislation but also for voting information for years past.

5-18. *Congressional Yearbook.* Annual. Washington, DC: Congressional Quarterly, 1993–1996. Index. ISSN: 1079-8129.

Like many other publications of Congressional Quarterly, this work describes the activities of the U.S. Congress. Appearing annually, the text is divided into chapters reflecting major topic areas addressed by Congress. Some examples include "Spending," "Environment and Agriculture," and "Defense and Foreign Policy." These chapters are further subdivided into more specific topics. For instance, the chapter on the environment has subheadings relating to nuclear waste, farm policy, and public lands. Within each of these specific categories, the reader finds descriptions of major bills and laws relevant to that topic, including bill numbers, sponsors, key dates and actions, and a narrative explanation usually a page or two in length. The back of the volume includes supplementary information, such as a glossary, listings of that year's public laws and vetoes, and members of the House and Senate. The publisher's *Congressional Quarterly Almanac* [entry 5-16] covers this same subject matter in much greater detail; this work is therefore suitable for those researchers needing a briefer and perhaps more accessible source for congressional actions.

5-19. *CQ Guide to Current American Government.* Biannual. Washington, DC: Congressional Quarterly, 1962–. Index. ISSN: 0196-612X.

A spin-off of *CQ Weekly* [entry 5-20], this publication reprints articles from its parent service and arranges them in a topical format. Each issue is divided into four sections: "Foundations of American Government," "Political Participation," "Government Institutions," and "Politics and Public Policy." Each of these four sections begins with a page-long introduction; this is followed by a number of relevant articles, including illustrations, sidebars, and a citation to the initial publication. Each issue also includes an index and several appendixes. The appendixes describe the legislative and budget processes, provide a glossary of congressional terminology, and reprint the text of the U.S. Constitution and its amendments. This publication can be used by those students seeking examples of recent issues pertaining to political participation, government institutions, and public policy, but perhaps its most valuable components are the descriptions of the legislative and budget processes, both frequently sought pieces of information.

5-20. *CQ Weekly.* Weekly. Washington, DC: Congressional Quarterly, 1945–. Indexes. ISSN: 1521-5997.

Familiar to reference librarians since 1945, this publication (formerly known as *Congressional Quarterly Weekly Report*) updates users about happenings in Congress and with the administration.

Special reports, analysis, and news are combined with colorful graphics and illustrations in an attractive package. There are regular listings of House and Senate votes, the status of appropriations, and the status of legislation. Each issue includes a topical index, and there are cumulative indexes throughout the year. The writing style is suitable for general readers, including high-school students. Any researcher delving into current affairs in Congress and with the presidency should consult this source. This publication is a useful complement to *National Journal* [entry 5-21], which also reports on the current political scene but takes an entirely different approach. (Note: The electronic version was not seen.) 🖥

5-21. *National Journal.* Weekly. Washington, DC: National Journal Group, 1969–. ISSN: 0360-4217.

As is the case with its competitor, *CQ Weekly* [entry 5-20], this publication informs the reader of happenings in government, particularly Congress, the presidency, and political events. The approaches of the two are quite different, however. Whereas *CQ Weekly* has a strong orientation toward specific recent political and congressional actions, *National Journal* favors approaches by topic. Each issue begins with one or more special reports of subjects that represent trends or policy issues. These might include education, the possibility of a woman president, minority groups, labor unions, radioactive waste, and others of a similar nature. These reports are fol-

lowed by sections dealing with Congress, the administration, lobbying, issues, and politics. Each of these sections includes one or more relevant articles. Numerous photographs accompany the text. Approximately every six issues, there is a two-page listing of "Recent Articles," arranged by subject. Unlike *CQ Weekly*, which somewhat lends itself to browsing when information on recent legislation is sought, *National Journal* more closely resembles a weekly newsmagazine and is best approached through standard indexing services. (Note: The electronic version was not seen.) 🖥

5-22. Makinson, Larry, and Joshua Goldstein. *Open Secrets: The Encyclopedia of Congressional Money and Politics.* 4th ed. Washington, DC: Congressional Quarterly, 1996. 1348 pp. Indexes. ISBN: 1-568-02229-8.

The role that money plays in American politics is clearly delineated in this reference source, which draws upon records of the Federal Election Commission for the bulk of its material. The major portion of the volume is devoted to listings for each senator and representative in the U.S. Congress. Two pages of information on each indicate the leading monetary contributors to that individual. Contributors are arranged by major categories, such as "Business," and are further subdivided into smaller categories. For example, under "Business," one finds the category "Construction," which is further subdivided into "General Contractors," "Home Builders," "Construction Services," and "Building Materials and Equipment." Within these smaller categories, one then finds names of business firms and organizations that have contributed to that particular member of Congress, along with the amount of the contribution. Graphic displays supplement the statistical figures. Names of individual contributors were excluded, as were contributors who donated $200 or less. Other major components of this work are an introductory chapter on political spending, profiles of major industries that contribute heavily, and profiles of congressional committees. The latter section indicates major donors to committee members. There is a general index as well as an index to state delegations, necessary because the listing within each chamber is alphabetical by name of member. This unique source is of value to all levels of research.

Directories

5-23. Piacente, Steve, ed. *Almanac of the Unelected: Staff of the U.S. Congress.* 15th ed. Washington, DC: Almanac Publishing, 2002. 622 pp. Index. ISBN: 0-890-59571-2.

As the subtitle indicates, this is a biographical directory to staff of the U.S. Congress. There are sections for both the House of Representatives and the Senate. Each of these is further subdivided into listings for those staff associated with the leadership positions and those staff associated with committees. Committees are arranged alphabetically. There is a separate section for joint committees. Within this structure, each unit listing begins with the description of the committee and its jurisdiction. Listings for staff members then follow and are arranged alphabetically. Each is a page in length and includes background information, date and place of birth, education, and professional highlights. The most substantive part of the listing is a column delineating the expertise of the individual, often including quotations from the biographee as well as issues with which he or she is familiar. Most listings include a photograph of the individual. A name index concludes the volume. While only a small number of researchers will consult this work, it compiles much information that would be difficult or impossible to find otherwise.

5-24. *American Lobbyists Directory.* Detroit: Gale Research, 1990–. Indexes. ISSN: 1045-3679.

The first edition of this directory, published in 1990, compiles the names of 65,000 individuals and groups registered as lobbyists at the federal or state level. Also included are the nearly 30,000 businesses and organizations sponsoring said lobbyists. The directory begins with an alphabetical listing of organizations that lobby at the federal level. Each listing includes the address of the business or organization as well as the names and addresses of the lobbyists employed by them. This is followed by similar listings for each of the states as well as the District of Columbia. There are three indexes that give access to the directory listings. One index is arranged by name of lobbyist, while the second index is by name of organization. The final index provides a subject approach and includes useful cross-references to related subjects. For example, the reader who consults "Livestock" in the subject index will find a number of listings there, but will also see cross-references to "Agriculture," "Grain/Feed," and "Ranching." All three of the indexes provide an entry number that leads the reader to the organization and its lobbyist listing in the directories. Although no biographical or organizational information can be found here, this publication will be useful to any researcher interested in a compilation of lobbyist groups or lobbyists.

5-25. Ornstein, Norman J., Thomas E. Mann, and Michael J. Malbin. *Vital Statistics on Congress*. Washington, DC: AEI Press, 1980–. Index. ISSN: 0896-9469.

This compilation, published since the early 1980s, provides the reader with a statistical picture of Congress. For example, the edition published in 1998 had the following chapters: "Members of Congress," "Elections," "Campaign Finance," "Committees," "Congressional Staff and Operating Expense," "Workload," "Budgeting," and "Voting Alignments." Each chapter begins with several pages of explanatory text. The text is then followed by a number of statistical tables and graphic displays illustrating the subject of that chapter. Sources for the data are indicated; they represent a mixture of government and nongovernment publications. Notes to the statistical tables explain discrepancies and complications. Most tables include a range of

years, in some cases extending back to the 1940s. The audience for this work will be those researchers requiring quantitative data on the U.S. Congress and its members.

5-26. *Washington Representatives*. Washington, DC: Columbia Books, 1977–. Indexes. ISSN: 0192-060X.

The lobbying effort in Washington is massive, as a glance at this volume indicates. The "representatives" listed here are not elected officials but rather individuals and groups that represent special interests. This work goes beyond the usual lobbyist listing to encompass those who represent foreign-governmental interests and members of the federal executive branch who represent their agencies to Congress. There are four major components to the directory. The first is a listing of firms that act as advocates for special interests. The second is a listing of the clientele of these firms, namely, the special interests themselves. A third component is relatively brief, showing the executive branch representatives. The final component is a listing of individuals who work for the firms, clients, and government offices in the first three components. All these four components are arranged alphabetically and provide addresses, phone numbers, fax numbers, e-mail addresses, Web sites, and personnel listings. There are also several indexes. Those of foreign clients and political action groups are obviously quite specific, while indexes by subject and industry and by legislative issues offer a broader access to the directories. Although no narrative or background is provided for these groups and individuals, this publication nevertheless represents perhaps the most detailed listing for the lobbyist industry.

Bibliographies

5-27. Goehlert, Robert U., and Fenton S. Martin. *Congress and Law-Making: Researching the Legislative Process.* 2nd ed. Santa Barbara, CA: ABC-CLIO, 1989. 306 pp. Indexes. ISBN: 0-874-36509-0.

Combining narrative text with annotated bibliographic entries, this volume "is designed to help users trace congressional legislation and to familiarize them with the major sources of information about Congress" (Goehlert and Martin 1989, introduction). The second edition adds to the first by providing greater detail on the progression of bills through the legislative process and greater detail in regard to committee membership. The nine chapters discuss not only the legislative process but also administrative law, the budget process, congressional agencies, foreign affairs, elections, the various categories of secondary sources, and background on government-document collections found in libraries. The general emphasis is upon secondary sources. Annotations range in length from a sentence to a paragraph. There are indexes by author, title, and subject. This volume is suitable for undergraduates as well as more advanced researchers. These same two authors have also written *How to Research Congress* [entry 5-29], a shorter but more recent

guide that will help to update the information in this work.

5-28. Reams, Bernard D., Jr, comp. *Federal Legislative Histories: An Annotated Bibliography and Index to Officially Published Sources.* Westport, CT: Greenwood Press, 1994. 595 pp. Indexes. ISBN: 0-313-23092-7.

Approximately 255 legislative histories are annotated in this volume, which covers congressional terms from 1862 through 1990. These legislative histories originally appeared as congressional committee prints, insertions in hearings, or studies or briefs of the Congressional Research Service. Among the information provided for each legislative history is its public-law number, bill number, *Statutes at Large* citation, title, bibliographic information, a listing of bills for which the legislative history is relevant, and the annotation itself. Arrangement of entries is by a unique numerical "record number." All the indexes refer the reader to these record numbers. There are indexes by author, popular name, congressional session, and public-law and bill numbers. There is also a table that allows the user to find the appropriate record number when only the *Statutes at Large* citation is known. Optimum use of this work presupposes that the reader has access to texts of bills or statutes.

5-29. Martin, Fenton S., and Robert U. Goehlert. *How to Research Congress.* Washington, DC: Congressional Quarterly, 1996. 107 pp. Indexes. ISBN: 0-871-87870-4.

This short guide is similar to *How to Research the Presidency* [entry 5-94] in that it is aimed at the beginning researcher. An introductory section briefly describes types of legal resources and research methodology. A section on secondary resources and search tools then follows and includes such categories as almanacs, dictionaries, handbooks, bibliographies, databases, and journals. The next section is devoted to primary sources and covers statutory law, case law, administrative law, and congressional-information resources. Some are electronic, including Internet sites. The items in these sections are either annotated or receive explanatory text. The final portion of the book is a bibliography on Congress dealing with subjects such as congressional processes, reforms, powers, committees, leadership, and the like. Items included in this section are restricted to books, and there are no annotations. A short glossary of congressional terms appears at the back of the volume. There are indexes by both title and author. This publication is suitable for high-school and undergraduate students alike.

5-30. Kennon, Donald R., ed. *Speakers of the U.S. House of Representatives: A Bibliography, 1789–1984.* Baltimore: Johns Hopkins University Press, 1986. 323 pp. Indexes. ISBN: 0-801-82786-8.

The office of Speaker of the House of Representatives is potentially one of great power; this scholarly and detailed bibliography provides an entry point for research upon the individuals who have held that office. The text begins with an overview and bibliography of the Speakership itself. Four parts then follow, each representing a specific chronological time frame and each beginning with a general bibliography. Bibliographies for each of the Speakers during that time frame follow. Brief biographical background precedes each Speaker bibliography. Items chosen for inclusion must provide significant information on either the institution or one or more of the Speakers. Most of the items included are books, articles, and dissertations, but brief information is also provided in relation to location and scope of manuscript collections. Autobiographical works are included in the listings. Very brief annotations accompany the bibliographic entries. There are indexes by author and subject. The last Speaker to be included is Tip O'Neill.

5-31. Goehlert, Robert U., and Fenton S. Martin. *United States Congress: An Annotated Bibliography, 1980–1993.* Washington, DC: Congressional Quarterly, 1995. 640 pp. Indexes. ISBN: 0-871-87810-0.

This work presents 3,200 annotated items pertaining to Congress during the period 1980 through 1993. Emphasis is upon items that are analytical and scholarly rather than descriptive. For that reason, research monographs, journal articles, and dissertations were sought for inclusion. Biographical articles and newspaper articles were excluded, as were publications of the federal government other than those of the Congressional Research Service. The volume is divided into fourteen chapters, each relating to a different subject. Examples include "Congressional Reform," "Legislative Analysis," and "Leadership in Congress." Annotations are largely descriptive but do occasionally offer some analysis of the item in question. There are indexes by author and subject. The authors state that their work is aimed at students, general readers, and other researchers, and, indeed, this publication can be used profitably by undergraduates as well as those with more advanced needs.

Dictionaries

5-32. Dickson, Paul, and Paul Clancy. *Congress Dictionary: The Ways and Meanings of Capital Hill.* New York: John Wiley, 1993. 400 pp. ISBN: 0-471-58064-3.

In this volume, the authors offer a guide to the slang and jargon used in Congress from early days to the present. Some examples include "Dirty Tricks," "God Squad," "Pay as You Go," and "Rainmaker." Definitions are arranged alphabetically and range in length from a sentence to a paragraph. Definitions are often enlivened by brief anecdotes. The illustrations that accompany the text are derived from the nineteenth century as well as the twentieth century. Occasional sidebars supplement some definitions. There are a number of entries for standard congressional and official terminology, but this volume is really more valuable for its concentration upon "unofficial" language. A short bibliography at the end of the volume will lead the reader to other sources, some in the same somewhat irreverent vein.

5-33. Kravitz, Walter. *Congressional Quarterly's American Congressional Dictionary.* 3rd ed. Washington, DC: Congressional Quarterly, 2001. 280 pp. ISBN: 1-568-02611-0.

As one would expect from the title, this dictionary provides definitions and brief explanations of terms in current use in the U.S. Congress. There is particular emphasis on the legislative process and congressional procedures. In those instances where differences are apparent between the House of Representatives and the Senate, those differences are explained. Entries are arranged alphabetically; most are about a paragraph in length, but more substantive matters receive several paragraphs. There are numerous cross-references to other related entries. Most of the terms defined are standard English or official terminology, but there are also occasional definitions of jargon. Compared to *CQ's Pocket Guide to the Language of Congress* [entry 5-34], this work is twice as long and was published more recently, presumably making it more up to date.

5-34. *CQ's Pocket Guide to the Language of Congress.* Washington, DC: Congressional Quarterly, 1994. 127 pp. ISBN: 0-871-87995-6.

Hundreds of definitions pertaining to congressional activity appear in this short volume. Most relate to the legislative process and congressional procedures. Most are standard English, but a few originate in jargon. Where differences exist between the Senate and the House, such differences are indicated. Most definitions are relatively brief, from a sentence to a paragraph, but a few of greater complexity or significance receive two or three paragraphs of explanation. While much of this information might be available from dictionaries or legislative manuals, this compilation provides a handy single-volume source for congressional researchers.

Encyclopedias

5-35. Tarr, David R., and Ann O'Connor, eds. *Congress A to Z.* 4th ed. Washington, DC: CQ Press, 2003. 605 pp. Index. ISBN: 1-568-02800-8.

Congressional Quarterly has been reporting on national legislation for approximately fifty years. This work is one of several Congressional Quarterly volumes that provide an A-to-Z approach to American government. This volume provides readers with basic information needed to understand the legislative branch of the federal government. Individual entries vary a good deal in length. Some are only a few paragraphs, while others run for several pages. Cross-references to other entries are indicated in uppercase. Among the entries are short articles on important individuals and significant congressional committees. All time periods are included. Numerous photographs, usually of members of Congress, make for an attractive format. Major entries include a list of books for additional reading. A series of appendixes provides rosters of congressional leaders and other useful information. The writing style is suitable for both high-school and undergraduate students; all who need beginning information on Congress and its work can refer to this volume.

5-36. Bacon, Donald C., Roger H. Davidson, and Morton Keller, eds. *Encyclopedia of the United States Congress.* 4 vols. New York: Simon and Schuster, 1985. 2359 pp. Index. ISBN: 0-132-76361-3.

The U.S. Congress is arguably the most successful legislative body in the history of the world, yet it is often the butt of jokes and scorn. This encyclopedia provides both general readers and specialists with a detailed review of this important body and its work. The encyclopedia includes over 1,000 articles arranged alphabetically and ranging in length from 250 to about 6,000 words. The longer essays are assigned to major topics such as those that describe Congress as an institution, including constitutional powers, procedures, committees, budget process, and staffing. Other articles discuss lives of legislators, the relationship between Congress and other elements of the American political system, elections, policy in many areas of interest, landmark laws, and essays on all of the fifty American states and their contribution to this institution. Cross-references and bibliographies are provided, and each article is signed by its contributor; contributors are generally political scientists, historians, and journalists. Many photographs and other illustrations supplement the text. The first volume includes an alphabetical list of the entries, while the final volume includes the text of the U.S. Constitution, a glossary, a synoptic outline of the contents, and a general index. The writing style makes this work accessible to students and specialists alike.

Guides and Handbooks

5-37. *Biographical Directory of the American Congress, 1774–1996.* Quadrennial. Alexandria, VA: CQ Staff Directories, 1994–. ISSN: 1091-0859.

This massive directory is based upon the previous edition published by the Government Printing Office that ceased publication in 1988. Congressional Quarterly has updated the earlier edition with information through September 30, 1996. The volume begins with a listing of presidents and their cabinet officers. This is followed by directory information for the Continental Congress and tabular information on apportionment of representatives. The next section is a listing for each Congress, showing officers and senators and representatives from each state. These listings also indicate party affiliation and city of residence. The final part of the work, and by far the most extensive, is the listing of biographies. These are arranged alphabetically and include information somewhat similar to that found in a Who's Who directory. Those members of Congress who are of some renown also receive a bibliographic listing of additional sources. This standard directory will be consulted by all researchers requiring basic information on the members of Congress. 🖳

5-38. Deering, Christopher J., and Steven S. Smith. *Committees in Congress.* 3rd ed. Washington, DC: Congressional Quarterly, 1997. 254 pp. Index. ISBN: 0-871-87818-6.

Much of the work in Congress is accomplished within committees. The five chapters in this volume cover the following subjects: "Committees in Congress," "Evolution and Change in Committees," "Member Goals and Committee Assignments," "Inside Committees: Leaders, Subcommittees, and Staff," and "Committees in the Postreform Congress." Emphasis is on general procedures rather than specific committees. Compared to earlier editions, this edition provides less on historical background and more on theories relating to committee power and recent efforts at reform. Examples illustrating committee politics are usually drawn from recent years. Numerous sidebars and tables supplement the text, and each chapter provides endnotes that will lead interested readers to other sources. The audience for this work will include undergraduates and other academic researchers seeking introductory information on congressional committee structure and its political background.

5-39. Canon, David T., Garrison Nelson, and Charles Stewart III. *Committees in the U.S. Congress, 1789–1946.* 4 vols. Washington, DC: Congressional Quarterly, 2002. ISBN: 1-568-02171-2.

A companion to *Committees in the U.S. Congress, 1947–1992* [entry 5-40], this set is an extremely valuable source that should be in any library that supports retrospective research in regard to Congress. The general format is similar to the companion set. Altogether, approximately 100,000 appointments to congressional committees can be found here, representing a work of compilation that eliminates tedious searching by librarians and their patrons alike.

5-40. Nelson, Garrison, and Clark H. Bensen. *Committees in the U.S. Congress, 1947–1992.* 2 vols. Washington, DC: Congressional Quarterly, 1993–1994. 1048 pp. Index. ISBN: 0-871-87729-5 (Vol. 1); ISBN: 0-871-87611-6 (Vol. 2).

These are the first two volumes in a projected multivolume set that will document all committee assignments in Congress from 1789 to the present; this set is made up of individual volumes that provide separate sets of information. The first volume describes committee jurisdictions and provides member rosters for each. All committees are described, including select, special, and joint committees. Brief information is provided on each committee member, including their party affiliation, the state they represent, and their number of years in the congressional body in question and on the committee. An index to committees and members concludes the volume. The second volume concentrates upon committee histories and includes an alphabetical listing of members with their assignments. These listings show the Congress member's committee ranking, the terms in the body and on the committee, and the date of assignment.

Committee histories are relatively brief, usually about half a page. Compilation of this information from other sources would be tedious, so consultation of these two works can be recommended to all those researchers dealing with congressional committees in the second half of the twentieth century. The companion set covering 1789 to 1946 is described previously [entry 5-39].

5-41. Davidson, Roger H., and Walter J. Oleszek. *Congress and Its Members.* 8th ed. Washington, DC: Congressional Quarterly, 2001. 510 pp. Index. ISBN: 1-568-02649-8.

The thesis of this volume is "the dual nature of Congress as a collection of career-maximizing politicians and the forum for shaping and refining national policy" (Davidson and Oleszek 2001, preface). As such, it also serves general readers and college students with a general introduction to that body. There are four major sections to this work. The first provides a historical introduction, while the second part examines recruitment of members, elections, and the relationship of members to their constituents. The third part discusses procedural aspects of Congress, including committees. The fourth deals with policy issues, including the relationships of Congress with the president, the courts, organized interests, budgets, and national security. A number of tables, sidebars, and illustrations accompany the text, and footnotes and a bibliography appear at the back. Examples of congressional action and behavior are usually drawn from recent events. Although this is as much a textbook as it is a reference book, its engaging style and coverage of many basic aspects of Congress recommend it to student researchers.

5-42. *Congressional Districts in the 2000s: A Portrait of America.* Washington, DC: Congressional Quarterly, 2003. 900 pp. Indexes. ISBN: 1-568-02849-0.

This is the third volume on congressional districts published by Congressional Quarterly; these titles appear about once a decade and provide a snapshot of districting in the latter part of the twentieth century. The arrangement is alphabetical by state. Short narrative and tabular information, as well as an outline map of counties and districts, begin each listing. This is followed by a numerical listing of districts in the state. For each district, there is a narrative description and other information in regard to recent election returns and demographics. The latter encompasses many categories in addition to the usual population demographics. For example, each district receives a listing of institutions of higher education, newspapers and their circulation, other media listings, military installations, and major businesses and employers. There are indexes by city, county, university and college, cable television, military installation, and business. An introductory chapter also provides the reader with background on the subject of reapportionment and redistricting. Some of this information, such as the narratives that

describe individual districts, can be found in other Congressional Quarterly publications, such as *Congressional Quarterly's Politics in America* [entry 5-117], but the demographic information is more unique. Collectively, the volumes in this series will be useful to researchers who are investigating congressional districts over the long term.

5-43. *Congressional Quarterly's Guide to Congress.* 5th ed. Washington, DC: Congressional Quarterly, 2000. 1354 pp. Index. ISBN: 0-871-87584-5.

This thick volume provides the following chapters: "Origins and Development of Congress," "Powers of Congress," "Congressional Procedures," "Pressures on Congress," "Housing and Support," "Pay and Perquisite," "Congress and the Electorate," and "Qualifications and Conduct." These individual sections are quite detailed, ranging up to 150 pages in length. Although theoretical matters receive some discussion, emphasis is upon politics and the practical workings of Congress. Recent administrations generally receive more attention than do those in the eighteenth and nineteenth centuries and the earlier part of the twentieth century. Some of the text is drawn from other Congressional Quarterly publications. Illustrations, statistical tables, and sidebars supplement the main text. Each chapter concludes with a bibliography. An extensive series of appendixes, with page numbering separate from the main text, concludes the volume and includes listings for leadership, party affiliations, general-election results, and the texts of the Constitution and the rules of both bodies of Congress. Very brief biographical information is also provided on each member of Congress through 1991. Those researchers particularly interested in congressional political happenings in the last few decades should take note of this work.

5-44. Bosnich, Victor W. *Congressional Voting Guide: A Ten Year Compilation.* 5th ed. Dallas, TX: CVG Press, 1994. 621 pp. Indexes. ISBN: 0-961-89585-3.

Approximately 154 major bills dating from 1984 to 1993 are included in this voting summary. The majority are actually from 1990 to 1993. There are separate sections for the House and the Senate. Each begins with a listing of the measures on which the members were voting that includes a brief summary, allowing the reader to obtain an idea of the contents. Each is also numbered; these numbers serve as a key in the list of votes by each member. Representatives and senators are then listed by state. For each measure for which the member recorded a vote, that vote, either "yes" or "no," is indicated. Very short biographical information is included for each member, as is a percentage indication of his or her support of the president in 1992 and 1993. There are indexes by both name and subject. Only major and controversial bills were included in this compilation, and because it concentrates on just a few years, it is of more limited value than other voting compilations. Earlier editions of Bosnich's work can be

consulted for voting records in years prior to this volume.

5-45. Sharp, J. Michael. *Directory of Congressional Voting Scores and Interest Group Ratings.* 3rd ed. 2 vols. Washington, DC: Congressional Quarterly, 2000. 1676 pp. ISBN: 1-568-02565-3.

There is a twofold value to this reference work. First, it includes all members of Congress since 1947, when the Americans for Democratic Action first began rating congressional representatives in terms of their voting patterns. Second, it offers a snapshot of voting patterns that gives the reader insight into the political stance and ideology of members of Congress. The arrangement is alphabetical by name. Basic background is provided for each member, including education, occupation, political career, and election record. This is followed by a table that provides annual data for two categories of information: "Voting Scores" and "Group Ratings." The first category indicates the member's support or opposition in terms of the "Conservative Coalition" (a group including Republicans and Southern Democrats), party unity, support of the president, and voting participation. All are defined in terms of percentage. The second category indicates the member's score as ranked by ten major interest groups: Americans for Democratic Action, American Conservative Union, American Civil Liberties Union, American Security Council, Chamber of Commerce of the United States, Consumer Federation of America, Committee on Political Education of the AFL-CIO, League of Conservation Voters, National Education Association, and National Taxpayers Union. An appendix in the second volume lists members by Congress and by state and chamber from 1947 through January 3, 1995. The user new to this volume will need to consult the introductory matter to understand the format, but the information to be obtained is well worth the effort.

5-46. Christianson, Stephen G. *Facts about the Congress.* New York: H. W. Wilson, 1996. 635 pp. Index. ISBN: 0-824-20883-8.

The intent of this volume is to present basic information about each Congress from the 1st (1787–1791) through the first session of the 104th Congress (1995–1996). Basic information for each Congress includes background, leadership, a chronology, major legislation, relationship with the president, nominations, key votes, constitutional amendments (if any), and a brief bibliography. Some information appears in tabular form. Earlier Congresses receive about four pages of treatment; later Congresses receive about twice as much. Introductory matter provides an overview of Congress, while a number of appendixes provide such information as the text of the Constitution, leadership in the two houses, apportionment, pay rates, and congressional buildings. Occasional illustrations and photographs supplement the text. This is a handy volume for those researchers requiring brief information on each Congress throughout the history of

that body. It is suitable for both high-school and undergraduate students.

5-47. *How Congress Works.* 3rd ed. Washington, DC: Congressional Quarterly, 1998. 184 pp. Index. ISBN: 1-568-02391-X.

Those student researchers seeking an overview of Congress and its functions in "clear and non-technical language" (*How Congress Works* 1998, introduction) can turn to this publication. The three major components of the volume examine party leadership, the legislative process, and the workings of the committee system. Illustrations and sidebars supplement the text. Endnotes and bibliographies appear at the end of each of the three major sections. The volume also includes about fifteen pages of materials for reference, such as listings of leadership positions, vetoes, and sources for Internet information. Like other volumes published by Congressional Quarterly, this work seeks to introduce the reader to government functions in a format that is concise but reasonably analytical and that displays respect for the workings of the democratic process. It can be used by both high-school and undergraduate students.

5-48. Smock, Raymond W., ed. *Landmark Documents on the U.S. Congress.* Washington, DC: Congressional Quarterly, 1999. 642 pp. Index. ISBN: 1-568-02399-5.

The author, official historian of the House of Representatives, has compiled almost 200 documents that illustrate the workings of the U.S. Congress. The variety is great: debates, speeches, declarations of war, committee hearings, Supreme Court decisions, and citizen petitions are among those items included. The intent is to show Congress in many aspects, not merely to provide those documents of official nature pertaining to its establishment or powers. Documents are arranged chronologically, and each begins with an explanation by Smock of its significance. Many are included in full text; others are partial text, with omissions indicated with ellipses. Each document concludes with a reference to the source for the complete text. A short bibliography at the back of the volume will lead the reader to additional material. This compilation will be of use at both the high-school and collegiate levels for students and teachers seeking historical background on Congress with an emphasis upon original sources. 💻

5-49. Parsons, Stanley B. *United States Congressional Districts, 1788–1841.* Westport, CT: Greenwood Press, 1978. 416 pp. Index. ISBN: 0-837-19828-3.

This volume addresses itself to both legislative and aggregate electoral behavior, and is the first in a series that provides historical data on this subject. In terms of legislative behavior, this work intends to complement Congressional Quarterly's *Guide to U.S. Elections* [entry 5-182] and data available from the Inter-University Consortium for Social and Political Research. Electoral behavior is explicated here through the tabulation of county

and district population figures. The volume is arranged into several time periods, each representing several Congresses. Within these time segments, states are arranged alphabetically. Each includes an outline map indicating county and district boundaries. The map is accompanied by population statistics and a listing of congressional representatives. The latter information includes party, address, county, and numbers indicating the Congresses to which the individual was elected. An appendix lists names and creation dates of counties; these are arranged by name of state. A bibliography of several pages and an index of names of congressional representatives conclude the volume. Not only is this reference work of value for historical data on districts, it also has peripheral use for county boundaries and creation dates. Other volumes in this series are described next [entries 5-50 and 5-51].

5-50. Parsons, Stanley B., Michael J. Dubin, and Karen Toombs Parsons. *United States Congressional Districts, 1883–1913.* New York: Greenwood Press, 1990. 439 pp. ISBN: 0-313-26482-1.

One of a series of volumes that use demographic and statistical data in conjunction with maps to assist the researcher in analyzing legislative and electoral behavior in congressional districts and counties in the American past, this work is essentially similar in format to its immediate predecessor, which dealt with the time frame from 1843 to 1883. For a description of that volume, described next, see entry [5-51].

5-51. Parsons, Stanley B., William W. Beach, and Michael J. Dubin. *United States Congressional Districts and Data, 1843–1883.* New York: Greenwood Press, 1986. 226 pp. ISBN: 0-313-22045-X.

One in a series of volumes that cumulatively describe past congressional districts, this work differs somewhat from its predecessor, which encompassed the time period from 1788 to 1841. A comparative scarcity of statistics for the earlier time frame induced the compilers to include personal information on congressional representatives on a district-by-district basis. In contrast, the availability of additional data led to the elimination of "representative" background in this volume. Instead, the reader finds additional statistics on each county and district. Data on manufacturing and agricultural production are among the new series found here. Otherwise, the format is similar to the preceding work, described in more detail previously [entry 5-49].

5-52. Kaptur, Marcy. *Women of Congress: A Twentieth Century Odyssey.* Washington, DC: Congressional Quarterly, 1996. 256 pp. Index. ISBN: 0-871-87989-1.

Part monograph and part reference work, this volume provides a comparatively brief overview of women in the U.S. Congress. The author, herself a congressional representative, divides her account into three portions. The first part deals with the period from 1917 to World War II, the second covers the period from that war through the 1960s,

while the final part brings the reader up to the 1990s. Each of the three parts includes an overview of the situation; this is followed by biographies of key women. The biographies range from five to about sixteen pages. The first biography deals with Jeannette Rankin; the last is about Nancy Landon Kassebaum. This text is followed by nearly fifty pages of tabular information about all women who have served in the Congress. Endnotes accompany the main text, and there is also a short bibliography at the back of the volume. Also included in the text are a number of photographs, including one for each of the biographees. This work is lively in tone and suitable for both high-school and college researchers.

Atlases

5-53. Archer, J. Clark, et al. *Atlas of American Politics, 1960–2000.* Washington, DC: CQ Press, 2002. 242 pp. Index. ISBN: 1-568-02665-X.

Approximately 200 maps form the backbone of this atlas, which is divided into eight chapters that discuss topics such as "Presidential Elections," "Congress," "The Political Culture of States," and "Social and Economic Policy." Extensive narratives accompany the maps. Most maps display boundaries at either the state or county levels, with a few indicating congressional-district boundaries. A four-page reference list at the back of the volume indicates sources for maps, and each chapter concludes with a brief bibliography for those who wish to explore further. To a certain extent, this atlas serves as an update to the atlases by Martis described elsewhere in this section [entries 5-54, 5-55, and 5-56].

5-54. Martis, Kenneth C., ed. *Historical Atlas of Political Parties in the United States Congress, 1789–1989*. New York: Macmillan, 1989. 518 pp. Indexes. ISBN: 0-029-20170-5.

This atlas differs from most in that the maps are accompanied by a scholarly and detailed narrative, complete with notes. The maps themselves are multicolored and show party representation by state and district. Lists of members of Congress accompany the maps, and extensive information is provided for party affiliation, which is particularly important for the earlier years of the U.S. Congress. The sections on affiliation indicate sources by which said affiliation can be determined. An introductory section of almost seventy pages describes the history of political parties. Erudite and complex, this atlas demands close attention from its users and will have its greatest appeal for a specialized audience, which will benefit from its wealth of detail.

5-55. Martis, Kenneth C., and Gregory A. Elmes. *Historical Atlas of State Power in Congress, 1790–1990*. Washington, DC: Congressional Quarterly, 1993. 190 pp. Index. ISBN: 0-871-87742-2.

This is another in a series of atlases published by Congressional Quarterly. It displays information pertaining to congressional apportionment. Normally, apportionment takes place after each census, and this volume includes maps that display gains and losses by state during this period since 1790. Maps are only a portion of this work, however; a good deal of statistical information is presented, and there is extensive textual analysis of the results of apportionment. Included are discussions of original versus new states, slave versus Free states, and rural versus urban areas. A three-page bibliography will lead interested readers to other sources on this subject. This specialized atlas provides a good deal of information that could be tedious to assemble by other means. Its primary audience will be graduate students, scholars, and other serious researchers.

5-56. Martis, Kenneth C. *Historical Atlas of United States Congressional Districts, 1789–1983*. New York: Free Press, 1982. 302 pp. Indexes. ISBN: 0-029-20150-0.

The introductory section of this atlas describes the background of congressional districts with particular emphasis upon their geography and mapping. The bulk of the volume is devoted to black-and-white maps indicating state and district boundaries for each Congress; the maps are accompanied by listings of members. The final part of this work, which targets a scholarly audience, provides legal descriptions of the districts. Users of this atlas will also want to be aware of the *Historical Atlas of Political Parties in the United States Congress* [entry 5-54]. Neither atlas, however, reflects changes in the last two decades. (Note: The Bureau of the Census has published congressional district atlases for a number of years; these are not described here due to their Government Printing Office provenance.)

Executive Branch of Government

Compared to the presidency, the agencies of the executive branch have received relatively little attention from reference-book publishers, despite their importance in the promulgation of federal regulations. There are a couple of exceptions to this rule, however. A number of works have been devoted to the examination of military agencies, and they are covered in this section. U.S. intelligence and cold war literature will be found in the chapter on "International Relations."

Directories

5-57. Eng, Vincent. *Almanac of the Executive Branch*. 5th ed. Washington, DC: Bernan Associates, 2001. 600 pp. Indexes. ISBN: 0-890-59285-3.

This publication provides biographies of officials appointed by the president to positions in the executive branch. There are separate chapters for the Executive Office of the President, independent agencies, and each of the departments in the cabinet. Within each chapter, a reader will find brief information on the jurisdiction and history of the agency as well as an organizational chart. Biographies are generally about a column in length and include education and professional background of the appointee as well as several paragraphs describing his or her career. Appropriate contact information is provided along with a photograph of the individual. There are indexes of names and subjects; as biographies are not arranged alphabetically, it is necessary to consult the index if one is seeking a particular individual. This is not a source for beginning students but rather for those researchers requiring a certain degree of depth on the personnel of a particular presidential administration.

5-58. Evinger, William R. *Directory of U.S. Military Bases Worldwide*. 3rd ed. Phoenix: Oryx Press, 1998. 441 pp. Indexes. ISBN: 1-573-56049-9.

Almost 1,200 military bases and installations are listed in this directory. The first portion of the text is an arrangement by state, while the second portion is a listing of overseas bases. Within each state, bases are arranged by locality, while overseas bases are arranged by name of unit within each country. Major installations and bases receive extensive coverage, including the history of the base, information on units at the station, and personnel services. All listings include contact information, such as postal and Internet addresses. Recent base closures are indicated in two appendixes. There are indexes by base, branch of service, locality and branch of service, and unit. While many bases can now be identified and contacted through the Internet, this volume is still useful because it is so comprehensive, encompassing reserve units that might otherwise be overlooked.

5-59. *Federal Regulatory Directory*. 11th ed. Washington, DC: Congressional

Quarterly, 2003. 830 pp. Indexes. ISBN: 1-568-02812-1.

More than just a directory, this standard work also assists the reader with background information. The volume opens with an introductory chapter that outlines the history and rationale of federal regulatory agencies. Most of the work is devoted to discussion of the agencies themselves, beginning with major organizations, such as the Federal Reserve System. This is followed by a listing of each of the federal departments, each with its own array of agencies. For example, the Forest Service is described within the section for the Department of Agriculture. The section for each agency usually includes contact information (such as postal address and Internet site), narrative background, key personnel and phone numbers, information sources, brief descriptions of relevant legislation, and listings for state and regional offices. A final chapter examines regulatory oversight, while a number of appendixes provide text of acts and executive orders pertinent to regulatory agencies. There are indexes.

5-60. *Federal Yellow Book: Who's Who in Federal Departments and Agencies.* Quarterly. New York: Leadership Directories, 1976–. Indexes. ISSN: 0145-6202.

One of a series of "Yellow Books," this directory concentrates upon the federal executive branch. Agencies are divided into three major sections. The first section covers the offices of the president and vice president. The second is devoted to the departments, while the third

section covers independent agencies. The second and third sections are arranged alphabetically by name of department or agency. Listings of personnel are quite extensive and usually include telephone numbers, postal addresses, and e-mail addresses. There are indexes by subject, organization, and name. Unlike some directories, this volume provides no information about the agencies themselves; its real strength is rooted in the personnel listings, which will be of value to those researchers requiring detailed directory assistance for federal agencies.

Bibliographies

5-61. Goehlert, Robert, and Hugh Reynolds, comps. *Executive Branch of the U.S. Government: A Bibliography.* Westport, CT: Greenwood Press, 1989. 380 pp. Index. ISBN: 0-313-26568-2.

About 4,000 citations appear in this work, which focuses upon "the executive branch, including the history, development, organization, procedures, rulings, and policy of the departments" (Goehlert and Reynolds 1989, introduction). Although emphasis is on cabinet-level departments, materials have also been included for some subagencies, particularly those well known to the public, such as the Federal Bureau of Investigation, National Park Service, and Social Security Administration. There are fifteen chapters. The first chapter includes material relating to the executive branch in general. The following chapters are devoted to individual departments, with a separate chapter for the U.S. Postal Service.

The items selected for the bibliography include books, scholarly articles, dissertations, and some research reports. Government publications were excluded. Within each chapter, citations are arranged alphabetically by author, and indexes are provided of authors and subjects. There are no annotations. Given that the time frame for inclusion extended from 1945 to about 1985, this bibliography will be of interest primarily to historians and political scientists researching the executive branch during the decades following World War II and concluding with the first Reagan administration.

5-62. Unsworth, Michael E., ed. *Military Periodicals: United States and Selected International Journals and Newspapers.* New York: Greenwood Press, 1990. 404 pp. Index. ISBN: 0-313-25920-8.

Considerably more erudite than the usual annotated bibliography, this work provides detailed information in regard to a selected number of periodicals that have had an "impact on the armed forces of the United States and on American military thought" (Unsworth 1990, preface). The volume is divided into three parts: "Long Profiles," "Short Profiles," and "Multiple-Edition Profiles." Major military journals are described in the first part. Here, the descriptions go far beyond the usual annotation; most are several pages in length and describe the publication history of the periodical and assess its significance. Endnotes and bibliographies lead readers to additional sources of information. More concise information is provided in

the other two parts of the volume, but even here the annotations are more detailed than is usually the case. A chronology of nearly forty pages and an appendix of journals arranged by subject matter conclude this work. While this is obviously a specialized subject, readers requiring a scholarly introduction to the field of military periodicals will be well rewarded by starting here.

Dictionaries

5-63. Polmar, Norman, Mark Warren, and Eric Wertheim. *Dictionary of Military Abbreviations.* Annapolis, MD: Naval Institute Press, 1994. 307 pp. ISBN: 1-557-50680-9.

The U.S. armed forces make use of a truly formidable set of abbreviations. Since there are several branches of the military, each has developed its own peculiar language, so officers working with more than one branch must have a guide such as this one in order to understand all the vocabulary. There are no definitions here, only the complete terminology for each abbreviation. There are actually six different parts to the dictionary. Most definitions appear in the main body of the text, but there are also separate listings for "Aircraft Designations," "Aviation Unit Designations," "Military Ranks," "Missile and Rocket Designations," and "Ship Designations." For this reason, users must be alert to check all portions of the dictionary; it would be easy to overlook the appropriate category.

5-64. Dupuy, Trevor Nevitt, comp. *Dictionary of Military Terms: U.S. Dept. of*

Defense; A Guide to the Language of Warfare and Military Institutions. 2nd ed. New York: H. W. Wilson, 2003. 271 pp. ISBN: 0-824-21025-5.

This dictionary is substantially based upon a federal government publication, the *Department of Defense Dictionary of Military and Associated Terms;* any changes from the original appear to be insignificant. The definitions themselves are relatively short, usually a sentence or two. Emphasis is on avoiding jargon, for this work is intended to be of assistance to members of all the military services, each of which has its own "language." Cross-references are provided to other relevant entries. Separate listings of NATO terms and acronyms and abbreviations do not include definitions. Military terminology, like that of other occupations, changes frequently, but this dictionary will be useful thanks to its relatively recent publication date. However, most readers will be served equally well by consulting the original federal government publication.

5-65. Tomajczyk, S. F. *Dictionary of the Modern United States Military: Over 15,000 Weapons, Agencies, Acronyms, Slang, Installations, Medical Terms and Other Lexical Units of Warfare.* Jefferson, NC: McFarland, 1996. 785 pp. Index. ISBN: 0-786-40127-3.

As the subtitle indicates, this volume goes beyond the usual dictionaries that concentrate on official terminology, abbreviations, and acronyms. A good deal of the dictionary entries here consist of informal terms, occasionally including vulgar and

sexist language. There are also entries for subject matter, such as "Aircraft Accidents," "Divorce," and "Homosexual." Entries range in length from a single sentence to several paragraphs. There are also appendixes in regard to chemical agents, military designations and ranks, and music appropriate to the arrival and departure of dignitaries. An extensive bibliography indicates source materials; many are articles that appeared in military periodicals. This is not only a useful supplement to official terminology; it serves as a guide to the culture of the U.S. military establishment.

5-66. Jessup, John E., ed. *Encyclopedia of the American Military: Studies of the History, Traditions, Policies, Institutions, and Roles of the Armed Forces in War and Peace.* 3 vols. New York: Charles Scribner's Sons, 1994. 2255 pp. Index. ISBN: 0-684-19255-1.

This encyclopedia concentrates on the U.S. military and uses a topical rather than an alphabetical arrangement of its entries. Essay-length articles are grouped under six major parts: "War in the American Experience," "Formulation of American Military Policy," "The Roles of the Armed Forces," "The American Military in War and Peace," "Military Arts and Sciences," and "Military Practices." Articles range in length from about ten pages up to about thirty. The articles conclude with cross-references and long bibliographies. The first volume includes a detailed chronology that displays military episodes in conjunction with other events and prominent personalities. Contributors are for the most part drawn from the ranks of the American academic community. There are no illustrations other than a number of maps. The level of readership for this reference work is more likely to be at the collegiate rather than high-school level. The *Encyclopedia of the American Military* provides the reader with conceptual information in regard to military affairs in the United States from the beginning to the present.

Guides and Handbooks

5-67. Foundation for Public Affairs. *Public Interest Profiles.* Washington, DC: Congressional Quarterly, 1978–. Indexes. ISSN: 1058-627X.

Approximately 200 public-interest groups are described in this reference work. Organizations were selected for inclusion if they have a major impact on national policy or are well known to the news media and the public at large. Organizations are arranged into twelve chapters, each representing a particular topic. Some examples include "Community/ Grassroots," "Environmental," "Religious," and "Think Tanks." Within these twelve categories, the groups are arranged alphabetically. Entries range in length from a single page to as much as five pages. A basic listing includes contact information, staff listings, tax status, budget and funding, and membership. Other pieces of information include a listing of publications and methods by which the group operates, including advertising, litigation, and research. Better known groups also are accorded quota-

tions from third parties that attest to their effectiveness and political orientation. Naturally, fewer such quotations appear for those groups less in the public eye. Although this reference publication is selective in its approach, its detailed descriptions will be of value to students and researchers not only for individual groups but for the lobbying picture as a whole.

5-68. Watson, Cynthia. *U.S. National Security Policy Groups: Institutional Profiles.* Westport, CT: Greenwood Press, 1990. 289 pp. Index. ISBN: 0-313-25733-7.

Profiles of 135 policy groups appear in this volume. All were involved in some way in national security and strategy, both of which connote defense. Foreign policy groups were excluded. Those that were selected for inclusion generally were nonprofit, educational, and nonpartisan, as defined by the Internal Revenue Service for tax purposes. Defense contractors and their political action committees were excluded. The arrangement is alphabetical by name of organization. Each includes the following pieces of information: "Introductory Note," "Origins," "Organization and Funding," "Electoral Politics," "Policy Concerns and Tactics," and a listing for additional information. A couple of examples of the organizations to be found here are the American Enterprise Institute and the American Friends Service Committee. A major caveat about this volume is that it describes the policy situation as it existed in the 1980s and therefore is of value for historical purposes rather than for current information.

Judicial Branch of the Government and Criminal Justice

Not surprisingly, this section is dominated by reference publications devoted to the U.S. Supreme Court. However, a number of other topics receive a modicum of treatment as well. Some are directories of the bench. Others are encyclopedic treatments of U.S. law and justice and are aimed at the student and interested layperson. Descriptions of significant court cases also receive their due. Those volumes focusing upon the U.S. Supreme Court itself discuss the justices past and present, the workings of the Court, its history, and its major decisions over the years. All in all, the works described in this section substantially assist the researcher who lacks a legal background to better gain an understanding of the U.S. judicial system.

Literature Guides

5-69. Benamati, Dennis C. *Criminal Justice Information: How to Find It, How to Use It.* Phoenix: Oryx Press, 1998. 236 pp. Index. ISBN: 0-897-74957-X.

This reference work seeks to incorporate advances in recent technology in terms of information gathering in the field of criminal justice; indeed, the preface states that researchers may no longer need to consult with a reference librarian or even enter a library building in order to fulfill their information needs. Despite that, this compilation still provides the user with reference to standard sources: abstracting services, indexes, statistical sources, government agencies, and the like. Many Internet sites are included. There is also a chapter on criminal justice information at the international level. Compiling a bibliographic reference source like this one in an age when technology is creating rapid change among sources is a difficult process, but this work should be of assistance to those doing research in regard to criminal justice.

Abstracting and Indexing Services

5-70. *Criminal Justice Abstracts.* Quarterly. Monsey, NY: Willow Tree Press, 1968–. Indexes. ISSN: 0146-9177.

At present, this indexing service presents approximately 1,600 abstracts annually on topics relating to criminal justice. Abstracts in each issue are arranged into several major categories: "Crime, the Offender, and the Victim," "Juvenile Justice and Delinquency," "Police," "Courts and the Legal Process," "Adult Corrections," and "Crime Prevention and Control Strategies." Coverage extends to books, journals, and publications of government agencies, some fairly esoteric. Although most are English-language publications, there are also occasional references to those in other languages, as the intent is to ensure a cross-cultural perspective to criminal justice when possible. Each quarterly issue includes an index of authors and another of subjects and geography. These cumulate in the final issue of the year. This final issue also includes a list of the journals abstracted through the course of the year. This abstracting service and its electronic analog (not seen) will be of interest to advanced scholars and professionals rather than to a more general audience. 🖳

Annuals and Yearbooks

5-71. *American Law Yearbook.* Annual. Detroit: Gale Research, 1999–. Indexes. ISSN: 1521-0901.

Published as a supplement to *West's Encyclopedia of American Law* [entry 5-80], this work updates the original set with articles on topics initially omitted and with articles on current happenings on the legal scene. For example, the 1998 volume includes articles on Ralph Abernathy and Sonny Bono, noting their deaths and indicating their contributions to the legal and political world. There are also articles on subjects such as "Endangered Species," "Freedom of Information Act," and "Labor Law." These help to update the parent set. There are two indexes, one of cases and the other of names and subjects. Otherwise, the format of this annual volume is very similar to that of the *Encyclopedia*.

5-72. *Supreme Court Yearbook.* Annual. Washington, DC: Congressional Quarterly, 1990–2001. Index. ISSN: 1054-2701.

This Supreme Court compendium is divided into four major parts. The first part is an overview of the most recent term of the Court. The second part is a more detailed account of some of the Court's major decisions, while the third part provides case summaries. These case summaries are divided into categories, such

as "Business Law," "Environmental Law," "First Amendment," and "Individual Rights." The final section is a preview of the upcoming term. In addition, there are several appendixes. One lengthy appendix provides excerpts from opinions. The others describe the workings of the Court, provide brief biographies of the current justices, and provide a glossary and the text of the U.S. Constitution. This work can be consulted by several levels of researchers. Students and interested citizens will find the introductory and summary materials written in an accessible fashion, while those individuals with greater legal background or a need for more detail can turn to the opinion excerpts for a more comprehensive treatment.

Directories

5-73. *American Bench: Judges of the Nation.* Biennial. Minneapolis: Reginald Bishop Forster and Associates, 1977–. Index. ISSN: 0160-2578.

Those researchers requiring biographical details on judges, as well as directory information, can turn to this volume. The work begins with a description of the federal court system, including addresses, phone numbers, and biographies of judges. The rest of the volume is devoted to a state-by-state description of the courts, including federal, state, and sometimes local. Again, the information provided usually includes addresses, telephone numbers, and judicial biographies. The biographies vary in length, and in a number of cases biographical information is lacking. The biographies concentrate on education and career activities. Each state section also includes maps with boundaries of federal and state judicial districts. A name index appears at the beginning of the publication; references here are not to pages but rather to the specific court system. Compared to the *Want's Federal–State Court Directory* [entry 5-75], this work provides biographies and a good deal of additional detail; *Want's* is perhaps a better choice for those researchers requiring organizational structures and briefer listings.

5-74. *Judicial Staff Directory.* Biannual. Washington, DC: CQ Press, 1986–. Index. ISSN: 1091-3742.

This directory is divided into seven color-coded parts. The first section, "The Federal Courts," is the longest of the seven and provides the usual name and contact information, including for staff members. Bankruptcy courts, U.S. Attorneys, and U.S. Marshals also appear in this section. The second section, "The Department of Justice," is a directory for key offices and individuals of that agency. The third section is an alphabetical list, by state, of counties and cities that includes census counts and appropriate circuit and district court indications. The fourth section provides maps of each state indicating jurisdictional boundaries. The fifth section is an index of judges, while the sixth section provides short biographies of 2,200 judges and core staff deemed of significance. The final section is an index to all individuals, some 17,500 persons as of 1999, listed in the volume. Compared to its competi-

tors, *American Bench* [entry 5-73] and *Want's Federal–State Court Directory* [entry 5-75], this directory provides access to staff members not found in the others, which concentrate upon the courts and their judges. 🖳

5-75. Want, Robert S., ed. *Want's Federal–State Court Directory.* Annual. Washington, DC: Want Publishing Company, 1984–. Index. ISSN: 0742-1095.

Utilizing a relatively brief format, this directory provides the reader with names and contact information for federal and state courts as well as very short listings for Canada. Most of the volume is devoted to federal courts. The listings here include federal judges and clerks, bankruptcy judges and clerks, magistrate judges, U.S. attorneys, places of holding court, vacancies and nominations, administrative law judges, and record centers. The usual contact information encompasses postal addresses, phone numbers, and fax numbers. Electronic access and addresses are included when they exist. The section on state courts is considerably briefer, with each state accorded a single page. The listings here include major judicial and executive offices. Organizational charts indicate how lawsuits and cases flow from one court to another. The final portion of this directory includes miscellaneous information, such as electronic access to federal court records, a federal government directory, a guide to the federal court system, and the like. Those researchers requiring biographies or staff listings can turn to the *American Bench* [entry 5-73] or the *Ju-*

dicial Staff Directory [entry 5-74], but this directory should suffice for those requiring only directory listings.

Bibliographies

5-76. Martin, Fenton S., and Robert U. Goehlert. *How to Research the Supreme Court*. Washington, DC: Congressional Quarterly, 1992. 140 pp. Indexes. ISBN: 0-871-87697-3.

Targeting an audience requiring basic introductory information in regard to researching the U.S. Supreme Court, this volume is divided into three parts. The first part describes search tools and secondary sources, such as dictionaries, encyclopedias, indexes, and databases. The second part emphasizes primary sources, including case law, statutory law, and administrative law. The items in these first two sections are either annotated or described in general. The final section is a bibliography divided into two portions. The first lists works on the Supreme Court and its powers and procedures, while the second lists justices alphabetically by name and indicates publications relevant to each. This bibliography section is not annotated. A set of appendixes provides background on nominations, very brief biographies, and a glossary. This volume can be used by high-school and undergraduate students but will be of value to more advanced researchers who lack prior knowledge of the Supreme Court.

Encyclopedias

5-77. Bessette, Joseph M., ed. *American Justice*. 3 vols. Pasadena, CA: Salem Press, 1996. 932 pp. Indexes. ISBN: 0-893-56761-2.

This three-volume set includes 843 articles that range in length from 200 to about 3,000 words. The arrangement is alphabetical through the three volumes. Typical subjects include "Banking Law," "Child Abuse," "Insanity Defense," "Probation," and "Sting Operation." Among the categories of articles are Supreme Court cases, federal legislation, the criminal justice system, individuals, organizations, types of crimes, historical events, and contemporary issues. Entries often begin with a brief definition and indication of significance of the topic. There are numerous cross-references to other relevant entries, and more substantive entries include a bibliography. A number of photographs, often of dramatic situations, accompany the text. Each volume includes an alphabetical list of entries in all three volumes and a similar listing of entries by category. The final volume includes a number of appendixes; among them are a time line, a glossary, a bibliography, listings of major Supreme Court cases, and the text of the U.S. Constitution. The contributors, drawn from the U.S. academic community, have written this work at a level accessible to high-school and college students alike.

5-78. Janosik, Robert J., ed. *Encyclopedia of the American Judicial System: Studies of the Principal Institutions and Processes of Law*. 3 vols. New York: Charles Scribner's Sons, 1987. 1420 pp. Index. ISBN: 0-684-17807-9.

The workings of the legal system are a mystery to many laypersons. This reference work seeks to explain the U.S. legal system to those readers not versed in the law. The arrangement is topical, not alphabetical, and the set is divided into six major parts, each with its own grouping of separate articles. The six parts are "Legal History," "Substantive Law" (such as criminal and family law), "Institutions and Personnel," "Process and Behavior," "Constitutional Law and Issues" (such as due process and free speech), and "Methodology." Within this framework, most separate articles number from about ten to twenty pages. The contributors are all scholars in their respective specialties and provide the reader with listings of cases and an indicated bibliography. Cross-references lead the reader to other relevant articles, and a table of contents appears in all three volumes. The final volume also includes an alphabetical listing of the articles as well as a general index, so several access points are available to the reader. There are no illustrations, and the writing, while as jargon-free as possible, of necessity requires close reading. For that reason, this set is more likely to be of value to experienced researchers (including many undergraduates) than to those looking for brief, basic information.

5-79. Hall, Timothy L., ed. *Magill's Legal Guide.* 3 vols. Pasadena, CA: Salem Press, 2000. 1019 pp. Index. ISBN: 0-893-56165-7.

Compared to this publisher's *American Justice* [entry 5-77], which focuses upon

the philosophical, constitutional, and historical aspects of U.S. law, this set concentrates more upon the everyday workings of the law as encountered by the average citizen. Altogether, the set includes 594 essays ranging up to 3,000 words in length and arranged alphabetically by entry. While some articles discuss issues, such as abortion and drunk driving, many others concern particular actions (arrest, divorce, bail, and deportation), and still others deal with topics such as "Common-Law Marriage," "Defendant Self-Representation," "Small Claims Court," and "Summons." Others describe legal terminology: "Statute of Limitations," "Torts," and "Wrongful Death." Numerous cross-references are provided, and more substantive articles include an annotated bibliography. Sidebars and illustrations supplement the text, as do a series of appendixes that provide background on important laws and cases, organizations, a glossary, and a bibliography arranged by category of law. This will be a welcome set for high-school and undergraduate students researching common legal topics as well as for laypersons investigating the law.

5-80. *West's Encyclopedia of American Law.* 2nd ed. 12 vols. Minneapolis/St. Paul: West Publishing, 2003. Indexes. ISBN: 0-787-66367-0.

As stated in the preface, this set "contains over 4,000 entries devoted to terms, concepts, events, movements, cases, and persons significant to U.S. law" and replaces its predecessor, *The Guide to American Law.* The arrangement is alphabetical through the first ten volumes. Each of these volumes includes its own bibliography and indexes of cases, names, and subjects; all appear at the back. Cross-references are indicated in uppercase within the text of the articles. Very complete legal citations are provided to statutes and cases. The set includes many sidebars and numerous color illustrations and graphics. Some volumes include a section entitled "Milestones in the Law," which presents very thorough documentation in regard to certain major court cases in U.S. history. The eleventh volume, entitled *Appendix,* outlines U.S. legal history and includes the full text of important documents, among them acts of Congress, speeches, and court cases. The twelfth volume includes a "Dictionary of Legal Terms," and comprehensive indexes of cases, names, and subjects. This set is a welcome replacement for its predecessor, although the complicated arrangement of material can be somewhat annoying to those first approaching this work. (Note: The new edition to be published in late 2004 was not seen.)

Guides and Handbooks

5-81. Barnes, Patricia G. *Congressional Quarterly's Desk Reference on American Courts.* Washington, DC: CQ Press, 2000. 301 pp. Index. ISBN: 1-568-02435-5.

Utilizing a question-and-answer format, this volume presents 595 pieces of information on the courts. The arrangement includes five chapters, titled as follows: "The Law," "The U.S. Constitution,"

"The Federal Court System," "State Constitutions," and "The State Court System." As the chapter titles indicate, state as well as federal jurisdictions are discussed. The questions address themselves to judicial history, forms and functions of courts, political processes pertaining to the courts, and legal terminology. A reference section at the back of the volume includes the text of the U.S. Constitution, sources for online decisions, the interpretation of court citations, a glossary, and a short bibliography. Other than a few graphic displays, there are no illustrations. Although the question-and-answer format is awkward, the index does assist in identifying specific topics, and the writing style is accessible to laypersons and high-school and college students alike.

5-82. Mikula, Mark, ed. *Great American Court Cases.* 4 vols. Detroit: Gale Group, 1999. 2644 pp. Index. ISBN: 0-787-62947-2.

While there are a number of other reference works that provide comparatively brief information on significant U.S. court cases, this set, with its multivolume approach, allows for greater depth of treatment of individual cases. Altogether, about 800 cases are profiled here. About sixty derive from state or lower level federal jurisdictions, but the rest are U.S. Supreme Court decisions. Fundamental cases from earlier times are included, but emphasis is on case law from the latter part of the twentieth century. The four volumes are arranged by broad topic areas: "Individual Liberties,"

"Criminal Justice," "Equal Protection and Family Law," and "Business and Government." Each volume is further subdivided by subject matter. For example, the first volume, "Individual Liberties," includes a section entitled "Right to Bear Arms," under which the reader finds descriptions of three key cases. Each of the subdivisions includes an introductory overview, and the text allocated to each case ranges from 750 to 2,000 words in length. Background, issues at stake, dissenting opinions (if any), and the impact of the decision are among the usual items discussed in each case. Sidebars provide additional information, and there are listings for related cases and bibliographies. The final volume includes an index and alphabetical and chronological listings of cases. The format is attractive and the text is suitable for both high-school and undergraduate students.

5-83. Knappman, Edward W., ed. *Great American Trials*. 2nd ed. 2 vols. Detroit: Gale Research, 2002. 1675 pp. Index. ISBN: 0-787-64901-5.

Approximately 200 significant and celebrated trials were selected for inclusion in this volume. The arrangement is chronological, but the table of contents provides access not only chronologically but also alphabetically and by subject. The first case dates from 1637 and 1638, while the last to be included was the Rodney King trial. The section for each trial begins with basic information of the "who, when, where, why, and how" variety. This is followed by a narrative text describing events leading up the trial, the trial itself, and its significance. Most also include a bibliography of articles and books for additional reading. A number of illustrations supplement the text, and the author has made an effort to avoid legal jargon and to appeal to the general reader. A glossary and an index conclude the volume. While it is unlikely that student researchers will be writing term papers on individual trials, many of the cases found here will be of value to those writing on subjects such as civil rights, education, family issues, racial issues, and the like. The text is suitable for both high-school and college students.

5-84. Biskupic, Joan, and Elder Witt. *Guide to the U.S. Supreme Court*. 3rd ed. 2 vols. Washington, DC: Congressional Quarterly, 1997. 1172 pp. Index. ISBN: 1-568-02130-5.

From relatively humble beginnings, the Supreme Court has developed into an institution of great power, one that in recent decades has worked to ensure individual rights. This set examines the Court in considerable depth. Altogether, the two volumes include six major parts. "Origins and Development of the Court," "The Court and the Federal System," and "The Court and the Individual" make up the first volume, while the second volume is devoted to "Pressures on the Court," "The Court at Work," and "Members of the Court." Each of these six parts is further subdivided into a number of components for easier access by the reader. Numerous sidebars and illustrations supplement the main narrative. Each of the volumes also includes a detailed table of contents for the entire set. Detailed endnotes appear throughout the work, and a bibliography of about ten pages can be found at the end of the second volume. There are indexes of cases and subjects, as well as lengthy appendixes that provide text of important documents and statistical and tabular data on the Court. The text is suitable for undergraduates, but this work will be consulted by more advanced researchers as well.

5-85. Johnson, John W., ed. *Historic U.S. Court Cases, 1690–1990: An Encyclopedia.* New York: Garland, 1992. 754 pp. Indexes. ISBN: 0-824-04430-4.

The 171 cases described here illuminate many aspects of U.S. law, politics, and policy. The court cases were selected through the application of several criteria. Some of the cases included are important precedents, others have achieved historical fame, some represent a particular body of litigation, and many discuss significant issues in the law. The volume is arranged into six major parts, focusing upon such broad topics as crime, economics, race and gender, and civil liberties. Within each of these six major parts, the reader finds additional subdivision so that cases treating the same subject matter appear together. Within these subdivisions, the arrangement is chronological. Essays are written by individual scholars and range in length from about 1,000 words to about 5,000, depending upon the importance of the case. The essays generally provide both a narrative to the background of the case as well as analysis in regard to its impact. Short bibliographies to key resources conclude each essay. Access to the text is provided by an index of cases as well as a second index of names and subjects. The level of writing is suitable for undergraduates, but this work can be consulted profitably by scholars as well.

5-86. McWhirter, Darien A. *Legal 100: A Ranking of the Individuals Who Have Most Influenced the Law.* Secaucus, NJ: Kensington Publishing/Citadel Press, 1997. 416 pp. ISBN: 0-806-51860-X.

In an effort to demonstrate individual impact upon the evolution of Western and Anglo-American law, the author provides biographies of 100 individuals influential in that respect. Most are lawyers, but there are representatives from other professions and occupations as well. Although some individuals profiled lived millennia ago, most are from the most recent two centuries. Many names will be familiar to readers, but there also biographies of those who might otherwise be known only to legal specialists. Biographies are usually three or four pages in length and include at least one portrait. There are cross-references to other biographies in the volume. The writing level is suitable for high-school as well as undergraduate students. The ranking of the individuals by the degree of their influence is of dubious value, but otherwise this book will be of use to beginning students needing a biographical approach to legal history.

5-87. Hall, Kermit L., ed. *Oxford Companion to the Supreme Court of the United States.* New York: Oxford University Press, 1992. 1032 pp. Indexes. ISBN: 0-195-05835-6.

Entries in this compendium are arranged alphabetically and include several categories. Biographies represent one category and include not only the Supreme Court justices themselves but also those whose nominations have been rejected, prominent lawyers who presented arguments before the court, and other key figures. A second category treats concepts of constitutional interest, such as due process of law and separation of powers. The third category describes the day-to-day operations of the Supreme Court, while a fourth category, that for major cases, numbers about 400 items. Interpretive entries represent yet another category, and here the focus is upon substantive national topics, such as abortion, censorship, race, and school prayer. Within this category is a series of chronological essays on the history of the Court that amounts to approximately thirty pages. The final category explains the vocabulary of the Court. Most entries are a half page or a full page in length and include cross-references to other relevant articles. More substantive subjects often include a short bibliography. The entries are signed by the contributors, who are members of the American academic community. Portraits of the justices accompany their biography, and access to the text is provided through an index of cases and another of topics. The writing style makes this work appropriate for un-dergraduates and other higher-education researchers. ⌨

5-88. Hall, Kermit L, ed. *Oxford Guide to United States Supreme Court Decisions.* New York: Oxford University Press, 1999. 428 pp. Indexes. ISBN: 0-195-11883-9.

The decisions of the U.S. Supreme Court have frequently impacted American society and politics. This guide presents significant cases throughout the history of the court. The arrangement is alphabetical by name of case. All cases receive at least a paragraph of explanation, and the more significant are accorded up to three pages. Citations allow the reader to refer to the original text if necessary, but the explanations found here, which discuss both the background and the significance of the case, will be sufficient for many researchers. Cross-references are indicated for other cases to be found in this volume, and there are indexes by both case name and topic. Other appendixes provide a glossary, the text of the U.S. Constitution, and chronologies in regard to Supreme Court justices. Most of the contributors are drawn from the U.S. academic community, but the writing style is suitable for the researcher new to the subject.

5-89. Wagman, Robert J. *Supreme Court: A Citizen's Guide.* New York: World Almanac Books, 1993. 342 pp. Index. ISBN: 0-886-87692-3.

As the subtitle indicates, this reference work targets an audience of general readers and nonexpert researchers.

Some of the chapters cover topics found in similar reference works. These include court processes, the history of the Supreme Court, short biographies of the justices, and summaries of major cases. Perhaps the most unusual chapter is that which deals with "The Supreme Court's Ten Worst Decisions." As the author admits, a compilation of "worst" decisions is necessarily subjective; still, this unusual listing will intrigue readers. Citations are included for those who wish to examine texts of cases in other works. A twelve-page bibliography will also assist those seeking other references. The major value of this work lies in its relatively brief history of the Supreme Court as well as its delineation of significant cases. Both will be of use to readers requiring an introductory approach to the subject.

5-90. Jost, Kenneth, ed. *Supreme Court A to Z.* 3rd ed. Washington, DC: CQ Press, 2003. 576 pp. Index. ISBN: 1-568-02802-4.

Among the several hundred entries in this volume are articles on justices, noteworthy cases, legal terminology, and subjects such as "Affirmative Action," "Child Labor," "Open Housing," and "Police Power." The arrangement is alphabetical, with most entries ranging from a page in length to several. Cross-references to other entries are indicated in uppercase. The table of contents assists the reader in gaining an overview of the volume, while a bibliography of approximately ten pages at the back of the work will lead the reader to other core re-

sources. Additional reference material includes listings of nominations and the text of the Constitution. A number of illustrations supplement the articles. Compared to Congressional Quarterly's *Guide to the U.S. Supreme Court* [entry 5-84] and the *Oxford Companion to the Supreme Court of the United States* [entry 5-87], this publication is more suitable for an audience that encompasses high-school students as well as researchers in higher education.

5-91. Epstein, Lee. *Supreme Court Compendium: Data, Decisions, and Developments.* 3rd ed. Washington, DC: CQ Press, 2003. 780 pp. Index. ISBN: 1-568-02592-0.

Most reference works dealing with the Supreme Court concentrate upon biographies of the justices or a narrative of the history of the Court and the issues that it has addressed. This publication has a different focus; it presents statistical data pertaining to a number of aspects of the Court. There are nine chapters, each with its own set of tables. The Supreme Court as an institution, its processes, outcomes, political and legal environment, and its impact represent the subject matter of several chapters, while other chapters address themselves to collective and individual data in regard to the justices. Each table cites a source or sources. These include both printed publications and databases. A bibliography at the back of the volume will also assist the interested reader who wishes to pursue particular subjects. A detailed table of contents and an index also help the user find specific topics within this volume, which will be of interest to advanced researchers rather than those just beginning to delve into the Supreme Court.

Presidency of the U.S. Government

The U.S. presidency is the subject of a vast literature, and even in the realm of reference works there are numerous choices. Martin and Goehlert have provided readers with volumes that are useful for both neophytes and veteran researchers who are just beginning to explore the bibliographic dimensions of this topic. There are also many choices among dictionaries and encyclopedias that assess the presidency and its many ramifications. Naturally, many are biographical in approach, with some devoting themselves to unsuccessful candidates, vice presidents, and first ladies. Other categories include campaigns, statistics, and even scandals. Finally, those who desire easy access to collections of significant speeches and historic documents have a number of different options.

Bibliographies

5-92. Martin, Fenton S., and Robert U. Goehlert. *American Presidency: A Bibliography.* Washington, DC: Congressional Quarterly, 1987. 506 pp. Indexes. ISBN: 0-871-87415-6.

A companion to these two authors' *American Presidents: A Bibliography* [entry 5-93], which focuses upon the individual presidents, this work takes as its subject the office of the presidency. Most of the listings pertain to mono-graphs, journal articles, and dissertations; inclusion of popular literature is much more selective. Federal government documents were omitted. The arrangement is topical, with chapters on subjects such as the media, foreign affairs, domestic and economic policy, and elections, among a number of others. There are no annotations. All entries are in the English language and were published from 1885 to 1986. There are separate indexes by author and by subject. Although this bibliography, which contains over 8,000 listings, is now a number of years old, it still serves as an access point for scholarly researchers who are seeking literature published in the era before computers.

5-93. Martin, Fenton S., and Robert U. Goehlert. *American Presidents: A Bibliography.* Washington, DC: Congressional Quarterly, 1987. 756 pp. Indexes. ISBN: 0-871-87416-4.

A companion to *American Presidency: A Bibliography* [entry 5-92], this work follows much the same format, differing in the fact that it discusses the individual presidents and their administrations rather than focusing upon the presidential office as an institution. According to the introduction, items selected for inclusion were "analytical, scholarly, and not merely descriptive." Hence, most of the entries represent monographs, journals, and dissertations. The arrangement is chronological, beginning with George Washington and ending with Ronald Reagan; the vast majority of citations are to items published from 1885 to 1986.

Each presidential section includes categories for "Biographies," "Private Life," "Public Career," "Presidential Years," and "Writings." In the instance of more significant presidents, the section on "Presidential Years" includes a categorization by topics of interest during that administration. No annotations are provided. There are separate indexes by author and by subject. This bibliography will be of use both to undergraduates and to more advanced researchers.

5-94. Martin, Fenton S., and Robert U. Goehlert. *How to Research the Presidency.* Washington, DC: Congressional Quarterly, 1996. 134 pp. Index. ISBN: 1-568-02029-5.

This short book provides a useful introduction to beginning researchers tackling the topic of the presidency. There are three parts to the volume. The first examines secondary sources and search tools, including such familiar items as almanacs, handbooks, and newsmagazines. Electronic resources are also described. The second part concentrates upon primary sources, such as the various official publications of the president, political party platforms, archival sources, and case law. Items in these first two parts receive annotations designed to be readily understood by all readers. The final part, an extensive bibliography on the presidency and the individual presidents, makes up about half the volume. Listings in this part do not receive annotations. Among the topics covered are presidential powers, the executive branch, and presidential selection, as well as separate listings for each of the presidents. Advanced scholars will probably need a more comprehensive approach than is available here.

Encyclopedias

5-95. Magill, Frank N., ed. *The American Presidents: The Office and the Men.* rev. ed. 3 vols. Danbury, CT: Grolier Educational Corporation, 1989. Index. ISBN: 0-717-27166-8.

Among the number of reference works dealing with the American presidents, this set recommends itself to students more than to specialists. Each president from Washington through the first George Bush is accorded an encyclopedia-length article that concentrates on discussion of the important happenings during each administration, along with an assessment of the personal and political contributions of each president. A brief bibliography at the end of each article points the reader toward major secondary and primary sources. A portrait of each president and other illustrations are scattered throughout the text. Articles are signed, and the affiliation of each contributor is listed at the beginning of the first volume; unfortunately, no other indication of the contributor's expertise is given. The third volume concludes with an index to all three. High-school and college students requiring a basic, accessible biography of a president can be directed to this set.

5-96. Levy, Leonard W., and Louis Fisher, eds. *Encyclopedia of the American Presidency.* 4 vols. New York: Simon and Schuster, 1994. 1827 pp. Indexes. ISBN: 0-132-75983-7.

The U.S. presidency is perhaps the most important office in contemporary world affairs. This encyclopedia discusses the presidency in depth from its beginning to the present. The set includes over 1,000 articles arranged alphabetically and ranging in length from several paragraphs to several pages. General categories of topics include biographies of all the presidents and significant other individuals, the powers of the office, the roles of the president, the relationship of the office with Congress and the judiciary, public policies, and the president as party leader, among others. Cross-references are indicated in uppercase, and short bibliographies are provided with each article. The contributors are drawn from the ranks of American scholars and include historians, political scientists, economists, and other experts in the field. An appendix in the final volume includes the text of the U.S. Constitution. The final volume also includes several tables outlining the structure of the individual presidencies and a synoptic outline of the contents of the encyclopedia. There are two indexes, one of cases and one a general index. The writing style is suitable for undergraduates and for more advanced researchers, and this set can be recommended to all those needing reasonably detailed information on the presidency.

5-97. Nelson, Michael, ed. *Guide to the Presidency*. 3rd ed. 2 vols. Washington, DC: CQ Press, 2002. 1764 pp. Index. ISBN: 1-568-02714-1.

The arrangement of this set is a bit unorthodox compared to most reference books. Rather than an alphabetical arrangement of articles, the contents more closely resemble that of a highly detailed textbook. There are seven parts to the two volumes, with each part containing several chapters. The parts deal with the "Origins and Development of the Presidency," "Selection and Removal of the President," "Powers of the Presidency," "The President, the Public, and the Parties," "The White House and the Executive Branch," "Chief Executive and Federal Government," and "Biographies of the Presidents and Vice Presidents." In addition, a series of appendixes provides the full text of a number of relevant documents as well as tables and graphs pertaining to the presidential office. The chapters within each part provide a good deal of detail regarding their specific topics. Numerous photographs enliven the text. Each volume includes an index to the entire set. Compared to the *Encyclopedia of the American Presidency* [entry 5-96], this set is somewhat less detailed and perhaps a bit less analytical in its approach and therefore might be more approachable by high-school students and beginning undergraduates.

5-98. Havel, James T., ed. *U.S. Presidential Candidates in the Elections: A Biographical and Historical Guide*. 2 vols. New York: Macmillan Library Reference, 1996. 1073 pp. ISBN: 0-028-97134-5.

Havel takes a somewhat unusual approach to the topic of presidential candidates and elections. The first volume of this set is devoted to Who's Who biographies of all presidential candidates (including some who never actively ran for office) that the author could identify, including those from third parties. As a result, the reader can find here details about the lives of many otherwise obscure individuals. The biographies include parentage, spouse, career activities, and political activities, with information as to the individual's candidacy placed in boldface. The second volume is a listing of election results from 1789 through 1992. For each election, there is a listing of the candidates and election results. As time advances from election to election, detail increases with the number of parties involved. Whenever possible, platforms are given for all parties.

Guides and Handbooks

5-99. Whitney, Gleaves, ed. *American Presidents: Farewell Messages to the Nation, 1796–2001.* Lanham, MD: Lexington Books, 2003. ISBN: 0-739-10393-8.

This work is a compilation of former U.S. presidents and their respective farewell addresses. There are actually three different types of farewell addresses included here. There are the formal farewell addresses to the nation as a whole, final annual messages to the Congress, and other addresses that served as a farewell message intended for "significant" audiences. Nine formal presidential addresses are included in this work. Collectively, they do indeed provide an interesting perspective of American history.

5-100. Bush, Gregory, ed. *Campaign Speeches of American Presidential Candidates, 1948–1984.* rev. ed. New York: Frederick Ungar Publishing, 1985. 343 pp. ISBN: 0-804-41137-9.

Asserting that campaign speeches by presidential candidates receive little attention due to the advance of televised political advertising, Bush presents here a selection of speeches that provide the interested reader with an overview of campaign rhetoric in the decades following World War II. The arrangement is chronological by campaign. Candidates from the two major parties are represented by two speeches apiece. Significant third-party candidates are represented by a single speech. Each campaign receives introductory comments by Bush that help to place the speeches in context. The editor admits that many speeches are simplistic in tone, but believes that researchers who consult this volume can trace themes on major subjects such as civil rights, defense, and government spending through many years of rhetorical attention and analysis. An earlier edition embraces speeches from 1928 through 1972 and is worth continued use despite the overlap between the two.

5-101. Nelson, Michael, ed. *Historic Documents on the Presidency: 1776–1989.* Washington, DC: Congressional Quarterly, 1989. 528 pp. Index. ISBN: 0-871-87518-7.

Almost seventy-five documents are reproduced here, beginning with the Declaration of Independence and concluding with the inaugural speech of George Bush in 1989. The documents were selected to illustrate significant activities of individual presidents and the institutional development of the presidency. For that reason, the documents demonstrate interactions with the Supreme Court and Congress, the evolution of the president's power, and the president's activities as commander in chief, chief diplomat, and chief legislator. Each document receives an introduction that places it in context. The index leads readers to particular topics. Regrettably, there are no bibliographic references; on the other hand, this work serves students as a useful documentary introduction to the institutional history of the presidency. Researchers may also wish to consult a companion volume, *Historic Documents on Presidential Elections, 1787–1988* [entry 5-184].

5-102. Nelson, Michael, ed. *The Presidency A to Z.* 3rd ed. Washington, DC: CQ Press, 2003. 603 pp. ISBN: 1-568-02803-2.

Over 300 entries give biographical information on each of the presidents as well as information on the powers of the presidency. This work also provides election results and examines presidential relations with the Supreme Court, Congress, the political parties, media, and civil service. Each president's major policy initiatives have also been highlighted. Altogether, this is a helpful brief overview for the beginning student.

5-103. Justice, Keith L., comp. *Presidents, Vice-Presidents, Cabinet Members, Supreme Court Justices, 1789–2003: Vital and Official Data.* Jefferson, NC: McFarland, 2003. 297 pp. Index. ISBN: 0-786-41044-2.

Strictly a listing lacking biographical narratives, this volume nevertheless is a very handy source for dates for and names of key officials in every administration through the beginning of that of George W. Bush. Among the groupings of information are "Presidential Succession," "Vice Presidential Succession," and "Cabinet Succession." Several appendixes provide other interesting components of presidential officialdom, including a listing of women in the cabinet. The inclusion of Supreme Court appointees helps to round out this work, a real time saver for researchers requiring this information for more than one administration.

5-104. Ragsdale, Lyn. *Vital Statistics on the Presidency: Washington to Clinton.* rev. ed. Washington, DC: Congressional Quarterly, 1998. 464 pp. Index. ISBN: 1-568-02393-6.

This volume provides a statistical description of the presidency, emphasizing the impact of the institution upon its holders rather than the reverse. Such a presentation can illuminate patterns, change, and continuity within the institution. There are nine chapters dealing with subjects such as selection of the president, elections, public opinion, policy making, and congressional relations. Each chapter opens with a narrative that assists in an explanation of the statistical tables that follow. Sources for each table or graphic display are indicated. A six-page list of references is included. While there are many reference volumes that describe the biographical and political background of the various presidents, this work instead takes a quantitative approach to the subject. Although it is not likely to be consulted by beginning students, Ragsdale's volume will be a valuable compilation for more advanced researchers examining the office of the American president. 💻

5-105. Shields-West MacNelly, Eileen. *World Almanac of Presidential Campaigns.* New York: World Almanac, 1992. 250 pp. Index. ISBN: 0-886-87610-9.

Obviously aimed at a popular audience, this work introduces the reader to presidential elections from 1788 through 1988. Each election receives several pages of text. A portion is a narrative of the campaign, while the remainder provides information that might fall into the category of trivia. The latter includes symbols, slogans, songs, trends, and quotations. However, vote totals are summarized, and the user who reads through the entire text devoted to a particular campaign can certainly get an initial idea of politics of the time. A bibliography of several pages will refer interested researchers to additional sources. Not a first choice for graduate students and other advanced researchers, this book can instead be recommended to high-school and undergraduate audiences.

U.S. Constitution and Its Amendments

Recent high-profile controversies over the impeachment of Bill Clinton and the disputed presidential election of 2000 have quickened public attention in regard to the U.S. Constitution and its amendments. A useful compilation of constitutional texts, including those of the individual states, can be found in *Constitutions of the United States: National and State.* There are a number of encyclopedias and dictionaries devoted to discussion of constitutional law. Among them, the *Constitutional Law Dictionary* and its supplements and the *Encyclopedia of the American Constitution* and its supplements provide the researcher with multivolume and erudite treatment of the subject. Conversely, beginning students can turn to the *Constitution and Its Amendments* and the *Companion to the United States Constitution and Its Amendments: 1789 to the Present.* Other useful works discuss the origins of the Bill of Rights, proposed amendments and concomitant issues, and constitutional concepts both here and abroad.

Annuals and Yearbooks

5-106. *Constitutions of the United States: National and State.* Dobbs Ferry, NY: Oceana Publications, 1974–. Indexes. ISSN: 0572-8274.

As the title indicates, this publication presents current texts of state constitutions. Constitutions are arranged alphabetically by state, with constitutions for territories following the fifty-state array.

Each volume includes a title page indicating the contents. Brief notes accompany the constitutions and provide the reader with significant dates in regard to constitutional history within that state. The final volume includes indexes for all fifty states in regard to "Laws, Legislature, Legislative Procedure" and "Fundamental Liberties and Rights." These date from the 1980s. No other annotations or commentary are provided. State constitutions are often available through the Internet, but this set does gather reasonably authoritative texts for all jurisdictions.

Encyclopedias

5-107. Vile, John R. *Companion to the United States Constitution and Its Amendments.* 3rd ed. Westport, CT: Praeger Publishers, 2001. 308 pp. Index. ISBN: 0-275-97251-8.

Vile, a political science professor at Middle Tennessee State University, has written this volume to provide the general reader with an overview of the Constitution that is both detailed and nontechnical. An introductory chapter provides historical background, while the following chapters discuss the various articles of the Constitution and its amendments in a fashion that allows the reader to readily grasp the issues and contexts of these documents. Each chapter also includes a listing of important cases and a bibliography of useful books. At the back of the volume, the reader finds brief summaries of fifty important cases, a glossary, and complete texts of the Constitution, the Declaration of Independence, and the Articles of Confedera-

tion. While there are a number of reference works that provide greater detail and a more erudite examination of the Constitution, this book can be used by many researchers, including those at the high-school level, to gain an initial overview of the topic.

5-108. Cogan, Neil H., ed. *Complete Bill of Rights: The Drafts, Debates, Sources, and Origins.* New York: Oxford University Press, 1997. 707 pp. ISBN: 0-195-10322-X.

Feeling that there was no single place in which to find original texts pertaining to the Bill of Rights, Cogan here attempts to remedy that problem. Each of the ten amendments is accorded one or more complete chapters. Within each chapter, the reader finds excerpts from specific documents bearing upon a particular aspect of the amendment. The texts include drafts presented in the first Congress; proposals from state conventions; state and colonial constitutions, charters, and laws; and discussions of drafts and proposals that took place in the first Congress, state conventions, the Philadelphia Convention, and appropriate newspapers and pamphlets. Texts vary in length, with some relatively short and others more extensive. Within each grouping of texts, the arrangement is chronological. References are provided for those readers who wish to locate the complete document. Whereas most reference books devoted to the Bill of Rights describe and analyze the salient points of the various amendments in terms of past and present issues, this work allows the reader access to the documents and ideas that influenced those who drafted the Bill of Rights. Cogan intends his work for an audience of lawyers, judges, scholars, and the lay public. It will also be of value to undergraduates researching topics relating to one of the first ten amendments.

5-109. Palmer, Kris E. *Constitutional Amendments: 1789 to the Present*. Detroit: Gale Group, 2000. 716 pp. Index. ISBN: 0-787-60782-7.

As of the date of publication of this volume, there had been twenty-seven amendments to the U.S. Constitution. This book discusses all twenty-seven and also devotes a chapter to those amendments that have failed for one reason or another. Each of the existing amendments receives its own chapter; these average twenty-two pages in length. Each of the chapters begins with the text of the amendment itself. This is followed by an "Overview" that analyzes the significance and potential controversies surrounding that amendment. The rest of the chapter describes the evolution of the amendment in historic context, beginning with the eighteenth century and continuing into the present. Some amendments, such as the Fifth, are more complex than others and receive more extensive treatment. Each chapter concludes with a list of sources for additional consultation. Occasional illustrations, usually of individuals pertinent to the discussion at hand, accompany the text, and a number of sidebars provide further information. A detailed chronology, the text of the Constitution, a glossary, a table of law cases, and a bibliography of ten pages all offer further assistance to the reader. This helpful work can be consulted by high-school and undergraduate students alike.

5-110. Chandler, Ralph C., Richard A. Enslen, and Peter G. Renstrom. *Constitutional Law Dictionary*. Vol. 1, *Individual Rights*. Santa Barbara, CA: ABC-CLIO, 1985. 507 pp. Index. ISBN: 0-874-36031-5.

Hoping to reach an audience that includes general readers, practitioners, and academics alike, the authors of this work attempt to describe concepts, terms, and cases relating to individual rights in the United States. Cases were chosen if they were felt to be landmark decisions or if they were important recent decisions. The volume begins with an introductory chapter on constitutionalism. This is followed by five separate chapters describing cases relevant to the First, Fourth, Fifth, Sixth, and Eighth amendments. Within these chapters, cases are arranged chronologically. Each chapter begins with an overview and a listing of the cases, coupled with the concept that each case represents. Descriptions of cases are generally about two pages in length. The final two chapters describe "Equal Protection and Privacy" and "Legal Words and Phrases," respectively. Several appendixes provide the text of the Constitution and information about Supreme Court justices. An alphabetical list of the cases and an index help provide access to the text, which is more suitable for an academic audience than for high-school students. Undergraduate students doing research on individual constitutional rights will profit by consulting this volume. The second volume in this set is described below [entry 5-111].

5-111. Chandler, Ralph C., Richard A. Enslen, and Peter G. Renstrom. *Constitutional Law Dictionary*, Vol. 2, *Governmental Powers*. Santa Barbara, CA: ABC-CLIO, 1987. 715 pp. Index. ISBN: 0-874-36440-X.

Whereas the first volume of this set, described previously [entry 5-110], discusses individual rights protected by the U.S. Constitution, this volume concentrates upon the powers of the federal government. The initial chapter provides an overview of constitutionalism, while succeeding chapters describe court cases pertaining to the various powers. These chapters are entitled "Judicial Power," "Executive Power, Foreign Affairs, War Powers and Citizenship," "Legislative Power," "Federalism," "The Commerce Power," "The Federal Taxing and Spending Power," "State Economic Regulation and Due Process," and "The Contract Clause." The final two chapters describe important Supreme Court justices and relevant legal words and phrases. Each of the chapters dealing with powers begins with an overview and with a listing of the cases described in that chapter along with the concept that they illustrate. Court cases are arranged in chronological order and generally are about two pages in length. The authors attempted to include cases that were considered to be landmarks as well as

relevant cases of recent vintage. The writing style is accessible to general readers as well as to specialists, but this volume will be of greater value in academic libraries than in high schools.

5-112. Newman, Roger K., ed. *Constitution and Its Amendments*. 4 vols. New York: Macmillan Reference, 1999. Index. ISBN: 0-028-64858-7.

Although several reference volumes are devoted to the U.S. Constitution, this set will have its greatest appeal for novice researchers. The four volumes discuss the articles and amendments to the Constitution in consecutive order. The more controversial and significant provisions receive the most detailed treatment. Altogether, there are 165 articles, none longer than 2,500 words. Numerous sidebars, subdivisions within the text, definitions, and illustrations will all assist readers in interpreting the subject matter. The final volume includes an index to the entire set. The editor admits that the text is aimed at younger readers and seeks to render the Constitution understandable rather than to employ a more analytical approach. Still, this is a handy source for general readers, high-school students, and many undergraduates alike. More sophisticated researchers will want to turn to other works, such as the *Encyclopedia of the American Constitution* [entry 5-113] and the *Constitutional Law Dictionary* [entries 5-110 and 5-111].

5-113. Levy, Leonard W., and Kenneth L. Karst, eds. *Encyclopedia of the American Constitution*. 2nd ed. 6 vols. New

York: Macmillan Reference, 2000. 3164 pp. Indexes. ISBN: 0-028-64880-3.

The original edition, published in 1986, numbered about 2,200 pages, so this second edition is about 1,000 pages longer. The set seeks to interpret and explain the U.S. Constitution to the general reader lacking any legal or constitutional background. Articles are arranged alphabetically and are up to 6,000 words in length. Typical articles include "Abortion and the Constitution," "Capital Punishment," "Term Limits," and "Warren Court." Among the categories of entries are articles on important cases and significant individuals. Articles are signed by the contributors, who are professionals and scholars in their field, and short bibliographies often appear as well. The final volume includes the texts of the Articles of Confederation and the Constitution and its amendments, as well as separate indexes of cases and subjects. Articles reprinted in their entirety from the original edition and its supplements are indicated with dates, as is the material written specifically for the second edition; this new material focuses on Constitutional issues that arose in the 1990s. The mix of articles from the first and second editions and the supplements to the first edition is a bit distracting, but otherwise this encyclopedia is an excellent resource for both beginning students and more advanced researchers as well.

5-114. Mitchell, Ralph. *Guide to the U.S. Constitution.* 2nd rev. ed. Washington, DC: Congressional Quarterly, 1998. 106 pp. Index. ISBN: 1-568-02040-6.

The U.S. Constitution is a short document that has generated a vast and erudite literature. In contrast, this volume is aimed at students and laypeople who wish to consult the Constitution in regard to specific subjects. The first half of the volume provides historical background in regard to the Constitution and the Declaration of Independence. The second volume consists of the text of the Constitution and its amendments, followed by a detailed index. This index is the heart of this work, allowing the reader to search for a specific topic and then follow that topic to the relevant constitutional provisions. A glossary explains terms that may be unfamiliar. Those researchers requiring greater detail will turn to other reference works, but this guide is a good starting point for those new to the subject.

5-115. Maddex, Robert L. *Illustrated Dictionary of Constitutional Concepts.* Washington, DC: Congressional Quarterly, 1996. 335 pp. Index. ISBN: 1-568-02170-4.

There are a number of reference sources that discuss the U.S. Constitution, its amendments, and its sources. This volume is unusual in that it concentrates upon concepts common to constitutions around the world. The author provides a brief introduction that describes the development of constitutional theory from the ancient Greeks to the present day. The main portion of the text is an alphabetical listing of short entries in regard to terms, concepts, events, and individuals having an impact on constitution making.

Some examples of entries include confirmation, economy, housing, legislative branch, majority rule, privilege, secession, and war. Most entries range in length from a couple of paragraphs to an entire page. Definitions are accompanied by excerpts from individual national constitutions that aptly illustrate the definition or concepts. The author deliberately avoids discussion about whether the nations in question actually enforce the provisions in their respective constitutions. Occasional black-and-white photographs help make the text more attractive. The constitutions themselves provide most of the source material, but the author also indicates monographs and other works used to compile this volume. This is a handy starting point for both high-school and college students needing background on the general subject of national constitutions. 🖥

U.S. Politics and Government

Among the standard starting points for this arena are the *Almanac of American Politics* and *CQ's Politics in America,* both of which provide narrative information on congressional representatives and their states and districts. Dictionaries reflecting American political terminology and jargon are another standby; one of the better among these is the *American Political Dictionary,* edited by Plano. Three multivolume encyclopedias treat the U.S. political system in some depth for levels of researchers ranging from middle school to advanced undergraduates: *Encyclopedia of American Government, Encyclopedia of American Political History,* and *Encyclopedia of the American Legislative System.* A number of reference works present biographical information on political leaders past and present, with increasing emphasis upon women and minorities. In short, the beginning researcher has a wide array of reference sources from which to choose when investigating U.S. politics, its structure, and political landscape.

Annuals and Yearbooks

5-116. *Almanac of American Politics.* Biennial. Washington, DC: National Journal, 1972–. Index. ISSN: 0362-076X.

This standard source is arranged alphabetically by state. Each state section begins with a detailed overview of state politics, including information on the governor and the two senators. Information on the congressional districts and their representatives follows and includes election results, group ratings, key votes, and a photograph of the representative. Compared to *CQ's Politics in America* [entry 5-117], this publication has somewhat less information on the individual senators and congressional districts, but more information on the governor's office and the state political environment. Both publications are excellent, and both should be consulted by beginning students and more advanced researchers alike; the two publications complement one another rather than competing outright. (Note: The electronic version was not seen.) 🖥

5-117. *CQ's Politics in America.* Biennial. Washington, DC: CQ Press, 2000–. Index. ISSN: 1527-8913. Title varies: 1981–1998.

Along with the *Almanac of American Politics* [entry 5-116], *CQ's Politics in America* is a standby for those seeking detailed current information on members of Congress and their districts. The basic arrangement is alphabetical by state. Each state section begins with tabular information pertaining to politics and demographics, and also includes an outline map showing counties and congressional districts. Each senator and representative then receives a "warts and all" biographical essay emphasizing his or her political career, state or district politics, and appropriate information about the individual's place in Congress. There are also descriptions of individual districts with emphasis upon their political flavor. Brief statistical tables emphasizing election and voting information also accompany each profile. An invaluable resource, this work provides the reader with political nuances not often found in other reference books.

5-118. *Encyclopedia of Governmental Advisory Organizations.* Annual. Detroit, MI: Gale Research, 1973–. Indexes. ISSN: 0092-8380.

Government-advisory groups have been in existence in the United States since 1794. This volume provides descriptions of approximately 7,000 such groups, most of them active today. There are several major categories of these groups: presidential-advisory committees, ad hoc committees, White House and other coordinating committees, departmental and agency committees, congressional-advisory committees, public-advisory committees, consultative organizations and conferences, and interagency committees. The listings are arranged into ten chapters that reflect major areas of interest to the government, such as agriculture, defense, education, science and technology, and transportation. Listings include the history and authorization for each group, its program, its membership, and contact information. The latter includes phone, fax, e-mail address, and postal address. Among the appendixes is one that lists regional depository libraries and another that provides the text of the Federal Advisory Committee Act, which established the rules and regulations that govern these committees. There are also five indexes: personnel, publications and reports, a listing by presidential administration, a listing by department or agency, and an alphabetical and keyword index.

Directories

5-119. *Capital Source: The Who's Who, What, Where in Washington.* Biannual. Washington, DC: National Journal, 1986–. ISSN: 0898-6916.

A product of the publishers of *National Journal,* this publication provides directory information twice annually. There are four major sections. The first, on government, includes officials from the executive, legislative, and judicial branches of the federal government, foreign embassies, and state government. The next section deals with corporations, financial institutions, labor unions, think tanks, interest groups, and real estate. The third section, "Professional," incorporates trade and professional groups, consultants, lobbying groups, advertising and public relations firms, and law firms. The final section, on media, encompasses both broadcast and print publications as well as news services and the foreign press. Throughout the directory, most listings include a contact person, postal address, phone number, fax number, and a Web address. While much of this information can be found in other directories, this resource has the advantage of combining a number of areas that are often spread among several directories.

Bibliographies

5-120. Martin, Fenton S., and Robert U. Goehlert. *American Government and Politics: A Guide to Books for Teachers, Librarians, and Students.* Washington, DC: Congressional Quarterly, 1997. 204 pp. Indexes. ISBN: 1-568-02221-2.

The books that are included in this volume are those considered suitable for high-school students, but many can be used with beginning undergraduates as well. The volume is arranged into chapters that generally correspond to topics that appear in high-school government textbooks. Among the subject areas covered are the Constitution, civil rights, interest groups, political parties, elections, the three branches of the federal government, federalism, and public policy in several major areas. Several areas were excluded from consideration. These include collections of documents, certain classics in the field of political science, those works based on statistical methodology, high-school textbooks, and reference books. Annotations are brief and descriptive in nature. A short chapter listing fiction sources appears at the end of the volume; these listings are not annotated. Indexes by author and subject provide additional access to the annotations. This work will be of use not only to teachers working with political science students, but also to librarians developing collections in this field.

5-121. Weiskel, Timothy C., and Richard A. Gray. *Environmental Decline and Public Policy: Pattern, Trend and Prospect.* Ann Arbor, MI: Pierian Press, 1992. 224 pp. Indexes. ISBN: 0-876-50289-3.

Something of a hybrid, this volume grew out of testimony that Weiskel, who has a background in history and anthropology, offered a congressional hearing in 1988 in regard to the global environment. The work includes five chapters that discuss public policy, the history of environmental decline, environmental decline in the third world and in Africa, and future prospects. Most chapters include an annotated bibliography of relevant books, journal articles, and government publications. These bibliographies are highly selective; only about seventy-five items are included altogether. On the other hand, the accompanying annotations are quite detailed, usually at least a page in length. The annotations are descriptive rather than analytical. Still, this work does an excellent job of directing the reader to the most relevant literature on this subject as of the early 1990s. Indexes of both authors and titles are included.

5-122. Hollings, Robert L. *Nonprofit Public Policy Research Organizations: A Sourcebook on Think Tanks in Government.* New York: Garland, 1993. 217 pp. Indexes. ISBN: 0-815-30766-7.

As the subtitle indicates, this volume considers "think tanks" to be nonprofit public-policy research organizations; in addition, this title's definition of think tanks further restricts inclusion to those that are private rather than government-affiliated groups. The bibliographic entries are arranged into nine chapters, each with its own brief introductory essay. The chapters reflect specific topics, such as "Role in American Public Policy Making" and "Funding." Annotations range in length from a sentence to a paragraph. The author attempted to include all literature on the topic, including books, articles, and dissertations. Most have been published since 1960. A series of appendixes provides a directory to think tanks, including those associated with institutions of higher education. There are also indexes of authors and of major think tanks discussed in the annotations. While the directory information is now dated, this bibliography is useful for its compilation of literature on this sometimes ill-defined topic.

5-123. Olson, Laura R., comp. *The Religious Dimension of Political Behavior: A Critical Analysis and Annotated Bibliography.* Westport, CT: Greenwood Press, 1998. 150 pp. Index. ISBN: 0-313-28484-9.

The intent of this highly relevant bibliography is to offer guidance and interpretation to various works published in the area of American politics and religion. The compiler has decided to omit ethical concerns and issues of constitutional law. There is an interpretative essay entitled "The Religion Dimensions of Political Behavior" and an annotated bibliography including approximately 410 entries, each with extensive write-ups. The bibliography contains only journal articles and monographs. The overall arrangement of the bibliography is by author under main subject headings. There is an index.

Dictionaries

5-124. Plano, Jack C., and Milton Greenberg. *American Political Dictionary.* 11th ed. Fort Worth, TX: Harcourt College Publishers, 2002. 759 pp. Index. ISBN: 0-155-06867-9.

This eleventh edition defines about 1,300 terms, agencies, court cases, statutes, and issues that are pertinent to U.S. government. State and local government is included as well as that at the national level. Rather than an alphabetical array, the authors have instead chosen to arrange their work in fourteen chapters that roughly correlate to chapters that correspond to an introductory textbook on the subject. For example, there are chapters on the Constitution, party politics and elections, the branches of the federal government, civil rights, and major areas to which federal agencies devote themselves, such as agriculture and health. Each chapter begins with an alphabetical listing of definitions. The definitions themselves are about a paragraph in length and are followed by another paragraph pointing out the significance of the term being defined. Cross-references lead the reader to other relevant terms. Each chapter also includes information on important agencies, cases, and statutes relevant to the terms defined in that chapter. The back of the volume includes the complete text of the Constitution as well as an index. There are no illustrations or bibliographic references; nevertheless, this is an excellent dictionary for those studying the governmental institutions and politics of the United States.

5-125. Whisker, James Biser. *A Glossary of U.S. Government Vocabulary.* Lewiston, NY: Edwin Mellon Press, 1992. 261 pp. Index. ISBN: 0-773-49242-9.

Whisker, a faculty member at West Virginia University, compiled this dictionary in an attempt to establish precise definitions for U.S. politics and its terminology. He notes that usage among political practitioners generally ignores that of political scientists, exacerbating the lack of precision in the field. Rather than an alphabetical arrangement of terms, Whisker instead has chosen to group definitions by broader categories. Thus, there are twelve chapters ranging from "Ideology" to "Political Socialization" and including "Politics and Political Parties," "Public Administration," and "Civil Liberties and Civil Rights," among others. The definitions, evidently all written by the author, are usually a short paragraph in length. Each chapter concludes with listings and descriptions of relevant court cases, including the citation to the original refer-

ence. The index includes the usual alphabetical listing of topics, followed by a separate listing of cases. There is no bibliography, and Whisker does not indicate his sources. Although this dictionary is not without value, its idiosyncrasies, including the categorization of definitions by chapter, make it a less-useful source than it might be otherwise.

5-126. Shafritz, Jay M. *HarperCollins Dictionary of American Government and Politics.* New York: HarperCollins Publishers, 1992. 656 pp. ISBN: 0-062-70031-6.

This dictionary may be the most comprehensive of all those devoted to the field of American politics and government. It includes approximately 5,000 entries. Entries were chosen in part on the author's examination of scholarly journals, newspapers, and general periodicals. Terms of only historical interest were excluded. Among the categories included are biographies, court cases, federal laws, federal agencies, and slang. The arrangement is alphabetical; most entries receive a sentence to a paragraph in treatment. The texts of the Declaration of Independence and the U.S. Constitution appear at the back. There is no index, but an appendix includes a number of key concepts, each with a listing of pertinent terms defined in the dictionary. Illustrations and side-bars make this a more attractive dictionary than many. About half the material here first appeared in the *Dorsey Dictionary of American Government and Politics.* This is a useful source for those readers who need comparatively brief information on standard political and government terminology.

5-127. Hill, Kathleen Thompson, and Gerald N. Hill. *Real Life Dictionary of American Politics: What They're Saying and What It Really Means.* Los Angeles: General Publishing Group, 1994. 414 pp. ISBN: 1-881-64941-5.

Asserting that television has reduced the vocabulary of Americans and that politicians generally communicate to the electorate through television, the Hills hope to raise the level of thought and participation by defining terminology used by political figures. The arrangement is alphabetical, with most definitions one or two paragraphs in length. Rather than "official" terminology, the emphasis here tends to be upon jargon terms and catch phrases. Some examples include "Brain Drain," "Democratic Wimp Factor," "Friendly Fire," "Outsider," and "Reinventing Government." Occasional cross-references direct the reader to related terms. There are a number of appendixes, some reprinting important documents such as the Declaration of Independence and others providing directory information for government officials both elected and appointed. There are no bibliographic references. The greatest value of this work lies in its definitions of American political jargon in use during the latter half of the twentieth century.

Encyclopedias

5-128. Halsey, Richard S. *The Citizen Action Encyclopedia: Groups and Move-* *ments That Have Changed America.* Westport, CT: Oryx Press, 2002. 385 pp. Index. ISBN: 1-573-56291-2.

This encyclopedia lists over 150 organizations that have somehow succeeded in causing change in the U.S. legal system, societal values, or the overall political landscape. Entries include information about the individuals, organizations, and notable events that make up the history of the U.S. citizens' movement, and their attempt to raise the public's awareness of designated economic, ideological, or societal issues. Only groups that operated at the national level are included, so this leaves out local, state, and regional organizations. Also, global-action groups, like Amnesty International, are left out of these pages. Most entries are around one page in length, but over thirty-five articles have been designated as "umbrella" articles, and they are longer. The treatment is decidedly nonscholarly. There is an index.

5-129. Bessette, Joseph M., ed. *Encyclopedia of American Government.* Pasadena, CA: Salem Press, 1998. 4 vols. 896 pp. Index. ISBN: 0-893-56117-7.

This set, which is aimed at an audience of middle- and high-school students, also has application for neophyte undergraduates researching U.S. government. Altogether, there are 200 articles arranged alphabetically and varying from 500 to 2,500 words in length. Articles include such basic subjects as voting but also address contemporary issues and issues relating to justice. Some information appears in sidebars, and the text is also supplemented with numerous illustrations and graphic displays. Cross-references are provided to other relevant articles, and short bibliographies are included at the end of each entry. Examples of articles include "Antitrust Law," "Commerce Regulation," "Separation of Powers," and "Town Meetings." The latter exemplifies an effort to describe local as well as national political institutions. The final volume includes the text of the Constitution, a glossary, and a twenty-page bibliography, as well as a listing of articles by subject category and a comprehensive index. The contributors were drawn from the U.S. academic community; their emphasis is upon the practical workings of government rather than theory. Advanced researchers will probably prefer to consult more sophisticated reference works.

5-130. Greene, Jack P., ed. *Encyclopedia of American Political History: Studies of the Principal Movements and Ideas.* 3 vols. New York: Charles Scribner's Sons, 1984. 1420 pp. Index. ISBN: 0-684-17003-5.

Arguing that the first shared experience of Americans was political and that a single national culture had to wait until the original thirteen colonies united into a single entity, this set aids the reader in exploring the impact of politics and public life upon the history of the United States. The ninety articles in this set, which is paginated continuously throughout, average about fifteen pages in length and are arranged alphabetically with the exception of an initial article on the historiog-

raphy of political history. Typical articles include "Agricultural Policy," "Feminism," "Interstate Commerce," and "Transportation Policies." Each article concludes with an extended annotated bibliography highlighting core literature and a list of cross-references to other relevant articles in the set. There are no illustrations. Affiliations of contributors, all of whom are academicians, are listed in the final volume, which also includes a comprehensive index. This encyclopedia is now some years old and of course does not take into account historical approaches and events since the early 1980s. Aside from that caveat, it can be recommended to both students and specialists requiring thoughtful, in-depth introductory information to topics in U.S. political history.

5-131. Silbey, Joel H., ed. *Encyclopedia of the American Legislative System.* 3 vols. New York: Charles Scribner's Sons, 1994. Index. ISBN: 0-684-19243-8.

While there are many reference works that discuss the workings of the U.S. Congress, this encyclopedia differs from most in that it addresses the state legislatures as well. Articles are arranged in a thematic approach rather than alphabetically. There are six major groupings of articles: "The American Legislative System in Historical Context," "Legislative Recruitment, Personnel, and Elections," "Legislative Structures and Processes," "Legislative Behavior," "Legislatures and Public Policy," and "Legislatures within the Political System." Each of these major categories includes more than ten essays of article length, each discussing a separate component of the larger topic area. Articles are generally from ten to twenty pages in length. Coverage is historic as well as contemporary. Each ends with cross-references to other articles and an annotated bibliography. Each of the three volumes includes a complete table of contents for the entire set, and the final volume includes a comprehensive index. There are no illustrations. The contributors are drawn from the U.S. academic community. The writing style is thorough and erudite, but not beyond the comprehension of undergraduate students. This is a thorough source that can serve as a starting point for any researcher dealing with the U.S. legislative system.

5-132. Grossman, Mark. *Political Corruption in America: An Encyclopedia of Scandals, Power, and Greed.* Santa Barbara, CA: ABC-CLIO, 2003. 466 pp. Index. ISBN: 1-576-07060-3.

The 250 entries that ended up in this encyclopedia have been chosen on a selective basis. Political scandals and corruption entries lie next to ones on the history of political reformers, reform measures, and related court cases. Sex scandals have been eschewed. This A-to-Z work runs from ABSCAM to Zenger (John Peter). Many of the entries are on crimes, criminal investigations, political cartoons, and individuals. Entries average about one-half to one-page long and tend to be quite heavy on essential facts and dates. A few typical entries are "Boss Tweed,"

"Edwin Washington Edwards," "Teapot Dome Scandal," and others. The breezy journalistic prose makes this work perfect for general readers, high-school students, and lower-division undergraduates. There is an index and a bibliography.

Guides and Handbooks

5-133. Martin, Mart. *Almanac of Women and Minorities in American Politics.* Boulder, CO: Westview Press, 1999–. Index. ISSN: 1544-8614.

As the title indicates, this work is in almanac format, combining statistics and brief text to give the reader a snapshot of women and minorities in American politics. Six of the seven chapters are devoted to particular groups: women, African Americans, Hispanics, Asian Americans, Native minorities, and gays and lesbians. In general, the information in each chapter repeats for that particular group. Included are statistics and tables relating to officeholders at state and national levels as well as election statistics. Data for the local level is much briefer, with an emphasis upon "firsts." The section on gays and lesbians is considerably briefer than that for the other groups because self-identification only began in the 1970s. A final chapter provides milestones for other ethnic and religious groups. A bibliography at the back of the volume identifies additional sources. While this publication lacks a narrative structure, its listings of officeholders, election statistics, and numerous "firsts" will make it of value to those researchers seeking such information, which might otherwise be difficult to find.

5-134. Duffy, Bernard K., and Halford R. Ryan, eds. *American Orators before 1900: Critical Studies and Sources.* Westport, CT: Greenwood Press, 1987. 481 pp. Index. ISBN: 0-313-25129-0.

Of the more than fifty individuals profiled here, many are from the political arena and include such well-known names as Thomas Hart Benton, John C. Calhoun, Benjamin Franklin, Patrick Henry, Abraham Lincoln, and Daniel Webster. The format is the same as that for the companion volume, *American Orators of the Twentieth Century* [entry 5-135]; see that entry for a more detailed description.

5-135. Duffy, Bernard K., and Halford R. Ryan, eds. *American Orators of the Twentieth Century: Critical Studies and Sources.* New York: Greenwood Press, 1987. 468 pp. Indexes. ISBN: 0-313-24843-5.

Most of the fifty-eight individuals profiled in this volume are drawn from the ranks of politicians and include such prominent individuals as William Jennings Bryan, Dwight Eisenhower, Herbert Hoover, and Ronald Reagan. Articles are arranged alphabetically and present brief biographical information, but the major focus is upon the individual's rhetorical style and his or her effectiveness as a speaker. Each biography concludes with listings of primary sources, bibliographies of critical studies and biographies, and a chronology of major speeches. A glossary and a bibliographic essay in regard to sources for American public address conclude the work. There is an index by subject matter and another of speakers and speeches.

Contributors are drawn from the fields of communication and political science. Although the focus of this volume is rhetoric studies, it has multidisciplinary value for political scientists examining communication issues. Researchers may also be interested in the companion volume *American Orators before 1900* [entry 5-134].

5-136. Nelson, Richard Alan. *Chronology and Glossary of Propaganda in the United States.* Westport, CT: Greenwood Press, 1996. 340 pp. Index. ISBN: 0-313-29261-2.

This reference work defines propaganda broadly to include not merely the usual connotations involving political entities, but also other forms of advocacy, including public relations and advertising. The volume is divided into two major portions. The first is a chronology of events relating to propaganda. This chronology is 115 pages in length and often provides paragraph-length detail on the events described. The second half of the volume is a glossary, arranged alphabetically. Once again, most entries receive about a paragraph of explanation. There are numerous cross-references indicated in uppercase. An extensive list of references concludes the volume. The index provides access to the text. This specialized work will be of value to those scholars and undergraduate researchers dealing with propaganda as it occurs in government, communications, and public relations.

5-137. Wetterau, Bruce. *Desk Reference on American Government.* 2nd ed.

Washington, DC: Congressional Quarterly, 2000. 344 pp. Index. ISBN: 1-568-02549-1.

Answers to approximately 600 questions regarding the federal government are provided in this volume. Questions and answers are arranged into five major chapters: "The Government," "The Presidency," "Congress," "Campaigns and Elections," and "The Supreme Court." Within each chapter, questions and answers are then arranged by category; for example, the chapter on the presidency has sections for the first ladies and the vice presidents, among others. Answers are usually about a paragraph in length. When appropriate, cross-references are provided to other relevant entries. Each answer also includes references keyed to the source or sources for that answer. Many of the sources are other Congressional Quarterly publications. Complete citations and a bibliography appear at the back, and here the reader can also find the text of the Constitution. The organization of this reference work is obviously somewhat complex, so reference to the index will be necessary as a first step for most users consulting it.

5-138. Wetterau, Bruce. *Desk Reference on the Federal Budget*. Washington, DC: Congressional Quarterly, 1998. 344 pp. Index. ISBN: 1-568-02378-2.

The federal budget, and the process by which it is implemented, is undeniably a complex matter. This reference work is intended to fill a gap between those articles that appear in current media sources, and relate to specific budgetary issues, and scholarly articles that are beyond the understanding of most laypersons. The six chapters of this volume describe the budget, the economy, the sources of federal income, the sources of spending, the budget process, budgeting since 1933, and the federal role in banking. Rather than provide the reader with the usual narrative text, Wetterau instead utilizes a question-and-answer format. This can be a bit disconcerting; while some questions are obvious in nature, others appear quite narrow when taken out of context, for instance, "What first appeared in President Carter's annual economic report?" For that reason, most readers will probably benefit by beginning with the initial question in the chapter of interest to them, then working through the next series of questions and answers. Cross-references that are provided with each answer assist in the process of finding relevant information. Numerous graphic displays and tables help to explain the subject. A bibliography of five pages leads the readers to more esoteric sources. The writing style of this work is suitable for both high-school and college students.

5-139. Clucas, Richard A. *Encyclopedia of American Political Reform*. Santa Barbara, CA: ABC-CLIO, 1996. 346 pp. Index. ISBN: 0-874-36855-3.

Clucas compiled this reference work after becoming frustrated at the difficulty students often experienced in finding basic information on political-reform issues. As he states in the preface, "I limited my focus to reform proposals that seek to change either the structure or role of American government," avoiding narrowly defined policy debates. Most entries are relatively brief, ranging from a paragraph to a page, or perhaps two, in length. Typical entries include "capital gains tax," "federal-state relations," and "referendum." Each entry concludes with a listing of cross-references and a list of references. The latter are partial in nature; to obtain the complete references, the reader must turn to a lengthy bibliography at the end of the text. Although the information given here tends to be brief, it does provide a start for the beginning researcher, and the references lead one to more detailed resources.

5-140. Schultz, Jeffrey D., et al., eds. *Encyclopedia of Minorities in American Politics.* 2 vols. Phoenix: Oryx Press, 2000. 774 pp. Index. ISBN: 1-573-56129-0.

The two volumes in this set, part of the American Political Landscape series, divide four major minority groups among its volumes. The first volume discusses African Americans and Asian Americans, while the second is devoted to Hispanic Americans and Native Americans. Within this framework, the format for each group is the same. An introductory chapter is followed by a set of alphabetically arranged entries that average close to 150 pages in length. Articles in these sections range from a paragraph to several pages in length and include cross-references and a bibliography. Typical entries describe individuals, organizations, issues, and topics such as "Political

Leadership" and "Political Participation." Next is a group of appendixes pertinent to that minority group. Here, the reader finds the full text of significant documents, information on organizations, and tables that list minority members of Congress both historical and contemporary. Each volume concludes with a timeline and an index; these are duplicates of one another, allowing the reader to consult either volume to ascertain the contents of the other. The set includes numerous illustrations and will be of value to both high-school and undergraduate researchers.

5-141. Schultz, Jeffrey D., John G. West Jr, and Iain Maclean, eds. *Encyclopedia of Religion in American Politics.* Phoenix: Oryx Press, 1999. 389 pp. Index. ISBN: 1-573-56130-4.

This volume is similar in format to others in the American Political Landscape series. An introductory chapter provides an overview of the topic. Next, the reader finds an alphabetical array of articles on the subject of religion in U.S. politics; this section occupies close to 300 pages. Among the categories of entries are short biographies of individuals, court cases, and topics such as "Foreign Policy and Religion in Politics," "Liberation Theology," and "Social Justice." Many entries are relatively short, one or two paragraphs in length, but more significant topics receive a couple of pages. There are numerous cross-references, and bibliographies accompany each entry. Many illustrations supplement the text. The encyclopedia portion of the volume is followed by an appendix that provides full text of twenty-five significant speeches and documents, while briefer appendixes provide a listing of organizations and a timeline. The writing style is suitable for both high-school and undergraduate students.

5-142. Schultz, Jeffrey D., and Laura van Assendelft, eds. *Encyclopedia of Women in American Politics.* Phoenix: Oryx Press, 1999. 354 pp. Index. ISBN: 1-573-56131-2.

Approximately 700 alphabetically arranged entries appear in this volume, which seeks within its scope to be comprehensive. Some of the entries are biographies: suffragettes, feminists, antifeminists, and politicians are among those included. There are also entries on events, legal cases, concepts, and political issues. The latter include abortion, education, and welfare. Each entry includes a bibliography, and cross-references to related entries appear in boldface. Many entries, particularly those dealing with individuals, are brief, no more than a paragraph. Articles on concepts and issues provide greater substance and are often two or three pages long. An introductory section also provides historical context for women in American politics, as do several appendixes. These include the full text of important speeches and documents, statistical tables, organizations, and a detailed timeline. This work is a useful starting point for those students, high school and undergraduate alike, who need grounding in this subject.

5-143. Bickers, Kenneth N., and Robert M. Stein. *Federal Domestic Outlays, 1983–1990: A Data Book.* Armonk, NY: M. E. Sharpe, 1991. 294 pp. Indexes. ISBN: 0-873-32840-X.

Taking the position that distribution of federal dollars to congressional districts is a key component of the political scene, the compilers of this volume examined domestic outlays not only for the 435 congressional districts but also for the 50 states and major regions of the United States during the period 1983 through 1990. This approach allows for comparisons of spending categories among the constituencies involved. The statistical tables are presented in four chapters. The first indicates trends in outlays to recipient categories. The second displays recipient categories by district and year. The next chapter displays outlays for policy categories, while the final chapter indicates policy categories by congressional district. Programs are described in two appendixes, while two additional indexes provide supporting information. Essentially, this is a statistical compilation that will be of interest to those scholars and researchers dealing with federal domestic spending.

5-144. Stempel, Guido H., III, and Jacqueline Nash Gifford, eds. *Historical Dictionary of Political Communication in the United States.* Westport, CT: Greenwood Press, 1999. 171 pp. Index. ISBN: 0-313-29545-X.

According to the editors, "political communication is communication about politics and government, about or within political campaigns, and about or by politicians" (Stempel and Gifford 1999, introduction). Although political communication has been around for centuries, only recently has it been the topic of systematic research. The entries in this encyclopedia briefly discuss significant persons, organizations, events, and ideas pertinent to political communication throughout the history of the United States. The arrangement is alphabetical, with most entries ranging from a single paragraph to a about a page in length. Each includes a list of sources for additional information. A short bibliographic essay at the back of the volume will also lead readers further into the subject matter. Most of the contributors are journalism and communications professors in U.S. institutions. Although there are no illustrations, the writing style is suitable for undergraduates as well as more advanced researchers. The greatest value of this work will probably be its attention to the development and terminology of political communication.

5-145. Kurian, George Thomas, ed. *A Historical Guide to the U.S. Government.* New York: Oxford University Press, 1998. 741 pp. Index. ISBN: 0-195-10230-4.

As defined in this volume, the U.S. government consists of the executive branch and its agencies; the legislative and judicial branches are excluded. Most of the volume consists of an alphabetical array of articles describing the various agencies of the executive branch. There are also occasional articles on subjects such as "Advising the President" and "Women and the Executive Branch." Articles range in length from a couple of pages up to about eight. The emphasis is on historical activities of the agencies rather than upon their current mission and activities. Bibliographies are provided for most agencies, as are cross-references when appropriate. There are occasional illustrations, and agencies that possess seals have those seals reproduced at the beginning of the relevant article. The contributors are drawn from the American academic community and from the ranks of the federal government. A series of appendixes reproduce approximately twenty-five documents pertinent to the establishment of agencies within the executive branch and range in date from 1789 to 1993. The writing style makes this a suitable work for both undergraduates and more advanced researchers.

5-146. Austin, Erik W. *Political Facts of the United States since 1789.* New York: Columbia University Press, 1986. 518 pp. ISBN: 0-231-06094-7.

This volume seeks to compile data in regard to U.S. political circumstances in a modest format unlike the massive works often found in library reference collections. There are seven chapters: "National Leadership," "State Politics," "Parties and Elections," "Foreign Affairs," "Armed Forces," "Wealth, Revenue, Taxation, and Public Expenditure," and "Demographic Information." Each of these chapters includes several statistical tables, some quite lengthy, that compile relevant data pertaining to the topic in question.

Many of the tables compile basic data over the course of a century or more. As the titles of the chapters indicate, emphasis is on national rather than state or local statistics. Austin's work is now almost twenty years old, so your up-to-date information will have to be sought elsewhere; nevertheless, there is some value to having long runs of statistics in a desktop work such as this.

5-147. Schultz, Jeffrey D. *Presidential Scandals.* Washington, DC: CQ Press, 2000. 480 pp. Index. ISBN: 1-568-02414-2.

Those seeking scandalous episodes involving presidents or their major appointees need look no further than this book. "Scandal," as defined here, is "any action that was considered dishonest or a violation of propriety at the time of the presidency or that would have been considered as such had it come to light at the time" (Schultz 2000, preface). Scandals are arranged by presidency, beginning with George Washington and concluding with Bill Clinton. Entries range from a single page to several pages in the case of major episodes such as Watergate. Each presidential section concludes with a bibliography referring the reader to additional sources. Few presidents are untainted, although some of the episodes recorded here might more appropriately be labeled controversial rather than scandalous. Given the recent focus upon the misbehavior of Clinton, this volume provides both high-school and undergraduate students with a good entry point for shady episodes in the White House.

5-148. *U.S. Government Leaders.* 3 vols. Pasadena, CA: Salem Press, 1997. 934 pp. Indexes. ISBN: 0-893-56954-2.

Altogether, this set provides essays on 124 political and government leaders in American history, concentrating upon those most frequently examined in the curriculum. Among them are all the U.S. presidents, as well as individuals from the colonial era, members of Congress, cabinet officers, significant women and members of minority groups, and others with major impact upon the U.S. political scene. The biographies are ranged alphabetically through the three volumes. They average about seven pages in length, and comprise five elements. The first element provides birth and death information and a brief statement summarizing the individual's significance. The second component, "Early Life," describes that portion of the biographee's life story. The next component, "Life's Work," examines the individual's career, with emphasis on his or her achievements. The following component summarizes the contributions of the individual, while the final component is an annotated bibliography of important works by or about the biographee. These bibliographies will be useful in directing students to other core resources. All but eleven of the biographies found here have been republished from two other reference sets from this publisher: *Great Lives from History: American Series* and *Great Lives from History: American Women Series.* The eleven additional biographies represent individuals active in recent decades. Contributors to this set are drawn from the U.S. academic community, but the narrative style is suitable for both high-school and undergraduate students.

5-149. Stanley, Harold W., and Richard G. Niemi. *Vital Statistics on American Politics.* Biennial. Washington, DC: CQ Press, 1988–. 446 pp. Index. ISSN: 1534-4762.

Published biennially, this work is a useful resource for students and other researchers seeking to make sense of statistical data pertaining to politics. Stanley and Niemi, who were responsible for the 2003–2004 edition, state in their introduction: "our goal has always been to provide broad coverage that spans, whenever possible, a lengthy time perspective." Chapters cover such topics as elections, campaign finance, the media, Congress, federalism, and social policy, among others. Each chapter begins with a couple of pages of explanatory text that help place the numerous statistical tables in context. A twenty-page bibliography at the back of the volume leads readers to other core resources, including Internet sites, and the tables themselves have source notes. This publication is a good starting point for those needing introductory information or a grounding before plunging into more detailed political statistics.

Elections, Political Parties, and Public Opinion

The election process in the United States includes a number of components, each of which has received attention in the reference-book literature. The elections themselves are a focus of much attention.

Some works merely compile election data, while others provide some analytical background. Presidential elections have received an inordinate amount of attention, but interested researchers can also find works devoted to congressional, gubernatorial, and state election results. Political parties have played a central role in the election process throughout U.S. history, and several reference works delve into party background. Emphasis is of course on the major parties, but some reference works discuss third parties as well. Public opinion, as represented through polling, has been an important factor in political life during the latter part of the twentieth century, and several reference publications provide access to polling results.

Abstracting and Indexing Services

5-150. *American Public Opinion Index.* Annual. Bethesda, MD: Opinion Research Service, 1981–2000. ISSN: 0740-8978.

This publication serves as the index for a companion microfiche set entitled *American Public Opinion Data.* The index is arranged alphabetically by subject; the user finds the appropriate subject, under which are listed questions asked in one or more polling efforts. Abbreviations and dates accompanying the question can then be correlated with a listing at the back of the second volume that indicates specifics for the poll in question. These specifics include a citation for the name of the poll, a source from which information about the poll is available, and the date, sample size, method, and universe, as well as notes pertaining to that poll. Some of the surveys are national in scope, while others were conducted within individual states. Topics cover the gamut; some are political in nature, while others relate to more personal interests, such as "Sex" and "Shopping." (Note: The electronic version was not seen.) 🖥

5-151. *The Gallup Poll: Public Opinion.* Annual. Wilmington, DE: Scholarly Resources, 1971–. Index. ISSN: 0195-962X.

This series of volumes presents the findings of Gallup polls from 1935 to the present. Earlier years were compiled in multivolume sets. Since 1978, poll results have appeared in annual volumes. The basic arrangement each year is chronological. Both the questions and the responses are included. The index leads the reader to polls on a particular subject. One cannot help but notice that a great many more polls are conducted in the late twentieth century than was the case in earlier decades. In addition, recent years included much more analysis and demographic breakdown of results than was the case earlier in the century. By the late 1990s, the annual volumes also included results from CNN/*USA Today* Gallup surveys. These appear as a separate appendix and receive less analysis than the main Gallup findings. Although the multitude of volumes makes this set somewhat clumsy to consult, it does reproduce survey findings of this famous polling organization in a format that is readily understood by users at all levels. Earlier compilations

are listed below [entries 5-152 and 5-153].

5-152. *The Gallup Poll: Public Opinion 1935–1971.* 3 vols. New York: Random House, 1972. 2388 pp. Index. ISBN: 0-394-47270-5.

See entry 5-151.

5-153. *The Gallup Poll: Public Opinion 1972–1977.* 2 vols. Wilmington, DE: Scholarly Resources, 1978. 1334 pp. Index. ISBN: 0-842-02129-9.

See entry 5-151.

5-154. Smith, Tom W. *General Social Surveys, 1972–1994: Cumulative Code Book.* Chicago: National Opinion Research Center, 1994. 1073 pp. Index. ISBN: 0-932-13251-0.

This code book accompanies the database that cumulates the results of the General Social Surveys. The surveys have been conducted twice a year almost annually since 1972. Respondents are interviewed over the course of approximately one-and-a-half hours; those surveyed are "English-speaking persons 18 years of age or over, living in non-institutional arrangements within the United States" (Smith 1994, introduction). Questions are quite wide ranging, covering not just the usual political questions, but also questions dealing with employment, friendship, relatives, and religion, among many other topics. Responses for each question are shown and additionally are grouped by year. A final column totals the responses over the years. Altogether, there are approximately 800 questions. A number of appendixes assist the user who possesses technical background in sampling. Casual readers, such as undergraduates, should be able to derive useful assistance from consultation of this code book without having to resort to the data file itself. More advanced researchers may prefer to use the complete data. (Note: The microfiche and electronic versions were not seen.) 💻

Annuals and Yearbooks

5-155. Zuckerman, Edward. *Almanac of Federal PACs*. Biennial. Washington, DC: Amward Publications, 1986–. Index. ISSN: 0886-2567.

Earlier editions of this work included only those political action committees (PACs) that gave at least $50,000 to congressional candidates. Beginning with the 1996–1997 edition, coverage was expanded to include all such groups that contributed at least $5,000. For that reason, the coverage went from approximately 650 to over 2,400 PACs. PACs are arranged into six major categories: "Business," "Lobbying and Law Firm," "National Trade Association," "Labor Union," "State and Regional Association," and "Miscellaneous Interest Group." The final category is further subdivided into eleven groupings. These relate to such subjects as abortion, defense policy, the environment, and gun ownership. The PACs are arranged alphabetically within each chapter or relevant subdivision. Each listing includes contact information, explanatory text, and financial information. This data is arranged into two-year cycles that correspond with elections to the House of Representatives. In some cases, as many as five years worth of data is provided; in others, there may be only a single year. Explanatory text also varies in length from one PAC to another. The index provides access for those readers who are searching for a particular group.

5-156. *America at the Polls: A Roper Center Databook*. Biennial. Storrs, CT: Roper Center for Public Opinion Research, 1994–1998. ISSN: 1081-2644.

Initiated in 1994, this series provides an in-depth examination of presidential and midterm elections, drawing upon polls conducted by the Gallup Organization, and Election Day exit surveys of voters taken by Voter News Service. The volume is a combination of narrative analysis, statistical data, and graphic displays. Each issue discusses topics of interest to the particular election campaign in question. For example, the seven chapters making up the 1998 edition covered such subjects as the views and mood of Americans, the demographics of the electorate, and the role of money in the election process. Most of the contributors are members of the Roper Center or other individuals with experience in the polling industry. This work is attractively arranged and will be of use to all levels of researchers, from high-school students to scholars. Unfortunately, as of 2004 there appear to be no new editions.

5-157. *America Votes*. Biennial. Washington, DC: CQ Press, 1956–. ISSN: 0065-678X.

A publication long associated with Richard M. Scammon, this series has for many years provided a reliable source for presidential and midterm election statistics. Recent issues begin with introductory material that summarizes election results in a series of tables. The bulk of the volumes, however, are devoted to state-by-state data. State chapters begin with profile information listing the current governor and congressional members as well as tables that summarize statewide votes for president, governor, and senator from the 1940s to the present. Next, one finds a map with the boundaries of counties and congressional districts delineated. Tables detailing county and district voting data are then presented, and these are followed with basic statistics in regard to general and primary elections. Although election statistics can be garnered from other sources, this series represents a core resource, given its detail and the fact that it has been published over several decades.

5-158. *Congressional Quarterly's Federal PACs Directory.* Biennial. Washington, DC: Congressional Quarterly, 1999–. Indexes. ISSN: 1099-0097.

All federal PACs that contributed at least $5,000 to one or more congressional candidates during a particular two-year election cycle appear in this volume. The listings are divided into thirteen chapters, each representing a particular topic area. Some examples include "Agriculture," "Construction," "Health," and "Transportation." These chapters are further subdivided into topics; those dealing with subjects such as abortion, the environment, and gun control appear in the chapter entitled "Ideological/Single Issue." Within each subdivision, PACs are arranged alphabetically. Information for each includes brief explanatory text, contact information, and financial data. The latter usually encompasses the three most recent election cycles. An introductory chapter describes the development of the PAC system, and a series of appendixes provide rankings of PACs in a number of categories. There are indexes by geography, name, and sponsor/PAC. This publication is similar to the *Almanac of Federal PACs* [entry 5-155]; most researchers will want to consult both.

Directories

5-159. *Black Elected Officials: A Statistical Summary.* Annual. Washington, DC: Joint Center for Political and Economic Studies, 1997–. Index. ISSN: 1546-4385. Supersedes: *Black Elected Officials: A National Register.*

Beyond acting as a roster of black elected officials, this work also provides the reader with a certain amount of background information. The volume begins with a series of tables and figures that demonstrate statistical data for black officials. The bulk of the work consists of rosters arranged by name of state. The number of black elected officials is indicated, and brief background information is provided on the following subjects: population; federal congressional districts; state legislative districts; county and municipal government; and numbers pertaining to officials in the judiciary, law enforcement, school districts, and special districts. Names and addresses for officials from the federal to the local level are then provided. The index allows the user to search for individual officials when the name is known. This specialized source is most valuable for the fact that it provides names and information on all black elected officials regardless of level of government. 💻

5-160. *Election Results Directory.* Annual. Denver, CO: National Conference of State Legislatures, 1993–. Index. ISBN: 1-555-16741-1.

The title of this publication is somewhat misleading; rather than a compilation of election statistics, it is instead a directory of elected officials associated with state legislatures. Annual publication normally coincides with January in order to reflect results of November elections. There are alphabetically arranged sections for each of the fifty states. Similar sections for other jurisdictions, such as the District of Columbia and Puerto Rico, follow the state array. Within each of these sections, the reader finds basic contact information, including legislative addresses and phone numbers, as well as brief background regarding the political makeup of the legislature and other pertinent facts. Addresses and phone numbers for major elected officials of the executive branch also are provided. However, the major listing for each jurisdiction is that which indicates addresses, phone numbers, party affiliation, district number, and

gender for all state legislators by house. Newly elected individuals are indicated with an asterisk. All officials are listed by name in the index.

Dictionaries

5-161. Young, Michael L. *American Dictionary of Campaigns and Elections.* Lanham, MD: Hamilton Press, 1987. 246 pp. Index. ISBN: 0-819-15446-6.

Approximately 725 terms are defined in this dictionary. All were selected on the basis of Young's knowledge of the field or their use by scholars or political professionals. Rather than an alphabetical arrangement, the terms are arranged into seven chapters, each representing a particular category: "Campaign Processes," "Media and Politics," "Polling and Public Opinion," "Electoral Strategies and Tactics," "Parties and PACs," "Voting and Political Behavior," and "Money and Politics." The index consists of an alphabetical listing of all terms that provides reference to the chapter in which they are defined. Entries are generally one or two paragraphs in length and include cross-references to other relevant entries. A five-page bibliography directs the reader to other sources. Emphasis is on terms used in the latter part of the twentieth century rather than the entire history of U.S. politics. Given the fact that this dictionary is now nearly twenty years old, it is perhaps of greater value to scholars in political science and history than to students researching term papers.

5-162. Renstrom, Peter G., and Chester B. Rogers. *Electoral Politics Dictionary.*

Santa Barbara, CA: ABC-CLIO, 1989. 365 pp. Index. ISBN: 0-874-36517-1.

Rather than utilizing the alphabetical sequence found in most dictionaries, this volume arranges its definitions into seven chapters, each reflecting subject matter appearing in chapters in introductory textbooks on the subject. These seven chapters include "Political Culture and Public Opinion," "Political Participation," "Elections," "Political Campaigns," "Political Parties," "Interest Groups," and "The Mass Media." Definitions are then arranged alphabetically within each chapter. Definitions are usually several sentences in length and are followed by a separate paragraph explaining the significance of the term. Each definition is assigned a unique entry number; these numbers are important because they are used in cross-references. The cross-references appear with the definitions and include both the cross-reference itself and its entry number. This could be confusing to users who might assume that the numbers stand for page numbers. The index allows access to the entire text; again, index listings refer the reader to the entry number. Although the format of this work is a bit complex, it does provide the reader with definitions of many ideas, concepts, and legal cases relevant to the election process.

Encyclopedias

5-163. Shade, William G., and Ballard C. Campbell, eds. *American Presidential Campaigns and Elections.* 3 vols. Armonk, NY: M. E. Sharpe Reference,

2003. 1137 pp. Index. ISBN: 0-765-68042-4.

This encyclopedia has the virtue of including all presidential elections other than that of 2004. Each election is accorded about fifteen pages of coverage. Standard information for each includes a chronology, highlights of the campaign, vote data, a map of the United States displaying the states carried by each candidate, and several short primary-source documents. Sidebars, illustrations, and political cartoons enliven the text. The first volume includes several essays on topics such as the Electoral College, suffrage, third parties, and campaign finance, while the final volume provides appendixes and a twelve-page bibliography. The writing style is suitable for both high-school and undergraduate students. Any researcher seeking a brief introduction to a particular political campaign will profit by consulting this encyclopedia.

5-164. Moore, John L. *Elections A to Z.* 2nd ed. Washington, DC: CQ Press, 2003. 614 pp. Index. ISBN: 1-568-02801-6.

The 220 entries contained in this encyclopedia give a large amount of information on all aspects of U.S. elections as a political process and as an area of study. There are election terms, articles on the U.S. electorate, major and minor political parties, campaign finance laws, landmark court cases related to elections, and the like. There are also numerous charts, tables, graphs, and photographs. Entries contain cross-references to other related entries. There is an index and a bibliography.

5-165. Ness, Immanuel. *Encyclopedia of Interest Groups and Lobbyists in the United States.* 2 vols. Armonk, NY: M. E. Sharpe Reference, 2000. 786 pp. Index. ISBN: 0-765-68022-X.

Lobbyists are an important component of the governing process, and this reference work provides a detailed guide to the most significant groups among them. Altogether, there are entries on 197 interest groups, divided into thirteen sections. These sections describe such areas as banking and finance, media, health, agriculture, environment, and civil rights. Each of the thirteen sections begins with a general introduction of several pages, including a bibliography of significant sources. Descriptions of individual groups are about two to three pages long, and concentrate upon history, activities, and finances. In most cases, a bibliography leads the reader to relevant books, articles, and Web sites about that organization. The second volume includes an extensive array of statistics and graphical displays as well as a lengthy bibliography. This set is a valuable resource in a topic area where there are relatively few reference books; it can be used by both high-school and undergraduate researchers.

5-166. Kurian, George Thomas, ed. *Encyclopedia of the Republican Party and Encyclopedia of the Democratic Party.* 4 vols. Armonk, NY: M. E. Sharpe, 1997. 1864 pp. Indexes. ISBN: 1-563-24729-1.

The organization of this four-volume set is a bit complicated. The first two volumes deal with the Republican Party, while the second two volumes are devoted to the Democrats. Although format is the same for each two-volume subset, each has its own separate paging and indexes. For example, the first volume includes a detailed history of the Republicans, followed by discussion of their positions on individual issues, such as crime, drug policy, health care, welfare, and many others. This is followed by biographies of Republican presidents, vice presidents, and losing presidential candidates, as well as Speakers and other notables. Tabular information is then presented on Republican members of Congress and governors. The second volume includes information on conventions, texts of platforms, and election information, as well as appendixes that delineate details about the party. The second volume also includes indexes for subjects, biographies, geographical locale, and minorities and women. The third and fourth volumes replicate the first two, but with reference to the Democrats. Illustrations, cross-references, and bibliographies at the end of each entry assist the reader in understanding the subject. Contributors in general are political scientists from the U.S. academic realm. The text is suitable for high-school and undergraduate students alike; this set is valuable for compiling a large amount of information that otherwise might have to be sought in a number of different reference works.

5-167. Ness, Immanuel, and James Ciment, eds. *Encyclopedia of Third Parties in America.* 3 vols. Armonk, NY: M. E. Sharpe Reference, 2000. 816 pp. Indexes. ISBN: 0-765-68020-3.

This encyclopedia, a companion to the *Encyclopedia of the Republican Party and Encyclopedia of the Democratic Party* [entry 5-166], follows a thematic arrangement rather than the usual alphabetical array. Initially, the reader finds a set of essays describing the role of third parties in U.S. history and arranged chronologically. The next section presents a group of multicolored maps that indicate the percentage of total votes received by significant third parties by county and presidential election. Next, an extensive section presents narrative histories of over 100 third parties, including the Federalists, Anti-Federalists, and Whigs prominent in the early days of the nation. In general, these essays range in length from two pages to five, with a few parties receiving more lengthy treatment. Short biographies of individuals noteworthy in third-party movements make up the next section. A glossary, a twenty-five-page bibliography, and indexes arranged by subject, biography, and geographical locales conclude the set. Entries other than biographies usually receive a bibliography as well. Cross-references and occasional illustrations supplement the text. This work is suitable for both high-school and undergraduate students and provides greater depth of treatment on this subject than does the *Encyclopedia of Third Parties in the United States* [entry 5-168].

5-168. Kruschke, Earl R. *Encyclopedia of Third Parties in the United States.* Santa Barbara, CA: ABC-CLIO, 1991. 223 pp. Index. ISBN: 0-874-36236-9.

Kruschke, a political science professor at California State University–Chico, indicates that he has been interested in third parties for a quarter of a century. Here, he compiles background information on eighty-one such parties that are significant or representative of all such parties throughout U.S. history. Some are relatively well known: the Black Panther Party, Free Soil Party, Greenback Party, and the various Progressive parties. Others are more obscure but nonetheless intriguing: the Jobless Party, Poor Man's Party, and Straight-Out Democratic Party. The more significant entries receive several pages of text, while lesser known or less-important groups receive a few paragraphs. References to other books and articles are included with each entry. The arrangement is alphabetical, but an appendix gives a chronology indicating the foundation of the parties from 1823 through 1988. The writing style is appropriate for high-school as well as undergraduate students. Although information on some of these groups can be found elsewhere, this volume is a handy starting point for all levels of researchers.

5-169. Maisel, L. Sandy, ed. *Political Parties and Elections in the United States: An Encyclopedia.* 2 vols. New York: Garland, 1991. 1345 pp. Index. ISBN: 0-824-07975-2.

Approximately 250 scholars from a number of fields, including political science, history, and sociology, contributed to this work, which takes as its subject those aspects of American politics directly relevant to political parties and elections. The arrangement is alphabetical, with most entries ranging in length from a column to a couple of pages. Some articles, such as one on "Legislative Government in the United States Congress, 1800–1900," are considerably longer, however. In addition to articles on individual parties, political movements, and significant presidential elections, there are also short biographies of numerous individuals who have played a role in parties and elections. Cross-references are provided, as are listings of relevant books and articles pertaining to each article. The second volume includes a number of appendixes, most of which are rosters of officeholders or members of ethnic and gender groups. The writing style makes this work of value to an undergraduate audience as well as more advanced researchers.

Guides and Handbooks
5-170. McGillivray, Alice V., comp. *America at the Polls.* 2 vols. Washington DC: CQ Press, 2001. ISBN: 1-568-02058-9 (Vol. 1); 1-568-02604-8 (Vol. 2).

The first volume of this set reproduces presidential election statistics from Harding to Eisenhower, while the second volume encompasses the time period from Kennedy to the election of George W. Bush in 2000. Each volume begins with summary statistics showing state-by-state electoral and popular totals, pluralities, and percentages for each

election and each candidate. This is followed by sections devoted to each state and including data on each election. Among the pieces of information included are popular vote, Electoral College vote, and statistics for each county. The latter includes census population, total vote, votes by party, plurality, and percentage. Also included is an outline map showing county boundaries and names. A page of "Election Notes" explains complications resulting from third-party contestants in each state. Also included is information on primaries in each election cycle. This is a basic resource for researchers requiring county and state data for presidential elections from 1920 forward, excluding 2004.

5-171. Glashan, Roy R., comp. *American Governors and Gubernatorial Elections, 1775–1978.* Westport, CT: Meckler Books, 1979. 370 pp. ISBN: 0-930-46617-9.

Basic information on approximately 2,300 individuals elected to the post of governor in the United States over a period of two centuries appears in this volume, along with brief data on elections. Territorial as well as state governors are included. The information appears in tabular form and is arranged alphabetically by state. Information for each governor includes the following: name, date of birth, place of birth, date of assumption of office, age at assumption of office, party, occupation, residence, date of death, and age at death. Election information includes date of election, a tabulation of votes and percentage of votes by candidate and party, and voting totals for third-party candidates. Footnotes explain discrepancies in the tabulations. Quotations illustrating the thoughts of the various governors are scattered throughout the text. The volume concludes with a bibliography and a listing of sources for quotations. Although the information found here is brief, this volume does provide a quick source for facts about the American governors. For a description of a supplementary volume, edited by Mullaney, see below [entry 5-172].

5-172. Mullaney, Marie Marmo, comp. *American Governors and Gubernatorial Elections, 1979–1987.* Westport, CT: Greenwood Press, 1988. 103 pp. ISBN: 0-887-36316-4.

This volume updates a work compiled by Glashan a decade earlier and provides the same type of information in the same format. For a description of the earlier work, see the previous entry [entry 5-171].

5-173. Miller, Warren E., and Santa Traugott. *American National Election Studies Data Source Book, 1952–1986.* Cambridge, MA: Harvard University Press, 1989. 375 pp. ISBN: 0-674-02636-5.

This statistical compilation is based in large part upon data sets available at the Inter-University Consortium for Political and Social Research at the University of Michigan. In general, the volume hopes to analyze American elections and voter behavior. There are six chapters. The first examines the social com-

position of the electorate. The second focuses upon political partisanship, while the third sets forth voter opinions in regard to public policy issues. The fourth is devoted to attitudes of citizens toward government institutions and political figures, while the fifth chapter concerns itself with political participation. The final chapter assists in understanding and summarizing data appearing in earlier chapters. The intended audience for this work will be political scientists, graduate students, and other advanced researchers, all of whom will probably profit by reading the introductory material before plunging into the tables.

5-174. Utter, Glenn H., and Ruth Ann Strickland. *Campaign and Election Reform: A Reference Handbook.* Santa Barbara, CA: ABC-CLIO, 1997. 351 pp. Index. ISBN: 0-874-36862-6.

As is the case with other volumes in the Contemporary World Issues series, this work aims to provide high-school and college students with beginning information on a topic of current interest. An introductory chapter is followed by a lengthy chronology, biographies, statistical data and tables, appropriate quotations, a directory of organizations and agencies, and a long annotated bibliography that includes both print and nonprint resources. Among the important topics covered in this volume are those that deal with campaign finance, term limits, and efforts to improve participation by citizens in the voting process. The authors are both American political scientists. The introductory chapter and the chronology may be the most important portions of the work for those students seeking basic information on campaign and election reform.

5-175. McGillivray, Alice V. *Congressional and Gubernatorial Primaries, 1993–1994: A Handbook of Election Statistics.* Washington, DC: Congressional Quarterly, 1995. 352 pp. ISBN: 0-871-87899-2.

As stated in the introduction, this volume "details the Republican and Democratic primaries that nominated the major party candidates for Governor, Senator and members of the U.S. House of Representatives in each state." Similar information is also reported for the District of Columbia. The arrangement is alphabetical by state. Data for primaries for House members are reported only at the district level and include vote totals and percentages for each candidate. Data for governor and senator is more detailed, with reporting extending to the county level. Here, the data includes number of registrations, vote totals, and percentages of total votes. State maps with district and county boundaries round out the information. This volume has been superseded by Congressional Quarterly's *U.S. Primary Elections* [entry 5-194].

5-176. *Congressional Elections, 1946–1996.* Washington, DC: Congressional Quarterly, 1998. Indexes. ISBN: 1-568-02248-4.

Combining data obtained from the Inter-University Consortium for Political and Social Research and information appearing in Congressional Quarterly publications, such as *America Votes* [entry 5-157], this work presents a half century of election statistics for the U.S. Congress. An introductory narrative of almost sixty pages discusses issues and elections during that time frame. An extensive section on Senate elections follows. It includes names of senators, their political affiliation, their dates of service, and separate tabulations of election results and candidates. Both popular and primary vote returns are included. The final major portions deal with House elections. Because these elections occur more frequently and involve many more candidates, the data here is presented by year of election beginning with 1946. This portion of the volume also includes narrative details in regard to reapportionment and redistricting. A short bibliography directs the reader to other sources, both scholarly and more general in nature. There are indexes to Senate candidates, to Senate primary candidates, to House candidates, and a general index. While the election statistics provided here can be found in other sources, their compilation in a single volume is useful, as is the narrative outline of political events and major issues, which will be of special value to beginning students.

5-177. Brace, Kimball W., comp. *Election Data Book: A Statistical Portrait of Voting in America.* Lanham, MD: Bernan Press, 1993. 1026 pp. ISBN: 0-890-59011-7.

Brace's compilation differs from others

in that it reports election returns at the county level as well as the state and national, and combines its figures with demographic information. Each state, and the District of Columbia, is accorded a separate chapter. Each chapter includes as many as ten categories of information. Some pertain to population figures and voter participation and registration. Others show votes for president, senator, governor, and U.S. representative. Presidential primary returns are also shown. Each chapter includes an outline map of counties and districts as well as graphic displays and maps that assist the reader in interpreting election results. A number of full-color maps appear at the end of the volume, displaying and interpreting the results of the 1992 election nationwide. Thanks to its detailed election returns and use of graphics, this work recommends itself to those researchers requiring in-depth information.

5-178. Dubin, Michael J. *Gubernatorial Elections, 1776–1860: The Official Results by State and County.* Jefferson, NC: McFarland, 2003. 300 pp. Index. ISBN: 0-786-41439-1.

The information contained in this work is derived from three sources: legislative journals, original manuscript data, and published newspaper reports. The gubernatorial election results have been organized in a state-by-state summary. The main body is by election year and then arranged by county. Votes are then tabulated along with the percentage results. There is a candidate index by state.

5-179. *Gubernatorial Elections, 1787–1997.* Washington, DC: Congressional Quarterly, 1998. 183 pp. Indexes. ISBN: 1-568-02396-0.

Congressional Quarterly publishes a number of works relating to election statistics; this volume is useful because it summarizes election data for governors over a period of more than two centuries. There are several parts to the work. Introductory material provides general information and a listing of governors by state, including party affiliation and dates of service. The two major sections provide general-election returns from 1787 through 1997 and primary-election returns from 1919 through 1997. The data here includes year of election, names of candidates and their party affiliations, vote totals, and percentages of vote. The section that presents primary returns includes important third parties as well as the two major parties. Primary information extends through 1956 in the case of most states. However, in the case of the Southern United States, where politics was dominated by the Democratic Party in the first half of this century, Democratic primary data extends back to 1920; in effect, the primary replaced the general election in these states. There are separate indexes for general-election candidates and primary candidates.

5-180. Wilcox, Laird, ed. *Guide to the American Right.* Annual. Olathe, KS: Editorial Research Service, 1984–1999/ 2000. Index. ISSN: 8756-0216. Subtitle varies for older volumes.

The researcher interested in directory

information for right-wing organizations can turn to this volume for assistance. Many hundreds of organizations are included. The basic listing is alphabetical and includes an address and a brief characterization of the intent of the organization. As part of the latter, each group is assigned a two-letter code that indicates its major thrust. Some of the categorizations include "Campus Conservative," "Christian Right," "Gun Control Opposition," "Immigration Opposition," and "Tax Rebellion." Wilcox also provides an index that lists organizations by their zip code, allowing the reader to locate groups in his or her own locale. The volume concludes with a lengthy bibliography of items pertaining to the right-wing and representing pro-and-con points of view. Each includes a very brief annotation. This compilation by Wilcox presupposes that the reader requiring more information on a particular organization will use the addresses provided to contact the group itself.

5-181. Goldstein, Michael L. *Guide to the . . . Presidential Election.* Quadrennial. Washington, DC: Congressional Quarterly, 1995. 93 pp. Index. ISBN: 0-871-87855-0.

Written before the 1996 presidential election, this volume is aimed at citizens with the intent of encouraging them to participate in the process. Five chapters provide political context, information on the primary system, nomination, the campaign, and potential controversies both current and future. Numerous statistical tables and graphic displays provide the reader with information both past and current that is pertinent to the 1996 election. Each chapter includes a short annotated bibliography to both print and nonprint resources. A series of short candidate biographies describes potential presidential-office seekers, including some from third parties. If this volume is produced during every presidential election year, it should prove to be a useful resource for students needing information on election situations past and present.

5-182. *Guide to U.S. Elections.* 4th ed. 2 vols. Washington, DC: CQ Press, 2001. 1700 pp. Indexes. ISBN: 1-568-02603-X.

A massive work, this publication provides the reader with a single place to locate election returns and associated data in regard to U.S. elections from 1789 through the early 1990s. The major portion of the volume is divided into three sections. The first, almost 300 pages long, is a combination of text and tabular information relating to political parties, with much emphasis upon convention politics. The second section pertains to presidential elections, including electoral votes, popular vote, and primaries. The third section is similar in approach, with concentration upon gubernatorial and congressional elections. An appendix includes information relevant to the entire election process, including congressional leadership, congressional terms, U.S. population, and the like. There are indexes of presidential, gubernatorial, Senate, and House candidates, as well as indexes of gubernatorial and Senate primary candidates and a general index. Some of the data in this reference work was obtained from the Inter-University Consortium for Political and Social Research. In fact, the reader could probably find some of this same material in other publications of Congressional Quarterly, but there is an advantage to having it gathered in a single source. For popular voting returns for the U.S. Senate and the House of Representatives before 1913 and 1824, respectively, one must look elsewhere; see the entry for *United States Congressional Elections, 1788–1997* [entry 5-193].

5-183. *Handbook of Campaign Spending: Money in the 1992 Congressional Races.* Biennial. Washington, DC: Congressional Quarterly, 1990–1994. Index. ISSN: 1085-8059.

Complementing Congressional Quarterly's *Open Secrets* [entry 5-22], which profiles contributors to members of Congress, this work details how congressional candidates spend their money during political campaigns. The 1992 edition, for example, is divided into three parts. The first is a lengthy introduction to the world of campaign spending. The second and third parts provide specific information on Senate and House races, respectively. Within these last two parts, the arrangement is alphabetical by name of state. Each winning candidate receives a page of narrative text and statistics on campaign expenditures, including those of the loser. Campaign expenditures are divided into eight major categories: "Overhead," "Fund Raising," "Polling," "Advertising,"

"Other Campaign Activity," "Constituent Gifts/Entertainment," "Donations," and "Unitemized Expenses." Some of the major categories are further subdivided for additional detail. The narratives help to place the dollar amounts in context and to provide insights into campaign practices.

5-184. Nelson, Michael. *Historic Documents on Presidential Elections, 1787–1988.* Washington, DC: Congressional Quarterly, 1991. 902 pp. Index. ISBN: 0-871-87607-8.

Approximately seventy documents are reprinted in this volume, beginning with debates that took place during the Constitutional Convention and concluding with a debate between presidential contenders Bush and Dukakis in 1988. Documents were selected in order to highlight particular elections for the institutional development of presidential elections. There are a number of different types of documents, including party platforms, major speeches, debates, and items shedding light on third parties, among others. Some entries are quite lengthy; Jimmy Carter's interview with *Playboy* takes up twenty pages. Entries are arranged chronologically and begin with introductory text that places the document in context. An appendix provides tabular information on presidents, vice presidents, and presidential elections. The probable audience for this volume will be high-school and undergraduate students requiring original-source material in regard to the American presidency. A companion volume is *Historic*

Documents on the Presidency, 1776–1989 [entry 5-101].

5-185. *National Party Conventions, 1831–* . Washington, DC: Congressional Quarterly, 1972–. Index. ISSN: 1520-7978.

Nominating conventions have been a fixture of American politics since 1831; this publication describes all conventions for parties that received at least two percent of the popular vote in a presidential election. There are several parts to the volume. The first, and relatively brief, section describes politics before the convention system. The next section, on the conventions themselves, is by far the longest. It is arranged chronologically by election. For each election, there is a narrative describing the political context of each party as well as relevant excerpts from major planks in the party platforms. Detail for more recent conventions tends to be lengthier, especially in regard to platforms. A third section provides statistics on key ballots. Again, these are arranged chronologically and by party. A final section compiles information on parties and candidates. Particularly useful are the short narratives on third parties. A brief bibliography and an index conclude the volume. High-school and undergraduate students will benefit from this work, but it will be of value to more advanced researchers as well.

5-186. Schapsmeier, Edward L., and Frederick H. Schapsmeier. *Political Parties and Civic Action Groups.* Westport, CT: Greenwood Press, 1981. 554 pp. Index. ISBN: 0-313-21442-5.

Several hundred political parties and groups are described in this volume. Selection was based upon three criteria. First, those groups selected must have had a formal structure or existence. Second, the group must have engaged in activities with political implications. Finally, their activities must have had relevance to the national scene, rather than simply being local in nature. The result is eclectic: "John Birch Society," "Black Panther Party," "Bonus Army," "Brookings Institution," and "Christian Crusade" are some of the organizations that rub elbows here. The arrangement is alphabetical by name of organization. Entries range in length from a couple of paragraphs to a couple of pages. Cross-references to other relevant organizations are indicated with an asterisk. Most entries include references to sources for more detailed information. There are two appendixes. The first lists organizations by their primary function, such as business, civil rights, or reform, while the second is a chronology extending from 1765 through 1979. This chronology is restricted to simply listing the formation of groups by year. Because of its publication date, this work is now primarily useful for historical information on this subject.

5-187. *Presidential Elections, 1789–2000.* Washington, DC: Congressional Quarterly, 1992. Index. ISBN 1-56802-790-7.

Researchers requiring a single-volume approach to basic presidential election statistics can turn to this work. Included is data on the Electoral College, electoral votes for the president, popular vote, primaries, and nominating conventions. In the case of electoral votes, maps of the United States accompany the tables, allowing the reader to see the results at a glance. Popular votes and primary voting are shown to the state level, and, in the case of national elections, there are returns for third-party candidates. Percentages and pluralities are indicated along with vote totals. In some instances, explanatory text is included. Very brief background information is given for candidates, and those portions of the Constitution pertaining to presidential selection are reproduced at the back of the volume. Researchers requiring vote totals below the state level will have to seek out other sources; otherwise, this is a good starting point for presidential-election statistics.

5-188. McGillivray, Alice V. *Presidential Primaries and Caucuses 1992: A Handbook of Election Statistics.* Washington, DC: Congressional Quarterly, 1992. 294 pp. ISBN: 0-871-87890-9.

As the title indicates, this volume compiles statistics on the 1992 primary season. An initial section reproduces statistics at the state level for both Democratic and Republican primaries from 1984 through 1992, including all candidates. The bulk of the volume is devoted to a state-by-state listing of statistics for 1992. Basic information includes the date of the primary, registration, procedural details, total registration, total

vote, and percentage of total vote. These figures are given by county and by candidate. Pledged delegate totals are also reproduced. State maps indicate county names and boundaries. For those states not using primaries, the volume describes instead the caucus/convention system and delegate counts. This work appeared first in 1992 with the intention of publication during every election cycle. Similar volumes, *Congressional and Gubernatorial Primaries* [entry 5-175] and *U.S. Primary Elections* [entry 5-194], complement this work, as does *America Votes* [entry 5-157].

5-189. Powers, Roger S., and William B. Vogele. *Protest, Power, and Change: An Encyclopedia of Nonviolent Action from ACT-UP to Women's Suffrage.* New York: Garland, 1997. 610 pp. Index. ISBN: 0-815-30913-9.

Although their general focus is upon the United States in the twentieth century, the editors of this work maintain that nonviolence is an activity that can be found in many cultures over many centuries. Some examples, such as those of Gandhi and Martin Luther King Jr, are well known, but this work provides the reader with information on many others as well. Some examples include the gay rights movement, nonviolent action in Mexico, and the resistance movement in Tibet. In addition to episodes such as those mentioned, there are also entries for methods of nonviolence, organizations, individuals, and a number of related topics, such as conflict resolution, pacifism, and strategy. A topical list of entries that appears at the beginning of the volume will assist the reader in navigating the contents. Entries are a single page to several pages in length and include cross-references to other relevant entries as well as a bibliography. Print size is somewhat small, but this allows for greater detail than would be the case otherwise. Occasional photographs supplement the text. This excellent volume will be of value for undergraduates or more advanced scholars.

5-190. Thomas, G. Scott. *Pursuit of the White House: A Handbook of Presidential Election Statistics and History.* Westport, CT: Greenwood Press, 1987. 485 pp. Index. ISBN: 0-313-25795-7.

Utilizing a somewhat complex format, this volume presents statistics relating to presidential conventions, primaries, and elections from 1789 through 1984. The first six chapters arrange those elections into six time periods. Each includes an extensive narrative introduction, followed by statistical charts. The final three chapters discuss the participants, who are defined not only as major-party candidates; the major parties themselves; and the states. Again, these chapters feature a combination of text and statistics. In general, statistics for primaries and conventions are provided only for the major parties, and statistics for candidates exclude those who failed to obtain at least a few percentage points of the entire vote. Notes appear at the end of the volume, along with a brief bibliography. The value of this work lies in the fact that it does provide basic statistics on conventions, primaries, and elections alike; the disadvantage is a complicated format that may discourage beginning students.

5-191. Wolfe, Gregory. *Right Minds: A Source Book of American Conservative Thought.* Lake Bluff, IL: Regnery Gateway, 1987. 245 pp. Index. ISBN: 0-895-26583-4.

In essence, this is a bibliography and directory to the U.S. conservative movement. The volume is divided into three parts. The first part is a bibliography of writings pertaining to conservatism and arranged by topic. The topics not only include government and politics per se but also issues such as crime, urban studies, abortion, race, and education. Emphasis is upon items published after 1945. Entries are briefly annotated. This section is about 100 pages long. The next section, about sixty pages in length, presents biographies of significant conservatives from 1763 through 1985. The final section is a directory of journals and periodicals, think tanks, foundations, publishers, and relevant manuscript collections. This latter section is now obviously outdated, but the bibliography is still useful for its overview of conservative thinking, particularly in the period encompassing most of the cold war epoch.

5-192. Barone, Michael, William Lilley III, and Laurence J. DeFranco. *State Legislative Elections: Voting Patterns and Demographics.* Washington, DC: Congressional Quarterly, 1998. 403 pp. ISBN: 1-568-02200-X.

Demographic and statistical information in regard to state legislatures is less easy to find than the same data at the federal level, but this volume and two companion works, *The Almanac of State Legislatures* [entry 5-220] and *The State Atlas of Political and Cultural Diversity* [entry 5-221], assist greatly in providing the researcher with such information. A brief introduction precedes state-by-state data, with states arranged alphabetically. Each state entry begins with a narrative that briefly describes demographics and election and party trends throughout the state. The reader then finds recent election data and demographics listed separately for state senate and house districts. The demographic data includes average household income, level of college education, those households receiving social security, and population statistics for major ethnic groups. The tables are accompanied by eye-catching maps and bright colors. These show district boundaries as well as variation among urban, suburban, world, and mixed populations. The narrative information will be of value to all levels of investigation, including beginning students, but the statistical and demographic data will be of special interest to those researchers requiring detailed information on state politics. 💻

5-193. Dubin, Michael J. *United States Congressional Elections, 1788–1997: The Official Results.* Jefferson, NC: McFarland, 1998. 1005 pp. Indexes. ISBN: 0-786-40283-0.

This reference work supplements the various election resources published by Congressional Quarterly by providing popular-vote election returns to the U.S. Congress from 1788 through the fall of 1996. The arrangement is chronological, with each Congress receiving its own section. The returns for the House appear first and are arranged by state and district. The winning candidate is indicated along with his or her party affiliation, popular-vote total, and percentage of vote. The same information is provided for losing candidates. A statistical summary follows; it provides an overview of the entire House results. Popular returns for the Senate then appear and follow the same format. Information on runoff and special elections also appears when such contests took place. Notes and source listings are provided for each congressional section. Bibliographic information and indexes for political parties and candidates conclude the volume. This compilation will be especially useful to those researchers dealing with elections held in earlier epochs of American history.

5-194. *U.S. Primary Elections, 1995– .* Biennial. Washington, DC: Congressional Quarterly, 1996–. ISSN: 1525-1241.

Beginning with a volume covering primary elections in 1995–1996, this work succeeds two separate publications: *Presidential Primaries and Caucuses* [entry 5-188], and *Congressional and Gubernatorial Primaries* [entry 5-175]. The basic arrangement is by state. Each state section includes an outline map indicating boundaries of counties and congressional districts. Statistics on the various primaries follow. Data on presidential, senatorial, and gubernatorial races are detailed to the county level, but data for candidates for House of Representatives is only presented at the district level. In all cases, statistics indicate vote totals and percentages for both winning and losing candidates. An introductory section provides composite data for presidential primaries from 1984 through 1996 as well as convention ballots for 1996. This publication complements *America Votes* [entry 5-157], which concentrates upon general elections and historical figures.

State and Local Government

The number of reference works devoted to state and local government is reasonably extensive, although a certain number of those publications consist of directories that can now be supplemented by information available on the Internet. For those researchers requiring a bibliographic approach to publications about states, the two volumes compiled by Hellebust are excellent starting points. Publications of the Council of State Governments and Congressional Quarterly provide ongoing information on activities of state governments. Also highly useful is the *National Survey of State Laws,* which allows for comparisons among the states in regard to legislation dealing with potentially controversial issues. The volume by Maddex also allows for comparisons among state constitutions. Reference publications pertaining to municipalities are significantly fewer in number that those for the states;

among them, the standard is the *Municipal Year Book.*

Annuals and Yearbooks

5-195. Council of State Governments. *Book of the States.* Biennial. Lexington, KY: Council of State Governments, 1935–. 507 pp. Index. ISSN: 0068-0125.

A standard source for information on state government, this reference work provides the reader with a great deal of factual and statistical data. The first several chapters cover such subjects as constitutions, executive branches, legislatures, and the judiciary. The remaining chapters deal with elections, finances, management issues, programs, and intergovernmental affairs. The chapter on programs encompasses topics such as education, criminal justice, the environment, and highways. There is very little narrative text; chapters are composed of tables that generally provide data on individual states. There are two strengths to this work. First, it allows the reader to find specifics in regard to a particular state. Second, it allows for comparison among the states in numerous categories. The audience for this publication is likely to be more advanced students and researchers rather than beginners, although the data certainly can be of interest to general readers.

5-196. National Governors' Association. *Governors of the American States, Commonwealths, and Territories.* Annual. Washington, DC: National Governors' Association, 1950s–. ISSN: 1065-9552.

The basic arrangement of this unpretentious booklet is alphabetical by name of jurisdiction. For each jurisdiction, the reader finds a paragraph-length biography of the governor accompanied by tabular information relating to birth date, family, religion, party, date elected, and expiration of term. Photographs of each governor and his or her spouse are also included. The back of the volume presents tabular information in regard to political affiliations and terms of office, along with a directory of chiefs of staff and media contacts with address and phone number. The biographical detail provided in this volume is perhaps its strongest recommendation.

5-197. International City/County Management Association. *Municipal Year Book.* Annual. Chicago: International City Management Association, 1934–. Index. ISSN: 0077-2186.

The *Municipal Year Book* serves a twofold function. First, it is a scholarly resource for those researchers seeking analysis of recent trends and events in municipal government. Synthesizing information gathered for the purposes of the volume, contributors (most of them academicians) provide articles on topics such as workplace violence, performance measurement, and perceptions of women chief administrative officers. These articles are gathered into three sections annually: "Management Issues and Trends," "The Intergovernmental Dimension," and "Staffing and Compensation." Topics of articles of course vary

from year to year. Two further sections appear in each volume. The first is a directory of officials, while the second is an annotated bibliography. The directory is of mixed value; it includes all counties and all municipalities that have a population over 2,500, thus incorporating smaller cities not always included in other directories. On the other hand, the directory information is quite brief, including only a main phone number and names of several major officers. No addresses are included. The arrangement of the directory for both cities and counties is by name of state. Each annual volume includes a cumulative index that covers not only that volume but also those for the four preceding years. This work is always a useful starting point for those delving into the state of the art of urban government.

5-198. Beyle, Thad L. *State and Local Government.* Annual. Washington, DC: CQ Press, 1999–. Index. ISSN: 0888-8590.

Although the title of this reference work might lead the reader to believe that it includes state-by-state information, it is instead a collection of articles discussing comparative politics and common issues. The organization corresponds roughly to that of textbooks on state government. There are approximately ten major chapters dealing with subjects such as politics, the news media, legislatures, governors, bureaucracies, state courts, local government, and current issues. Each chapter includes two or more articles written by different contributors, and each article discusses a particular issue presently agitating state and local governments. This series is of use not only to those researchers investigating current state and local government but also to those who wish to examine trends over a period of time by consulting the various editions. (Note: The title before 1999 was *State Government.*)

Directories

5-199. *BNA's Directory of State Administrative Codes and Registers: A State-by-State Listing.* 2nd ed. Washington, DC: BNA Books, 1995. 432 pp. ISBN: 1-570-18002-4.

State regulatory sources are often difficult to use and expensive to obtain, either in print or through electronic resources. Regulatory and administrative codes have generally lagged behind state constitutions and statutes in terms of their availability through the Internet. Thus, this volume is quite helpful because it enables the user to identify the codes and initiate research. The volume is arranged alphabetically by state, and the District of Columbia and the various territories are included as well. Each state section begins with detailed bibliographic information that includes such data points as format, cost, contact information, and discussion of search aids and tips. Electronic access, if any, is indicated. This is followed by a table of contents for the entire code, enabling the reader to determine which section or sections might be relevant. Finally, there is a description of the state register,

which in most cases updates the administrative codes on a regular basis. An appendix provides search information in regard to opinions by attorneys general. While this source does not provide the full text of codes (a mammoth task), it is a helpful starting point for those researchers approaching this thorny topic.

5-200. *Carroll's Municipal/County Directory.* Annual. Washington, DC: Carroll Publishing, 1995–2001. Indexes. ISSN: 1093-2054. (Split into two separate publications with 2002 *Carroll's Municipal Directory* and *Carroll's County Directory.*)

As of 1999, this directory encompassed approximately 7,800 municipalities and 3,100 counties. The municipal portion is divided into two sections, one for municipalities with populations over 15,000 and the other for places with populations below that figure. The latter includes contact information for only the chief elected official. Municipalities over 15,000 receive more detailed listings, with the most complete information appearing for those places with populations over 25,000. Addresses and phone numbers are the chief components of the listings. The municipal directory also includes an alphabetical listing of executives and a geographic index. The section on county governments is somewhat similar. Again, counties with smaller populations (under 50,000) have a listing only for the chief elected and administrative officials, while counties above that level of population receive more detailed listings. Also provided are alphabetical listings of executives and counties. Although some of this information is available through the Internet, it is useful to have a single printed source available for consultation.

5-201. *Carroll's State Directory.* Annual. Washington, DC: Carroll Publishing, 1995–. Indexes. ISSN: 1093-2070.

This directory is divided into several sections. Initially, the reader finds brief listings for subjects such as governors, legislative sessions, and state home pages. This is followed by an alphabetical listing of all individuals in the entire volume, with their phone numbers and e-mail addresses. The next section is a state-by-state listing by organization and agency. This is followed by listings for each state legislature. The final section provides directory information for supreme and appellate courts, including justices, chief justices, and clerks of court. A keyword index encompasses the entire volume. In general, the listings provide phone numbers for individuals, and addresses, fax numbers, and Internet sites for agencies. As is the case with other print directories of government agencies, this work provides a single-volume source for information that otherwise might have to be compiled from a number of electronic sources and sites. 💻

5-202. Council of State Governments. *Directory I—Elective Officials.* Annual. Lexington, KY: Council of State Governments, 1998–. ISSN: 1521-7272.

One of three directories published by the Council of State Governments, this source concentrates on elected officials. The basic arrangement is by name of state or other jurisdiction, such as the District of Columbia or Guam. Each state section begins with such factual matter as a state's chief executive officer, legislative membership by party, term limits, and election dates. The state directory portion includes the major officials of the executive branch: governor, lieutenant governor, secretary of state, attorney general, and treasurer. The judiciary then receives a brief listing, focusing upon the court of last resort. The bulk of the directory is devoted to legislatures, encompassing both bodies. Directory information for all elected officials usually includes addresses and phone numbers. In some instances, the reader can also find fax numbers and e-mail addresses. National maps at the beginning of the volume indicate party control of governorships and legislatures. See the following entries for descriptions of the other two volumes [entries 5-203 and 5-204]. (Note: The electronic version was not seen.) 💻

5-203. Council of State Governments. *Directory II—Legislative Leadership, Committees and Staff.* Biennial. Lexington, KY: Council of State Governments, 1998–. ISSN: 1536-4666.

There are four major parts to this directory. The first, "Legislative Organization," is arranged by name of state or jurisdiction (such as District of Columbia or American Samoa). Directory information for each state includes address and phone numbers for the state capitol, and officers, principal staff, and committees for each legislative body. The second section, "Selected Officers," provides contact information for ten major officers, such as senate majority and minority leaders. This allows the reader to see at a glance officeholders in similar positions in all the states and jurisdictions. The format of this second section is repeated in the final two sections, "Selected Committees" and "Selected Legislative Functions." For example, the latter includes computer and library services. Thus, this directory provides the user with two major approaches to directory information, one by name of jurisdiction and the other by subject matter. The Council of State Governments publishes two related directories as well. Descriptions of the other two volumes in this set appear above and below [entries 5-202 and 5-204]. (Note: The electronic version was not seen.) 🖥

5-204. Council of State Governments. *State Directory: Directory III—Administrative Officials.* Annual. Lexington, KY: Council of State Governments, 1998–. 448 pp. ISSN: 1521-7264.

Unlike two other directories published by the Council of State Governments [entries 5-202 and 5-203], this source is arranged by function rather than principally by state or jurisdiction. The volume includes approximately 150 such functions, arranged alphabetically by name of function. Examples of functions include "Aging," "Banking," "Drinking Water," "Lottery," and "State Fair." Within the categories, the states or jurisdictions (such

as District of Columbia and Puerto Rico) are arranged alphabetically. Normally, each state receives only a single directory listing within each category. Typically, the directory listing is for the chief officer of the agency. The listing includes name, address, phone number, fax number, and often an e-mail address. This directory is especially useful for those researchers seeking major-agency contact information across all jurisdictions. One drawback is the fact that there is no subject index, so the user must browse through the table of contents to ascertain the names of relevant categories. For example, there is no listing for "taxation"; instead, the relevant category is "Revenue." (Note: The electronic version was not seen.) 🖥

5-205. *Municipal Staff Directory.* Biannual. Alexandria, VA: CQ Staff Directories, 1998–. Indexes. ISSN: 1092-4019.

This work provides directory information for approximately 80,000 officials in municipalities that have populations of 10,000 and greater. Altogether, there are approximately 3,000 such municipalities. The arrangement is alphabetical by name of municipality. Each listing begins with brief demographic and political statistics. This is followed by directory information for the mayor's office, city councils, and major city departments. Addresses are included only for the mayor's office in most instances; however, departmental information does include the name of the chief executive, his or her title, and a phone number. The directory portion of the volume is followed by a biographical section that includes brief background on approximately 600 of the individuals listed in the directory. The fact that so few are included among the biographies may be disappointing for those researchers preferring a more comprehensive approach. There are two indexes. The first lists municipalities by state, while the second is a listing of individuals by name, along with a phone number and a page reference. There are three major sections to the volume: municipalities, counties, and "Authorities." The latter is a general rubric for those local units not otherwise classified. Entries include chief elected officials and their staff, as well as other elected officials and departments. Listings are structured to indicate office hierarchies. The listings include postal address, phone numbers, fax numbers, teletype numbers, and e-mail addresses, if available. For elected officials, one can also find an expiration date for the term in office. Short background appears for major officials and includes education, occupation, and career information. Selection of a particular directory is a matter of user preference; this resource is nicely arranged and provides some details not always found in its competitors.

Bibliographies

5-206. Hellebust, Lynn, ed. *State Legislative Sourcebook: A Resource Guide to Legislative Information in the Fifty States*. Annual. Topeka, KS: Government Research Service, 1986–. ISSN: 0898-7297.

Unlike a companion volume, *State Reference Publications* [entry 5-207], which discusses state reference publications in general, this work focuses upon the state legislatures in some detail. The arrangement is alphabetical by state, including the District of Columbia and Puerto Rico. There are six major categories for each state: "Legislative Organization and Process," "Legislator Information," "Session Information," "Interim Study Information," "Lobbying Information," and "General State Government Information." Each of these categories usually includes a number of annotated bibliographic entries. Along with standard print sources, one also finds Internet sites and occasional oddities, such as videos. Three appendixes provide additional directory assistance for those seeking to obtain information on bills through the telephone or who are interested in influencing state legislatures. This has always been a helpful source, and it is now even more valuable thanks to inclusion of Internet information.

5-207. Hellebust, Lynn, ed. *State Reference Publications: A Bibliographic Guide to State Blue Books, Legislative Manuals and Other General Reference Sources*. Topeka, KS: Government Research Service, 1998. ISSN: 1057-0586.

Reference publications created by state governments in regard to themselves have always been difficult to identify. This source is probably the best place to determine if a particular reference work can be found for any one of the fifty states or for Puerto Rico or the District of Columbia. The arrangement is alphabetical by name of state or jurisdiction.

There are seven possible categories for each state: "Internet Sites," "Books and General Reference," "Legislative Manuals and Handbooks," "Directories and Biographies," "Statistical Abstracts," "Government and Politics Books," and "Other Reference Sources." The categories have some tendency to overlap, so the reader is advised to check carefully under all possible headings. Each item receives a brief descriptive annotation. Although there are seven potential categories, there are not necessarily listings in each category for each state. Most items are products of state government, but some are produced by commercial publishers. Prices and addresses are included in most cases. An appendix provides an annotated bibliography directing the reader to a number of other useful sources in regard to state government. Although much state government information is now available through the Internet, this remains an excellent source for identifying print publications.

Dictionaries

5-208. Elliot, Jeffrey M., and Sheikh R. Ali. *State and Local Government Political Dictionary.* Santa Barbara, CA: ABC-CLIO, 1988. 325 pp. Index. ISBN: 0-874-36417-5.

This dictionary intends "to present factual information about state and local political institutions, processes, and practices" (Elliot and Sheikh 1988, preface), with the added hope that the interested reader will be inspired to take a greater interest in the local political scene. Altogether, there are 290 entries. Rather

than the usual alphabetical dictionary arrangement, the contents are instead arranged into eleven topical chapters. These are intended to reflect the contents of standard textbooks. Constitutions, intergovernmental relations, elections, the three branches of government, bureaucracy, finances, local jurisdictions, and policy issues are among the subjects covered. Each definition is about a paragraph long and is accompanied by a second paragraph that points out the significance of the term. Cross-references to other relevant terms are provided. Each definition is assigned a unique entry number, allowing the reader to turn directly to a cross-reference without having to consult the index. Several pages of notes at the back of the volume will assist the user in finding other sources. Most political dictionaries concentrate upon the national scene, so this volume is handy for its focus upon state and local governments.

Guides and Handbooks

5-209. Mullaney, Marie Marmo. *Biographical Directory of the Governors of the United States, 1988–1994.* Westport, CT: Greenwood Press, 1994. 425 pp. Index. ISBN: 0-313-28312-5.

The late 1980s and early 1990s were a difficult time in state government, featuring a recessionary economy and transfer of federal functions to the states at the behest of the Reagan administration. This volume provides a snapshot of that era. The arrangement is alphabetical by name of state; territories and similar entities are excluded. Each state section includes a biography of the governor ranging from two to five pages in length. There is considerable emphasis upon the state political situation and how it was handled by that governor. Each biography is accompanied by a photograph of the individual and a bibliography. The latter includes references to local newspapers that might be difficult for readers to retrieve. Those consulting this work will be limited to researchers requiring background on one of the governors found here or those investigating politics at the state level during this time frame. Several previously published volumes cover an additional ten years back to the late 1970s.

5-210. Hovey, Kendra A., and Harold A. Hovey. *CQ's State Fact Finder: Rankings across America.* Annual. Washington, DC: Congressional Quarterly, 1993–. Index. ISSN: 1079-7149.

One of several different publications that provides state rankings and comparisons on an ongoing basis, this reference work attempts to differentiate itself from its competitors by focusing upon "many statistics that are not included in standard statistical reports of government agencies, and thus don't appear in compilations of statistics which rely solely on such published reports" (Hovey and Hovey 1993, introduction). The format is somewhat complicated. First, introductory text attempts to direct the reader to those tables that will assist in making personal decisions about relocation of either a household or a business. This is followed by almost 300 pages of rankings

arranged by topics such as population, economies, geography, government, and the like. Each table includes an alphabetical array of the states with the appropriate statistical information for each, as well as a ranking in order from highest (or largest) to lowest (or smallest). A final major section includes two pages devoted to each state, with numerical rankings shown for nearly 200 categories. The subject tables include references to sources, many originating with the federal government, but do not provide complete bibliographic references. An index facilitates additional access to subjects of interest. Users may initially be somewhat daunted by the general arrangement of this volume, but it includes a wealth of information and can be recommended to both students and more advanced researchers.

5-211. Frymier, Jack. *Cultures of the States: A Handbook on the Effectiveness of State Governments.* Lanham, MD: Scarecrow Press, 2003. 411 pp. ISBN: 0-810-84768-X.

There are three major features to this handbook on state governments. First is a study of the effectiveness of the fifty state governments. The second is a methodology of research, and the third component is represented by the printed results of a database. There are eleven main chapters on broad topics related to the evaluation of the fifty states on "Race and Gender," "Economic Factors," "Tax Factors," and eight others. Appendixes make up the bulk of the book; these represent tables and other statistical data on such categories as deaths, farm income, birth rates, and unmarried teenagers, in various rank-order placements. As a snapshot approach to state rankings, this volume will provide ammunition for those researchers wishing to find states that rank low or high in a number of categories, but its usefulness will diminish as time goes by.

5-212. *Mason's Manual of Legislative Procedure.* Denver, CO: National Conference of State Legislatures, 2000. 707 pp. Index. ISBN: 1-580-24116-6.

The original compiler of this volume, Paul Mason, died in 1985. This is a joint project of the American Society of Legislative Clerks and Secretaries and the National Conference of State Legislatures. It differs from other parliamentary procedure manuals in its emphasis upon procedures within elected legislative bodies. In addition to extensive information on rules covering motions, the reader can find here rules dealing with debates, rules pertaining to legislative administrative bodies (including internal elections and details on committees), "Relations with the Executive and with the Other House," "Investigations and Public Order," and other matters particular to legislatures. The text is supplemented by an extensive listing of citations to legal cases and a listing of common motions.

5-213. *National Survey of State Laws.* 4th ed. Detroit: Gale Research, 2003. 693 pp. ISBN: 0-787-65694-1.

Students and general library users alike are often interested in finding compara-

tive state laws in regard to well-known and controversial topics. This volume provides a quick starting point for such research. The various laws are categorized into eight major subject areas, including business and consumer, criminal, education, employment, family, general civil, real estate, and tax. Within these major categories, the reader finds additional subdivisions. For example, the section on criminal law includes subdivisions for capital punishment, drunk driving, gun control, and a number of others. Specific laws are then shown through tables, which are arranged alphabetically by name of state. Relevant code sections are cited, and a summary of the statute appears as well. Sentencing and penalty information appears as appropriate. Most users will consult the table of contents, but a "Topic Cross Reference Table" will assist in providing cross-references to additional relevant topics. An appendix provides names of the statutory compilations in each state. Some researchers will find all the information they need in this volume; others seeking greater detail can use the references provided here to locate the specific statutes, many of which are now available through the Internet.

5-214. Pattarozzi, Chris, comp. *Selected State Enactments: Fifty-State Survey of Enacted Legislation on Priority Issues.* Annual. Denver, CO: National Conference of State Legislatures, 1989–. 100 pp. Index. ISSN: 1063-2549. (Title Varies: *Selected State Attachments.*)

The National Conference of State Legislatures compiles this volume through the use of questionnaires distributed to appropriate state agencies. Respondents were queried in eighteen major subject areas. These include such policy issues as agriculture, education, health care, law enforcement, and transportation. Within each of these categories, there are further subdivisions. For example, under the major heading of "Civil Rights and Civil Law," one finds some headings for "Discrimination," "Abortion," "Hate Crimes," and others. Within these subdivisions, the researcher finds references to session laws that were enacted by the various states during the previous year. The citations are to a chapter and number. There are no summaries or discussion of enactments. There are several appendixes, including one for pending legislation that is similar to the enactments sections. Now that many states are providing their statutes online, the value of this work will be enhanced, although it will remain of value primarily to knowledgeable researchers rather than to beginners.

5-215. Maddex, Robert L. *State Constitutions of the United States.* Washington, DC: Congressional Quarterly, 1998. 518 pp. Index. ISBN: 1-568-02373-1.

The average state constitution is nearly ten times the length of the U.S. Constitution and has been amended far more frequently, yet this body of legal documents is much less frequently described in reference publications than is the federal Constitution. This work provides the general user with a starting point for state constitutional background. Introductory

material describes state constitutions and their structure. The bulk of the volume consists of summaries of major constitutional provisions, arranged by state. The constitutions of three U.S. territories follow this section. The discussions of the individual constitutions average about nine pages in length. Discussion focuses upon such subjects as constitutional history, rights of citizens, the three branches of government, and topics such as impeachment, local government, and taxation. Citations to specific code sections are included. The information varies a bit from state to state; significant provisions specific to a particular constitution receive a certain amount of attention. The front matter includes tables that allow for easy comparison. Several appendixes provide the text of the U.S. Constitution, a table of cases, and a bibliography of several pages. In many cases, texts of state constitutions are now available through the Internet, but most researchers will be better served by consulting this volume first.

5-216. Appleton, Andrew M., and Daniel S. Ward, eds. *State Party Profiles: A Fifty-State Guide to Development, Organization, and Resources.* Washington, DC: Congressional Quarterly, 1997. 388 pp. Index. ISBN: 1-568-02150-X.

While information on national parties and party politics is relatively easy to find, there is a greater dearth of reference sources for parties at the state level. This book helps to fill that gap. The arrangement is alphabetical by state, with each state receiving about seven pages of text. Within each state chapter, there are four major subdivisions: "Party History," "Organizational Development," "Current Party Organization," and "Resource Guide." Emphasis is on the time frame from 1960 to the present, although brief background on pre-1960s developments is also provided. The "Resource Guide" not only includes bibliographic references to published sources, it also outlines the availability and location of archival materials. An appendix tabulates information in regard to individual state laws and regulations governing political parties. The individual chapters are written by scholars who specialize in the party politics of the state in question. This is a highly useful volume; it can be recommended to students needing only introductory information on state political parties and will be of value to scholars seeking a starting point for more in-depth research.

5-217. *State Rankings: A Statistical View of the Fifty United States.* Annual. Lawrence, KS: Morgan Quitno, 1990–. Index. ISSN: 1057-3623.

This publication is somewhat similar to *CQ's State Fact Finder* [entry 5-210]. There are 527 tables of comparisons among the states divided into a number of major categories. These include agriculture, defense, economy, geography, health, social welfare, and several others. A typical table shows the rankings of the states accompanied by figures and percentages for each. Like *CQ's State Fact Finder,* this volume also provides information for the District of Columbia.

Each table includes a reference to the source or sources from which it was compiled. Addresses and phone numbers for the source agencies are provided at the back of the volume. Access to the rankings is provided by a detailed table of contents and an index by subject. The format is straightforward and easy to use, and the provision of complete bibliographic citations to sources is welcome. The information found here complements that found in some of the competing publications; many libraries will probably want to subscribe to several.

5-218. Foster, Lynn, et al., eds. *Subject Compilations of State Laws, 1995–1996: An Annotated Bibliography.* Westport, CT: Greenwood Press, 1960–. 275 pp. Indexes. ISSN: 1062-5682.

The sixth in a series of volumes by the same title, this work continues to use the same format to provide a compilation of articles and books relevant to laws appearing in state statutes. The arrangement is somewhat complex. There are over 200 major subject headings, such as "Brain Death," "Flags," "Insanity Defense," "Smoking," and "Whistleblowers." Each of these headings includes one or more bibliographic entries and annotations. The annotations refer the reader to specific locations within the articles where there are citations back to the individual state codes. Each entry is also assigned a unique accession number; these numbers began with the first volume, so that each volume includes unique numbers. There are numerous cross-references to both other entries within this volume and entries in earlier volumes. There are indexes by both author and publisher. The greater accessibility of electronic databases has perhaps limited the value of this set; on the other hand, it still provides reference to articles and books now of historical interest and is helpful for its specificity in regard to treatises pertinent to comparative law among the states.

5-219. Cox, Elizabeth M. *Women State and Territorial Legislators, 1895–1995: A State-by-State Analysis, with Rosters of 6,000 Women.* Jefferson, NC: McFarland, 1996. 398 pp. Index. ISBN: 0-786-40078-1.

Cox compiled this volume after finding that information on women legislators at the territorial and state levels was quite lacking. The bulk of the volume is arranged by state and territory. Within each, one finds alphabetical listings of the women who have served in the bodies of the state legislature. Each listing also includes the city and county represented, party affiliation, and the legislative years that were served. The jurisdictional sections also include brief demographic data in regard to women legislators. Lengthy introductory comments also discuss demographics and the organization of the volume, all supplemented by graphic displays. There are several appendixes, including one that provides numbers and percentages of women in these legislative bodies from 1895 through 1995 and several that indicate "firsts." A useful bibliography will lead researchers to other relevant sources. A name index assists those readers seeking a particular individual.

While there is no biographical information here, this volume is an excellent starting point for those political scientists interested in gender issues or state legislatures.

Atlases

5-220. *The Almanac of State Legislatures.* 2nd ed. Washington, DC: Congressional Quarterly, 1998. 387 pp. ISBN: 1-568-02434-7.

Through the use of multicolor maps and statistical charts, this atlas provides political and socioeconomic information on 6,743 state house and senate legislative districts. The maps and data are arranged by state. There are two statewide maps showing senate and house districts, and a number of more detailed maps displaying districts in major urban areas. Each map is accompanied by a demographic table displaying thirteen pieces of information for each district. The major categories of information include household income, college education, employment, aged population, and ethnic population. Data is based upon the 1990 census. The arrangement allows for ready comparison among districts; one can easily determine how rich or poor a particular district is or how it compares with other districts in terms of ethnicity. The audience for this volume will be that of the more specialized researcher, but journalists and politicians will have an interest in the data also.

5-221. Lilley, William, III, Laurence J. DeFranco, and William M. Diefenderfer III. *The State Atlas of Political and Cultural Diversity.* Washington, DC:

Congressional Quarterly, 1997. 290 pp. ISBN: 1-568-02177-1.

Believing that race and ancestry are playing an increasingly important role in politics and that there is a shift in political power from the national to the state level, the three authors created this atlas to visually demonstrate American cultural diversity. The arrangement is too complicated to completely explain in a brief annotation. Basically, a series of maps shows populations of fourteen ethnic groups where they predominate in particular state house and senate districts. The fourteen groups include African American; American Indian, Eskimo, or Aleut; Asian or Pacific Islander; Chinese; Japanese; Korean; Hispanic; Mexican; Puerto Rican; Cuban; German; Irish; Italian; and Polish. A series of introductory maps showing the entire United States is followed by more detailed maps displaying district data for each of the ethnic groups. These maps are accompanied by demographic statistics for each district. Data is based on 1990 for 1994 census statistics. Users may benefit from consulting this volume in tandem with the *Almanac of State Legislatures* [entry 5-220]. This is a complex and specialized work, one that will appeal to researchers in the field of state or ethnic politics rather than to most undergraduates or general readers. ▢

6

International Relations and International Organization Reference Sources

The discipline of international relations has been one of the major subcomponents of political science for a number of years. Generally, it is regarded as the study of states and their foreign policies and the way they interact with one another either as individual units or collectively within intergovernmental organizations. Over the years, several schools of thought have been attached to the study of international relations. Political science dictionaries describe some of these schools as (1) realism, the so-called liberal tradition, and (2) various other approaches that eschew the central role of sovereign state government and focus instead on other factors, such as the Marxist approach stressing economic production or world-systems theory that takes on a more internationalist perspective. These are just two such examples of different directions international relations research has taken over time. Others will certainly follow.

International Relations
Directories
6-1. Seymore, Bruce, ed. *International Affairs Directory of Organizations: The ACCESS Resource Guide.* Santa Barbara, CA: ABC-CLIO, 1992. 326 pp. Indexes. ISBN: 0-874-36686-0.

This is a revised edition of the *Review of ACCESS Resource Guide* (1988). It is one in a series of ACCESS directories, guides, and the like that exists to open the door to resources for those undertaking research in world events. ACCESS attempts to identify and then track on a selective basis those organizations and specialists that cover the entire political spectrum on foreign affairs topics. There are only nongovernmental bodies listed for the United States. In addition to more traditional resources, it also lists archives and special collections in libraries. The main body is arranged alphabetically by country. Basic directory-type information precedes every entry. Entries are in a standardized format broken down into such categories as purpose, resources, audience, membership, and others. There are several indexes.

6-2. Bahamonde, Ramon, comp. *International Policy Institutions around the Pacific Rim: A Directory of Resources in East Asia, Australia, and the Americas.* Boulder, CO: Lynne Rienner, 1998. 317 pp. Indexes. ISBN: 1-555-87795-8.

This straightforward directory offers the reader a list of 289 institutions located around the Pacific basin that are important resource centers for understanding the political, economic, and social issues pervading this dynamic region of the world, especially ones related to international relations policy matters. This directory of nongovernmental organizations is one of the first publications distributed by the Pacific Council on International Policy, founded in 1995 in cooperation with the Council on Foreign Relations. This work should assist those requiring Pacific Rim–focused issues of international economics, sociology, and politics. The arrangement of the main body is alphabetical by country within each larger geographical region of the globe. The directory portion follows a standard format of name, background and objectives, programs, publications, funding sources, staffing, head, contact person, address, e-mail, and so forth. The two indexes available are by institute name and by head of the organization. 🖳

Bibliographies
6-3. *Current World Affairs: A Quarterly Bibliography.* Alexandria, VA: John C. Damon, 1990–. ISSN: 1050-4850.

The intent of this quarterly publication is to provide quick access to English-language publications in world affairs. Each issue contains approximately 1,000 articles that have appeared in 4 major newspapers and 50 to 100 periodicals. The periodicals are listed in alphabetical order with relevant articles numbered in sequence thereafter. Article citations include title, date, page numbers, location, and article summary. Each issue has a very short section for books and congressional publications. A short glossary of terms appears in each issue. This publication is best for high-school students, undergraduates, and the general public.

6-4. Wang, James C. F. *Ocean Politics and Law: An Annotated Bibliography.* New York: Greenwood Press, 1991. 243 pp. Indexes. ISBN: 0-313-27925-X.

This bibliography contains approximately 2,081 entries that include a selective lineup of English-language books, journal articles, yearbook chapters, and conference proceedings. The book is divided into twelve categories on various broad aspects of ocean politics and the law. Typical chapters are on deep seabed mining, regional approaches to marine environmental control, development of general international principles, and nine others. The works are arranged in alphabetical sequence by author within each chapter. Roughly 5 percent of the citations receive any type of annotation. There are author and subject indexes.

Dictionaries

6-5. Berridge, Geoff. *A Dictionary of Diplomacy*. 2nd ed. New York: Palgrave Macmillan, 2003. 296 pp. ISBN: 1-403-91535-0.

This dictionary was designed mainly for undergraduate and even some graduate-level students who must deal with research and/or readings in matters pertaining to diplomacy. Entries are short and in standard dictionary arrangement. The second edition contains a significant number of new entries over the previous one. Individuals who have had a profound impact on the history of diplomacy are included as well as terms relating to basic international law, diplomatic initiatives, basis treaties, events, and the like. Typical entries are "Klemens von Metternich," "sovereignty," and "reciprocity."

6-6. O'Loughlin, John. *Dictionary of Geopolitics*. Westport, CT: Greenwood Press, 1994. 284 pp. ISBN: 0-313-26313-2.

This dictionary has signed entries written mostly by international scholars on all aspects of geopolitics. While core geopolitical terms are all dutifully included and well written, determining the criteria for the other terms appearing in this book is more problematic. Some terms deal with places, diplomats, political terms, peace conferences, and so on. A number of the entries are included in their original foreign language. Typical terms are: "Antisubmarine Warfare," "Decolonization," "Domino Theory," "Hideki Tojo," and "Organization of American States (OAS)." Would one normally consider using a dictionary of geopolitical terms for some of those entries? While highly eclectic in content, the strength is in core geopolitical concepts and in "Geopolitikers."

6-7. Fox, James R. *Dictionary of International and Comparative Law*. 3rd ed. Dobbs Ferry, NY: Oceana Publications, 2003. 369 pp. ISBN: 0-379-21501-2.

This alphabetically arranged international and comparative law dictionary provides very brief entries on acronyms and international legal terms. This is a highly specialized dictionary that does not replace a more general legal dictionary. It provides the names of some international treaties, events, terms, and the like. There are also Permanent Court of International Justice (PCIJ) and International Court of Justice (ICJ) deliberations and decisions listed.

6-8. *Dictionary of International Relations Terms*. 3rd ed. Washington, DC: Department of State Library, 1987. 115 pp. S1.2: IN8/30/98.

This relatively concise work is an alphabetical dictionary of international relations terms that were infused with new meaning or perspective. The overarching goal is to establish a contextual framework to these international relations definitions. Cross-references establish links to other terms. Each term listed has one or more sources for the international relations terms being examined. Entries usually include a historical dimension to the term itself. Definitions do not connote official State Department policy.

6-9. Shafritz, Jay M. *The Dictionary of Twentieth-Century World Politics.* New York: Holt, 1993. 756 pp. ISBN: 0-805-01976-6.

Listed here are the events, history, key political players, philosophies, and ideas that have had a significant impact on twentieth-century politics. The people included in this dictionary tend to be kings, prime ministers, presidents, or others who are regarded as serious international political thinkers. Entries are fairly brief but do have cross-references. Biographical entries have a number of black-and-white pictures. The book's appendixes are arranged by "Key Concepts Organized by Subject." There are also some useful chronologies such as U.S.-USSR summit meetings, events that happened during the Six Days' War, and much more.

6-10. Feltham, Ralph George. *Diplomatic Handbook.* New York: Longman, 1998. 7th ed. 206 pp. ISBN: 0-582-31716-9.

The purpose of this book is a narrow one, and that is to provide information to men and women who are determined to find either international or diplomatic careers. There is discussion about the history and context of diplomatic relations, the Ministry of Foreign Affairs, the diplomatic mission, protocol and procedures, consular offices, the United Nations, and so on. The information printed varies in importance. It can talk about diplomatic immunity in time of war or the proper location of the host and hostess at an international banquet for ten, including choice of proper wine. This book is best for presenting the more nitty-gritty information on the diplomatic mission, its role, duties, and privileges of office.

6-11. Freeman, Charles W. *The Diplomat's Dictionary.* rev. ed. Washington, DC: United States Institute of Peace Press, 1997. 451 pp. Index. ISBN: 1-878-37966-6.

This work was written with the singular purpose of meeting the requirements of those called upon to serve as mediators, negotiators, governmental envoys, consuls, ambassadors, and foreign policy officials. In fact, this is a combination of quote book and diplomatic-terminology dictionary. Many of the quotes are assigned originators, if known. Most of the definitions are short and to the point. There is a list of preeminent people associated with the global foreign policy–making establishment in short, one-sentence descriptive statements. The index includes terms and sources of quotes. Unfortunately, it is very incomplete and subjective as to inclusions and exclusions of people, quotes, and terms.

6-12. Hing, Bill Ong. *Immigration and the Law: A Dictionary.* Santa Barbara, CA: ABC-CLIO, 1999. 400 pp. Index. ISBN: 1-576-07120-0.

This is a basic-level dictionary of immigration terms as they relate to U.S. law. Entries cite court cases, define legal terms, identify advocate groups, note individuals, provide language from select congressional acts, give Immigration and Naturalization Service regulations, and more. The dictionary is written for the general reader or person who wants to understand better the terms and legal authority related to U.S. immigration law for whatever reason. Entries can be several sentences or multiple pages long. There is a "Table of Cases" and an index. This work might be helpful to those desiring to become U.S. citizens or to those working with advocate groups that involve immigration matters.

6-13. Ziring, Lawrence. *International Relations: A Political Dictionary.* 5th ed. Santa Barbara, CA: ABC-CLIO, 1995. 458 pp. Index. ISBN: 0-874-36791-3.

This dictionary contains twelve broad international relations chapters. Some of them are "International Organization," "U.S. Foreign Policy," and "Ideology and Communication." There are a total of 714 entries alphabetically ordered under all of the dozen broad chapters. Individual terms are defined and then appraised for historical significance within the field of international relations. There are numerous "see" and "see also" references interspersed throughout the text. The index is indispensable for most efficient use of this reference work. This work is best suited for general readers and undergraduate students.

6-14. Griffiths, Martin. *International Relations: The Key Concepts.* New York: Routledge, 2002. 399 pp. ISBN: 0-415-22882-4.

The emphasis of this international relations dictionary is to present to the general reader and lower-division under-graduate or high-school student a set of 150 contemporary issues that should be quite familiar to most international relations students. It contains concepts, institutions, and terms. A few typical entries are: "Balance of Power," "Hegemony," "Free Trade," and "Regionalism." These are basic international relations terms treated in a very straightforward manner. The average entry is two to three pages and contains adequate cross-referencing. Entries provide both historical and more contemporary perspectives of the term or issue examined.

6-15. Parry, Clive. *Parry and Grant Encyclopedic Dictionary of International Law.* New York: Oceana Publications, 1986. 564 pp. ISBN: 0-379-20828-8.

The emphasis of this work is on international law, not international organization. Terms are strictly alphabetically ordered. The definitions of terms or words can be quite lengthy, and these definitions frequently cite law cases, encyclopedias, journals, International Court of Justice reports, and the like. The authority for definitions is usually plainly cited. While highly authoritative, the dictionary's entries tend to have a plodding feel to them. One hundred pages are devoted to reprinting documents ranging from the United Nations Charter to the Vienna Convention on Diplomatic Relations, and a number of others. (Note: A second edition [2004] has just been published, but was not seen.)

6-16. Evans, Graham, comp. *Penguin Dictionary of International Relations.*

New York: Penguin, 1998. 623 pp. ISBN: 0-140-51397-3.

This work serves two purposes. It is a dictionary dedicated to the overall restructuring of the study of international relations, which has been transformed due to the end of the cold war era. The bipolar world has changed the framework for analyzing world politics. Also, this book is a substantial revision of *The Dictionary of World Politics*, published previously in both 1989 and 1992. The main body is arranged in standard alphabetical format. Many entries are several pages in length. There is heavy use of cross-references and "see also" notes. Some fairly current terms appearing in the news, such as "Ethnic Cleansing," are included. The definitions offer not only examples of the terms but also explanations of how a term was used over history within different contexts. There is a fairly long, general, unannotated bibliography of works on various international relations works included.

6-17. *What's What in World Politics: A Reference Book.* Moscow: Progress Publishers, 1987. 461 pp. No ISBN.

This international affairs dictionary brings the superpower era alive again with definitions of terms that are reminiscent of the world order in the post–cold war era. All entries are in English. Many of the terms included here are supposedly those used in the daily newspapers, radio, television, and other mass media of the middle to late 1980s. Many of the terms chosen are quite standard, such as the "Arab League," "Col-lective Security," and "Geopolitics." Other terms appear to lie closer to Soviet interests, like "class struggle," "Socialist International," "Reaganomics," and so on. There appears to be little effort to show an objective definition of terms, and a pointed anti-Western bias does emerge. The work's overriding value is to offer the English-language reader a glimpse into Soviet thinking and worldview just a few years before the collapse of the USSR and the European Communist states.

Encyclopedias

6-18. Clements, John. *Clements' Encyclopedia of World Governments.* Dallas: Political Research, 2002. 539 pp. ISSN: 0145-9678.

This work has no introduction, and this makes divining its scope and mission difficult. It does make lavish use of statistics, but consistently fails to cite sources. The work is kept updated through a series of supplements. There appears to be an idiosyncratic air to this publication.

6-19. *Encyclopedia of International Boundaries.* In Collaboration with the International Boundaries Research Unit, University of Durham, England. New York: Facts on File, 1995. 543 pp. ISBN: 0-816-03233-5.

The field of border studies is a growing and dynamic area of study within international relations today. This book examines international land boundaries only. Excluded are both maritime boundaries and internal state divisions. Where boundary disputes do exist, there is an honest attempt made to explain all sides of the issue. Ethnic divisions are often the geographical fault line that leads to most border disputes among nations. Even the change in the flow of a river has had consequences on land claims. The book is organized alphabetically by country, and the entries then give a full account of every border issue regarding that country. Entries are factual and to the point, stressing the historical links to the border issue at hand. The accompanying maps are an integral part of understanding many of the border disputes. The bibliography includes many older materials that may be difficult to locate in one's typical local library setting.

6-20. Weigall, David. *International Relations: A Concise Companion.* London: Arnold, 2002. 256 pp. ISBN: 0-340-76332-9.

This is a basic international relations encyclopedia with 1,500 alphabetically arranged entries intended to meet many ready-reference-type questions. It is aimed at those studying international relations within its modern historical context and for the general reader. Its emphasis is on the concepts, organizations, treaties, doctrines, diplomacy, and the environment. Biographical entries have been excluded. Typical entries are on "acid rain," "China card," "House Un-American Activities Committee (HUAC)," and "Desert Storm (1991)." Most definitions get several sentences, with longer ones hitting a full page or so. Entries are liberally cross-referenced. A few black-and-white pictures appear scat-

tered throughout the pages. A three-part bibliography at the end includes works with historical background, introductory texts and theory, and a highly selective list of Web sites. There is no index. 💻

Guides and Handbooks

6-21. Cossolotto, Matthew. *The Almanac of Transatlantic Politics, 1991–92.* Washington, DC: Brassey's, 1991. 428 pp. ISBN: 0-080-35978-7.

The main focus here is on the twenty-one individual nations making up Western Europe and North America. Political developments, institutions of government, political parties, and political leaders in these twenty-one democratic nations are highlighted. This work also includes separate chapters on the European Community and NATO. There are also sections on the six former Warsaw Pact countries and the European Free Trade Association (EFTA). There are data tables, electoral and statistical profiles, recent election results, discussion of the various governments and their programs, short biographies of major leaders, and so on. There is some lack of focus here, and the work does not differentiate itself from other works where similar information resides.

6-22. Williams, Tim Guyse, ed. *BBC World Service Glossary of Current Affairs.* Chicago: St. James Press, 1991. 813 pp. ISBN: 1-558-62108-3.

This handbook is alphabetically arranged by individual country. It includes not just the major countries, but the many smaller island nations as well. Each country has a listing of people, political parties, dates, governmental bodies, and the like. There is no preface or introduction defining the scope of the work or its criteria for inclusion or exclusion. Each country warrants about six to seven pages of information. A forty-page "International Section" provides terms of international organizations, regional groups, European Community units, and so forth.

6-23. *Careers in International Affairs.* Washington, DC: Georgetown University Press, 2003. 7th ed. 371 pp. Index. ISBN: 0-878-40391-4.

This work was written to assist those searching for jobs in business, government, world organizations, and nongovernmental organizations (NGOs) where they will both serve and represent their respective nations or membership within the international community. It should have a particularly strong appeal to those people who feel quite comfortable in shifting over time from public to private to nonprofit sectors. Tips and insights are provided into the skills and requirements many different employers find necessary for a successful career. This edition appears to focus somewhat more on the "interpersonal dynamics" of the job search. This includes the ability to communicate well, combined with productive mentoring relationships. Over 300 various organizations are listed that have a reputation for hiring people in the area of international affairs. They are listed in broad categories, and complete contact information is given for

every one of them. A few of the organizations listed here are WorldWatch Institute, General Electric, the Institute for Policy Studies, and many more. An index is included.

6-24. CIAO: Columbia International Affairs Online. http://www.ciaonet.org/.

This fee-based service was established in 1997. It is designed for undergraduate students and perhaps others interested in both the research and more theoretical aspects of international affairs. Links have been established to a number of full-text publications including think tank policy briefs, occasional papers, nongovernmental organization publications, foundation-funded research reports, and conference proceedings. There are also ample links to domestic and foreign media outlets. Several course packs are available to teaching faculty, as well as sample syllabi for such courses as "Globalization and Public Policy." Links have been made for items published from 1991 to date. CIAO is a collaborative effort between Columbia University and the Columbia University Press. 💻

6-25. Council on Foreign Relations. http://cfr.org.

This highly respected organization concentrates on foreign affairs and U.S. foreign relations with other countries or international organizations. Relevant links are arranged according to continent or region (e.g., Middle East) or other broad categories, such as "Peace and Conflict," "Globalization," and one on media and public opinion. The links here are generally transcripts of speeches, journal articles, other research-center reports, the foreign press, and the like. Searching for back files of material is permitted for this Web site and the council's major publication, *Foreign Affairs*, in full-text version. 🖳

6-26. Women in International Security. *Fellowships in International Affairs: A Guide to Opportunities in the United States and Abroad.* Boulder, CO: Lynne Rienner Publishers, 1994. 195 pp. ISBN: 1-555-87517-3.

This handbook offers the opportunity to locate fellowships, grants, and other awards available primarily to those planning to enter a career in some aspect of international affairs. It is a basic alphabetically arranged listing of institutions and foundations that funnel money to potential international affairs careerists. Each entry offers the fund seeker a brief background of the organization, its qualifications, duration, stipends, deadlines, and contact information. Many of the organizations listed are major ones that could be found in standard grant directories, but this work targets those that support international relations–related projects. An appendix offers tips on proposal writing.

6-27. Foreign Policy Association (FPA). Foreign Policy Association: Resource Library. http://www.fpa.org/.

The Foreign Policy Association's resource library Web site is a rather wide-ranging assortment of representative speeches, research reports, organizations, news media, and more on a number of foreign policy issues or regional analysis. There are preselected categories, or the user can take advantage of the dialogue box by entering a desired search term. Results to either search method are in the form of links to full-text articles appearing in journals, reports, news stories, and the like. These links are frequently made to comparatively more establishment-oriented Web sites. Articles often contain a link to other electronic resources on the same topic for the FPA and from external sources. Many entries lead to additional media reports and opinion pieces. 🖳

6-28. Levinson, David. *The Global Village Companion: An A-to-Z Guide to Understanding Current World Affairs.* Santa Barbara, CA: ABC-CLIO, 1996. 438 pp. Index. ISBN: 0-874-36829-4.

The ultimate goal of this author, who is an anthropologist, is to write a work that helps readers comprehend the emerging global influences at work in the modern world that have an immediate impact on a raft of contemporary social issues and cultures. Not only is it seen as a way to better understand print, radio, television, and other news reporting, but it also helps to create a roadmap of sorts for examining issues people confront in their daily living experiences, political situations, and communities at large. Each entry is about a page or two. A number of terms are defined, and the history of those terms explained along with information on their global importance. These terms include concepts, trends, events, organizations, and others. The emphasis falls into eight major topical classes, some of which are "Women's Role and Status," "Conflict," and "Communications." Readers are encouraged to look for a complex set of relationships when analyzing sociocultural issues. While a number of sources were consulted in compiling this handbook, the finished product will appeal and be most valuable for general readers and those in high-school, junior college, and lower-division undergraduate classes. This book is heavily cross-referenced and contains several useful appendixes, a chronology of events for 1945 through 1995, a fairly substantial bibliography, and a comprehensive index.

6-29. Serow, William J., ed. *Handbook on International Migration.* Westport, CT: Greenwood Press, 1990. 385 pp. Index. ISBN: 0-313-26117-2.

A total of nineteen countries and regions of the world are surveyed on how immigration and/or emigration have shaped those respective areas' politics or economy. The narratives that make up the main entries are largely in the form of bibliographic essays that include current research done by authors on the topic of migration in the country being covered. There are ample statistical tables, charts, and graphics included. Most chapters conclude with a list of readings, which are often in the native language of the country at hand. Chapters seem especially well written and informative, and they provide the reader with ample data and reasons for significant population

moves inside a particular nation or region, or from one country to another. Of the nineteen countries chosen, about half are developing nations, and the other half are some of the more affluent countries of the world. A subject index is included.

6-30. ISN: International Relations and Security Network. http://www.isn.ethz .ch/.

This is a fine Web site for finding very current news reports on security issues, world affairs, and various regional surveys. There are links to full-text articles and research reports on various foreign affairs topics, security and arms preparations or activities, and other areas of similar interest. This site is maintained by the Zurich-based Center for Security Studies (CSS) and the Swiss Federal Institute of Technology (ETH Zurich). The section on "Links Library" has a large concentration of different topics covered, such as international intergovernmental organizations (IGOs), international organizations in Asia, international development organizations, and more. These links have a clear propensity for homing in on more established international organizations. Many of these links do get helpful one- or two-sentence annotations. Topic lists can be so large as to be subdivided into additional categories. 💻

6-31. Nolan, Cathal J. *The Longman Guide to World Affairs.* White Plains, NY: Longman, 1995. 450 pp. ISBN: 0-801-31298-1.

This is a one-volume directory of biographical information, elements of diplomacy, major international conferences, international law, international political economy, as well as fundamental political science concepts and other related terms in alphabetical sequence. There are approximately 4,600 total main entries. Typical entries are "GATT," "International Monetary Fund (IMF)," "Bretton Woods 1944," "Sphere of Influence," and the like. Entries are succinct, but crisply written, and pack a lot of information into such limited space. The work contains cross-references and "see also" references. The lack of an index is a detriment to use given the work's breadth of scope.

6-32. Krieger, Joel, ed. *Oxford Companion to Politics of the World.* 2nd ed. New York: Oxford University Press, 2001. 1018 pp. Index. ISBN: 0-195-11739-5.

The perspective on this Oxford handbook is decidedly post–cold war, much more so than the first edition that was published just at the end of the bipolar era that overshadowed international affairs over the previous forty years. Over 500 international contributors have generated approximately 670 articles, including 87 that are totally new essays for the second edition. There are numerous entries that delve into the study of globalism and the dynamics of capitalism in their abilities to provide for various universal needs, such as social justice, security, equality, and sustainable development. The essays emphasize an interdisciplinary approach to international politics. Each one is signed, and there is a detailed index. This is truly

an exemplary work that provides students, faculty, and general readers with key global issues in the contemporary world order.

6-33. Virtual Resources: International Relations Research Resources on the Web. http://mitpress.mit.edu/journals/inor/deibert-guide/toc.html.

This Web site is especially useful for both international relations and comparative government–related topics. It is quite selective in determining what to link, but it is a good basic starting point for those who do not wish to be overwhelmed with a large, complex listing of Web sites. When tested, a number of dead links had not been changed, deleted, or redirected. Ronald J. Deibert at the University of Toronto maintains this site. 💻

6-34. Segal, Gerald. *The World Affairs Companion: The Essential Guide to Global Issues.* rev. and updated ed. New York: Simon and Schuster, 1993. 296 pp. ISBN: 0-671-88020-9.

This handbook was designed to help undergraduate students and the more general reader make some sense out of the way the global political landscape is unfolding in the post–cold war era by providing them with a wide range of key facts, data, information, and analysis. The work itself is divided into major international geographic areas. Much of the work discusses past, current, and possibly future global conflicts. There are nine broad chapters on various themes and regional issues. Such chapters as "Modern Warfare," "New Europe," and "Africa" are broken down further into five to ten subdivisions or topics. There are many statistical tables, charts, and figures. Short reading lists follow this. The author has published widely on security matters, Asian politics, and other topics related to this work. This is less a scholarly work than one evincing solid journalism.

6-35. The WWW Virtual Library: International Affairs Resources. http://vlib .org/InternationalAffairs.html.

This is a very good place to begin for a solid and wide-ranging annotated listing of international relations/affairs materials appearing on the Web. Most sites are in English, but many on topics of particular interest to studies of the developing world are in various foreign languages. There are media links, from popular U.S. sources like CNN to the BBC, EuroNews, and the Zona Latina site. There are links to international radio and television stations, international relations journals, international organizations of every stripe, research institutes, and U.S. government sites. There is also a section on regions and countries, such as Eastern Europe and the Middle East. The largest category is for such topics as those in public health, human rights, American foreign policy, and several major European languages, including German, French, and Spanish. Every Web listing is annotated, and these write-ups are quite helpful. The site was created and maintained by Professor Wayne A. Selcher, a member of the Political Science Department at Elizabethtown College. ▣

Atlases

6-36. Boyd, Andrew. *An Atlas of World Affairs*. 10th ed. New York: Routledge, 1998. 252 pp. ISBN: 0-415-10670-2.

This current affairs atlas has been around for ten editions since 1957. It is designed for students and teachers who want to know about post–World War II history or contemporary international political events. The seventy-five chapters, only several pages each, describe the people, factions, and major events that have helped shape the world we live in today. International issues and areas of conflict are placed within their geographical contexts with the 100 or so maps published in this atlas. The various chapters include countries, regions, and a few more general topics, such as "Oil" or "Nuclear Geography." All maps are in black and white with bold outlines making them excellent for photocopying. The textual portion is quite concise, its sole purpose being to assist in the interpretation of the maps themselves. ▣

6-37. Anderson, Ewan W. *International Boundaries: A Geopolitical Atlas*. New York: Routledge/Taylor and Francis, 2003. 941 pp. ISBN: 1-579-58375-X.

Not seen.

United States Foreign Relations
Directories
6-38. Howard, A. D. Dick. *Democracy's Dawn: A Directory of American Initiatives on Constitutionalism, Democracy, and the Rule of Law in Central and Eastern Europe*. Charlottesville: University

Press of Virginia (for the United States Institute of Peace), 1991. 225 pp. ISBN: 0-813-91352-7.

The main part of this book is the chapter entitled "American Organizations and Their Programs in Central and Eastern Europe," which is a survey of private and some publicly supported agencies that are attempting to assist this region to establish democratic institutions and a constitutional democracy. Each alphabetically posted agency is divided into nine standardized parts, including the name of the agency, address, telephone number, description, contact person, publications, conferences, programs, and so forth. There are two appendixes. One is a guide to programs arranged by country, while the second serves as a guide to programs by type of assistance, such as grants or technical assistance. Many of these organizations may be found in other standard directories, but the work has been done here in focusing on a particular dynamic region of the globe. This directory is destined to go out of date fairly quickly unless subsequent editions are published.

Bibliographies

6-39. Lincove, David A., comp. *The Anglo-American Relationship: An Annotated Bibliography of Scholarship, 1945–1985.* New York: Greenwood Press, 1988. 415 pp. Indexes. ISBN: 0-313-25854-6.

This fully annotated bibliography tracks the literature documenting the changing relationship between the United States and the United Kingdom in the post–World War II era. The books, collections of essays, journal articles, and U.S./U.K. doctoral dissertations appearing between 1945 and 1985 cover the evolving relationship between the United States and United Kingdom, an age of the rise of the United States to superpower status that eclipsed both Europe and the United Kingdom in military and economic power. With a few exceptions, works dealing with art, literature, music, and law are excluded from consideration. The core of the book is divided into two parts. Part 1 presents the bibliography of nondiplomatic interactions by topic, such as "Foreign Investments and Trade," "Immigration and Emigration," and so forth. Part 2 centers squarely on diplomacy and makes up two-thirds of the total book. It is arranged chronologically, based on a sequence of major historical events. There is an author index and a subject index.

6-40. Doenecke, Justus D., ed. *Anti-Intervention: A Bibliographical Introduction to Isolationism and Pacifism from World War I to the Early Cold War.* New York: Garland, 1987. 421 pp. Indexes. ISBN: 0-824-08482-9.

This bibliography covers the anti-intervention literature beginning with opposition to the U.S. entry into World War I up to the mid-1950s. Included is literature on both pacifist and isolationist perspectives. The bibliography provides works that are books, journal articles, and dissertations, and all these works are in English. Many of the entries are annotated.

The organization of the book is in five main sections: "General Works," "World War I and its Aftermath," "The Twenties, Thirties, World War II and the Cold War," "Opinion-Making Elements," and "Interest and Ideological Groups and Leaders." There are author and subject indexes.

6-41. Tarrago, Rafael E. *Early U.S.-Hispanic Relations, 1776–1860: An Annotated Bibliography.* Metuchen, NJ: Scarecrow Press, 1994. 171 pp. Indexes. ISBN: 0-810-82882-0.

This bibliography covers the early days of the United States as an independent country up until the pre–Civil War era. The topic of this work is the set of relations between the U.S. republic in its infancy and the Hispanic nations and peoples of the era. It is selective and does not list manuscripts, textbooks, dissertations, government publications, or pamphlet materials. The main chapters are arranged in either chronological or thematic headings. All chapters are subdivided in greater detail and placed into alphabetical sequence by author. Each of the 783 citations is annotated. Some chapters have a number of Spanish-language materials listed. There is only an author and a geographic index. Political scientists may quibble over inclusion of this work because it may indeed be more suitable as a guide to historical literature. Its uniqueness in the bibliographic literature of U.S. foreign relations offers ample reason for its inclusion.

6-42. Silverburg, Sanford R. *United States Foreign Policy and the Middle East/North Africa: A Bibliography of Twentieth-Century Research.* New York: Garland, 1990. 407 pp. Index. ISBN: 0-824-04613-7.

This geographically focused bibliography examines U.S. foreign policy toward the nations of the Middle East and North Africa during the entire period of the twentieth century. Citations are to books, essays, journal articles, and selected dissertations and master's theses taken from U.S. or British universities. Some National Technical Information Service reports are also included. The goal is to make this work as comprehensive as possible in the topics actually covered. The researchers were primarily American. There is one alphabetical arrangement of citations, none of which are annotated. The overwhelming number of works cited in this bibliography were published in the 1980s and tend to be mainstream items that should be available to some extent at most medium-sized or larger academic libraries. The subject index is surprisingly sparse given the size of the book and the level of comprehensiveness claimed.

Dictionaries

6-43. Findling, John E. *Dictionary of American Diplomatic History.* 2nd rev. and exp. ed. New York: Greenwood Press, 1989. 674 pp. ISBN: 0-313-26024-9.

There are a total of 1,200 entries included in this diplomatic-history dictionary. One-half are biographical and one-half are events, terms, treaties, and the like. Biographies are selectively chosen, but always included are the ministers or ambassadors to Great Britain or the USSR from 1933 to the date of publication, as well as most chiefs of mission to France, Germany, Japan, and China, and selective representatives to Mexico, Italy, Spain, and other selective countries especially in South and Central America. Specifically excluded are U.S. wars and presidents who were not directly active in diplomatic negotiations with foreign nations. All entries are arranged in standard A-to-Z dictionary style. Each entry is fairly short and contains readings and reference entries. This source is terrific for finding dates. There are appendixes for "Chronology of American Diplomatic History," "Diplomatic Personnel Listed by Presidential Administration," "Initiation, Suspension, and Termination of Diplomatic Relations," and so forth. Cross-references are embedded within each entry.

6-44. Flanders, Stephen A. *Dictionary of American Foreign Affairs.* New York: Macmillan, 1993. 833 pp. ISBN: 0-028-97146-9.

From the Alamo to the Invasion of Grenada, it's all here in short entries of about one-half to one page in length. This dictionary contains well-written and contextualized entries on diplomatic agreements, events, ideas, organizations, and the like related to U.S. foreign affairs. The emphasis is decidedly on contemporary U.S. foreign affairs within these 1,400 entries. All secretaries of state and the general foreign policy direction of each U.S. presidential administration are given. Concentration is on

fundamental details, dates, names, and specific events. There are several appendixes, including ones for timelines of U.S. foreign affairs from 1776 to date of publication, executive branch secretaries of the air force and Central Intelligence, and the diplomatic corps to France, Germany, the German Democratic Republic, Great Britain, Japan, Mexico, NATO, OAS, Russia/USSR, Spain, and the United Nations. Also listed are all the relevant congressional committees who oversaw U.S. foreign policy matters, such as the House Foreign Affairs Committee, the Senate Armed Forces Committee, and so forth.

6-45. Shavit, David. *The United States in Asia: A Historical Dictionary.* Westport, CT: Greenwood Press, 1990. 620 pp. Index. ISBN: 0-313-26788-X.

This work is quite similar in scope and content to the author's other work on the Middle East for the same publisher [entry 6-47]. Most of what is noted for Shavit's Middle East work holds true for this entry, except its focus is on Asia. This book, however, has an index.

6-46. Shavit, David. *The United States in Latin America: A Historical Dictionary.* New York: Greenwood Press, 1992. 471 pp. Index. ISBN: 0-313-27595-5.

The entries contained in this historical dictionary provide limited information about the people, institutions, and events that affected the relationship between the United States and any nation within Latin America. The work is especially devoted to bringing to light the individuals who were actually in Latin America and those who left behind written and/or visual records of their stay in that part of the world. It also is good for providing information on those organizations in Latin America itself, as well as the events that occurred in the region. All countries of Latin America are covered south of the United States including Mexico, Central America, the various Caribbean islands, and the continent of South America. U.S. diplomats have been added on a highly selective basis. There is a preliminary section on abbreviations used and another on the chronology of U.S./Latin relations for 1794 through 1990. Entries are arranged in alphabetical order, each containing a one-paragraph block of information. The crux of each entry is the person's, organization's, or event's link to Latin America. The overwhelming number of entries are for individuals. An appendix lists the chiefs of the American diplomatic missions throughout Latin America from 1823 to 1990. A short bibliographic essay and an index round out this work.

6-47. Shavit, David. *The United States in the Middle East: A Historical Dictionary.* Westport, CT: Greenwood Press, 1988. 441 pp. ISBN: 0-313-25341-2.

This wide-ranging historical dictionary gives relatively concise levels of information on the people, events, and institutions that have helped define the relationship between the United States and the nations of the Middle East. The author's original goal was to be fairly comprehensive in scope, but the work ended up being more in the selective category, even by admission in his own introductory statements. American military personnel who were sent to North Africa during World War II have been determined to be outside the purview of this dictionary. There are also relatively few government agencies or business firms listed. Most entries, approximately 90 percent, seem to be individuals. Entries are one-paragraph long and provide dates, a sentence or two on that person's link to the Middle East, and works either written by or written about the individual. Some representational terms that are not individuals are for "ARAMCO (Arabian American Oil Company)" and "Camp David Accords." There are separate listings of chiefs of the American diplomatic missions to the Middle East countries from 1831 to 1986 and for individuals arranged by their profession. The work concludes with a short bibliographic essay of books written on the region and their respective or collective relations with the United States.

Encyclopedias

6-48. De Conde, Alexander. *Encyclopedia of American Foreign Policy.* 2nd ed. 3 vols. New York: Charles Scribner's Sons/ Gale Group, 2002. Index. ISBN: 0-684-80657-6.

The second edition of this encyclopedia has moved away from short entries arranged strictly in alphabetical order to ones that are more in-depth and interpretive in quality. The essays in the second edition are intended to supplement and/or to enrich those American foreign policy treatises published in standard textbooks, monographs, and journal articles. Many of the articles are quite lengthy, often reaching journal-article length or longer. There are 121 such essays, of which 44 are new to this particular edition. All but one of the other essays from the previous edition have been thoroughly updated. The editorial policy here is to refrain from devoting separate essays to accounts of many major subjects of American foreign policy and/or diplomacy, such as the Louisiana Purchase, the War of 1812, World War II, and the Korean War. While these topics are still indexed and discussed in depth, that is now done within the context of articles with a broader nature and scope. The book contains a chronology of American foreign policy from 1607 to 2001. The essays are all signed by international affairs scholars. There are no pictures, maps, graphs, or other visuals. A thorough index is available and highly useful for this set.

6-49. Jentleson, Bruce W., ed. *Encyclopedia of U.S. Foreign Relations*. 4 vols. New York: Oxford University Press, 1997. ISBN: 0-195-11055-2.

Prepared under the auspices of the venerable Council on Foreign Relations, this book has put together a number of articles by U.S. and international scholars who examine the people, ideas, policies, major events, and key decisions that largely shaped U.S. foreign relations. Essays numbering 1,024 explain how American foreign policies developed over time. There is in-depth treatment of

a number of topics, including World War II, the cold war, and the environment. Numerous cross-references are an integral design component for leading readers through various threads of related topics. The work employs numerous maps, charts, figures, and detailed chronologies. The introduction to the work on the discussion of U.S. foreign affairs is a good essay in its own right. Entries are all signed and include a set of suggested readings. Some entries in this work, such as the one on the Constitution, are scholarly overviews of the subject and have an air of authority to them. This is a unique and well-researched work.

6-50. DeRouen, Karl R. *Historical Encyclopedia of U.S. Presidential Use of Force, 1789–2000*. Westport, CT: Greenwood Press, 2001. 313 pp. ISBN: 0-313-30732-6.

Not seen.

Guides and Handbooks

6-51. Leonard, Thomas M. *Central America and United States Policies, 1820s–1980s: A Guide to Issues and Reference*. Claremont, CA: Regina Books, 1985. 133 pp. Index. ISBN: 0-941-69014-8.

The goal of this book is to place the problems of Central America and their impact on U.S. foreign policy into some semblance of historical perspective. Chapter 1 reviews Central American history, while Chapter 2 traces the ongoing evolution of U.S. foreign policy toward this region. There is also a relatively large chapter entitled "Selective Bibliography," which makes up approximately one-third of the entire work. All works cited in this chapter are in the English language and cover Central American history and the economic/political relations with not only the United States but also Costa Rica, El Salvador, Guatemala, Honduras, and Nicaragua. This "Selective Bibliography" attempts to parallel the same topics covered in Chapters 1 and 2. There is only an author index.

6-52. Brune, Lester H., ed. *Chronological History of U.S. Foreign Relations.* 2nd ed. 3 vols. New York: Routledge, 2003. 1488 pp. ISBN: 0-415-93914-3.

This work is a very down-to-earth examination of events surrounding U.S. foreign relations with other countries over time. It also notes events in those other foreign nations that had a definite impact on U.S. policy-making decisions and issues. There are a number of black-and-white line maps and pictures printed to assist students, general researchers, and nonspecialists in understanding central events within the context of U.S. foreign relations. Most entries are one or two paragraphs, but they can be several paragraphs longer at times. This is a wonderful source for dates and understanding the role of historical events in U.S. foreign policy matters. The more recent second edition of this work covers the period from about 1763 through early 2001 and 30 percent of the material contained is new since the first edition.

Foreign Relations of Other Countries
Bibliographies

6-53. Silverburg, Sanford R. *Asian States' Relations with the Middle East and North Africa: A Bibliography, 1950–1993.* Metuchen, NJ: Scarecrow, 1994. 158 pp. Index. ISBN: 0-810-82872-3.

This unannotated bibliography concentrates not only on the relations among countries and within regions but on a number of important topics such as oil, trade, Islam, and so forth. Asian countries are seen as showing increasing interest in the Middle East and North Africa because of oil politics. Emphasis is clearly on the diplomatic, political, economic, and religious components of these relationships. Not surprisingly, the bulk of the literature aims at the larger political entities. The main body of the bibliography is arranged alphabetically by broad subject heading, such as "Asia-Saudi Arabia-Oil," "Australia-Zionism," and "Japan-Persian Gulf." Most entries are in English, but some are in other European and non-European languages. There are no cross-references and only an author index. This does create some inefficiency in pulling out desired topics from the body of the bibliography. In the main body of the work, there is a heading for "India-Palestine," but no cross-reference from "Palestine-Asia." Despite the access issue, this bibliography does fill in a gap in the literature.

6-54. McNenly, Jennifer, comp. *A Bibliography of Works on Canadian Foreign*

Relations, 1991–1995. Toronto: Canadian Institute of International Affairs, 1998. 104 pp. ISBN: 0-919-08465-6.

This series of bibliographies of Canadian foreign affairs has been coming out regularly for nearly forty years. Bibliography listings are in English or French and include Canadian as well as non-Canadian monographs, journal articles, theses, research papers, government documents, and conference papers. There are two parts to the bibliography: subject and personal name. This five-year cumulative work indexes approximately 250 different international journals. Full bibliographic citations are offered. This bibliography is especially good for those wanting the Canadian perspective as seen through using Canadian resources.

6-55. Aster, Sidney, ed. *British Foreign Policy 1918–1945: A Guide to Research and Research Materials.* rev. ed. Wilmington, DE: Scholarly Resources, 1991. 391 pp. Index. ISBN: 0-842-02310-0.

This work is part of a publisher's series that includes France, Germany, Great Britain, Italy, the Soviet Union, international organizations, and international economic relations. This work is designed for students and scholars doing research on European diplomatic history between the First and Second World Wars. Each book within this series is arranged in a similar pattern. Chapter 1 is a guide to the organization and history of the British Foreign Office and its foreign policy. Chapter 2 provides information on library resources, archives, newspaper collections, and other repositories

of information germane to the topic of British foreign policy. The remainder of the book is a bibliography of general and more specialized works such as bibliographies, reference works, journals, parliamentary publications, memoirs, and biographies. Part of this bibliographic section also deals with various aspects of foreign policy and provides a chronology section broken down into several broad categories. Sources listed in this bibliography are in English and other major European languages. About 15 percent of the material is annotated. A "unified" index is offered for authors, editors, and compilers only. The lack of a subject index is a drawback given the size and arrangement of this work.

6-56. Echard, William E., comp. and ed. *Foreign Policy of the French Second Empire: A Bibliography.* Westport, CT: Greenwood Press, 1988. 416 pp. Indexes. ISBN: 0-313-23799-9.

Over 4,100 bibliographic citations drawn from books, dissertations, and 679 journals have been included in this work. Chapters arranged by country, region, or topic represent the main feature of this work. Entries related to foreign policy matters with other nations represent the overwhelming number of these unannotated citations. A significant number of the entries are in French, Spanish, German, and languages other than English. The chapter on topical entries includes "Disarmament/Peace Movements/Pacifism," and "Economic Policies and Role of France," among others. There is a standard author index and a subject index that may induce some level of confusion among some readers. There is no introduction to this bibliography. The typeface is a bit hard on the eyes.

6-57. Young, Robert J., comp. and ed. *French Foreign Policy 1918–1945: A Guide to Research and Research Materials.* rev. ed. Wilmington, DE: Scholarly Resources, 1991. 339 pp. ISBN: 0-842-02308-9.

Three main chapters constitute this work. They are "Foreign Ministry and Foreign Policy," "Archives and Libraries," and "Bibliography." The last chapter is by far the longest one. The French Empire and colonial possessions/administration are deemed inappropriate for inclusion. This book does, however, introduce its readers to research materials written in or available in France. The central government of France by far receives the most attention. An essay on the French foreign policy–making establishment and the growth of the foreign ministry opens this research guide. The substantial bibliography is by general subject, while annotations were quite sparse throughout this section. 🖳

6-58. Cassels, Alan, ed. *Italian Foreign Policy 1918–1945: A Guide to Research and Research Materials.* rev. ed. Wilmington, DE: Scholarly Resources, 1991. 261 pp. ISBN: 0-842-02307-0.

The arrangement of this work is quite similar to all the others in this series. Materials listed are all in English, French, German, and Italian. Part 1 discusses

Italy's Foreign Ministry and foreign policy, while part 2 examines the archives, libraries, and newspapers available on the topic. Part 3 is a bibliography broken down into ample subdivisions, and this is by far the largest part of this book. This guide includes a larger-than-typical number of non-English-language sources. 🖳

6-59. Hoadley, Steve. *The New Zealand Foreign Affairs Handbook.* 2nd ed. New York: Oxford University Press, 1992. 176 pp. ISBN: 0-195-58248-9.

This is a handbook compiled for those interested in New Zealand's foreign relations in several ways. It contains facts, serves as a guidebook for those seeking information on the topic, and has a textbook component for students beginning to study the issues. There are fifteen chapters averaging about ten pages each. The first chapter is general in nature and examines New Zealand from a global perspective. Following this general introductory chapter are fourteen others on more specific topics, such as aid, trade, multilateral diplomacy, and government. There are plentiful charts, tables, maps, and other visual devices, with most of this data drawn from official New Zealand government sources. Each chapter is arranged in a totally different manner. This is a very idiosyncratic work, but unique as a synthesizer for this area.

6-60. Andor, Lydia Eve, comp. *The Small and the New in Southern Africa: The Foreign Relations of Botswana, Lesotho, Namibia and Swaziland since their Independence.* Johannesburg: South African

Institute of International Affairs, 1993. 526 pp. ISBN: 1-874-89021-8.

This bibliography was not examined.

6-61. Johnston, Robert H. *Soviet Foreign Policy 1918–1945: A Guide to Research and Research Materials.* Wilmington, DE: Scholarly Resources, 1991. 236 pp. Indexes. ISBN: 0-842-02312-7.

This work's organization is similar to other works in this publisher series. Chapter 2 is a short essay on the Soviet government's Foreign Ministry and its foreign policy history. There is also a list of former Soviet diplomats and other major officials. Chapter 3 identifies mostly non-Soviet research archives and libraries, followed by a bibliographic section of selective reference works, bibliographies, journal articles, and other resources. The listing of official Soviet publications is highly selective. The 907 citations are listed under broad categories such as "Leninist Decade," "Stalinist Diplomacy," and others. Indexes are available by title and author only. 🖳

Dictionaries
6-62. Weigall, David. *Britain and the World 1815–1986: A Dictionary of International Relations.* New York: Oxford University Press, 1987. 240 pp. ISBN: 0-195-20610-X.

The author's lofty goal is to serve as a "standard" reference work on British foreign policy and international relations. Included are historical and biographical entries, definitions, and concepts of international relations and/or diplomacy.

Its time frame is for modern history beginning with the Battle of Waterloo. The articles on British relations with major powers are particularly long. In the entries on individuals, their contributions to diplomacy and international affairs are highlighted. This is an excellent work for dates and factual information. Most entries end with a short reading list. The text can read a bit on the stuffy side but is authoritative. There is also a chronology of events that involve Britain, and there are several historical maps. Articles are heavily cross-referenced. 🖳

6-63. Palmer, Alan Warwick. *Dictionary of the British Empire and Commonwealth.* London: Murray, 1996. 395 pp. ISBN: 0-719-55650-3.

This is a reference companion for students of the British Empire and Commonwealth political events, history, and current affairs. While political and historical events within Great Britain itself receive some space, the emphasis here is on overseas British territories or the Commonwealth nations. Biographies are included, but again, individuals from Britain itself garner scant attention unless their political lives have been inextricably linked to overseas British lands. Most entries within this alphabetically arranged dictionary reflect the time period after 1788 up to the mid-1990s. Each entry is fairly short, only about one paragraph, but the entries do have cross-references built into them. There is a modest reading list attached. The author of this work has written a number of books on modern history.

Peace Research, Arms Control, and Disarmament

Abstracting and Indexing Services

6-64. *Peace Research Abstracts Journal.* Bimonthly. Thousand Oaks, CA: Sage Publications, 1964–. Indexes. ISSN: 0031-3599.

Conflict resolution and all aspects of peace research are covered in this unique abstracting service. The publication is sponsored by the Peace Research Institute in Canada. Topics indexed cover the broadest possible context of peace research, conflict resolution, and international affairs in general. Typical subject categories are "Environmental Law," "Foreign Policy," "International Law," "World Economy and Trade," and "Military Policy." There is keyword access in addition to an author and a subject index. Each bimonthly issue contains approximately 600 separate abstracts. These abstracts are drawn from journal articles, books, government publications, dissertations, newsletters, and international research studies. 🖳

Annuals and Yearbooks

6-65. *Disarmament and Security Yearbook/USSR Academy of Sciences, Institute of World Economy and International Relations* [*Razorvzhenie I Bezopasnost*]. 2nd ed. Moscow: Novosti Press Agency; Boulder, CO: Westview Press, 1988.

Not surprisingly, the United States and the Soviet Union both individually and in the context of their superpower interrelationship receive the most attention here. There is an honest attempt to deal with disarmament issues in the spirit of "glas-

nost'" and democratization. The articles contained within are mainly by Soviet and Russian experts in the field. There are chapters on various aspects of disarmament, regional conflicts, weapons systems, nuclear arms, and so forth. The style of prose can be absolutely leaden at times, but it does give a glimpse into Soviet-style thinking during the transitional Gorbachev years. There are numerous statistical tables, graphs, maps, charts, and the like, but text predominates. Overall, this work is less of a statistical compendium than a collection of survey articles on disarmament and security issues from the Soviet perspective.

6-66. *SIPRI Yearbook: Armaments, Disarmament and International Security.* Annual. New York: Oxford University Press, 1972–. ISSN: 0953-0282. Title and Subtitle Vary.

According to the thirty-third edition (2002), the Stockholm International Peace Research Institute's (SIPRI) three main areas of interest are in security and conflict; military spending and armaments; and, in the area of nonproliferation, arms control and disarmament. Part 1 is a survey of security and conflicts for the year 2001. This is broken down further into major armed conflict, conflict prevention, military divisions of the European Union (EU), and security-sector reform within the EU and United Nations. Part 2 gives military spending on arms, arms production figures, arms industry data, and international arms transfers. Part 3 centers on all aspects of nuclear nonproliferation, ballistic-missile-defense systems, arms control, military uses of outer space, chemical and biological weapons development, and more. Contributors are an international group of authoritative and highly regarded researchers and scholars.

Directories

6-67. Woodhouse, T., ed. *International Peace Directory.* Plymouth, UK: Northcote House, 1988. 189 pp. ISBN: 0-746-30379-3.

This is an alphabetically arranged, country-by-country survey of organizations existing within each nation's borders that promote peace research and peace education. It also includes various associations dedicated to the ultimate goal of peace. Only groups advocating peaceful relationships and conflict-resolution techniques are listed in this directory. Groups envisioning peace exclusively through the prism of military power are excluded from consideration. Each entry is fairly well standardized as to format. This work identifies which particular peace issues are important to each respective peace organization, whether it is arms control, disarmament, or other peace-related activities.

6-68. Fenton, Thomas P., comp. and ed. *Third World Struggle for Peace with Justice: A Directory of Resources.* Maryknoll, NY: Orbis Books, 1990. 188 pp. ISBN: 0-883-44660-X.

This is an openly partisan handbook of resources for teaching Western high-school and undergraduate students to appreciate alternative viewpoints on the world's developing nations in general and the United States in particular. This handbook highlights third world–related organizations and brings to light monographs, periodical articles, and audio-visual materials to people in the industrialized countries of the world in order to correct injustice in the manner their governments and international corporations treat third world nations and peoples. The organizations and resources included have been chosen to educate people about third world struggles, economic oppression and military repression, and its dream of self-determination. Materials that emphasize any aspect of the East-West conflict are excluded. The third world sources picked for this handbook tend toward the more popular materials that are generally accessible. Many of the sources covered are partisan and openly biased in favor of an activist view of the world.

Bibliographies

6-69. Atkins, Stephen E. *Arms Control and Disarmament, Defense and Military, International Security and Peace: An Annotated Guide to Sources 1980–1987.* Santa Barbara, CA: ABC-CLIO, 1988. 411 pp. Indexes. ISBN: 0-874-36488-4.

This is a successful attempt to establish a semblance of bibliographic control over the monographic literature rather than the journal literature on the topic of arms control and related subjects. It includes books, hearings, papers, reference works, and microforms, primarily in English. The time period chosen covers the transition from the Carter era to the Reagan administration, especially Reagan's change in approach to defense and security policy matters and spending. There are a total of 1,596 fully annotated citations placed under one of the appropriate topical chapters. Four of the larger chapters are additionally broken down into genre of publication: dictionary, guidebook, monograph, bibliography, and so forth. The annotations are truly excellent and illuminating. There is an author/title index and a separate subject index.

6-70. Fermann, Gunnar. *Bibliography on International Peacekeeping.* Dordrecht, Neth: Martinus Nijhoff, 1992. 304 pp. Indexes. ISBN: 0-792-32011-5.

This is a topical bibliography of academic resources drawn from books, reports, and journal articles. There are no newspaper article entries. The works listed are mostly, but not exclusively, English-language materials. The contributors are international in scope. Entries are annotated selectively, and these serve as a "recommendation" from the compiler. The organization is by topic, arranged in fourteen sections. These topics pertain to the financial, political, and military aspects of international peacekeeping efforts. Each of the 1,148 entries has one or more subject-heading terms, and often may state where a book has been reviewed or reprinted. There is a subject and a general index of names.

6-71. Ridinger, Robert B. Marks. *The Peace Corps: An Annotated Bibliography.* Boston: G. K. Hall, 1989. 366 pp. Index. ISBN: 0-816-18912-9.

This is a bibliography that provides a quarter-century overview of the Peace Corps literature published since 1961, the year President Kennedy announced its organization, until 1986. Most of the literature consists of memoirs of returned Peace Corps volunteer workers, agency publications, coverage in the popular and scholarly presses, and more. The bibliography is arranged in three major segments. The first section is on the creation and development of the agency and on the description of its programmatic emphasis. The second part examines the programs targeted at individual recipient countries. Finally, the last section looks at the active roles and influence for change played by returning Peace Corps volunteers. There are government and other agency publications, books, dissertations, memoirs, periodical articles, and videotapes included for listing in the bibliography. There are a total of 1,432 bibliographic entries, all annotated and often lengthy. The index is sparse.

6-72. Lofland, John. *Peace Movement Organizations and Activists in the US: An Analytical Bibliography.* Binghamton, NY: Haworth Press, 1991. 141 pp. ISBN: 1-560-24075-X.

This is a bibliography of more contemporary English-language monographs on the activities of American peace movement organizations and activists. The context is a look at organized citizens and their efforts to alter governmental policy on issues of war and peace toward ones that stress a less militaristic course of action. The bibliography includes biographies and autobiographies, insider accounts, books, and scholarly histories of the peace movement. The time period covered is primarily the post–World War II era through the 1980s. There is some pre–World War II material included as well. The work is especially rich in uncovering material on the anti–Vietnam War movement in the United States. The book is alphabetically arranged by individual author. There are no annotations with the exception of an occasional descriptive sentence.

Dictionaries

6-73. Roberts, Nancy L. *American Peace Writers, Editors, and Periodicals: A Dictionary*. Westport, CT: Greenwood Press, 1991. 362 pp. Index. ISBN: 0-313-26842-8.

Approximately 400 individuals living from the American colonial period up to 1990 who sought to encourage others through their writings in the cause of peace are listed. This selective work includes people who were inspired by both religious and secular peace ideals. All were activists in the cause of peace. The purpose of this particular reference work is to emphasize the link between journalism and the U.S. peace movement. The arrangement of the book is strictly alphabetical in order. Some entries have individual archival sites noted. All entries are fairly brief and in a format akin to the well-known Who's Who series of biographical dictionaries. Information provided includes birth and death dates, places of birth and death, where published, a short paragraph on their lives, their activist ori-

entation and affiliation, works citing those listed, and so forth. One section lists "Peace Advocacy Periodicals," while an appendix concludes with a selective chronology of the U.S. peace movement from 1815 to 1982. There is also a highly selective bibliography of secondary works and a bare-bones index.

6-74. Elliot, Jeffrey M. *The Arms Control, Disarmament, and Military Security Dictionary*. Santa Barbara, CA: ABC-CLIO, 1989. 349 pp. Index. ISBN: 0-874-36430-2.

This dictionary is arranged around broad subject chapters, such as "War and Peace," "Nuclear Weapons," and "Arms Control and Disarmament," and then by a string of terms in alphabetical sequence within these topic headings. Entries average approximately one page and are quite substantive. Each entry has background information followed by its "Significance," which is a standard arrangement in the Clio Dictionaries of Political Science series. The scope tends to be selective rather than exhaustive. It is heavily footnoted, which is a bit unusual for a dictionary of this kind. Terms selected for inclusion would appear to be best for undergraduate students. A good index is quite useful.

6-75. Mays, Terry M. *Historical Dictionary of Multinational Peacekeeping*. Lanham, MD: Scarecrow Press, 1996. 340 pp. ISBN: 0-810-83031-0.

This publication is meant to fill the void in the international peacekeeping literature outside of the abundance of information on United Nations operations. Peace-keeping is used here in its broadest possible context, which is a neutral military action. The time period covered is 1920 to the mid-1990s. It traces the evolution of international peacekeeping from the use of cease-fire observers to the more multi-faceted contemporary role of refugee aid, forced separation of warring parties, disarmament actions, and in some instances the actual supervision of elections. A chronology of peacekeeping events from 1920 to June 16, 1995, is available for examination. The main body is strictly alphabetical and contains fairly brief entries that center on diplomats, military forces, agreements, peacekeeping bodies, and the many cities, regions, and countries often associated with international peace-keeping efforts, such as Kuwait, the Congo, Cyprus, and others. There is a lengthy bibliography attached to this work on all aspects of international peacekeeping and military forces. The absence of an index could hamper the effective use of this otherwise valuable work. (Note: A second edition was scheduled to be published in 2004 but was not seen.)

6-76. Ali, Sheikh Rustum. *The Peace and Nuclear War Dictionary.* Santa Barbara, CA: ABC-CLIO, 1989. 294 pp. ISBN: 0-874-365531-7.

A specialized dictionary of over 300 main entries growing out of the rapid changes in the new technical and global language related to both nuclear weaponry and the international peace process. Each selected term has its "significance" explained right after the definition of that word or phrase has been rendered. The entry terms are related exclusively to the concepts, events, weapons, armaments, and policies that go into weighing the balance between nuclear hardware and strategic options on one side and international peace on the other. Entries are well written with sample topics including the MX Missile and SALT I and II.

Encyclopedias

6-77. Burns, Richard Dean, ed. *Encyclopedia of Arms Control and Disarmament.* 3 vols. New York: Charles Scribner's Sons/Macmillan International, 1993. 1692 pp. ISBN: 0-684-19281-0.

Each of the set's three volumes examines arms control from a different perspective. Volume 1 is largely a country-by-country or regional survey on the history of war, peace, and arms control up to the present date. There are essays on nuclear weapon–free zones, security issues, treaties, the role of nonviolence in various cultures, the United Nations, nuclear test ban initiatives, the SALT talks, peace movements, and much more. The introduction defines the terms quite well. The latter half of volume 1 has a section entitled "Themes and Institutions," which is a collection of essays of eight to twenty pages each done by experts in the field. Some of these themes are arms control treaty verification, international atomic energy agency and arms control, and the like. Volume 2 has articles pertaining to "The Historical Dimensions to 1945." These are substantive articles on the League of Nations, Kellogg-Briand Pact, early aerial-bombing regulations, the

Versailles Treaty, and so forth. Volume 2 also contains such topics as arms control activities since 1945, Antarctica, outer space treaties, antisatellite weapons, the Strategic Defense Initiative, and more contemporary issues. Volume 3 contains the text of various treaties related to arms control and disarmament. This is an excellent source of information for high-school and undergraduate students written in a clear style with wide appeal.

6-78. Ramsbotham. Oliver. *Encyclopedia of International Peacekeeping Operations.* Santa Barbara, CA: ABC-CLIO, 1999. 356 pp. ISBN: 0-874-36892-8.

Those seeking theoretical knowledge or the more pragmatic elements of international peacekeeping activities will find this work useful. It was written in reaction to the significant increase in peacekeeping employing a multilateral conflict-management approach. The time period is anchored in the modern world. Many of the entries from 1945 to date have been organized under United Nations auspices. The reader searching information about underlying policy factors, or perhaps the organizational and/or regional contexts of the peacekeeping initiative itself, will find this and other information throughout the pages of this alphabetically arranged work. Entries can be nations, United Nations agencies, specific peacekeeping actions, biographies, and the like. Several peacekeeping-related appendixes are included.

6-79. Rosenberg, Jerry M. *Encyclopedia of the Middle East Peace Process and the Middle East/North Africa Economic Community.* Greenwich, CT: JAI Press, 1997. 451 pp. ISBN: 0-762-30350-6.

Because the political situation in the Middle East has remained so intractable, this is a work that may unfortunately stay relevant during the lifetime of all who consult its pages. It was compiled to provide its readers a historic perspective of the events leading up to the current attempts at working through a regional peace process. The pages cover facts, events, issues, ideologies, controversies, and the actions all necessary to better the user's understanding in the continued quest for peace, cooperation, and productivity within the region. The arrangement is by alphabetical short entries drawn largely from official sources of information. Both relatively standard and the more unusual entries in the areas of politics and economic development are included. Some entries are on the very chronology of the peace process, the work done over the years by the Council on Foreign Relations, and the numerous treaties and trade pacts that have been penned over time. Useful cross-references are employed throughout the work.

6-80. Pauling, Linus, ed. *World Encyclopedia of Peace.* New York: Pergamon Press, 1986. 4 vols. Indexes. ISBN: 0-080-32685-4.

This is one of the first attempts to put together such a comprehensive reference encyclopedia on all aspects of peace. The two predominant themes of this work are peace research and peace activism. The topic of peace is examined from all sides, including the perspectives of realists, global idealists, and so on. The encyclopedia reflects the bias that much peace research shows from having been done in either North America or Europe. The four-volume set was published as commemoration for the fortieth anniversary of the United Nations and the International Year of Peace (1986). Volumes 1 and 2 form the main body of this work. These two volumes contain several-page articles in alphabetical order on people, theories, perspectives on war and peace, international relations terms, international organization, and the like. Volume 3 has major international treaties from 1919 (Treaty of Versailles) to 1981 (Convention on Prohibition on Restoration of the Use of Certain Conventional Weapons . . .). This is followed by a peace chronology ensued by Nobel Peace Prize Laureates. The final volume is a directory of peace organizations and institutions. There is also a sixty-five-page bibliography broken down by topic and journals in the field of peace research, and various indexes to the work as a whole. (Note: The second edition (1999–) in eight volumes was published, but was unseen by the reviewer.)

Guides and Handbooks
6-81. Lunardini, Christine A. *The ABC-CLIO Companion to the American Peace Movement in the Twentieth Century.* Denver, CO: ABC-CLIO, 1994. 269 pp. ISBN: 0-874-36714-X.

This work's purpose is to demonstrate to readers the very wide range of philoso-phies underlying the U.S. peace movement and the individuals associated with them. People and organizations that have been especially prominent in the U.S. peace movement from the late 1800s to the present constitute the bulk of the entries in this book. A concise introduction to the first 100 years of the peace movement offers the reader a chance to understand the context of the social and political milieu in which these people and groups operated. Entries are strictly alphabetical and average about one-half to one page long and are done in style that may appeal more strongly to the general reader. Entries for individuals provide information on their education, work experience, and peace-advocacy activities, and conclude with a short list of additional readings. A number of black-and-white pictures are interspersed throughout. The work appears to be especially strong in Vietnam era organizations, events, and terminology. Women are well represented as entries. Some typical terms are "Port Huron Statement" and "Jane Fonda."

6-82. Howlett, Charles F. *The American Peace Movement: References and Resources.* Boston: G. K. Hall, 1991. 416 pp. ISBN: 0-816-11836-1.

This work spans 300 years of peace activism in the United States. There are a total of twelve chapters, each covering a different aspect of the American peace movement. There are 1,600 citations overall, including primary and secondary sources of information. A forty-page historical overview precedes the bibliographic portion of Chapter 1. Typical chapters are "International Peace Movements," "Peace, Patriotism, and the Judicial Process," and many others. The arrangement is alphabetical by author within each section. Each citation contains a one- or two-sentence annotation of the work. The appendix is a short historiography of the U.S. peace movement.

6-83. Grenville, J. A. S. *The Major International Treaties, 1914–1945: A History and Guide with Texts.* New York: Methuen, 1987. 268 pp. ISBN: 0-416-08092-8.

See annotation for entry 6-84.

6-84. *The Major International Treaties since 1945: A History and Guide with Texts.* New York: Methuen, 1987. 528 pp. ISBN: 0-416-38080-8.

Only the earlier of these two works was examined. It offers a short history and analysis of a number of international treaties and agreements from 1914 to 1945. The complete or partial text from landmark treaties is given. Most of the research that went into this guide was culled from the League of Nations Treaty series and the United Nations Treaty series. The volume is arranged into ten chapters, and each of these is subdivided into smaller sections. The treaties are ordered chronologically within the subdivisions. The major provisions of treaties are printed. This is reprinted material from *Major International Treaties, 1914–1973*, except for a new introduction and a revision of Chapter 10, "The Alliances and Alignments of the United States: From the League of Nations to the United Nations." (Note: A 2001 revision of these two works has been published in two volumes as *The Major International Treaties of the Twentieth Century* [ISBN: 0-415-14125-7].)

6-85. Abrams, Irwin. *The Nobel Peace Prize and the Laureates: An Illustrated Biographical History, 1901–1987.* Boston: G. K. Hall, 1988. 269 pp. ISBN: 0-816-18609-X.

The introduction to this work declares that this historical handbook was compiled to provide the reader with accurate information on the Nobel Peace Prize itself in order to counter any misconceptions that may surround it. In part 1, the book attempts to clarify the process for selecting the Nobel Peace Prize candidates and to give some history on the prize's origin. The first eighty years of the existence of the committee that runs this program also is examined. Part 2 looks at the actual laureates themselves by providing a biographical essay and bibliography for every individual who has won the prize. There are black-and-white pictures of each winner. The bibliography cites both primary and secondary sources. Individual entries average around two pages. (Note: A 2001 edition covering the 1901–2001 century has been published [ISBN: 0-881-35388-4], but was unseen.)

6-86. Day, Alan J., ed. *Peace Movements of the World.* Phoenix: Oryx Press, 1987. 398 pp. ISBN: 0-897-74438-1.

This handbook is a country-by-country listing of the various groups that have or are currently fighting for peace and disarmament at least up until the time of publication. The majority of these movements are from North America and Western Europe rather than from the developing countries of the world. In order to be included, the group in question must stress the global threat of the nuclear arms race. Groups whose major focus falls outside this singular area of concern are excluded. The time frame is 1945 to the 1980s. There is an article entitled "International Movements" directly preceding the main body of the work, which is the alphabetical order of individual countries. These one-half-page entries provide the movement's address, formation history, activities, membership, publications, aims and objectives, and its affiliations. The movement's name is given in both English and its native tongue.

6-87. Meyer, Robert S. *Peace Organizations, Past and Present: A Survey and Directory.* Jefferson, NC: McFarland, 1988. 266 pp. ISBN: 0-899-50340-3.

The organizations tracked in this directory may demonstrate differences in approach to issues of peace and nonviolence, but they all support it strongly. The peace organizations have been divided into three separate categories. The first are those groups using personal approaches to peace. They stress pacifism, friendship, and assistance programs. The second category is for organizations using an instructional approach, such as promoting peace through research, publication, and educational efforts. The

third set includes groups that have opted for a structural approach to peace by trying to reform the United Nations into a more effective body or by striving to work for a world federation of nations. Each entry is in prose format and does not follow any standardized pattern of organization throughout the book. The final result is a quirky presentation with great variety in detail and length of entry.

6-88. Janes, Robert W. *Scholars' Guide to Washington, D.C., for Peace and International Security Studies.* Washington, DC: Woodrow Wilson Center Press; Baltimore: Johns Hopkins University Press, 1995. 407 pp. Indexes. ISBN: 0-801-85218-8.

This guide is arranged into three primary parts. The first part on "Collections" discusses hours of operations, collection sizes and strengths, data files, maps, and other types of resources for the libraries, archives, and information centers in the Washington, D.C., area. These organizations are lumped together by category. The second major part of this work identifies the organizations, research centers, academic programs, government agencies, and independent associations in the same region. Such information as addresses, contact people, focus of the organization, and publications put out by the organization is given. The third part is composed of various appendixes on the media, bookstores, Library of Congress class numbers, and more. Included are indexes to personal papers, library subject strengths, general subjects, and organizations/institutions, all related to the quest for peace and international studies.

6-89. SIPRI: Stockholm International Peace Research Institute. http://www .sipri.se/.

This organization has been around for almost forty years, and it has dedicated itself to the establishment of a stable peace regime and peaceful solutions to major international problems. The Stockholm International Peace Research Institute (SIPRI) is also heavily involved in studying arms limitations, reduction, and control in general. It is well known and respected for its work in gathering detailed statistics and figures on weapon development, arms shipments, and military expenditures among the world's nations. Some of SIPRI's own data is on this Web site. A number of databases are available pertaining to both international relations and comparative politics that can be searched individually or in groups for up to six different countries for concurrent analysis. See also the *SIPRI Yearbook* [entry 6-66]. 💻

6-90. Rengger, N. J., comp. *Treaties and Alliances of the World.* 6th ed. New York: Stockton; London: Cartermill, 1995. 538 pp. ISBN: 1-860-67021-0.

This work is organized around three primary chapters: "International Organization," "Regional Agreements," "and "Transregional Alliances and Other Informal Groupings." The "Regional Agreements" chapter is the longest. This is a terrific tool for teaching treaties and agreements over time or in determining

who the signatories were. Some entries are quite short, perhaps one sentence in length. Other entries are lengthier and include analysis and historical context. There is no statement on the scope of this work or which treaties are still in force. Agreements among the developing nations are included as well.

Atlases

6-91. Barnaby, Frank, ed. *GAIA Peace Atlas.* New York: Doubleday, 1988. 271 pp. ISBN: 0-385-24190-9.

This is a heavily illustrated and popular work that prints articles about global nuclear proliferation, United Nations peacekeeping activities, the role of military proxies during the ongoing battle between the United States and the Soviet Union, global economics and natural resources, and nonviolence. These and other topics serve ultimately as background to the book's real intent of pushing for a redirection of world politics toward planning for a sustainable future.

6-92. Smith, Dan. *The State of War and Peace Atlas.* rev. 3rd ed. London: Penguin, 1997. 128 pp. ISBN: 0-140-51373-6.

The end of the cold war did not usher in an age of peace and tranquility around the globe, and neither did it end the concentration of weapons in the hands of just a few countries, although the list of countries with weapons of mass destruction continues to grow apace. This situation has led to an ongoing readjustment of international politics and alliances that will have to evolve over time in the arena of world public opinion and multilateral security arrangements. This unique atlas charts these and other changes on the international level. This edition has opted for stressing local and regional conflicts rather than global systems of power and influence typical of the cold war's framework of analysis. There are thirty-four chapters broken down into five parts. Typical chapters cover such topics as the dynamics of war, wars of identity and belief, the military world and peace dynamics, and so on. Each chapter is nicely colored, contains high-quality graphics, and is eye-catching and easy to read and interpret for a number of uses. Text, however, is minimal and is clearly a secondary aspect of this work. There are individual pages of regions, continents, and other geographic areas, along with more thematic graphical representations of terrorism, NATO, general military spending, and more. (Note: A fourth edition was made available in 2003 under the title *Penguin Atlas of War and Peace* but was not examined.)

Human Rights Issues
Annuals and Yearbooks
6-93. *Amnesty International Report*. Annual. London: Amnesty International Publications, 1976–. ISSN: 1070-0781.

This highly respected annual published several short articles on Amnesty International (AI) and its work in the field of international human rights along with United Nations and other intergovernmental organizations. Each issue examines roughly 150 nations for evidence of human rights or civil rights violations of all types. Each entry is several pages long and certainly pulls no punches. It names individuals who have been tortured, ethnic groups brutalized, and the like. There are several appendixes related to the work being done by AI, and there is a list of countries who are signatories to the seven major human rights treaties and international conventions.

6-94. *Critique: Review of the U.S. Department of State's* Country Reports on Human Rights Practices *for 1995.* New York: Lawyers Committee for Human Rights, 1996. 256 pp. ISBN: 0-934-14382-X.

This perhaps irregularly published work monitors twenty-seven countries regarding the U.S. State Department's *Country Reports on Human Rights Practices* for 1995. These twenty-seven nations tend to be ones that the U.S. State Department has accused of more serious human rights violations. Since some of these twenty-seven countries are U.S. allies, this book monitors State Department coverage to ensure there are no ulterior political motives intervening in order to make fair assessments of human rights violations. This book attempts to pick up where the U.S. State Department leaves off in detailing human and civil rights abuses. The Lawyers Committee for Human Rights does, however, give the State Department credit in making changes in their publication to be more forthcoming. The organization putting this book together works closely with many other international human rights activist and monitoring groups.

Bibliographies

6-95. *Human Rights Bibliography: United Nations Documents and Publications, 1980–1990.* 5 vols. New York: United Nations, 1993. 2048 pp. Indexes. ISBN: 9-211-00377-6.

This 9,000-entry bibliography is extracted from the United Nations Bibliographic Information System (UNBIS) and was published to coincide with the June 1993 World Conference on Human Rights held in Vienna, Austria. This project was intended to include the numerous United Nations–sponsored or United Nations–published documents put out on human rights issues. Annual volumes were originally planned as supplemental works to the basic decennial set noted here. Volume 1 has all the documents included arranged in very broad subject categories, and Volume 2 serves only as an author index. Volumes 3 through 5 are subject indexes and are probably the most useful part. United Nations document numbers are provided for each entry.

Dictionaries

6-96. Robertson, David. *A Dictionary of Human Rights.* London: Europa Publications, 1997. 301 pp. ISBN: 1-857-43023-9.

This is indeed a welcome reference work given the steadily increasing concern and interest in international human rights issues. Supranational legal institutions such as the European Court of Justice have been prime movers in this area. The bulk of the terms and other entries selected for this alphabetically arranged dictionary are rooted in U.S. Supreme Court decisions, European human rights documents, and the German constitution. Entries are in the one-half- to one-page range, replete with cross-references done in bold typeface. The level of detail is good, and there is a highly successful effort to target core meanings, arguments, legal decisions, and history for the user. Sample entries are as follows: "Freedom of Association," "First Amendment," and "Reproductive Freedom." There are very few terms relating to the third world entries in this reference work. A lengthy appendix, approximately one-third of the entire book, includes such seminal human rights documents as the Magna Carta, U.S. Bill of Rights, Universal Declaration of Human Rights, and others.

6-97. Saha, Santosh C. *Dictionary of Human Rights Advocacy Organizations in Africa.* Westport, CT: Greenwood Press, 1999. 200 pp. ISBN: 0-313-30945-0.

The key goal for this book is demonstrating the extent to which the indigenous peoples of Africa have organized human rights groups that in turn cater to Africans and their needs. This dictionary, in standard A-to-Z format, examines international as well as African-based human rights groups. Only nongovernmental organizations were included. The author has included certain socioeconomic rights often stated by advocacy groups to be linked to the broader concept of human rights. Examples of these entries include: freedom of economic development and right to information. A number of women's groups are also recounted here. Entries give the date the human rights group was founded, who established it, sources of funding, major activities, and so forth. Entries do vary in length, some offering minimal information. A ten-page bibliography is included and serves as a fine introduction to the English-language literature on the topic of African human rights work.

6-98. Gibson, John S. *Dictionary of International Human Rights Law.* Lanham, MD: Scarecrow Press, 1996. 225 pp. ISBN: 0-810-83118-X.

This human rights dictionary was designed to provide its users the sources, definitions, and key events in international treaties and human rights issues. Part 1, "Issue and Contexts," relates to most of the human rights in this dictionary. Part 2 arranges these rights into categories such as civil and political, legal, economic, social, cultural, and so forth. Each entry contains five parts: the right, other sources of the right, expanded definitions of the right, landmarks in the evolution of the right, and cross-references to other similar human rights. This is not really a dictionary, but almost a summary of basic international human rights laws categorized by subject. The lack of an index is a real drawback here, but extensive use of cross-references within the entries themselves somewhat mitigates this loss.

6-99. Gorman, Robert F. *Historical Dictionary of Human Rights and Humanitarian Organizations.* Lanham, MD:

Scarecrow Press, 1997. 296 pp. ISBN: 0-810-83263-1.

This is a wide-ranging work that lists a large number of public, private, international, national, governmental, and grassroots activist human rights organizations and their work. There is information available on the differing goals and actions of these groups as well as those of some people identified with the causes of human rights. The book opens up with a list of acronyms and abbreviations employed throughout the dictionary and then offers a fairly detailed timeline of many human rights events that have transpired since 1900. A lengthy narrative on the global history of human rights gives a substantive introduction to the topic. A few of the representative main entries in this alphabetically arranged work are those on such terms as the Holocaust, housing, and international law, all as they relate directly to the advancement of human rights issues. There is good use made of cross-referencing to related ideas, topics, or organizations. A substantial bibliography is included and classified into seventeen distinct sections. The entries appearing in the bibliography all seem to be in English.

Encyclopedias
6-100. Lawson, Edward. *Encyclopedia of Human Rights.* 2nd ed. Washington, DC: Taylor and Francis, 1996. 1715 pp. Index. ISBN: 1-560-32362-0.

This should be regarded as a standard reference work touching upon all aspects of the human rights workings of the United Nations and its numerous related agencies. Written in the spirit of the 1995–2005 Decade of Human Rights Education, this work is comprehensive in its coverage on human rights topics pertaining to what has been accomplished by the United Nations organizations with active human rights records. Contents include international organizations, the state of human rights, biographical information on Nobel Peace Prize winners, international agencies, and so on. The text of a number of international human rights documents is printed in this alphabetically arranged work. Many of the entries veer toward the shorter side of the spectrum, but they are authoritative in scope and content. The work's topical entries are the longest ones. Bibliographies are often attached to the individual entries for additional reading. The publications of some United Nations bodies are listed selectively. A major appendix is a chronological list of international human rights documents, while another appendix posts the signatory status of all major United Nations human rights treaties and conventions.

6-101. Langley, Winston. *Encyclopedia of Human Rights Issues since 1945.* Westport, CT: Greenwood Press, 1999. 392 pp. Index. ISBN: 0-313-30163-8.

The goal of this work is to assist readers in gaining access to a wide spectrum of substantive human rights issues since World War II. Entries are about one page long and are arranged alphabetically. The entries range widely from "Abortion" to "Organization of African Unity" to "Uni-

versal Declaration of Human Rights." Only a few biographies are included. This work is quite good for bringing to light dates, historical contexts, related issues, status, and the like. Many of the individual nations serve as entries, and this work provides its readers with a nation-by-nation human rights survey of each country. A general index appears as the last element of the book. 💻

Guides and Handbooks

6-102. Devine, Carol. *Human Rights: The Essential Reference.* Phoenix: Oryx Press, 1999. 311 pp. ISBN: 1-573-56205-X.

Not seen.

6-103. Humana, Charles, comp. *World Human Rights Guide.* 3rd ed. New York: Oxford University Press, 1992. 396 pp. ISBN: 0-195-07674-5.

Humana takes an unusual approach to the discussion of human rights around the world. Forty inquiries are made in regard to each nation with a population over one million. Examples include the freedom to travel in one's own country or another country, freedom from torture, equality for women, freedom from secret trials, and the like. For each of these forty items, individual countries are rated on a four-point scale. In each case where rights are not respected, individual comments are appended. The arrangement is alphabetical by name of country. Brief statistical information for each nation is also provided. Most of the forty parameters are drawn from United Nations covenants; the full text of two of these, "The Universal Declaration of Human

Rights" and the "International Covenant on Civil and Political Rights," is provided. A table at the front of the volume shows how each country rates (in terms of a percentage) in comparison with all others. Several maps conclude the volume. While the format is somewhat complicated, this work provides brief and handy information for high-school and undergraduate students as well as more advanced researchers. The author is a human rights activist who formerly was employed by Amnesty International.

International Economic Relations
Directories
6-104. Welsh, Brian W. W., ed. *Dictionary of Development: Third World Economy, Environment, Society.* 2 vols. New York: Garland, 1990. 1194 pp. ISBN: 0-824-01447-2.

The aim of publishing this work is to bring together in one physical volume the definitions, in standard A-to-Z dictionary format, of the major facts, concepts, events, and various issues that pertain to the study of development in third world countries. The relatively short section on developing-country indicators presents basic social and economic information about these countries' economies and societies. The main part of the text is an alphabetical array of terms used in the development process, its research writings, and its policy statements. Each entry is cross-referenced to others as an aid for both general readers and many specialists in the field. There is an admitted slant in examining issues related to poverty, environmental conservation, and future trends in development. Most entries are of rather modest size and scope, and include such examples as "Development Theory," "Export Processing Zone," "Family Planning," and "Self-Reliance." A list of journals publishing articles on development issues is printed. There is no index.

6-105. Arnold, Guy. *Historical Dictionary of Aid and Development Organizations.* Lanham, MD: Scarecrow, 1996. 196 pp. ISBN: 0-810-83040-X.

Here, general readers and undergraduate students will discover the principal organizations and countries that provide a high percentage of all aid and development assistance throughout the world. Other entries include a selective number of individuals, important meetings, and conferences, while still other entries demonstrate the various forms of aid that are available. The arrangement of this dictionary is strictly alphabetical. While many entries may reach a full page in length, most are closer to being simply a single paragraph of text. Cross-references appear frequently within the entries. There is a good but highly selective bibliography of books on aid to developing nations. This serves as a respectable source for undergraduates looking up basic definitions of the World Bank, Food and Agricultural Organization, or the Columbo Plan. The work is definitely best for information on aid and development since World War II, although this is never made explicit.

6-106. Fry, Gerald. *The International Development Dictionary.* Santa Barbara, CA: ABC-CLIO, 1991. 445 pp. Index. ISBN: 0-874-36545-7.

This work follows a familiar pattern for ABC-CLIO political dictionaries. It is arranged like the others, in alphabetical order within a number of broad topical chapters and subchapters. Chapters run from those on development theorists and leaders to fundamental development concepts, then specific development movements, organizations, and projects, and others. There are 500 entries with an index to assist in using this work. Entries are about one-half to one page long. About 50 percent of each entry's space is devoted to describing the individual concept or term, while the remaining paragraph interprets the actual "significance" of the person or event being discussed. This work perceives international development work as linked to the more traditional disciplines of political science, history, economics, and geography. There appears to be a particular emphasis here on sustainable development policies and social justice ramifications.

6-107. East, Roger, comp. and ed. *World Development Directory.* Chicago: St. James Press, 1990. 568 pp. ISBN: 1-558-62067-2.

This directory attempts to examine international development assistance primarily from intergovernmental organizations (IGOs), nongovernmental organizations (NGOs), and the public and private agencies operating within the developing countries themselves. It covers official development assistance from various multilateral organizations and official government bodies along with the context of distributing foreign aid to the countries of the developing nations of the world. This directory stresses the work carried out by NGOs. Part 1, which is relatively brief, looks at United Nations and other regional NGO agencies, such as the Andean Development Corporation. Parts 2 and 3 form the heart of the book. Part 2 is a list of donor country profiles, giving official foreign aid statistics and an alphabetical listing of private development agencies like OXFAM Canada and Australian Catholic Relief. The scope of these organizations' activities, their aims, criteria, publications, and contact people are provided. Part 3 enumerates in alphabetical order similar locally based NGOs and some governmental agencies working out of the developing countries themselves. This work is intended mostly for those who are international development specialists.

Encyclopedias

6-108. Jones, R. J. Barry, ed. *Routledge Encyclopedia of International Political Economy.* 3 vols. New York: Routledge, 2001. 1818 pp. Index. ISBN: 0-415-14532-5.

Interest in the area of democracy and the international economy has heightened since the cessation of the cold war. Included here are individuals, concepts, and terms associated with international political economy. Articles on Milton

Friedman and Hans Wolfgang Singer sit next to those on various topical components. The articles are arranged in standard alphabetical order, but they vary tremendously in length. Cross-referencing is built into the articles. There appears to have been a shift toward greater use of mathematics and the use of complex equations in this subdiscipline. The article on Picro Sraffa (1898–1983) epitomizes this trend toward quantitative analysis. This work was done half by U.S. scholars and half by English scholars, and it should be valuable to students of economics interested in economic development issues. An index is included. 🖳

National Security, Intelligence Activities, and Defense
Annuals and Yearbooks
6-109. Henderson, Robert D. A. *Brassey's International Intelligence Yearbook.* Annual. Dulles, VA: Brassey's, 2002–. Index. ISBN: 1-574-88549-9.

Since the September 11 twin Trade Towers terrorist attack in New York City, many countries around the world have created new intelligence agencies or made drastic reforms in their existing intelligence communities. There has also been a fairly well-publicized amount of intelligence-sharing information among different countries since that date. This annual publication examines the new intelligence deployment and the way it functions inside fifty countries. The major portion of this work is individual country surveys that contain organization charts, Internet addresses, agencies, legislative actions, oversight committees, and further readings. An index is included.

6-110. Sivard, Ruth Leger. *World Military and Social Expenditures.* Annual. Leesburg, VA: WMSA Publications. 1974–. ISSN: 0363-4795.

According to the author, the purpose of this singular publication is "to provide an annual accounting of the use of world resources for social and military purposes, and an objective basis for assessing relative priorities." It attempts to fold together social and military costs for comparative purposes. An examination of the global military expenditure is followed by a similar analysis of government spending on social, health, and welfare programs. The arrangement is extraordinary in result with a number of comparative tables printed up. Both global and country-by-country analysis and cost figures are given. Military costs are put into human terms. (Note: The 1996 sixteenth edition was the latest seen.)

Bibliographies
6-111. Petersen, Neal H. *American Intelligence, 1775–1990: A Bibliographic Guide.* Claremont, CA: Regina Books, 1992. 406 pp. Indexes. ISBN: 0-941-69045-8.

Over 6,000 entries make up this bibliography on intelligence in its broadest possible context. The scope of topical coverage includes domestic intelligence, internal security, military intelligence, and the like, and is wide enough to provide any researcher with as broad a spectrum as possible of the available literature on intelligence. Both monographs and journal articles have been selected for inclusion in this bibliographic guide that spans approximately 215 years of history. The organization of the book is mainly chronological and by historical event, such as the "Vietnam Era," "Atomic Energy Intelligence," "Joseph R. McCarthy and McCarthyism," the "Civil War," "CIA," and many others. Entries are alphabetical by author and are not annotated. Each chapter and subchapter begins with a short introduction. There is an author and a subject index.

6-112. Rocca, Raymond G. *Bibliography on Soviet Intelligence and Security Services.* Boulder, CO: Westview Press, 1985. 203 pp. ISBN: 0-813-37048-5.

This author knows his business, since he was an intelligence officer for the U.S. government. More than 500 books, articles, congressional publications, and other materials are annotated into five sections: "Bibliographies and Reference Works," "Russian/Soviet Accounts," "Defector/First Hand Accounts," "Secondary Accounts," and "Congressional and Other Official Documents." The defector section is by far the longest and is broken down into two sections. One section is for books, and the other section is for journal articles and book chapters in mainly English-language sources, but some Russian, French, and other languages are represented here. Most works included are from the 1960s and 1970s. The superb annotations speak

well of the knowledge of the author in being critical, informative, and interesting in their content and style.

6-113. Tillema, Herbert K. *International Armed Conflict since 1945: A Bibliographic Handbook of Wars and Military Interventions.* Boulder, CO: Westview Press, 1991. 360 pp. Index. ISBN: 0-813-38311-0.

This is a handbook in a single volume that supposedly enumerates and describes every one of the 269 international wars and other conflicts that took place between 1945 and 1988. Another aspect of this handbook is a 1,000-work bibliography of books, essays, and journal articles on this same topic. The list of wars and conflicts is exhaustive, including each international conflict, no matter how small it was at the time of occurrence. Conflicts that raged within a solitary nation-state are largely omitted except when another country intervenes. Each main chapter is arranged by geographic area, with military conflicts organized by date. Every synopsis explains who intervened, where, when, how, under what circumstances, and with what ultimate effect. There are also estimates of the numbers of people killed. There are cross-references to other related conflicts. The bibliography is replete with English-language materials. An index is attached.

6-114. Lowenthal, Mark M. *U.S. Intelligence Community: An Annotated Bibliography.* Garland Reference Library of the Humanities, Vol. 1765. New York: Garland, 1994. 206 pp. Indexes. ISBN: 0-815-31423-X.

This selective bibliography concentrates on the "specific roles that intelligence plays in the national security policy process, and the strengths and weaknesses of intelligence's contribution to that process" (Lowenthal 1994, introduction). In addition, there is also something of an emphasis on analysis rather than operations. The five parts of the volume cover theory and practice, history and organization, oversight, published compilations of documents, and other bibliographies. In total, there are 225 entries, with each receiving a brief annotation of one or two sentences. There are indexes for author and subject. Over half the volume, however, consists of appendixes; most are reproductions of texts of relevant legislation and executive orders, while others provide organizational information in regard to the U.S. intelligence community. Obviously selective in approach, this work has value for the fact that it attempts coverage of the scholarly literature on the subject more than sensational accounts of spies.

Dictionaries

6-115. Carl, Leo D. *CIA Insider's Dictionary of U.S. and Foreign Intelligence, Counterintelligence and Tradecraft.* Washington, DC: NIBC Press, 1996. 743 pp. ISBN: 1-878-29211-0.

Carl, a veteran of several U.S. intelligence agencies, here presents a dictionary derived from the second edition of the *International Dictionary of Intelligence,* published in 1992. He targets an audience that includes students of intelligence, professionals, fiction writers, and others interested in the subject. Definitions range in length from a single sentence to a half page. Many definitions relate to agencies, acronyms, and jargon. Among the latter, the interested reader can learn about "God disease," "hot mike," "making a pass," and "ringing the gong," among many others. Also included are transliterations of intelligence terms from agencies other than those in the English-speaking world. Biographies, however, have been excluded. Definitions refer to events from World War II to the present. Bibliographies at the back of the volume refer the reader to secondary literature and to federal government publications. The vast number of definitions compiled here recommends this work to those researchers specializing in intelligence operations.

6-116. Becket, Henry S. A. *Dictionary of Espionage: Spookspeak into English.* New York: Stein and Day, 1986. 203 pp. ISBN: 0-812-83068-7.

This dictionary of spy terms borrows mostly from the cold war era or from U.S. and Soviet espionage operations. Entries run from one line to one page in length. The author claims that active and retired agency personnel and Soviet defectors contributed many of the definitions supplied in this dictionary. No cross-references and no subject index make this nonscholarly work best for the general public. The writing style is on a very basic level.

6-117. Luttwak, Edward. *The Dictionary of Modern War.* New York: Harper-Collins, 1991. 680 pp. ISBN: 0-062-70021-9.

Readers who are looking for a reference work offering short definitions of the ideas, institutions, weapons of modern military might, and the like will find this work an appropriate choice. It is in alphabetical order. There is a plethora of facts, dates, and numbers, but no pictures of any sort. Most entries are related to the United States, NATO, and the USSR. Types of missiles, military theories, treaties, and security organs all receive coverage, but wars do not account for any entries.

6-118. Waldman, Harry. *The Dictionary of SDI.* Wilmington, DE: Scholarly Resources, 1988. 182 pp. ISBN: 0-842-02281-3.

The aim of this tightly focused dictionary on Strategic Defense Initiative (SDI) is "to clarify and simplify SDI's complex terrain, lay out technology involved, and identify those areas under debate" (Waldman 1988, introduction). While the term "SDI" is no longer a household word, it was definitely a topic of acrimonious debate during the years of the Reagan administration. Over 800 main entries accentuating the technical aspects of armaments over the political values surrounding SDI constitute the bulk of this alphabetically arranged lexicon. Sample entries are "Delta Rocket," "Thermal Kill," and "Architecture." The pictures accompanying some of the entries can be exceptionally helpful in grasping their conceptual underpinnings. There is no index available. 🖳

6-119. Wilson, William. *Dictionary of the United States Intelligence Services: Over 1500 Terms, Programs and Agencies.* Jefferson, NC: McFarland, 1996. 191 pp. ISBN: 0-786-40180-X.

Wilson, himself a former intelligence officer, says in his introduction that he compiled this dictionary "to consolidate all the various United States intelligence services' terms, definitions, and concepts: one document which would deal exclusively with United States' intelligence." Defense agencies and their terminology were included. Terms were selected from government publications and civilian resources. None were obtained from classified materials. In general, terms older than the era of the Vietnam War were excluded, as well as most pertaining to foreign intelligence agencies. Definitions are usually brief, no more than a sentence or a short paragraph. No sources are indicated for the individual definitions, but Wilson does provide a three-page bibliography to relevant publications. There are no illustrations. Compared to the work by Carl [entry 6-115], this book is less comprehensive and detailed, but is more suitable for the general reader needing basic definitions.

6-120. Kohn, George. *Dictionary of Wars.* rev. ed. New York: Facts on File, 1999. 614 pp. Indexes. ISBN: 0-816-03928-3.

This edition revises the 1986 one by providing seventy new articles and some revised older ones. The new ones were mostly related to twentieth-century events. There are approximately 1,800 main entries, probably enough to fill most people's need for a one-volume source of concise information on wars and battles throughout history. The work is not meant to be comprehensive and looks at battles from 2000 BC to date. A war is defined as being an open, armed conflict between nations or states, parties, factions, or people within the same state (i.e., a civil war). The entries have been written to highlight the military, political, and social factors for each conflict. Each alphabetically arranged main entry contains the name of the battle, dates spanned, how it originated, the opposing sides, a summary of events, and the general outcome of the war. Entries rarely extend beyond a single paragraph. The entire globe is covered. There are two indexes. One is a geographical index, and the other is a general one without the geographic entities.

Encyclopedias

6-121. Parrish, Thomas. *The Cold War Encyclopedia.* New York: H. Holt, 1996. 490 pp. Index. ISBN: 0-805-02778-5.

Prominent people and events in mostly foreign affairs matters make up this work aimed at general readers and lower-division undergraduates or high-school students. Specialists in the field of history, political science, or military science would be better served by using the other numerous cold war dictionaries and encyclopedias that have been published over the last decade or so. Domes-

tic politics, social trends, novels, and movies are outside the scope of coverage here. Terms and people related to intelligence activities and/or espionage receive extensive coverage. Entries are ordered in alphabetical sequence and are generally one to four paragraphs long. There are black-and-white maps and pictures interspersed throughout the pages. A few of the more standard entries here are "Summit," "Imre Nagy," "Kitchen Debate," "China Lobby," and "U-2." There is a "Cold War Chronology" for the years 1917 to 1991. There is an index.

6-122. O'Toole, G. J. A. *Encyclopedia of American Intelligence and Espionage; from the Revolutionary War to the Present.* New York: Facts on File, 1988. 539 pp. Index. ISBN: 0-816-01011-0.

As the author of this reference work points out in his introduction, the world of espionage is more frequently portrayed by journalists and novelists than it is examined in scholarly literature. The purpose of his work is to help fill this gap by compiling for the reader that information that is not actually still classified. Five major categories of articles are included in an alphabetical array. The categories include organizations, major wars, important subjects such as "Overhead Reconnaissance" and "Covert Action," events and incidents, and biographies. Entries range in length from a single paragraph to several pages. There are plentiful cross-references, and most entries include brief citations for additional reading; complete references are found at the back of the work. There are numerous photographs to supplement the text. This work will be useful to researchers in higher education who require basic information on U.S. intelligence operations and personalities. Perhaps its chief drawback lies in the fact that it can only be used for events up through the mid-1980s.

6-123. Szajkowski, Bogdan. *Encyclopedia of Conflicts, Disputes and Flashpoints in Eastern Europe, Russia and the Successor States.* Harlow, Essex, UK: Longman, 1993. 489 pp. Index. ISBN: 0-582-21002-X.

The author of this handbook has identified over 70 ethnoterritorial disputes in Central and East Europe and another 204 in the former Soviet Union. He breaks down all the conflicts listed into three major classifications: economic, political, and ethnic/cultural/religious. The book is alphabetically arranged and supports its discussions with numerous statistics, tables, facts, percentages, and so forth. Cross-references are liberally included within the entries. There are maps that accompany a small number of entries. Each entry is well written, with typical ones being "Russian Armed Forces," "Kosovo," and "North Ossetian Soviet Socialist Republic." An index is provided.

6-124. Hill, Kenneth, ed. *Encyclopedia of Conflicts since World War II.* 2 vols. Armonk, NY: M. E. Sharpe Reference, 1999. 1400 pp. Indexes. ISBN: 0-765-68004-1.

This ambitious encyclopedia purports to list every major international and civil conflict since World War II anyplace around the globe. There are a total of over 180 separate entries divided into three sections. The first section, "Roots of War," contains eight entries that outline the major types of conflicts and causes of war. The second section is on "Alliances and Treaties," and offers a number of different ways that countries, regions, political blocs, or the international community can deal with threats to their security, resolve the conflict at hand, and maintain the peace. The third section is on "Conflicts" and is the largest of the three sections, containing roughly 151 of the entries, arranged by most important country involved in the conflict. It then lists the type of conflict and participants. A number of black-and-white pictures and maps are included. This work is aimed mainly at high-school students and lower-division undergraduates. There are several appendixes: one on biographical data, a glossary of terms, and a bibliography. There are several indexes to work with in using this book to find information on recent conflicts and related issues.

6-125. Lerner, K. Lee, ed. *Encyclopedia of Espionage, Intelligence, and Security.* 3 vols. Detroit: Gale, 2004. Index. ISBN: 0-787-67546-6.

This encyclopedia does not carry daring accounts of spy work and espionage, but it does serve as a good source for learning more about those terms people read about on a daily basis in their regular newspapers and magazines. The work claims to examine scientific foundations and the application of technology, and to analyze the organizational structure of the modern world of espionage. It recommends itself to be used as an adjunct for high-school and undergraduate students in the study of contemporary issues. Not surprisingly, much is devoted to the United States and its Homeland Security issues. Entries are all alphabetical and are replete with cross-references. All articles are duly signed and do tend to be written by scholars and specialists in the fields covered, all drawn from the United States and Europe. There are some black-and-white pictures and a list of additional readings for each entry. Typical entries are one-and-one-half pages and include: "Chechen-Russian Conflict," "Cyber Security," and "Terror Alert Systems." There is a chronology of espionage from 6000 BC to date of publication and an index covering all three physical volumes.

6-126. Arms, Thomas S. *Encyclopedia of the Cold War.* New York: Facts on File, 1994. 628 pp. ISBN: 0-816-01975-4.

This is one of several such encyclopedias or dictionaries that have been published on the cold war since the cessation of the superpower rivalry between the United States and the Soviet Union. Cold war events since 1945 are included. There is a clear preponderance of Americans listed as biographical entries. All individuals so listed have been done so mainly with regard to their cold war context. Entries are arranged in a simple A-to-Z format. Entries range in scope from cold war events, individual countries, battles and wars, major weapon system, and the

like. More specific topics are the "Cuban Missile Crisis," the "MX Missile System," "SALT Treaty," government agencies, and others. A good number of pictures are interspersed throughout the text. Pieces are quite well written and average about one page in length. Looking for a cold war person, date, or event? This is a good first choice.

6-127. Tucker, Spencer C., ed. *Encyclopedia of the Korean War: A Political, Social, and Military History.* 3 vols. Santa Barbara, CA: ABC-CLIO, 2000. 1123 pp. Index. ISBN: 1-576-07029-8.

Reference works on the Korean War have taken a back seat in number and variety to those on the Vietnam War. This is probably the most comprehensive encyclopedia on the topic available in English up to the date of publication. A wide section of topics and individuals make up the bulk of the entries in the first two volumes. Volume 3 reprints in whole or in part a number of telegrams, messages, excerpts of the Far Eastern Economic Assistance Act and other laws, United Nations Security Council resolutions, and military reports. This documentary section is arranged chronologically up to 1953. All entries are signed, and there are a number of references as well. The work is designed to provide general readers with a firm feel for the historical currents existing during the period. There is an index covering the entire set. 🖥

6-128. Grossman, Mark. *Encyclopedia of the Persian Gulf War.* Santa Barbara,

CA: ABC-CLIO, 1995. 522 pp. ISBN: 0-874-36684-4.

While this book does indeed carry a number of entries pertaining to armaments, rockets, missiles, air attack fighters, and the like, it does an equally creditable job in underscoring the political dimensions so critical for the complete understanding of the Gulf War. Discussions within the United Nations and with the United States and its interesting assortment of allies are also given here. Entries are arranged strictly alphabetically and include political alliances, weapons, individuals, and the bombing sites that made the Gulf War so unique an event. Each entry, no matter how brief, carries with it a short reading list of materials. The work as a whole is profusely illustrated, especially for airplanes and maps. Several interesting appendixes included are a "scorecard" of SCUD missile attacks, the total number of U.S. coalition forces by country, full U.S. casualty list, and a detailed chronology of documents related to this conflict. 💻

6-129. Tucker, Spencer C., ed. *Encyclopedia of the Vietnam War: A Political, Social, and Military History.* 3 vols. Santa Barbara, CA: ABC-CLIO, 1998. 1196 pp. Index. ISBN: 0-874-36983-5.

Over 900 entries in three physical volumes make this encyclopedia of the Vietnam War one of the more comprehensive ones published to date. A large number of maps and illustrations accompany the straightforward, nonscholarly text. The encyclopedia is laden with biographical entries, a majority drawn

from the Communist sides of the military engagements. Vietnamese history also serves as one of the strengths of this publication. The military-related entries cover well the arms and equipment used by the U.S. military branches while pursuing the war effort over the years of engagement. Typical entries are on battles, geographic locations, and the antiwar movement. Most entries average roughly a page or more in print. Volume 2 includes literature and film bibliographies, while Volume 3 is a documentary history republishing speeches, statements, television addresses, and so forth. An index is available to the entire set. 💻

6-130. Jessup, John E. *An Encyclopedic Dictionary of Conflict and Conflict Resolution, 1945–1996.* Westport, CT: Greenwood Press, 1998. 887 pp. Index. ISBN: 0-313-28112-2.

Religion, territory, perceived and anticipated rights, and conquest and attainment of political power are regarded here as the most easily seen antagonisms that haunt humanity over the ages. While antagonism without violence is possible, the forms of physical force include wars, invasions, assassinations, massacres, and genocide. This work serves as a companion volume to *A Chronology of Conflict and Resolution, 1945–1985*, published in 1989. It is in alphabetical order, and each entry can be one paragraph or up to several pages long. Entries can be people, organizations, religious sects, countries (except the United States or USSR), political parties, treaties, and the like. Longer entries may carry suggested reading lists. There is a significant amount of information on historical background to reasons for modern outbreaks of violence. Typical entries are "Gulf of Aqaba," "Kashmir," and "Ndabaningi Sithole." The index is appropriately in-depth.

6-131. Dupuy, Trevor, ed. *International Military and Defense Encyclopedia.* 6 vols. Washington, DC: Brassey's, 1993. 3132 pp. Index. ISBN: 0-028-81011-2.

An authoritative work in six volumes put out by the defense-specialist publisher Brassey's. It includes 786 articles aimed at faculty and students at all academic levels, military officers, enlisted personnel, reservists, and others. This work is a terrific subject encyclopedia for those with any interest in the study or research of international security, foreign policy analysis, defense issues, and military matters. This book avoids the U.S.-centric view of the world by utilizing many English, German, Egyptian, and other international scholars as contributors. Indeed, gaining an international perspective on a number of key security and military issues appears to be a desired intent of the editor. The signed articles vary tremendously in length, from a low of about 100 to a high of 10,000 words. This book is not devoted exclusively to the study of contemporary military and defense issues. There is an entry on the American Revolutionary War, and another one on the military history of Assyria. The individual country studies are especially interesting. They provide information on the civil air fleet, total armed forces, numbers for each branch of military service, and forces residing abroad. Some biographical information and topical survey articles constitute part of this work. There are bibliographies at the end of every article. The index to this work must be cited as an excellent example of the craft.

6-132. Polmar, Norman. *Spy Book: The Encyclopedia of Espionage.* 2nd ed. New York: Random House, 2004. 719 pp. ISBN: 0-375-72025-1.

This is a dictionary of the people, places, hardware, codes, and operations associated with spying activities. The spy histories of China, the United Kingdom, France, Germany, Israel, Japan, Russia/USSR, the United States, Cuba, and Vietnam are included. The length of the entries can vary from a single sentence to a six-page encyclopedic one. Most entries are replete with cross-references. The author has published a number of previous works on topics related to military espionage and intelligence-gathering operations. There are about 2,000 entries in this encyclopedia. They are quite literate for its genre. This book meets the needs of researchers and others who require a serious reference encyclopedia on espionage. There are a few scattered pictures and photographs and a short bibliography of recommended reading materials. The heads of the CIA, Russia's Narodny Kommissariat Vnutrkennikh Del (Peoples' Commissariat of Internal Affairs), Israel's MOSSAD, or ha-Mossad Le-Modiin ule-Tatkidim Meyuhadim (The Institute for Intelligence and Special Tasks), and several other major government intelligence agencies are listed. The work evinces significantly less coverage for related intelligence topics within the borders of the developing countries.

6-133. Watson, Bruce W., ed. *United States Intelligence: An Encyclopedia.* New York: Garland, 1990. 792 pp. ISBN: 0-824-03713-8.

This is a reference work that is certain to please the more serious researcher or student in the field of U.S. intelligence. The goal is to bring together in one physical volume all the major terms and entities currently in use mainly from the post–World War II environment until the end of the 1980s. It covers both the worlds of strategic intelligence and tactical intelligence. Within these pages, the reader will find listings of major weapon systems, a chronology, a bibliography, and more. Entries are cross-referenced, and there are several appendixes, including one that prints up verbatim public laws, executive orders, letters, and so forth. Even the shortest entries in this work get a one- or two-item further-reading list. The style is straightforward, tending toward an almost military-like cadence.

Guides and Handbooks
6-134. Allcock, John B. *Border and Territorial Disputes.* 3rd ed. Harlow, Essex, UK: Longman, 1992. 630 pp. ISBN: 0-582-20931-5.

Approximately ninety border disputes are organized here by regions of the globe. Numerous maps provide graphic representation of the nature of the dispute. Europe is a focal point, with the demise of the Soviet Union and the rise of nationalist sentiments in the Balkan area, especially around what had been Yugoslavia. Maritime border disputes are not covered here. Each of the entries gives the overview and a history of the disputed border area. The current political situation and issues are also recounted. Many of the disputes underscore the critical nature of transborder ethnic issues in today's world. International Court of Justice advisory rulings are noted where relevant. The longer-standing border issues between more important political players receive lengthier coverage and greater levels of detail. Included are some multilateral border disputes, not just bilateral ones.

6-135. Jessup, John E. *A Chronology of Conflict and Resolution, 1945–1985.* New York: Greenwood Press, 1989. 942 pp. Index. ISBN: 0-313-24308-5.

This chronology covers the period specifically from the end of World War II to 1985. It is a day-by-day articulation of events, military actions, troop withdrawals, regional conflicts, military accords, coup d'etats, and civil wars. Entries follow the country's name in which the event occurred and are typically one-sentence-long definitions. An abbreviation glossary is included for those used within the book. A general index appears, but is weak for finding pertinent material on more heavily covered countries such as the United States or Israel.

6-136. Polmar, Norman. *Chronology of the Cold War at Sea, 1945–1991.* Annapolis, MD: Naval Institute Press, 1998. 241 pp. Index. ISBN: 1-557-50685-X.

September 2, 1945, to December 30, 1991, forms the coverage period for this chronology of cold war naval information. It is a day-by-day log of various cold war naval events ranging from destroyer actions, minesweeper hits, naval aircraft engagements, status of Defense Authorization Acts, and Secretary of Defense actions. A glossary of ship designations and listings of the Soviet and U.S. military leaders are also included. The index is for ships and people only.

6-137. Hill, Kenneth L. *Cold War Chronology: Soviet-American Relations, 1945–1991.* Washington, DC: Congressional Quarterly, 1993. 362 pp. Index. ISBN: 0-871-87921-2.

This Congressional Quarterly publication is a chronology of the cold war covering U.S.-Soviet relations and events for almost fifty years. The author perceives one consistent pattern in U.S.-Soviet relations during the cold war, and that was the tendency to apply conflicting interpretations to treaties signed by both nations. This was especially true of Yalta and Potsdam. The chronology is quite detailed and covers the period on a day-by-day basis. Included within the chronology are military, political, and diplomatic events between the United States and the Soviet Union. Entries are short, perhaps one or two sentences long, but each entry gives an abbreviation that serves as a source document for

that particular entry. The excellent index is essential here. The sources-consulted list is not very long, but it is highly authoritative in what it includes.

6-138. Schwartz, Richard Alan. *The Cold War Reference Guide: A General History and Annotated Chronology, with Selected Biographies.* Jefferson, NC. McFarland, 1997. 321 pp. ISBN: 0-786-40173-7.

This guide concentrates on the two superpowers, the United States and Soviet Union, during the cold war. There is much less attention paid to the other major players, such as the People's Republic of China, Great Britain, France, or Germany. This work is clearly intended to offer the U.S. perspective and, as such, includes events that were deemed especially significant from the U.S. point of view. Chapters include an overview of the cold war era and individual chapters on the more noteworthy events during the cold war, such as the Korean War, the Cuban Missile Crisis, and so forth. Another chapter serves up an annotated chronology of the cold war, and another one explores the concurrent international political leadership at the time. Next is a section of highly selective biographies, many of which are drawn from the United States. A final chapter includes an introductory bibliography of the cold war. This work is best for high-school students and lower-division undergraduates.

6-139. Kort, Michael, ed. *Columbia Guide to the Cold War.* New York: Columbia University Press, 1998. 366 pp. Index. ISBN: 0-231-10772-2.

This guide is written for high-school and undergraduate students to help them study the cold war era. The book is divided into four parts. Part 1 constitutes the first six chapters and is a series of narrative essays that discuss and analyze the cold war in decade-long chunks of history. It introduces the reader to Yalta, the Hungarian uprisings, Sputnik, the Berlin Wall, détente, and finally, the fall of Communism. Part 2, the largest parcel of the book, is an alphabetical encyclopedia of the people, events, and terms that were used to define this era. Entries in this part are highly selective and average one page in length. Part 3 is a day-by-day chronology from 1945 to 1991. The last part is a listing of resources, such as books and journal articles, on topics ranging from the general to the more specialized. Most topics are further subdivided for in-depth coverage and include memoirs, biographies, bibliographies, reference works, primary-source materials, and more. All entries are annotated in this section and reflect a distinctly American point of view. An index is available for consultation.

6-140. Schooley, Helen. *Conflict in Central America.* Harlow, Essex, UK: Longman, 1987. 326 pp. Index. ISBN: 0-582-90274-6.

While most information in this work touches upon events occurring since the late 1970s, the book emphasizes the various differences in perception of the nature of the conflict in Central America.

The book is organized into six chapters. The first deals with the political history of the area. It provides short articles on the political events in the region or by individual country. The second chapter examines the economic and social dimensions of conflict in the area. Chapter 3 discusses the conflict from an internal and transborder perspective. The following chapter looks at human rights and refugees. Chapter 5 examines the foreign involvement in Central America, and the last chapter covers various Central American peace initiatives. Each article or entry is laced with dates, rosters of political parties, statistics, and the like. Unfortunately, the subject index is virtually useless. A highly selective list of readings is included.

6-141. Lord, Mary E., ed. *Foundations in International Affairs: $earch for $ecurity.* Washington, DC: ACCESS, 1996. 183 pp. ISBN: 1-878-59714-0.

This is a study on grants making in international security and constitutes the third in a series of similar works. It details how international fund-raising entities have reacted to various global transformations. About 388 donors drawn from nearly ninety countries around the world are listed in this work. Contemporary fund-raisers are interested in more than arms control and international conflicts. They also are equally interested in a wide range of transnational issues, such as economic development, environmental problems, ethnic conflict, and refugee status. Analysis done at the time seems to indicate a trend away from funding U.S.-based organizations, and establishing preference instead to more collaborative arrangements between U.S. and international organizations. Listings include private, public, governmental, corporate, and community grants makers. The opening chapter is an introduction to a global look at international affairs grants. The main body has about thirty uniform subdivisions per entry that include deadline, range of grant amounts, assets, and the like. Most listings are of U.S. organizations.

6-142. Hoover Institution on War, Revolution, and Peace. http://www-hoover.stanford.edu/.

This organization is widely associated with conservative thinking. In its mission statement, the Hoover Institution states: "By collecting knowledge, generating ideas, and disseminating both, the Institution seeks to secure and safeguard peace, improve the human condition, and limit government intrusion into the lives of individuals." Despite the reputation of the parent institution, the Web site is somewhat disappointing. There is comparably very little full-text available on such typical topics as "American Public Education," "American Individualism and Values," and "Accountability of Government to Society." Perhaps the best resource is the "Weekly Essays" written by Hoover Fellows and consisting of opinion pieces in a newspaper-column format. 🖥

6-143. Mitrokhin, Vasily, ed. *KGB Lexicon: The Soviet Intelligence Officer's Handbook.* Portland, OR: Frank Cass, 2002. 451 pp. Index. ISBN: 0-714-65257-1.

This unique handbook provides over 1,600 words and terms that give a standard accepted definition of a wide range of intelligence terms used by the KGB and its agents during its existence as the premier intelligence-gathering unit within the defunct Soviet Union. The work is divided up into two parts. The first part is an "Intelligence Lexicon" and the second part is a "Counter-Intelligence Lexicon." Terms are arranged alphabetically by the Russian-language term, but all of them are translated into English. The index will be most useful here.

6-144. Bahmueller, Charles F., ed. *World Conflicts and Confrontations.* 4 vols. Pasadena, CA: Salem Press, 2000. Index. ISBN: 0-893-56219-X.

Each physical volume concerns a specific geographical region of the globe, and within each volume, entries are arranged alphabetically by individual country. The intent here is to identify those areas that constitute "hot spots" in terms of armed conflict. There are a total of 104 essays and ten regional survey articles. Each entry begins with a statement highlighting the country's most pressing problem, and this is followed by an examination of the origins, nature, and history of the problem at a high-school or lower-division undergraduate analysis level. Basic facts, statistics, and dates are provided for each country, and many of the entries also have at least one black-and-white photograph. There are appendixes of foreign embassies in the United States, international organizations, news sources, a glossary of terms, and a chronology for 1453 through 1999. There is a general index.

6-145. Kerr, Donald. *World Directory of Defense and Security.* New York: Stockton, 1995. 527 pp. ISBN: 1-561-59145-9.

This is an alphabetical listing of the world's nations and provides information relating to the defense and security for each one. The primary emphasis is on defense and the size of the military and the equipment used by each country's own military force. There is a separate list for a country's major weaponry. Each country entry is divided into the following standard subdivisions: "Geography," "External Threats," "Agreements, Alliances and Affiliations," "Arms Control," "Internal Dynamics," "Defense," and "Foreign Commitments and Foreign Forces In." A number of the world's smaller island nations are not included, and the former Soviet republics are regarded as separate countries. This work is good for the comparative analysis of the relative strengths of each country's armed forces, demographics, economic resources, and infrastructure. It also brings forth any fault line pertaining to internal schisms derived from language or religious differences, active separatist movements, major tribal histories, and others. There is some overlap in content with the *SIPRI Yearbook* [entry 6-66].

6-146. Munro, David. *A World Record of Major Conflict Areas.* Chicago: St. James Press, 1990. 373 pp. ISBN: 1-558-62066-4.

This work describes about twenty-eight different current conflicts in various parts of the world. Both the historical and contemporary aspects of the ongoing issues are elucidated for the general reader and undergraduate student. The outline of the book follows a geographical arrangement. There are five main sections: Africa, Middle East, Asia and the Far East, the Americas, and Europe. Within each of these broad chapters, sections on specific conflicts follow a standardized pattern, including map, profile of the country/area, introduction to the historical and current status of the conflict, and a chronology, which emphasizes more recent events. After this information, there are three directory parts giving personalities, geographic locations, and other ingredients of the conflict, such as treaties, ethnic groups, and the like. Each entry has a short section on additional readings. A typical entry is ten to fourteen pages long. Maps are somewhat short of detail and specificity.

Atlases

6-147. Anderson, Ewan W. *An Atlas of World Political Flashpoints: A Sourcebook in Geopolitical Crisis.* New York: Facts on File, 1993. 243 pp. ISBN: 0-816-02885-0.

This topical atlas examines major conflict or potential conflict zones around the globe. A total of eighty political flash-points are included, and each entry provides the general geographic situation, history, background information, relative importance, and the current status. Each entry ends with a short list of readings on the subject. The maps depict the flash-points in a graphic mode. These are typical Facts on File maps, in black-and-white created for ease of photocopying. Articles emphasize the geographic elements of the political situation for the locale detailed. This work is best suited for high-school and undergraduate students as well as the general public. Some assessments, such as that of Northern Ireland, tend to border on the gloomy side of the equation.

6-148. Gilbert, Martin, ed. *Routledge Atlas of the Arab-Israeli Conflict*. 7th ed. New York: Routledge, 2002. Unpaginated. ISBN: 0-415-28117-2.

This work traces the Arab-Jewish conflict from 1900 to time of the publication date. Maps are the key content here, with all text appearing inside the 146 maps. The editor's goal is to demonstrate how this seemingly endless conflict has generated such bitterness and hostility to the political actors in the region and also to examine the types of incidents these emotions have set off. The majority of maps represent conflict and war, but several of them recall attempts to bring this conflict to a close. Those maps tend to show boundary lines and cease-fire accords. Maps are black and white only, but project strong graphic qualities. Every map is packed with information and dates.

Terrorism
Bibliographies
6-149. Ontiveros, Suzanne Robitaille, ed. *Global Terrorism: A Historical Bibliography*. Santa Barbara, CA: ABC-CLIO, 1986. 168 pp. Indexes. ISBN: 0-874-36453-1.

Based on the contents of ABC-CLIO's historical databases, this bibliography includes 598 citations along with full abstracts from journal articles only. Over 2,000 different periodicals published in over ninety countries around the globe provide the citation base. There are seven chapters that represent the standard geographic regions of the world, such as North America, Europe, the Middle East, and four others. The abstracts can vary in length from merely one sentence to a whole paragraph. Each entry is in English, and foreign-language works have had their article titles translated into the English language. Entries are all signed, and the annotations are quite good. There are two indexes available: subject and author. A chronology of terrorist events from 1975 to 1985 is included.

6-150. Lakos, Amos. *International Terrorism: A Bibliography*. Boulder, CO: Westview Press, 1986. 481 pp. Index. ISBN: 0-813-7157-0.

The coverage for this bibliography on the literature of terrorism is for 1965 to 1985 and includes monographs, journal articles, various government publications, conference reports, and doctoral dissertations. This unannotated bibliography is divided into several fairly broad chapters such as "Reference Works,"

"Theories of Terrorism," "Psychological and Social Aspects of Terrorism," and a large last section on "Geographic Subdivision," which is the largest section of them all, sporting 1,200 entries. The order of the listings in this major section is by region and then format of material being cited. Materials earmarked for inclusion in this bibliography are all English-language. There is an author and subject index.

6-151. Lakos, Amos. *Terrorism, 1980–1990: A Bibliography.* Boulder, CO: Westview Press, 1991. 443 pp. Indexes. ISBN: 0-813-38035-9.

The main body of this bibliography has ten chapters, most with additional subdivisions on all aspects of terrorism. Works cited are books, journal articles, documents, and various reports, all alphabetically arranged by author. There are a total of 5,850 entries, with journal-article entries clearly predominating in number. None of the entries are annotated. This is the second bibliography on terrorism compiled by this author. This work covers English-language materials published from 1980 to 1990, while his previous bibliography spanned the mid-1960s to the mid-1980s. Items that were omitted from the previous bibliography are included in this one. The largest chapter is on geographic headings. There is an author index and a subject index.

6-152. Bhan, Susheela. *Terrorism: An Annotated Bibliography.* New Delhi, India: Concept Publishing, 1989. 338 pp. Indexes. ISBN: 8-170-22256-7.

This bibliography on terrorism is arranged in several parts: abstracts, addenda, and reference and forthcoming publications. There are just over 800 total citations, with most of those under the heading of "Abstracts." These abstracts were either lifted from other standard indexing/abstracting sources or penned exclusively for this one. Those that were used originally by other sources came from the *International Political Science Abstracts* [entry 3-6], *PAIS International in Print* [entry 3-7], or *Sociological Abstracts* [entry 2-272]. Therefore, the materials chosen for this bibliography do not necessarily reflect the regional collective thinking or literature of the country of publication, India. There are some citations to or abstracts of newspaper articles and dissertations scattered throughout the pages. There is an author and a subject index, both linked only to citations with abstracts.

6-153. Wilcox, Laird M. *Terrorism, Assassination, Espionage, and Propaganda: A Master Bibliography.* Olathe, KS: L. Wilcox, 1989. Unpaginated. ISBN: 0-933-59256-8.

This is a straight, across-the-board dictionary-arrangement bibliography by author. There are no subject chapters to this work, a real drawback. Included in this offbeat bibliography are books and journal articles. Books from the early 1930s are listed, but the majority of book entries were published from 1960 through the 1970s. Bibliographic information is minimal, but there is usually enough to locate an item. The annotations are usually one-sentence statements about the book. Altogether, over 3,200 items are listed in this work, all in English and primarily from U.S. publishers. Works from European countries are the second-largest group of materials.

Dictionaries

6-154. Rosie, George. *The Directory of International Terrorism.* New York: Paragon House, 1987. 310 pp. ISBN: 0-913-72929-9.

The introduction of this dictionary on terrorism grapples with the definitions and characteristics of international terrorism. While not stated explicitly in the introduction, this work's strength lies in its coverage of twentieth-century international terrorism. This book includes in its alphabetically arranged pages entries on bombing incidents, international terrorists, hijackings, individual terrorist groups, and their political parties. Entries are fairly short, often about one-quarter page long. This is an especially good source for dates and factual ready-reference-type information. No subject index is the one weakness.

Encyclopedias

6-155. Combs, Cindy C. *Encyclopedia of Terrorism.* New York: Facts on File, 2002. 339 pp. Index. ISBN: 0-816-04455-4.

An expert on terrorism has compiled this encyclopedia and notes the long history of terrorism in international politics. Terrorism's more modern incarnation is seen as based largely in the fall of the Soviet Union, the cessation of the cold war,

the growth and intensification of ethnic conflicts, and the rise of religious fanaticism in some parts of the world. The open borders prevalent in many democratic countries combined with the general openness of civil society in those nations also are contributing factors leading to the increase in terrorist activities. New types of terrorism linked directly to computer networks and electronic technology, such as cyber terrorism, are also on the rise today. This single volume claims to include the most serious and most significant victims of modern terrorism. The entries are highly cross-referenced and average about one-quarter to one-half a page in length. Typical entries are "Christian Identity Movement," "Tupamaros," "Turner Diaries," and "Hamas." High-school students, undergraduates, and the general public will all find this work useful. There are a number of helpful appendixes, such as the type of facilities struck by terrorists, yearly counts of terrorist acts, and the like. An index is included.

6-156. Thackrah, John Richard. *Encyclopedia of Terrorism and Political Violence.* New York: Routledge and Kegan Paul/Methuen, 1987. 308 pp. Index. ISBN: 0-710-20659-3.

This is an alphabetically arranged handbook written in a fairly popular style aimed at the layperson and nonspecialist. Inclusions are highly selective and average about one-half to one page in length. There is probably little here that could not be found in more detail in some other reference source. The subject index is subpar, but there are some "see" and "see also" references in the articles themselves.

6-157. Crenshaw, Martha, ed. *Encyclopedia of World Terrorism.* 3 vols. Armonk, NY: M. E. Sharpe Reference, 1997. 768 pp. ISBN: 1-563-24806-9.

This work is oriented toward general readers, high-school students, and lower-division undergraduates who are looking for several-page articles on global terrorism. Each entry on terrorism has six major headings, all of which have several subdivisions. These six major sections are "Historical Background," "Background to Modern Terrorist Campaigns," "General Background to Modern Terrorism," "Terrorist Groups and Campaigns," "Terrorism in the Industrialized World," and finally, "Responses to Terrorism." This is a good introductory source for gaining information about terrorism throughout history and around the globe, including in developing and industrialized nations. Articles are heavily illustrated with plenty of maps. The writing style tends to be nonacademic and more journalistic, good for the nonspecialist in terrorist studies. There are a couple of appendixes, including one that is a chronology of terrorism.

6-158. Shanty, Frank G., ed. *Encyclopedia of World Terrorism: 1996–2002,* and *Encyclopedia of World Terrorism: Documents.* 2 vols. Armonk, NY: M. E. Sharpe, 2003. ISBN: 1-563-24807-7.

These two volumes continue a set in conjunction with Crenshaw's work [entry 6-157]. It both supplements the encyclopedia articles on terrorism and provides a number of key document sources on the topic. (Note: This continuation set was unseen.)

Guides and Handbooks

6-159. Shafritz, Jay M. *Almanac of Modern Terrorism.* New York: Facts on File, 1991. 290 pp. ISBN: 0-816-02123-6.

This compendium of ready-reference facts and information about terrorism includes terms, events, people, and organizations related to terrorism. There are several main sections including a chronology of major terrorist incidents since World War II; the largest chapter on terrorism giving definitions, events, and the like; a sampling of statements made by various political figures on terrorism today; a chronology of numerous definitions of terrorism; and a bibliography of readings. There is a good introduction that discusses the difficulty in defining who a terrorist is or what constitutes a terrorist event or attack. Examining the national or political perspective of the analyst is often a crucial factor here. Entries are short, dictionary style. This work is not nearly as comprehensive as the *Encyclopedia of World Terrorism* [entry 6-157], but is aimed only at the last fifty years or so. The bibliography includes classics of the literature and is a good core reading list for modern terrorist studies.

6-160. Mickolus, Edward F. *International Terrorism in the 1980s: A Chronology of Events.* 2 vols. Ames: Iowa State

University Press, 1989. 541 pp. Index. ISBN: 0-813-80024-2.

Volume 1 chronicles terrorist events for the years 1980 through 1983, while Volume 2 covers 1984 through 1987. This work carries on the work done by Edward F. Mickolus in *Transnational Terrorism: A Chronology of Events, 1968–1979.* In defining what terrorism is, emphasis here is placed on the overall political goals of the act. This chronological guide enumerates terrorist incidents for 1980 through 1987. The author uses an eight-digit code to categorize all international terrorist events and skyjackings. The introduction contains a good bibliographic essay entitled "Theoretical Models of Terrorism." Naturally, the chronology is arranged by date. Entries give the date, country involved, value of the terrorist act, individuals or groups involved, casualties, and more. Appendix 1 functions as a list of terrorist organizations. The index is in three components: by country, by type of terrorist incident, or by terrorist group.

6-161. Schmid, Alex Peter. *Political Terrorism: A New Guide to Actors, Authors, Concepts, Data Bases, Theories and Literature.* rev., exp., and updated ed. New York: North-Holland, 1988. 700 pp. ISBN: 0-444-85659-5.

This handbook is half directory of major terrorist organizations and half bibliography of works on the topic. The directory portion gives short, thumbnail sketches of terrorist groups by country. It then provides their general mission, goals, and recent activities. The bibliography portion, which takes up about 50 percent of the entire volume, has over 6,000 entries. The databases noted in this work have undergone dramatic change since publication.

6-162. Mickolus, Edward F. *Terrorism: 1988–1991: A Chronology of Events and a Selectively Annotated Bibliography.* Westport, CT: Greenwood Press, 1993. 913 pp. ISBN: 0-313-28970-0.

See entry 6-163.

6-163. Mickolus, Edward F. *Terrorism, 1992–1995: A Chronology of Events and a Selectively Annotated Bibliography.* Westport, CT: Greenwood Press, 1997. 958 pp. ISBN: 0-313-30468-8.

These two related bibliographies on terrorism are both organized in the same manner and are meant to portray a comprehensive view of terrorism and terrorist activities. The bibliography is arranged by region of the globe, such as Africa, Latin America, and so forth and includes books, journal articles, and selected U.S. government publications. Foreign-language materials represent perhaps 5 percent of the total works listed. There are several special topics on such subjects as nuclear and high-technology threats. Items are annotated.

6-164. Atkins, Stephen E. *Terrorism: A Reference Handbook.* Santa Barbara, CA: ABC-CLIO, 1992. 199 pp. Index. ISBN: 0-874-36670-4.

This handbook is aimed at teachers, students, and the general public, and attempts to be objective in how terrorism is defined and treated. The work opens with several short introductory sections on terrorism, including its philosophy, the notion of state terrorism, the meaning of counterrevolution, and the like. It offers basic guidelines and analysis of terrorist organizations, methods, and terminology. This is followed by a selected chronology of terrorist events from 1894 to 1992. Next, there are biographical profiles of high-profile terrorists from 1945 to 1992. These are also highly selective. After this is a section on selected publications, usually just a few excerpts, of such agreements or historic documents as the Palestinian National Charter or the 1987 Venice Statement on Terrorism. The next section of this handbook is the part that serves as a directory of terrorist organizations from 1940 to 1992. It lists both current and defunct organizations. A number of standard reference works and books on terrorism are included. There is a basic index.

International Organization
Literature Guides
6-165. *International Information: Documents, Publications, and Electronic Information of International Governmental Organizations.* 2nd ed. Englewood, CO: Libraries Unlimited, 1997. 528 pp. ISBN: 1-563-08147-4.

This book examines traditional print and electronic sources of information as compiled, organized, and distributed by a number of larger international organizations. The changes in international docu-

mentation and electronic information have been affected by a number of technological, social, political, and economic factors that continue to interact apace. The chapters go on to discuss the United Nations, European Union, Organisation for Economic Co-operation and Development (OECD), and other international organizations and their respective publications and electronic information sources. Other chapters examine research methods, the International Documentation Research Center (IDRC), and the many agencies that make up the European Parliament and the corresponding documents, legislative papers, committee documents, session documents, opinions, and debates of these specialized units. The work concludes with a lengthy and substantial bibliography on international organizations and the publications and electronic materials they issue.

Annuals and Yearbooks
6-166. *Yearbook of International Organizations: Guide to Global and Civil Society Networks.* Munich: Union of International Associations, 1967–. 5 vols. ISBN: 3-598-24512-2.

This venerable library standard has been providing comprehensive listings of organizations from around the globe for almost forty years. While many of the organizations show a clear link to politics and government, many do not do so. Entries give full expanded directory-type information, including paragraphs on founding, organizational structure, core activities, sponsored events, and membership information. Phone numbers and e-mail addresses are included. Most organizations are located in the United States or Europe, but those in the developing countries are not excluded. Volume 1, Parts A and B, constitutes the main body of the work, while the remaining volumes allow subject or country access, bibliography, and statistical information. (Note: Only Volume 1, Parts A and B were seen.)

Directories

6-167. Schraepler, Hans-Albrecht. *Directory of International Organizations.* Washington, DC: Georgetown University Press, 1996. 424 pp. ISBN: 0-878-40607-7.

This directory was compiled by the former head of information of the Council of Europe in Strasbourg, who is also an ex-German diplomat. Its intent is to provide core information about a wide circle of international organizations. Each entry is in a standardized format: (1) legal basis (charters, etc.), (2) objectives and functions (political, scientific, military, cultural, etc.), (3) membership (members and auxiliary members), and (4) structures (general assembly, executive council, commissions, etc.). The initial chapters begin with the "United Nations" and its specialized agencies, followed by "NATO," then "Regional Organizations of Worldwide Importance" by region (OAS, EU, OAU, ANZUS, etc.), "Economic Organizations of Worldwide Relevance" (OECD), "Commonwealth and Commonwealth of Independent States," and "Other Organizations of Worldwide Relevance." Entries

are consistent in providing directory-type information and text. An appendix offers a country listing and indicates which international groups each nation has membership in. This work is best for finding out information on the more important or larger international organizations in existence.

6-168. *The Europa Directory of International Organizations.* 5th ed. London: Europa Publications, 1999–. Index. ISSN: 1465-4628.

This is intended to serve as a comprehensive guide to international organizations and their international affairs framework. It includes coverage of the more important intergovernmental organizations as well as containing over 1,500 other related entries. Historical and legal perspectives are given when relevant. Part 1 is a listing of various special days, weeks, years, and decades as sponsored by some international organization. World Space Week and International Literacy Day are just two such examples. Part 2 is a directory of the United Nations in some depth. Part 3 is a similar directory, but for non–United Nations organizations. Part 4 gives more abbreviated entries for other international organizations arranged by subject or area of interest, and Part 5 is a Who's Who section. The major international organizational bodies receive the full treatment of purpose, members, activities, statistical information, publications, and so on. The biographies are extremely selective, but give e-mail addresses. There is an index. (Note: The 2003 edition was examined.)

Dictionaries

6-169. Schlechter, Michael G. *Historical Dictionary of International Organizations.* Lanham, MD: Scarecrow Press, 1998. 247 pp. ISBN: 0-810-83479-0.

This work is somewhat similar in format to both Gorman [entry 6-99] and Urwin [entry 6-184] , but covers a different set of organizations, in this instance ones that present information on the international organizations themselves as well as their respective leaders and important activities. The chronological focus is on 1800 to the very late twentieth century. An introductory essay of note on the history and possible future direction of international organizations is included. An attached bibliography leads off with a short bibliographic essay and then follows with an unannotated but substantial list of works arranged in broad categories. Many books selected for the bibliography were relatively recent when this dictionary was originally published.

6-170. Schiavone, Giuseppe. *International Organizations: A Dictionary and Directory.* 4th ed. New York: St. Martin's Press, 1997. 334 pp. ISBN: 1-561-59195-5.

This work has identified just over 100 intergovernmental organizations (IGOs) that the author anticipates will play an increasingly larger role in the post–cold war era. The book commences with an essay on previous multilateral efforts aimed at bringing about peace, fighting the war on drugs, coordinating how to handle foreign debt, and so forth. The main body of the book ensues, and it is an alphabetical listing of the major IGOs. Each entry provides the organization's objectives, functions, powers, and primary activities. Most entries also give address, main officer, publications, and a short bibliography. There is also a small amount of space devoted to the IGO's historical background. Entries vary in length from about one to fifteen pages. Larger entries tend to be some of the world's largest and most active IGO bodies, such as the United Nations and the European Communities. At the rear of the book, the reader will find a highly selective directory of less eminent IGOs.

6-171. Ali, Sheikh Rustum. *The International Organizations and World Order Dictionary.* Santa Barbara, CA: ABC-CLIO, 1992. 283 pp. ISBN: 0-874-36572-4.

This specialized dictionary has over 300 entries on various international agencies and their political and economic activities primarily over the last fifty-year period. The focus is clearly the United Nations and its myriad political- and economic-development bodies that have been put into place since World War II ended. These alphabetically ordered entries are extremely selective, perhaps overly so. Entries average roughly one page in length and contain many cross-references. The bifurcated entries provide a descriptive summary of the organization or term and then proceed to draw out its significance regarding its development, major players, and historical context, all in a highly concise manner.

Guides and Handbooks

6-172. Baer, George W., comp. and ed. *International Organizations 1918–1945: A Guide to Research and Research Materials.* rev. ed. Wilmington, DE: Scholarly Resources, 1991. 212 pp. Index. ISBN: 0-842-02309-7.

This work is intended to serve the needs of researchers who require use of archival resources on international organization during the League of Nations period, give or take a couple of years. This introduction to archival sources is accomplished by breaking down the chapters into broad topics, international organization, or national archive. A number of narrow research collections are highlighted. Approximately 25 percent of the book is devoted to listing archival repositories from around the world. The remainder of the work is the publication of a lengthy and authoritative bibliography arranged by topic and subtopics, and then alphabetically by author of the work cited. The bibliography includes both monographs and journal articles, many of which are in languages other than English. There are 1,725 entries making up this bibliography of high-quality entries. An index of authors is attached. 💻

6-173. Owen, Richard. *The Times Guide to World Organisations: Their Role and Reach in the New World Order.* London: Times Books, 1996. 254 pp. ISBN: 0-723-00789-6.

This work is intended to be a "compact guide" to international organizations and their acronyms. There is a special attempt to deal with United Nations agen-

cies and nongovernmental organizations with a global reach and an international mandate of operations. A high percentage of the organizations in this work were originally created to reconstruct Europe after World War II. Many of these same organizations slowly evolved during the 1960s to be in a position to assist the new former-colonial states now emerging with independent governments. The main body is broken up into twenty-three subject chapters with such headings as "Environmental," "Regional," "Women's," and the like. Each entry is about one-and-one-half pages long in a standard editorial format that includes background, objective, main activities, leadership, scope, budget, and affiliations. This is akin to the *Fortune 500* of international agencies. Only the largest and most notable are included.

European Organization
Annuals and Yearbooks

6-174. Johnson, Justin. *Directory of Political Lobbying.* Annual. London: Politico, 1999–. ISBN: 1-842-75000-3.

This yearly publication lists only those companies that devote a considerable amount of their time and energy to political lobbying activities. There are only several chapters, but the main ones are "United Kingdom Lobbying Directory" (over 50 percent of the entire book), "Who's Who in Lobbying," and the "European Union Lobbying Directory." The United Kingdom Lobbying Directory section is an A-to-Z listing of companies with full contact information including Web address and e-mail, a clients list, general company information, and much more for larger businesses. The other sections are equally straightforward in subject and presentation. (Note: The most recent edition seen was dated 2001/2002.)

6-175. *The European Union: Annual Review of Activities.* Cambridge, MA: Blackwell Publishers, 1994–. (Published annually as a special issue of *The Journal of Common Market Studies.*)

This yearbook contains review-length articles of the major events that took place within the European Union states over the previous year. The last year seen was for 1996, and the lead story then was on Mad Cow Disease, followed by a detailed chronology of events related to the British government's response to this epidemic within the United Kingdom. There are other broad chapters included in this annual publication, including "Governance and Institutional Developments," "Internal Policy Developments," "Legal Developments," and others. There is a listing of publications put out by the European Union and its agencies over the last year. Also, a lengthy list of books on European political and economic integration is included.

6-176. Council of Europe. *European Yearbook* [*Annuaire Europeen*]. Annual. The Hague: Nijhoff, 1955–. ISSN: 0167-6717.

This yearly guide has a goal of examining various European organizations and the Organisation for Economic Co-operation and Development (OECD) but of excluding any organization related to the United Nations or any of its specialized agencies. The body of this work is divided into twenty-one main sections, usually subdivided into several additional parts. Entries can be in French, English, or both languages. The entries are written by technical experts writing for others of the same ilk who share such similar interests and backgrounds. Typical headings are "Organization of Security and Co-Operation in Europe (OSCE)," "Council of Europe," "European Laboratory for Particle Physics (CERN)," and many others. Entries for any annual volume review accomplishments for that past year. There is a lengthy bibliography of European books, journals, and the like in English, French, German, and several other major Western European languages. An index is lacking.

6-177. *Eurostat Yearbook.* Annual. Luxembourg: Office for Official Publications of the European Communities, 1995–. ISSN: 1681-4789.

This publication bills itself as a yearbook "for and about Europeans." This annual compares the major features of every European Union country to one another, to non-EU countries, to those in the European Free Trade Association (EFTA), and to the United States, Canada, and Japan. The work is designed primarily to allow for the comparative analysis of statistical and other figures. The body of the work is organized into five broad topics, each broken down into numerous subcategories. There is a good number of useful color maps tied to much of the statistical data. The tables are mostly eleven-year compilations. This book offers a unique way to begin to envision Europe as a political and economic entity and to compare it as a unit to other OECD and developed countries. (Note: This source is issued also in a trilingual edition on CD-ROM.) 💻

Directories

6-178. *The Directory of EU Information Sources.* 11th ed. Genval, Belgium: Euroconfidential, 2000. Index. (Former title: *Directory of EC Information Sources.*)

This directory is divided up into ten sections and provides access to the key people of the European Commission, European Parliament, various European Union institutions, foreign representatives in Brussels, press agencies, journalists and think tanks specializing in foreign affairs, EU consultants and lawyers, and trade/professional associations that surround the EU in its operations. The thirteen different appendixes and keyword index place this directory at the less facile end of the ease-of-use spectrum, especially for first-time users.

6-179. Day, Alan J., comp. and ed. *Directory of European Union Political Parties.* London: John Harper, 2000. 267 pp. Index. ISBN: 0-953-62786-1.

This directory is arranged by European Union country. It lists roughly 140 political parties that hold seats in the fifteen EU member national parliaments. Information is given on these political parties through the end of 1999. All entries include contact data, e-mail, Web site, leadership information, policy orientations, history, current political status, and the like. Political parties are arranged in one alphabetical order. The dependencies of any EU country are also included here. There is an index.

6-180. Philip, Alan Butt, ed. *Directory of Pressure Groups in the EU.* 2nd ed. London: Catermill, 1996. 569 pp. ISBN: 1-860-67073-3. (Former Title: *Directory of Pressure Groups in the European Community.*)

Compiled by several specialists in European Union affairs, this reference book includes listings for over 800 groups and 200 consultancies. While pressure groups are the centerpiece here, other groups are also included that are considered to have some influence on the EU. All listings derive from a 1991 questionnaire that was eventually supplemented. An introduction to the work gives a decent description of the EU's governance structure and apparatus. Entries in the main body are strictly alphabetical and range in length from very brief directory-type informational packets to more detailed background on an organization's structure, scope, assessment of lobbying prowess, and more. All entries provide name, acronym, address, phone number, fax number, date founded, and officers. The section on consultants at the rear of book provides only the most minimal information.

Bibliographies

6-181. Paxton, John, comp. *European Communities.* New Brunswick, NJ:

Transaction Publishers, 1992. 182 pp. ISBN: 1-560-60052-X.

This work is a bibliography that covers monographs, journal articles, pamphlets, directories, databases, and theses. The topics of the works listed are on materials about the European Community (EC) organizations rather than on materials issued by them. While there is some historical coverage, most of the works cited are for more contemporary or future EC activities. There are a total of twenty chapters, some of which are "Member States," "Political Union," "Transport Policy," and "Energy Policy." There are roughly 700 bibliographic entries given. A goal of this bibliography is to generate a bibliography of core works on the EC aimed at general readers, students, and people in business. One section is devoted to selective reference materials on the EC. The great majority of works cited were published in the decade prior to the publication of this bibliography.

Dictionaries

6-182. Ramsay, Anne, ed. *Eurojargon: A Dictionary of European Union Acronyms, Abbreviations and Sobriquets.* 6th ed. Chicago: F. Dearborn, 2000. 376 pp. ISBN: 1-898-86967-7. (Former Title: *Eurojargon: A Dictionary of EC Acronyms, Abbreviations and Sobriquets.*)

This increasingly thickening work brings together abbreviations and acronyms used with the European Union and the former European Community. The selection criterion is simple pragmatism. This dictionary is designed for a broad spectrum of different users. There are a couple of thousand entries bundled together mostly, but not exclusively, in English. Special emphasis is given to terms pulled out of EU documents. It is arranged alphabetically by abbreviation/acronym. Entries for associations frequently provide an address. There are some "see" references included. This is a useful work for EU students.

6-183. DeFouloy, Christian. *Glossary of EC Terms and Acronyms.* London: Butterworths, 1992. 421 pp. ISBN: 0-406-00463-3.

Here is a glossary in alphabetical order providing the full name of the acronym spelled out first in its original language and then in several other Western European languages, including French, German, Italian, and Spanish. Definitions of a word or term are done generally only for that word's original language. Other languages receive a literal translation of the term into that tongue. Then, the user of this glossary would look up this term in the book for its translated meaning in the other European language. For example, "Comfort Letter" has a definition printed in English, the originating language for that term. If you seek out the French equivalent, then look up this same term in its French translation, "Lettre de Classement." It is a polyglot dictionary with a twist. Many of the terms listed are fairly technical ones, and definitions are adequate but severe.

6-184. Urwin, Derek W. *Historical Dictionary of European Organizations.*

Lanham, MD: Scarecrow Press, 1994. 389 pp. ISBN: 0-810-82838-3.

This dictionary provides a number of major and some lesser known European-based organizations. The work details these organizations' multifaceted activities and underscores the leaders and other people who played a prominent role in the historical development of these bodies. Since World War II and its aftermath were such catalysts for cooperative organizational efforts in Europe, most of the entries in this work arise from that period or later. Individuals who promoted the cause of European unity and cooperative actions also receive space as main entries in this alphabetically arranged dictionary. Entries are prone to be fairly brief but quite informative given their length. Some entries, such as those on the "cold war" or "Winston Churchill" tend to be considerably longer than the standard entry. There is a seventy-page bibliography divided into various subtopics. This bibliography contains books and journal articles in the English language only.

Encyclopedias

6-185. Dinan, Desmond, ed. *Encyclopedia of the European Union.* Boulder, CO: Lynne Rienner, 1998. 565 pp. Index. ISBN: 1-555-87634-X.

The goal of this encyclopedia, as stated in its introduction, is to be "an authoritative and comprehensive reference work" on the European Union. Over 700 issues, ideas, events, institutions, treaties, personalities, and other EU-related terms were selected for inclusion by a team of U.S. and European scholars and experts. While the lengthier articles tend to be signed, the entries throughout this work are uniformly well written, and a number of the entries have short bibliographies attached. This work is designed to track issues, examine country relations with the EU or other EU member states, bring to light major policy initiatives, and provide dates for needed information. Several appendixes are printed, including ones on abbreviations, an EU chronology, various statistical tables, and a listing of summit meetings. Top this off with a thorough index, and this would appear to be the authoritative encyclopedia of this topic up until its date of publication.

6-186. *The European Communities Encyclopedia and Directory 1992.* London: Europa, 1991. 390 pp. ISBN: 0-946-65365-8.

This work serves as a comprehensive guide to the European Community countries and provides ample factual information on the institutions within that intergovernmental organization. The study of the EC was done in both its historical and current contexts. The encyclopedia includes information on its member countries, individuals, acronyms, and terms. There are also six essays on the EC that scrutinize the legal, social, and economic framework and the organization's external affairs. A separate and lengthy statistical-survey section is included that gives data on agriculture, demographics, industry, trade figures, finance, and more. The source for all of these statistics is Eurostat. A "Directory" section provides information on each EC institution, including names of officers, addresses, and other standard directory-type information.

6-187. *The European Union Encyclopedia and Directory.* 3rd ed. London: Europa Publications, 1999. 520 pp. ISBN: 1-857-43056-5.

This work is published every few years and strives to be a comprehensive guide to the European Union both in a contemporary and historical perspective, and it appears to do much of what it claims. Full details of any newly created European institution are given. The "A–Z of the European Union" section has short entries on the EU institutions, their operations, member states, key people, and organizations of importance to the EU. The "Essays on the European Union" portion provides more substantive articles on major EU topics including economic integration and its political/legal frameworks. These longer articles are all signed. The "Directory" segment, the longest, lists each EU institution, giving its address, telephone and fax numbers, e-mail address, Web site, key officers, and the like. A statistical survey of the EU regarding its agriculture, trade information, financial data, and more round out this book.

Guides and Handbooks
6-188. Westlake, Martin. *The Council of European Union.* rev. ed. London: John Harper, 1999. 417 pp. ISBN: 0-953-62780-2.

This is an example of a successful effort that strove to present the council in its hierarchical structure, from the European Council and going down the bureaucratic layers to its working parties. The goal of comprehensiveness seems to be within the ballpark here, as the reader is introduced to the council, its organization, constituent units, history, work accomplished, membership, decisions, rules and procedures, vote-weighting formula, and so forth. The writing is rich in detail and paints an illuminating portrait of the council's inner workings. Included within is a very good bibliography of English-language sources. This handbook is the definitive work of its type in English up to its publication date.

6-189. Thomson, Ian. *The Documentation of the European Communities: A Guide.* New York: Mansell, 1989. 382 pp. Index. ISBN: 0-720-12022-5.

The aim of this work is to describe the existing range of publicly available printed documentation sources produced by the European Communities. Much of the information here is based on research done at the European Documentation Centre at the University of Wales, College of Cardiff. There are four categories of documentation: (1) legislation—the laws and founding treaties, (2) documentation of the legislative process—much of it working documentation, (3) research— European Commission publications research for its own internal policy analysis needs and externally commissioned research pertaining to economic activities and Europe's position in the world, and

(4) explanatory and background documentation—informing citizens of the EC and what they are doing. This book continues the efforts of John Jeffries in his *Guide to the Official Publications of the European Communities.* Use of the index is essential for most effective use of this guide.

6-190. *EU Information Handbook.* Annual. Brussels: EU Committee of the American Chamber of Commerce, 1996–. No ISBN. No ISSN. (Former Title: *EC Information Handbook.*)

This is a handbook offering the organizational structure and staff of the various institutes of the European Union. There is a chapter on other world organizations, such as the International Monetary Fund (IMF), World Bank, World Intellectual Property Organization (WIPO), and the like, and another on nongovernmental organizations, such as the American National Standards Institute (ANSI), the European Patent Office, ISO, and so forth. All information given is standard directory type, but e-mail addresses are conspicuously lacking. The handbook provides good graphic representations of the EU and its various organizations.

6-191. Corbett, Richard. *The European Parliament.* 5th ed. London: John Harper, 2003. 363 pp. Index. ISBN: 0-954-38111-4.

Compiled by several European Parliament (EP) insiders, this book presents itself as an authoritative source on the organization, powers, and processes that go into this body. The provisions of the Maastricht Treaty are incorporated into the contents of this work. Part 1 covers the institutional and historical contexts in which the EP works. Part 2 examines the structure and operations of the EP from the vantage point of individuals, political groups, and administrative organs. Part 3 looks at the actual powers of the EP. The work as a whole is interspersed with various charts, tables, and figures. There are also EP election results for 1979 through 1994 by country. A short bibliography arranged into several broad categories is included. An index is attached.

6-192. Barbour, Philippe, ed. *The European Union Handbook.* Chicago: Fitzroy Dearborn Publishers, 1996. 349 pp. Index. ISBN: 1-884-96428-1.

Aimed at the general reader and lower-division undergraduate, this handbook is an introduction to the European Union and its development out of the European Communities. There are four main chapters, several of which have additional subdivisions. They are "History and Context," "Politics," "Economics," and "Law and Society." A fifth relatively brief chapter looks at the possible future of the EU. Each of the four chapters is written by a different scholar, and all chapters lead off with an essay on the topic. After this essay, there is a short reading list. The subdivisions to some of these chapters include chronologies, tables, charts, partial texts of key documents, and other relevant ones. Emphasis, however, is clearly on the text. Several appendixes, including a 1947–July 1995 chronology; a glossary of terms; as well as an annotated general bibliography and index round out this book.

6-193. Hasenknopf-Reknes, Adelheid. *European Union Handbook and Business Titles.* Los Angeles: Americas Group, 1995. 128 pp. ISBN: 0-935-04718-2.

Here is a reference work aimed perhaps more at people in the business world rather than academe. This is particularly true for addressing the communication needs of North Americans involved in international commerce and trade. This is a compact guide that offers a short overview of the European Union, its many organizations, officers, calendars, statistics, and other information. The "Titles" section provides all the European-language equivalents of a U.S. title. For instance, a job title such as chief training officer will have its Danish-, Dutch-, French-, German-, Italian-, Norwegian-, Portuguese-, Spanish-, and Swedish-language equivalents. A brief style manual covering syntax, metric conversion, tipping, tipping hints, clothing size conversions, and so forth may be of marginal value to some.

6-194. Freeman, Lawrence, ed. *Europe Transformed: Documents on the End of the Cold War.* New York: St. Martin's Press, 1990. 516 pp. ISBN: 0-312-05225-1.

This sourcebook of documents related to the end game of cold war politics and history includes such topics as German unification, Eastern Europe's economic condition, relations among the former Eastern bloc countries or with the European Community, the future of NATO, arms control prospects, and the like. The reprints of major treaties, agreements, and statements all related to these topics compose the primary contents of this sourcebook. These reprints are intended both to provide a historical perspective and to follow the ideas at play during this dynamic period. This is all organized to serve less as an analysis of history than an examination of the diplomatic processes at work during the era. The main body of the book is separated into 3 parts: "Major Treaties and Agreements," "Mandates and Proposals for Arms Control," and "Proposals and Statements by Political Leaders." Be advised that even the editor has admonished readers that a number of the documents reprinted within this book were already dated, and that was in 1990.

6-195. Blair, Alasdair. *The Longman Companion to the European Union since 1945.* New York: Longman, 1999. 384 pp. Index. ISBN: 0-582-36885-5.

This is basically a long chronology of European Union events, history, actions, and policies from 1945 to 1998. There are a number of chapters of about five-year spans of time given names evocative of the period covered. The 1945–1949 period is entitled the "Cold War," while the 1955–1960 one is "Road to Rome." Information on the entries themselves falls into these broad chapters. Readers are provided with institutional history and the development of the European Commission, European Parliament,

European Council of Ministers and European Council, the European Court of Justice and Court of First Instance, Economic and Social Committee, and so on. There are chapters on major EU policies, such as "Agriculture," where it gives an overview and a history, and discusses reforms and budget information. There are also chapters on social policy, economic policy, monetary policy, single-market policy, foreign and security policies, and development policy. The various summits from Bremen (July 6–7, 1978) up to Vienna (December 11–12, 1998) are covered. There is a very short section of biographical entries of major European statespersons, heads of government, and key ministerial positions. There is member state contact information and an index.

6-196. Cox, Andrew. *A Modern Companion to the European Community: A Guide to Key Facts, Institutions and Terms.* Aldershot, UK: Edward Elgar, 1992. 327 pp. ISBN: 1-852-78516-0.

This work was published to be a "practical" guide to identifying the institutions and specialized terminology of the European Community. A short, introductory chapter contains a historical sketch of EC developmental growth over the years. Chapter 2 functions as the main body of this book, and it is a series of country studies giving directory information, highly selective economic data from 1989, and individual country overviews in four sections. These four sections are general introduction, postwar economic growth, postwar recession, and challenges envisioned for the 1990s. Articles clearly lack a scholarly tone and level of analysis. This particular EC guide is best suited for the general reader or lower-division undergraduate.

6-197. Rosenberg, Jerry M. *The New Europe: An A to Z Compendium on the European Community.* Washington, DC: Bureau of National Affairs, 1991. 206 pp. ISBN: 0-871-79669-4.

This handbook contains over 2,500 short entries on all aspects of the European Community. It includes prominent individuals, events, and a myriad of EC agencies that do much of this body's work. The work begins with an introduction to the EC and its organizational structure. There is also a chronology of the EC from 1957 to 1990. The descriptions devoted to the main entries are nontechnical in nature and perfect for the general public, high-school students, and freshmen and sophomores in college.

6-198. Bainbridge, Timothy. *The Penguin Companion to European Union.* 3rd ed. London: Penguin Books, 2002. 573 pp. ISBN: 0-141-00769-9.

The primary focus of this book is on the institutions, policies, and procedures of the European Union. The scope also includes other European institutions, while others may predate it or overlap in time with it. Only the major European organizations are covered. The book also has included a number of biographical entries of individuals who have made a notable contribution to the course of European integration. There are fifty new entries in this third edition. While the arrangement of the book is alphabetical, a number of the more substantive entries, such as the "Court of Justice," are quite long and serve as gateways to related topics by using a liberal dose of "see also" links. A highly selective fifteen-page unannotated bibliography of various aspects of the EU appears at the end of the book. There is no index. The book appears to display a strong dose of pro-EU enthusiasm.

United Nations
Annuals and Yearbooks
6-199. *Global Agenda: Issues before the . . . General Assembly of the United Nations.* Annual. Lanham, MD: Rowman and Littlefield for United Nations Association of the United States of America, 1976/1977–. ISSN: 1057-1213.

The annual issues are subdivided into approximately ten broad topical chapters such as those on peace, arms control and disarmament, global resource management, social and humanitarian issues, and others. These broad headings are in turn broken down into even more specific subjects. Each entry offers a general overview of current events, and then proceeds to expound on the United Nations (UN) response to that particular issue, region, or event. The narrative responses tend to put the UN and its agencies in the best possible light most of the time. The volume does, however, provide a glimpse of the tremendous amount of work covered by the UN and its related agencies in virtually every corner of the globe.

6-200. *Yearbook of the United Nations.* Annual. New York: Columbia University Press in cooperation with the United Nations, 1947–. Index. ISSN: 0082-8521.

This annual appears to be no longer published, but older editions of this standard work provide authoritative accounts of events and details of many actions that have been taken at the United Nations or throughout one of its myriad agencies. Key points of important committee reports, follow-up information, General Assembly resolutions, and voting tabulations are all made available for readers. The main part of the work is arranged into seven major parts, including those in the areas of peacekeeping, human rights, legal questions, international organizations, and more. The longest chapter is the one on economic and social questions. There is an index of resolutions and decisions. (Note: The 1995 edition was the latest examined.)

Bibliographies
6-201. Baratta, Joseph Preston. *United Nations System.* New Brunswick, NJ: Transaction Publishers, 1995. 511 pp. Indexes. ISBN: 1-560-00201-8.

This is another bibliography that is part of the publisher's International Organization series (see *North Atlantic Treaty Organization* [entry 6-209]. According to the introduction, the audience is quite broad, starting with "informed citizens" and then progressing on to students, scholars, and "international civil servants." The organization of the book as a whole begins with the general and moves on to the more specific. It is arranged to correspond to a particular point of view, and that is the United Nations organization's declining level of international consensus on the means and ends for addressing major global problems. The works cited in this bibliography are meant to be representational of what is actually available. The 1,400 entries have an extensive set of well-crafted annotations. Chapters are arranged by United Nations functions or along the lines of its numerous organs, but mostly the former. Typical headings include "Peacekeeping," "Human Rights," "NIEO," and "Labor." The book comes with both an author and a subject index.

Dictionaries

6-202. Boczek, Boleslaw Adam. *Historical Dictionary of International Tribunals.* Metuchen, NJ: Scarecrow Press, 1994. 361 pp. ISBN: 0-810-82903-7.

This work will cater to a highly specialized band of lawyers, students, researchers, educators, and journalists who require information on international tribunals and courts. The main body is prefaced with a chapter delineating a number of tribunal or court events and/or decisions. There are 200 entries forming the main body of this work, and they provide insights into both former and current tribunals. It also covers those bodies that were set up but never became operational for one reason or another. A large number of the main entries are on significant judicial or international tribunal decisions. All International Court of Justice (ICJ) decisions are included. A number of selective biographical entries are also provided, especially on those who were major people within the international judiciary, frequently from the former Permanent Court of International Justice (PCIJ) and from the current World Court. A listing of all PCIJ and all ICJ judgments and advisory opinions appears within. This handbook contains a very good bibliography broken down into various subject divisions. The lack of an index may pose a problem to some users of this work.

6-203. Bennett, A. LeRoy. *Historical Dictionary of the United Nations.* Lanham, MD: Scarecrow Press, 1995. 244 pp. ISBN: 0-810-82992-4.

This work furnishes a look at the United Nations and its work over the body's first fifty years. It includes information on the various UN units and organizational subunits, topics related to the UN, and the people associated with the events and history of the UN for its first half-century. A chronology of UN events is available followed by a twenty-three-page introduction to the UN and its great achievements or notable failures for the time covered. It is arranged alphabetically, and entries are loaded with "see" and "see also" references. While the work may not be comprehensive in its treatment of the topic, it does appear to manage to cover virtually all of the UN's major efforts and its principal personalities who have served in leadership roles for this organization. The bibliography of official and reference works along with books on the UN and its history is quite useful. Several seminal UN documents make up the book's appendixes. These include the Universal Declaration of Human Rights, the United Nations Charter, and others.

Encyclopedias

6-204. Moore, John Allphin. *Encyclopedia of the United Nations.* New York: Facts on File, 2002. 484 pp. Index. ISBN: 0-816-04417-1.

This encyclopedia's stated purpose is to serve as a comprehensive guide to the United Nations and its institutions, procedures, major policies, operating procedures, specialized agencies, people, decisions, and overall involvement in world affairs. This is an encyclopedia about a "new" UN, exemplified best by people such as Kofi Annan. The new UN and the people behind it are both part of what is seen as an emerging international civil society. General topics that are the nexus to this "new" orientation are seen in the UN's increasing interest in women, globalization, sustainable development, terrorism, and indigenous peoples of the globe. It is no longer a body that tracks primarily the issues of peace and international security as was true during the bulk of the cold war era. A total of about twenty-five contributors have written entries laid out in alphabetical order. Each entry contains a number of "see" and "see also" references. Most entries are relatively short, averaging one page in length. More important or longer-standing issues receive up to six-page entries, such as the one on the

"Arab-Israeli Dispute." Several useful appendixes are attached, including ones on the UN Charter, Universal Declaration of Human Rights, UN member states as of June 2002, select UN resolutions, and a UN chronology. A complete index completes the work. See also Osmanczyk [entry 6-205].

6-205. Osmanczyk, Edmund Jan, ed. *Encyclopedia of the United Nations and International Relations.* 2nd ed. New York: Taylor and Francis, 1990. 1220 pp. ISBN: 0-850-66833-6.

This is the authoritative encyclopedic work on the United Nations (UN), its specialized agencies, and its myriad nongovernmental, intergovernmental, international, and regional groups that all work together under the UN umbrella. There are thousands of entries on various international agreements, conventions, and treaties from the late 1800s to date. Economic, political, military, sociology, and diplomatic terms and international law are all defined within their UN system context. The work does rely on heavy use of cross-referencing. The relatively smallish print may have some readers running for their bifocals or magnifying glasses. Entries are excellent in quality, and some are lengthier essays, such as the ones on the General Agreement on Tariffs and Trade (GATT) and the International Court of Justice (ICJ). The caliber of the piece on the 1982 Sea Law is typical of this as well. (Note: A new third edition packaged in a four-volume set has been published in 2003 under a minor title variation.)

Guides and Handbooks

6-206. Chamberlin, Waldo. *Chronology and Fact Book of the United Nations.* New York: Oceana Publications, 1961–1991. ISBN: 0-379-21200-5. ISSN: 0888-370X.

This chronology covers the periods from 1941 through 1991. It serves primarily as a supplement to the *Annual Review of United Nations Affairs.* The chronology is a fairly complete summary of the United Nations' last fifty years in existence. There are three major parts to this book: "Chronology," "Tables of Data," and "Main Documents of the UN." Included here are not only the General Assembly but also the rules and general procedures of the International Court of Justice. The purpose of each United Nations agency is clearly outlined. (Note: The latest issue seen was dated for the year 1992.)

Other Intergovernmental Organizations
Bibliographies

6-207. Clements, Frank A. *Arab Regional Organizations.* New Brunswick, NJ: Transaction Publishers, 1992. 198 pp. Indexes. ISBN: 1-560-00057-0.

This publication lists materials about Arab regional organizations, not by them. Excluded from this work are specialized agencies of the Arab League and learned or professional societies. There are several main sections to this book. The first part is a directory of Arab regional organizations, composed mainly of headings for the Arab League and its various sub-units, but also providing information on the Arab Monetary Fund, the Arab Organization of Petroleum Exporting Countries (AOPEC), and the Gulf Cooperation Council. The second part concentrates on Arab sources of aid or assistance, and the third section lists international organizations and both Arab and non-Arab sources, especially United Nations agencies and the International Monetary Fund (IMF). Each entry is annotated in several concise, well-written sentences. While English-language materials clearly predominate, there are foreign-language materials included. Most entries are for journal articles. There are three separate indexes of authors, titles, and subjects. This work is very similar in scope and audience to *European Communities* [entry 6–181] and other titles in the Transaction Press series.

6-208. *Bibliography on the Organization of African Unity (O.A.U.).* Addis Ababa, Ethiopia: O.A.U. Library, 1993. 113 pp. No ISBN.

This is the first bibliography published by the Organization of African Unity (OAU) and was prepared for diplomats, researchers, and students to assist them with their research on this intergovernmental organization. All citations included for publication pertain to some aspect of the OAU or its work. The arrangement of the bibliography is alphabetical by author or title. Half of the cited works are in French, and the other half are in English. None of the entries are annotated.

6-209. Williams, Phil, comp. *North Atlantic Treaty Organization.* New Brunswick, NJ: Transaction Publishers, 1994. 283 pp. Indexes. ISBN: 1-560-00154-2.

This is one work among several in the publisher's series on international organizations. All of them are similar in that they are annotated bibliographies made up of books, journal articles, pamphlets, directories, databases, and theses on their respective topics, in this case the North Atlantic Treaty Organization (NATO). All of these works cite NATO as the subject being studied. Only the most essential official publications put out by NATO are included. Every entry is annotated except the dissertations. These annotations are lengthy and very informative; they tend to include a high level of expertise and a sense of historical context. The main body of the work has nineteen chapters, the longest of which are "History of NATO," "Evolution of NATO Strategy," and "European Nations and the Alliance." A preponderance of the bibliographic entries is dedicated to NATO's political and international activities, not its military operations. There are around 900 citations total. The journal titles included in this number are overwhelmingly drawn from a core of about ten standard political science journals, such as *Foreign Affairs* and *International Organization*. There are author, subject, and title indexes.

6-210. Sheinin, David. *Organization of American States*. New Brunswick, NJ: Transaction Publishers, 1996. 209 pp. Indexes. ISBN: 1-560-00243-3.

This work is similar in scope and treatment to the bibliographic series noted for other books in this publisher series

on international organization. The main entries are English-language books and journal articles broken down into a number of broad categories and subcategories. Chapters range from history to events, the Organization of American States (OAS) in Inter-American politics, and issues. Some of the issues are agriculture, women, security, human rights, and others. All citations have been fully annotated, and these annotations should serve the user well. There are author, subject, and title indexes.

6-211. Welch, Thomas L. *The Organization of American States: A Bibliography*. Washington, DC: Columbus Memorial Library, OAS, 1990. 102 pp. Indexes. No ISBN.

This bibliography on the Organization of American States is somewhat different than Sheinin's work [entry 6-210]. Books, journal articles, and an occasional dissertation written since the 1948 founding of OAS make up the core bibliography. These works were written by people outside the OAS system. A number of articles on either side of 1948 on the topic of Pan-Americanism have been included when appropriate. There are no official OAS documents in this bibliography. The main body has two sections, one for books and another for journal articles. Each section is arranged alphabetically by author's name. A number of works cited are from languages other than English that go into the makeup of the OAS member states. Also, there are no annotations. There is a title and a subject index available.

Dictionaries

6-212. Wilson, Larman C. *Historical Dictionary of Inter-American Organizations*. Lanham, MD: Scarecrow Press, 1998. 361 pp. ISBN: 0-810-83381-6.

This work captures the essential issues, problems, people, and chronology of the Inter-American geopolitical zone from approximately 1800 to July 1997. Entries are drawn predominantly from the post–World War II era. This work argues that international organizations have served as major actors in inter-American relations and diplomatic history for at least 200 years. In this particular handbook, over 100 regional and subregional international organizations are examined. Entries provide these organizations' respective histories, functions, locations, and ultimate significance within the Inter-American political process. The main body is arranged in standard alphabetical format, and these entries include international bodies with special importance within the Western hemisphere, political and economic leaders, diplomacy, international law, wars, historical events, and more. In addition, there is a 1,200-work bibliography of books, articles, government documents, and organization reports arranged in a hierarchical subject context. Some non-English-language materials are cited.

6-213. McDougall, Derek. *Historical Dictionary of International Organizations in Asia and the Pacific*. Lanham, MD: Scarecrow, 2002. 232 pp. ISBN: 0-810-84093-6.

Part of a larger publisher series, this work was designed to provide information on a large number of organizations and on the roles of crucial individuals and nations in creating and operating these international bodies. It is intended to serve as a tool for those people studying international organization in Pacific Asia. There is a list of the numerous abbreviations and acronyms used throughout. The lead chapter examines each organization's history and type since 1900. Not all of the groups listed focus exclusively on Pacific Asia. Amnesty International and the International Bank for Reconstruction and Development (IBRD) are two such examples. In the main body of the work are some terms and broad subjects, such as peace, globalization, and collective security. Most entries, however, are those international organizations that center more squarely on Pacific Asia as their prime area of interest. These entries offer the history, meetings, participants, critical dates, and more. A number of United Nations–related organizations are also listed.

6-214. DeLancey, Mark W. *Historical Dictionary of International Organizations in Sub-Sahara Africa*. Metuchen, NJ: Scarecrow, 1994. 517 pp. ISBN: 0-810-82751-4.

Not seen.

Encyclopedias

6-215. Atkins, G. Pope. *Encyclopedia of the Inter-American System*. Westport, CT: Greenwood Press, 1997. 561 pp. ISBN: 0-313-28600-0.

The goal of this work is to serve as a one-volume reference encyclopedia on the entire Inter-American System from 1889 to the mid-1990s. Students and researchers who maintain a special interest in Inter-American organization, international organization, or international relations in general should find this book helpful. Entries include but are not limited to multilateral institutions, policy evolution from the 1889 era, membership and observers in different organizations, treaties, conventions, protocols, resolutions, conflicts, and individuals. Entries can be highly interdisciplinary and include elements of foreign policies, international analysis, international law, political economics, and history. The bulk of the 250 listings arranged alphabetically in this encyclopedia range from very brief to longer, interpretive essays. The introduction to the Inter-American System as a whole gives key historical and geographic contexts. While most articles have a short reading list, some have more substantial listings of English-language works. Other elements of the encyclopedia include a chronology of major events, the charter of the Organization of American States, and a short bibliographic essay that highlights Inter-American system information. Some of these works are in Spanish.

Guides and Handbooks

6-216. Lane, Jan-Erik, ed. *Political Data Handbook: OECD Countries.* 2nd ed. Oxford: Oxford University Press, 1997. 357 pp. ISBN: 0-198-28053-X.

This handbook strives to serve as a single-volume statistical compendium to governments and politics of the Organisation for Economic Co-operation and Development (OECD) countries. This purpose is supplemented with background social and economic information. The book encompasses the member countries of Western Europe and the non-European OECD members that include the United States, Japan, Canada, New Zealand, and Australia. The handbook is bifurcated into a section on comparative tabular data by topic and one that covers the most significant aspects of government and policies in the individual OECD countries. The section on comparative tables is for population, employment, and a wide range of economic figures supplied by government agencies, political parties, and election results. All of this is decidedly post–World War II in time-period coverage. The other section proffers information on state structure, offices, political parties, government, and constitution. The work is aimed at political scientists, journalists, teachers, and students.

7

Comparative Politics and Comparative Government Reference Sources

This is a major subfield of political science that applies a comparative analysis to the study of government institutions and systems, constitutions, various political developments, and individual countries. Area studies are generally considered either a part of comparative politics or related to it with a historical dimension added.. Accordingly, this chapter has subdivisions for Africa, Asia/Middle East, Europe, and Central and South America. A student will most likely associate the term "Comparative Politics and Comparative Government" with the study of one country's governmental structure and system of government against another country's. This is probably too narrow a focus, but it can be the major component of a specialty in comparative study of politics and/or countries. The political process itself, especially the electoral process and its study of voting behavior and interest groups from one country to another, is another major area of study in the field of comparative politics. The U.S. component often ends up being taught in American

politics and government classes and U.S. foreign policy in international relations ones. The relative importance of this very traditional subfield in political science departments varies somewhat from campus to campus.

Comparative Politics and Comparative Government in General
Annuals and Yearbooks

7-1. *Canadian Annual Review of Politics and Public Affairs.* Toronto: University of Toronto Press, 1960–. Index. ISSN: 0315-1433.

This is an annual publication that covers a lot of ground in Canadian federal and provincial political processes over the last twelve-month period. It kicks off with a detailed calendar of the year's Canadian events. The main body then ensues and is packaged into two parcels. The first part examines Canada exclusively at the federal level, while the second part covers the provincial political landscape. They tend to be roughly equal in length and coverage. Essays appearing in the federal part could touch upon any of the following: the economy, federal government agencies, taxes, political parties, foreign affairs, multilateral agreements, and the like. The second part contains survey articles that have a purely provincial flavor. The Yukon and the Northwest Territories are both included in the second part. Contributors to the review articles are all Canadian academics. There is an obituary of the more prominent Canadians who died over the last year. An index is included for names and subjects.

7-2. *Freedom in the World.* New York: Freedom House, 1978–. ISSN: 0732-6610.

This is an annual publication put out by Freedom House, a relatively conservative political think tank. Freedom House monitors how the earth's many nations and dependent territories are doing regarding their respective progress in fostering human and political rights for their citizens. The number of people walking the earth is perceived by Freedom House as being "Free," "Partly Free," or "Not Free." The worst offenders of human rights are listed separately. The main body is a country-by-country survey on human and political rights and the status of individual freedom. Each survey article is several pages long and in a set format for easy comparative purposes. Ratings are assigned to each country or territory. The lack of explicitly defined criteria used for assigning these ratings is a weakness.

7-3. *Human Rights Watch World Reports.* New York: Human Rights Watch, n.d., ca. 1991–. ISSN: 1054-948X.

This annual publication investigates human rights violations and reports of abuse in seventy countries by Human Rights Watch, an advocacy group. The publication states that it defends freedom of thought and expression, due process, and equal protection of the law, among other things. The main body of the work is laid out by region and then by individual nation. Every country chapter receives about a four- or five-page report arranged for comparative analysis by using standardized entry formats. Each country entry contains a summary of recent human rights developments and details what Human Right Watch is doing in that particular country to fight human rights abuses. See also entries 6-93, 6-94, and 6-103.

7-4. *Index to International Public Opinion.* Annual. Westport, CT: Greenwood Press, 1978/1979–. ISSN: 0193-905X.

This annual publication collects questions asked in a number of public-opinion polls. The answers to the questions appear in a companion microfiche set, available from the same publisher. For 1986 and after, both index and response data are on CD-ROM. The main index is alphabetically arranged by polling topic. Many of the questions deal with political officials, labor, candidates, voting behavior, and the like. Fairly comprehensive information is provided on the polling source, whether privately or publicly commissioned, sample size, method employed, sampling universe, and more. The actual polling took place in roughly sixty-eight countries. It is an interesting source for political candidates to tailor remarks to specific target audiences in the United States or other countries.

7-5. *The Military Balance.* Annual. London: International Institute for Strategic Studies, 1960–. ISSN: 0459-7222.

This standard reference source is issued annually in order to provide an expert assessment of the relative armed forces and defense expenditures of 169 different countries. In Part 1, the individual countries of the world are grouped together by region. Each grouping starts off with a short essay describing the military issues confronting that particular region. Tables of data depicting nuclear delivery, warhead holdings, and military satellites are major parts of this work. Part 2 analyzes macroeconomic and more defense-related economic data of countries, again clustered by region. It examines the overall military strength of a country and examines how well its economic base may indeed support that level of armed forces and equipment. Arms-trade data is also covered in this section. The assessments of comparative military strengths are mostly done using quantitative methods. The data published is not based on data culled from previously published data as generated by the nation-states. Instead, the International Institute for Strategic Studies (IISS) staff compiles all of the data used

in most of this work. Some of this data admittedly falls into the estimate category. The level of specificity for arms and weapons owned by the nations of the world is quite surprising given the secrecy that often surrounds arms procurement and nuclear weapons programs. (Note: The 2002/2003 volume was inspected.) 💻

7-6. *Political Risk Yearbook.* Annual. E. Syracuse, NY: PRS Group, 1989–. ISSN: 1054-6294. Web version: http://www.prs-group.com. 1999–. Updated Annually.

This impressive ongoing work has become an authoritative source of political and economic risk analysis information for about 106 different countries. There are current data tables and time-series figures, probability analysis for regime and/or political party changes, new and influential political men and women, investment climate scans, trade policies and agreements, and background information on foreign affairs, social conditions, history, and political currents. Maps are available in both print and Web formats, and the information is updated annually. The print version is arranged by volumes corresponding to either whole continents or other large geographic units, such as Central America, and then by individual country. 💻

7-7. *Yearbook on International Communist Affairs.* Stanford, CA: Stanford Institution Press, 1966–1991. Index. ISSN: 0084-4101.

The twenty-fifth anniversary issue for

1991 marked the last annual volume of this memorable Hoover Institution survey of Communism around the globe. The last issue profiles 125 countries and discusses the various Communist governments, political parties, and events within each of those nations over the last twelve months prior to publication. Included in this final annual are several essays on international Communist organization and a single essay on Soviet propaganda themes. A register of Communist parties ensues, giving country populations, Communist Party membership, party leader, political status, dates of last party congress, and how the Communist parties fared at the ballot box in the last election. The main body is arranged by continent or region of the globe, then alphabetically by country within that organization. Most entries are several pages in length. These entries are fairly well structured in a similar manner, including individual Communist Party, date founded, membership information, general secretary, front groups, and more. The work is indexed by subject and by personal name. While the Hoover Institution has a fairly conservative reputation, this work was widely regarded as authoritative for the years published.

Directories

7-8. *The International Directory of Government.* 3rd ed. London: Europa, 1999. 901 pp. ISBN: 1-857-43057-3.

This directory is published approximately every five years or so and includes all the nations on the earth at time of publication. Each entry gets similar treatment by providing head of state, legislative system currently in place, full listing of ministers, addresses, phone numbers, and an outline of activities undertaken. Other possible subheadings include those for agriculture, business, the economy, employment, and international affairs. E-mail addresses are few and far between. A new feature for the third edition is the complete listing of the main organ of government in the states and territories not under effective central control. This information appears at the end of each chapter, when relevant. For the United States, this includes the fifty state governments, U.S. Commonwealth territories, and U.S. external territories. For Israel, this would include the Palestinian Autonomous Areas.

7-9. Welborn, Deborah. *International Directory of Women's Political Leadership: Women's Organizations and Women Leaders.* College Park, MD: Center for Political Leadership and Participation (CPLP), 1992–.

This book draws heavily from a file compiled and maintained by the Center for Political Leadership and Participation at the University of Maryland. There are several major and a few minor chapters all dealing with women from around the world and their relative success in joining their country's political elite as determined by their ability to become elected members of their respective national legislatures. Brief chapters, such as the one discussing the status of women in Africa, are typical ones, and they contain a series of short essays of several pages long. One such short essay examines the democratization of Africa in terms of women's transitional status there. The credentials of these writers are not always clear. Much of the text in this work centers on the use of bibliographic essays that cite the literature as well as the authors' findings. There is also a bibliography at the conclusion of each chapter. A directory of women political leaders from across the globe is arranged by continent and then by individual country. There is no e-mail or Web site information provided in this chapter, the largest in the book. A number of statistics were gathered and compiled by the Inter-Parliamentary Union on both the relative status and gains forged by women holding office in legislative bodies in developed and developing countries. There is also a country-by-country survey of the percentage of women in these national legislatures for comparative purposes.

7-10. National Institute for Research Advancement, ed. *NIRA's World Directory of Think Tanks.* 4th ed. Tokyo: National Institute for Research, 2002. 508 pp. Indexes. ISBN: 0-333-99415-9.

A total of 320 think tanks from roughly seventy-seven different countries and regions are listed in this directory. The intention is to post only the "most prominent" public policy research organizations. Every think tank listed must be an institute having a certain degree of independent decision-making latitude. No government agencies or bodies are included. Also, only organizations that make that research generally available to the public are covered. This eliminates from consideration those think tanks doing primarily contract research work for special clients. Each entry is structured around a uniform format, beginning with name of organization, location, contact information, organizational status, background and scope of activities, areas of research, and geographic focus. Entries provide e-mail addresses and URLs. There are several indexes at the back, including ones by English name, by country, and another by non-English name.

7-11. Minority Rights Group, ed. *World Directory of Minorities.* 2nd ed. London: Minority Rights Group International, 1997. 840 pp. ISBN: 1-873-19436-6.

The world's minorities are arranged into eleven geographical regions, all subdivided by individual country. This arrangement requires readers to look up multiple entries in those instances where a particular minority may straddle two or more nations, such as the Kurds. The country entries with more significant minority rights issues and/or larger minority populations receive relatively more print. Minority groups are listed in a statistical profile and discussed in descending order by population size. The minority groups covered in this work focus on ethnic, religious, and linguistic groups. Neither sexual minorities nor peoples with disabilities are included. Minorities are analyzed from a political perspective in recounting their relative human rights history and status among the world's nations. Finally, this work can be used as a resource book for listing a number of private organizations that serve as advocacy groups for minority populations. This is an interesting and often overlooked work with a rich yet easy to read narrative.

Bibliographies

7-12. Schaffner, Bradley L. *Bibliography of the Soviet Union, Its Predecessors, and Successors.* Metuchen, NJ: Scarecrow, 1995. 569 pp. Index. ISBN: 0-810-82620-X.

Over the last decade, much has been written on this book's topic due to the access given to scholars requiring a range of materials previously restricted. The bibliography covers a fairly broad range of topics in the area's social, political, and cultural developments, but special stress is placed on the more contemporary period and the area's dynamic transition from Communism to some form of capitalism. The books listed are largely in major Western European languages, often English. The book is arranged by Library of Congress subject headings, but books are listed only once. Biographies and reference works are excluded. Most of the books selected cover the Soviet Union as a whole, not as individual republics. Entries are not annotated and there are no journal articles. The bibliography is especially rich for those seeking secondary materials from the 1980s and 1990s. There is an author index only.

7-13. Larby, Patricia. *Commonwealth.* New Brunswick, NJ: Transaction Pub-

lishers, 1993. 254 pp. ISBN: 1-560-00110-0.

This is a bibliography broken down into a number of broad categories, such as, "Britain and the Commonwealth," "Constitutional Development," "Politics and Government," "Women," "Education," "Public Health and Medicare," and many others. The intent of this bibliography is to trace the evolution, structure, functions and everyday workings of the Commonwealth at both the official and unofficial levels of operation. Many of the citations are from the 1970s. Excluded from consideration here are materials on individual Commonwealth nations and much of the literature on regional Commonwealth activities. The Secretariat's own publications also are generally excluded from consideration here. There is an introductory essay on the history and evolution of the British Commonwealth. Each citation is annotated with one or several sentences. Entries are arranged alphabetically by author within each of the broad categories noted above. These entries are all books, journal articles, and a highly selective amount of official publications. Included are several black-and-white maps on the Commonwealth today.

7-14. Mahler, Gregory, comp. *Contemporary Canadian Politics, 1988–1994: An Annotated Bibliography.* Westport, CT: Greenwood Press, 1995. 204 pp. ISBN: 0-313-28924-7.

Scholars and researchers from Canada, the United States, the United Kingdom, Australia, and other countries update the compiler's previous work that covered the years 1970 through 1987. The parameters covering the two works are basically the same for each. Several areas are outside the scope of both works. They are biographies, political histories, documents, and government reports. A few traditional Canadian political concerns are given special attention. These relate to the Canadian legal and constitutional system of government, the Canadian model of federalism, regionalism, the relations between English-speaking and Francophone provinces, and other similar topics. Thematic chapters are all subdivided by genre of publication. Books are listed alphabetically, followed by an alphabetical listing of journals, and so on. A number of the works are in French. Approximately 50 percent of the citations are fully annotated. This work generally meets the goals of the compiler, whose desire it was to generate a bibliographic tool useful equally to advanced researchers and undergraduate students.

7-15. Shaaban, Marian. American Library Association, Government Documents Round Table, comp. *Guide to Country Information in International Governmental Organization Publications.* [Bethesda, MD?]: CIS, 1996. 343 pp. Indexes. ISBN: 0-886-92336-0.

The goal of this publication is to give the user an orderly and comprehensive roadmap to the many vital serials, monographs, and monographic series put out by intergovernmental organizations (IGOs) pertaining to the world's individual nation-states. These publications are noted for often containing comparative data on specific countries within a single volume. Most of the publications listed have an English-language edition, and many of them are also issued in at least one other language as part of a multilingual edition. The main body of this annotated bibliography is arranged by the world and regional areas, and then subdivided by broad subject arrays. There are indexes for issuing body and for title of work.

7-16. Sukhwal, B. L. *Political Geography: A Comprehensive Systematic Bibliography.* New York: AMS Press, 1996. 715 pp. Index. ISBN: 0-404-63151-7.

The goal of this fairly comprehensive work was to gather together virtually everything published in the English language on the topic of political geography. The bibliography also includes materials in the major European and other languages of the world. The work was compiled by consulting more than 270 journals, periodicals, and bibliographies appearing in monographs. There are also some theses and dissertations listed. The main body of the bibliography is divided into seventeen chapters, each of which is further subdivided into "General and Theoretical Works" and "Political Geography of Regions." The regional divisions are again broken down to genre of publishing format, including government documents. Some typical major chapters of the seventeen are "Frontiers, Boundaries, Landlocked States and Buffer Zones," "Geography of International Relations," and "Political Geography of

Oceans." The entire work is unannotated. There is only an author index. The lack of a more general index will make access to this body of literature somewhat more difficult and time-consuming.

Dictionaries

7-17. Chandler, Ralph C. *The Constitutional Law Dictionary.* 2 vols. Santa Barbara, CA: ABC-CLIO, 1985–1987. ISBN: 0-874-36031-5.

Volume 1 covers the law on individual rights, while the second volume examines government powers. Several supplements have been published for Volume 1 and at least one supplement has come out for Volume 2.

7-18. Collin, P. H., ed. *Dictionary of Government and Politics.* 2nd ed. Chicago: Fitzroy Dearborn Publishers, 1998. 303 pp. ISBN: 1-579-58072-6.

Among the various dictionaries of government vocabulary, this one differs from most in that it tends to cover both British and American usage. This second edition also includes expanded coverage of the terminology of the European Union. Approximately 5,000 terms and phrases are explained in basic English that should be readily understood by those readers not having a background in government. Definitions are brief, similar to those found in an ordinary dictionary. Examples that show the defined term in the context of a sentence are displayed in boldface. Some definitions also include commentary. There are no illustrations. Because this volume was initially published in Great

Britain, its greatest value probably lies in the fact that it provides American readers with explanations of government language used in that country. For example, a "Supplement" that appears at the end of the volume reproduces several legislative documents found in the United Kingdom, such as a "Notice of Whipping."

7-19. Cashmore, E. Ellis. *Dictionary of Race and Ethnic Relations.* 2nd ed. London: Routledge, 1988. 325 pp. ISBN: 0-415-02511-7.

This second edition contains updated text and readings, new events, new research and findings, and even some relatively newer theories of race and ethnicity. The author's admitted bias is his belief that any serious study of race and ethnic relations must be based squarely on one key issue, and that is how any inequality was perpetuated over time by various means of discrimination. The concentration of this book is mostly on the United Kingdom, while the United States does receive secondary although ample treatment. The main body is in standard A-to-Z format and contains useful cross-references throughout the signed entries. Entries average about two to four pages, which elevates this work perhaps to encyclopedic dictionary status. Entries include terms, individuals, ethnic groups, and relevant topics. Terms demonstrate a breadth of scope that would make this work more applicable to the needs of undergraduates and the general reader rather than scholars. Some of these terms are "Police and

Racism," "Civil Rights Movement," "Joseph A. de Gobineau," and "Marxism and Racism." Some may detect a somewhat leftist perspective here. (Note: A third edition was published in 1994, but was not seen.)

7-20. Greve, Brent. *Historical Dictionary of the Welfare State.* Lanham, MD: Scarecrow Press, 1998. 159 pp. ISBN: 0-810-83332-8.

This historical dictionary provides the reader with a broad historical background on the social welfare system of the Western world along with other developed economies, such as Japan. It assists in defining basic terms and concepts of the welfare state. The main criterion for selecting a term for a main entry is the historical importance of that concept. There are very few entries of a biographical nature. A chronology of the welfare state from 1388 through 1997 is included. Statistical data does not appear to form a significant portion of this work. Near the end of the work is a very good and fairly lengthy bibliography that has been subdivided into subtopic or geographic areas. The lack of a subject index may prove inconvenient for some users.

7-21. Jaensch, Dean. *The Macmillan Dictionary of Australian Politics.* South Melbourne: Macmillan, 1992. 4th ed. 246 pp. ISBN: 0-732-91445-0.

Not seen. See also entry7-72 for *The Penguin McQuarie Dictionary of Australian Politics* in the Guides and Handbooks section.

7-22. Shimoni, Yaacov. *Political Dictionary of the Arab World.* New York: Macmillan, 1987. 520 pp. ISBN: 0-029-16422-2.

This is a single-volume political compendium to the entire Arab world from its recent history up to the time of publication. Please note that since this work deals with the Arab world and not simply the Middle East region, excluded are the countries of Israel, Turkey, Iran, and Cyprus. This work strives for impartiality even though it is written under the auspices of the Dayan Center, Shiloah Institute of the University of Tel Aviv. The historical time period covered is from around 1900 AD to the mid-1980s, with the emphasis on the time period following World War II. Organization of the dictionary-style main entries is purely alphabetical. Terms can be nations, political movements, political parties and their leaders, ideologies, wars, territorial disputes, or alliances. The entries are concise and very well written yet pack a lot of information into a relatively small print space. Entries on "Arab-Israel Conflict" and "Arab-Israeli Wars" are lengthy and serve as an excellent introduction to the complex range of issues surrounding these events.

Encyclopedias

7-23. Bogdanor, Vernon. *Blackwell Encyclopaedia of Political Institutions.* New York: Blackwell Reference, 1987. 667 pp. ISBN: 0-631-13841-2.

This is a publication complementary to *The Blackwell Encyclopaedia of Political Thought* [entry 4-11] in Chapter 4.

Entries focus exclusively on core concepts applied to examination of developed nations, especially those in the United States and Europe. Other nations receive scattered treatment. Analysis is on political institutions, political organizations, and political community. Included are major political scientists no longer living at the time of publication. International relations materials are omitted. Contributors are predominantly European, with British and U.S. scholars in the majority. Good reading lists, some relatively extensive, are included at the conclusion of each entry, and the entries are heavily cross-referenced but well-written pieces. Entries range in the one-to-two-page zone. One unique feature included here is that it often tells who coined a particular political term or phrase.

7-24. Lipset, Seymour Martin, ed. *Democracy in Asia and Africa.* Washington, DC: Congressional Quarterly, 1997. 237 pp. ISBN: 1-568-02123-2.

This work, edited by an eminent social scientist, is a survey of democracy in the regions of Asia and Africa, including each nation-state appearing on these two continents. Contributors are primarily U.S. academics, but the work is targeting high-school and undergraduate students. The book purports to avoid examining democracy as a static object but instead focuses upon the policies, election results, constitutional developments, general economic conditions, class and/or race relations, and ethnic, religious, and other factors. Included within the covers of these books are articles on individual nations and broader articles on the democratic-development process by region or continent or on the more theoretical aspects of democracy as a living idea. A number of documents that serve as milestones of the progress democracy has made over the years have been reproduced. Some of these are Constitution of Japan (1947), Israeli Declaration of Independence (1948), and the African Charter on Human and People's Rights.

7-25. Lipset, Seymour Martin, ed. *Democracy in Europe and the Americas.* Washington, DC: Congressional Quarterly, 1998. 280 pp. Index. ISBN: 1-568-02122-4.

Something of a spin-off of *The Encyclopedia of Democracy* [entry 4-19], this work updates its predecessor and concentrates upon Europe and North and South America. There are individual articles, usually several pages in length, on either countries or regions. These are supplemented by two articles that discuss democratic theory in Europe and the Anglo-American world. Each article includes a bibliography with most citations dating from the 1980s and 1990s. Individual articles describe the evolution of democracy over the centuries and bring the story down to the late 1990s. There are numerous maps but no other illustrations. At the back of the volume can be found text of a number of relevant documents, from the Magna Carta to the Summit of the Americas Declaration of Principles, promulgated in 1994. Also useful is a listing of articles by region; this appears in the front matter. Contributors are drawn from the academic community in the United States and abroad. Compared to the *Encyclopedia of Democracy,* this work is somewhat more up to date and has the advantage of concentrating on particular areas of the world. For a description of the companion volume, consult *Democracy in Asia and Africa* [entry 7-24].

7-26. Leoussi, Athena S., ed. *Encyclopaedia of Nationalism.* New Brunswick, NJ: Transaction Publishers, 2001. 314 pp. ISBN: 0-765-80002-0.

This encyclopedic guide attempts to pack a wide range of issues and debates into the study of nationalism. These areas include the study of the nature of nations and nationalist movements, the role of ethnicity in shaping the foreign policy of democratic countries, and the role of the nation-state in this emerging world order. While the main body is primarily alphabetical in order, entries can be grouped into six distinct categories. These six groupings are the defining figures of eighteenth- and nineteenth-century nationalism (such as Fichte and Rousseau), entries on the diverse aspects of nationality (such as decolonization and national symbols), relations between nationalism and other collective phenomena (such as art and language), relations between nationalism and other ideologies (such as Communism and liberalism), various theories of nationalism (such as ethnosymbolism and kin selection), and finally the various accounts of

the nations. Articles are on the long side and offer several layers of analysis ideal for future discussion. Articles have a scholarly tone and tend to read like a partial review of the literature published in the field. Each article is signed, and short reading lists are provided. See also Snyder and Motyl [entries 7-29 and 7-30].

7-27. Green, Jonathon. *Encyclopedia of Censorship.* New York: Facts on File, 1990. 388 pp. Index. ISBN: 0-816-01594-5.

This encyclopedia attempts to trace the development of censorship over history and in its present-day state. Censorship is perceived within this work as being continuous and pervasive, yet not monolithic in nature. The focus is on the United States and United Kingdom, but discussion includes other Western nations, South Africa, Europe, the former Communist bloc countries, and the third world. All aspects of wartime censorship are eliminated from consideration. Entries are alphabetically arranged, and range from one or two sentences to several pages in length. The main entries could be countries, people, publications, organizations of all stripes, court cases, laws, congressional committees, and so forth. Each entry has a number of cross-references embedded in it. There is a list of banned films in the United States, and another section on book burnings and the first date a book was actually torched. The print that was used in producing the index is extremely small.

7-28. Charny, Israel W., ed. *Encyclopedia of Genocide.* 2 vols. Santa Barbara, CA: ABC-CLIO, 1999. ISBN: 0-874-36928-2.

This work goes well beyond many readers' initial thoughts of the pogrom directed at the Jewish people and others at the hands of the German Nazis during the middle of the twentieth century. Truly global and historical perspectives are provided for all peoples of the earth, including Cambodians, Armenians, and Native Americans. The work serves as a poignant reminder that such a vile impulse as genocide repeats itself throughout history in many different parts of the world. The main part of the work is arranged around groups of entries under a broader topic related to some aspect of genocide. Part 1 is quite brief and gives definitions of genocide and its current study. Part 2, the main portion of the book, provides articles on genocide-related events, intervention, and its prevention. There are traditional entries, feature-length entries, and source documents. The pages contain maps, statistical tables, and more. There are listings of films of the Holocaust and ample information on German concentration camps and on individuals like Elie Wiesel and Simon Wiesenthal, who, after World War II, hunted down the Nazis who were responsible for some of the more egregious official acts of genocide. 🖳

7-29. Snyder, Louis L. *Encyclopedia of Nationalism.* New York: Paragon House, 1990. 445 pp. ISBN: 1-557-78167-2.

Nationalism has played a pivotal role in world history and politics over the past two centuries. Snyder here provides the reader with introductory information on many aspects of the subject. Entries are arranged alphabetically and include topics such as "Asian Nationalism" and "Autonomy" as well as biographical listings for individuals such as Kemal Ataturk. Entries are generally about a page or two in length and include bibliographic references. There are no illustrations; more seriously, there is no index. However, thanks to its broad coverage, this work will be of value to those high-school students and undergraduates needing introductory information on nationalism and its components, and the bibliographic listings (as well as a bibliography at the back of the volume) will lead researchers to other academic resources published before 1990. See Leoussi [entry 7-26] for a different approach to the study of nationalism.

7-30. Motyl, Alexander, ed. *Encyclopedia of Nationalism.* 2 vols. San Diego, CA: Academic, 2001. Index. ISBN: 0-122-27230-7.

In this multivolume set, Volume 1 contains full-length articles on the fundamental themes in the study of nationalism throughout history up to the modern era. Each of these substantive writings is classified into one of three broad areas. These three areas are disciplinary approaches, historical overviews, and thematic issues, with the latter category receiving the most treatment. These articles follow a standard format: title of article, author's name and affiliation, outline, glossary, defining statement, main body, cross-references, and further readings. The entries tend to be penned by U.S. academics and researchers, with perhaps 10 percent authored by international scholars. Articles are ten pages or longer and are written for undergraduates and the general reader with a serious interest in the study of nationalism. Volume 1 has its own index. Volume 2 lists leaders, movements, and concepts, and its entries are significantly shorter than those appearing in the first volume's pages. It contains entries on people such as Chief Joseph and Karel Dillen, national movements such as Iranian nationalism and Moroccan nationalism, and concepts such as patriotism and terrorism. There are fewer cross-references, no index, and the entries are unsigned. Volume 1 appears as though it may have received more editorial attention than did Volume 2. See Snyder [entry 7-29] and Leoussi [entry 7-26] for varying perspectives on the study of nationalism. 💻

7-31. Wuthnow, Robert, ed. *Encyclopedia of Politics and Religion.* 2 vols. Washington, DC: Congressional Quarterly, 1998. Index. ISBN: 1-568-02164-X.

An alphabetical array of 256 signed articles make up this encyclopedia on the interplay of politics and religion in the modern world. Articles range from 800 to 8,000 words in length and were written by a number of international scholars. The articles themselves strive to describe both the historical linkage between religion and politics and any set of global relationships that may exist over time. Most of the entries are drawn from the nineteenth and twentieth centuries.

Individual entries include countries or regions of the globe, major international religions, traditions, movements, events, and people. There are some maps, texts of selected documents, and pictures accompanying the articles. Some entries may be unexpected in a work with this title, such as "Feminism," "Human Rights," and "Voting." Several appendixes join with an excellent index at the rear of this encyclopedia.

7-32. Cole, Robert, ed. *The Encyclopedia of Propaganda.* 3 vols. Armonk, NY: M. E. Sharpe Reference, 1998. 961 pp. ISBN: 0-765-68009-2.

Not seen.

7-33. Minahan, James. *Encyclopedia of Stateless Nations: Ethnic and National Groups around the World.* 4 vols. Westport, CT: Greenwood Press, 2002. 2241 pp. Indexes. ISBN: 0-313-31617-1.

This work is an "expanded sequel" to J. Minahan's, *Nations without States* [entry 7-38]. The author of this guide believes that nationality and ethnic relations are major factors determining much of international and regional relations in contemporary world affairs. This work provides the reader with an "accurate and up-to-date" guide to the national groups operating as political actors in today's dynamic world (Minahan 2002, introduction). Over 300 national groups from the historical era to the millennium are covered here. This is a highly selective group since there may be approximately up to 9,000 such national groups overall that could have been included. Each national survey is divided into several parts or headings, beginning with its name or alternate names, population statistics, the homeland, the people and culture, the language and religion, brief historical sketches, and present status. Flags and maps are also printed up for the reader. Not surprisingly, this guide is devoted mainly to those nationalities that are at the forefront of the post–cold war nationalist resurgence. A short bibliography of works concludes each entry. There are several indexes for quick access to various aspects of information on nationalities. 💻

7-34. Burg, David F. *Encyclopedia of Student and Youth Movements.* New York: Facts on File, 1998. 254 pp. ISBN: 0-816-03375-7.

This work attempts to reveal to the nonspecialist who the various student and youth groups are and how widespread they appear to be around the world. Some countries, such as Germany and China, have an inordinate number of entries because of the relative large number of youth groups over time in those two countries. There is no claim to be exhaustive in treatment here, but entries do go back to the Middle Ages. The focus of the alphabetically sequenced entries is on events, organizations, and people. Specific listings are "Copenhagen University Protest," "National Student League (NSL)," and "Weatherman," among others. The exact dates and number of participants are frequently given. Much of the focus of this work is for people and groups from outside the United States. The style is lively and

should appeal to the general reader or lower-division undergraduate or high-school student. The individual entries tend to be relatively short.

7-35. Rudolph, Joseph R., ed. *Ethnic Conflicts.* Westport, CT: Greenwood Press, 2003. 375 pp. Index. ISBN: 0-313-31381-4.

Approximately fifty different ethnic conflicts drawn from around the world have been placed into alphabetical order by country or by geographic area. There has been no attempt to capture in print a comprehensive picture of the history of ethnic violence and conflict. The time frame is mainly for the twentieth-century period, with the latter half of that century receiving the heavier emphasis due to various factors unleashed during the breakup of the colonial era and the subsequent quest for independence and self-determination. In general, only the most important examples of ethnic violence in the 1900s were included as "case studies." Under countries with a history of ethnic violence, there are generally only one or two specific conflicts examined. Mexico, for instance, has one entry only, and that is on the Zapatista Rebellion centered in Chiapas. The Soviet Union has three (Chechnya, Georgia, and Nagorno-Karabakh). Each entry follows a common structure. The first part is the general timeline; the second part is the historical background; the third part discusses management of the conflict; the fourth part notes the conflict's significance; and the final part is a listing of readings, apparently all in English despite the mother tongue of the country. There are a few maps, black-and-white pictures, and an index. This work is best suited for high-school students and undergraduates.

7-36. Rose, Richard. *International Encyclopedia of Elections.* Washington, DC: CQ Press, 2000. 392 pp. Index. ISBN: 1-568-02415-0. http://www.ipu.org.

The entries emphasize contemporary events, but historical references to elections are certainly included. Elections of all kinds are examined, including free elections and ones that are not free, elections to unique offices, national parliaments, elections within various levels of federated systems, and generally nonpartisan local elections. Some of the articles discuss ways of making political or other choices without using voting methods, such as consumer behavior. The main entries tend to be fairly generic terms found all over the literature of campaigning, counting votes, and so forth. Each entry is signed and ends with a short reading list. Some entries are up to ten pages long and were written mainly by Commonwealth country and U.S. scholars. This is definitely not the place to hunt for election results, but should be quite valuable to those researchers requiring fairly scholarly information on all aspects of elections as political, social, or cultural phenomena. An index is included. 💻

7-37. McMenemy, John. *The Language of Canadian Politics: A Guide to Important Terms and Concepts.* 3rd ed. Waterloo,

ONT: Wilfred Laurier University Press, 2001. 314 pp. ISBN: 0-889-20372-5.

Canadian political terms are written up in brief essay formats. Over 500 such topics relevant to Canadian political life are included. Specifically, an entry typically covers that country's institutions, ideas, programs, laws, events, and more. Entries are drawn from both contemporary and historical Canadian political life. Typical specific items are "Proportional Representation," "Social Credit Party," "Continentalism," and "Charlottetown Accord (1992)." Entries average out at about one-eighth to one page in length. There is no index.

7-38. Minahan, James. *Nations without States: A Historical Dictionary of Contemporary National Movements.* Westport, CT: Greenwood Press, 1996. 692 pp. ISBN: 0-313-28354-0

This dictionary includes approximately 210 nations from around the world who share a common theme, and that is a deep pride in their unique culture and belief systems. These nations also are or have been under the dominion of another state or political entity. The vast majority of these nations yearn for some semblance of political independence. The entries appearing in the main body of the dictionary are in standard alphabetical order. Each entry includes the nation's leaders, language, geography, demographics, a description of the flag, and a short history of the group and its interactions with other ethnic groups and cultures. There is no attempt to claim comprehensiveness for this work.

The book concentrates fairly exclusively on a time frame related directly to the post–cold war nationalist resurgence in many parts of the world. There is a selective bibliography at the end of each of the three-page entries. The population dispersions are especially noteworthy. See Minahan's *Encyclopedia of Stateless Nations* [entry 7-33].

7-39. Segal, Gerald. *Political and Economic Encyclopaedia of the Pacific.* Chicago: St. James Press, 1989. 293 pp. Index. ISBN: 0-582-05161-4.

This information source purports to offer a "genuinely Pacific" perspective of the politics, economics, and security it covers. Two broad types of entries are for national and international terms. The entries for individual countries constitute the largest part of the book, and these write-ups are subdivided in a uniform manner. The international relations entries cover bilateral and multilateral issues for security, economic, ideological affairs, and natural resources discussions. Most main entries pertain to the 1945-to-date time period. All entries are signed and can vary in length from a couple of sentences up to ten-page articles. This particular work is aimed at general readers and undergraduate students who need abbreviated yet factual information on political personalities, political parties, and the like. An index is attached.

7-40. Kurian, Thomas George, ed. *World Encyclopedia of Parliaments and Legislatures.* 2 vols. Washington, DC: Congressional Quarterly, 1998. 878 pp. ISBN: 0-871-87987-5.

This two-volume encyclopedic set was written to offer the reader a record of the state of parliamentary-style democracy around the globe for over 190 countries. The parliamentary systems studied in this work fall into one of two categories, "evolved" or "imposed." Entries are arranged strictly alphabetically and follow a rather standard format, including a parliament's historical background, constitutional provisions on parliament, elections, sessions, annual calendar, how laws are made and enacted, committee structure, political parties, relations with the executive, and more. In the latter portion of Volume 2, there is a collection of fourteen topical essays related to parliamentary systems, including legislative voting behavior, parliaments of new democracies, and others. These essays are signed and are excellent introductions to the subject of this encyclopedia. Essays average five to ten pages in length. The main body of this work is a narrative, not simply short, directory-like entries. This is a very apt choice for comparative parliament-system analyses across historical and more current perspectives. See also *Parliaments of the World* [entry 7-69] in this chapter's Guides and Handbooks section.

7-41. Kaple, Deborah A., ed. *World Encyclopedia of Political Systems and Parties.* 3rd ed. 2 vols. New York: Facts on File, 1999. 1269 pp. ISBN: 0-816-02874-5.

One volume lists medium and major countries in one alphabetical sequence, while the second volume contains entries in the same arrangement on smaller countries and the microstates and is very similar to Derbyshire's *Encyclopedia of World Political Systems* [entry 7-54], published thirteen years later. The content matter under each country is a signed article written by a U.S. or European scholar or specialist. Each entry describes the branches of government, regional and local government, the electoral system, and the existing political party system and provides a party-by-party examination of each political party currently operating in that nation. There is a short reading list, several charts, and a few tables of data. Chapters on the smaller countries are decidedly more concise.

Guides and Handbooks

7-42. Eagles, D. Munroe. *The Almanac of Canadian Politics.* 2nd ed. New York: Oxford University Press, 1995. 765 pp. ISBN: 0-195-41140-4.

Anyone interested in a more serious approach to the analysis of Canadian voting behavior will find this information on the 295 individual constituencies in Canada that vote a good fit. The core of this reference book is the examination of all these constituencies beginning with an analytical overview of the topic. A number of "Highest/Lowest" tables have been compiled for this task. Profiles of all the voting constituencies have been arranged in standardized format, allowing comparative analysis. Some of these statistics could have appeal to students of Canadian marketing assignments as well. This work is not for those who need quick access to Canadian voting results at any level.

7-43. Nash, Kate, ed. *The Blackwell Companion to Political Sociology.* Malden, MA: Blackwell, 2001. 478 pp. Index. ISBN: 0-631-21050-4.

This string of essays features articles on those emerging topics in sociology that take into account some of the traditional domain of political science as a discipline, including the nation-state, legitimacy, citizenship, and other issues. Sociology here injects research regarding popular culture and social policy issues. The main body contains four parts, each of which is subdivided into between eight and thirteen parts. These four parts are "Approach to Power and the Political," "The State and Governance," "The Political and the Social," and "Political Transformation." Changing boundaries of research and study are the fundamental principles underlying these articles put together by an international group of academics. The articles are better described as bibliographic essays and literature reviews, and all begin with a concise summary paragraph. This work is aimed at scholars, researchers, graduate students, and upper-division undergraduates. A bibliography of more than fifty pages and including books and journal articles is available for the reader. An index is included. See also *The Blackwell Dictionary of Social Policy* [entry 7-44].

7-44. Alcock, Peter, ed. *The Blackwell Dictionary of Social Policy.* Malden, MA: Blackwell, 2002. 290 pp. Index. ISBN: 0-631-21847-5.

This is a dictionary of British social policy by English academics who are members of the Social Policy Association (SPA). It was commissioned mainly to accompany the *Students Companion to Social Policy.* Done in collaboration with the SPA, the aim of this publication is to provide a clear and accessible guide to the major terms and ideas students and others are likely to encounter in studying various aspects of social policy. The audience here is British. This is definitely not to be regarded as an international social policy text. This work also does not attempt to provide any element of coverage from the other major English-speaking countries of the globe. It does, however, serve as a guide to the major terms and concepts based on the events of supranational and international agencies that have a definite impact on policy development and practice within the United Kingdom. The book is in alphabetical order with entries averaging about one or two sentences up to one-half page. Entries are adequately cross-referenced and signed. Several typical entries are "Adoption Policies," "Disability," "Family Planning," and "Pensions." There are also some biographical entries. There is an index.

7-45. Feigert, Frank B. *Canada Votes, 1935–1988.* Durham, NC: Duke University Press, 1989. 351 pp. ISBN: 0-822-30894-0.

This book serves as an update to Howard A. Scarrow's *Canada Votes: A Handbook of Federal and Provincial Election Data* (not listed), which covers the period from 1878 through 1960. The main body of the book is arranged from national- to regional- and then to provincial-level election results. Provincial election statistics are allotted by far the most space, perhaps up to 70 percent of the pages. This book is composed primarily of Canadian election results over time. This information can often be somewhat difficult to locate quickly but is arranged nicely here. Voting results from the Northwest Territories and the Yukon are also given. This is an exceptionally well-written and edited work, and quite informative. Narrative, however, is sparse here and does no more than give basic information and context. There is a good basic bibliography of journal articles on Canadian politics and government culled from Canadian and U.S. journals, as well as a few monographs, mostly published in Canada.

7-46. Bejermi, John, comp. *Canadian Parliamentary Handbook* [*Repertoire Parlementaire Canadien*]. Annual. Ottawa: Borealis Press, 1982–. ISSN: 0714-8143.

This handbook provides historical background on various Canadian political institutions, such as the elected House of Commons and the appointed Senate and the members of these institutions. All current (as of publication) members' biographies include photographs, constituencies, mailing addresses, and other standard biographical data. Not surprisingly, this book will be most useful for Canadian libraries, U.S. libraries near the Canadian border, and business and academic programs where Canada is a major focal point. There is very little information regarding Canadian federal regulatory agencies or central administration. The legislative branch of government receives most of the attention here.

7-47. Blaustein, Albert P., ed. *Constitutions of Dependencies and Special Sovereignties.* 11 vols. (loose-leaf service). Dobbs Ferry, NY: Oceana Publications, 1977–. ISBN: 0-080-19848-1.

This is a large, multivolume set maintained in loose-leaf binders that includes virtually every dependency, territory, province, autonomous region, state, and the like that possesses its own constitution. Most of the entries are from European dependencies. The entire text of the dependency's constitution is written out in its original language. Arrangement of this large set is simply alphabetical by political unit dependency.

7-48. Blaustein, Albert P., and G. H. Flanz. *Constitutions of the Countries of the World: A Series of Updated Texts, Constitutional Chronologies and Annotated Bibliographies.* 20 vols. (loose-leaf service). Dobbs Ferry, NY: Oceana Publications, 1971–.

This is a loose-leaf binder set with an alphabetical listing of countries from Afghanistan to Zimbabwe and the full text of their respective constitutions. Many, but not all, of the constitutions have been translated into English. A number of the constitutional texts are in their original language with a translation into French or some other language. Constitutional chronologies for each nation are given. Some of the nations listed here have short bibliographies of reading materials appended to them. Many of the constitutions from the former Soviet republics are included. This work is continuously updated on a more or less regular basis. This is a monumental work in this field.

7-49. Maddex, Robert L. *Constitutions of the World.* 2nd ed. Washington, DC: CQ Press, 2001. 417 pp. ISBN: 1-568-02682-X.

This reference book includes a summarization of eighty world constitutions including their constitutional histories. The countries selected for inclusion tend to be the larger nation-states or important political actors. Arrangement is alphabetical by country, and entries are all printed in a standard format. The entries begin with some brief information about the general economy, then provide a historical overview, a survey on the country's historical and legal development, and background information on the indigenous population and early political and social organizations. All this is followed by the country's most current constitution or a draft version for those undergoing substantive change in the document. None of the constitutions included here are reprinted in their entirety. Entries are limited to approximately eight pages, with each individual nation's constitution broken down into a functional format including: fundamental rights, structure of government, branches of government, and the amending process. See also Blaustein and Flanz's *Constitutions of the Countries of the World* [entry 7-48].

7-50. Morby, John E. *Dynasties of the World: A Chronological and Genealogical Handbook.* rev. ed. Oxford: Oxford University Press, 2002. 254 pp. Index. ISBN: 0-198-60473-4.

This handbook gives the years of rule and family relationships for the major dynasties around the world. The treatment offered to European royalty is especially comprehensive. Some dynasties, such as the Medes and Hindu royal lines, have been omitted because of insufficient information. Names are either close to their original or in a standardized English-language equivalent. The main body has about ten geographic sections, subdivided by kingdom or political unit. All rulers have their dates and the full name of the dynasty included. Any calendar discrepancy is brought out in the notes section. Bibliographies are attached to most entries for additional reading if desired. An index is included.

7-51. Gorvin, Ian, ed. *Elections since 1945: A Worldwide Reference Compendium.* Chicago: St. James Press, 1989. 420 pp. ISBN: 1-558-62017-6.

Election results from all national presidential and legislative elections in sovereign states since the year 1945 are included in this work. The election results

in the world's colonies are listed only after the individual colony reached independent status. The editor advises users of this reference work that there was heavy reliance placed on *Keesing's Record of World Events* [2-141], a British source of record. Information for each country includes a discussion of the electoral system, evolution of the right to vote, and main political parties. There are numerous tables and graphs displaying each election's results and the relative political party strengths. Election results in the United States are included as well as a special section on the European Parliament. See also the *International Encyclopedia of Elections* [entry 7-36] and an Internet resource [7-52].

7-52. Electionworld.Org/Elections around the World. http://www.election world.org.

This Web site is the standard by which all other election/voting sites should be measured. It is international in scope and sufficiently detailed for virtually every national-level election being held around the world since 1996. The navigator may search by electoral calendar year or for political party by country from Afghanistan to Zimbabwe. Links have been established to databases, calendars, government leaders, international news agencies, and much more. 🖳

7-53. Mattar, Phillip, ed. *The Encyclopedia of the Palestinians.* New York: Facts on File, 2000. 514 pp. ISBN: 0-816-03043-X.

A total of forty-eight American, Palestinian, and Israeli scholars contributed to this one-volume compendium of knowledge about contemporary Palestinian history and society. The work is conceptualized into three historical periods: 1831 to 1917, 1917 to 1948, and 1948 and after, with the birth of the State of Israel. One-third of all entries listed are for individuals. Articles are all signed, with most being less than one-half page long. A few wide-ranging entries, such as "Arab-Israeli Conflict," are considerably longer, about ten pages, and attempt to emphasize the political activities, world players, and individual stakeholders for that issue. Several other more lengthy articles include those on "Arab-Israeli War of 1948," "Yasir Arafat," "Palestine Liberation Organization," "Zionism," and others that may have been in the news recently. There is an annotated bibliography of books that focuses on the political issues, groups, problems, and parties, as well as significant politicians participating within this crucible of conflicting visions of this region's future status.

7-54. Derbyshire, J. Denis. *Encyclopedia of World Political Systems.* 2 vols. Armonk, NY: M. E. Sharpe Reference, 2000. 930 pp. ISBN: 0-765-68025-4.

This encyclopedic handbook examines the globe's 192 existing nation-states and how their respective political systems arose out of their unique social and ethnic backgrounds that helped create them. The nation-states are divided into those where the citizens control the government and levers of power in multiparty or pluralistic societies, and those that have one-party or monistic systems. While historical information is given, the historical frame of reference is contemporary. The nation-states are arranged in regional chapters. Entries all receive a standard format for arrangement and give basic data, a map of the country and surrounding region, ethnic composition, religions, political features, local and regional government, political system, political parties, latest election results, and political history. There is a brief regional analysis at the beginning of each chapter. This work is especially detailed for political history and political party information. See *Political Systems of the World* [entry 7-82] for a different perspective.

7-55. O'Mara, Michael, ed. *Facts about the World's Nations.* New York: H. W. Wilson, 1999. 1065 pp. ISBN: 0-824-20955-9.

This handbook is an alphabetical arrangement of countries and their dependencies covering the countries' respective geography, history, constitution and government, international relations, economics, education, and welfare. Entries are structured using the same categories for each. The use of statistics is highly selective and includes those for individual sectors, armed forces, national finance, larger population centers, and others. The section on a country's "History" tends to be the longest section of most entries. There are some potential ready-reference-related questions that could be answered by printing the length of railroads and roads in kilometers; the number of telephones, radios, and television sets; literacy rates; amount of land under cultivation; and the like. No index is available, but this is still one of the better all-purpose, one-volume works on the countries of the world.

7-56. Cook, Chris. *The Facts on File World Political Almanac: From 1945 to the Present.* 4th ed. Revised by Whitney Walker. New York: Facts on File, 2001. 600 pp. ISBN: 0-816-04295-0.

Not seen.

7-57. Elazar, Daniel Judah, ed. *Federal Systems of the World: A Handbook of Federal, Confederal, and Autonomy Arrangements.* 2nd rev. and exp. ed. New York: Stockton Press, 1994. 364 pp. ISBN: 1-561-59086-X.

This handbook is designed to provide a comparative survey of contemporary forms of federalism that have taken root around the globe in countries that maintain self-rule and political autonomy. Data for this effort has been compiled by the Jerusalem Center for Public Affairs. Each entry scrutinizes the type of federalism that evolved within each country. Each entry, arranged alphabetically by country, follows a standardized format with these subdivisions: "Introduction," "Territorial Structures and Population," "General Government Structure," "Constitutional Principles and Design," "Political Culture," and "Political Dynamics/Recent Constitutional Dynamics," and concludes with some references. Most country entries have black-and-white maps and selectively chosen demographic data. There are various appendixes assisting in any comparative

examination of the concept of federalism and its characteristics by individual nations. See *Handbook of Federal Countries, 2002* [entry 7-58] by Ann L. Griffiths for a different perspective.

7-58. Griffiths, Ann L., ed. *Handbook of Federal Countries, 2002.* Montreal: McGill-Queens University Press, 2002. 513 pp. ISBN: 0-773-52419-3.

The idea behind this handbook is to share information to aid in the spread and ultimate strengthening of democracy around the entire world. It is published for the Forum of Federation, an international nonprofit clearinghouse for all types of information and resources on the concept of federalism. The main body of the work consists of articles on twenty-five countries either claiming to be federations or demonstrating enough elements of federalism to include them in this examination. Each article has four parts: "History and Development of Federalism," "Constitutional Provisions," "Recent Political Dynamics," and finally, "Sources for Further Information." There are also a couple of statistical tables highlighting political and geographic indicators, and others on economic and social indicators. Also, there are four essays printed on various components in the study of federalism. There is neither an index nor an appendix of any sort.

7-59. Da Graca, John V. *Heads of State and Government.* New York: New York University Press, 1985. 265 pp. ISBN: 0-814-71778-0.

The heads of state and leaders of the government for contemporary nation-states, regional and territorial governments, and self-governing colonies make up the 500 entries in this alphabetically ordered work. A few states that have recently disappeared from existence are also included. A selectively picked number of international organizations also appear within. Main entries are all subdivided into a number of regional and political categories. As an example, Germany has all its emperors, presidents, and chancellors listed first, followed by similar information on the contemporaneous or defunct German states such as Baden, Bavaria, and Hesse. The 1985 publication date means that many current heads of governments or states will not be listed. This work does, however, go well beyond the scope of Europe and the United States in coverage. (Note: The newer 2000 [second] edition was not seen, but has bulked up to 1,222 pages.)

7-60. Lentz, Harris M. *Heads of State and Governments: A Worldwide Encyclopedia of over 2,300 Leaders, 1945–1992.* Jefferson, NC: McFarland, 1994. 912 pp. ISBN: 0-899-50926-6.

This work looks at all countries with "independent" governments. A country's acceptance into the United Nations or other international agencies, along with full diplomatic relations granted by most nations, constitutes the major grounds for inclusion. The arrangement of this work is alphabetical by common English name for a particular country. Each entry has a comparable format that starts off with a very brief geographical and historical statement that is followed by biographical information on the heads of state or government. More than just a biographical listing along the lines of Da Graca's work [entry 7-59], this book aims to serve a more encyclopedic function, offering information beyond the listing of heads of government and state by providing dates and historical or political facts. The work takes into account the breakup of the Soviet Union.

7-61. Lewis, James R., ed. *The Human Rights Encyclopedia.* 3 vols. Armonk, NY: M. E. Sharpe Reference, 2001. Indexes. ISBN: 0-765-68023-8.

The study of human rights has moved steadily from a relatively theoretical study of itself to a more thorough examination of real life issues affecting largely but not exclusively the women, children, and disabled of the earth's population. This encyclopedia reflects this shift in study. The overriding purpose of this multivolume set is to bring knowledge of human rights–related concerns to a wider audience and to serve as a basic resource for students, educators, and the general public. The main body of the encyclopedia is divided into two halves, the first half examining countries, and the second, issues and individual people. Each country is briefly outlined for its history, society, and political makeup, and this serves as the context for the second part of the entry, which presents an introductory picture of human rights in that specific country.

Entries are generally on the short side and appear to be aimed at high-school and lower-division undergraduates. The remaining space devoted to topical articles is longer and offers a more substantive result than the first part. Appearing in this latter section are articles on reproductive rights, law and justice, and torture. Some may find several of the accompanying black-and-white photographs a tad too graphic for their tastes. There are several appendixes. There is a general index and a name index. See Chapter 6 on International Relations for the international perspective on human rights, and see Maddex's *International Encyclopedia of Human Rights* [entry 7-65] and Donnelly's *International Handbook of Human Rights* [entry 7-66].

7-62. *Human Rights Internet Reporter/ HRI.* Ottawa, ONT: Human Rights Internet Quarterly, 1976–. ISSN: 0275-049X. http://www.hri.ca.

This work was founded in 1976 and caters to the needs of the human rights community. Topics vary considerably from issue to issue. One will be a directory of African human rights organizations, while another will be a special issue on human rights education. The issue on education is a review of Web sites, programs, and materials on all aspects of human rights education programs. URLs and/or e-mail addresses are given when known. Listings for directory-type information are worldwide in scope. The information is in a print version as well as online. ⌨

7-63. Maddex, Robert L. *Illustrated Dictionary of Constitutional Concepts.* Washington, DC: Congressional Quarterly, 1996. 335 pp. ISBN: 1-568-02170-4.

This work was written at a time when the renewal of constitutional study was rising, partly as a result of the fall of the Communist regimes of Eastern Europe and the USSR. The entries tend to stress the uniqueness of each nation's path to developing a valid constitutional framework for its government and people. This work is aimed squarely at the more general reader and lower-division undergraduate student. It is heavily illustrated, and its entries are alphabetically ordered. The many terms used and defined in this work are often placed in their geographic or national setting. ⌨

7-64. Mackie, Thomas T. *The International Almanac of Electoral History.* 3rd ed. Washington, DC: Congressional Quarterly, 1991. 511 pp. ISBN: 0-871-87575-6.

This compendium to election results from twenty-five Western nations plus Japan was devised to distribute a complete and exact rendering of election returns since the beginning of competitive voting. More than 600 elections are covered for all national elections excluding only national referenda and European Community voting tabulations. Each country serves as a main entry, using a format that is applied universally throughout the main body of this work. This information begins with the evolution of the election system in that particular country and then provides a historical slate of political parties and the actual election results using four tables. Of the four tables, two give the percentage of seats each party won in the national election and two give the percentage voting returns by political party. These entries average about a dozen pages each. This work has potential use for comparative election analysis and the charting of political trends.

7-65. Maddex, Robert L. *International Encyclopedia of Human Rights: Freedoms, Abuses, and Remedies.* Washington, DC: CQ Press, 2000. 404 pp. Index. ISBN: 1-568-02490-8.

The editor of this encyclopedia envisions it as a first step in the identification, organization, and definition of the varied concepts, terminology, documents, institutions, and individuals who have all played a major role in some aspect of human rights issues at either a national, regional, or international level. Over 150 concepts and human rights–related terms form the basis of substantive main entries. These terms are considered basic to all human beings or those accepted only by certain peoples of the world. Many of the latter are derived from the decisions of regional and/or international bodies. Each entry discusses the term, its history, and its more contemporary human rights context. Some of the excerpts from important documents are those from constitutions, international human rights agreements, court decisions, commissions, and the like. There are about 100 sections of sig-

nificant international human rights documents printed here that include text from treaties, declarations, and statements of principle. A few select national human rights documents, such as the Magna Carta (1215), are also included. There is a list of agencies, organizations, and biographies (about fifty) that provide directory-type information complete with e-mail and Web site addresses. There is an index.

7-66. Donnelly, Jack, ed. *International Handbook of Human Rights.* New York: Greenwood Press, 1987. 495 pp. ISBN: 0-313-24788-9.

This handbook is a survey of nineteen countries where human rights abuses are documented to have occurred on an ongoing basis to a country's own citizen body. The overriding assumption of this work is that human rights are universal and a basic right of every individual as outlined in *The Universal Declaration of Human Rights.* The book consists of fifteen- to twenty-page articles that look at the cultural, historical, political, and economic backgrounds for each of the nineteen examined countries. It then goes on to measure the results of these backgrounds on each country's human rights record. There is a modest list of publications intended to serve as suggested reading at the end of each chapter. The contributors to this work are very well qualified and are usually social scientists residing in North and South American institutions of higher learning or research centers.

7-67. Norton, Alan. *International Handbook of Local and Regional Government: A Comparative Analysis of Advanced Democracies.* Brookfield, VT: Edward Elgar/Ashgate Publishing, 1994. 559 pp. ISBN: 1-852-78005-3.

The source material for this handbook is taken from two comparative studies authorized by the Institute of Local Government Studies at the University of Birmingham in the United Kingdom. The purpose of this work is to present, in largely comparative format, information about local and regional governments existing in the world's developed countries to be used by policy makers within Great Britain. Part 1 is a general survey of local and regional governmental bodies in mostly the Organisation for Economic Co-operation and Development (OECD) countries. Part 2 is the main chapter of this handbook and consists of a nation-by-nation recounting of local government and its administration in a standard arrangement that promotes comparisons of many sorts by breaking down chapters into various subcomponents of history, organization, finance, citizen participation, and others. There is a lengthy bibliography appearing at the back of the work for books and journal articles in many different languages. Japan is the only country included from outside of Europe or North America.

7-68. Sullivan, Michael J. *Measuring Global Values: The Ranking of 162 Countries.* Westport, CT: Greenwood Press, 1991. 423 pp. ISBN: 0-313-27649-8.

The results given in this work are based on research carried on at Drexel University's World Policy Institute and the Pew Foundation Glenmede Trust Program for the Implementation of Microcomputer Technology in College Curricula. The study makes use of a certain database-management software program used to compare 162 countries using over 100 various global indicators, such as peace, economics, ecological balance, social justice, political participation, and many others. The goal of the work is to develop a set of political and social indicators by plugging in a number of values. These would be used to develop a set of measures to compare and analyze national policy among the world's nation-states. The results are seen in the numerous tables of calculations providing comparative data for analysis. There is also insightful textual commentary that puts everything into perspective when analyzing for comparisons.

7-69. International Centre for Parliamentary Documentation of the Inter-Parliamentary Union. *Parliaments of the World: A Comparative Reference Compendium.* 2nd ed. 2 vols. New York: Facts on File, 1986. 1422 pp. ISBN: 0-816-01186-9.

This is one of the more comprehensive reference handbooks on all aspects of the modern world's parliaments. Text is accompanied by numerous statistical tables that together provide information on terms of office, electoral systems, member totals, immunity and privileges, salaries, perks, subsidized benefits, rules of procedures, session facts, voting majority requirements, constitutional amendments, publications of parliamentary debates, legislation, roles of committees, the budget process, and much more. Parts of this work will probably be somewhat out of date, but it still gives an excellent historical perspective of parliamentary operations in the mid-1980s.

7-70. Woldendorp, Jaap. *Party Government in Forty-Eight Democracies (1945–1998): Composition, Duration, Personnel.* Boston: Kluwer Academic Publishers, 2000. 580 pp. ISBN: 0-792-36727-8.

Data handbooks can serve as excellent vehicles for carrying out different methods of comparative research techniques emphasizing qualitative analysis. This handbook is no exception and includes data for forty-six parliamentary and two presidential democracies, all arranged in alphabetical order. Its purpose is to provide compact and wide-ranging data collection of a complete and comparative nature on the basis of these chosen democratic governments in terms of their respective political parties, ministers, parliamentary support, and duration periods and reasons for termination. This work was designed as a way to facilitate the research being conducted in political institutions, especially the "new" institutionalism that is committed to the systematic empirical testing of such data-driven assumptions. Information pertaining to the executive branch of government is especially important to this work, especially as it ties to the active political parties. This is a unique research tool for upper-division students and researchers.

7-71. Katz, Richard S., ed. *Party Organizations: A Data Handbook on Party Organizations in Western Democracies, 1960–1990.* London: Sage, 1992. 973 pp. ISBN: 0-803-98783-8.

This handbook presents cross-national comparable data tables for Western democracies over a thirty-year period. The internal organizational structure of nearly eighty political parties in twelve countries is examined for a wide range of data, traits, and operational characteristics. The twelve countries are Austria, Belgium, Denmark, Finland, Germany, Ireland, Italy, the Netherlands, Norway, Sweden, the United Kingdom, and the United States. Each nation's data tables and information on their respective political parties are displayed in a highly organized manner. Each country entry includes a short introduction on that country's political parties and the government system within which they operate. Also discussed are the electoral systems, election results, party membership, allied organizational units, organization charts, and much more.

7-72. Tardif, Richard. *The Penguin MacQuarie Dictionary of Australian Politics.* New York: Viking Penguin Books, 1988. 376 pp. ISBN: 0-949-75744-6.

Here is a concise handbook to Australian politics, government apparatuses, political parties, institutions, pressure groups, the electoral system, and the country's politicians. It includes colloquial terms, and its emphasis is clearly twentieth-century politics, government, and events. This strictly alphabetical work is aimed at general readers and undergraduate students. Many entries have "see also" references. There are several short appendixes on "Prime and Federal Ministers," "Federal Opposition Leaders," and "Federal Election Results." A short section on additional readings, mostly Australian sources, rounds out the resources of this book.

7-73. *Political Atlas and Handbook of the World.* Annual. Published for the Center for Comparative Political Research of the State University of New York at Binghamton and for the Council on Foreign Relations. New York: McGraw-Hill, 1975–. Index. ISSN: 0193-175X.

This is a longtime denizen of many ready-reference shelves in academic libraries and larger public libraries, and it has gone through several minor title changes. The work is in two parts, by country and by intergovernmental organization. The country entries offer brief factual information about official language, monetary units, political status, population information, and the like as a start. More narrative information follows in standardized sections of current overview, government and constitution, foreign relations, current issues, political parties and their orientation, the legislature, the news media, and a few country-specific categories. The section on organizations gives membership information, purpose, history, bureaucratic structure, and primary activities. These organizations tend to be the larger, better known, and more influential ones. An index is attached. (Note: The volume for 2000/2002 was the latest seen.)

7-74. *A Political Chronology of Central, South and East Asia.* London: Europa, 2001. 309 pp. ISBN: 1-857-43114-6.

See entry 7-77.

7-75. *A Political Chronology of Europe.* London: Europa, 2001. 364 pp. ISBN: 1-857-43113-8.

See entry 7-77.

7-76. *A Political Chronology of South-East Asia and Oceania.* London: Europa, 2001. 233 pp. ISBN: 1-857-43117-0.

See entry 7-77.

7-77. *A Political Chronology of the Middle East.* London: Europa, 2001. 282 pp. ISBN: 1-857-43115-4.

All of these works make up the publisher's Political Chronology series. They follow a similar format and provide details for both current and historical events. The coverage definitely emphasizes the last fifty years. The events listed are political, economic, cultural, and social highlights. The main body is arranged around the countries listed for the region, including any autonomous areas. The only one in this series examined in great detail was *A Political Chronology of the Middle East.* This one includes Turkey, Israel, and Azerbaijan. There are no bibliographies and there are no indexes included.

7-78. Ameringer, Charles D., ed. *Political Parties of the Americas, 1980s to 1990s: Canada, Latin America, and the West Indies.* Westport, CT: Greenwood Press, 1992. 697 pp. ISBN: 0-313-27418-5.

This book is intended both to serve alone as an individual publication and to complement Robert J. Alexander's *Political Parties of the Americas: Canada, Latin America, and the West Indies,* published in 1982 (see F. Holler, 4th edition, entry 2107). The 1992 work incorporates new developments in the various political parties operating in the Americas since 1980. It also presents updated background data. The arrangement of this work is alphabetical by country. Each chapter follows a similar outline. There is a general introduction on political developments of the 1980s and early 1990s, a revised bibliography, a list of active political parties along with a description of each emphasizing any recent changes, and a list of political parties for historical purposes that have ceased to exist prior to 1980. One-party states, like Cuba, are included in the fifty main entries.

7-79. Day, Alan J., ed. *Political Parties of the World.* 5th ed. London: John Harper, 2002. 604 pp. Indexes. ISBN: 0-953-62787-X.

The editor notes the increasing importance of racial and/or religious affiliation as a determinant of political party membership in the contemporary world. There is also a very strong antiglobal current flowing in some countries. The number of political parties considered has increased for this fifth edition to 2,550, 400 of which have been created since the previous edition published in 1996. Defunct parties have been removed from the pages of this edition. A large amount of the information provided in this guide has been obtained directly from the political parties themselves. The work is laid out in a standard alphabetical order by country. Entries are preformatted, beginning with an overview of the form of government and the role of the political parties, followed by a listing of all the political parties, giving name, address, telephone number, fax number, e-mail address, Web site, and leadership. A narrative on the history of the party, its alliances, former candidates for office, dates, and the like ensues. Any country that has a political party operating, even if just a ruling party, is included. Countries with no political parties at time of publication, such as Saudi Arabia, have a one-paragraph statement noting that this country is a kingdom with no parties. There are several useful appendixes. There are two indexes, one for personal names and another for political party names. See also *World Encyclopedia of Political Systems and Parties* [entry 7-41].

7-80. Danopoulus, Constantine, ed. *The Political Role of the Military: An International Handbook.* Westport, CT: Greenwood Press, 1996. 517 pp. Index. ISBN: 0-313-28837-2.

This relatively unique reference handbook examines the world's military from

1989 to the mid-1990s, the first half decade after the fall of Communism in Europe. The work is predicated upon the sound assumption that changes in a nation's military can have a large impact on society, or vice versa. Its purpose is to analyze the very role played by the military in their respective societies and the historical forces that have helped determine those roles and to understand the socioeconomic constraints in which they have been operating over time. Only the larger countries are included here to represent the various different regions of the world in Africa, Europe, Asia, the Middle East, and Latin America. There are a total of twenty-five distinct studies formatted in a manner to facilitate several levels of comparative analyses. Entries are arranged by country and are all signed. Both bibliographies and an index are available. 💻

7-81. Allen, Louis. *Political Scandals and Causes Celebres since 1945: An International Reference Compendium.* Chicago: St. James Press, 1991. 478 pp. ISBN: 1-558-62009-5.

The scandals and other incidents contained in this handbook must pass two fundamental criteria. First, the affair in question must be truly "political" in nature, or be so by close implication. This opens the door to a number of politicians and those involved in espionage. The second criterion is that the affair must be generally regarded as a "self-contained" episode. This eliminates a number of standard graft and corruption cases. The work as a whole is concerned primarily with the politics of the world's major democracies. Therefore, an inordinate number of entries pertain to France, the United States, and the United Kingdom. Individual entries are arranged by date of occurrence under the country in which they transpired. Most entries happened over the last fifty years and are a couple of pages per incident. Several typical entries are "Watergate Affair (1972–1974)," "Raoul Wallenberg Affair (1945–1990)," and the "Dikko Affair (1983–1984)." The entries are nonscholarly, almost chatty at times.

7-82. Derbyshire, J. Denis. *Political Systems of the World.* 2nd ed. New York: St. Martin's Press, 1996. 684 pp. ISBN: 0-312-16172-2.

This guide attempts to offer an analysis of the political institutions existing in the world today and to identify those events that have made an impact on the political landscape. The fairly unique goal here is to link an individual nation's overall political system with its historical, social, and economic backgrounds. It includes virtually every state on the surface of the globe, even tiny ones like Monaco and the Saint-Pierre and Miquelon islands. Examination of the dynamics of the political systems includes each country's political parties and state institutions. The main portion of the book is arranged in broad regional groupings of countries. Also, entries do touch upon how sovereign states interact with one another. The book's game plan is to be apportioned into two parts. The first part looks at sundry constitutional forms that can be adapted for political units and then it turns its attention to their respective philosophers or ideologies. It then goes on to compare executives, heads of state, and heads of government, along with voting methods and political parties. The second part depicts these political units in action with a country-by-country analysis. There are over seventy-five tables of statistical data and a map for each entry. See also *Encyclopedia of World Political Systems* [entry 7-54] for a different view of this topic, also by Derbyshire. (Note: A third edition, published in two volumes in 1999, was not seen.)

7-83. Arnold, Guy. *The Third World Handbook*. 2nd ed. London: Cassell, 1994. 213 pp. ISBN: 0-304-32837-5.

This handbook of the developing nations of the world attempts to keep current by redefining the parameters of what it means to be third world. It examines which countries belong to this grouping and the problems common to the third world nations for the mid-1980s to mid-1990s. This handbook addresses three broad concerns. They are the emergence of third world nations, membership and regional collaborations, and the problems faced by individual member states. This second edition includes the successor states to the former Soviet Union, such as Kazakhstan and Georgia. A chronology of decolonization and political hegemony over third world areas is included. There follows a short essay on the role of the United Nations and the third world proclivity toward nonalign-

ment. Various intergovernmental organizations are traced, such as the Organization of African Unity, and the regional politics of the comparable area are analyzed. A highly select sampling of articles and statistics pertaining to the Organization of Petroleum Exporting Countries (OPEC) follow. This is followed by a short section on biographical notes of major third world leaders since 1945.

7-84. Niemi, Richard G. *Trends in Public Opinion: A Compendium of Survey Data*. New York: Greenwood Press, 1989. 325 pp. Index. ISBN: 0-313-25426-5.

The ultimate purpose of this handbook is to provide access to a large and relevant list of questions that have been repeated in exactly the same or a very similar manner over a given period of time. The survey is centered on the General Social Survey (GSS), an ongoing set of surveys done at the time by the National Opinion Research Center (NORC) located at the University of Chicago. It was designed specifically to spot trends in public opinion results. Additional sources of survey data examined for this work were the *American Public Opinion Index* [entry 5-150], *The Gallup Poll* [entry 5-151], and other standard instruments. There are fifteen categories of survey questions, all with several subdivisions each. Some of the major categories are "Confidence in Institutions," "Politics," "International Affairs," and "Race Relations." Results are given in tabular format. There is an index.

7-85. Endres, Kathleen L., ed. *Women's Periodicals in the United States: Social* *and Political Issues.* Westport, CT: Greenwood Press, 1996. 529 pp. ISBN: 0-313-28632-9.

This work was designed to serve as guide to the field of magazines published by women of all social and political views. The reader will find the reactionary and radical leftist entries side by side. The approach used for inclusion is admittedly eclectic, with only seventy-six magazine titles actually chosen for inclusion. These tended to be the leading titles of their genre. The main body is arranged alphabetically by title of the magazine. Each entry is constructed in a largely similar pattern. The entry begins with a short history of the publication followed by an examination of how, why, and by whom it was launched. It then examines where the initial funding was obtained and the magazine's philosophy and mission. It also recounts some of the better known stories or authors appearing in the publication. A short bibliography appears at the end of each entry. Articles are all signed and are written mainly by faculty members in journalism or communication departments. There is a lengthy bibliography at the back of the book.

7-86. *The World: A Third World Guide.* Montevideo, Uruguay: Instituto del Tercer Mundo, 1984–. ISBN: 1-869-84742-3 (for 1997/1998).

This is a decidedly third world analysis of the world and all the countries on the planet. There are two distinct parts in this annual publication. The first part contains twenty-two introductory essays on such key topics as the arms race, water, global warming, indigenous peoples, debt, refugees, health, and others. Each one takes up several pages and provides an overview of the topic, statistics, charts, maps, and more. The second part is the larger of the two and is a country-by-country survey and economic profile of the nation. Treatment here stresses the environment, society, and the state/politics. Each entry is structured into a standardized format permitting quick comparative analyses. Even some of the earth's tiniest island nations, such as Kiribati, Palau, and the Pitcairn Islands are included in the second part. (Note: The 1997/1998 volume was the most recent one seen.)

7-87. *World at Risk: A Global Issues Sourcebook.* Washington, DC: CQ Press, 2002. 692 pp. ISBN: 1-568-02707-9.

Broad survey-type articles and basic reference materials in thirty critical contemporary global issues have been written in the fields of economics, human development, law, politics, security, and the environment. Each of these articles starts out with a general analysis and then proceeds to more detailed assessments at the regional and national levels. The entries are sequenced in the following manner: historical background and development, current status, regional summaries around the globe, tables of pertinent data, extremely selective and short biographical sketches, directory of organizations, and further research in both traditional and online formats. Chapters average approximately twenty-five pages and are all pointedly cross-disciplinary in approach to the topic. This work is intended for high-school students, undergraduates, and members of the general public.

7-88. Taylor, Peter J., ed. *World Government.* rev. ed. New York: Oxford University Press, 1994. 256 pp. ISBN: 0-195-20861-7.

This heavily illustrated work offers a broad, comparative analysis of the different regions and governments that represent the world's post–cold war global system. Three themes are addressed throughout the first part of this work. They are the questions of formal state power, how states are actually governed, and how states interact with one another. Part 2 is a regional survey of the world's countries broken down by individual nation. This section is replete with maps, colored photographs, and more. The larger states receive comparably more space. The photographs are of particularly high quality and give a real flavor for what is being described in the accompanying text portion. This is a fine tool for general readers, high-school students, and lower-division undergraduates in comparative government classes. It is not a work about world government, international organization, or global agencies such as the United Nations.

Atlases

7-89. Anderson, Ewan W. *Global Geopolitical Flashpoints: An Atlas of Conflict.* Chicago: Fitzroy Dearborn Publishers, 2000. 391 pp. Index. ISBN: 1-579-58137-4.

This highly specialized atlas includes all current and potential armed flashpoints since 1989 to nearly the date of publication. It traces the relative importance of the location and development of the specific set of geopolitical issues at stake, and it analyzes the status of the current situation. Each entry has a fairly detailed map that one would expect in a work describing itself as an atlas. These maps depict those spots of geopolitical instability, whether arising from strategic, political, economic, or social factors. The majority of these entries pertain to Africa and Asia. The main entries are alphabetical by the name of the flashpoint, such as "Bosnia," "Palestine," "Spratly Islands," and others. Each entry conforms to a standardized format that starts off with background, situation, issues, status, and readings. Some entries are for entire countries. There are a total of 123 entries. An index accompanies the atlas.

7-90. Kidron, Michael. *The New State of the World Atlas.* 4th ed. New York: Simon and Schuster, 1991. 159 pp. ISBN: 0-671-74556-5.

This is a unique atlas that, in the introduction, calls itself an example of "cartojournalism," displaying through the use of maps the visual background to a number of major events or situations. The atlas includes approximately 50 two-page color maps, each with a different perspective, on such demographic, social, and economic indicators as population, marketing muscle, national income, food power, plagues, quality of life, and a number of others. The maps use a combination of color and size scaling to represent a wide range of social, political, economic, and demographic conditions. Global imbalances are depicted by the use of the visual designs displayed in these maps. Following the maps portion of the atlas are fifty short entries describing what the reader has actually looked at and giving some background to the displays. A comparative set of world tables arranged by country rounds out the contents of this reference work.

7-91. Leonard, R. L. *World Atlas of Elections: Voting Patterns in Thirty-Nine Democracies.* London: Economist Publications, 1986. 159 pp. ISBN: 0-850-58089-7.

This specialized atlas serves up voting and election results for most of the then-recent parliamentary and presidential races for the thirty-nine democratic countries functioning about twenty years ago. Maps depict the actual election areas and victorious political parties are shown for each individual national seat. Maps are available for percentage of votes cast, voting tables, charts, and trends for over a forty-year period. There are no local or regional election results in this work. There is a chapter on European Parliament voting results for 1979 and some years later. Entries are arranged alphabetically by country with the different maps appearing within these chapters. See the Guides and Handbooks section that precedes this Atlases section for additional global electoral works.

Africa
Literature Guides
7-92. Zell, Hans M., ed. *The African Studies Companion: A Guide to Information Sources.* 3rd rev. and exp. ed. Glais Bheinn, Scotland: Hans Zell, 2003. 545 pp. ISBN: 0-954-10291-6.

The third edition contains a number of new online resources lacking in the previous one, and the entries have approximately doubled in total count. The main body of the book contains twenty-three major sections, most with several subdivisions. Some of these major sections are arts, politics, news sources, organizations, agencies, and library collections. New sections include biographical resources, audio-visual aids, and maps, among others. Sources listed throughout this work tend to be more general or multidisciplinary in scope as well as in the English language exclusively. The goal of this work is to list journal articles, books, maps, reference works, and the like that examine African studies in its broadest context. It does not include any work that covers a single African country or a specific topic related to the African continent. The works chosen discuss either Africa as a whole or multiple areas of it. Entries receive lengthy annotations. According to the editor, the publication intent is to publish a "new and fully updated edition of *African Studies Companion*" every two years in both print and electronic formats, and then perhaps update the product to those willing to pay extra on a subscription basis. 🖥

Annuals and Yearbooks

7-93. Legum, Colin, ed. *Africa Contemporary Record: Annual Survey and Documentation.* New York: Africana Publishing, 1968/1969–. ISSN: 0065-3845.

This was an annual publication through Volume 22, but with Volume 23 it became a biennial. After several cycles of two-year formats, the publication hopes to revert to its annual publication schedule. Most volumes have three main sections. The first section is "Current Issues," which provides essays on the recent political and economic developments in Africa, including articles on African regionalism, French policy in Africa, Africa's political economy in the future, and the like. The second section is a "Country-by-Country Review," which is especially good for the comparative government or current affairs students and others. It is the largest section of the work. Every entry examines in a structured manner the politics, social affairs, foreign policy, and economic affairs of each African nation. Entries are all signed. Political parties currently operating and their respective leaders are listed for each country along with election news and results, government officials, budget discussions, and more. The third section is "Text of Documents," with various resolutions, protocols, and agreements pertaining to African nations, regional groups, international accords, and so forth. A number of useful statistical tables are provided that give such information as demographic information, economic figures, military expenditures, national debt totals, and others.

Bibliographies

7-94. Scheven, Yvette. *Bibliographies for African Studies, 1970–1986.* London: Hans Zell, 1988. 550 pp. Index. ISBN: 0-905-45033-7.

This book lists separately published bibliographies relating to sub-Saharan Africa in the social sciences and humanities. It cumulates the author's earlier volumes and adds bibliographies for 1984 through 1986. Bibliographies can be books, articles, or parts of edited works. Most materials are in English or French. Some items are also in the other major European languages or Afrikaans. The Sudan and Somalia are included for the first time in this cumulation. Archival materials are listed, but only on a highly selective basis. The book is organized into two major sections: "Topical" and "Geographical." Entries are arranged alphabetically by author or main entry. Most citations have a one or two-sentence descriptive annotation. Entries all indicate how many numbers of items are included in each bibliography, whether or not they are annotated, the scope, the arrangement, and types of indexes. There are roughly 3,280 entries altogether. The "Topical" section is broken down into forty areas of interest, such as labor, geography, politics, and social issues. The content of the materials listed extends well beyond the boundaries of purely political science issues. A thorough index is included.

7-95. Mahadeven, Vijitha, ed. *Contemporary African Politics and Development: A Comprehensive Bibliography, 1981–1990.* Boulder, CO: Lynne Rienner, 1994. 1314 pp. ISBN: 1-555-87334-0.

The goal of this bibliography is to compile a comprehensive and fully annotated list of materials for researchers, students, and policy analysts. It lists over 17,000 English- and French-language scholarly citations found in UCLA's library system and originally published as a monograph, academic journal article, edited volume, reference work, or government publication. Entries are arranged geographically by country and/or region of Africa, and then topically within each individual country. Entries include both cross-references and "see also" references. This was the most comprehensive work of its kind when originally published. Each country's topical subdivision entry organization follows a similar pattern, such as labor, agriculture, planning and development, politics, and military affairs. Entries are alphabetical within these subdivisions. An editorial decision was made to exclude materials on Egypt.

7-96. *Current Bibliography on African Affairs.* Farmingdale, NY: Baywood Publishing, 1962–. ISSN: 0011-3255.

This is a standard quarterly bibliography on Africa in all its facets, including studies on international relations, politics and government, economics, society, military affairs, development issues, and many other areas. While not exclusively a political science bibliography, many of the articles do in fact relate to either politics or economic/social development. Citations are culled from books, journals, and an occasional major newspaper entry. One-half of this bibliography is broken down into various broad subject headings, including "Foreign Economic Relations," "Labor," "Foreign Assistance," "Development," and "Gender." The other one-half of the book is arranged by country, by regional groupings.

7-97. Musiker, Naomi, comp. *Kaunda's Zambia, 1964–1991: A Selected and Annotated Bibliography.* Johannesburg: South African Institute of International Affairs, 1993. 426 pp. Indexes.

This annotated bibliography contains over 1,650 entries and includes books, journal articles, government publications, various reports, and occasional conference proceedings on Zambia stretching from the country's date of independence to the forced end of the Kenneth Kaunda era in government and politics. Entries listed in alphabetical order are chosen overwhelmingly from major sources. Newspaper articles are excluded from this bibliography. The journal titles chosen for indexing represent a fairly good international mix of originating countries and languages. Bibliographic citations drawn from foreign-language materials are translated into English. The annotations are generally limited to one- or two-sentence descriptive information packets. There are author and subject indexes. The subject index can be somewhat confusing and relatively weak given its importance to the success in using this bibliography in a successful and efficacious way.

7-98. Strachan, Beth, comp. *Mozambique, the Quest for Peace: The Political, Social and Economic Context, 1980–1994: A Select and Annotated Bibliography.* Johannesburg: South African Institute of International Affairs, 1996. 821 pp. ISBN: 1-874-89066-8.

Not seen.

7-99. Williams, Michael W. *Pan-Africanism: An Annotated Bibliography.* Pasadena, CA: Salem Press, 1992. 142 pp. ISBN: 0-893-56674-8.

This is a bibliography of books, chapters, and journal articles that are relatively easily accessible to students doing undergraduate levels of research on Pan-Africanism. The work starts off with an overview of the history of Pan-Africanism and is then divided up into three major parts. Part 1 provides a list of materials on the broad background and history of African-based pannational movements. Part 2 contains more specific topics such as political and cultural ties, the historical development of various organizations and movements, and so forth. Part 3 is devoted to biographical sketches of twenty of the so-called greats of Pan-Africanism, such as Frantz Fanon and Patrice Lumumba. Several women are included in this list of twenty. One such person is Barbara Ransby. There are also many short biographical entries for the "lesser known" Pan-Africanists. Mbiyu Koinange falls into that category.

7-100. Stultz, Newell Maynard. *South Africa as Apartheid Ends: An Annotated Bibliography with Analytical Introductions.* Ann Arbor, MI: Pierian Press, 1993. 228 pp. Indexes. ISBN: 0-876-50330-X.

The purpose of this bibliography is to provide a selective listing of annotated social science materials on contemporary South African public affairs. The citations chosen for this work are all in English. The time frame emphasizes the period since the Sharpeville Massacre in 1960. The intended target audience is mainly U.S. college students doing research on South African politics and public policies. There are eight major chapters, each one of which is broken down into several subdivisions. The chapters open with a short, yet spirited introduction to the chapter topics, which include "African Majority," "Minority Communities," "Race and Race Relations," and "Reform and Political Change." Annotations average about one paragraph and are scholarly in orientation. The books and journal articles cited in the bibliography portions are intended to be housed at most average-sized U.S. academic libraries. There is an author and a title index.

7-101. Kalley, Jacqueline A. *South Africa's Road to Change, 1987–1990: A Select and Annotated Bibliography.* New York: Greenwood Press, 1991. 432 pp. Indexes. ISBN: 0-313-28117-3.

This annotated bibliography continues the work done by a previous book, *South Africa under Apartheid.* This work chronicles South African events from

1987 through 1990. What makes this bibliography unique is that it was regarded as an opportunity to present the South African viewpoint from a number of different political perspectives. Citations are mostly for international journals and total around 1,500 entries in one straight alphabetical index by author or main entry title. Annotations run from one sentence to lengthy paragraphs. There is an author index and a subject index at the end.

Dictionaries and Encyclopedias

7-102. Williams, Gwyneth. *The Dictionary of Contemporary Politics of Southern Africa.* New York: Macmillan, 1989. 339 pp. ISBN: 0-028-97471-9.

While this dictionary of politics for southern Africa was written before the advent of majority rule in South Africa, it is still quite useful since other countries are included, ranging in geographic scope from Tanzania on the northern perimeter to South Africa on the southern end. Included are biographies of major figures, short histories, key demographic information, economics, geographical information, party policies, political systems, maps, and more. Arrangement is strictly alphabetical, and entries tend to be fairly short but loaded with cross-references. South Africa receives the highest number of related entries, Botswana the least. The entries are concise yet very well written and content useful.

7-103. Arnold, Guy. *Political and Economic Encyclopedia of Africa.* Harlow, Essex, UK: Longman Current Affairs,

1993. 342 pp. Index. ISBN: 0-582-20995-1.

This book is similar in title, content, and organization to the other political and economic encyclopedias of other parts of the world. Four types of entries constitute the main body of this alphabetically arranged encyclopedic dictionary. They are fifty-four individual countries all subdivided in a standard manner, organizational entries, individuals, and general entries. Each entry averages about half a page. This encyclopedia is good for facts, dates, basic information, and more. The country entries are by far the longest and include a discussion of each nation's geography, peoples, history, political developments, and economy. It is heavily cross-referenced and also has an index. This is a good basic reference source.

Guides and Handbooks

7-104. Cook, Chris. *African Political Facts since 1945.* 2nd ed. New York: Facts on File, 1991. 280 pp. ISBN: 0-816-02418-9.

This compendium covers the period from 1945 through 1990 and includes information on the entire continent of Africa. The work is aimed at nonspecialists and attempts to provide information about Africa across a broad spectrum of areas. The book begins with a chronology of major events by year. Then there is a listing of governors and heads of state for each country, even those political dependencies now defunct, such as Tanganyika. There is then a list of major ministerial appointments by country, followed by a discussion of the constitutions and parliaments of each nation in a narrative format, and then a complete roster of active political parties, including notes about when they were active and any major actions those parties may have undertaken. Cook also delineates what armed conflicts and political coups took place from 1945 through 1990, and there is a brief synopsis of each war with participants, dates, reasons for the conflict, results, and more. Rounding out the book is a look at the foreign affairs and treaties concluded by the African nations, a survey of the continent's ethnic groups, and a brief section of succinct biographical entries.

7-105. Morrison, Donald George. *Black Africa: A Comparative Handbook.* 2nd ed. New York: Paragon House, 1989. 716 pp. ISBN: 0-887-02042-9.

This work is a fairly unique attempt to provide researchers both topical and other relevant data that would lend itself well to a comparative analysis and profile of black Africa. This would include such areas as cultural pluralism, economic development, political participation, foreign policy, and the like. The work includes text, analysis, charts, and tables, and it is indeed the quantitative analysis elements of this work that are its strength and raison d'etre. There are measurements of urban populations, ethnic groups, history of political parties, elections, and more. The statistics are all derived from the black Africa database that was available at the time.

7-106. Bute, E. L. *The Black Handbook: The People, History, and Politics of*

Africa and the African Diaspora. Washington, DC: Cassell, 1997. 392 pp. Index. ISBN: 0-304-33542-8.

While this work is not devoted exclusively to politics or political affairs, about 40 percent of the entries are in fact in these areas. The main body contains about ten separate chapters, including "Inter-Governmental Organizations and Treaties" and "Terror Movements and Ideas." Entries are ordered alphabetically within each chapter. Many of the historical and other nonpolitical entries appear to be written up with a nose to the political situation surrounding the person or event listed. A "Chronology of Africa and the Diaspora" for the time period 1494 through 1997 is drawn out. An index is available.

7-107. Nohlen, Dieter, ed. *Elections in Africa: A Data Handbook.* New York: Oxford University Press, 1999. 984 pp. ISBN: 0-198-29645-2.

Election data has been compiled and presented in the same systematic way for each country listed. Tables are organized into ten parts, including electoral participation of parties and alliances, distribution in votes in national referendums, elections to the constitutional assembly, parliamentary and presidential offices, and the composition of Parliament. The data handbook begins with an introductory chapter on African elections and discusses the various electoral systems across the continent. This is followed by the main portion of the book, the country-by-country surveys in alphabetical order, all with short introductions to the numerous data and statistical tables. The result is a considerably comprehensive work for a single-volume handbook. This compendium of election results is virtually similar in topic and style to *Elections in Asia and the Pacific: A Data Handbook* [entry 7-131].

7-108. DeLancey, Mark W., ed. *Handbook of Political Science Research on Sub-Saharan Africa: Trends from the 1960s to the 1990s.* Westport, CT: Greenwood Press, 1992. 427 pp. Indexes. ISBN: 0-313-27509-2.

The handbook starts out with three general surveys leading into the main part of the book that is divided into "Regional Surveys" and then into "Country Surveys." The general surveys are good bibliographic essays on several relevant topics. In addition, there are five regional chapters: "Lusophone (Portuguese) Africa," "Southern Africa," "East Africa," "Horn of Africa," and "Cameroon and Equatorial Africa." The country-based surveys are for South Africa, Ivory Coast, Ghana, and Nigeria. All of these chapters are in the form of bibliographic essay. A number of the works cited within the bibliographic essays are for works written in languages other than English. One of the appendixes is a directory of social science research centers in sub-Saharan Africa, including their national archives, libraries, and so forth, arranged by country. Many of the contributors have ties to the University of South Carolina-Columbia's International Studies program. There are indexes by name and by subject.

7-109. Riley, Eileen. *Major Political Events in South Africa 1948–1990.* New York: Facts on File, 1991. 250 pp. ISBN: 0-816-02310-7.

Similar in format and content to the other works in this publisher's series, this work looks at South Africa from 1948 through 1990. It starts off with a short overview of the history of the area, the first Europeans, British colonial rule, and so forth. The chronology, the main body of the book, ends with Nelson Mandela's release from prison on February 11, 1990. The biography section includes entries for both black and white prominent politicians.

7-110. Kalley, Jacqueline A, comp. *Southern African Political History: A Chronology of Key Political Events from Independence to Mid-1997.* Westport, CT: Greenwood Press, 1999. 904 pp. Index. ISBN: 0-313-30247-2.

The goal of this work is to bring together information on the political development of the South African Development Community (SADC) and its member states since their independence from colonial rule. Emphasis is clearly on the time period from 1961 to the date of publication, when South Africa gained republican status. The main body is arranged alphabetically by country, and then information is listed in chronological order. Each specific entry provides dates and a relatively short one-page summary of what happened on a particular date over the last forty years or so. Entries are mainly political events, agreements signed, diplomatic moves, state visits, United Nations actions, troop movements, and actions carried out by the political parties of all ideological stripes. A subject index is available and carries some interesting indexing terms.

Asia and the Middle East
Annuals and Yearbooks

7-111. Maddy-Weitzman, Bruce, ed. *Middle East Contemporary Survey.* Annual. New York: Holmes and Meier, 1977–. Index. ISSN: 0163-5476.

This annual survey of the Middle East region is often a couple of years behind, but worth the wait. Each yearly volume is in two main parts. First is a string of broad essays on regional issues and relations with other parts of the world. This first part has two major headings: "International, Regional and Palestinian Affairs" and "Middle East Economic and Demographic Issues." Both of these major headings are broken down into numerous, more specific subdivisions. The second part of the book is a country-by-country review of all the Middle Eastern Arab states, plus Turkey, Israel, and Iran. Each of these country's politics and society are scrutinized here, in an easy-reading yet authoritative manner, regarding major contemporary developments of interest since the previous edition was released. Each chapter was written by a different specialist in Middle East affairs, with the country-by-country articles being especially detailed and thorough. Maps are included as helpful supplemental material. An index is included.

Bibliographies

7-112. Mahler, Gregory S. *Bibliography of Israeli Politics.* Boulder, CO: Westview Press, 1985. 133 pp. Index. ISBN: 0-813-37042-6.

This bibliography includes 1,500 entries on books and journal articles published in the United States, Europe, or Israel. All are in the English language regardless of place of publication. Studies that focus purely on the economy, history, or military are excluded unless they have a clear political science perspective. There are no annotations, but there is an author and keyword index. The book is arranged in one straight alphabetical sequence without additional subdivisions, which makes the index all the more critical for effective use of the volume.

7-113. Chan, Gerald. *International Studies in China: An Annotated Bibliography.* Commack, NY: Nova Science Publishers, 1998. 100 pp. ISBN: 1-560-72588-5.

The purpose of this work was to present the Chinese international relations perspective to scholars rather than the more prevalent Western-based version. About one-quarter of this work consists of a reprint of a February 1997 issue of *Issues and Studies* on the origins and development of the study of international relations within the People's Republic of China's academic and research centers. The remaining portion of the book constitutes the bibliography section. All works listed are Chinese books, journal articles, and other publications in the Chinese language. The titles of these

Chinese works have been translated into English. About 20 percent of the works cited in this international relations bibliography have been designated to receive short annotations. There is a short section or two on works written in English, not all of which were written by someone of Chinese extraction. The majority of works within the bibliographic section are fairly recent publications. This work will serve best the needs of researchers using larger academic libraries, preferably those with exceptionally strong East Asian studies or Chinese foreign affairs programs.

7-114. Fenton, Thomas P., comp. and ed. *Middle East: A Directory of Resources.* Mary Knoll, NY: Orbis Books, 1988. 144 pp. ISBN: 0-883-44533-6.

This work is both a directory and a bibliography of resources intended to set up five objectives that assist third world nations through outside intervention. The bibliographic portion lists books, journal articles, and audio-visual materials to "concerned citizens in First World countries . . . in order to take informed and effective action to correct injustices in the ways governments and business treat Third World nations and peoples" (Fenton 1988, introduction). While many of the organizations may have by now vanished, moved, merged, or changed focus, the bibliography section consumes 90 percent of the pages and still has value. All entries are heavily annotated, but at a price of displaying a partisan bias for providing aid to the Middle East countries without the usual political or economic strings attached. A few other third world regions of the world were covered by this publisher, but they were all done prior to 1986.

7-115. Silverburg, Sanford R. *Middle East Bibliography.* Metuchen, NJ: Scarecrow Press, 1992. 564 pp. Index. ISBN: 0-810-82469-8.

This is a well-researched bibliography meant to highlight books published from 1980 to the early 1990s, but older materials are included. Most of the books selected are in English, but monographs in Hebrew, Arabic, Persian, and Turkish are also listed. The introduction is in reality an excellent bibliographic essay on the history of the Middle East region. Again, most works are in English, but works cited extend to bibliographies, journals, published papers, manuscripts, and collections in addition to book-format materials. The main body is arranged by broad subject category and entries are unannotated. Typical headings are "Egypt—Women," "Iraq—Human Rights," "Israel—Politics," and others of this ilk. While some non-political-science topics are covered, the bibliography is especially rich in history, politics, and foreign relations of the Middle Eastern nations. There is an author index only, which could be a bit of a problem when more detailed subject searching is required.

7-116. Middle East Research and Information Project (MERIP). http://www.merip.org.

This Web site serves as an excellent and current source of news analysis and commentary on the politics, culture, and society of the lands of the Middle East. Much of the data contained in this site are in fact full-text articles drawn from *MERIP REPORTS,* which began publication in May 1971. Researchers can undertake research on a topic across the database by using the search command. Back issues of material are available by subscription only. Op-eds are also available in full text, and they are culled from a wide range of U.S. and a highly selective roster of foreign-based newspapers. 💻

7-117. I-Mu, comp. *Unofficial Documents of the Democracy Movement in Communist China 1978–1981: A Checklist of Chinese Materials in the Hoover Institution on War, Revolution and Peace.* Stanford, CA: Hoover Institution Press, 1986. 100 pp. ISBN: 0-817-92672-0.

This is a unique bibliography of materials related directly to the short-lived Democracy Movement that went on in the People's Republic of China from 1978 through 1981. The Hoover Institution made a concerted effort to collect as many of these prodemocracy documents as possible. This book serves as a checklist for those publications. Included in this checklist are citations for 162 unofficial Chinese journals, 32 pamphlets, 28 items taken down from Democracy Wall in Tiananmen Square, 3 reels of microfilm, and 15 volumes of various underground materials.

Dictionaries
7-118. Hiro, Dilip. *Dictionary of the Middle East.* New York: St. Martin's

Press, 1996. 376 pp. ISBN: 0-312-12554-2.

This author of a number of books dealing with the Middle East and Islamic affairs has put together a specialized subject dictionary that covers the area's politics, history, literature, leading figures, religious groups, and more. Entries could include country profiles, the history of the Gulf War, religious groups in the region, regional conflicts and border disagreements, the role of the United Nations in the region, and the like. Biographical entries are limited primarily to those who have made a major political, military, religious, or literary impact on the country where that individual reached adulthood by the year 1900 AD. Similarly, only twentieth-century peace agreements and protocols are included. Entries are fairly short, ranging from about one-third to one-half a page each. There are several black-and-white maps. This book serves as a great fairly up-to-date ready-reference source of information for dates, biographies, events, wars, and more. The bulk of the entries pertain to the politics of the region.

7-119. Stockwin, J. A. A. *Dictionary of the Modern Politics of Japan.* New York: RoutledgeCurzon, 2003. 291 pp. ISBN: 0-415-15170-8.

The topic of Japanese politics generally gets short shrift in the Western literature compared to the pervasive interest in this Asian country's economic policies and trade balances. This dictionary provides a broad look at Japanese prime ministers, political parties and party leaders, major politicians, central government agencies, the judicial system, various political crises, the electoral process, constitutional issues, public policy matters, and much more. An introductory essay on the politics and political history of Japan precedes the main body of the work. Entries are arranged in alphabetical order and average approximately one page of information each. Each listing contains a short history and a list of additional readings. Several entries, such as "Election System," receive especially long coverage. The great majority of entries contain cross-references.

7-120. Leifer, Michael. *Dictionary of the Modern Politics of South-East Asia.* 3rd ed. New York: Routledge, 2001. 312 pp. Index. ISBN: 0-415-23875-7.

This reference work identifies the ten countries it considers making up Southeast Asia, with the exception of East Timor. Resistance to Western-style democracy has tended to be fairly strong in this part of the world. The book opens up with capsule political overviews of all ten Southeast Asian nations. These overviews average several pages in length. Other entries include events, treaties, political parties and their ideas, political movements, regional organizations, and more. Biographies appear for major contemporary or historical figures only. There is a good, solid, contemporary focus to this work. Many entries can be several pages. At the end of the book is a selective reading list. There is only one index, and that is by country.

7-121. He, Henry Yuhuai. *Dictionary of the Political Thought of the People's Republic of China.* Armonk, NY: M. E. Sharpe, 2001. 727 pp. Index. ISBN: 0-765-60569-4.

Anyone needing help interpreting the frequently recondite political thoughts and terms originating from the People's Republic of China (PRC) will find this work most useful in understanding this Byzantine political language. Political thoughts and terms are covered from the very founding days of the PRC, but this dictionary is especially rich in the political language published since the fall of the Gang of Four in 1976. The individual entries can be several pages long and the author is systematic about providing the history of a term, the people who may have been involved, activities surrounding the term or event, and the role of the Chinese leadership. Each entry is in four distinct parts. Part one is the term written in the original Chinese characters, and part two is the term written down in the Chinese phonetic alphabet. Part three is the English translation, and the last part is an explanation and discussion in English. The English translation is a bit stilted but readable in short or moderate doses as was its primary intent. The index is absolutely essential for efficient use.

7-122. MacKerras, Colin, ed. *The Dictionary of the Politics of the People's Republic of China.* New York: Routledge, 1998. 267 pp. Index. ISBN: 0-415-15450-2.

This work covers a fairly narrow slice of

history, specifically from 1978 up to September 1997. These years ending with 1997, the year of the Fiftieth Party Congress, is seen by the editors as the so-called reform period. The work begins with nine introductory essays on China's political, social, economic, and geographical realities. Boldface type within each essay is designed to lead the reader to an appropriate entry in the main body of the book. The essays and dictionary entries both are capable of possessing many of these cross-references. Entries are rarely less than one page long, frequently even longer. Typical terms appearing in the main dictionary touch upon individual political agencies, major nationalities, domestic and foreign policy issues, and more. Entries provide the reader with a good feel for the flavor of the era and the topic being examined. The entry for the "Hundred Flowers Movement" exemplifies this spirit. Each entry is signed by the author, who more often than not is a faculty member from one of Australia's universities. There is an index, and there is also a short annotated list of additional readings made available to the reader.

7-123. Olson, James S. *Dictionary of the Vietnam War.* New York: Greenwood Press, 1988. 585 pp. ISBN: 0-313-24943-1.

This dictionary serves as a ready-reference tool for the period covering 1945 through 1975. It includes the people, military operations, and the controversies that were important to the politics in the United States during this undeclared war. All entries are signed and vary in length from a single paragraph to several pages. Remember such terms as tiger cage, napalm, and the Tet Offensive? They are all here, and this book evokes a very tumultuous era in American history and government. The editor is to be commended for attempting to bring balance to such an emotionally charged topic, even with the passing of a quarter of a century since the Vietnamese peace accords. The entry on William L. Calley Jr. best exemplifies this neutrality. There are a number of appendixes in this dictionary, including a selected bibliography on the Vietnam War broken down into subtopics, a Vietnam War chronology, and various maps of South Vietnamese military regions.

7-124. Ziring, Lawrence. *The Middle East: A Political Dictionary.* Santa Barbara, CA: ABC-CLIO, 1992. 401 pp. Index. ISBN: 0-874-36612-7.

This is a revised edition of *The Middle East Political Dictionary* (see entry 2202 in 4th edition of Ziring). The Middle East is defined here as all countries from Morocco to Pakistan and India, and from Turkey to the Sudan, or twenty-two countries in all. All are Muslim states except Israel. The time covered is the latter half of the twentieth century. Special attention is given to the Arab-Israeli conflict. The work is organized into seven broad chapters, including "Islam," "Political Parties and Movements," and "Israelis and Palestinians." Within each chapter, entries are arranged alphabetically. Each entry begins with the topic's historical context and ends with a section on that entry's "significance" as tied to major international relations–related issues. There are numerous cross-references within most entries. The 257 main entries tend to average out at one to three pages. The index is good and quite necessary given the overall arrangement of the work.

7-125. Reich, Bernard. *Political Dictionary of Israel.* Lanham, MD: Scarecrow Press, 2000. 448 pp. ISBN: 0-810-83778-1.

The goal of this dictionary is to provide a comprehensive and up-to-date single reference volume on all facets of the political life of what is contemporary Israel. While this work builds upon the author's previous work, *Historical Dictionary of Israel* (1992), the emphasis in this publication is politics. The book is intended for students, scholars, general readers, and journalists. There is a brief chronology of Israel's modern era. There are also ten tables that give such information as prime minister, immigration totals, and the like. The main portion of the book is alphabetically arranged and entries can be up to several pages long. Entries with longer definitions have a bibliography attached. This dictionary can be used to find biographies, political parties, Kibbutzim, military terms, educational resources, major newspapers, the Knesset, Jewish settlements, the various military episodes (such as the Sinai War), and more. A bibliography at the end of the book contains works on Israeli relations with foreign nations, especially its Arab

neighbors. This is neither a Jewish American dictionary nor one on the Middle East, but one that focuses on the State of Israel and its political life.

7-126. Korbani, Agnes G. *Political Dictionary of Modern Middle East.* Lanham, MD: University Press of America, 1995. 258 pp. ISBN: 0-819-19579-0.

A total of just over 900 entries give a wealth of information on the people, nations, wars, coups, and conflicts that go into making up this often volatile region of the globe. Entries tend to be highly concise, but some of them can be over one full page in length. Some sample terms taken from the book include "Camp David Accords," "Likud Party," and the "Palestinian Liberation Organization (PLO)." There is a short bibliography at the back of the book. This bibliography as well as the work itself is acceptable for casual use by high-school students, lower-division undergraduates, and general audiences.

7-127. Rolef, Susan Hattis, ed. *Political Dictionary of the State of Israel.* 2nd ed. New York: Macmillan, 1993. 417 pp. ISBN: 0-028-97193-0.

Israel and the Middle East in general receive a lot of attention in the reference-publication world, given their ability to grab and hold headlines for weeks and months at a time. This particular A-to-Z dictionary provides mostly basic levels of information on Israeli politics. Approximately 450 articles, each averaging about one page long, present the personalities, the political parties, the major events, wars, the Knesset, the electoral system, the role of the media in politics, and economic and foreign policy. Each entry contains one or more cross-references. A "supplement" of roughly seventy pages covers the last five-year period. Some of these entries are new; others are continued from the main section. A few maps and statistical tables are included. Some people may find the format of the main pages somewhat distracting and/or cluttered. See also the *Political Dictionary of Israel* [entry 7-125] by Reich.

Encyclopedias

7-128. Sela, Avraham, ed. *The Continuum Political Encyclopedia of the Middle East.* rev. and updated ed. New York: Continuum Publishing, 2002. 944 pp. Index. ISBN: 0-826-41413-3.

While the events from 1980 through 2000 receive the emphasis, events and articles are infused with a distinctly historical perspective. There is notably special treatment for events occurring in the post–Gulf War and post–cold war eras. The relationship between the Israelis and the Arabs garners much attention here. Entries are in standard alphabetical order, and all entries have cross-references. Contributors are mostly Israeli scholars drawn from Israeli universities. Entries include noted individuals, countries, nationalities, political terms, and can be up to ten pages long for such specific items as "Palestinian Guerrilla Organizations" and "Intifada." The index is unusual in that it cites cross-references, not page numbers. See also several similar entries above in "dictionaries" section.

7-129. Ke-Wen, Wang, ed. *Modern China: An Encyclopedia of History, Culture, and Nationalism.* New York: Garland, 1998. 442 pp. Index. ISBN: 0-815-30720-9.

According to the editor, Wang Ke-Wen, almost every significant Chinese political leader and movement over the past couple of centuries has been considered to be "nationalist." Strict definition of this concept is elusive, however, and is complicated by ideas of the Chinese nation-state, ethnicity, and culture. This reference work seeks to elucidate the issue by discussing individuals, cultural affairs, and political affairs in the larger context of nationalism. Entries are arranged alphabetically and generally are from a page to three pages long. Each includes a list of references. The front matter includes a listing of entries by subject. Some of these include "Communist Revolution," "External Conflicts," "Intellectual Currents," "Literature," and "Personalities." The index also assists in access to the text. There are occasional photographs, usually of individuals. Two maps and a chronology extending from 1839 to 1997 further enhance the volume. The contributors are drawn from the U.S. academic community with an occasional bow to other countries, including China. This work will be of value to scholars and to undergraduate students studying modern China. 💻

7-130. Huffman, James L. *Modern Japan: An Encyclopedia of History, Culture, and Nationalism.* New York:

Garland, 1998. 316 pp. Index. ISBN: 0-815-32525-8.

The author of this specialized encyclopedia argues that nationalism lies at the core of Japan's modern development. There is a subject list of thirty broad categories, each with three to fifty-five or so encyclopedic entries placed into those categories. The longest subject lists are for the following: "Military," "Politics and Government," and "Ultranationalism." Most of the contributors are from Canada and the United States, and their academic affiliations are listed. There are surprisingly few contributors from Japan. The actual main body of the work is a straight alphabetical arrangement of entries. Each entry attempts to include at least one book for additional reading. Some photographs are interspersed between the covers of the book. The articles tend to be quite well written and often cover topics one might be surprised to find within the scope of this work, such as the superb piece on anti-Semitism. There is one index.

Guides and Handbooks

7-131. Nohlen, Dieter, ed. *Elections in Asia and the Pacific: A Data Handbook.* 2 vols. New York: Oxford University Press, 2001. ISBN: 0-199-24958-X.

This is virtually the same work as *Elections in Africa: A Data Handbook* [entry 7-107], but with the geographical focus shifted to Asia and the Pacific areas. The main body has a slightly different arrangement from its African counterpart. This Asian and Pacific data handbook is broken down into wide geographical area and then arranged alphabetically by country. Voting results here go back about 100 years for a few select countries, such as Australia and New Zealand. Many of the former Soviet Socialist Republics are listed and properly represented as independent states. There is no index.

7-132. Cook, Chris, comp. *Facts on File Asian Political Almanac.* New York: Facts on File, 1994. 264 pp. ISBN: 0-816-02585-1.

The overriding intent of this handbook is to publish a large amount of factual information and figures on the important political events and trends on the continent of Asia from 1945 to the early 1990s. A large percentage of the data contained in this work is in tabular format. This almanac also gives very brief biographical sketches of the major Asian political leaders and statespersons, a glossary of political terminology, and a chronology of noteworthy happenings. Excluded from consideration are the Middle Eastern countries, the Persian Gulf states, and the former Soviet republics located in the Caucasus and central Asia. The chapter on "Heads of State and Government" is arranged by country and gives full names and dates in a position of authority. A listing of current and former political parties complete with their philosophical leanings is included.

7-133. Li, Kwok-Sing, comp. *Glossary of Political Terms of the People's Repub-*

lic of China. Shatin, Hong Kong: Chinese University Press, 1995. 639 pp. Indexes. ISBN: 9-622-01615-4.

This is a most unusual lexicon of the People's Republic of China political terms because Mao and the ruling party tended to rely so heavily on the use of slogans over the years. Chinese political terms may often have a different meaning to them than what may be apparent to a Westerner. Some of the political terms included here are policies of the party, while others are ideas or events. It is arranged in A-to-Z pattern. Entries provide original Chinese characters, their transliterations, and English-language translations for terms only. The definitions are in English only. The entry definitions often cite the term as it is used in the Chinese press and give the appropriate historical context. Entries average about one page each. The terms included here are unlike the ones found in more traditional glossaries of English-language political phrases and include such terms as "Four Not-To-Do, Four Allowances," "Spiritual Pollution," and the infamous "The East Wind Prevails over the West Wind." All indexes are in Chinese and English languages. There is definitely some editorial opinion interjected throughout about personal feelings toward the People's Republic of China and Mao as a leader.

7-134. Sagar, Darren. *Major Political Events in Indo-China, 1945–1990.* New York: Facts on File, 1991. 230 pp. ISBN: 0-816-02308-5.

This handbook is one in a series put out by Facts on File on major events for several key developing countries and regions of the globe. It begins with an eighteen-page introduction to the topic by discussing the history of this important area, the Indo-China Wars and the ill-fated French and American military involvement there. The bulk of the book is a chronology of events that took place in the region from 1945 through 1990. There also is a selective list of biographical entries as well as a couple of appendixes ranging from the Gulf of Tonkin Resolution (1964) to the number of casualties in the Vietnam War. A short bibliography is attached.

7-135. Mostyn, Trevor. *Major Political Events in Iran, Iraq and the Arabian Peninsula 1945–1990.* New York: Facts on File, 1991. 308 pp. ISBN: 0-816-02189-9.

Similar in format and content to the Darren Sagar work on Indo-China [entry 7-134], this work looks instead at Iran, Iraq, Saudi Arabia and the six small oil-producing countries of Qatar, Kuwait, United Arab Emirates, Bahrain, Oman, and Yemen. There is a short introductory article on the region's history, politics, and religion. The primary purpose of this and the other books in the series is the chronology of political events, military actions, peace agreements, international politics, and actions regarding the State of Israel and its security or military forces. Biographical names are mostly those of either major political figures or more prominent members of the various royal families in Arabia.

7-136. Diller, Daniel C., ed. *Middle East*. 9th ed. Washington, DC: Congressional Quarterly, 2000. 596 pp. Index. ISBN: 1-568-02101-1.

This Congressional Quarterly publication is divided into three main parts. The first part is an overview of the Middle East subdivided into the Arab-Israeli conflict, U.S. Middle East policy, the Persian Gulf, Mideast oil, fourteen centuries of Islam, and several other chapters. All entries are essay formats and are rich in facts, dates, statistics, and names. The second part serves as individual country profiles for Egypt, Iran, Iraq, Israel, Jordan, Kuwait, Lebanon, Libya, Saudi Arabia, the Persian Gulf nations, Syria, and Yemen. The third part is an appendix of document passages. The overarching audience spans high-school students, undergraduates, and general readers. Maps and pictures are selectively included. There is a chronicle of events for 1945 through 1999 that is relatively high in level of detail. There is an index.

7-137. Brom, Shlomo, ed. *The Middle East Military Balance, 2001/2002*. Cambridge, MA: MIT Press, 2002. 465 pp. ISBN: 0-262-06231-3.

The editor claims that the facts and figures given in this work are the "best estimate" of military armed forces levels within the various nations forming the Middle East lands. The first part is a qualitative assessment in the form of a narrative essay of all the air, land, and sea

forces throughout the area in an overall perspective. The second part, the main core of the book, is a country-by-country survey of each nation's military might. These surveys give a complete roster of arms procurements both to and from other countries of the world. Look here to find weapons totals, missiles, warships, and other weapons used by that country's military. The third part provides various charts and data tables for comparative analysis of air, ground, and sea forces. The fourth part is a glossary of weapons terms ranging from "Jericho II surface-to-surface missile" to the "Bradley M-3 infantry fighting vehicle." (Note: The description here is based on the 1999/2000 edition, the latest seen.)

7-138. Lewis, D. S. *Political Parties of Asia and the Pacific: A Reference Guide*. Detroit, MI: Gale Research, 1992. 369 pp. Index. ISBN: 0-582-09811-4.

The intent of this guide is to provide both accurate and fairly detailed information on the political parties now operating across the countries of Asia and the Pacific region in the modern world. The main body of the work is divided into countries, with each entry including basic background information on the constitutional organization, electoral systems, election results, and so forth of each country. Each individual party listing contains full party name, address, leaders, political orientation, and more. Listings for those relatively major political parties also include historical evolution, membership, and international affiliations. Some of the major defunct political parties are also listed, as are the major guerrilla organizations. There is one index for political parties. This guide will be of value mainly to undergraduates seeking contextual or comparative information on the political parties of these regions.

7-139. Tachau, Frank, ed. *Political Parties of the Middle East and North Africa.* Westport, CT: Greenwood Press, 1994. 711 pp. ISBN: 0-313-26649-2.

This handbook provides ample information on the various political parties of the Middle East and North Africa over the last century. The author claims that the emphasis is directed at the "formation, evolution, and impact" of each political party listed and the manner in which these political parties interact with each other and with society as a whole. For the purposes of this work, the Middle East is delimited to Morocco to the west, Iran to the east, the Sahara Desert to the south and east of the Mediterranean Sea and Turkey. Each chapter follows a specific format, starting with an introductory essay on the political party system within a particular country. Information is then given for both contemporary and defunct political parties. Short but reputable bibliographies are attached to the entries. Most works are in English. One appendix includes a chronology of the region's notable political events arranged by a country's last 100 years. Another appendix is a genealogy of the political parties, showing how their respective names have changed over time and who has risen to lead that party. Contributors are

mostly scholars from the United States and the Middle East.

7-140. Dixson, D. S. Sung, ed. *Republic of China: A Reference Book.* New York: Highlight International New York, 1988. 582 pp.

This is a compendium of information on the Republic of China (ROC). The country's major events are listed in a way that touches upon the economics, politics, current events, and public policies of the Taiwan government. The work is heavily illustrated and tilts toward the official government line. The guide offers much information about the country, including the powers of the government and its branches; the relationship between the central and local governments; the various political parties, including the opposition; data on economic and industrial development, transportation, science, and technology issues; and a chronology of major events from 1911 through June 1986. The work concludes with a Who's Who in the ROC and the ROC Constitution.

7-141. *Southeast Asian Affairs.* Singapore: Institute of Southeast Asian Studies, 1974–. ISSN: 0377-5437.

This highly irregularly published serial covers a wide range of both domestic and political issues from the regional perspective that includes Southeastern Asia as a whole in essay format in Chapters 1 through 4. Following this is a country-by-country survey of the small and larger polities that make up Southeast Asia. Economic and political events in China appear to be getting greater and greater coverage in this publication. Events across the Southeast Asian landscape affected by international conflicts and cooperative efforts, economic growth and development, diplomatic initiatives, and more all vie for space in this serial publication. Articles are all signed and of relatively high quality for this type of publication, which can often take on the feel of a vehicle for official cheerleading. The last issue seen by the author was for 2004.

7-142. *Territories of the Russian Federation 2003.* 4th ed. London: Europa, 1999–. 305 pp. Indexes. ISBN: 1-857-43191-X.

In the latest edition examined, the federal components of modern-day Russia were presented along with various other insights into this part of the world. Russia is still emerging as a federal state and this work homes in on the continuously evolving balance of power relationship developing between what is now the center and the eighty-nine or so constituent territories within Russia. The work is divided up into four parts. Part 1 is an introduction providing the overall perspective of regional politics and a look at the Russian territories within the context of the national economy. There is also a chronology of Russian history and politics along with some economic data. Part 2 is the heart of this enterprise and consists of individual chapters on each of the eighty-nine federal units. This section offers the land's geography and historical background, current political out-

look, economic factors, and maps. Parts 3 and 4 consist of a select bibliography of books and the indexes. One of the indexes gives an alphabetical listing of terms including relevant historical and/or alternative spellings. (Note: This description is based on an examination of the fourth edition, the last seen.)

7-143. Benvenisti, Meron. *The West Bank Handbook: A Political Lexicon.* Boulder, CO: Westview Press, 1986. 228 pp. ISBN: 0-813-30473-3.

This is a glossary of social, economic, legal, cultural, and political topics pertaining to one of the world's intractable hot spots, the West Bank. It is a translation of a Hebrew/Arabic edition, and it is aimed largely at the people actually living in this region. Typical entries include "Camp David Accords," "Community Settlement," "Refugee Camps," and "Rejection Front." There are various line-drawing maps, many of which are tied to the growth of the Israeli settlements. This handbook represents an honest attempt to get beyond political eyeglasses that color much of the way both the Israelis and the Arabs perceive and interpret things in that part of the world.

Europe
Annuals and Yearbooks
7-144. *Britain.* Annual. London: Stationery Office, 1949/1950–. Index. ISSN: 0068-1075.

Since 1997, this annual publication has been issued by the Office for National Statistics and covers England, Scotland, Wales, and Northern Ireland. It is intended to present snapshot views of the government, health system, education system, transportation, social and cultural events, and the many economic figures that go into what makes Britain a country today. This official work contains a raft of maps, interesting statistics, charts, color photographs, and much more. The pages of this work seem to portray issues and events through the spectrum of rose-colored lenses. There is one appendix and an index. 💻

7-145. *Dod's Parliamentary Companion.* Hailsham, UK: Dod's Parliamentary Companion Ltd., 1832–. Index. ISSN: 0070-7007.

This is quite similar to Dod's sister publication, *Dod's Scotland, Wales and Northern Ireland Companion (2003)* [entry 7-175], and serves pretty much the same function. All members of the United Kingdom's House of Commons and Lords are listed in short directory-type fashion including thumbnail black-and-white snapshots. There are also lists of executive agencies, British embassies, high commissioners, and others. There is an index.

Directories
7-146. Mercer, Paul. *Directory of British Political Organisations.* 3rd ed. London: Politico's, 2001. 464 pp. ISBN: 1-902-30186-2.

This directory serves as an introduction to the many British political organizations or the organizations associated in some manner with British politicians. The goal was to identify as many of these types of British organizations as possible. Entries are designed to answer a number of questions regarding what the organization does, its beliefs, which people run it, what publications it puts out, the size of membership, where is it located, and when and how it was founded. A shift over time is seen from the heyday of British political parties to the modern rise of more single-issue pressure groups. Altogether, approximately 3,000 organizations are listed. These organizations are broken down into a number of broad categories as an appendix to the work. Terms such as those on animal rights, consumer, foreign, and youth make up these categories to locate groups of common interest, if not common philosophical approach.

Bibliographies
7-147. *The American Bibliography of Slavic and East European Studies.* Annual. Stanford, CA: American Association for the Advancement of Slavic Studies, 1956–. Indexes. ISSN: 0094-3770.

This annual publication attempts to list all English-language materials published in either the United States or Canada in the social sciences or humanities related to Eastern Europe and the former USSR. A small number of foreign-language materials published in the United States or Canada have found their way into the bibliography's pages. Works about Communism in general not directly linked to one or more of the Eastern European or former Soviet states are excluded. Newspaper articles, translation journals, nonprint media sources, videos, and computer software have also been eliminated. The core of the work is made up of nineteen chapters, most of which have geographical subdivisions. Entries are placed within context of these chapters. Approximately 35 percent of these chapters are devoted to the politics, government, and economics of the region. Entries are unannotated, except that some entries have a one sentence or phrase-long note along with them. There is an especially large chapter on reviews of relevant books. There are three separate indexes: author, subject, and title. (Note: The latest edition seen was for 1993, and this included 6,260 entries.) 💻

7-148. *Bibliographic Guide to Soviet and East European Studies.* Boston: G. K. Hall, 1978–. ISSN: 0162-5322.

This dictionary catalog is culled from the holdings of the research libraries of the New York Public Library (NYPL) and the Library of Congress. All entries are interfiled in one alphabetical sequence, typical of dictionary catalog formats. Entries include titles published in the Soviet Union or in Eastern Europe, in the Russian, Latvian, Bulgarian, Polish, and other languages. All entries must have as their topic some aspect of the former Soviet Union or Eastern Europe. This publication serves as an annual supplement to the *Dictionary Catalog of the Slavonic Division* at NYPL's research libraries. This is a superb source with complete bibliographic data and should prove excellent for political scientists and those in other disciplines with an interest in this dynamic region.

7-149. Narkiewicz, Olga A. *Eurocommunism, 1968–1986: A Select Bibliography.* New York: Mansell, 1987. 188 pp. ISBN: 0-720-11801-8.

This bibliography covers the period 1968 through 1986 when the interest in Euro-Communist leaders and parties was quite high. The introduction is a good essay examining the East European Communist parties and determining if the impact of Euro-Communism was making inroads into their political styles or policies. This bibliography is a selective listing of books, symposia, major newspaper stories, and journal articles. While most bibliographic items are in the English language, there was some effort to include French, German, and Spanish works. An editorial decision was made to inject this bibliography with a number of varying viewpoints on the essence of Euro-Communism. There are two main parts; each one is format driven. About 40 percent of the entries are annotated. This bibliography appears to be especially well designed to find materials on the individual Euro-Communist parties. The use of neither a subject index nor cross-references could be a potential problem depending on use.

Dictionaries

7-150. Stevenson, John, ed. *The Columbia Dictionary of European Political History since 1914.* New York: Columbia University Press, 1992. 437 pp. ISBN: 0-231-07880-3. (Original title: *Dictionary of British and European History since 1914.*)

This alphabetically arranged dictionary

lists the people, events, political groups, and topics that center on British and European political history since 1914. It is intended to be selective in scope and inclusion. Some American figures with particularly close ties to British or continental European history, such as Dwight D. Eisenhower and John Foster Dulles, are included. The entries are quite concise with appropriate cross-references. Some entries have short reading lists; others do not. This source is best for ready-reference facts, dates, contexts, and quickly accessible biographical information.

7-151. Aplin, Richard. *A Dictionary of Contemporary France.* 2nd ed. Chicago: Fitzroy Dearborn Publishers, 1999. 488 pp. ISBN: 1-579-58115-3.

See entry 7-153.

7-152. Carrington-Windo, Tristam. *A Dictionary of Contemporary Germany.* Chicago: Fitzroy Dearborn Publishers, 1996. 456 pp. ISBN: 1-579-58114-5.

See entry 7-153.

7-153. Triuscott, Sandra. *A Dictionary of Contemporary Spain.* Chicago: Fitzroy Dearborn Publishers, 1998. 301 pp. ISBN: 1-579-58113-7.

Each of these three books [entries 7-151, 7-152, and 7-153] is very similar to one another in content and organization even though each covers a different European nation. Only the book on Germany is reviewed, but with the exception of purely German topics, everything else can be said for the works on France and Spain. There are over 2,000 entries in alphabetical order providing definitions of terms and abbreviations generally encountered in any research conducted using the modern German media. Information on the institutions and people who make up contemporary German society and politics is included. Particular attention has been devoted to terms pertaining to the national and local governments and educational system. There is a special emphasis here on highlighting the regional differences that weave through all aspects of public life and cultural fabric of the nation. The guiding principal for inclusion is "usefulness." East German concepts have been omitted. Individuals listed must have been alive as of publication. The main entries are arranged by German-language term accompanied by an English-language definition of one to several paragraphs. Representative entries are *"die Gruenen," "die Zeit,"* and *"Bundespraesident."* There are no cross-references for these or any terms, and there is no index, a real problem in efficacious usage of this work.

7-154. Urwin, Derek W. *Dictionary of European History and Politics, 1945–1995.* New York: Longman, 1996. 423 pp. ISBN: 0-582-25874-X.

This is a straightforward dictionary of historical terms related to major events in European history and politics from 1945 through 1995. Entries tend to fall into one of four categories: events and issues, territories, national and international organizations, and biographies. The author states in his introduction that there is a definite bias for inclusion of those entries that pertain to the larger European states. Armenia, Azerbaijan, and Georgia were included as part of the breakup of the former Soviet Union. Overall, the author was highly selective in deciding which terms to include in this dictionary. Definitions are on the succinct side and are heavily cross referenced. The page format and general page layout can be somewhat distracting. The lack of an index could hinder some people's effective use of this work.

7-155. Pribylovskii, Vladimir. *Dictionary of Political Parties and Organizations in Russia.* Moscow: Postfactum/Interlegal; Washington, DC: Center for Strategic and International Studies, 1992. 129 pp. Index. ISBN: 0-892-06180-4.

This work was published just after the collapse of the Communist system in the Soviet Union. It lists about 120 political parties and movements that have come into existence since 1987. Information contained in this work was gathered either directly from the listed political groups themselves or was gleaned from articles appearing in the Russian press. Each alphabetically arranged main entry contains the following data: contacts, address, telephone number, founding date, and size of membership. It also includes very short biographical sketches of the leaders of these groups. An index is provided.

7-156. Jackson, George, ed. *Dictionary of the Russian Revolution.* New York:

Greenwood Press, 1989. 704 pp. ISBN: 0-313-21131-0.

This is an ambitious work by the editor, whose stated goal is to publish in one English-language reference work all the major institutions, people, and movements that were associated in any way with the Russian Revolution of 1917–1921. These well-written entries contain up to a maximum of 2,500 words and cover such topics as social classes in Russia, social problems and issues, workers, agrarian issues, members of minority groups, religious overviews, and more. Each entry is signed by one of over 100 contributors, mostly international academics. Surprisingly, none of the contributors are scholars living in the former USSR. There is a short bibliography at the end of the relatively longer entries. A chronology of events pertaining to the Russian Revolution makes up one of the appendixes. Several maps are printed, including one of the Brest-Litovsk Settlement. Also, there is the result of the 1897 census of the Russian Empire and a later 1926 census of the Soviet Union for comparative purposes. This reference work is superb for undergraduate students.

7-157. Townley, Edward. *Dictionary of Twentieth-Century European History.* Chicago: Fitzroy Dearborn Publishers, 1999. 283 pp. ISBN: 1-579-58127-7.

Despite the title, this dictionary is fairly evenly divided between entries related to history and entries related to politics. Every entry begins with a relatively short definition and then proceeds to provide greater amounts of information depending on the overall historical importance of the entry. Entries range from "Slobodan Milosevic" to "Janos Kadar," "Gdansk," and the "Spanish Civil War." The cross-references embedded in the text are not as numerous as would be desired, but they are quite helpful when present in leading the reader to other pertinent information or topics. The great majority of entries are on the pithy side, perhaps a couple of sentences at the most. Some maps and tables are dispersed throughout and do not make up a significant portion of the work. This work is best for budding historians or political scientists and especially general readers.

7-158. Rossi, Ernest E. *The European Political Dictionary.* Santa Barbara, CA: ABC-CLIO, 1985. 408 pp. Index. ISBN: 0-874-36046-3.

This dictionary, like all the others in the ABC-CLIO Dictionaries in Political Science series, follows a standardized format throughout. Chapters are clustered around the major European nations, with each entry consisting of two paragraphs. The first paragraph contains a definition plus additional information, and the second one provides the term's "Significance" by placing the topic into some sort of historical and political perspective. Overall coverage begins mostly with the post–World War II era, extending to the early 1980s. This work could stand an update given the dramatic changes in and around Europe over

nearly the last two decades. The articles are well done, however, and there is an adequate index.

7-159. Wilson, Andrew. *Russia and the Commonwealth A to Z.* New York: Harper Perennial, 1992. 258 pp. ISBN: 0-062-71551-8.

This dictionary has roughly 1,000 entries ranging in length from one sentence to a long paragraph. Main entries explore individuals, organizations, or various terms. A team of journalists visiting the area was mainly responsible for deciding which terms to include in this dictionary. Both individuals and/or organizations must have been regarded as an essential component of current historical events. Terms must have proven significant or widely in use in the not-so-distant past, and they must have been deemed likely to be used again in the immediate future. There is a clear streak of irreverence running through many of the entries. A sample of some of the many political terms included here are "Politburo," "Perestroika," and "Komsomol." All terms appearing in the main body of the work are arranged under thematic concepts such as "Agriculture," "Armed Forces," "Political Life," "Parties and Movements," and the like.

Encyclopedias

7-160. Brown, Archie, ed. *The Cambridge Encyclopedia of Russia and the Former Soviet Union.* 2nd ed. New York: Cambridge University Press, 1994. 604 pp. ISBN: 0-522-35593-1.

This Cambridge University Press product focuses in on Russia and is much more heavily illustrated than the previous 1982 edition. While this encyclopedia is of a general nature, there are a number of chapters of interest to political science students and general audiences, such as "Politics," "Economy," "Society," "Military Power," and "International Relations." These chapters make up roughly one-fourth of the entire book. Because so many former Soviet sources of information that were formerly off limits to Westerners have been opened up to the scholarly community, there are a number of reinterpretations and reevaluations of the Soviet years and rule. New maps reflect the post-USSR names. There are short reading lists, which are adequate for the nonspecialist, appended to each entry. This work is a nice introduction to Russian and Soviet life for high-school and undergraduate students, and the general public.

7-161. Altschiller, Donald. *The Conflict in Northern Ireland: An Encyclopedia.* Santa Barbara, CA: ABC-CLIO, 1999. 730 pp. ISBN: 0-874-3693-7.

The work is divided into eight chapters, each containing an alphabetical listing of bombing incidents, Unionists, various organizations, Catholic groups and individuals, political parties, instances of foreign involvement, and the like. The chapter entitled "Dictionary of Northern Ireland Politics" takes up almost 50 percent of the entire book. Other chapters include a 1921–1999 chronology of events and discussions of election results, systems of government, and more. The section on election results is detailed enough for the average student needing this data. The statistics chapter offers the number of shootings, explosions, devices defused, injuries by affiliation, deaths, and houses searched by the British army, as well as information on the value of stolen property, and so on. The entries are uniformly well written and informative and tend to range in length between several sentences and three or four pages.

7-162. Frucht, Richard, ed. *Encyclopedia of Eastern Europe: From the Congress of Vienna to the Fall of Communism.* New York: Garland, 2000. 958 pp. Index. ISBN: 0-815-30092-1.

While most may categorize this work as history, a number of the entries are indeed political terms, politicians, government and political party leaders, and more. The longer survey articles on each of the individual Eastern European nations are especially informative pieces. All entries are signed and written by a stable of international scholars, many of whom live in the United States or Eastern Europe today. Short further-reading lists are attached to virtually every entry, no matter how short. The clean, basic writing style will appeal well to the general reader as well as a researcher hunting for some background dates or facts. There are a number of "see also" references at the end of all the articles. There is a section on historical maps and an index.

7-163. Zemstov, Ilya. *Encyclopedia of Soviet Life.* New Brunswick, NJ: Transaction Publishers, 1991. 376 pp. ISBN: 0-887-38350-5.

This book was written just before the demise of the Soviet state and the Communist Party's grip on power. Zemstov, an author of several other books on the Soviet political system, has put together this work to help define the terms given the political, economic, and social upheaval in the last days of the USSR. This political dictionary of Soviet life is conceived of as a "lexicon of glasnost," and it strives to measure the impact of this transitional era on the Russian language. A total reconceptualization is needed in order to examine Soviet life in the post-USSR era. The introduction is a good gateway into the world of Soviet politics and language. Entries are all in English, although the Russian-language version of the term is also supplied. Some of the terminology gets a bit bogged down in detail, but overall the general tenor reflects well the subtleties and changes of meaning of terms during the Soviet Empire's final days. There are no biographies included in this particular work.

7-164. White, Stephen, ed. *Political and Economic Encyclopaedia of the Soviet Union and Eastern Europe.* Harlow, Essex, UK: Longman Current Affairs, 1990. 328 pp. Index. ISBN: 0-582-06036-2.

This work was written during the transitional period from Communist rule to experimentations with more democratic methods of popular government that occurred in those heady days of optimism. Most main entries tend to be individual countries, ruling political parties, politicians and government leaders, geographic entities, and an array of broad subjects, such as those on energy, environmental protection, Soviet relations with the West, and Stalinism. Entries are in standard alphabetical order and are all signed. A number of cross-references are embedded within the articles. This is a good place to seek out facts, dates, and other useful information. There are some scattered charts and statistical tables, all of marginal value. The abbreviated index is of minimal help in using this resource effectively.

7-165. Nicholson, Frances, ed. *Political and Economic Encyclopaedia of Western Europe.* Harlow, Essex, UK: Longman, 1990. 411 pp. Index. ISBN: 1-558-62072-9.

This is primarily an encyclopedia of contemporary European politics. It endeavors to explain terms and concepts central to the European debate, the European economic space, the common European home, and how the Single European Act fits into the process of establishing a unified economic market by 1992. The area coverage includes Lappland to Cyprus but excludes East Germany, all former Soviet bloc nations, Yugoslavia, and Turkey. There are articles on political parties in national parliaments, trade unions, employer federations, and major economic institutions. The key political issues facing individual nation-states have individual entries, as do all of the biographical entries of the leading politicians. Other main entries fall into the categories of political philosophies ("Gaullism") or topical issues ("AIDS," "Global Warming"). The bulk of the contributors are European specialists and writers. All entries are signed. The country entries are by far the longest and most detailed. Cross-referencing within the articles is heavily used. There are maps and highly selective election returns. An index is available. (Note: A 2003 edition has been published by Europa as *Political and Economic Dictionary of Western Europe* but was unseen.)

Guides and Handbooks

7-166. Seymore, Bruce, ed. *The Access Guide to Ethnic Conflicts in Europe and the Former Soviet Union.* Washington, DC: Access, 1994. 171 pp. Index. ISBN: 1-878-59708-6.

This publication profiles fifteen of the new nations that were carved out of the former Soviet Empire and discusses the various political, military, religious, and economic issues that confront these countries and the world community at large. This work was specifically designed to aid students and researchers searching for information on the religious and ethnic fault lines within the former USSR. It was selective in determining which countries were included for examination. The book is divided into three parts, of which the second part constitutes the main body of the work. Part 1 is an essay on nationalism and ethnic conflict authored by Paul Goble, then senior associate at the Carnegie Endowment for International Peace. Part 2 presents the reader with a look at the various ethnic conflict points in Europe and the former Yugoslavia and Soviet Union. Transnational conflicts, such as anti-Semitism, xenophobia, gypsies, and the like are also included. Each entry receives uniform treatment and is arranged by "Participants," "Location," "Populations," "Goals," "Leadership," "History," "Current Status," and "Chronology." Part 3 is simply a directory of relevant organizations. The book is indexed.

7-167. Waller, Robert. *The Almanac of British Politics.* 7th ed. London: Routledge, 2002. 929 pp. ISBN: 0-415-26833-8.

This book strives to describe the political geography and election anatomy of the United Kingdom. The analysis is based on individual constituency profiles with certain assessments being made on the voting results. Variables examined are economic and social characteristics, local and national political issues, and various regional factors. Biographies of members of Parliament (MPs) are provided. There are numerous tables of data regarding the districts and percentage of seats, and socioeconomic information about each election district. Other information gives the religious, economic, social, and political history of every election district. The profiles of the individual MPs are both informative and surprisingly amusing. Basic black-and-white maps outline individual election districts. There is an index listing MPs only. The *Atlas of British Politics* [entry 7-198] is a companion volume for this work.

7-168. Cossolotto, Matthew. *Almanac of European Politics, 1995.* Washington, DC: Congressional Quarterly, 1995. 321 pp. ISBN: 0-871-87914-X.

This handbook covers the nineteen European democracies with populations of at least one million people. It omits all of the Eastern European countries. Each chapter is arranged in a similar manner, beginning with a country profile that gives information on the capital, language, religion, and international memberships of each democracy. Following this is a complete look at all the major and minor political parties operating in that country and how the election processes work and the results of the previous election voting results. This work is best for high-school and lower-division undergraduate students since treatment is fairly superficial.

7-169. Hassan, Gary. *Almanac of Scottish Politics.* London: Politico's, 2001. 452 pp. ISBN: 1-902-30153-6.

This publication is somewhat similar to the Dod's series for England, Scotland, Wales, and Northern Ireland [entry 7-175]. This publication uses sixteen sections to divide the main body into constituency surveys, voting results, opinion-polling results, chronologies, local elections, and more.

7-170. Rallings, Colin, comp. and ed. *Britain Votes 6: British Parliamentary Election Results, 1997.* Brookfield, VT: Ashgate Publications, 1998. 229 pp. ISBN: 1-840-14054-2.

Number 6 in this ongoing series gives comprehensive British parliamentary electoral results from the 1997 election, which changed the face of British politics on a grand scale by ushering in a Labour government and racking up a huge majority of Members of Parliament (MPs). The work serves as an "interim supplement" to the British Parliamentary Election Results series. It includes results from all 659 constituencies. Each entry gets a standard format and provides voter turnout by candidate and party affiliation, percentages of votes, 1992 results, and more. A number of supplemental statistical tables are given, such as "Seats Changing Hands," "Highest Conservative Share of Vote," "Labour Change of Vote Share 1992/97," and so forth. There is no narrative text or analysis of election results.

7-171. Norris, Pippa, ed. *Britain Votes 2001.* Oxford: Oxford University Press in association with Hansard Society Series in Politics and Government, 2001. 276 pp. ISBN: 0-198-51049-7.

The main body of this handbook is divided equally between sections on "The Campaign" and those on "The Analysis of the Results" of the millennial election within the confines of the United Kingdom. There are also several more general articles on the voting results. Some statistical tables are included within the articles. The articles touch upon polling results, voter perceptions, how the major political parties (the Tories and Labour) are reacting to these polls and results, and so forth. Articles also include information on voter turnout, the election's potential effect on the British economy, the impact of and on Northern Ireland and Scotland, and much more. The overall tone is decidedly scholarly, and statistical data is clearly of secondary importance in this work. This work should not be confused with the ongoing Britain Votes series, which tends to place elections under the eyes of those more interested in conducting statistical analysis.

7-172. Rallings, Colin. *British Electoral Facts, 1832–1999.* 5th ed. Aldershot, Hants., UK; Brookfield, VT: Ashgate, 2000. 313 pp. ISBN: 1-840-14053-4.

This work began publication in 1968. The fifth edition employs some new tables and appendixes not appearing in the previous four editions. The single goal is to provide a reference compendium of British election facts and statistics all in one physical volume. These facts are related solely to the national election results and not to the regional or local ones. These national election results are given for the countries that comprise the United Kingdom for all general elections from 1832 through 1999. There are numerous tables of data that give voter turnout, expenditures, analysis of major political party election returns, public-opinion poll results, members of Parliament who are women, and more.

7-173. Crewe, Ivor. *The British Electorate 1963–1992: A Compendium of Data from the British Election Studies.* rev. ed. New

York: Cambridge University Press, 1995. 501 pp. ISBN: 0-521-49646-2.

This book includes the results of the 1992 British Election Study. One can use it to look up votes or political party distribution. There is neither analysis nor attempts at interpretation. Each table presents British election results in a standardized format for virtually every social, economic, or demographic variable imaginable. The tables are usually presented as a time series for comparative purposes. Political indications through polling on certain issues are also in tabular format. The lack of an index may slow some users down a bit in tracking needed data or information.

7-174. King, Anthony, ed. *British Political Opinion, 1937–2000: The Gallup Polls.* London: Politico's, 2001. 367 pp. Index. ISBN: 1-902-30188-9.

The Gallup Poll for Great Britain first appeared in a 1937 issue of *Cavalcade.* In this volume, there are a total of seventeen chapters that include such headings as: "Voting Intentions," "Political Parties," "Prime Ministers," the "Monarchy and Royal Family," and more. These polls are invaluable in tracking British public opinion on a wide range of social issues, news events, political and economic developments, religious beliefs, family size, and even international travel. An especially large part of this work is taken up with Gallup's measuring voter sentiment and intentions relating to the performance of the prime minister in office during the survey. There appears to be a fairly good track record in predicting many future British elections. Most of the opinion polls have been conducted on a monthly basis and include the original questions. There is a brief index available.

7-175. *Dod's Scotland, Wales and Northern Ireland Companion (2003).* London: Dod, 2003. 677 pp. Index. ISBN: 0-905-70241-7.

This relatively recent publication covers the institutions of and personalities who work in the Scottish Parliament, the National Assembly for Wales, or the Northern Ireland Assembly. There is an individual chapter devoted to each of these three special institutions. Each chapter begins with an essay on that nation's parliamentary history, political parties, and political history in general. All the members of these three governing bodies are listed in straight alphabetical order complete with a small black-and-white photo and areas of the person's particular legislative interests. Also listed are the members of the cabinets, ministers, and legislative committees. Each of the election constituencies are profiled along with their respective electoral histories and voting patterns. There is an index.

7-176. Caratani, Danele. *Elections in Western Europe since 1815: Electoral Results by Constituencies.* London: Macmillan Reference, 2000. 1090 pp. ISBN: 0-333-77111-7.

This compendium is the first in a whole series of volumes about election results. It is a collection of voting tabulations to the lower houses of eighteen European

countries beginning in the year 1815 and ending with the most recent election at time of publication. A companion CD-ROM should be used to access the most comprehensive data collected for this project. Election results data are used to track the evolution of each country's electoral system, road to democratization, equalization of voting conditions, as well as relative successes or failures of the competing political parties and the voting changes in various political constituencies. The main body of the book is arranged in three parts. Part 1 is "Election Law Mechanics," Part 2 is "Country Chapters," and the third part is made up of several appendixes. 💻

7-177. Barberis, Peter. *Encyclopedia of British and Irish Political Organizations: Parties, Groups, and Movements of the Twentieth Century.* New York: Pinter, 2000. 562 pp. Indexes. ISBN: 1-855-67264-2.

This encyclopedic handbook was compiled to provide swift and relatively easy access to all the political organizations and movements that were considered to be significant in Britain and Ireland during the period from 1900 through 2000. The work is intended for use by students, researchers, general readers, and the practitioners of politics. Over 2,500 political organizations are listed, and they are arranged over the entire gamut of the political spectrum. The author warns readers not to confuse this work with an encyclopedia of pressure groups. Local, international, and statutory groups are excluded from coverage. The book is divided into twenty different sections. Seven of these sections are on the major political parties and contain an introductory essay on the topic and a chronology of select events from 1900 through 1998. Most entries offer the organization's name, dates active, journals published, and a short history of its leaders and political life. Other chapters are on the "Far Right," "Wales," "Labour Party," "Europe," and so forth. There is a substantive thirty-five-page bibliography of books and articles. A scholarly tone pervades this work's pages. There is an index by name and one by parties, groups, and movements.

7-178. Bogajski, Janusz. *Ethnic Politics in Eastern Europe: A Guide to Nationality Policies, Organizations, and Parties.* Armonk, NY: M. E. Sharpe, 1994. 493 pp. Index. ISBN: 1-563-24282-6.

This is a guidebook to the more recently formed politically oriented ethnic and nationalistic groups that have become most prominent in the Eastern European nations since the fall of the Communist regimes throughout the area. Each entry examines the official government policy with respect to the numerous ethnic groups that dot the region. Also, the book recounts the origins, leadership, makeup, action programs, and the effects of these ethnic and nationalistic organizations on both a country's domestic and foreign policies. About 50 percent of the book is taken up with countries associated with the union that formerly made up the country of Yugoslavia. The other countries analyzed

here are Albania, the Czech Republic, Slovakia, Poland, and Hungary. All Soviet republics lie outside the scope of this work. An index has been put together.

7-179. Cook, Chris. *European Political Facts of the Twentieth Century.* 5th ed. New York: Palgrave, 2001. 481 pp. Index. ISBN: 0-333-79203-3. (Revised edition of *European Political Facts, 1900–1996.*)

This handbook examines Europe in its broadest context from the Atlantic to the Ural Mountains. The fifth edition includes the breakup of the Soviet Union and the Eastern bloc. The starting date of European political facts has been pushed back to 1900 from the third edition's 1916. There is little major change in the overall organization of the main body of the book, however, and there are still ten primary chapters. They cover the "Heads of State," "Parliaments," "Elections," "Justice," "Political Parties," and more. While much of this handbook's directory listings are now strictly of historical interest, the tables on election results can be used to analyze trends or shifts in political sentiment over time. These election results appear in an especially long chapter. There is an index. 💻

7-180. Newton, Kenneth. *Handbook of Central and East European Political Science.* Essex, UK: European Consortium for Political Research, University of Essex, 1994. 145 pp. Index. ISBN: N/A.

This book was designed and written to meet the growing demand about the field of political science for those political scientists who find themselves in the Central and Eastern European area today. It is hoped to have value for Western scholars as well. It is to be regarded as a companion volume to *Political Science in Europe,* which covers Western Europe. The definition of Central and Eastern Europe is relatively broad, including such countries as the Ukraine, Estonia, and Kyrgyzstan. The term "political science" is also defined with the widest latitude. Public and private research organizations are included. The main body is arranged by country and is then followed by national-level institutions, minority departments, centers, and institutes. After this, the private organizations are listed. Within each entry, there is the name and directory-type information for the institute or organization, including contact person, publications issued, a brief description of the group, and research interests of members. There is an index to names/institutions that looks like it was hastily put together.

7-181. Webb, Adran. *The Longman Companion to Germany since 1945.* New York: Longman, 1998. 335 pp. Index. ISBN: 0-582-30736-8.

The information in this handbook ranges from Adolf Hitler's death in 1945 until mid-1998, the date of publication. Included is a half century of politics and history culminating in the unification of East Germany with West Germany to form a single German republic. This work includes events, individuals, and politics in both Germanys before the unification period. Postunification poli-

tics are also included, and these highlight some of the past and ongoing problems that must be faced by political leaders from the eastern and western parts of Germany. Some of the topics included are those on election results, immigration statistics, economic data, officeholders, and the like. A short bibliographic essay concludes the work. An index is available.

7-182. Karatnycky, Adrian, ed. *Nations in Transit, 2002: Civil Society, Democracy and Markets in East Central Europe and the Newly Independent States.* New Brunswick, NJ: Transaction Publishers, 2002. 445 pp. ISBN: 0-765-80976-1.

This work is a byproduct of a 1995 study commissioned by the United States Agency for International Development's (AID) Bureau for Europe and the New Independent States (NIS). The book was published in association with Freedom House, which is a conservatively oriented think tank that has tracked the notion of freedom around the globe for years. It examines the fundamental trends in politics, administration, media, civil society, and economic change in Eastern and Central Europe as well as in a number of nations linked to the former Soviet Union. The ultimate goal of this study is to establish some correlation between democratization and the unfolding economic transition in this area. Much of this work was carried out using survey instruments asking forty-six questions. The main body of this work is made up of the answers to these forty-six questions by Eastern/Central Europe and NIS states in alphabetical order. The length of space devoted to answering these forty-six questions varies from country to country. Russia's section is the longest and contains the most complex set of responses. (Note: There is a change in subtitle with the 2003 edition. This was not examined by the author.)

7-183. Szajkowski, Bogdan, ed. *New Political Parties of Eastern Europe and the Soviet Union.* Harlow, Essex, UK: Longman Group, 1991. 404 pp. ISBN: 0-582-08575-6.

This book presents a comprehensive snapshot of the recent historical development and current state of the political parties that were emerging from the ashes of what had been the Soviet Union and its Eastern Europe allies. The following countries are included: Albania, Bulgaria, Czechoslovakia, Estonia, East Germany, Hungary, Latvia, Lithuania, Poland, Romania, the USSR, and finally, Yugoslavia. There is a relatively short introductory essay on the history of the political parties in this region, then statistics on levels of popular support among the various parties, election results, and a directory of the political parties themselves.

7-184. Ramsden, John, ed. *The Oxford Companion to Twentieth-Century British Politics.* New York: Oxford University Press, 2002. 714 pp. ISBN: 0-198-60134-4.

A rather wide swath of topics, ranging from economics to the military and then

sociology, has been entered here if they pertain somehow to British politics. Scotland and Wales have been treated as separate political systems, and there is some coverage of Northern Ireland. A classified contents list has been organized into a number of broad political categories and then sequenced alphabetically by an individual's name or topical entry. The actual main body of the work is primarily a standard alphabetical arrangement. Entries have ample "see" and "see also" references. Bibliographies appear at the end of longer entries only. Several appendixes include those on the dates of ministers from 1895 through 2001, major national officeholders and dates, and on general election results for 1895 through 2001 for all the larger political parties. Entries are uniformly succinct and infuse the work with a pleasant brew of English wit and humor. This work should be regarded as highly authoritative in nature. The contributors are virtually entirely from England, and each article is signed. There is no index.

7-185. Bugajski, Janus. *Political Parties of Eastern Europe: A Guide to Politics in the Post-Communist Era.* Armonk, NY: M. E. Sharpe, 2002. 1055 pp. Index. ISBN: 1-563-24674-7.

This guide offers a fairly detailed look at the recent political events unfolding in the eighteen Eastern European countries along with Montenegro and Kosovo. In the wake of the 1989 revolutions, many political analysts assumed that democracy, civil society, and more freewheeling, market-driven economies were so closely interrelated that the demise of single-party rule would herald all three of these pillars of liberal democracies. Other essential variables ended up being the legacies of Communism and the Communist Party, the social and cultural contexts in which the newly created institutions were to function, their relative effectiveness, and the new threats and challenges to democratic reform movements and government. The book provides the reader with an overview of each European country by examining its respective major political developments during the critical period of the 1990s. This includes looking at the structure of the political system, the relative strength and roles of the most important political formations, and significant issues confronting each country. The individual nations are arranged in alphabetical order and templated by "History," "Overview," "Post-Communist Developments," "Political Parties," "Political Data," and "Election Results." Entries for the individual nations total roughly forty pages each. The part on political parties is usually by far the longest section. There is an index for individual names and for political party names.

7-186. Szajkowski, Bogdan, ed. *Political Parties of Eastern Europe, Russia and the Successor States.* New York: Stockton Press, 1994. 735 pp. ISBN: 1-561-59079-7.

This guide to political parties of Eastern Europe, Russia, and the successor states has a first section arranged alphabetically by country, from Albania to Yugoslavia. Entries give the last decade's historical overview and the role of political parties, election results, percentages of seats won, news on the party leaders, coalition governments, and more. The second component of the book is its "Directory of Major Parties." This directory follows a standard format listing name, address, telephone number, date founded, leaders, membership, history, programs, and party organization. The largest chapters are on Bulgaria, Hungary, Romania, and the Russian Federation. This book argues that eight broad categories of political parties have emerged in Central Europe, Russia, and the successor states. They are dissident groups, nationalist parties, right-wing parties, issue-based parties, religious parties, reformed former Communist parties, and more traditional hard-line Communist parties.

7-187. Boothroyd, David. *Politico's Guide to the History of British Political Parties.* London: Politico's, 2001. 338 pp. ISBN: 1-902-30159-5.

This is a handy guide to approximately 250 different British political parties, listed for the most part in fairly brief alphabetical fashion. The scope of this work includes political parties operating within the United Kingdom or Northern Ireland since 1922, or from 1801 through 1922 for all of Ireland. All of the entries listed have vied for a seat in the U.K. Parliament through the electoral process. Entries provide the name of the person founding the political party, the date established, the main plank of the party, its history, and its e-mail address and Web site if still operating. Britain's major political parties (Conservative, Liberal, and Labour) tend to get the largest amount of space devoted to their respective entries. There are a number of cross-references to assist the reader in tracking parties that have merged, split off, or vanished into the sunset of history. Even some of the more humorous and tongue-in-cheek political parties are included in this handbook, such as the Official Monster Raving Loony Party.

7-188. Parry, Richard. *Scottish Political Facts.* Edinburgh: T. and T. Clark, 1988. 160 pp. ISBN: 0-567-29123-5.

The intent for publishing this work was to produce a work comparable to *British Political Facts* but for Scottish politics and government. The time frame for this work is 1832 through 1987. Found within the covers of this handbook are detailed election results for each parliamentary constituency in Scotland and its boundaries. There is also economic census data for each of these constituencies, as well as a list of all Scottish members of Parliament. All local election results from 1974 to date of publication are available.

7-189. Cook, Chris. *Sources in European Political History.* 3 vols. New York: Facts on File, 1987–1991. ISBN: 0-816-01016-1 (Vol. 1); 0-816-01756-5 (Vol. 2); 0-816-01757-3 (Vol. 3).

A total of three volumes were published in this set over a five-year span. Volume 1 was on the "European Left." Volume 2

was devoted to "Diplomacy and Imperialism," and the third volume covered "War and Resistance." Only Volume 1 was examined. It was a guide to existing personal papers written by over 1,000 people who were important in Socialist, labor, radical, or revolutionary movements somewhere in Europe. The time period for inclusion ran from 1848 through the end of World War II in 1945. Papers that were written by people belonging to the British or Irish Left have been treated elsewhere in *Sources in British Political History 1900–1951.* Leftist political activists from Eastern Europe have also been omitted from this work. The main portion of the book is an alphabetical listing by individual. The very short entries do give birth and death dates, political party affiliations, where the individual was active, and the like. The location of the personal papers is given. Volume 2 is dedicated to diplomacy and international affairs, while Volume 3 examines war and resistance.

7-190. Laird, Rod D. *A Soviet Lexicon: Important Concepts, Terms, and Phrases.* Lexington, MA: Lexington Books/D. C. Heath, 1988. 201 pp. ISBN: 0-669-16738-X.

This book was designed and written to offer a basic level of understanding of the Soviet system's terms, concepts, and phrases necessary to interpreting this former superpower's politics, economics, and social issues. The work opens with a short article on the Soviet system as a whole, including its roots, history, and modern institutions. It is in strict alphabetical dictionary format and has extremely concise one- or two-sentence definitions of most terms, events, Soviet agencies, and more. Geographical place names and Soviet personalities outside those who served on the Politburo are lacking. There are several lengthy appendixes included, such as those on "Field and Candidate Members of the Politburo: 1917–1987" and "Constitution of USSR: Rules of the CPSU."

7-191. Pockney, B. P. *Soviet Statistics since 1950.* New York: St. Martin's Press, 1991. 333 pp. ISBN: 0-312-04003-2.

There are five main sections to this statistical compendium. They are "Population and Labour," "Industry," "Energy," "Agriculture," and "Foreign Trade." Each chapter has approximately twenty to thirty tables of statistical data and figures. Some are short time series. Some sets of tabular data have brief introductions preceding them, attempting to put these figures into some type of relevant perspective. There are very few statistics available after 1985. Sources used for statistics gathering were mainly primary Soviet ones. Lacking these, Western statistical sources were consulted.

7-192. Konn, Tania, ed. *Soviet Studies Guide.* London: Bowker-Saur, 1992. 237 pp. ISBN: 0-862-91790-5.

This work is a combination of short survey articles on various aspects of the USSR. The contributors are all specialists in Soviet and/or Eastern European affairs. While many of the entries deal with culture, history, and society, at least

50 percent of the book addresses the politics and economics of the former Soviet Union. The articles themselves are highly interdisciplinary and are in fact bibliographic essays highlighting the literature that has been published on the topic. Some examples of the articles included are "Government and Politics," "International Relations," and "Armed Forces." One-sentence evaluative annotations accompany these citations. Bibliographies of works appearing at the conclusion of each survey article are mostly English-language monographs.

7-193. Schoepfin, George, ed. *The Soviet Union and Eastern Europe.* New York: Facts on File, 1985. 637 pp. Index. ISBN: 0-816-01260-1.

This handbook provides basic information on the USSR and its former Eastern European bloc allies. The introduction serves as a country-by-country analysis of all these countries, from Albania to Yugoslavia, and provides information on each nation's geography with maps, demographics, history, economy, social welfare, education, mass media, and highly selective biographical sketches. After this introduction, there are a number of tables of comparative data. The bulk of the handbook, however, consists of signed articles by European, Commonwealth, and U.K. academics giving surveys on topics ranging from "Nationalism in Eastern Europe" to "Agriculture," "Soviet Social Policies," and "Religion in the Soviet Union and Eastern Europe." Articles can reach up to twenty pages in length and can have substantial reading lists attached. This is a good reference tool for doing "before" and "after" research on the fall of Communism in Europe. There is a good multipurpose index.

7-194. Butler, David. *Twentieth-Century British Political Facts, 1900–2000.* 8th ed. New York: St. Martin's Press, 2000. 584 pp. Index. ISBN: 0-312-22947-X. (Superseded *British Political Facts . . .* with the 8th ed.)

This handbook has twenty-two chapters of facts arranged in a number of different categories, such as political parties, the economy, international relations, royalty, the armed forces, and local government. Each of these main headings is broken down further into another five to ten subdivisions. This is the place to look if one is seeking listings of names, dates, election results, social security laws, revenues, newspapers, and much more for Great Britain, including Northern Ireland. Internet addresses for a number of British governmental units, political parties, Parliament, and newspapers are found within these pages. It is not intended to be comprehensive, but it covers a lot of ground. It should be useful for students, journalists, and others needing a good, basic, centralized compilation of British and Northern Ireland political facts and figures for the last century. An index is included.

7-195. Jacobs, Francis, ed. *Western European Political Parties: A Comprehensive Guide.* Harlow, Essex, UK: Longman, 1989. 730 pp. ISBN: 0-582-00113-7.

This handbook on the political parties of Western Europe covers a broad spectrum of political and social views. There are three parts, all arranged in a similar pattern. Part 1 is for the European Community (EC) nations, Part 2 is for the non-EC countries, and Part 3 is for various selective Western European political groupings, which include party groups within the European Parliament, such as the Nordic Council and Council of Europe. For each Western European country, there is a brief introduction about the nation, its politics, political history, and political system. Election results back to 1945 are given. The individual political parties are described in some detail, with the emphasis being on parties that are currently active in a national parliament. There is a clear attempt made here to give relatively greater treatment to the smaller countries or to the regional or green political parties. The political parties are lumped together under appropriate political leanings, like liberal, regional, or far left. The text throughout this work is quite well done and highly informative. It is an excellent political snapshot of the time period.

7-196. Drost, Harry. *What's What and Who's Who in Europe.* New York: Simon and Schuster, 1995. 646 pp. ISBN: 0-139-55030-5.

This is a handbook on the leaders and current affairs of Europe. The definition of Europe for this book includes the Baltic States but not the Commonwealth of Independent States (CIS). The general reader and nonspecialist will find this work a treasure trove for biographies, facts, dates, organizations, economic indicators, and more related to European interests. The main body is arranged in one alphabetical sequence. Most entries fall within the category of political science terms, such as political parties, politicos, constitutions, countries, intergovernmental organizations (IGOs), and so forth. This work is quite good for discovering statistics and factual data, but finding them in nontabular formats can be challenging at times. France, Germany, Italy, and the United Kingdom each receive a relatively large amount of space. Entries are loaded with cross-references.

7-197. Shaw, Warren. *The World Almanac of the Soviet Union: From 1905 to the Present.* New York: World Almanac, 1990. 360 pp. ISBN: 0-886-87565-X.

Put out by the publishers of the familiar *World Almanac,* this publication is a survey of events, individuals, and chronology of the Soviet Union written for a general audience. The topical section contains entries that vary significantly in size. The article under "Agriculture" is one of the longer entries, while other entries, such as "Komsomol" and "Détente," receive much shorter treatment, but could have benefited from greater historical context and political dimension. The main body of the work is alphabetical. Other entries are short, one-sentence, with minimal information. The section on biographies gives one-paragraph capsule comments on people inside and outside of the political arena.

The chronological section starts with 1905 and concludes with June 1990. This work is best for high-school students, lower-division undergraduates, and the general public.

Atlases

7-198. *Atlas of British Politics.* Dover, NH: Longwood, 1985. 205 pp. ISBN: 0-709-93608-7.

Not seen.

7-199. Henig, Simon. *The Political Map of Britain.* London: Politico's, 2002. 1011 pp. ISBN: 1-842-75015-1.

This book was designed to provide readers with an overview of Britain's political landscape after the 2001 general election results were tabulated. It looks at the national, regional, and county units of the United Kingdom and gives the results of the previous two elections for comparative analysis and trend spotting. The coverage is for the entire United Kingdom, including Wales, Scotland, and Northern Ireland. The book itself is a compilation of statistical tables with no maps. The entries for the political units begin with voting results and then offer a short discussion of the geographical unit and the candidate and the final vote itself. There is a supplementary colored map included with several permutations of the voting results.

Central and South America
Annuals and Yearbooks
7-200. *Latin America and Caribbean Contemporary Record.* New York:

Holmes and Meier, 1983–. ISSN: 0736-9700.

This now-defunct annual publication was similar in organization and scope to the other titles in the Contemporary Record series. Part 1 is a collection of essays on key current issues in the region or on a specific country. The essays are very well written by academic writers and other experts in the field. Part 2 is a nation-by-nation survey of political events, election results, coup attempts, important legislation passed, ruling party news, and foreign affairs. Part 3 is a compilation of highly selective primary documents drawn from around South America or the Caribbean nations. Many of these documents are speeches, declarations, resolutions, and local/foreign broadcasts. The last part of this substantive reference work is the social, political, and economic data provided in the numerous tables. Figures on debt payments, population trends, trade statistics, and other information are just a partial inventory of what is included in this chapter.

7-201. Breene, Robert G., ed. *Latin American Political Yearbook.* New Brunswick, NJ: Transaction Publishers, 1998–. ISSN: 1097-4997.

The intended purpose of this annual is to provide a wide overview and review of the year's major political and economic events that transpired in Central America, South America, and the Caribbean nations. There are seven main chapters. Essays appear to be relatively subjective in nature and lack analytical balance.

This is not an authoritative work and should be used with some caution. (Note: Volume 3 for 2000 was the last year inspected.)

Bibliographies

7-202. Vanden, Harry E. *Latin American Marxism: A Bibliography.* New York: Garland, 1991. 869 pp. Index. ISBN: 0-824-09193-0.

This is a rather inclusive, if not comprehensive, bibliography on Marxist activities in Latin America from 1920 up until the late 1980s. There are over 6,300 entries in a number of languages, although English by far predominates. The book is arranged into four historic eras, each one of which corresponds to a particular epoch in the history of Marxism throughout Latin America. The overwhelming number of bibliographic entries are nonannotated. Most of the works cited were published from the mid-1940s until the date of publication, but a number of them do go back to around 1900. The arrangement is most suitable for tracking Marxist movements within a particular country or in doing some aspect of comparative analysis. There is only one index, and that one is for authors.

7-203. Dow, Hugh. *Popular Participation and Development: A Bibliography on Africa and Latin America.* Toronto: Centre for Urban and Community Studies, University of Toronto, and CERLAC, the Centre for Research on Latin America and the Caribbean, York University, 1992. 145 pp. ISBN: 0-772-71361-8.

Not seen.

Dictionaries

7-204. Gunson, Phil. *The Dictionary of Contemporary Politics of Central America and the Caribbean.* New York: Simon and Schuster, 1991. 397 pp. ISBN: 0-132-13372-5.

The lack of an introduction and a preface make it somewhat difficult to define the goal of this book or its scope. Entries, mostly ranging from several sentences up to two pages, include individuals, political parties, nations, terms, organizations, and the like. The time period covered appears to be mainly the latter half of the twentieth century. There is liberal use of "see" and "see also" references throughout the work. Many of the entries are biographical in nature. Various black-and-white maps of no particular merit are included. This work is best for high-school and undergraduate students.

7-205. Gunson, Phil. *The Dictionary of Contemporary Politics of South America.* New York: Macmillan, 1989. 314 pp. ISBN: 0-029-13145-6.

The bias of the authors here was for longer entries rather than a larger number of shorter ones. The relative length of the entry is intended to demonstrate the comparative relative importance of that particular entry. Biographies are included for political leaders, political movements and workers groups, events, treaties, and the like. The entries are heavily cross-referenced. Many of the entries are quite interesting and appear to be taken mainly from the modern era of the last fifty years or so prior to publication. The sole appendix is by country.

7-206. Russi, Ernest E. *Latin America: A Political Dictionary.* 2nd ed. Santa Barbara, CA: ABC-CLIO, 1992. 242 pp. Index. ISBN: 0-874-36608-9.

The central focus of this subject dictionary is Latin countries in the Americas and how the United States has related to these specific countries. These 284 entries arranged by eleven broad topic chapters are designed to meet the needs of undergraduate students or general researchers who do not require an exhaustive treatment of the topic. Entries within the eleven broad chapters are alphabetical. Some of the headings included are "Political Culture and Ideology," "Economic Integration," and "United States-Latin American Relations," among others. Each of the main terms are fully defined and then placed into context by noting their relative significance. There are numerous "see" and "see also" references. The index is above average in utility value.

Encyclopedias

7-207. Borderlands Encyclopedia: A Digital Educational Resource on Contemporary United States-Mexico Border Issues. 1998–. http://www.utep.edu/border.

This Web site has been put together by the University of Texas, El Paso, Office of Technical Planning and Distance Learning. It provides audio-visual access via the Internet to a wide range of borderland issues facing the United States and Mexico. A number of different full-text items have been divided into six main categories. They are "Culture and

Media," "Economics and Business," "Education and Training," "Family Life and Population Groups," "Government and Politics," and "Health and Environment." Full-text materials include newspaper articles, books, short and long journal articles, and more. A sound card will definitely augment the overall value of this Web site because of the large number of audio pieces available. The target audience appears to be high-school students as well as undergraduates, but anyone interested in seeing what the big-picture issues are regarding U.S.-Mexican borderlands studies should uncover some value in this Web site. 🖳

7-208. Kapiszewski, Diana, ed. *Encyclopedia of Latin American Politics.* Westport, CT: Oryx Press, 2002. 358 pp. Index. ISBN: 1-573-56306-4.

The intent of this encyclopedia is to dispel the myriad misconceptions that many people hold toward the politics and history of Latin America. For the purposes of this work, Latin America includes the eighteen Spanish-speaking republics, along with Portuguese-speaking Brazil and French-speaking Haiti. A chapter on Puerto Rico has also been written up for the encyclopedia. Emphasis is clearly on the last century's historical and political events. Every chapter is a country profile providing the economics, politics, social data, a brief historical overview, a listing of heads of state, and a bibliography to be used for additional reading matter. Articles all begin with a country profile that offers roughly

twenty categories of headings on such topics as that nation's legislative and judicial systems, population figures, religious makeup, ethnic groups, and the like. Peru and Mexico have the largest chapters. At the end of the bibliography, there is a good primary listing of electronic resources for foreign and international organizations, newspapers, biographies, government sites, and more. An index is available for use by the reader.

7-209. Calvert, Peter, ed. *Political and Economic Encyclopaedia of South America and the Caribbean.* Harlow, Essex, UK: Longman Group, 1991. 363 pp. Index. ISBN: 0-582-08528-4.

This Longman encyclopedia has only three types of entries. They are forty-seven individual countries, general topics, and individuals. The "Chronology for 2300 BC–1991 AD" is included as part of the general entries. It is best used to gather information on countries and their political parties. Entries on individuals vary considerably in size and quality. Salvador Allende gets a single paragraph. All entries are signed, but contributor information and affiliations are lacking. The index is inadequate.

Guides and Handbooks
7-210. Gross, Liza. *Handbook of Leftist Guerrilla Groups in Latin America and the Caribbean.* Boulder, CO: Westview Press, 1995. 165 pp. ISBN: 0-813-38494-X.

This handbook is intended to systemize the current information available on leftist guerrilla movements throughout Latin

America and the Caribbean. The organizations listed here have all taken up arms and do not employ legal means to bring about a change in a government's composition or policies. There are four established criteria for inclusion in this handbook. The group must adhere to some type of leftist ideology, have some desire to bring down the existing sociopolitical structure and replace it with some variation of a Marxist-oriented state, be fully committed to armed struggle, and act generally in a clandestine manner. The book is arranged alphabetically by country, with each leftist group enumerated within the appropriate country. Entries follow a general pattern giving the date founded and when the group was in existence, the type of Marxist orientation (such as Trotskyite or Guevarist), the regions of the country where the group was most active, the names of the leaders, a short history, and the group's major actions. Each chapter begins with a "Bibliographical Commentary," which is a one-paragraph bibliographic essay listing and commenting upon books written on the topic. A larger and more general bibliography appears at the end of the handbook. The lack of an index can present some difficulty for use. 💻

7-211. Dent, David W., ed. *Handbook of Political Science Research on Latin America: Trends from the 1960s to the 1990s.* New York: Greenwood Press, 1990. 448 pp. Indexes. ISBN: 0-313-26446-5.

Sixteen Latin American scholars, many associated with the well-known *Hand-book of Latin American Studies,* have combined to produce a set of bibliographic essays from the general to the more specific aspects of Latin American political science research. These authors note that Latin American research really blossomed during the 1960s with the Cuban Revolution and the Alliance for Progress. The basis of this handbook is a *Handbook* data file going back to 1950. This data file includes monographs, journal articles, government documents, and dissertations. The bibliographic essays assist the reader in comprehending the political and social changes in Latin America. An introductory chapter covers political science research in Latin America for both comparative politics and international relations. All of the bibliographic essays are broken down into topical subdivisions, such as agrarian issues, education, church and state, and the like. A high percentage of the works cited are in Spanish. There are several appendixes and two indexes available.

7-212. Radu, Michael. *Latin American Revolutionaries: Groups, Goals, Methods.* McLean, VA: Pergamon-Brassey's International Defense, 1990. 386 pp. Index. ISBN: 0-080-37429-8.

The main body of this handbook is organized into two related parts. Part 1 contains essays on various facets of Latin American revolutionary movements and ideology. These essays are uniformly well written and are aimed at undergraduates and informed general readers. Part 2, the main part of the book, is a catalog of terrorist and insurgent movement activities taking place in South and Central America since Castro rose to power in 1959. The eight countries that are regarded as being fairly free of leftist guerilla threats or attacks are excluded from this book. Also excluded are all of the islands dotting the Caribbean. The thirteen countries that are examined are listed alphabetically, and then in turn these countries are each subdivided by group. Main entries of individual groups have a standard arrangement, beginning with location, then continuing with origins, front organizations, membership information, leadership, ideology, propaganda, positions on violence, external support, and others. A select bibliography made up of English and non-English-language books is attached. There is a good index of adequate depth, which will assist users of this work in bringing out its full potential.

8

Public Administration and
Policy Studies Reference Sources

This lengthy chapter combines public administration and mainly domestic policy issues. Public administration is frequently, but not always, part of a political science department's offerings and deals with administrative rules and regulations, practices, performance, and individuals who are prominent in the field. Public administration also looks at public-sector administration at all government levels in the United States as well as abroad.

Policy studies look at the results of decisions made by governmental agencies and units on various economic, political, social, environmental, health, and a number of other topics within the public domain. These studies examine decisions made by elected and nonelected people in office and in academics, and by think tank analysts. These decisions could be new policies, revised ones, or exploratory studies and analyses of a particular policy matter. Policy making can involve administrators and/or committee members in its discussion and eventual implementation.

General Public Administration and Policy Studies
Literature Guides

8-1. Simpson, Anthony E. *Information-Finding and the Research Process: A Guide to Sources and Methods for Public Administration and the Policy Sciences.* Westport, CT: Greenwood Press, 1993. 491 pp. ISBN: 0-313-25251-3.

This resource guide was designed to meet the needs of researchers in the fields of social and policy sciences, especially those researchers working in areas related to public administration. It discusses a wide variety of library resources in disciplines that are linked intellectually to public administration and/or policy science studies. Law and government resources are not covered in this guide. This work begins with general chapters on research problems and strategies, proper use of print and online library catalogs, journal-literature searching, and proper use of relevant indexes, abstracts, CD-ROMs, bibliographies, and statistical sources of information. Many of the bibliographic entries are annotated. The introductory remark for each chapter drives home the need for having an orderly research strategy in place when using library or other resource materials.

8-2. McCurdy, Howard E. *Public Administration: A Bibliographic Guide to the Literature.* New York: Marcel Dekker, 1986. 311 pp. Index. ISBN: 0-824-77518-X.

The intent of this bibliographic guide is to support students, researchers, and practitioners by providing an orientation to the literature of public administration. A major portion of this guide is the identification of 181 important public administration monographs that are cited frequently and considered authoritative works in the overall corpus of public administration literature. Each of these 181 books is reviewed, its main findings highlighted, and its overall contribution to the field evaluated. The bibliography section is divided into thirty-three topical sections and subdivisions, such as "State and Local Administration" and "Budgeting and Finance." These 1,200 entries are unannotated. Most of the titles were drawn from the 181 seminal works noted above. There are also two essays on the field of public administration over time. Only an author index is attached.

8-3. Cherry, Virginia R. *Public Administration Research Guide.* Hamden, CT: Garland, 1992. 253 pp. ISBN: 0-824-07643-5.

This guide to the public administration literature is organized into fifteen separate chapters, most of which are arranged by genre of material, such as encyclopedias, dictionaries, handbooks, government documents, and others. This guide goes well beyond this in that it also has additional sections on writing aids, style manuals, finding sources, quantitative methods and sources, and more. Much of these latter chapters are filler pages replete with information widely available elsewhere. The lack of an introduction does little to define the scope of this work and its overall criteria for inclusion and exclusion of materials. Annotations, when done, are quite short.

Abstracting and Indexing Services

8-4. *Sage Public Administration Abstracts.* Quarterly. Beverly Hills, CA: Sage, 1974–. Indexes. ISSN: 0094-6958.

This is a quarterly issued publication that has been in existence for about thirty years. The main body has a total of fourteen separate chapters including "Administration and Politics," "Administration and Society," and "Public Service Personnel." There are numerous subdivisions within each chapter, and all articles are listed alphabetically by author within this subdivision. Each entry is numbered in the sequence listed. Only journal articles are included as citations, replete with lengthy abstracts for each one. The "Related Citations" section indexes without abstracts those articles that are related to various public administration issues. Some nonjournal articles do populate this section. The last issue for each volume has cumulative indexes for all previous four issues. The abstracts stand out as exceptionally well written and informative. There is a separate author index and subject index. 🖳

Directories

8-5. Atwood, Thomas C., ed. *Guide to Public Policy Experts, 1997–1998.* Annual. Washington, DC: Heritage Foundation, 1997. 695 pp. ISBN: 0-891-95068-0.

The people listed in this directory tend to work with the Heritage Foundation and constitute a kind of resource bank for them. The members of the Heritage Foundation tend to share a conservative political philosophy. The guide itself is published annually and is broken down into twelve different categories, such as "Energy and the Environment," "Crime and Security," and "International Experts." Each entry is in standard directory-type format. The only information provided for individuals are affiliation, address, phone number, and areas of specialization. The section on "International Experts" lists the majority of foreign-based policy experts. There are several auxiliary listings by geographic region and Canada. The experts listed in this directory are overwhelmingly men. This publication would be a good way to find speakers who represent the right-of-center political ground on a wide range of topics.

8-6. Hellebust, Lynn, ed. *Think Tank Directory: A Guide to Nonprofit Public Policy Research Organizations.* Topeka, KS: Government Research Service, 1996–. Indexes. ISSN: 1063-3340.

Think tanks are vaguely defined organizations that nevertheless appear with some frequency in the news. As defined in the preface to this directory, think tanks are "nonprofit public policy research organizations, both independent and university-affiliated." Government research agencies and profit-making entities were excluded. Altogether, 1,212 think tanks can be found here; about half are affiliated with colleges and universities. The arrangement is alphabetical by name of organization, with contact information and sixteen other categories of information provided for each organization. Of the latter, some of the more important categories tell the reader the purpose of the think tank, its areas of policy interest, its methods of operation, its size of budget, and its sources of funding. Entries are generally about a half page long. There are four indexes: geographic, policy areas, alternate names, and subsidiaries. This will be a valuable resource for the think tank "industry" if new editions are forthcoming periodically.

Bibliographies

8-7. Jreisat, Jamil E. *Administration and Development in the Arab World: An Annotated Bibliography.* New York: Garland, 1986. 259 pp. Indexes. ISBN: 0-824-08593-0.

This bibliography lists various resources on administration, human resources, and development in the Arab World. The literature cited ranges from works published from 1970 through 1985. It includes books, articles, and dissertations. A grand total of 746 works are cited on the more current aspects of Arab public affairs. The terms "Administration" and "Development" connote the social-, economic-, and political-development aspects of overall national planning. Sources written in Arabic are excluded from this bibliography. Chapter 1 lists books and articles on administration. Chapter 2 is on human resources, and Chapter 3 on sociopolitical factors. Chapter 4 lines up works on economic development and national planning, and the fifth chapter contains doctoral dissertations on administration, human resources, and development issues. Most citations have up to a three-sentence annotation. Citations are arranged alphabetically within each separate chapter. There is an author index and one by country.

8-8. Murin, William F. *Delivering Government Services: An Annotated Bibliography.* New York: Garland, 1988. 315 pp. Indexes. ISBN: 0-824-06618-9.

Here is an annotated bibliography of over 900 citations that focus on the many aspects of government service and the delivery of these services. Relatively few of the citations chosen for inclusion are theoretical or conceptual in nature. The government services covered here include: education, engineering, parks, garbage collection, and others. Also examined is who provides the government service, who pays for future services, who benefits, and a determination of whether or not these public goods are delivered in an equitable manner. The primary emphasis of this bibliography is the delivery of government services at the local and county levels in the United States, but it does not totally exclude state or national government services. Also, a number of other major countries are cited as well. The citations are drawn mostly from the academic side of the literature rather than from the professional or popular literature. There are seven chapters, some with subchapters. While citations are overwhelmingly journal articles, there are some monographs included. All cites are dated from 1970 through 1987. There is both a name index and a subject index.

8-9. Bergerson, Peter J. *Ethics and Public Policy: An Annotated Bibliography.* New York: Garland, 1988. 200 pp. Index. ISBN: 0-824-06632-4.

This bibliography was compiled in response to a heightened interest in academe in political ethics and scandals since such events as Watergate and the Iran-Contra episode. Works listed in this bibliography cover the early 1960s up to 1987. Only scholarly materials are included, and they can be books, journal articles, or dissertations. The selection of entries scans a wide swath from purely procedural to weighty public policy issues of various topics. Each entry, mostly journal articles, contains a paragraph or two as an annotation. The overall arrangement of this bibliography is around broad classification categories such as "Codes of Ethics for Policy Analysis" and "Case Study Applications."

There is only one index, and that is for authors.

8-10. Martin, Daniel W. *The Guide to the Foundations of Public Administration.* New York: Marcel Dekker, 1989. 454 pp. Index. ISBN: 0-824-78284-4.

This is an excellent research guide to the literature of public administration. It is an annotated bibliography that leads the user through the development of public administration literature. There are two main parts. Part 1 is "The Emergence and Impacts of Public Administration," while Part 2 is "Internal Operations of Public Administration," which makes up two-thirds of the entire book. Each part of the book is further subdivided into subject chapters. Within each of these chapters, the works are discussed chronologically utilizing a bibliographic essay that links the influence of one author or work on another, later author in a continuous chain. The annotations are notably good. The bibliography includes both books and journal articles numbering about 1,400 in all. Some foreign-language materials are scattered throughout the citations. The value of this work is having placed relevant books and journal articles into the intellectual development of public administration literature. The index adds minimal value to the book's contents or goal.

8-11. Payad, Aurora T. *Organization Behavior in American Public Administration: An Annotated Bibliography.* New York: Garland, 1986. 264 pp. ISBN: 0-824-08685-6.

The publication of this work is taken as evidence that organizational-behavior literature is relevant to the public sector. The 620 entries cover books, articles, chapters, reviews, and dissertations. The period of study is 1940 through 1984, but the bulk of the citations run from 1974 through 1984. The 1940 starting date coincides with the first year of publication of *Public Administration Review.* There are five main chapters, each having several subdivisions. Annotations are written up for every entry included in this bibliography. This work is not intended to be comprehensive in its listings.

8-12. Rabin, Jack. *Public Budgeting and Financial Management: Annotated Bibliography.* Hamden, CT: Garland, 1991. 160 pp. Indexes. ISBN: 0-824-07595-1.

This annotated bibliography brings together the literature of public budgeting, decision making, and financial management by concentrating on their political, decisional, and economic aspects. Works cited include monographs, journal articles, databases, and more for the years 1940 through 1990. Scholarly publications are especially well represented in the bibliography. Newspaper and magazine articles and speeches are excluded from the 525 citations. The annotated bibliography is not dictionary style but, rather, is arranged by broad subject chapters. Annotations tend to be descriptive rather than critical in nature but are quite helpful and succinct. There are indexes for authors and subjects, with the subject index being relatively sparse of terms.

8-13. Bowman, Sarah Y. *Public Personnel Administration: An Annotated Bibliography.* New York: Garland, 1985. 209 pp. Index. ISBN: 0-824-09151-5.

This is an index to fifty-five public administration and some political science journals published in the United States. Some monographs and court cases are mixed in. There are eleven topical chapters with such headings as "Civil Service Reform," "Human Resources Planning," and "Productivity." Each chapter's bibliography is arranged alphabetically by author listings. There are nearly 700 citations, of which 661 are nicely annotated. Availability of an author index only makes access somewhat problematic. The works chosen are selective, but well chosen.

8-14. Holzer, Marc. *Public Sector Productivity: A Resource Guide.* New York: Garland, 1988. 166 pp. Index. ISBN: 0-824-09458-1.

This is a bibliography created to introduce both the practitioner and the individual specialist to a broad range of resources that could be used to assist the research processes devoted to seeking new methods to improve the overall delivery of public services. The work commences with a several-page definition of "productivity." The work is selectively annotated and includes books, government publications, journal articles, and newsletter items. The bibliography is arranged alphabetically by author for each of the various formats of materials included. A listing of relevant U.S. organizations is included to round out the "resource guide" component of this work. There is an index.

8-15. Hollings, Robert L. *Reinventing Government: An Analysis and Annotated Bibliography.* Commack, NY: Nova Science Publishers, 1996. 113 pp. Indexes. ISBN: 1-560-72264-9.

This rather selective bibliography reflects the author's opinion that the "two goals of accountability and productivity are often diametrically at odds with one another" (Hollings 1996, preface) when efforts are made to improve government. The first twenty pages of this book examine the subject in a narrative fashion, although many bibliographic references are included. Most of the work, however, is an annotated bibliography arranged in a somewhat unorthodox fashion. For example, one category encompasses both books and videos, while another category addresses itself to "National Level Attempts at Implementation," and yet a third category examines "Uses in Advertising." Three appendixes direct the reader to other sources of information, and there are indexes by author and subject. Annotations are usually a paragraph long, and the items selected represent books, journals, and popular magazine articles, among others. This idiosyncratic bibliography has limited usefulness for those researchers dealing with this specific topic.

8-16. VCU Libraries Public Administration Resources. http://www.library.vcu.edu.

This list is fairly selective, but it does do

its intended job in pointing to those Web sites that are major resources in the world of public administration and the policy sciences. 💻

Dictionaries and Encyclopedias

8-17. Jackson, Byron M. *Encyclopedia of American Public Policy.* Santa Barbara, CA: ABC-CLIO, 1999. 230 pp. ISBN: 1-576-07023-9.

The first fifty pages of this work present about eighty "key concepts" of public policy. These could be people, events, or terms, with one-half- to one-page entries on such concepts as the balance of payments, block grants, and policy cycle. The core of the book contains thirteen broad areas, such as "Economics," "Agriculture," "Labor," and "Housing," all broken down into twenty to fifty subdivisions of one-quarter to one page in length. Chronologies appear at the beginning of every heading. There are also lists of readings, which include relatively recent works. The book is a nice resource for the nonspecialist and for lower-division undergraduate students.

8-18. Nagel, Stuart S., ed. *Encyclopedia of Policy Studies.* 2nd exp. and rev. ed. New York: Marcel Dekker, 1994. 956 pp. Indexes. ISBN: 0-824-79142-8.

Defining policy studies "as the study of the nature, causes, and effects of alternative public policies for dealing with specific social problems" (Nagel 1994, introduction to the first edition), this encyclopedia introduces the reader to a field that has an obvious relationship to political science, but which is cross-disciplinary in nature. This multidisciplinary approach is evident from the arrangement of the volume; the major portion of the work is devoted to analysis of specific policy problems with emphasis in areas including political science, economics, sociology, psychology, and the like. Altogether, there are thirty-five chapters, each written by a specialist in the field. Each chapter provides a detailed discussion accompanied by an extensive list of references. Subject and author indexes provide additional access to the text. The second edition attempts to provide more discussion in regard to cross-national analysis, interdisciplinary analysis, and evaluation of alternative public policies than did the first edition. Although contributors were asked to discuss basic issues in order to reach an audience of nonexperts, this reference work will be of greater value to more advanced students than to beginners.

8-19. Rabin, Jack, ed. *Encyclopedia of Public Administration and Public Policy.* 2 vols. New York: Marcel Dekker, 2003. Index. ISBN: 0-824-70946-2 (Vol. 1); 0-824-74299-0 (Vol. 2).

This encyclopedia contains relatively scholarly material on the fundamental themes, issues, and concepts pertinent to the study of both public policy and public administration. The entries offer much more in the way of comprehensive information and subject background than other dictionaries/encyclopedias of public administration and policy studies. Entries are still, however, in alphabetical order, but are signed by specialists in the field. The entries do not serve as a general introduction to the terms, but provide a more scholarly perspective in examining their constituent parts. The reference citations exemplify the quality of this work. Typical entries are "Sustainable Development," "Fiscal Transparency," "Policy Sciences Approach," and "Learning Organizations." The work is available in toto on the Internet as well as in print format. The intent of the editors and publishers is to keep this work current with quarterly updates. An index covers both volumes. 💻

8-20. Schultz, David, ed. *Encyclopedia of Public Administration and Public Policy.* New York: Facts on File, 2004. 526 pp. Index. ISBN: 0-816-04799-5.

This dictionary/encyclopedia is aimed at general readers, high-school students, and undergraduates requiring definitions of basic public administration and public policy terms and concepts. It also includes some agencies, federal programs, and biographical items. Entries are arranged alphabetically. Some typical entries include "performance auditing," "revenue sharing," and "drug policy." There is an index.

8-21. Rowley, Charles K., ed. *Encyclopedia of Public Choice.* 2 vols. Boston: Kluwer Publishers, 2004. ISBN: 0-792-38607-8.

Not seen, but this work appears to be an encyclopedia of the policy sciences. 💻

8-22. Shafritz, Jay M. *The Facts on File Dictionary of Public Administration.*

New York: Facts on File, 1985. 610 pp. ISBN: 0-816-01266-0.

This lexicon of public administration–related materials covers the standard terms expected in a decent public administration dictionary. It also includes biographies of well-known people in the field and history of public administration. Entries could be key U.S. Supreme Court rulings on public administration–related issues; or its theory, concepts, practices, and laws; or institutions found in public administration or related academic fields of inquiry. A listing of public administration journal titles is given. There is ample use made of cross-references and "see also" references. Some solid bibliographies are contained within many of the entries. All entries are alphabetically arranged, and the longer ones are often one or two pages.

8-23. Shafritz, Jay M., ed. *International Encyclopedia of Public Policy and Administration.* 4 vols. Boulder, CO: Westview Press, 1998. 2504 pp. Index. ISBN: 0-813-39973-4 (Vol. 1); 0-813-39974-2 (Vol. 2); 0-813-39975-0 (Vol. 3); 0-813-39976-9 (Vol. 4).

This is a relatively comprehensive encyclopedia on the fundamental concepts, practices, and issues that touch upon all aspects of public policy, including its analysis, evaluation, management, and implementation. There are also articles on individuals, commissions, and various organizations in this multivolume work that contains over 900 articles in just over 2,500 pages. The work serves to be valuable both in its historical and contemporary perspectives. Each entry begins with a definition of the topic. More detailed information follows. The attempt to stay away from more technical levels of discourse and reach out instead to nonexperts in various walks of public affairs life was generally successful. This work offers extensive coverage of international policy and public administration. It is all alphabetically arranged, and short bibliographies are attached to each of the signed entries. Articles are often several pages long. The sections on budgeting are especially strong. An excellent index accompanies the work.

8-24. Chandler, Ralph C. *The Public Administration Dictionary.* 2nd ed. Santa Barbara, CA: ABC-CLIO, 1988. 430 pp. Index. ISBN: 0-874-36498-1.

This is a departure from the standard alphabetically arranged dictionary. This one has been organized around seven basic components of public administration: "Fundamentals," "Public Policy," "Public Management," "Bureaucracy," "Personnel Administration," "Financial Administration," and "Public Law and Regulation." Numerous cross-references within the entries facilitate use. Each entry concludes with a paragraph or two on the term's significance. An index is included and important to this type of broad subject format. This work appears to be geared toward serving as a study guide or course aid.

8-25. Fox, William. *Public Administration Dictionary.* n.p.: Juta, 1995. 139 pp. ISBN: 0-702-13219-5.

This is a standard subject dictionary on the study of public administration. It uses South African English spellings throughout the work. It is arranged in standard alphabetical format. Entries are quite short and to the point. There is no claim to be comprehensive here, and it certainly is far from that. The style is a bit stiff, especially for American speakers of the English language.

8-26. Kruschke, Earl R. *The Public Policy Dictionary.* Santa Barbara, CA: ABC-CLIO, 1987. 159 pp. Index. ISBN: 0-873-46443-4.

This work has a multipurpose of serving as a dictionary and reference guide, a study guide for introductory public policy courses, a supplement to textbooks, and a source of review materials for policy science majors. It attempts to blend together terms drawn from both the study and practice of public policy matters. All terms chosen are limited mainly to U.S. public policy, with an occasional foray into the broader Western political tradition. Each term has a definition and a paragraph on its significance. Entries average out at about one-half a page each. The terms defined tend to be very basic ones, such as "performance indicators," "impact studies," and "environmental policy." A ten-page bibliography of more or less standard works and an index are both available.

Guides and Handbooks

8-27. *CQ Researcher.* 48 issues annually. Washington, DC: Congressional Quarterly, 1923–. Index. ISSN: 1056-2036.

Formerly entitled *Editorial Research Reports,* this reference service tends to receive heavy use and provides undergraduate researchers with an overview of current controversial topics. The reports are approximately 12,000 words in length and are issued four times a month, on Fridays. These weekly reports then appear in quarterly paperbacks and finally in an annual hardbound cumulation. The four major components of each report are "The Issues," "Background," "Current Situation," and "Outlook." An annotated bibliography and a chronology buttress the text. Numerous sidebars provide the reader with varying angles on the question. Illustrations and graphic displays appear on a frequent basis. Each report also includes a sidebar entitled "At Issue," which outlines pro-and-con statements regarding the topic of the report. Each hardbound volume includes a subject and title index that is cumulative from the January 1991 issues through the current volume. The selection of topics is quite wide ranging; some are issues that would occur to undergraduates (feminism, alcohol advertising, abortion, and gun control), while others, such as the future of Mexico or executive pay, reflect policy issues not necessarily on the front burner in today's headlines. Taken in all, this is an excellent resource for undergraduates needing a solid grounding on a term-paper topic or those searching for a subject about which to write or speak. ⌨

8-28. Bowman, James S., ed. *Ethics, Government and Public Policy: A Reference Guide.* New York: Greenwood Press, 1988. 341 pp. ISBN: 0-313-25192-4.

An arrangement of articles all signed and refereed has been broken down into four sections: "Analytical Approaches," "Ethical Dilemmas and Standards for Public Servants," "Techniques and Methods in Ethical Policy Making," and "Study of Systematic Issues in Government." The entries are aimed at all levels of readers, including scholars, students, and practitioners. The articles are creditable overviews accompanied by lengthy notes. There are short selective bibliographies appended to the end of every article.

8-29. *Grant$ for Public Policy and Public Affairs.* Annual. [New York?]: Foundation Center, 1990–. Indexes. ISSN: N/A.

This directory lists around 7,000 grants available over $10,000 that are offered by 617 foundations. The range of these grants is wide and includes those in the areas of public administration, leadership development, foreign policy, international peace and security issues, education, and others. All the grants listed here are also published in the Foundation Center's *Foundation Grants Index.* In this work, the grants are arranged alphabetically by state, then by foundation name and recipient name. Access is enhanced by three indexes, including geographical, recipient names, and subject words.

8-30. *The Guide to Graduate Education in Public Affairs and Public Administration: NASPAA Directory of Programs.* Washington, DC: National Association of Schools of Public Affairs and Administration, 1997–.

This is aimed at students who desire to pursue a career in public affairs or public administration and are looking for a way to select a good program that meets their individual needs. Career counselors should find this serial of some value as well. This guide offers tips on applying to graduate programs, financial aid packages, work experience suggestions, and more. It is arranged solely by alphabetical order by school listed. Each school's program is detailed with needed credits, tuition costs, contact people, addresses, and thesis requirements. (Note: This description is based on the 1997/1999 issue.)

8-31. Rabin, Jack, ed. *Handbook of Public Administration.* 2nd ed. New York: Marcel Dekker, 1998. 1246 pp. ISBN: 0-824-70086-4.

The new edition of this handbook is meant to contribute to the debate on how to reengineer public institutions to make them more responsive to their respective customers and citizens. Each chapter represents a key subfield of public administration as an endeavor of study. The opening bibliographic essay examines public administration from a historical context. It is a chronology of ideas and provides bibliographic footnotes within the essay. The second essay attempts to capture the five great ideas of public administration, and this serves as the organizational basis for the entire handbook. Chapters are then spread out over fourteen topical subfields that include "Public Administration Pedagogy," "Policy Sciences," and "Judicial Adminis-

tration." Each of these subfields is then broken down into two additional parts. The first part is a chronological history of the topic, while the second part is five great ideas within that particular subfield of study. Since different people have written the two subchapters, they do not always dovetail or build upon one another. Chapters are, however, very well written and clearly are written for those who study or teach public administration or for practitioners. 💻

8-32. Subramaniam, V., ed. *Public Administration in the Third World: An International Handbook.* Westport, CT: Greenwood Press, 1990. 447 pp. Indexes. ISBN: 0-313-24730-7.

The main body of this guide is arranged into four broad geographic areas: Asia, the Middle East and North Africa, sub-Saharan Africa, and the West Indies and Latin America. The first three are broken down even more by major country, while the last geographic area, the West Indies and Latin America, is broken down into a small subset by topic or area. The section on the Middle East includes only Egypt, Iran, Saudi Arabia, and Turkey, while the last section examines only the English-speaking Caribbean and the southern cone of Latin America. Each chapter is similar to one another, but there are a few differences related to the various subdivisions. Entries begin with an introduction to public administration, its historical background, the public administration structure and career civil service, postindependence structure, government branches, local government administration, reforms, and a conclusion. A bibliographic guide at the end of the handbook includes materials in the English language only. The contributors are mainly Canadian and third world scholars or specialists. There is a name index and a subject index.

8-33. Lynn, Naomi B., and Aaron Wildavsky, eds. *Public Administration: The State of the Discipline.* Chatham, NJ: Chatham House Publishers, 1990. 540 pp. Indexes. ISBN: 0-934-54062-4.

Feeling that public administration had been neglected in recent state-of-the-art overviews of the discipline of political science, this volume attempts to fill that gap. The contributors of the individual chapters are all members of both the American Society for Public Administration and the American Political Science Association. Contributed chapters are arranged into six parts: "Professional History and Theory," "Issues of Organization and Management," "Intergovernmental and Comparative," "Methodology," "Public Policy," and "Looking to the Future." Altogether, there are twenty separate chapters, as well as indexes by name and subject. Each chapter also includes extensive references. Although now some years old, this work can still serve as a guide for both students and practitioners requiring detailed discussion in regard to the state of the art of public administration as of 1990.

Applied Policy Analysis

This section presents a number of major topical policy studies arranged strictly al-phabetically by title within the subject area. These sections are not broken down into formats of dictionaries, bibliographies, literature guides, and so forth because there generally are relatively few entries per subject. There has been no attempt made to cover every significant public policy issue or to list every resource that may reasonably apply to the ones so listed. The public policy issues selected and the reference sources chosen do indeed reflect an air of selectivity above and beyond that already demonstrated in the other sections of this book.

Abortion

Despite its prominence as a policy controversy in the United States for more than a quarter century, the topic of abortion has garnered only a couple of reference publications devoted to it specifically, and both are already over a decade old. Of the two items, the United Nations set on abortion policies is perhaps the more valuable because it allows for a comparative approach among the various countries of the world. Students seeking more recent information can also turn to reference works dealing with women's issues in general.

8-34. Muldoon, Maureen. *Abortion Debate in the United States and Canada: A Source Book.* Hamden, CT: Garland, 1991. 238 pp. Index. ISBN: 0-824-05260-9.

Examining one of the most heated issues in American society, this volume surveys the abortion issue in its many ramifications. The book is divided into five chapters, some quite lengthy. The first chapter discusses demographics, sociological research, and public opinion. The next chapter provides philosophical discussion on the subject. The third chapter consists largely of text and summaries of statements on abortion emanating from religious denominations in both the United States and Canada. The fourth chapter discusses advocacy groups and includes official statements issued by a number of them. The final chapter is an overview of the legal and political situation, with commentary on appropriate documents. Each of the five chapters concludes with a bibliography. One of the strengths of this volume is the fact that it discusses the Canadian response to abortion as well as that in the United States, allowing for comparison between the two. On the other hand, most readers will want to supplement information derived from Muldoon's work with more recent information.

8-35. United Nations. Department of Economic and Social Development. *Abortion Policies: A Global Review.* 3 vols. New York: United Nations, 1992–1995. ISBN: 9-211-51246-8 (Vol. 1); 9-211-51258-1 (Vol. 2); 9-211-51296-4 (Vol. 3). http://www.un.org/esa/population/publications/abortion.

Abortion is obviously an issue of great contention in the United States, yet this practice occurs worldwide and there is value in learning how different nations and societies react to it. This three-volume set describes abortion policies in 174 countries, arranged alphabetically.

Information is up to several pages in length and includes four basic components: "Abortion Policy," "Fertility and Mortality Context," "Background," and "Incidence of Abortion." The component dealing with background provides text, while the other components provide statistical or tabular information. The amount of information, especially statistics, varies greatly from one nation to another. Each of the three volumes includes references for the nations described in that volume. In addition, each volume includes an introductory chapter that discusses the components in general. Although this work is not aimed specifically at students, its format is more user friendly than many United Nations publications and so can be used readily by both high-school and college students.

African Americans

As is the case with a number of other minority groups, African Americans have been the subject of a number of reference works. Those useful for discussion of policy issues are described in this chapter. Among the core items are the *African-American Almanac,* now in its seventh edition, and the *Encyclopedia of African-American Civil Rights: From Emancipation to the Present.*

8-36. Mabunda, L. Mpho, ed. *African-American Almanac.* Triennial. Detroit: Gale Research, 1967–. Index. ISSN: 1071-8710.

Formerly known as the *Negro Almanac,* this compilation continues to be a rich source of information on the African

American experience. The seventh edition, published in 1997, includes sections on history, law, politics, the family, education, literature, media, the arts, sports, science and technology, and the military, among others. Typically, each section describes both historical events and the current situation, and often provides biographies of noteworthy individuals. The text is complemented by numerous illustrations and photographs. A section on national organizations includes brief descriptions, addresses, and phone numbers, and there is a similar directory for the media. A lengthy bibliography identifies significant books published in the early 1990s for both Africana and African Americans. Among reference works that deal with ethnic minorities, this has been a standard source for some years, providing introductory information in a single-volume format; it should be found in most libraries.

8-37. Asante, Molefi K., and Mark T. Mattson. *African-American Atlas: Black History and Culture—An Illustrated Reference.* New York: Macmillan USA, 1998. 251 pp. Index. ISBN: 0-028-64984-2.

A revision of the *Historical and Cultural Atlas of African Americans,* published in 1991, this work updates the original by adding additional spatial information, maps, charts, and photographs. The thirteen chapters are arranged in chronological order, beginning with background on the continent of Africa and concluding with a social and economic examination of African Americans in the 1990s.

Strictly speaking, this is not an atlas but rather a basic historical text accompanied by numerous illustrations and graphics that include maps among them. Many of the illustrations are multi-colored. A chronology and a short list of references conclude the work. The audience for this publication will consist of high-school students and beginning undergraduates in need of an introduction to the topic.

8-38. Lowery, Charles D., and John F. Marszalek, eds. *Encyclopedia of African-American Civil Rights: From Emancipation to the Present.* rev. ed. 2 vols. New York: Greenwood Press, 2003. Index. ISBN: 0-313-32171-X.

Approximately 800 entries make up the contents of this reference work. In order to compress as much information as possible into a relatively short volume, the editors chose to exclude certain topics. These include groups and individuals opposed to civil rights and presidents of the United States. According to the introduction, entries chosen for inclusion generally were those that discussed "a significant positive contribution to the advancement of black civil rights." Major categories for entries include individuals, organizations, events, and court cases. The latter include citations to the legal reporter that includes the complete text of the case. Entries are generally brief, usually a paragraph to a page in length. Each entry includes a bibliography of references to appropriate articles and books. An asterisk indicates cross-references to other entries. Entries are signed by the contributors, who are members of the academic community. A number of illustrations accompany the text. A chronology, bibliography, and index conclude the volume. This work is suitable for undergraduate students or more advanced researchers needing brief information on the civil rights movement.

8-39. Smith, Jessie Carney, and Carrell Peterson Horton, eds. *Historical Statistics of Black America.* 2 vols. Detroit: Deal Research, 1995. 2244 pp. Indexes. ISBN: 0-810-38542-2.

According to the introduction, this set complements the publisher's *Statistical Record of Black America* [entry 8-40], which focuses upon current information through a "uniquely different presentation" that makes available data not found in that volume. Among the differences is the fact that the historical set presents statistics pertaining to agricultural pursuits and to slavery, neither of which is covered in the contemporary volume. Likewise, there is little here in regard to sports, which was of minimal importance in earlier centuries. Much of the data comes from federal government sources or from early volumes of the *Negro Year Book* and the *Negro Handbook*. Most of the statistics pertain to the twentieth century up to 1975, though there is coverage of the eighteenth and nineteenth centuries when data are available. Both volumes include a very lengthy table of contents, and the second volume provides additional access through indexes by subject and year. A brief bibliography indicates sources that were consulted.

Sources are also indicated for the statistical tables themselves. Although some of the statistical items reported are somewhat eclectic, this reference work will be of value to all those who desire quick access to a great range of historical data on African Americans.

8-40. Smith, Jessie Carney, and Robert L. Johns, eds. *Statistical Record of Black America.* Detroit: Gale Research, 1990–1997. Index. ISSN: 1051-8002.

Similar in nature to other ethnic statistical sources published by Gale, this volume compiles data pertaining to African Americans. Most of the statistics come from federal government sources. The preface indicates that users may have to consult earlier editions of this work for certain statistics, so libraries will need to retain the earlier editions.

Aging and the Elderly

As the U.S. population ages, it seems likely that requests for information and research on this group will increase. At the present, however, only a relatively small number of reference works target this subject area and all of them date from the first half of the decade of the 1990s. Among them, the *Encyclopedia of Aging* is more suitable for advanced researchers, while the *Older Americans Almanac* will appeal to high-school students and undergraduates with more basic needs.

8-41. Maddox, George L., ed. *Encyclopedia of Aging: A Comprehensive Resource in Gerontology and Geriatrics.*

3rd ed. New York: Springer Publishing, 2001. 1408 pp. Indexes. ISBN: 0-826-14842-5.

Researchers requiring a comparatively erudite source on aging that is nevertheless accessible to the nonspecialist can turn to this volume. The arrangement of entries is alphabetical; most are no more than two or three pages in length. Each article concludes with a listing of cross-references, and bibliographic references are included in the text. Complete references appear in a comprehensive listing at the back of the volume. The list of references is nearly 200 pages long and includes many entries from the 1980s as well as some from the early 1990s. The articles are signed by the contributors, most of whom are U.S. academicians. The approach is multidisciplinary, drawing upon fields such as anthropology, biology, history, psychology, public policy, and sociology. Access is enhanced by a listing of entries that appears at the front of the volume, as well as by a subject index. There is also an index of contributors. There are few illustrations other than some graphic displays, and users should also be aware that emphasis is upon U.S. circumstances. This is one of those handbooks that can be consulted by both undergraduates and more advanced inquirers.

8-42. Roy, F. Hampton, and Charles Russell. *Encyclopedia of Aging and the Elderly.* New York: Facts on File, 1992. 308 pp. Index. ISBN: 0-816-01869-3.

As the population of the United States continues to age, the number of re-searchers seeking information on the subject will probably rise. This reference, written by a physician and a social gerontologist, attempts to cover both medical and social and psychological aspects of aging. The arrangement of entries is alphabetical. Most are relatively brief and are written in a nontechnical style. Cross-references are indicated in uppercase, and many entries include a bibliography of one or more items. The alphabetical listing of entries is followed by an extensive group of appendixes that present tables, graphs, and other information resources. A bibliography and an index are included in the volume. There are no illustrations. This work will be of greatest value to those researchers requiring only brief information on aging that is written for the lay reader. As such, it will be useful to both high-school and undergraduate researchers; for greater and somewhat more up-to-date detail, inquirers can refer to *Encyclopedia of Aging* [entry 8-41].

8-43. Manheimer, Ronald J., ed. *Older Americans Almanac: A Reference Work on Seniors in the United States.* Detroit: Gale Research, 1994. 881 pp. Index. ISBN: 0-810-38348-9.

Whereas the volume by Maddox [entry 8-41] is meant for a more scholarly audience, this work focuses more on a general-interest audience, one that includes not only undergraduates but also aging Americans, their families, and those who provide service to them. For that reason, the writing style is somewhat more basic than that found in Maddox.

Rather than an alphabetical array of articles, this volume chooses a topical approach. The text is arranged into eleven sections, encompassing subjects such as history, aging processes, financial concerns, health concerns, and lifestyles. Emphasis is on the United States; there will be little here for the researcher looking for cross-cultural information. Numerous photographs, graphic displays, and sidebars supplement the text. A listing of references concludes most major entries, and a more general bibliography appears at the end of the volume. Entries are signed by the contributors, who are a mix of academicians, individuals from both the public and private sectors, and freelance writers. Many articles include a listing of relevant organizations and their addresses, but this information inevitably will become outdated. Undergraduates and the general public will find this work to be useful for their needs.

8-44. Rix, Sara E. *Older Workers.* Santa Barbara, CA: ABC-CLIO, 1990. 243 pp. Index. ISBN: 0-874-36259-8.

Although this work is targeted at older adults, it will be of use to high-school and college researchers as well. The first half of the volume is a narrative describing the situation (as of 1990) of older workers in the United States. Among the topics discussed are demography, age discrimination, work ability, training, and women older workers, among others. A detailed table of contents allows easy access to this portion of the volume. The second half of the book is a listing of resources, including a directory and a lengthy annotated bibliography of print and nonprint resources. Given the publication date, this portion of the volume may prove to be less valuable to current research than the narrative. The volume concludes with a glossary, a fifteen-page list of references, and an index. Most readers who consult this work will also want to update it with newer information.

8-45. Schick, Frank L., and Renee Schick, eds. *Statistical Handbook on Aging Americans.* Phoenix: Oryx Press, 1994. 335 pp. Index. ISBN: 0-897-74721-6.

Like the volume edited by Darnay [entry 8-46], this work compiles statistics published mainly by the federal government, primarily as a result of the 1990 census. There are chapters on demographics, "Social Characteristics," health, employment, "Economic Conditions," and "Expenditures for the Elderly." The defining point for the aging population is sixty-five. Most of the material consists of tables directly reproduced from federal sources, although there are also a number of graphic displays. Complete references to original sources appear at the end of the volume. Compared to the volume compiled by Darnay, this reference source is about half the length and, for that reason, presumably less comprehensive. The most obvious difference between the two is the fact that Darnay uses a larger typeface and is generally easier to read. As is the case with its competitor, this work will date rapidly unless new editions are published. In either case, advanced researchers may prefer to consult the original sources.

8-46. Darnay, Arsen J., ed. *Statistical Record of Older Americans.* Biennial. Detroit: Gale Research, 1994–1996. Index. ISSN: 1087-254X.

One of a series of volumes published by Gale, this work compiles statistical tables pertaining to older Americans, who are defined as those over sixty-five (although some tables do cover a broader age range). Most tables are reprinted from federal government sources produced in the late 1980s and early 1990s. Complete references are provided for those who wish to follow up by consulting the original source. The tables are divided into sixteen chapters, encompassing topics such as demographics, families, income, pensions, social security, housing, and health care. For those researchers seeking a shortcut to statistical information in regard to the aging U.S. population in the early 1990s, this resource will provide easy access to that data. Those wanting up-to-date statistics obviously will have to look elsewhere, and the volume itself will quickly lose its reference value unless new editions are forthcoming.

AIDS

8-47. Lerner, Eric K., and Mary Ellen Hombs. *AIDS Crisis in America: A Reference Handbook.* 2nd ed. Santa Barbara, CA: ABC-CLIO, 1998. 323 pp. Index. ISBN: 1-576-07070-0.

Like other volumes in the Contemporary World Issues series, this book follows a fairly standard format. An introductory chapter provides general background, and is followed by chapters dealing with chronology, biographies, and factual data. Two additional chapters provide brief full-text documents from a variety of sources and a discussion of the legal aspects of the AIDS epidemic. The final chapters encompass a directory of agencies and organizations, and an annotated bibliography of print and nonprint materials. The writing style is suitable for both high-school and undergraduate students. Though not as in-depth a treatment as provided by the *Encyclopedia of AIDS* [entry 8-48], this volume provides a useful and somewhat more up-to-date supplement to that work.

8-48. Smith, Raymond A., ed. *Encyclopedia of AIDS: A Social, Political, Cultural, and Scientific Record of the HIV Epidemic.* Chicago: Fitzroy Dearborn Publishers, 1998. 601 pp. Index. ISBN: 1-579-58007-6.

The AIDS epidemic has been a matter of public policy discussion since 1981. This encyclopedia covers the topic through 1996. The volume begins with an alphabetical list of the entries and a "Resource Guide" that lists organizations and Internet sites relevant to the subject. This is followed by eight short essays discussing aspects of the epidemic and providing references to relevant entries. The entries themselves number approximately 250 and are arranged alphabetically. Most articles range from a page to several pages in length and include cross-references and bibliographies. Numerous photographs supplement the text. Some typical articles include "Bacterial Infections," "Conspiracy Theories," "Court Cases," "Kidney Complications," "Maternal Transmission," and "Prostitution." Biographies were excluded. The text is suitable for both undergraduate researchers and specialists requiring additional relevant information. Readers needing a detailed introduction to the topic of AIDS will benefit by consulting this volume. 💻

Asian Americans

8-49. Gall, Susan, and Irene Natividad, eds. *Asian American Almanac: A Reference Work on Asians in the United States.* Detroit: Gale, 1995. 834 pp. Index. ISBN: 0-810-39193-7.

One of the values of this work is the fact that it addresses itself to more than the usual categories of Asian Americans. Along with those of Chinese, Japanese, and Pacific Island descent, the reader will find here capsule descriptions of peoples from Pakistan, the Philippines, Indonesia, Korea, Laos, Pakistan, Thailand, and Vietnam. The first portion of this work is devoted to these individual ethnic descriptions. This is followed by a lengthy chronology and reproductions of approximately thirty documents significant to Asian American history. Most of the rest of the volume comprises individual chapters on subjects such as "Population Growth and Distribution," "Voters and Voting Rights," "Family," "Work Force," and the various fine arts. Sidebars and illustrations accompany the text, which also encompasses statis-

tical figures. Lists of references appear throughout, and there is a bibliography at the end of the volume. The text is suitable for both high-school and undergraduate students, and will answer many questions in regard to this ethnic group.

8-50. Kim, Hyung-Chan, ed. *Dictionary of Asian American History.* New York: Greenwood Press, 1986. 627 pp. Index. ISBN: 0-313-23760-3.

This reference work is divided into two major components: a group of essays and a dictionary of brief entries. The essays begin the volume. Each is written by a separate contributor and has a specific focus. There are essays on each of the major Asian American groups: Chinese, Japanese, Koreans, Indians, Filipinos, Pacific Islanders, and Southeast Asians. These are followed by a number of essays focusing on topics such as immigration law, politics, education, and popular culture. The dictionary portion of this work includes about 800 entries dealing with events, persons, places, and concepts relevant to Asian American history. Entries are arranged alphabetically and range up to two pages in length. Cross-references are indicated with asterisks, and many entries include a short bibliography. The volume concludes with a bibliography, a chronology, statistics from the 1980 census, and an index to the entire volume. Although this work is now older than many other reference works on the market, its scholarly approach will recommend it to undergraduate students and more advanced researchers. 💻

8-51. Nakanishi, Don T. *Distinguished Asian American Political and Governmental Leaders*. Westport, CT: Oryx Press/Greenwood, 2002. 229 pp. ISBN: 1-573-56325-0.

Not seen.

8-52. Gall, Susan B., and Timothy L. Gall, eds. *Statistical Record of Asian Americans*. Detroit: Gale Research, 1993. 796 pp. Index. ISBN: 0-810-38918-5.

This reference volume compiles a wide, if disparate, collection of statistics pertaining to Asian Americans in both the United States and Canada. Much of the data originally appeared in government sources, but it is useful to have it appear in a single source, as it does here.

Bioethics

8-53. Post, Stephen Garrard, ed. *Encyclopedia of Bioethics*. 3rd. ed. 5 vols. New York: Macmillan Library Reference USA, 2004. 3062 pp. Index. ISBN: 0-028-65774-8.

Bioethics is a recent multidisciplinary field with implications in the realms of philosophy, theology, religion, and the law. This set, a revision of the 1978 edition, presents 464 articles on the subject. Most are several pages in length; some are quite extensive. A listing of some typical articles indicates the scope of coverage: "Abortion," "Animal Welfare and Rights," "Eastern Orthodox Christianity," "Informed Consent," "Population Policies," and "Warfare." Numerous cross-references to related articles are pro-

vided, and articles conclude with bibliographies (some quite lengthy) for those readers wishing to pursue the subject. The final volume includes a long appendix that encompasses full-text codes, oaths, and other ethical statements related to bioethics. There are no illustrations. The contributors are drawn from the academic community in the United States and abroad. This set is an excellent resource for collegiate researchers, including undergraduates, who need a thorough introduction to bioethical issues.

8-54. Jonsen, Albert R., Robert M. Veatch, and LeRoy Walters, eds. *Source Book in Bioethics*. Washington, DC: Georgetown University Press, 1998. 510 pp. Index. ISBN: 0-878-40683-2.

As the editors of this volume point out, the field of bioethics is relatively new, germinating only in the 1970s. In order to assist students researching issues in the field, the editors have gathered full-text pertinent documents in several categories. Those major categories include "The Ethics of Research with Human Subjects," "The Ethics of Death and Dying," "Ethical Issues in Human Genetics," "Ethical Issues Arising from Human Reproductive Technologies and Arrangements," and "Ethical Issues in the Changing Health Care System." Each of these major categories is supported by the text of relevant documents. These include government publications, reports of other agencies, and legal cases, among others. In some instances, the documents were of such length that certain portions were omitted, but court statements were retained. Altogether, the reader finds here approximately fifty such documents. Each of the five sections also begins with an introduction of several pages, including a short list of references. This work is suitable for a collegiate audience.

Children and Families

8-55. Moe, Barbara. *Adoption: A Reference Handbook.* Santa Barbara, CA: ABC-CLIO, 1998. 303 pp. Index. ISBN: 0-874-36898-7.

Adoption is a fairly narrowly defined subject compared to many others that students choose for term-paper topics; this volume will assist such researchers to obtain basic background on the subject. The initial chapter provides an overview, while succeeding chapters provide a chronology, biographies, data, texts of legal documents, a directory of organizations, and an extensive bibliography of print and nonprint resources. The latter includes a number of Internet sites, which could be of particular value for this issue. Items in the bibliography are annotated. The chapter on data is accompanied by a number of statistical tables and graphic displays. A glossary initiates the reader into the language of adoption. The reading level is suitable for both high-school and undergraduate students. 🖥

8-56. Iverson, Timothy J., and Marilyn Segal. *Child Abuse and Neglect: An Information and Reference Guide.* New York: Garland, 1990. 220 pp. Index. ISBN: 0-824-07776-8.

This work has three major goals. First, it describes the background of child abuse and neglect within society. Second, characteristics of abused children and their families are examined. Third, it hopes to be a resource for those professions dealing with this issue. The arrangement is essentially that of a monograph rather than that of a standard reference work. A number of graphic displays accompany the text, and each of the six chapters concludes with a listing of references. Two appendixes provide the reader with directory information and information on reporting child abuse state by state. Given the publication date, much of the information in the appendixes is now outdated. The major value of this work is its discussion of theoretical issues and the view of child abuse issues contemporaneous with 1990. Further, the text is directed to a scholarly and professional audience. For these reasons, this work is most likely to be of value to researchers, including some undergraduates, who are delving into this topic in some depth and need detailed background regardless of publication date.

8-57. Hobbs, Sandy, Jim McKechnie, and Michael Lavalette. *Child Labor: A World History Companion.* Santa Barbara, CA: ABC-CLIO, 1999. 292 pp. Index. ISBN: 0-874-36956-8.

As defined by this volume, "child labor" includes adolescents and young people as well as children. Emphasis is also upon work and tasks performed from the Industrial Revolution forward. Articles are arranged alphabetically and range in length from a paragraph to three pages. Cross-references appear at the end of articles, as does a listing of bibliographic references. These references are repeated in a single bibliography at the end of the volume. A number of illustrations supplement the text. The front matter includes a listing of "Entries by Category" that include such broad topics as jobs in industries, countries, economics, organizations, and biographies of reformers, among others. The authors are British academicians, and they admit that this publication has an inevitable focus upon the United Kingdom and the United States. Nevertheless, there are also a number of articles on specific countries and regions of the world, highlighting problems and circumstances particular to those places. The audience for this book will include both high-school and undergraduate students. 💻

8-58. Edmonds, Beverly C., and William R. Fernekes. *Children's Rights: A Reference Handbook*. Santa Barbara, CA: ABC-CLIO, 1996. 364 pp. Index. ISBN: 0-874-36764-6.

Another in the Contemporary World Issues series, this work follows the format of companion volumes. An introductory chapter discusses children's rights, first defining those rights, then going on to discuss specific issues such as education, violence, refugees, and child labor. The focus is upon children's rights in the United States, with some detail in regard to international conventions and activities. This is followed by chapters on chronology and biographies; approxi-

mately eighteen prominent individuals are profiled. The next chapter provides background and text on relevant international instruments pertaining to children's rights. A further chapter discusses U.S. policy issues and a number of pertinent Supreme Court rulings. The final chapters provide statistics, a directory, and annotated bibliographies of print and nonprint resources. The writing style is suitable for both high-school and undergraduate students. 💻

8-59. Lerner, Richard M., Anne C. Petersen, and Jeanne Brooks-Gunn, eds. *Encyclopedia of Adolescence*. 2 vols. New York: Garland, 1991. 1222 pp. Index. ISBN: 0-824-04378-2.

Adolescence, and the behavior of adolescents, engages the attention of researchers, government policy makers, and parents alike. This reference work provides a scholarly approach to the subject. Each of the 200 entries is written by a specialist; a complete list of these contributors, along with their affiliation and the titles of entries written by them, appears at the front of the first volume. Entries are usually several pages in length. References appear in the text, and are keyed to bibliographic listings at the end of each article. Cross-references appear after the bibliographic listings. The arrangement of articles is alphabetical, but the titles of some entries are not especially intuitive. Examples include "Life-Span View of Human Development and Adolescent Development," and "Smokeless Tobacco Use among Adolescents." For that reason, readers will derive most benefit from this set by making use of the cross-references and the index at the back of the second volume. No listing of article titles is provided; such a list would have been of value to users wishing to obtain an overview of the contents. There are no illustrations other than occasional graphic displays. The audience for this work is obviously of a professional and scholarly nature, but advanced undergraduates can also consult it profitably.

8-60. Clark, Robin E., and Judith Freeman Clark. *Encyclopedia of Child Abuse.* 2nd ed. New York: Facts on File, 2001. 344 pp. Index. ISBN: 0-816-04060-5.

Child abuse is a topic that receives attention from a number of professions and disciplines. This encyclopedia hopes to reflect varying approaches to child abuse, including legal, medical, psychological, sociological, economic, historical, and educational perspectives. Arrangement of entries is alphabetical. Most are relatively short, no more than a couple of paragraphs. However, cross-references are provided to other relevant entries, and there are also occasional bibliographic listings. Typical entries include "Custody," "Daughters and Sons United," and "Defect Model of Child Abuse." The dictionary portion of this volume is followed by a number of appendixes that total approximately 100 pages. Many of the appendixes reproduce statistical information, most of it gathered in the United States, which at the time of publication was more active than other nations in

gathering this data. Also among the appendixes, the reader can find summaries of laws and regulations, and documents originating at the United Nations and in Canada. A bibliography of approximately fifteen pages and an index conclude the work.

8-61. Bankston, Carl L., ed. *Encyclopedia of Family Life.* 5 vols. Pasadena, CA: Salem Press, 1999. 1498 pp. Index. ISBN: 0-893-56940-2.

Issues concerning the family are frequently the topic of student investigation. Those families in countries other than the United States and Canada are not discussed. Articles attempt to cover the entire field, at least in relation to family life in North America, and they range in length from 250 to 4,000 words. The longer articles cover such subjects as aging, education, love, marriage, religion, and work. Shorter essays of approximately 2,500 words discuss other important topics, including adoption, divorce, family law, poverty, and support groups. Longer articles include an annotated bibliography, and all articles conclude with cross-references. Articles are signed by the contributor; these are listed in the first volume. Most are academicians in the United States and Canada. Numerous photographs and graphic displays accompany the text. The final volume includes a listing of major legislation and court decisions, a chronology, a glossary, an annotated bibliography over thirty pages in length, a list of entries arranged by category, and an index. This set is more suitable for high-school students and beginning undergraduates than advanced researchers, but the bibliographies will assist in leading these students to more in-depth sources.

8-62. Levinson, David, ed. *Encyclopedia of Marriage and the Family.* 2 vols. New York: Macmillan Library Reference USA, 1995. 791 pp. Index. ISBN: 0-028-97235-X.

The topics of marriage and family are obviously of interest to many library users, including academic researchers at all levels as well as laypeople. This encyclopedia has all these groups as its audience. Most articles are several pages in length and conclude with a listing of cross-references as well as a bibliography that often includes twenty or more items. Articles are signed by the contributors, whose affiliations are listed at the front of the first volume. There are no illustrations other than occasional tables and graphic displays. A listing of articles appears in the first volume, and a comprehensive index can be found at the end of the second volume. Typical articles include "Abortion," "Child Care," "Gender Identity," "Self-Esteem," and "Teenage Parenting." Articles that discuss subjects with legal aspects include in the bibliography a useful list of citations to relevant court cases. In all, this encyclopedia is a fine resource for topics of interest to student researchers at both the high-school and collegiate levels.

8-63. Smith, Charles A., ed. *Encyclopedia of Parenting Theory and Research.* Westport, CT: Greenwood Press, 1999. 501 pp. Index. ISBN: 0-313-29699-5.

This work presents 244 entries on issues regarding parents and children. The entries are relatively brief, normally about 1,000 words. Typical articles include "Academic Achievement," "Competition," "Nightmares," "Physical Punishment," and "Throwaway Children." Each includes a brief list of bibliographic references as well as cross-references to related articles. The contributors are largely drawn from the U.S. academic community. There are no illustrations, but the writing style is suitable for non-specialists, including parents and undergraduate researchers. These two groups, as well as other researchers requiring a short but scholarly introduction to parenting topics, will wish to consult this reference book.

8-64. Sherrow, Victoria. *Encyclopedia of Youth and War: Young People as Participants and Victims.* Phoenix: Oryx Press, 2000. 366 pp. Index. ISBN: 1-573-56287-4.

Beginning with the Thirty Years' War in the seventeenth century, records on warfare have been detailed enough to examine its impact upon young people. This reference volume examines youth and war during that four-century period, defining "youth" as those individuals eighteen years or younger. There are approximately 300 entries, arranged alphabetically. Typical topics include "Biological Warfare," "Chinese Civil War," "Hunger/Malnutrition," and "Red Cross."

There are also many entries for individuals, either young people themselves or those who have come to their assistance. Entries conclude with a listing of cross-references and a short bibliography. Complete bibliographic references can be found in a comprehensive listing at the back of the volume. Most entries are short, approximately a page or less in length, but many are accompanied by photographs and other illustrations. There is an inevitable emphasis on the twentieth century, particularly from World War II to the present. The writing style is suitable for both high-school and undergraduate students.

8-65. Cline, Ruth K. J. *Focus on Families: A Reference Handbook.* Santa Barbara, CA: ABC-CLIO, 1990. 233 pp. Index. ISBN: 0-874-36508-2.

Like other volumes in this series, this work focuses on an audience of high-school students and discusses a topic of immediate interest to them. In this case, the subject is the family. There are chapters on the family in general, stepfamilies, single-parent families, relationships with other family members and relatives, adoption, family finances, divorce, and child abuse. Each chapter covers the basics and provides an annotated bibliography of other resources, including print, nonprint, and fiction. Information on relevant organizations is also included, but the addresses and telephone numbers may very well have changed, given the publication date. Although this book addresses itself to a beginning audience

in relatively simple language, the topic is of interest to undergraduates as well as high-school students, and novices to research in both cases can benefit from its use.

8-66. Poe, Elizabeth Ann. *Focus on Relationships: A Reference Handbook.* Santa Barbara, CA: ABC-CLIO, 1993. 257 pp. Index. ISBN: 0-874-36672-0.

Rather than researchers delving into the topic of relationships as experienced by teens, teenagers themselves are the intended audience for this volume. For that reason, the style of writing is fairly basic and could be understood by those at the middle-school as well as high-school level. Nevertheless, freshman college students also grapple with these issues and sometimes choose to write term papers on them, so this work can be a helpful resource at the collegiate level as well. Major sections discuss relationships within families, among peers, and with adults outside the family unit, particularly those in school systems. Each of these major sections is further subdivided into chapters on specifics. For example, the section on families has chapters on parents, siblings, and extended families. Each chapter includes a listing of additional resources, encompassing fiction and nonfiction, nonprint items, and organizations. This book would not be the best choice for students doing more advanced research on teen relationships but is handy for beginning papers for middle-school and high-school students.

8-67. Kagan, Jerome, ed. *Gale Encyclopedia of Childhood and Adolescence.* Detroit: Gale Research, 1998. 752 pp. Index. ISBN: 0-810-39884-2.

Approximately 800 entries appear in this single-volume encyclopedia, which is aimed at a broad audience including parents, librarians, students, and those in the social service professions. Some entries are quite short, but others range in length up to 5,000 words. Typical entries include "Contraception," "Desegregation," "Genetic Disorders," "Rabies," and "Social Competence." Each entry begins with a brief italicized definition. Cross-references are indicated in boldface. Longer articles include a bibliography, a listing of relevant organizations, and occasional Web sites. A group of approximately forty contributors assisted in writing the articles. Articles contributed by these individuals are signed and normally include the affiliation of the contributor. In some cases, no affiliation is indicated, nor is affiliation indicated elsewhere. Also, many articles are unsigned; presumably, these were written by an editorial group. Illustrations and sidebar information make this volume attractive to the beginning user. A lengthy bibliography and an index conclude the volume. The uncertainty regarding attribution of entries somewhat mars an otherwise handy resource for beginning information on childhood and adolescence topics.

8-68. Sanders, Rickie, and Mark T. Mattson. *Growing up in America: An Atlas of Youth in the USA.* New York: Macmillan Library Reference USA, 1998. 291 pp. Index. ISBN: 0-028-97262-7.

Statistical information on children is not difficult to find, but it is often scattered among a number of sources. This volume compiles statistics on a number of subjects. There are chapters on demographics, social and economic background of children, their health, their relation to the criminal justice system, and their education. Each chapter includes extensive text that introduces the subject. The text is followed by numerous multicolor maps and graphic displays that illustrate and explicate the data. A detailed table of contents lists the graphic displays, with additional access provided through the index. An appendix provides maps that indicate population at the county level for major ethnic groups. One drawback of this atlas is the fact that sources are not indicated with the individual graphic displays. However, a careful researcher can probably ascertain the source by looking through a bibliography, arranged by chapter, which appears at the back of the volume. If this work is updated periodically, it will provide a valuable source for a statistical overview of children in the United States.

8-69. O'Hare, William P., ed. *Kids Count Data Book: State Profiles of Child Well-Being.* Annual. Washington, DC: Center for the Study of Social Policy. 184 pp. ISSN: 1060-9814. http://bibpurl.oclc.org/web/619.

Although demographic and socioeconomic data on children are available from federal government sources, this annual volume is a welcome resource for those seeking to find the said data in a single location with particular emphasis on the individual states. The initial chapters provide an overview and a summary of statistics at the national level. The bulk of the volume, however, is devoted to individual "State Profiles," which provide two pages of statistics and graphs pertaining to each of the states and the District of Columbia. The data and tables cover demographics, social and economic characteristics, health, juvenile justice, and indicators such as infant mortality, suicide, dropout rates, and poverty. A set of appendixes provides additional rankings, and sources for each section are indicated in a ten-page listing at the back of the volume. Other than the initial chapters, the emphasis here is upon tables and graphs rather than narrative text. Nevertheless, this work will be of value to almost any researcher dealing with this topic. ⌨

8-70. Broude, Gwen J. *Marriage, Family, and Relationships: A Cross-Cultural Encyclopedia.* Santa Barbara, CA: ABC-CLIO, 1994. 372 pp. Index. ISBN: 0-874-36736-0.

As the preface to this volume states, "humans are profoundly social beings." Regardless of culture, humans everywhere engage in similar relationships but with differing customs. This work provides the reader with a starting point for cross-cultural comparisons. The arrangement is alphabetical, with articles ranging in length from a single page to as many as seven or eight. Some of the articles discuss subjects that will readily spring to mind: courtship, family, marriage, and rape. Others will be less familiar to readers; these include articles on "Joking Relationships," "Love Magic," and "Widow Remarriage." Cross-references appear at the end of most articles, and each article includes a bibliography of books and articles. These bibliographic entries are repeated in a general bibliography at the back of the volume. A listing of all the articles appears in the table of contents. A number of photographs accompany the text. The writing style is accessible to nonspecialists, including both high-school and college students.

8-71. Kinnear, Karen L. *Single Parents: A Reference Handbook.* Santa Barbara, CA: ABC-CLIO, 1999. 263 pp. Index. ISBN: 1-576-07033-6.

Like others in the Contemporary World Issues series, this volume presents high-school and undergraduate researchers with a basic introduction to a particular topic of current interest. In this instance, an initial chapter provides an overview on single-parent families, while succeeding chapters provide a detailed chronology, biographies of key figures, statistical and factual data (including background on significant Supreme Court decisions), a directory of organizations, and annotated bibliographies for both print and nonprint sources. Both the text itself and the annotated references will be of use to student researchers digging into this topic. ⌨

8-72. Schmittroth, Linda, ed. *Statistical Record of Children.* Detroit: Gale Research, 1994. 983 pp. Index. ISBN: 0-810-39196-1.

Like other statistical compilations published by Gale, this volume pulls together statistics that for the most part appeared in a great variety of federal government publications. In general, as defined here, children are those fourteen years or younger. There are ten chapters, each of which provides a grouping of tables pertaining to a particular subject. Some examples include population, education, health, child care, crime, and recreation. There are also a number of tables that provide comparison with other countries. References are included for those researchers who wish to avail themselves of the original source. Most of the data was gathered in the late 1980s or early 1990s, so those individuals wishing up-to-date statistics will have to go elsewhere; indeed, this volume, like others in the series, will only retain its reference value if new editions are published.

Civil Rights

8-73. Grossman, Mark. *ABC-CLIO Companion to the Civil Rights Movement.* Santa Barbara, CA: ABC-CLIO, 1993. 263 pp. Index. ISBN: 0-874-36696-8.

One of several competing reference works on the civil rights movement, this work provides the reader who needs relatively brief information with an attractive single-volume source. Entries are arranged alphabetically and deal with individuals, court decisions, legislation, or-

ganizations, concepts, events, and information on segregationists. Some entries are only a paragraph long; the more substantial topics are allotted about two pages. Cross-references are indicated to related entries, and there are occasional illustrations, usually of individuals active in the movement. A chronology and a bibliography conclude the work. Compared to Luker's volume [entry 8-79], this work, with its cross-references and index, is probably more suited to high-school students and undergraduates, while those desiring a somewhat more scholarly approach can turn to Luker.

8-74. Harrison, Maureen, and Steve Gilbert, eds. *Civil Rights Decisions of the United States Supreme Court: The Twentieth Century.* San Diego: Excellent Books, 1994. 273 pp. Index. ISBN: 1-880-78005-4.

A companion to a separate volume that describes nineteenth-century civil rights decisions of the Supreme Court, this work presents text of fifteen twentieth-century cases pertaining to civil rights. Two are in regard to the internment of Japanese Americans during World War II; all the rest are pertinent to African Americans. This latter group of decisions is wide ranging, involving school desegregation, public transportation, voting rights, housing, and affirmative action, among others. Each case receives a brief introduction, but most of the text consists of the original document. Decisions have been edited in order to reduce legalese and to explain terminology unfamiliar to the lay reader. Chapters devoted to specific cases average about fifteen pages in length. The text of the Constitution and a short bibliography conclude the volume. Those researchers seeking extensive interpretation and background information will have to consult other reference works, but those needing a handy compilation of this century's major civil rights decisions will find assistance in this volume.

8-75. Sigler, Jay A. *Civil Rights in America: 1500 to the Present.* Detroit: Gale Research, 1998. 710 pp. Index. ISBN: 0-787-60612-X.

Unlike many other reference works that discuss civil rights from the viewpoint of a particular ethnic or minority group, this work describes the subject from a more general viewpoint. An initial section presents the history of civil rights in the United States from the beginning of European colonization through the latter part of the twentieth century. The next section is devoted to individual groups, including African, Asian, Hispanic, and Native Americans. Other groups covered in this section include immigrants (specifically Irish, Italian, German, Polish, Jewish, Japanese, and Arab) and nonethnic groups such as women and children. The third section discusses the politics, policy, and legal ramifications of civil rights and the government. The final section presents text of important documents and court cases. Each of these four major sections includes a number of separate chapters, each with its own bibliography. An annotated general bibliography, as well as a table of

cases and a glossary, can be found at the back of the volume. The text is made more attractive by the use of sidebars and numerous illustrations. The writing style is suitable for both high-school and undergraduate researchers. Thanks to its broad coverage, this is one of the better starting points for information on civil rights.

8-76. Martin, Waldo E. Jr, and Patricia Sullivan, eds. *Civil Rights in the United States.* 2 vols. New York: Macmillan Reference USA, 2000. 850 pp. Index. ISBN: 0-028-64765-3.

The editors of this set explain in their preface that their work encompasses both American civil rights themselves and the struggle by individual groups to achieve those rights. Articles are arranged alphabetically and range up to three pages in length. Noteworthy individuals, organizations, and groups; major pieces of legislation; and well-known events all receive entries, along with articles on concepts such as "Ethnicity and Race," "Homeless Rights," and "Radicalism." Cross-references are indicated in uppercase, and articles conclude with a bibliography of relevant items, usually books and articles. There are numerous illustrations. Most of the contributors are drawn from the U.S. academic community. The time frame extends from 1791 to the present. Particularly useful are articles on the individual states; such background on civil rights on a detailed geographic basis like this is not easily found elsewhere. This set will be useful for both high-school and undergraduate students.

8-77. Levy, Peter B. *Civil Rights Movement.* Westport, CT: Greenwood Press, 1998. 226 pp. Index. ISBN: 0-313-29854-8.

This is one of a series of volumes published by Greenwood Press that intends to discuss significant twentieth-century events for a general audience. The volume begins with a chronology, followed by a chapter over 100 pages long that discusses the history and course of the civil rights movement. This chapter describes events in the South as well as court cases and concludes with sections that examine the role of women and assess the significance of the movement. Two final chapters provide biographies of civil rights leaders and excerpts from primary documents. The latter are derived from both federal and nonfederal sources. A short group of photographs can be found in the center of the volume. An annotated bibliography of approximately ten pages concludes the volume. This work presents a good deal of detailed information on the civil rights movement, yet simultaneously will be suited for both high-school and undergraduate students pursuing this subject for basic term papers.

8-78. Bradley, David, and Shelley Fisher Fishkin, eds. *Encyclopedia of Civil Rights in America.* 3 vols. Armonk, NY: M. E. Sharpe Reference, 1998. 1018 pp. Indexes. ISBN: 0-765-68000-9.

While reference works by Grossman [entry 8-73] and Luker [entry 8-79] deal with the civil rights movement from the point of view of African Americans, this reference set is broader in scope, de-

scribing other ethnic groups as well as gays, women, children, older Americans, and those with disabilities. The arrangement is alphabetical. Entries deal with events, issues, laws, government policies, political figures, court cases, organizations, and individuals. Some entries are relatively short, no more than a paragraph, but topics of substantive interest receive up to four pages of text. Longer articles include an annotated bibliography. Cross-references are indicated in uppercase. Each volume includes its own table of contents, and all three volumes include a listing of all entries by category. The final volume includes a table of court cases, a chronology, a general bibliography, an index of court cases, and a general index. The table of court cases is the only place where complete legal citations appear. The set is heavily illustrated. This encyclopedia provides a good starting point for both high-school students and undergraduates seeking introductory information on all aspects of civil rights.

8-79. Luker, Ralph E. *Historical Dictionary of the Civil Rights Movement.* Lanham, MD: Scarecrow Press, 1997. 329 pp. ISBN: 0-810-83163-5.

Luker, himself a veteran of the 1960s civil rights movement, here presents the reader with information on individuals, organizations, laws, regulations, and court decisions relevant to the movement. The volume begins with a detailed chronology extending from 1941 through 1995. The entries themselves are alphabetical and range from a paragraph to a full page in length. Legal citations are included with court cases. The volume concludes with an extensive bibliography. There are no illustrations, nor is there an index. Compared to the volume by Grossman, this work is a bit more scholarly in tone and more likely to appeal to researchers at the undergraduate level and beyond, particularly those desiring detailed bibliographic assistance.

Crime and Police

8-80. Lentz, Harris M. *Assassinations and Executions: An Encyclopedia of Political Violence, 1900 through 2000.* rev. ed. Jefferson, NC: McFarland, 2002. 291 pp. Index. ISBN: 0-786-41388-3.

Regrettably, assassinations of political figures are commonplace in the modern world. This volume provides a narrative that begins with the assassination of Abraham Lincoln in 1865. The basic arrangement is chronological, but there is also detail of the lives of the victims (and sometimes their murderers) and consequences of their deaths. In addition to those assassinated outright, those who were executed after having fallen from power are also included. Most of those chronicled can be termed major figures, such as heads of states, ambassadors, and military officers. The author was selective in dealing with some third world nations where political violence seems to be endemic. In effect, this is a short history of the last 150 years with emphasis on violence at the higher levels of politics. Many of those deaths described here can be found in other reference works, but this volume is useful for providing context for the assassinations

of lesser known figures. The likely audience will be beginning students rather than scholars.

8-81. Schmalleger, Frank, ed. *Crime and the Justice System in America: An Encyclopedia.* Westport, CT: Greenwood Press, 1997. 299 pp. Index. ISBN: 0-313-29409-7.

Despite its title, the format of this work more closely resembles a dictionary than an encyclopedia. Entries are arranged alphabetically, with most no more than a page in length; some are a single paragraph. Topics encompassed include "significant terminology, precedent-setting cases, key historical and contemporary figures, notable policy initiatives, and significant findings" (Schmalleger 1997, preface). One or more references to recommended readings are included with each entry. There are no illustrations. Entries are signed by the contributors, most of whom are associated with U.S. colleges and universities. There are no cross-references, but the user can consult the index to find references on a particular subject throughout the volume. Most students will make use of this volume as a supplement to other, more detailed sources. The writing style is appropriate for both high-school and college audiences.

8-82. Durham, Jennifer L. *Crime in America: A Reference Handbook.* Santa Barbara, CA: ABC-CLIO, 1986. 318 pp. Index. ISBN: 0-874-36841-3.

The student seeking information on crime in the United States will find in this volume a general overview of about forty pages followed by a lengthy chronology, biographies of important figures (a number from the federal government), a compilation of statistics, long excerpts from a pair of federal enactments, a directory of organizations, and a bibliography of both print and historical resources. There are few illustrations other than some statistical tables and graphic displays. While the introductory material will be of use to both high-school and college students requiring a concise overview of this topic, the main value of the work perhaps lies in the statistics and the bibliography. Detailed information on crime will have to be sought in other sources.

8-83. Williams, Vergil L. *Dictionary of American Penology.* rev. and exp. ed. 2 vols. Westport, CT: Greenwood Press, 1996. 488 pp. Index. ISBN: 0-313-26689-1.

The initial edition of this work appeared in 1979; noting that there was less interest in rehabilitation in the 1990s, Williams has dropped much of the information on that subject and focused on newer concepts and methods. Articles are arranged alphabetically and are usually about two pages long. Cross-references to other entries are indicated in uppercase, and articles include references to other relevant publications. Some of the entries deal with stock concerns, such as sentencing, the death penalty, and recidivism. There are also descriptive entries for correctional systems in each of the American states. Three appendixes

follow the dictionary portion of this work. Two are directories of prison reform organizations and addresses of prison systems, while the third reproduces statistical tables relevant to crime and prisons in the United States. Many of these are reproduced from federal government documents, and altogether this particular appendix represents approximately 200 pages, almost half the volume. Compared to the *Encyclopedia of American Prisons* [entry 8-84], this work provides more statistics and a less detailed text, but is more suitable for a general audience, including undergraduate students.

8-84. Sifakis, Carl. *Encyclopedia of American Prisons.* New York: Facts on File, 2003. 320 pp. Index. ISBN: 0-816-04511-9.

Although the target audience of this reference work is academicians and professionals in the field of penology, it can be of value for undergraduate researchers for certain topics. These include such subjects as AIDS, prison crowding, gangs, civil rights of prisoners, sexual exploitation, and others. Articles are arranged alphabetically; most are several pages in length. A complete list appears in the front matter. Articles conclude with a bibliography and often with references to relevant court cases. Most of the contributors are academics, but some are associated with the penal system. There are only a handful of illustrations. Cross-references appear at the end of the articles, and access to the text can also be gained through the index. The writing style is serious and professional, but is jargon free and therefore can be understood by the nonspecialist. 🖳 ˏ

8-85. Grossman, Mark. *Encyclopedia of Capital Punishment.* Santa Barbara, CA: ABC-CLIO, 1998. 330 pp. Index. ISBN: 0-874-36871-5.

Capital punishment has been the subject of ongoing debate in the United States for several decades and represents a common topic for student papers. The value of this reference work lies in its historical approach to the subject. Many of the entries describe the life and death of individuals noted for having been executed in the United States or elsewhere from the time of Socrates to the present. There are also biographical entries for individuals who both favored and opposed capital punishment, as well as legal cases and topics such as the role race plays in executions. Most articles are a page or two in length. Many include references to relevant books and articles. The volume concludes with a bibliography and a chronology. There are no illustrations other than a group appearing at the center of the volume; for the most part, these depict famous executions. This would have been a stronger work had it focused more on concepts and ideas rather than famed victims. Students looking for pro-and-con arguments on the subject must divine these from entries in the index. The writing style is suitable for high-school and college students alike.

8-86. Bailey, William G., ed. *Encyclopedia of Police Science.* 2nd ed. New York: Garland, 1995. 865 pp. Indexes. ISBN: 0-815-31331-4.

The view of police work presented through the news media and popular culture is exaggerated in many respects; this encyclopedia, aimed at the specialist and nonspecialist alike, attempts to compile and present information that gives the reader a more accurate picture of the field. Arranged alphabetically, the articles found here cover both the dramatic and mundane aspects of police science and benefit from lessons learned in the Rodney King episode, which took place as this edition was being prepared. Most articles are several pages long and include a bibliography. The contributors are individuals who are either associated with police work or academicians. There are very few illustrations, and the general tone is serious in nature. A bibliography relating to police history appears at the end of the volume along with a general index and an index to legal cases. This work will be of value to scholarly researchers more than to beginning students.

8-87. Theoharis, Athan G., ed. *The FBI: A Comprehensive Reference Guide.* Phoenix: Oryx Press, 1999. 409 pp. Index. ISBN: 0-897-74991-X.

Over its career, the Federal Bureau of Investigation (FBI) has garnered both praise and condemnation. In recent decades, its activities have become more known to the public through documents released under the auspices of the Freedom of Information Act. This reference work seeks to provide a balanced view of the agency that discusses all its aspects.

The arrangement is topical, not alphabetical. The ten chapters cover subjects such as the history of the FBI, well-known cases, controversies, the culture of the agency, its daily activities, and its image in popular culture. One chapter provides biographies of individuals associated with the agency, while another gives a detailed chronology. A ten-page annotated bibliography and an index conclude the volume. As there are no cross-references in the text, users will find it necessary to consult the index to find specific information. A number of illustrations supplement the text, which is written at a level suitable for college students and interested laypersons. Four contributors, including the editor, are responsible for the text of the various chapters; all are professors at U.S. universities. Any student researching the FBI will benefit by consulting this work. 💻

8-88. Sifakis, Carl. *Mafia Encyclopedia.* 2nd ed. New York: Facts on File, 1999. 414 pp. Index. ISBN: 0-816-03856-2.

The author of this volume believes that organized crime in the United States is largely in the hands of the Mafia, and therefore a reference work on the Mafia rather than organized crime makes more sense. The entries are arranged alphabetically by subject. Many of the entries are for slang terms or for individuals prominent in the Mafia. Many died in violent circumstances. Relatively few articles deal with general issues, although an introductory section of some length does provide an overview of Mafia activities. There are cross-references and a num-ber of illustrations but no bibliographic references. Those high-school and undergraduate students requiring background on the Mafia and organized crime will be the audience for this publication. The earlier edition of this work is an e-book. 💻.

8-89. Glenn, Leigh. *Victims' Rights: A Reference Handbook.* Santa Barbara, CA: ABC-CLIO, 1997. 231 pp. Index. ISBN: 0-874-36870-7.

As is the case with other works in this series, this publication hopes to provide the reader with an introductory overview to the subject at hand as well as bibliographic references for additional research. The initial chapter outlines the problem and is followed by an extensive chronology of relevant events. The next chapter provides biographies of about a dozen individuals, most of them active in the victims' rights movement. This is followed by a chapter that provides text for summaries of relevant policy statements, legislation, and court cases. The final chapters provide a directory and an annotated bibliography of print and non-print resources. The writing style is appropriate for both high-school and undergraduate students requiring beginning information on this topic. 💻

8-90. Kurian, George Thomas. *World Encyclopedia of Police Forces and Penal Systems.* New York: Facts on File, 1989. 582 pp. Index. ISBN: 0-816-01019-6.

This reference work takes a somewhat unusual approach to its topic by discussing both the beginning point of the criminal justice system (police forces) and the end point (penal systems). Information was compiled on 183 countries. Rather than an alphabetical approach, these nations were instead divided into two groupings. The first grouping consists of "major countries," generally those with a population over 500,000, or those for which information was readily available. The second grouping includes "smaller countries and microstates," where the reader can find places such as the Cook Islands or nations for which detailed information was not available. Each of these two groupings is arranged alphabetically with entries that combine text and statistics in a format similar to a general encyclopedia. A number of topics are covered for those nations for which reasonably complete information is available. These topics include the structure and organization of police forces, their recruitment and training, and an overview of the penal system. Statistics include numbers on crimes such as murder, rape, robbery, drug offenses, and a number of others. Several appendixes provide information on Interpol, a directory, a bibliography of two pages, and some comparative statistics. This volume is useful because it compiles a good deal of information that might otherwise be difficult to find without extensive searching; however, it is now a number of years old, and many users will want to consult additional sources for updated material.

Disabilities

8-91. Pelka, Fred. *ABC-CLIO Companion to the Disability Rights Movement.* Santa Barbara, CA: ABC-CLIO, 1997. 422 pp. Index. ISBN: 0-874-36834-0.

Among the topics covered in this volume are individuals, organizations, significant laws, court cases, and concepts relevant to disability rights. The arrangement of entries is alphabetical. They range in length from a paragraph to almost two pages. Many include cross-references and a listing of books and articles for additional research. These bibliographic listings are repeated in a comprehensive bibliography at the back of the volume. Also included is a chronology that begins with 1817 and concludes with events in 1996. A number of photographs, usually depicting disabled individuals both well known and unknown to the general public, accompany the text. While individual articles found here are relatively brief, this work provides a good starting point for those student researchers approaching the topic for the first time or those requiring an overview of many facets of the disability issue. The writing style is suitable for high-school and college students alike.

8-92. Dell Orto, Arthur E., and Robert P. Marinelli, eds. *Encyclopedia of Disability and Rehabilitation.* New York: Macmillan Library Reference USA, 1995. 820 pp. Index. ISBN: 0-028-97297-X.

Although this volume is aimed at an audience that includes the disabled and those who work with them, it has value for student researchers as well. A number of the articles deal with topics such as affirmative action, the use of animals in managing or treating disabilities, the Americans with Disabilities Act, homelessness, violence, employment, and the like, all of interest to researchers seeking basic information. The articles are arranged alphabetically, and a listing of them appears in the front matter. Contributors are also listed at the front; most are academicians or individuals who work directly with those with disabilities. Articles are generally several pages in length and conclude with cross-references and a bibliography to relevant books and articles. The style of writing is thorough but accessible to the general reader. The volume concludes with a listing of resource agencies (which is subject to obsolescence) and an index, which indicates main entries in boldface. Basic information for almost any disabilities-related topic can begin with this work.

8-93. Van Cleve, John V., ed. *Gallaudet Encyclopedia of Deaf People and Deafness.* 3 vols. New York: McGraw Hill, 1987. Index. ISBN: 0-070-79229-1.

This reference set pertains to that group of people having hearing impairments as well as to deafness itself, defined as a physical attribute. (The word "deaf" is considered potentially offensive if used as a noun, so in this work it appears instead as an adjective.) This set is multidisciplinary, drawing upon the sciences, social sciences, and humanities. Articles are arranged alphabetically and usually are at least several pages long. Altogether, there are 273 entries. Longer articles are broken into sections and sub-

sections. There are biographies of significant individuals suffering from deafness as well as those individuals whose activities had an impact upon the community of the hearing impaired. Most entries include cross-references and a bibliography. Occasional illustrations supplement the text. Contributors are members of the scholarly and professional worlds. The writing style is serious and scholarly, so this reference recommends itself to the more experienced researcher rather than to beginners; this is particularly true of those articles dealing with subjects with technical overtones. Despite its age, this encyclopedia nevertheless is an excellent source for those students and scholars requiring knowledgeable and detailed information about this particular handicap.

Drug Abuse
8-94. Woods, Geraldine. *Drug Abuse in Society: A Reference Handbook.* Santa Barbara, CA: ABC-CLIO, 1993. 269 pp. Index. ISBN: 0-874-36720-4.

The preface to this volume points out that drug abuse has been a scourge in American society for several decades and that those affected include not just drug users but also those institutions in society that deal with this overwhelming problem. Defining "drug" to include illegal psychoactive drugs, legal drugs taken improperly, and alcohol and tobacco, Woods first provides an overview chapter of the drug issue. This is followed by chapters that include a chronology, biographies, "Facts, Statistics, and Documents," a listing of relevant organizations and agencies, and bibliographies of both print and nonprint sources. The chapter entitled "Facts, Statistics, and Documents" is quite lengthy and discusses subjects such as a demographic profile of drug users, risk factors, drugs and crime, the law and drugs, and drugs on the job, as well as providing the full text of relevant documents. A number of statistical tables and graphic displays accompany the text. Like others in this series, this volume is written at a level suitable for both high-school and beginning college students.

8-95. O'Brien, Robert. *Encyclopedia of Drug Abuse.* 2nd ed. New York: Facts on File, 1992. 500 pp. Index. ISBN: 0-816-01956-8.

The first edition of this reference work appeared in 1984. The second edition was issued to expand and update its predecessor. Otherwise, the intent remains the same as it had been for the first edition. It provides "extensive data and information on not only drugs and drug abuse, both licit and illicit, but also on the vast number of social institutions, customs and sociopolitical-economic interrelations that have an impact on drug abuse" (O'Brien 1992, preface). The approximately 500 entries are arranged alphabetically. The topics are wide ranging, including the drugs themselves, medical and biological aspects of drugs, ethnicity, geography, organizations, and laws. Articles are usually brief, about a page or a bit more. Cross-references are indicated in uppercase. The alphabetical array of articles is followed by an exten-

sive series of appendixes. These include street language and slang pertaining to drugs, as well as many tables of statistics. A bibliography of about twenty-five pages follows the appendixes. Although this work is now some years old and should be used in conjunction with more recent reference sources, it still provides the general reader, including high-school and undergraduate students, with nontechnical introductory information on many aspects of drug abuse.

8-96. Jaffe, Jerome H., ed. *Encyclopedia of Drugs and Alcohol.* 4 vols. New York: Macmillan Library Reference USA, 1995. 1861 pp. Index. ISBN: 0-028-97185-X.

The reader scanning the contents of this encyclopedia realizes that drug use has many facets. In addition to the usual narcotic drugs, this work provides articles on such seemingly benign substances as beer, soft drinks, and coffee. Moreover, there is discussion of drugs used in societies other than the United States and Western Europe. There are articles on the effects of drugs: depression, drunk driving, homelessness, and physical dependence. In short, students needing introductory information on many aspects of drug use—social, economic, and political—can be directed to this set. The first three volumes are devoted to an alphabetical array of articles, some written at length, although subheadings are provided in order to keep the user from becoming overwhelmed by too much text. Some entries are much shorter, no more than a paragraph. All entries include cross-references and a bibliography. There are relatively few illustrations; many are chemical formulas or statistical tables. Most of the authors are U.S. academicians, but there are contributors from other countries as well. The final volume includes no articles, but is instead devoted to appendixes that provide directory information, statistics, and listings of controlled substances, as well as a comprehensive index. Although this set obviously lags behind current events, it does provide college students with thoughtful and reasonably in-depth information regarding issues related to drugs.

8-97. Hirschfelder, Arlene B. *Encyclopedia of Smoking and Tobacco.* Phoenix: Oryx Press, 1999. 411 pp. Index. ISBN: 1-573-56202-5.

The topic of smoking is one that frequently engages student researchers. This single-volume encyclopedia presents approximately 600 alphabetically arranged entries on that subject, covering such topics as advertising, legislation and court cases, various types and brands of cigars and cigarettes, the tobacco industry, and the role of the federal government in the controversy. Many entries are brief, sometimes no more than a paragraph, but more substantive articles receive several pages of coverage. Cross-references are plentiful, and more substantive articles provide short bibliographic references. Numerous illustrations enhance the text. In addition to a chronology and a comprehensive bibliography, the back matter

includes six appendixes that reproduce essays, surgeon general's reports, summaries of court cases, and other pertinent information. The audience for this helpful work will consist of both high-school and undergraduate students.

8-98. O'Brien, Robert, Morris Chafetz, and Sidney Cohen. *Encyclopedia of Understanding Alcohol and Other Drugs.* 2 vols. New York: Facts on File, 1999. 1108 pp. Index. ISBN: 0-816-03970-4.

The first volume of this set is an alphabetical arrangement of entries pertaining to various aspects of alcohol and other drugs. Typical entries include "Bourbon," "Disease Concepts," "Moderation Management," and "Sex." There are numerous entries for various types of drugs, including scientific names. Many of the entries are relatively short, perhaps a paragraph in length. Those articles dealing with concepts and subjects are more substantial and range up to three pages long. Many entries include cross-references and sometimes a bibliographic listing. There are numerous statistical tables and graphic displays but no other illustrations. The second volume provides a glossary, a directory, a bibliography of over thirty-pages length, and six appendixes that reproduce full-text documents and statistics. Unfortunately, the appendixes are not titled nor provided with a table of contents, so it is difficult to determine what documents are in each appendix or the rationale for their inclusion. However, users can turn to the index, which does list items in the appendixes by title. Undergraduates and other academic researchers will be the most likely audience for this work.

8-99. Chepesiuk, Ron. *War on Drugs: An International Encyclopedia.* Santa Barbara, CA: ABC-CLIO, 1999. 317 pp. Index. ISBN: 1-576-07037-9.

The involvement of the U.S. government against drug use began to focus in the 1970s and has been a policy issue ever since. This reference book provides almost 650 entries discussing the war on drugs here and in relevant nations abroad, such as Colombia. The entries are arranged alphabetically and range in length from a paragraph to a couple of pages. Each includes at least one bibliographic reference, and many provide cross-references, sometimes quite lengthy in number. Among the general topic areas discussed are legal, social, economic, and political ramifications of the drug trade. Many of the entries are for organizations and prominent individuals involved on both sides of the issue. A number of photographs supplement the text, and the back matter includes a chronology, a listing of Web sites, and a bibliography that replicates the references found with each article. This work would have been enhanced had there been separate articles for countries prominent in the drug trade, particularly Colombia; instead, information on such countries is scattered among a number of articles. Nevertheless, this should be a useful source for both high-school and undergraduate students researching this topic.

Education

8-100. Grant, Carl A., and Gloria Ladson-Billings, eds. *Dictionary of Multicultural Education.* Phoenix: Oryx Press 1997. 308 pp. Index. ISBN: 0-897-74798-4.

Hoping to provide the reader with definitions and explanations of terms relevant to multiculturalism, this dictionary presents entries that range in length from a couple of paragraphs to several pages. Entries are arranged alphabetically and describe concepts pertaining to individual ethnic groups, to court cases, and to theoretical issues, among other topics. Biographies are excluded, as are articles that describe ethnic groups themselves (as opposed to their intellectual traditions). Cross-references are provided, as are bibliographic listings at the end of each entry. There are no illustrations. Contributors are drawn from the U.S. academic community. An index provides additional access to the text. Some readers may find this work to be rather "politically correct"; more to the point, there is enough emphasis on theoretical issues to make this reference work more appropriate for advanced college students than for beginning researchers.

8-101. Jones-Wilson, Faustine C. *Encyclopedia of African American Education.* Westport, CT: Greenwood Press, 1996. 575 pp. Index. ISBN: 0-313-28931-X.

African American education differs historically from other ethnic groups in that legal barriers specifically forbade or separated African Americans from schooling available to the rest of the population.

This sourcebook is useful because it emphasizes historical as well as contemporary issues and topics. Entries are arranged alphabetically, with length ranging from a half page to several pages. There are entries for concepts, individuals, institutions, organizations, legal cases, and theoretical issues. Cross-references are provided, and entries include short bibliographic listings. A ten-page bibliography also appears at the conclusion of the volume. There are no illustrations. The contributors are drawn from among academicians and educators. The writing style is appropriate for college students, but is also accessible for the high-school level as well. Compared to the work by Raffel [entry 8-103], this publication has a somewhat broader scope; the two complement one another well. 💻

8-102. Baker, Colin, and Sylvia Prys Jones. *Encyclopedia of Bilingualism and Bilingual Education.* Philadelphia: Multilingual Matters, 1998. 758 pp. Indexes. ISBN: 1-853-59362-1.

More than just a sourcebook for bilingual education, this reference work introduces the reader to many aspects of bilingualism in the world today. There are four major sections to this work: "Individual Bilingualism," "Languages in Society," "Languages in Contact in the World," and "Bilingual Education." The latter section constitutes about one-third of the entire text. In each section, the arrangement of articles is topical rather than alphabetical, so many users will want to consult the subject index to find specific information. In addition, the table of contents is also quite detailed. The authors, educators at a university in Wales, have a twofold purpose in preparing their work. In the first place, they hope to promote bilingualism, and secondly, they wish to provide a text that meets academic standards but is accessible to general readers. To the latter end, the text is supplemented by many full-color photos, maps, and graphics, and by numerous sidebars. As a result, this is a work that will appeal to undergraduates and high-school students alike. Short listings for additional reading accompany the different articles, and the encyclopedia also concludes with a bibliography of over 2,000 listings. This will be a work of value to any researcher seeking introductory information on bilingualism; the only drawback is the fact that the topical approach makes the encyclopedia seem rather overwhelming. Use of the index and table of contents will be necessary for most of those consulting this work.

8-103. Raffel, Jeffrey A. *Historical Dictionary of School Segregation and Desegregation: The American Experience.* Westport, CT: Greenwood Press, 1998. 345 pp. Index. ISBN: 0-313-29502-6.

School segregation and desegregation have been a source of conflict and interest for several decades. This reference work includes approximately 270 brief articles describing court decisions, individuals, desegregation plans, legislation, organizations, concepts, and other items relevant to the issue. Descriptions of civil rights episodes and affirmative action that are not directly related to school segregation and desegregation are excluded. The entries are arranged alphabetically and range in length from a paragraph to a couple of pages. Cross-references to other entries are indicated with an asterisk, and brief references refer the reader to additional sources of information. Several lengthy bibliographies at the end of the volume give complete references to the sources. There are no illustrations. An index provides additional access to the text; major entries are indicated in boldface. The writing style is suitable for the collegiate level, but this work will be of value for high-school students as well. 💻

8-104. Matthews, Dawn D. *Learning Disabilities Sourcebook*. 2nd ed. Detroit: Omnigraphics, 2003. 621 pp. Index. ISBN: 0-780-80626-3.

Learning disabilities are increasingly a source of concern and attention at all levels of American education. This work provides introductory information for an audience composed of those with learning disabilities and for their parents, but it is useful for students researching the topic as well. The arrangement is topical and includes seven different parts: an introduction, assessment, three parts that describe various learning disabilities, and two concluding parts that provide information specifically for parents or for older students and adults with learning disabilities. The text is professional in tone, but accessible to the serious researcher. There are no illustrations other than occasional graphic displays. Biblio-

graphic references accompany a number of the topics. Directory information pertaining to organizations, agencies, and the Internet supplement the text. This work will be of greater value to undergraduates than to high-school students.

8-105. Van Scotter, Richard D. *Public Schooling in America: A Reference Handbook*. Santa Barbara, CA: ABC-CLIO, 1991. 240 pp. Index. ISBN: 0-874-36595-3.

Like others in the Contemporary World Issues series, this volume treats a current issue in a manner designed to be accessible to beginning researchers. The first two chapters discuss issues affecting public schools. These include desegregation, equality of opportunity, safety, values, and school choice, among others. Chronological and biographical chapters further elucidate the subject. A fifth chapter discusses noteworthy reports on the state of public schools, while the next chapter compiles factual and statistical data. The final chapters provide the reader with a directory of agencies and organizations and a bibliography of reference materials and journals. As is the case with volumes in this series, the writing style is suitable for both high-school and undergraduate students. Many of the issues discussed here are still relevant despite the fact that this book is now a decade old; in most instances, however, the reader will also wish to seek out more current resources.

8-106. Jurinski, James John. *Religion in the Schools: A Reference Handbook.*

Santa Barbara, CA: ABC-CLIO, 1998. 209 pp. Index. ISBN: 0-874-36868-5.

The role of religion in the public school system has been debated for many decades with no resolution yet in sight. This volume presents an overview for the student seeking basic information on the subject. An introductory chapter discusses such subjects as school prayer, flag salutes, religion in public school curriculum, and the voucher system. The following chapters provide a chronology, biographies, excerpts from relevant documents, a directory of organizations, and a thirty-page bibliography of print, nonprint, and Internet resources. Among the documents are portions of relevant court cases, with a legal reference to the original legal reporter volume. There are no illustrations other than a handful of tables. A glossary provides the reader with definitions pertaining to religion and the legal system. The text is suitable for both high-school and college students. ⌨

8-107. Kopka, Deborah L. *School Violence: A Reference Handbook*. Santa Barbara, CA: ABC-CLIO, 1997. 184 pp. Index. ISBN: 0-874-36861-8.

As is the case with other works in this ABC-CLIO series, this volume presents high-school and college students with an overview of the topic at hand. An initial chapter summarizing the issue of school violence is followed by a chronology, biographies, federal and state approaches to the situation, a listing of relevant organizations, and an extended bibliography of print, nonprint, and Internet sources. The volume concludes with a glossary and an index. Kopka is described as a developer of educational media, educational writer, and consultant. There are few illustrations, but the text will be suitable for students who are just approaching the topic and need basic background.

Environment

8-108. Grossman, Mark. *ABC-CLIO Companion to the Environmental Movement*. Santa Barbara, CA: ABC-CLIO, 1994. 445 pp. Index. ISBN: 0-874-36732-8.

Articles on individuals, government agencies, environmental legislation, and environmental organizations are among the strengths of this reference work, which emphasizes historical background rather than current activities. Entries are arranged alphabetically. Each receives at least a paragraph of discussion, with many subjects receiving a page or more of text. Cross-references to other relevant entries are included. Occasional photographs supplement the text. The volume concludes with a chronology that begins with 1626 and ends with 1994. Bibliographic listings are also found at the end of the text rather than with the entries themselves; the bibliography is approximately twenty pages in length. The audience for this volume will be students at both the high-school and college levels as well as interested laypersons. The biographies are a special strength, as is the fact that federal legislative enactments are cited to the *United States Statutes at Large*.

8-109. Becher, Anne. *Biodiversity: A Reference Handbook*. Santa Barbara,

CA: ABC-CLIO, 1998. 275 pp. Index. ISBN: 0-874-36923-1.

As defined in this volume, biodiversity encompasses genetic, species, and ecological concerns. The initial chapter describes these aspects of diversity, then goes on to discuss the current world situation, including threatened extinctions and efforts to avoid them. This chapter includes a useful listing of references. Other chapters provide a chronology, biographies, statistics and excerpts from relevant documents, a directory, and annotated bibliographies of print and nonprint resources. Biographies are of those individuals active in defense of biodiversity. This general format is the same as the many other volumes in the Contemporary World Issues series, and, like the others, this work will be handy for those students approaching the topic for the first time and requiring an overview of the subject. The writing style is suitable for high-school and college students alike. 🖳

8-110. Paehlke, Robert, ed. *Conservation and Environmentalism: An Encyclopedia.* New York: Garland, 1995. 771 pp. Index. ISBN: 0-824-06101-2.

Approximately 500 entries are included in this reference work. They discuss concepts, issues, places (including some individual nations and parks), organizations, legislation and case law, well-known individuals, species, pollutants, and sustainability. Examples include Edward Abbey, herbicides, Eastern Europe, mutation, and solar energy. Arrangement is alphabetical; individual

entries receive treatment that ranges from less than a page to several pages. Cross-references and short bibliographies are included with most entries. There are no illustrations other than a few tables. As much as possible, the writing style is geared to the general reader despite the complexity of certain subjects. The contributors for the most part are academicians in the United States, Great Britain, and Canada, so this work reflects emphasis upon those countries as well as Australia and New Zealand. This is a reference work that is more likely to be of value to experienced undergraduate researchers than to beginners.

8-111. Donahue, Debra L. *Conservation and the Law: A Dictionary.* Santa Barbara, CA: ABC-CLIO, 1998. 380 pp. Index. ISBN: 0-874-36771-9.

The legal ramifications of the environmental movement are quite extensive and complex, so this work should be of assistance to beginning readers attempting to research the subject. Entries describe statutes, cases, organizations, individuals, and terminology. All are listed in the table of contents. Entries are arranged alphabetically and range in length from a paragraph to a couple of pages. Cross-references are provided to other relevant entries. Brief legal citations are included for cases, statutes, and regulations. Many of these are listed in a series of appendixes at the back of the volume, but many nonspecialist readers will probably need assistance in interpreting the citations. Individual entries lack bibliographic references, but there is a bibliography of about six pages at the back of the book. There are no illustrations; on the other hand, the writing style should be suitable for both undergraduate and high-school students. While the information here is relatively brief, it provides a starting point for those unfamiliar with the law and just starting their research.

8-112. Allin, Craig W., ed. *Encyclopedia of Environmental Issues.* 3 vols. Pasadena, CA: Salem Press, 2000. 874 pp. Index. ISBN: 0-893-56994-1.

As stated in the publisher's note, this set "is a wide-ranging guide designed to meet the growing need for environmental literacy." Altogether, the set includes 475 articles arranged alphabetically and ranging in length from 500 to 3,000 words. Typical articles include "Acid Mine Drainage," "Boulder Dam," "Endangered Species," and "Sierra Club." Articles begin with a relevant date, a categorization, and a short summary that serves as an abstract of the entire article. Articles over 1,000 words also include an annotated list for additional reading. There are numerous cross-references and illustrations. Articles are signed by the contributors, who are mostly U.S. academicians. Each of the three volumes also includes a "List of Articles by Category" that allows the reader to see relevant groupings at a glance. Emphasis is upon the United States, although there is also some coverage of international environmental problems as well. *Natural Resources* [entry 8-123], by this same pub-

lisher, is somewhat similar in nature, but focuses more upon minerals and their application (or misuse). Many readers may wish to consult both. The readership for this set will consist of high-school and undergraduate students.

8-113. Coffel, Steve. *Encyclopedia of Garbage.* New York: Facts on File, 1996. 311 pp. Index. ISBN: 0-816-03135-5.

The coverage of this volume is somewhat broader than one might expect given the title. In addition to topics associated with garbage and solid waste, there are also entries for subjects such as acid rain, jet engines, social cost, and water pollution. Arrangement is alphabetical. Shorter entries receive about a paragraph; longer entries are about two pages in length. Cross-references are indicated in uppercase. The only illustrations are graphic displays. The volume concludes with a two-page bibliography and an index. This is a topic of scientific and technical complexity, but the author uses a style that is accessible to serious researchers, including undergraduates, who have relatively little familiarity with garbage and solid waste disposal, but who require beginning information in a brief format. Unfortunately, Coffel provides no introductory statement of intent, so criteria for inclusion of entries is unknown.

8-114. Folchi Guillen, Ramon. *Encyclopedia of the Biosphere.* 11 vols. Detroit: Gale Group, 2000. Index. ISBN: 0-787-64506-0.

This set appeared originally in 1993 as a production of the *Enciclopedia Catalana* but only appeared in an English translation as of 2000. Rather than an alphabetical array, each of the eleven volumes pursues a separate topic. The titles of the individual volumes are *Our Living Planet; Tropical Rainforests; Savannahs; Deserts; Mediterranean Woodlands; Temperate Rainforests; Deciduous Forests; Prairies and Boreal Forests; Lakes, Islands, and the Poles; Oceans and Seashores;* and *The Biosphere Concept and Index*. Each of the profusely illustrated volumes stands alone and discusses not only scientific topics but also the impacts of humanity upon the various biospheres. The writing style is suitable for undergraduates and other nonspecialists. One major drawback to this set is the fact that each volume concludes with a "Thematic Index" that acts as a table of contents; U.S. readers are more accustomed to look for this information at the beginning of a work rather than at the conclusion. Otherwise, readers will find this set, with its accessible text and color photography, to be a good starting point for this subject.

8-115. Davis, Lee. *Environmental Disasters: A Chronicle of Individual, Industrial, and Governmental Carelessness.* New York: Facts on File, 1998. 246 pp. Index. ISBN: 0-816-03265-3.

Student researchers seeking examples of environmental catastrophes need look no further than this volume. Numerous disasters are described here. The arrangement of entries is somewhat unorthodox. There are five chapters, titled as follows: "Collective and Individual Assaults against the Environment," "Industrial and Governmental Disasters," "Oil Spill Disasters," "Nuclear Disasters," and "War Crimes against the Environment." Each of the five chapters begins with a listing of the disasters described (arranged by nation), a chronology, and an introductory essay. The narratives of the disasters that follow are arranged by country. Those researchers seeking a particular disaster or subject will be best served by consulting the index. The individual disaster narratives vary in length from a column to several pages and are accompanied by numerous illustrations. There is an emphasis on events taking place in recent decades. A short bibliography concludes the volume, but there are no references with individual entries. The author's indignation in regard to environmental degradation is readily apparent throughout this work, which is suitable for both high-school and undergraduate levels. ⌨

8-116. Bortman, Marci. *Environmental Encyclopedia.* 3rd ed. Detroit: Gale/Thomson-Gale, 2003. 1641 pp. Index. ISBN: 0-787-65486-8.

This single-volume encyclopedia provides an alphabetical array of short articles dealing with the social, economic, and political aspects of environmental issues. Scientific topics are covered as well, but are written at a nontechnical level for a lay audience. Typical articles describe the Bureau of Land Management, cancer, power plants, and shanty towns. Also included are biographies of key figures in the field as well as summaries of important environmental legislation. Most articles conclude with a listing of items for further reading, and cross-references to other articles in the encyclopedia are noted in boldface. Articles are signed by the contributors, who are listed, with their affiliations, at the front of the volume. Illustrations accompany the text. The volume also includes a chronology and a listing of legislative enactments. The index provides another access point to the text. The primary audience for this useful work will be students at both the high-school and college levels.

8-117. Miller, E. Willard, and Ruby M. Miller. *Environmental Hazards; Toxic Waste and Hazardous Material: A Reference Handbook.* Santa Barbara, CA: ABC-CLIO, 1991. 286 pp. Index. ISBN: 0-874-36596-1.

This work begins with a chapter nearly 100 pages long that provides a detailed overview of the subject of toxic and hazardous wastes. Generation, cleanup, and control of such wastes are all examined. Major toxic chemicals are described, as are the effects of hazardous waste. There are also sections on oil pollution and asbestos control. This chapter is followed by a chapter on chronology and a chapter on laws and regulations pertaining to hazardous waste. For the most part, laws and regulations are summarized rather than reproduced in part or in whole. The final chapters provide directory and bibliographic information. There are no illustrations. Due to its publication date, this work is probably most valuable today for a historical summary of the toxic and

hazardous waste situation at the beginning of the 1990s; it can still be of use to high-school and undergraduate students with no prior background in the subject, but such researchers will probably wish to consult more recent publications as well.

8-118. Newton, David E. *Environmental Justice: A Reference Handbook.* Santa Barbara, CA: ABC-CLIO, 1996. 271 pp. Index. ISBN: 0-874-36848-0.

One of a number of volumes in the ABC-CLIO Contemporary World Issues series, this work, like the others, hopes to provide the reader with introductory information on a particular "hot topic." The format will be familiar to those who have used other volumes in the series: an introductory chapter is followed by chapters on chronology, biographies, excerpts from relevant documents, a directory, an annotated bibliography encompassing print and nonprint resources, and a glossary. The introductory chapter provides examples of environmental injustices, their relationship to civil rights, and legal and political responses. This chapter also includes some brief statistical data. The chapter on documents includes text from laws, treaties, bills, executive orders, legal cases, and policy statements. Readership for this work includes both high-school and undergraduate students desiring an overview of environmental justice issues.

8-119. Netzley, Patricia D. *Environmental Literature: An Encyclopedia of Works,*

Characters, Authors, and Themes. Santa Barbara, CA: ABC-CLIO, 1999. 337 pp. Index. ISBN: 1-576-07000-X.

As the title indicates, this reference work concentrates upon the literature of the environmental movement and its authors. The entries are arranged alphabetically and fall into three categories: authors, their works, and themes in environmental literature. Most of the authors and works under discussion date from the second half of the twentieth century, but some attention is also paid to earlier time periods. Most of the entries are relatively short, ranging from a paragraph to a page in length. Cross-references to relevant entries elsewhere are abundant, and references to a bibliography at the back of the volume also appear. There are numerous illustrations. Among the articles relating to themes are "Air Pollution," "Forest Management," "Nature Writing," and "Wildlife Conservation." More limited in scope than other environmental policy reference works, this book will find its greatest use among those high-school and undergraduate students studying the political ramifications of the literature of the environment.

8-120. *Environment Encyclopedia and Directory 2001.* 3rd ed. London: Europa Publications, 2001. 622 pp. Index. ISBN: 1-857-43089-1.

This reference work is composed of five major components. First, a set of twenty maps shows areas both globally and regionally that are of high interest in environmental affairs. A second section provides definitions of approximately 1,000 environmental terms. The third section, about half the entire contents, is a directory of environmental organizations arranged by nation. Both governmental and nongovernmental organizations are included. Information provided for each includes address, telephone, fax, major officers, and a very brief description of the mission of the agency. The fourth section is an extensive bibliography of periodicals in the field. Information here includes address, telephone, fax, editors or other important officers, and a brief mission statement. The final section is a listing of biographies of 700 noteworthy individuals in the environmental field. These concentrate upon career achievements, addresses, phone numbers, fax, and e-mail addresses. The index arranges organizations by their field of activity.

8-121. Franck, Irene M., and David M. Brownstone. *Green Encyclopedia.* New York: Prentice-Hall General Reference, 1992. 486 pp. ISBN: 0-133-65685-3.

Targeting an audience that includes the general reader as well as knowledgeable environmentalists, this reference work discusses issues, environmental disasters, well-known environmentalists, philosophies, laws, and treaties. There is special emphasis upon organizations and government agencies concerned with the environment. Entries are arranged alphabetically and range in length from a paragraph to a couple of pages. Graphic displays supplement the text, and sidebars provide directory information for practical advice. The final portion of the volume is a "Special Information Section" that provides listings of endangered species, reserves, Superfund sites, acronyms, and a bibliography, among other pieces of information. Much of the directory information may be outdated by now; the real value of this work is its success in describing topics such as acid rain or toxic chemicals in a nontechnical fashion that can be understood by student researchers and other interested readers. 🖳

8-122. Lund, Herbert F., ed. *McGraw-Hill Recycling Handbook*. 2nd ed. New York: McGraw-Hill, 2000. 1152 pp. Index. ISBN: 0-070-39096-7.

Recycling is one environmental topic that has obvious application for all individuals. Although this work is written by professional contributors for a professional audience, it includes much information that is accessible to a general audience, including students at the collegiate level. The initial chapters provide an overview of and background on subjects such as history, legislation, marketing, financial planning, and public awareness. The next group of chapters describes recycling of specific categories of materials. These include some categories that will be obvious to most readers, such as glass bottles and plastic, as well as some that might not spring to mind so readily. These include "Yard Waste" and "Construction and Demolition Debris." The final chapters collectively describe "how-to" procedures for recycling programs. Although there are

occasional illustrations and graphic displays, emphasis is on presentation of information through detailed text. Page numbering is by individual chapter. Although some topics in the field of recycling may have moved beyond the theory and analysis presented here, this volume is still worth consultation by researchers approaching the subject for the first time. 🖳

8-123. Coyne, Mark S., and Craig W. Allin, eds. *Natural Resources*. 3 vols. Pasadena, CA: Salem Press, 1998. 964 pp. Index. ISBN: 0-893-56912-7.

Natural resources and their use by the human race are topics of contemporary interest to many researchers. This three-volume set includes 438 alphabetically arranged articles on the subject. The articles describe various types of natural resources (including many minerals); their use; economic, political, and social ramifications of that use; history; environmental effects; and policy issues. Some articles are brief, no more than several hundred words, while others are up to several thousand words in length. Cross-references follow each article, leading the reader to other relevant topics. There are numerous illustrations, including both photographs and graphic displays. Articles are signed by the contributor. A listing of the contributors appears at the front of the first volume; most are academicians at U.S. colleges and universities. The final volume includes a chronology, a glossary, a bibliography, a listing of articles by subject categories, and an index. The primary audience for this set will be beginning students at both the high-school and collegiate levels. More advanced researchers will probably wish to turn to more detailed and sophisticated sources. The value of the set would have been enhanced had bibliographic entries been provided with each article rather than having been placed at the end of the third volume.

8-124. Gay, Kathlyn. *Rainforests of the World: A Reference Handbook.* Santa Barbara, CA: ABC-CLIO, 2002. 257 pp. Index. ISBN: 1-576-07424-2.

Another in the Contemporary World Issues series, this volume discusses the much-debated issue of rain forests. The initial chapter describes rain forests, including those in temperate regions such as the Pacific Northwest, then goes on to discuss deforestation and efforts at preservation. The next three chapters provide a chronology, biographies, and facts and statistics. This latter chapter includes a number of maps and graphic displays that further elucidate the situation. The final chapters point the reader to organizations and both print and nonprint resources for additional research. These bibliographies are annotated. A glossary briefly defines important terms in the field. Like others in the series, this work will be of use to high-school and college students requiring basic introductory information on the subject under discussion. ⌨

8-125. Strong, Debra L. *Recycling in America: A Reference Handbook.* 2nd ed. Santa Barbara, CA: ABC-CLIO, 1997. 330 pp. Index. ISBN: 0-874-36889-8.

Another in the Contemporary World Issues series, this volume is similar in format to the others. An introductory chapter provides the reader with an overview of recycling. This is followed by a chapter on chronology and another on biographies of individuals prominent in the field. The next chapter provides facts and statistics on various types of recycled materials: aluminum and steel cans, glass, plastic, paper, metal, and miscellaneous products. This is followed by a lengthy chapter that summarizes state laws and regulations pertaining to recycling. The final two chapters provide a directory and a bibliography. Given the publication date of this work, it is now more valuable for the first several overview chapters than it is for laws, regulations, directory information, and bibliographic references. Nevertheless, it still retains solid reference value.

8-126. Crawford, Mark. *Toxic Waste Sites: An Encyclopedia of Endangered America.* Santa Barbara, CA: ABC-CLIO, 1997. 324 pp. Index. ISBN: 0-874-36934-7.

The 1,310 toxic waste sites described in this volume represents the worst areas of pollution in the United States, those that are commonly called Superfund sites. Crawford presents a thumbnail description of each site. The arrangement is by state, then alphabetically by the name of the site. Descriptions include information about how the site was generated, the toxic materials it contains, and action under way to remedy the problem. Each description also includes the address of the agency responsible for the cleanup. Each state section is accompanied by an outline map that shows the sites and the county in which they are found. However, the name of the site is not on the map; the reader must discover this by checking the individual entries for the name of the county. An introduction of several pages discusses the problem of toxic wastes and the Superfund program. Several appendixes provide listings of contaminants, a glossary, and a short bibliography. This is a highly useful book, for the subject it discusses is complex and often found only through technical literature generated by the federal government. Here, the interested researcher can find brief information to begin his or her research. Obviously, the Superfund list is not static, but the author provides the address of the Internet site where updated information can be found.

8-127. Rosenberg, Kenneth A. *Wilderness Preservation: A Reference Handbook.* Santa Barbara, CA: ABC-CLIO, 1994. 292 pp. Index. ISBN: 0-874-36731-X.

One of a series of works entitled Contemporary World Issues, this book follows the general format of its companion volumes. An introductory chapter describes the wilderness concept and controversies that pertain to it. This is followed by chapters providing a chronology and short biographies; most of the latter sketch individuals promi-

nent in the fight to preserve wilderness. The next chapter includes statistics, quotations from both sides of the debate, and excerpts from relevant federal legislation, including the Wilderness Act. The next two chapters list federal protected lands (including acreage) arranged by type of unit and by state, and a directory of government and nongovernment organizations concerned with the issue. An annotated bibliography of both print and nonprint sources appears in the final two chapters. The volume concludes with a glossary and an index. As is the case with other works in this series, this book can be used by both high-school and undergraduate students requiring a basic overview along with suggestions for additional research. 💻

Gays

8-128. Hogan, Steve, and Lee Hudson. *Completely Queer: The Gay and Lesbian Encyclopedia.* New York: Henry Holt, 1998. 704 pp. Index. ISBN: 0-805-03629-6.

Although the focus of this work is the contemporary gay and lesbian communities in the Western world, it also provides information on the historical background of today's movement. Arrangement of entries is alphabetical and includes organizations, individuals, overviews of gay and lesbian life in twenty-five countries, issues, and concepts. Entries are relatively brief, ranging from a couple of paragraphs to a couple of pages. Cross-references are indicated in uppercase, and many entries include a short bibliography. There are many photographs and other illustrations. These are not explicit, but may offend some readers. The volume concludes with a chronology of approximately seventy pages. Compared to the *St. James Press Gay and Lesbian Almanac* [entry 8-131], this volume provides many more individual entries but less detailed discussion. Many users will want to consult both. The reading level is in general more suitable for undergraduates than for high-school students.

8-129. Ridinger, Robert B. Marks. *Gay and Lesbian Movement: References and Resources.* New York: G. K. Hall, 1996. 487 pp. Index. ISBN: 0-816-17373-7.

As Ridinger points out in his introduction, the gay and lesbian movement has remained on the fringes of society until recent decades; for that reason, a bibliography is more difficult to compile than is the case for most subject areas. This bibliography commences with the period 1864 through 1939, when defenders of homosexuality emerged in Germany and the United States. Works from this time are relatively few, so most entries represent later publications describing the history of the period. Succeeding sections deal with later times in a chronological sequence. As a result, the number of entries increases almost exponentially as one approaches the late twentieth century. Altogether, there are 1,939 entries, each with its own annotation. Most are from gay periodicals, although there are also entries from standard publishing sources, both books and periodicals. The chronological arrangement is further subdivided into topics of special interest.

For that reason, the overall arrangement is somewhat complicated, so most readers will turn to the index to find specific entries written by a particular author or on a particular subject. It is likely that only larger libraries will have older numbers of many of the periodicals cited.

8-130. Newton, David E. *Gay and Lesbian Rights: A Reference Handbook.* Santa Barbara, CA: ABC-CLIO, 1994. 214 pp. Index. ISBN: 0-874-36745-X.

As is the case with similar volumes in the Contemporary World Issues series, this work seeks to provide the reader with introductory information and guides to further research. The initial chapter sketches the topic of gay and lesbian rights, discussing such issues as the gay liberation movement, housing, sodomy laws, hate crimes, and HIV. This is followed by a detailed chronology and biographies of a number of individuals prominent on both sides of the debate. The next chapter includes viewpoints from both proponents and opponents, and legal and documentary information. The final chapters provide a directory and annotated bibliographies of print and nonprint resources. Although this issue is one that is evolving continually, this publication will provide both high-school and college students with useful background that can then be updated with current sources.

8-131. Schlager, Neil, ed. *St. James Press Gay and Lesbian Almanac.* Detroit: St. James Press, 1998. 680 pp. Index. ISBN: 1-558-62358-2.

Despite the greater visibility of the gay and lesbian movement in recent years, there is a relative dearth of reference sources in regard to this subject. For that reason, this work is a welcome addition to the shelves. It hopes to provide users with a "reliable place to access information about the gay and lesbian experience . . . [and] a useful starting point to additional serious research about the topics discussed herein" (Schlager 1998, "Editor's Note"). The volume is divided into twenty-three major subjects; these include a chronology, important documents, "Coming Out," family, health, AIDS, military, music, sports, and science, among others. Each of the twenty-three sections averages about twenty-eight pages in length. A number of the sections provide short biographies of prominent gay and lesbian individuals. Emphasis is on gay history and political activism in the United States from the 1920s to the present; happenings elsewhere in the world receive only passing attention. Each chapter concludes with a bibliography, and there is a general annotated bibliography at the end of the volume. Numerous photographs enliven the text. Contributors include academicians, journalists, librarians, and freelance writers, including a number from the University of Colorado. The tone is generally sympathetic to the gay movement. Undergraduate students in particular will find this a helpful starting point for research on gays and lesbians.

Health Care

8-132. Ropes, Linda Brubaker. *Health Care Crisis in America.* Santa Barbara,

CA: ABC-CLIO, 1991. 172 pp. Index. ISBN: 0-874-36616-X.

This work follows the standard format of the Contemporary World Issues series. An initial chapter introduces the crisis in health care. The next three chapters provide a chronology, biographies, and factual and statistical data, respectively. Another chapter is a listing of relevant organizations and agencies, while the final two chapters provide an extensive annotated bibliography of both print and nonprint sources. A glossary explains terminology relevant to the subject. The text is suitable for both high-school and undergraduate students; however, most will probably wish to search for more recent information to update that found here.

8-133. Rovner, Julie. *Health Care Policy and Politics A to Z.* 2nd ed. Washington, DC: CQ Press, 2003. 282 pp. Index. ISBN: 1-568-02852-0.

In her preface, the author of this volume states that her goal "is to provide background information on the broad array of health issues on the national agenda." As such, she discusses health care issues rather than focusing upon terminology only. The arrangement is alphabetical and incorporates well over 200 articles. Some describe federal government agencies, legislation, and programs. Still others provide the reader with background on specialized jargon, such as "Durable Power of Attorney for Health Care" and "Guaranteed Issue." Yet another category includes the issues themselves: AIDS, cloning, health maintenance organizations, and the medically uninsured. Some entries are comparatively short, perhaps a lengthy paragraph, but more substantive topics receive several pages of treatment. Cross-references to other relevant entries appear in uppercase. Many photographs and occasional graphic displays accompany the text. A glossary of terminology and a directory of congressional committees conclude the text, but there is no bibliography beyond a directory of interested organizations. Both high-school and undergraduate students will find this work of value. ⌨

8-134. *Statistical Record of Health and Medicine.* 2nd ed. Detroit: Gale Research, 1995–1998. Index. ISSN: 1078-6961.

As is the case with other statistical information, data on health care and medicine can be tedious to find thanks to the multitude of available sources. This volume compiles many statistical indicators and tables pertaining to the subject, most of them published by federal government agencies. The statistics are ranged into eleven chapters, each on a particular subject. Some examples include "Health Status of Americans," "Health Care Establishment," "Medical Professions," and "International Comparisons." There is almost no text; tables are simply reproduced from the original source. However, sources are indicated for those researchers who wish to pursue the topic, and there is also a bibliographic listing of approximately ten pages at the back of the volume. An ex-

tensive table of contents and the detailed index provide access to the tables themselves. This volume is a useful starting point, particularly for undergraduates and other beginning researchers who require an introduction to the subject.

Hispanics

8-135. Kanellos, Nicolas, ed. *Hispanic Almanac: From Columbus to Corporate America.* Detroit: Invisible Ink, 1994. 644 pp. Index. ISBN: 0-787-60030-X.

Many facets of the Hispanic contribution to the United States are delineated in this work. The twelve chapters describe topics such as history, the business world, politics, the arts, media, and sports. Biographies of significant individuals are included in each topical chapter. Approximately 200 illustrations accompany the text. While emphasis is upon a narrative treatment, the reader can also find statistical information here. Coverage extends not only to the continental United States, but also to Mexico and the Caribbean. The writing style is suitable for high-school students as well as researchers within higher education. This work is an abridgment of the *Hispanic-American Almanac,* published in 1993.

8-136. Smith, Carter, and David Lindroth, eds. *Hispanic-American Experience on File.* New York: Facts on File, 1999. Index. ISBN: 0-816-03695-0.

Like other Facts on File publications, this loose-leaf volume is intended for easy reproduction by the student researcher. The arrangement is essentially chronological, discussing first the pre-

Columbian cultures of present Latin America, then progressing to current issues. The table of contents indicates to the reader those pages on which a particular set of information can be found. The text itself is relatively brief; instead, emphasis is upon illustrations, maps, and graphic displays. A final chapter discusses Hispanic American culture. Lists of sources and a bibliography can be found at the back of the volume. Treatment here is not as in-depth as that found in some other reference works, but the format will appeal to high-school students and beginning undergraduates working on introductory papers.

8-137. Horner, Louise L., ed. *Hispanic Americans: A Statistical Sourcebook.* Annual. Palo Alto, CA: Information Publications, 2002. 264 pp. Index. ISBN: 0-929-96033-5.

As the introduction to this annual volume indicates, Hispanics are not a racial group, but rather the only ethnic or cultural group for which the federal government gathers statistical data. All of the sources found here are reproduced from federal tables and compilations. The ten chapters deal with "Demographics," "Social Characteristics," "Household and Family Characteristics," "Education: Preprimary through High School," "Education: Postsecondary and Educational Attainment," "Government and Elections," "The Labor Force, Employment and Unemployment," "Earnings, Income, Poverty, and Wealth," "Crime and Corrections," and "Special Topics." Each of these chapters reproduces a number of tables, each with a source indicated. In some cases, the source is a print publication, and in other instances, the source is a Web site. The index provides additional access, and a glossary includes definitions of terms used in federal demographic compilations. Although the data found here is also available through government publications, it is useful to have it available under a single cover.

8-138. *Latino Encyclopedia.* 6 vols. New York: Marshall Cavendish, 1996. 1821 pp. Index. ISBN: 0-761-40125-3.

"Latino" as used in this reference set includes persons of Mexican, Puerto Rican, Cuban, Central or South American, or other Spanish cultural origins. Topics addressed include people, organizations, history, entertainment, family life, and cultural movements, among others. Entries are arranged alphabetically and number approximately 230 articles. Of these, twenty-eight are about 4,000 words in length and discuss major topics, while the remaining entries range from 1,000 to 2,000 words. Only the longer articles include bibliographies. An attempt has been made to provide biographies of lesser known individuals, but the reader will also find entries for noted celebrities and sports figures as well. There are numerous photographs and other illustrations. The final volume includes a chronology, bibliographies, and listings of entries by subject and by Latino subgroup. In general, this is a set in that will be of use to high-school students and beginning undergraduates at the college level.

8-139. Reddy, Marlita A., ed. *Statistical Record of Hispanic Americans.* 2nd ed. Detroit: Gale Research, 1995. 1173 pp. Index. ISBN: 0-810-36422-0.

Like other volumes published by Gale with a similar title, this reference work compiles statistics pertaining to a particular ethnic group. Data is gathered from a variety of sources, although federal government statistical work bulks large. Statistical categories can be somewhat idiosyncratic, but it is useful to have this data in a single volume rather than having to consult many sources. Unlike some of the other volumes in this series, this one does not report data from Canada, where, presumably, Hispanics are not a major ethnic group.

Historical Issues

8-140. Allen, Larry. *ABC-CLIO World History Companion to Capitalism.* Santa Barbara, CA: ABC-CLIO, 1998. 404 pp. Index. ISBN: 0-874-36944-4.

The intent of this volume is best described in the preface by the author, a professor at Lamar University: "I wrote the book as the history of the development of capitalism as seen through the eyes of one trained in economic theory rather than in history, and chose the topics and their treatment accordingly." The approximately 300 entries in his work are arranged alphabetically. Some are fairly obvious inclusions. Among them are entries for "Corporation," "Double-Entry Bookkeeping," "Great Depression," and "Industrial Revolution." Others, such as "Iron Act of 1750" and "Portuguese Colonial Empire" are less likely to occur

to the reader. For this reason, consultation of the index is important for optimal use of this work. Most entries are about a page in length, with a few ranging up to two pages. Cross-references lead the reader to other relevant entries, and short bibliographies are provided with each article. Occasional illustrations enhance the text. A chronology and an extended bibliography are also provided. The reading level of the text is suitable for both high-school students and college undergraduates.

8-141. Miller, Randall M., and John David Smith, eds. *Dictionary of Afro-American Slavery.* updated ed. Westport, CT: Praeger/Greenwood Press, 1997. 892 pp. ISBN: 0-275-95799-3.

The first edition of this work appeared in 1988. This updated edition, although it takes into account scholarship published in the years intervening, is primarily a reissue rather than a revision. An article on the historiography of slavery helps the reader to orient himself or herself in regard to recent thinking on the subject. The format remains the same; articles (including the one on historiography) are arranged alphabetically and are often several pages long. Articles are signed by the contributor and include bibliographic references. There are no illustrations. There is a detailed chronology, and a comprehensive bibliography, arranged by topic and covering the years from 1988 through 1996, will assist readers in identifying additional reading. The writing style is suitable for both high-school and undergraduate students. Although the institution of slavery was abolished in the United States over a century ago, its effects still are with us, so this reference work will be of value for researchers dealing with contemporary ethnic issues.

8-142. Toropov, Brandon. *Encyclopedia of Cold War Politics.* New York: Facts on File, 2000. 242 pp. Index. ISBN: 0-816-03574-1

Among the various reference books devoted to the cold war, this work differs from its competitors in that it focuses upon the domestic situation in the United States from 1945 through 1990 and how it was influenced by the confrontation with the Communist world. The arrangement is alphabetical and includes articles on events, organizations, institutions, individuals, groups, and concepts. In particular, there are entries for the antiwar movement (during the Vietnam era), the civil rights movement, and the women's movement, all of which accompanied the cold war epoch. Articles are relatively short, ranging in length from a couple of paragraphs to about two pages. Numerous photographs accompany the text, and cross-references assist the reader in locating other relevant entries. An alphabetical list of entries at the beginning of the work also allows for a quick overview of the contents. Those who will benefit most from use of this work will be high-school students and undergraduates requiring beginning information in regard to the political impact of the cold war on the United States. See also entries in Chapter 5 for other cold war reference materials.

8-143. Gutman, Israel, ed. *Encyclopedia of the Holocaust.* 4 vols. New York: Macmillan, 1990. 1905 pp. Index. ISBN: 0-028-96090-4.

The Holocaust is one of the central events of the twentieth century. Those researchers seeking introductory information that is both comprehensive and in depth can turn to this encyclopedia for assistance. The articles found here discuss the rise of the Nazi regime, the process by which racist legislation became mass murder, and the fate of those in concentration camps. There are also articles on individual European countries and groups other than Jews that were victims of the Third Reich. Some entries are relatively short, perhaps a couple of paragraphs, but others are several pages in length. Most include a bibliography, and cross-references are indicated in uppercase. A number of black-and-white maps accompany text, and numerous photographs serve to reinforce the horror of this episode. The final volume includes a glossary, a chronology, several appendixes, and a comprehensive index. Although the writing style is perhaps more suitable for college students, this sobering work should be of value to high-school students as well.

8-144. Klingaman, William K. *Encyclopedia of the McCarthy Era.* New York: Facts on File, 1996. 502 pp. Index. ISBN: 0-816-03097-9.

The author states that he has attempted to provide "a general overview of the most prominent personalities and issues of this controversial period in U.S. history" (Klingaman 1996, introduction). There are entries for individuals, events, organizations, and significant publications and motion pictures, with biographies predominating. Articles vary in length from a couple of paragraphs to two or three pages. There are occasional photographs of the personalities under discussion. Cross-references are indicated in uppercase. The author also provides eighteen appendixes that reproduce important documents from the time. A two-page bibliography indicates important secondary sources. Given the continuing interest in the McCarthy era, this reference work will be a useful starting point for students and other researchers delving into the events of that time.

8-145. Levy, Peter B. *Encyclopedia of the Reagan-Bush Years.* Westport, CT: Greenwood Press, 1996. 442 pp. Index. ISBN: 0-313-29018-0.

For adults, the presidencies of Ronald Reagan and George H. W. Bush remain relatively fresh in memory, but for younger students, they are now part of the historical record. This work provides brief information on individuals and topics of relevance to those administrations. Entries are arranged alphabetically and range in length from about 100 words to about 2,000. Many of the entries concern individuals both within the two administrations and others of importance to the era. More important to the student researcher are the entries that deal with policy issues and events of note. These in-

clude such topics as arms control, the collapse of Communism, defense spending, elections, the Persian Gulf War, poverty, and the savings-and-loan crisis, among many others. There are also entries for important pieces of legislation. Occasional photographs, mostly of prominent individuals, supplement the text. Entries generally include cross-references and brief listings of articles and books for further reading. A chronology, statistical tables, and an index conclude the volume. The writing style is suitable for both college and high-school students. 💻

8-146. Zentner, Christian, and Friedemann Bedurftig, eds. *Encyclopedia of the Third Reich.* 2 vols. New York: Macmillan, 1991. 1150 pp. Index. ISBN: 0-028-97500-6.

The Third Reich remains a topic of grim fascination more than half a century after its defeat. This reference work, first published in Germany in 1985, attempts to describe the Hitler regime not only from a political and military point of view but also taking into consideration other facets of the National Socialist regime, including social and economic developments. It has been translated by Amy Hackett from *Grosse Lexicon des Dritten Reiches.* Most of the entries are relatively brief, from a single paragraph to a column. Longer articles are up to three or four pages in length. Subjects for these latter articles include education, the Final Solution, propaganda, social policy, and women, among others. There are also reasonably detailed entries for major military campaigns and for nations involved for or against the Hitler regime. There are numerous short biographies of individuals within and without Germany. Numerous photographs and illustrations enhance the text. Cross-references are indicated in uppercase. Individual entries lack bibliographies, but there is an extensive bibliography at the end of the second volume. Contributors appear to be members of the German academic community. Some articles were updated for the English translation. The writing style is suitable for undergraduate and advanced researchers.

8-147. Rodriquez, Junius P., ed. *Historical Encyclopedia of World Slavery.* 2 vols. Santa Barbara, CA: ABC-CLIO, 1997. 805 pp. Index. ISBN: 0-874-36885-5.

According to the introduction to this set, slavery as an institution is a practice found throughout human history. The introductory material then goes on to provide a historical overview of the institution. The individual articles that follow are arrayed alphabetically. Most are one or two pages in length. Articles are signed by the contributors, who also provide listings for additional reading. Cross-references also appear at the end of the articles. Most of the contributors are from the U.S. academy. A group of five black-and-white maps appears at the beginning of both volumes; the maps focus upon the slave experience in the Western Hemisphere, as do the numerous illustrations. The second volume concludes with a lengthy bibliography arranged by topic and an index to both

volumes. Compared to the *Macmillan Encyclopedia of World Slavery* [entry 8-151], which was published shortly after this work, the *Historical Encyclopedia of World Slavery* has somewhat greater emphasis on the slave experience in the Americas and is a bit more suitable for an audience that includes both high-school and college students. The two works complement one another and are both worth consulting. 🖳

8-148. Drescher, Seymour, and Stanley L. Engerman, eds. *Historical Guide to World Slavery.* New York: Oxford University Press, 1998. 429 pp. Index. ISBN: 0-195-12091-4.

Slavery as a global institution is increasingly attracting scholarly attention. This work focuses upon "regional approaches and perspectives, as well as the structures, processes, institutions, and concepts that have gained acceptance as distinguishing features of contemporary historiography" (Drescher and Engerman 1998, preface). There is also emphasis on larger processes rather than events and persons, as well as on recent analysis and interpretation. Articles are arranged alphabetically and are two to about ten pages in length. Some examples include "Anti-Slavery Literature," "Slave Trade," and "Biblical Literature." Longer articles begin with an introductory overview followed by more detailed discussion. Cross-references and bibliographies are included. Contributors are drawn from the ranks of those historians and others proficient in this topic. Compared to other recent reference works on world slavery, this volume has somewhat greater nuance and will probably have greater appeal for more knowledgeable researchers, although it can also be used by college undergraduates. 💻

8-149. Frankel, Benjamin, ed. *History in Dispute.* Vol. 1, *The Cold War.* First Series. Detroit: St. James Press, 2000. 347 pp. Index. ISBN: 1-558-62395-7.

This first volume in the History in Dispute series focuses on the cold war. Pro-and-con arguments are presented on forty different topics, arranged alphabetically. The first entry is for "Admirals' Revolt," while the last is for "Yom Kippur War." Example of other entries include "Berlin Crises," "Containment," "Human Rights," and "Nuclear Weapons." Entries average eight pages in length and begin with an introductory statement of about a page. The introductions are followed by arguments on both sides of the topic. The contributors for these statements are for the most part drawn from the U.S. academic community. Entries conclude with a listing of references, and there is a more extensive bibliography at the back of the volume. Sidebars, maps, and photographs accompany the text. The writing style is suitable for undergraduates; those requiring an adversarial approach to cold war topics will be especially interested in this reference work.

8-150. Newton, Michael, and Judy Ann Newton. *Ku Klux Klan: An Encyclopedia.* New York: Garland, 1991. 639 pp. ISBN: 0-824-02038-3.

The Ku Klux Klan (KKK) has had a shad-owy existence for over a century. It has often split into a number of competing groups and just as often is associated with native Nazi groups. This work hopes to bring some order to the subject by presenting the reader with information on all aspects of the Klan. Entries are arranged alphabetically and include organizations, individuals (victims among them), geographical entities where Klansmen have been resident, ethnic groups, events, and facilities associated with the Klan. Klan terminology and beliefs are among other topics covered. Entries are usually short, from a paragraph to a couple of pages. References to sources are indicated with entry numbers at the end of each article; these entry numbers correlate with items in the bibliography at the back of the volume. This is obviously a specialized work, but will be of use to those students and other researchers delving into the KKK.

8-151. Finkelman, Paul, and Joseph C. Miller, eds. *Macmillan Encyclopedia of World Slavery.* 2 vols. New York: Macmillan Reference USA, 1998. 1065 pp. Index. ISBN: 0-028-64607-X.

Describing slavery as ubiquitous throughout human history and societies, this reference work presents articles that attempt to describe the full experience of slavery. Articles are arranged alphabetically and range in length from a few paragraphs to as many as ten pages. Illustrations enhance the text; most are drawn from circumstances in the Western Hemisphere. A group of twenty-five black-and-white maps appears at the beginning of the first volume along with a listing of contributors and their affiliations, and an alphabetical list of the entries. Most of the contributors are U.S. academicians. The second volume concludes with a "Synoptic Outline of Entries," a chronology, a bibliography, and the index. Bibliographies and cross-references also accompany the entries themselves. The writing style is erudite but accessible to undergraduates. Compared to the *Historical Encyclopedia of World Slavery* [8-147], which appeared almost simultaneously, this work has somewhat more emphasis on slavery in non-Western societies and is more suitable for a collegiate audience.

8-152. Kurz, Kenneth Franklin. *Reagan Years A to Z: An Alphabetical History of Ronald Reagan's Presidency.* Los Angeles: Lowell House, 1996. 288 pp. Index. ISBN: 1-565-65462-5.

The Reagan presidency has seen the publication of more than one reference book. This volume differs from the competition in that it offers fewer entries but greater length for each entry. Altogether, one finds here approximately eighty articles arranged in alphabetical sequence, beginning with "Air-Traffic Controllers Strike" and concluding with "Zero-Zero Option." Entries were selected on the basis of their historical significance or their uniqueness. Among the categories of articles are biographies, military episodes, and policy issues. Inevitably, there are omissions. For example, the reader seeking information on the savings-and-loan crisis must check the index, which includes two page references to the subject, both in the article on "Deregulation." A section of photographs and a short bibliography supplement the text. The author's treatment of his subject appears balanced and even-handed, and this work recommends itself to undergraduates and others new to the topic.

8-153. Singleton, Carl, ed. *Sixties in America.* 3 vols. Pasadena, CA: Salem Press, 1999. 907 pp. Index. ISBN: 0-893-56982-8.

The decade of the 1960s holds a continuing fascination; this three-volume set provides the reader with 554 articles dealing with that subject. A number concentrate on major themes: civil rights, the Vietnam War, politics, and the social revolution. Others discuss the arts, media, music, the space race, and medicine, among others. Articles, which are arranged alphabetically, range in length from 250 words to as many as 3,000 for more significant topics. Many articles conclude with a brief annotated bibliography, and there are numerous cross-references. The authors of the individual articles are U.S. academicians, but the writing style is suitable for both high-school and undergraduate students, who will also appreciate the attractive format, which features numerous subheadings and many photographs. The final volume includes a comprehensive index and a number of appendixes that compile information on subjects such as television shows, best-selling books, the music scene, sports, demographic trends, and Supreme Court decisions.

Homelessness

8-154. Hombs, Mary Ellen. *American Homelessness: A Reference Handbook.* 3rd ed. Santa Barbara, CA: ABC-CLIO, 2001. 272 pp. Index. ISBN: 1-576-07247-9.

Another in the Contemporary World Issues series, this volume follows the general format of the companion works. An introductory chapter is followed by a chronology, biographies, and statistical information. The following three chapters are devoted to reproductions of significant documents, federal legislation, and important litigation. The final three chapters provide a directory of organizations and agencies, and an extensive annotated bibliography of print and nonprint resources. There are no illustrations. Compared to other reference works on homelessness, this provides less detail but is perhaps more suitable for undergraduate or high-school students who have no previous knowledge of the subject and who are seeking introductory information.

8-155. Isserman, Maurice, and Rick Fantasia. *Homelessness: A Sourcebook.* New York: Facts on File, 1994. 356 pp. Index. ISBN: 0-816-02571-1.

Homelessness has been a particular topic of discussion for nearly two decades. This work sums up the situation with brief encyclopedic information aimed at general users. An introductory section of approximately thirty pages provides an overview. An alphabetical listing of short entries constitutes the main text. These entries include government programs, important individuals, legislative facts, legal cases, and general subjects such as migratory labor, the poverty line, public housing, and urban renewal. Entries are short, ranging from a paragraph to a couple of pages. Cross-references to other relevant entries are indicated in uppercase. The volume concludes with several appendixes that provide statistics and text of relevant documents, as well as a bibliography nearly fifty pages in length. The bibliography is arranged into books, articles, federal publications, and book-length bibliographies. The index indicates main entries in boldface. There are no illustrations other than some graphic displays. The text is written at a level suitable for both high-school and college students. Compared to *Homelessness in America* [entry 8-156], this volume provides more basic information and would probably be a preferable starting point for many researchers, who could then go on to the other work for more detailed background.

8-156. Baumohl, Jim, ed. *Homelessness in America.* Phoenix: Oryx Press, 1996. 291 pp. Index. ISBN: 0-897-74869-7.

Asserting that discussions of homelessness must focus upon the subject as a socioeconomic matter rather than providing a discussion of the personality of the homeless, this work provides the reader with an overview of the subject generally sympathetic to those caught in this situation. The contents are arranged into three major categories. The first provides general background; the second discusses homelessness within various ethnic and demographic groups; and the final part describes government responses to the homeless. Each part includes several chapters, each written by a specialist or group of specialists. The contributors are academicians or professionals who deal with the homeless. All contributed their time and royalties to this volume for the benefit of the National Coalition for the Homeless. Each chapter includes footnotes that are referenced to complete citations that appear at the back of the volume. In addition, there is a listing of references that is over twenty pages in length. The text is supplemented by occasional statistical displays. This volume has a format more similar to a textbook than to the usual reference encyclopedia, so it is necessary to consult the index to find specific subjects. The writing style is generally jargon free but more suitable for undergraduates than for high-school students. Compared to *Homelessness: A Sourcebook* [entry 8-155], this work presents a more in-depth discussion but is somewhat less useful for beginning researchers.

Housing

8-157. Van Vliet, Willem, ed. *Encyclopedia of Housing.* Thousand Oaks, CA: Sage Publications, 1998. 712 pp. Indexes. ISBN: 0-761-91332-7.

In his introduction, the editor indicates that housing is a multidisciplinary field drawing upon political science, sociology, economics, geography, anthropology, and psychology. Hence, this work attempts to integrate basic information in the field in an effort to acquaint practitioners, academicians, and students alike

with issues and topics pertaining to housing. Entries are arranged alphabetically and vary in length from a paragraph to several pages. The more substantive articles conclude with a listing of items for additional reading. Cross-references are also indicated at the end of most entries; some of these are unique in that they represent a "nodal" concept. In other words, cross-references from core articles to those of more peripheral interest are numerous, while those from the peripheral articles are fewer in number and lead the reader back to the core "nodal" concept. The nodal cross-references appear in boldface. There are indexes of contributors, authors, and subjects. There are also several appendixes, including one that lists major federal legislation in regard to housing. Extensive background regarding the contributors appears at the back of the volume. Illustrations are relatively few, and the editor has deliberately avoided including biographical entries, a comprehensive history of housing, and comprehensive coverage of legislation, all to save space. Entries for organizations in the field are relatively frequent, and include addresses, phone numbers, and other contact information. Obviously, these listings will be outdated in a few years. Otherwise, this is an excellent resource for all levels of researchers requiring an introduction or overview of housing topics. 💻

8-158. Van Vliet, Willem, ed. *International Handbook of Housing Policies and Practices.* New York: Greenwood Press, 1990. 821 pp. Indexes. ISBN: 0-313-25427-3.

Housing construction typically is a very localized industry, so cross-cultural comparisons are not always readily available. This volume provides lengthy detail on housing policies and practices in twenty-three different nations around the world, including the United States. There are representative countries from Western, Southern, and Eastern Europe; Latin America; the Middle East; Africa; Asia; and Oceania. Each of the individual country reports is provided by an expert in the field and includes a list of references. Numerous statistical tables accompany the text. The editor provides a long introductory chapter analyzing research on cross-national housing. Two appendixes provide listings of housing research journals and addresses for organizations and other information resources. There are indexes of both names and subjects. The text is aimed at a scholarly audience and will be more accessible to researchers at the collegiate level than to high-school students. More recent information on housing in the United States can be found in Van Vliet's *Encyclopedia of Housing* [entry 8-157], but this work, with its information on housing in a number of other countries, remains useful despite its age. 🖳

Human Sexuality
8-159. Bullough, Vern L., and Bonnie Bullough, eds. *Human Sexuality: An Encyclopedia.* New York: Garland, 1994. 643 pp. Index. ISBN: 0-824-07972-8.

Human sexuality is an area of study that is sometimes controversial, but this single-volume reference work attempts to address the subject in a nonsensational and scientific fashion. Entries are arranged alphabetically and include topics such as anal sex, female genital mutilation, impotence, premarital sex, and transsexualism. Some articles are relatively brief, perhaps a page, but many are several pages in length. Most end with a brief list of references. There are no cross-references, but consultation of the index will help the reader to find related topics. Articles are signed by the contributor. Most are academicians or medical practitioners. There are almost no illustrations other than those that depict basic anatomy. This volume serves as a handy resource for all researchers who need introductory information regarding sexuality.

8-160. Francoeur, Robert T., ed. *International Encyclopedia of Sexuality.* 4 vols. New York: Continuum, 2001. Index. ISBN: 0-826-40838-9 (vols. 1–3); 0-826-40862-1 (vol. 4).

This encyclopedia is valuable for its comparisons among thirty-two nations in terms of the sexual behavior of their population. Many of the countries are from the industrialized world, but there is also representation from the Islamic world, South America, Africa, and East and South Asia. The countries are arranged alphabetically through the three volumes. Although the length of article varies from country to country (with Canada, the United Kingdom, and the United States receiving much more detailed attention than others), articles are arranged according to a common outline. The basic outline includes demographics, basic premises, religious and ethnic factors that affect sexuality, various sexual practices, various unconventional behaviors, contraception, abortion, diseases, counseling, and the current state of research. This allows for easy comparison among nations regarding topics such as child abuse, rape, pornography, and abortion. Each article concludes with an extensive bibliography. Articles are signed, and brief information is provided on contributors in the final volume. About half are women. Some are medical practitioners or junior faculty rather than senior scholars in the field. There are no illustrations other than tables and graphs. The general style of writing is accessible to undergraduate students. This is an arena that is not without controversy; in some instances, informants from particular societies asked not to be identified. To some extent, the contributions are a mixture of statistical and scientific data and subjective judgments, but researchers at all levels can use this work as a starting point for information on sexual behavior in a number of societies and nations.

Immigration

8-161. Cordasco, Francesco, ed. *Dictionary of American Immigration History.* Metuchen, NJ: Scarecrow Press, 1990. 784 pp. ISBN: 0-810-82241-5.

Not seen.

8-162. Haines, David W., ed. *Refugees in America in the 1990s: A Reference Handbook.* Westport, CT: Greenwood Press, 1996. 467 pp. Index. ISBN: 0-313-29344-9.

The United States has long beckoned to refugees from political and economic oppression elsewhere in the world. This volume provides a 1990s appraisal of the situation, focusing upon recent refugee groups, including Afghans, Cubans, Haitians, Vietnamese, and eight other groups mostly from East Asia, the Middle East, and Eastern Europe. Each of these refugee groups is accorded a separate chapter about twenty pages in length, written by an academician or member of the public sector familiar with the group and the circumstances it faces in the United States. Additionally, there are chapters providing a general introduction to the subject and a discussion of policy issues pertaining to refugees in America. The final chapter is an annotated bibliography approximately forty pages in length, highlighting book and periodical literature that should be available in larger libraries. The separate chapters also include notes and references. The writing style avoids jargon but is more suitable for a collegiate audience than it is for high-school students.

8-163. Miller, E. Willard, and Ruby M. Miller. *United States Immigration: A Reference Handbook.* Santa Barbara, CA: ABC-CLIO, 1996. 304 pp. Index. ISBN: 0-874-36845-6.

The format of this volume differs somewhat from that of others in the Contemporary World Issues series. The introductory chapter, rather than being brief, here is approximately seventy-five pages long and describes both historical and contemporary issues relating to immigration. This first chapter also includes almost twenty tabular displays. Unlike other volumes in the series, this one contains no chapter setting forth biographies. However, one still finds a chapter on chronology and another chapter dealing with laws and regulations pertaining to immigration, naturalization, and refugees. As usual, the final chapters provide a directory of organizations and an extensive bibliography of print and nonprint resources. A glossary explains unfamiliar terminology. There are no illustrations. Both high-school and undergraduate students researching current issues relating to immigration can be referred to this volume for a reasonably comprehensive overview. 🖳

International Development

8-164. Crump, Andy, comp., and Wayne Ellwood, eds. *A to Z of World Development.* Oxford, England: New Internationalist Publications, 1998. 293 pp. ISBN: 1-869-84746-6.

Published by staff associated with the *New Internationalist,* a magazine dealing with international development and social justice, this dictionary asserts that its idea is "to produce a reference book on the major themes, ideas and personalities that have shaped relations between rich and poor worlds . . . in a way which avoided the orthodox and bogus notions of objectivity which pervade mainstream journalism" (Crump and Ellwood 1998, introduction). This obvious bias will be apparent to even the most casual reader; whether it will be bothersome will vary from person to person. Entries are gen-

erally fairly brief, ranging in length from a paragraph to about a page. There are entries for topics such as diseases, economic theories, international agencies, noteworthy individuals in the field of development, and subjects such as "Land Reform," "Shining Path," "Sustainable Development," and "Wildlife Trade." Full-color photographs, graphics, and sidebars supplement the text and make for a lively format. A brief bibliography and four pages of statistical data conclude the volume, which would have been improved had it included an index for articles on individual countries. Nevertheless, this work is a highly useful introduction for students and laypeople alike.

8-165. Welsh, Brian W. W., and Pavel Butorin, ed. *Dictionary of Development: Third World Economy, Environment, Society.* 2 vols. New York: Garland, 1990. 1194 pp. ISBN: 0-824-01447-2.

Believing that international development often goes underreported or misunderstood in the nations of the West, the editors of this two-volume set have attempted to provide an overview that addresses the complexities of this subject. They have provided an alphabetical listing of facts, concepts, events, and issues that relate to development, with an emphasis on poverty, development economics, environmental conservation, and future trends. The set begins with some basic economic and social indicators for developing countries. This section is followed by the alphabetical array of entries, which includes subjects such as agricultural development, child labor, corruption, homelessness, the International Monetary Fund (IMF), and sustainable development, among many others. Some entries, particularly entries for organizations, are quite short, but more substantive topics receive two pages or more of coverage. The set ends with a listing of relevant periodicals and their addresses. There are no illustrations, and there is no index. This reference work will be of greater value to university-level researchers than to high-school students.

8-166. Savitt, William, and Paula Bottorf. *Global Development: A Reference Handbook*. Santa Barbara, CA: ABC-CLIO, 1995. 369 pp. Index. ISBN: 0-874-36774-3.

As the authors of this volume point out, international development commenced with great enthusiasm after the Second World War but in recent years has run into controversy in both the developed and underdeveloped worlds and faces an uncertain future given the end of the cold war. Nonetheless, their assumption is that development efforts will continue into the next century. The format of their work is similar to that of other volumes in the Contemporary World Issues series. The initial chapter provides the reader with an overview of this subject. This is followed by a detailed chronology, biographies, statistical background, a directory of organizations, and an extensive bibliography of both print and nonprint resources. The volume closes with a glossary and an index. There are numerous statistical tables but no other illustrations.

The writing style is suitable for either high-school or college students, or any other general readers requiring beginning information on this topic.

Labor

8-167. Taylor, Paul F. *ABC-CLIO Companion to the American Labor Movement*. Santa Barbara, CA: ABC-CLIO, 1993. 237 pp. Index. ISBN: 0-874-36687-9.

In Taylor's prefatory words, this work "assembles in one volume information on labor leaders, major unions, landmark court decisions and legislation, key events, and the opposition of American business." Entries are arranged alphabetically. Most entries are a half page to a page in length. Cross-references are provided to other relevant entries, and a three-page bibliography at the back of the volume refers the reader to important books on the subject of labor. A chronology describes events from 1828 through 1981. A number of photographs and illustrations supplement the text. Taylor is the author of *Bloody Harlan*, the story of the United Mine Workers in Harlan County, Kentucky, and his sympathies are with the laboring class. The reference work by Filippelli [entry 8-168] provides greater detail on individual strikes and lockouts, but this volume provides handy information on court cases, individuals, and other subjects less easily found in Filippelli; the two works complement one another nicely.

8-168. Filippelli, Ronald L., ed. *Labor Conflict in the United States: An Ency-*

clopedia. New York: Garland, 1990. 609 pp. Index. ISBN: 0-824-07968-X.

Defining labor conflict as incidents involving strikes and lockouts, the editor includes here descriptions of 254 such episodes. In addition to the traditional strike or lockout, there are also a number of entries discussing racially or politically motivated events. The arrangement is alphabetical by name of event with up to five pages devoted to major happenings, such as the Homestead Strike of 1892. In addition to such well-known strikes, the editor has also made an effort to include a broad spectrum of conflicts from a variety of trades, industries, and geographical locales. The contributors of the individual entries are, in general, scholars at U.S. colleges and universities. Each of the entries includes a brief bibliography. There are no illustrations. The time frame ranges from the colonial era to the 1980s. User aids include a chronology, a glossary, a general bibliography, and an index. Although labor strife is a less central issue than in the past, this will be a useful source for undergraduates and more advanced researchers approaching the subject for the first time.

Media and Mass Communications

8-169. Hollis, Daniel Webster. *ABC-CLIO Companion to the Media in America.* Santa Barbara, CA: ABC-CLIO, 1995. 352 pp. Index. ISBN: 0-874-36776-X.

The focus of this work is upon important "firsts" in the history of the American media, major media organizations and personalities, selections from colonial times to the present and from across the nation, and entries on the various forms and technologies of the media. The arrangement is alphabetical. Typical entries include William F. Buckley Jr, individual newspapers such as the *Chicago Tribune,* "Chain Newspapers," "Media Humorists," and "Prior Restraint." Entries are generally a page or a couple of pages long and include one or more references for additional reading. These references are repeated in a comprehensive bibliography at the conclusion of the volume. Occasional illustrations and cross-references assist the reader in interpreting the text. Hollis indicates in the preface that his volume is intended to complement other resources rather than to be comprehensive itself. While this is true, the value of this work is enhanced by the fact that the author has included a number of articles dealing with historical or conceptual topics along with entries for individuals, media outlets, and events. The text is suitable for student audiences at both the college and high-school level.

8-170. McCoy, Ralph E. *Freedom of the Press, a Bibliocyclopedia: A Ten-Year Supplement (1967–1977).* Carbondale: Southern Illinois University Press, 1979. 559 pp. Index. ISBN: 0-809-30844-4.

This supplement reflects changes in discussion of the freedom of the press evident since the initial work was published in 1968 [see entry 8-171]. Subjects of interest in the past, such as heresy and sedition, were replaced in the 1970s by topics such as access to government information, the right to privacy, regulation of the press by government, and violence in the media. In addition, there had been a tremendous outpouring of publications on the subject, approaching all that had been written in the prior 400 years that were covered by the initial volume. This supplement also provides corrections to the original work. Format and indexing is essentially the same.

8-171. McCoy, Ralph E. *Freedom of the Press: An Annotated Bibliography.* Carbondale: Southern Illinois University Press, 1968. 526 pp. Index. ISBN: N/A.

Altogether, this bibliography provides annotations of approximately 8,000 books, pamphlets, journal articles, films, and other items pertaining to freedom of the press. Geographically, it is limited to the English-speaking countries but does include publications from the beginning of printing to the 1960s. All forms of mass media are included, as are a wide variety of subjects that have been the target of censorship; heresy, sedition, obscenity, libel, and blasphemy are among those covered. Some subject areas were excluded; among these are legal texts, newspaper and newsmagazine articles, works on the general topic of civil liberties, and works on propaganda. Entries are arranged alphabetically by author or by title if there is no author. The subject index assists the reader to identify topics, countries, court decisions, individuals, and titles of works that have been censored. Because this work required more than a decade to compile, some items identified late in the process were included in an addendum. These items do

appear in the index, however. There is no paging; the index refers to entry numbers only. The annotations are descriptive rather than critical. For supplements, see entries 8-170 and 8-172. 💻

8-172. McCoy, Ralph E. *Freedom of the Press: An Annotated Bibliography; Second Supplement: 1978–1992.* Carbondale: Southern Illinois University Press, 1993. 441 pp. Index. ISBN: 0-809-31583-1.

Earlier volumes of this work appeared in 1968 [entry 8-171] and 1979 [entry 8-170]. The general format here is the same as that found in the prior two volumes, although more selectivity has been exercised in order to avoid much duplication for topics of great interest. Some of the new issues covered in this supplement include the struggle over the teaching and reading of children in public schools, developments relating to electronic media, and discussion of violence as a violation of the civil rights of women. The original volume and its two supplements collectively provide scholars with a thorough compilation of significant publications relating to censorship and freedom of the press from the sixteenth century almost to the twenty-first century. 💻

8-173. Foerstel, Herbert N. *Free Expression and Censorship in America: An Encyclopedia.* Westport, CT: Greenwood Press, 1997. 260 pp. Index. ISBN: 0-313-29231-0.

The value of this reference work lies in its emphasis upon contemporary free speech issues. There are articles about such topics as abortion, child pornography, homosexuality, and the Internet, among others. One also finds entries for individuals such as Jesse Helms and Frank Zappa as well as for agencies, legislation, and more traditional topics along the line of "Sedition." Entries are arranged alphabetically and vary from a couple of paragraphs to several pages in length. There are bibliographic references and cross-references to other entries. A short bibliography and a table of cases both appear at the back of the volume. There are no illustrations. The writing style is suitable for undergraduates and other researchers in the higher-education community. The author is a librarian; his work serves a useful purpose in updating the censorship debate through the mid-1990s.

8-174. Gardner, Robert, and Dennis Shortelle. *From Talking Drums to the Internet: An Encyclopedia of Communications Technology.* Santa Barbara, CA: ABC-CLIO, 1997. 355 pp. Index. ISBN: 0-874-36832-4.

The emphasis of this volume is on the history of communication among human beings, from cuneiform to the Internet. Some entries discuss important individuals or agencies, but most are on subjects or concepts. These include "Computers and Society," "Extension Service," "Language," "Photograph," and "Radio." Entries are up to about four pages in length and conclude with cross-references and a listing of books and articles for additional research. The bibliographic list-

ings are repeated in a comprehensive bibliography at the back of the volume. The index provides additional access to the text. Illustrations are plentiful. The value of this work would have been enhanced by the inclusion of a chronology, however. Compared to be *International Encyclopedia of Communications* [entry 8-176], this volume is obviously less comprehensive but probably a better starting point for beginning students at the high-school and college levels. 💻

8-175. Blanchard, Margaret A., ed. *History of the Mass Media in the United States: An Encyclopedia.* Chicago: Fitzroy Dearborn Publishers, 1998. 752 pp. Index. ISBN: 1-579-58012-2.

The time frame of this work extends from 1690 to 1990, with an occasional look at developments since the latter date. "Media" is defined quite broadly to include (among others) books, advertising, magazines, motion pictures, newspapers, public relations, radio, and television. Emphasis, however, is on the way the various media have interacted with society and government in ways that are technological, legal, legislative, economic, or political rather than on the entertainment side of the media. Entries for individuals and institutions have been kept to a minimum in order to focus on issues and trends. Articles range from a page to several pages in length and conclude with cross-references and a bibliography. The front of the volume includes both alphabetical and topical listings of the entries; the latter will be especially useful to those readers who might want to find all entries on magazines reporting or war, for example. Most of the contributors are drawn from the ranks of academe. The text is supplemented by the inclusion of illustrations and occasional sidebars and statistical tables. This single-volume work represents an excellent starting point for students at the high-school and college levels.

8-176. Barnouw, Erik, ed. *International Encyclopedia of Communications.* 4 vols. New York: Oxford University Press, 1989. 1960 pp. Index. ISBN: 0-195-04994-2.

Communications, its history, and its theory all have an impact on many scholarly disciplines. This encyclopedia, begun as a project at the Annenberg School of Communications, University of Pennsylvania, attempts to discuss the subject from the viewpoint of anthropology, education, history, journalism, law, political science, psychology, and sociology, as well as a number of disciplines associated with the humanities. Articles are arranged alphabetically and are often several pages long. In some instances, several subtopics are gathered under a common theme; for example, a group of articles on advertising provides an overview, a history, and entries on advertising agencies and advertising economics. Cross-references and bibliographies are provided, and there are many illustrations and photographs. The contributors are drawn from the academic world in the United States and abroad. While many of the articles are of greater interest to researchers in the liberal arts than

in the social sciences, there are a number of entries of interest to the latter. These can be readily identified because the final volume includes a "Topical Guide" that lists all entries by subject, such as education, government regulation, political communication, and the like. Particularly useful are articles on communications in the various continents of the world as well as those entries dealing with the different modes of technology involved in the communications scene. The writing level is scholarly and best suited for a college and university clientele.

Military

8-177. Margiotta, Franklin D., ed. *Brassey's Encyclopedia of Military History and Biography.* Washington, DC: Brassey's, 1994. 1197 pp. Index. ISBN: 0-028-81096-1.

Approximately 80 percent of the articles in this work have been reprinted from the *International Military and Defense Encyclopedia* [entry 6-131] and represent those subjects considered more popular in nature. The remaining 20 percent of the articles, some thirty-one in number, deal with general historical subjects such as "The Cold War," "Land Warfare," and "Aerospace Forces and Warfare." Most of the articles selected from the parent work discuss individual wars and military figures. Articles are usually several pages long and include cross-references and a bibliography. Surprisingly, there are few illustrations or maps. For additional details, see the entry for the *International Military and Defense Encyclopedia* [entry 6-131].

8-178. Corvisier, Andre, and John Childs, eds. *Dictionary of Military History and the Art of War.* rev. English ed. Oxford: Blackwell Publishers, 1994. 916 pp. Index. ISBN: 0-631-16848-6.

Unlike the *Harper Encyclopedia of Military History* [entry 2-157], which features a chronological description of battles, campaigns, and wars, this dictionary emphasizes instead a thematic approach to the subject. Although there are a number of entries for battles and individuals influencing the evolution of warfare, many articles here discuss subjects such as "Civil Contribution of Armies," "Disarmament," "Hierarchies," "Language," and "Prisoners of War." There are also a number of entries for individual countries significant to the development of war. In short, this reference work attempts to integrate military history with general historical theory and trends. Most articles include cross-references and brief bibliographic listings. Illustrations are relatively few. The original edition was published in France in 1988; this English edition (edited by Childs) adds a number of articles of interest to Anglo-American readers, including several on recent wars deemed of importance. Unlike some military history volumes, this work can be consulted with profit by scholars as well as by undergraduate readers.

8-179. Sherrow, Victoria. *Women and the Military: An Encyclopedia.* Santa Barbara, CA: ABC-CLIO, 1996. 381 pp. Index. ISBN: 0-874-36812-X.

The controversy over the role played by women in the armed services is unlikely to go away soon. This reference work provides the reader with an introduction to the subject that is both historical and contemporary in nature. The volume begins with an introductory chapter that provides an overview from the Revolutionary War to the 1990s. The articles that follow are arranged alphabetically and are up to two pages in length. Most include cross-references and brief biographical citations; complete citations can be found in the comprehensive bibliographies at the back. Many of the entries are for individual events, organizations, or individuals. Others, however, deal with more general subjects such as discrimination, harassment, motherhood, and recruitment. A number of photographs accompany the text, which is suitable for both high-school and undergraduate students. Those articles dealing with general subjects, as well as the introduction, will probably be of greater value to beginning researchers than those dealing with more specific topics.

Miscellaneous

8-180. Jones, Steve, Robert Martin, and David Pilbeam, eds. *Cambridge Encyclopedia of Human Evolution.* Cambridge: Cambridge University Press, 1992. 506 pp. Index. ISBN: 0-521-32370-3.

The theory of evolution continues to create controversy, and reliable reference works are a boon to those seeking more information on the subject. This work has been written by specialists with a general reader in mind. The contributors in general are members of academic institutions in the United States and Great Britain. The arrangement of the text is more similar to a monograph than to the usual encyclopedia. Ten chapters describe topics such as "Patterns of Primate Evolution," "The Brain and Language," and "Early Human Behavior and Ecology." The volume is heavily illustrated with graphic displays, maps, and photographs. Some information appears in sidebars. Three appendixes provide biographies of noted figures in the field, a geological timescale, and a map of important sites worldwide. A glossary and an extensive bibliography also appear at the back of the volume. The reading level of the text is probably more suitable for an audience of collegiate researchers than for high-school students. While this reference work may not settle all questions about the subject of evolution, it is a good starting point for those needing detailed background. ⌨

8-181. Bekoff, Marc. *Encyclopedia of Animal Rights and Animal Welfare.* Westport, CT: Greenwood Press, 1998. 446 pp. Index. ISBN: 0-313-29977-3.

Although controversies in regard to animal rights appear frequently in the news, reference books on the subject are relatively few in number. This reference work will provide a starting point for those new to the subject. Articles are arranged alphabetically, with length ranging from about one page to several. Cross-references are indicated in uppercase. Each article includes a brief bibli-

ography to relevant books and journal articles. Some of the contributors are from animal rights and welfare organizations, but many are academicians, ranging from graduate students to professors. Some articles deal with concrete subjects, such as use of laboratory animals, and others present brief biographies of important individuals in the field, but many discuss the ethical and philosophical overtones of animal rights. Occasional illustrations supplement the text, and a list of sources appearing at the back the volume indicates core books and periodicals on the subject. Although the contributors were asked to write at a level that can be understood by anyone with at least a background in high-school biology, the discussion of abstract philosophical issues makes this a work more suitable for college students than for those at the high-school level.

8-182. Brobeck, Stephen, ed. *Encyclopedia of the Consumer Movement.* Santa Barbara, CA: ABC-CLIO, 1997. 659 pp. Index. ISBN: 0-874-36987-8.

In recent decades, the consumer movement has gained increased prominence in both the United States and elsewhere. This reference work compiles information that might be difficult to find in a single source otherwise. There are approximately 200 entries arranged alphabetically and ranging up to 5,000 words in length. Longer articles are accorded subheadings. The front of the volume includes an alphabetical list of the entries as well as a listing of entries by subject. There are eight major categories:

"General," "Consumer Populations," "Consumer Movement Activities," "Government Agencies," "Consumer Organizations," "Consumer Leaders," "Consumer Protections," and "International Consumer Movement." The latter includes descriptions of consumer movements in other countries and regions of the world, including some, such as Albania and China, that might not spring to mind otherwise. Entries for leaders number only four; information on other individuals must be sought through the index. Cross-references and readings are included with each entry. The contributors are a mix of college professors and experts from both the private and public sectors. There are no illustrations. This work can be recommended to both high-school and undergraduate students working on consumer issues.

8-183. Kurian, George Thomas, and Graham T. Molitor, eds. *Encyclopedia of the Future.* 2 vols. New York: Macmillan Library Reference USA, 1996. 1115 pp. Index. ISBN: 0-028-97205-8.

Accurately describing the future might appear to be an impossible task, but this encyclopedia makes a game effort. Known experts were asked to write articles that assess contemporary issues and project possible developments in the future. The encyclopedia includes 450 such articles, arranged alphabetically. Many are several pages in length. Cross-references and bibliographies are provided for each. Examples of articles include "Acid Rain," "Batteries," "Criminal Punishment," "Fundamentalism," "Home Own-

ership," and "Native Americans." There are also articles on continents, regions, and certain countries of the world. In general, however, emphasis is upon the English-speaking nations and the arenas of the economy, energy, education, and the environment. There are no illustrations other than some graphic displays. The second volume includes chronologies of both the past and the future; the latter merely speculates on possible future events. Perhaps the greatest value of this work lies in the fact that it provides state-of-the-art assessments of many topics that tend to be policy issues, with extrapolation of possible eventualities into the near future. The text is suitable for undergraduates or more advanced researchers.

8-184. Roberts, Carolyn S., and Martha Gorman. *Euthanasia: A Reference Handbook.* Santa Barbara, CA: ABC-CLIO, 1996. 348 pp. Index. ISBN: 0-874-36831-6.

Readers familiar with the Contemporary World Issues series will recognize the format of this volume. The initial chapter provides an overview of the issue. It is followed by chapters supplying a chronology, biographies, factual and statistical background, a directory, and an extensive bibliography of print and non-print materials. The biographies include brief information on individuals on both sides of the issue as well as some persons who have been the subject of euthanasia. Like other volumes in the series, this work will be of use to high-school and undergraduate students both. 💻

8-185. Schlager, Neil, ed. *Science and Its Times: Understanding the Social Significance of Scientific Discovery.* 8 vols. Detroit: Gale Group, 2000–2001. Index. ISBN: 0-787-63932-X.

The eight volumes of this set are subdivided chronologically beginning with 2000 BC and advancing to the present. The first four volumes are divided by chapter categories that include "Exploration and Discovery," "Life Sciences and Medicine," "Mathematics," "Physical Sciences," and "Technology and Invention." In the final three volumes, there are separate chapters for life sciences and for medicine. Within these chapters, the reader will find a chronology, an overview essay, a series of articles describing individual scientific discoveries that had social impacts, biographies, and a bibliography listing primary sources. Articles on individual scientific achievements are usually two or three pages long. The individual articles also follow a standard format that provides the reader with a short overview, background information, a discussion on the impact of the event in question, and a short bibliography. The biographies highlight important scientific figures. Numerous illustrations accompany the text. This set has an unusual approach to the study of science and will be useful to both high-school and beginning undergraduate students. (Note: Only Volumes 5 and 7 were examined for this review. Volume 8 serves as the cumulative index for the entire set.) 🖳

8-186. Kaul, Chandrika, and Valerie Tomaselli-Moschovitis, eds. *Statistical Handbook on Consumption and Wealth in the United States.* Phoenix: Oryx Press, 1999. 290 pp. Index. ISBN: 1-573-56251-3.

As the introduction to this volume indicates, the United States is a wealthy nation with a high level of consumption and spending on discretionary items. Interest in this topic provides a rationale for the compilation of statistics in its regard. There are eight chapters, some of which encompass general statistics relating to individual and family income, general economic data, and corporate wealth. Several other chapters detail consumption in particular categories, such as "Material Goods" and "Services." A final chapter describes the role of government in the economy. Each chapter begins with a brief introductory essay; however, most of the content consists of tables and graphic displays reproduced from other sources, particularly those of the federal government. The *Statistical Abstract of the United States* is especially well represented. As is the case with most such compilations of this sort, the value to the reader lies in the fact that data on a particular topic appears in a single volume, eliminating the need to consult a number of sources.

8-187. Kaul, Chandrika, and Valerie Tomaselli-Moschovitis, eds. *Statistical Handbook on Poverty in the Developing World.* Phoenix: Oryx Press, 1999. 425 pp. Index. ISBN: 1-573-56249-1.

The purpose of this work, as stated in the introduction, is "to compile a comprehensive set of statistics from a wide variety of sources that explore the causes, effects, ramifications, and policies concerning poverty in developing countries in an organized format accessible to the non-specialist." An initial chapter provides data on "Key Indicators" such as land area, population, gross national product, and infant mortality. Succeeding chapters are devoted to individual topics. These include "Poverty Measures," "Health," "AIDS," "Women and Poverty," and "Cities," among others. Each chapter includes brief introductory text; however, most of the volume consists of tables (arranged by nation) reprinted from standard sources published by international agencies. Tables from the *World Development Indicators* appear frequently. Nevertheless, many users will find this compilation a handy alternative to consultation of a number of separate print and electronic sources that otherwise would have to be perused.

8-188. Kutzner, Patricia L. *World Hunger: A Reference Handbook.* Santa Barbara, CA: ABC-CLIO, 1991. 359 pp. Index. ISBN: 0-874-36558-9.

Kutzner, director of the World Hunger Education Service at the time of publication of this book, takes the position that world hunger can be solved provided that political, economic, and social concerns are addressed. The format of her volume is similar to that of others in the Contemporary World Issues series. An initial chapter provides the reader with an overview of the problem and its potential solutions. This is followed by a lengthy chronology, biographies of sig-

nificant individuals, and statistical data and text. The volume concludes with directory information and a long bibliography including print and nonprint items. A glossary assists the uninitiated in understanding the field of world hunger. Although this work is now some years old, a fair amount of the information provided will still be useful; readers will want to consult other sources in order to provide current background and references to recent literature. The text is suitable for both high-school and undergraduate researchers. ▣

Multiculturalism

8-189. Levinson, David, and Melvin Ember, eds. *American Immigrant Cultures: Builders of a Nation.* 2 vols. New York: Macmillan Reference USA, 1997. 1091 pp. Index. ISBN: 0-028-97208-2.

This reference set intends to be an "authoritative compendium of knowledge about the non-indigenous cultural groups of the United States" (Levinson and Ember 1997, preface). (Indigenous groups, such as Native Americans, are described in a companion set, the *Encyclopedia of World Cultures.*) Over 160 ethnic groups are described here, with each receiving a separate article of some length. In general, the articles describe immigration history, demographics, and cultural and socioeconomic attributes. Most articles are complemented by one or more photographs of the ethnic group or its pursuits. There are cross-references to other groups that share a similar ethnic or immigration background. Each article concludes with the bibliography of core books and articles. Affiliations of contributors appear near the front of the first volume, and a series of appendixes include demographic information and holidays. This is a highly useful set for information on ethnicity. It can be used by both undergraduates and advanced researchers alike.

8-190. Cashmore, Ellis. *Dictionary of Race and Ethnic Relations.* 4th ed. New York: Routledge, 1996. 412 pp. Index. ISBN: 0-415-15167-8.

Assimilating recent episodes in racial relations, such as the O. J. Simpson trial and challenges to affirmative action, this fourth edition of a work first published in 1984 provides short articles on subjects relating to race in both the United States and Great Britain. The arrangement is alphabetical; typical entries include "Assimilation," "Drugs and Racism," "Internal Colonialism," and "Rational Choice Theory." Articles generally range from one to several pages in length. In addition to the author, there are four other major contributors and over thirty other "specialist" contributors. All articles are signed by the authors, who are scholars in institutions in both countries. Brief annotated bibliographies conclude the articles. The index assists with access to the text, and there are cross-references from article to article as well. The writing style is somewhat academic, so this is a source that is more likely to be useful at the collegiate level than elsewhere. In general, the text is sympathetic toward ethnicity and also reflects recent theoretical trends in academe. 🖳

8-191. Auerbach, Susan, ed. *Encyclopedia of Multiculturalism.* 6 vols. New York: Marshall Cavendish, 1994. 1813 pp. Index. ISBN: 1-854-35670-4.

While there are many reference works that examine specific ethnic groups in the United States, relatively few address themselves to the multicultural world as a whole. This set provides a single place where a researcher can seek information about individual ethnic groups (including European nationalities), religious groups, Canadians, and older Americans. There also entries on places, concepts, events, laws, and organizations prominent in multiculturalism. Some entries are brief, perhaps a paragraph, but more substantial topics receive essays up to 5,000 words long. Cross-references are indicated in uppercase. Listings of readings are included with some articles but not all. Most contributors are drawn from the U.S. academic community. Numerous black-and-white photographs accompany the text. The final volume includes a chronology, a filmography, a general bibliography, a listing of entries by topic, and a general index. This is a resource suitable for high-school and college students alike; it provides a starting point for a wide variety of topics. A two-volume supplement was published in 1998 and consists of 575 pages in two physical volumes.

8-192. Dassanowsky, Robert, ed. *Gale Encyclopedia of Multicultural America.* 2nd ed. 3 vols. Detroit: Gale Group, 2000. 1974 pp. Index. ISBN: 0-787-63986-9.

This three-volume set targets an audience consisting of public, high-school, and academic libraries. The first edition included 101 articles; this second edition has been enlarged to include 152 essays ranging in length from 3,000 to 20,000 words. Groups large and small are among those included, ranging from Apaches to the Yupiat. Rather than a single article on Native Americans, there appear a number of separate articles on different tribal groups, such as the Cherokee. The articles address the immigration history of the group and devote a good deal of space to customs, social and family life, language, and political details. Brief information is provided on well-known individuals, and there are listings for sources for additional information. The latter includes not only a short bibliography but also contact information for organizations, associations, and museums. Photographs accompany many articles. Each article is signed by the contributor, with affiliations appearing in the first volume. This is a useful reference work that will probably appeal more to students than to scholars; the text is written at a level accessible to the general reader. ▱

8-193. Lehman, Jeffrey, ed. *Gale Encyclopedia of Multicultural America: Primary Documents.* 2 vols. Detroit: Gale Group, 1999. 820 pp. Index. ISBN: 0-787-63990-7.

This two-volume set is a companion to the *Gale Encyclopedia of Multicultural America* [entry 8-192]. It contains 210 primary documents pertaining to approximately ninety different cultures present in the United States. Among the types of documents represented are letters, poems, biographies, speeches, and photographs. The arrangement is alphabetical by name of group. Many are Native American tribes, but there are also numerous entries for such groups as Italian Americans, Brazilian Americans, and Tibetan Americans. The individual sections average about nine pages in length and include one or more documents, together with introductory material and bibliographic information indicating the source of the document. Both historic and contemporary situations are represented. Occasional photographs supplement the text. This set represents a handy source for high-school and undergraduate students requiring brief documentary evidence pertaining to individual ethnic groups.

8-194. Thernstrom, Stephan, ed. *Harvard Encyclopedia of American Ethnic Groups.* Cambridge, MA: Harvard University Press, 1980. 1076 pp. ISBN: 0-674- 37512-2.

This pioneering effort at a compilation of information pertaining to ethnic groups contains articles on 106 such groups. Articles vary in length; some, such as "Copts," receive only about a page, while articles on "American Indians" total over sixty pages. Each article concludes with a bibliography directing the reader to other sources, including many scholarly references. Arranged alphabetically throughout the text are "Thematic Essays" on topics such as "Family Patterns," "Folklore,"

"Language Maintenance," and "Prejudice." Articles are signed by their authors, whose credentials are given in the front matter. Numerous tables and maps are scattered throughout the text, and two appendixes present demographic information and an explanation of "Methods of Estimating the Size of Groups." Newer reference books on this subject are available, and readers will certainly wish to consult them. Nevertheless, this older work is still of value both for its scholarly approach and for its thematic essays, which help to sum up thinking on ethnic groups through the 1970s. 🖳

8-195. Bankston, Carl L., ed. *Racial and Ethnic Relations in America.* 3 vols. Pasadena, CA: Salem Press, 2000. 1148 pp. Index. ISBN: 0-893-56629-2.

Almost 900 articles appear in this three-volume set. The contributors, drawn from the U.S. academic community, discuss topics from the point of view of theory, history, and current issues and events. Articles are arranged alphabetically and range in length from 200 words to about 2,500. Many include an opening statement of one or two sentences that address the significance of the topic. Cross-references are numerous, and longer articles conclude with a listing of "Core Resources," usually books. There are numerous illustrations and occasional graphic displays. The final volume includes brief biographies of individuals who have worked for intergroup relations, a detailed chronology, and a bibliography of nearly fifty pages. The latter is arranged by topic. About half the arti-

cles pertain to the major groups of color: African Americans, Native Americans, Asian Americans, and Latinos. This set is valuable for both its historic and contemporary coverage of race and ethnicity in the United States; it will be particularly helpful to undergraduates.

8-196. Keever, Beverly Deepe, Carolyn Martindale, and Mary Ann Weston, eds. *U.S. News Coverage of Racial Minorities: A Sourcebook, 1934–1996.* Westport, CT: Greenwood Press, 1997. 387 pp. Index. ISBN: 0-313-29671-5.

This publication is something of a cross between a reference book and a monograph. An initial chapter describes the various forms of bias in the news media. This is followed by separate chapters on Native Americans, African Americans, Hispanic Americans, and Asian Americans, with the latter further subdivided among Chinese, other Asian Americans, and Pacific Islanders. Each of these chapters is further divided into six time segments that collectively discuss media coverage from 1934 through 1996. The last three chapters describe investigative reporting and the Federal Communications Commission, and provide concluding statements. Individual chapters include extensive endnotes and bibliographies. There are no illustrations. The editors and contributors are generally members of the academic disciplines of journalism and communications, and this publication is obviously aimed at a scholarly audience. Despite its comparatively narrow focus, it will be of value to undergraduates seeking detailed information on news coverage of the individual racial minorities in the United States throughout the latter part of the twentieth century.

Native Americans

8-197. Grossman, Mark. *ABC-CLIO Companion to the Native American Rights Movement.* Santa Barbara, CA: ABC-CLIO, 1996. 498 pp. Index. ISBN: 0-874-36822-7.

The American Indian people have been entangled in the legal system for centuries, resulting in a complexity of laws, regulations, and cases. This reference work provides the general reader with an entry point to the subject. The arrangement is alphabetical; there are entries for agencies, individuals, significant cases, organizations, and federal legislative enactments. Entries range in length from a couple of paragraphs to as many as five pages. Many entries include references to relevant literature, and there is also a comprehensive bibliography at the back of the volume. Occasional illustrations supplement the text. This publication will be of value to those high-school and college students searching for specific facts and people, but those seeking the conceptual framework of Indian law will probably want to turn to other resources as well. 💻

8-198. Tiller, Veronica E. Velarde, ed. *American Indian Reservations and Trust Areas.* Albuquerque, NM: U.S. Department of Commerce Economic Development Administration, 1996. 698 pp. Index.

Intended as a replacement for the federal government's *Federal and State Indian Reservations and Indian Trust Areas*, published in 1974, this reference work presents information on Indian tribes, whether living on formal reservations or on other tribal lands. The arrangement is by state, then by reservation or tribe in alphabetical order. In most cases, a map shows Indian lands in each state. The information for each reservation or tribal unit includes demographic, educational, and economic statistical data; descriptions of the government, economy, and culture of the tribe; and postal addresses, phone numbers, and fax numbers. The bibliography is particularly useful because it includes tribal and federal government publications. This work is handy for providing a snapshot of Native American communities in the late twentieth century. Librarians should be aware that it has been reprinted in a commercial version entitled *Tiller's Guide to Indian Country*. 💻

8-199. Markowitz, Harvey, ed. *American Indians.* 3 vols. Pasadena, CA: Salem Press, 1995. 953 pp. Index. ISBN: 0-894-56757-4.

A multitude of reference books have appeared in recent years in response to a need for multicultural resources. Among the better choices for resources on Native Americans is this three-volume set. Encyclopedic in nature, its articles cover a variety of topics, including tribal groups, well-known individuals, "Dance," "Education," and "Food Preparation and Cooking." Most articles are relatively brief, no more than a column or perhaps a few pages. There are numerous cross-references from one article to others, and many articles include a brief annotated bibliography. Frequent illustrations and maps complement the text. The final volume includes an index and several appendixes. In general, treatment of Native Americans is sympathetic but even-handed. More attention is paid to historical periods before 1900 than to the twentieth century. This set is more suitable for undergraduate students than for specialists but is a useful starting point for a reasonably comprehensive treatment of Native Americans.

8-200. Johansen, Bruce E., ed. *Encyclopedia of Native American Economic History.* Westport, CT: Greenwood Press, 1999. 301 pp. Index. ISBN: 0-313-30623-0.

The editor of this volume has attempted to describe Native American economic history not only as it stood in the past, but also in regard to current circumstances. He emphasizes that Native American economics often is quite different from the standard capitalism present in today's world and is less static than has often been assumed. This volume is arranged alphabetically by topic. Entries range in length from a single paragraph to several pages. Longer or more significant entries include a bibliography for additional reading. There are numerous entries for the economy of individual tribes, but there are also articles on subjects such as self-determination, slavery, uranium mining, and wage labor. A "Se-

lected Bibliography" at the back of the volume appears to compile the bibliographic references that appear with the articles. There are no illustrations. This specialized reference work can be used by undergraduates and other academic researchers delving into this topic. 🖳

8-201. Hoxie, Frederick E., ed. *Encyclopedia of North American Indians.* Boston: Houghton Mifflin, 1996. 756 pp. Indexes. ISBN: 0-395-66921-9.

The introduction to this volume asserts that scholarship has uncovered a great deal of information that belies the popular idea of American Indians but that stereotypes continue to dominate the public's opinions about this ethnic group. In an attempt to address the situation, this reference work tries to portray Native Americans both past and present and has made a concerted effort to include Indian people among the contributors. There are four major types of entries. One group includes descriptions of approximately 100 tribes. The second group consists of approximately the same number of biographies. Third, there are entries for topics, tribes, and cultural traditions, ranging from "Alcoholism" to "Voting." The last category provides definitions for terms such as cradleboards, grass houses, and peyote, as well as major treaties and battles. Entries are arranged alphabetically and range up to three pages in length. Short bibliographies are included with each entry, and the text is accompanied by numerous photographs, graphic displays, and maps.

Contributors are drawn from the ranks of the academic community and include a number of Native Americans. This work is suitable for both high-school and undergraduate students. 💻

8-202. Malinowski, Sharon, ed. *Gale Encyclopedia of Native American Tribes.* 4 vols. Detroit: Gale Research, 1998. 2604 pp. Indexes. ISBN: 0-787-61085-2.

Reference books that describe the Native American tribes of North America are not uncommon, but this set provides greater detail than most. Each of the four volumes addresses individual tribes in major regions: "The Northeast and Southeast," "The Southwest," "The Arctic, Subarctic, Plateau, and Great Plains," and "The Pacific Northwest and California." Approximately 400 tribes are described. Each description includes the following components: "Introduction," "History," "Religion," "Language," "Buildings," "Subsistence," "Clothing and Adornment," "Healing Practices," "Customs," "Oral Literature," "Current Tribal Issues," and "Bibliography and Further Reading." Some information is provided in sidebars. Numerous illustrations supplement the text. Because the arrangement is not alphabetical, each of the four volumes includes a comprehensive table of contents and a comprehensive index. Also included in each of the volumes is a listing of the tribes recognized by the federal government and a glossary. Entries are signed, but credentials are not listed for all contributors. Nevertheless, this set will be of value to students at both the high-school and undergraduate levels as well as to patrons of public libraries.

8-203. Johnson, Michael. *Macmillan Encyclopedia of Native American Tribes.* 2nd U.S. ed. New York: Macmillan Library Reference USA, 1999. 288 pp. Index. ISBN: 0-028-65409-9.

According to the introduction to this second edition, the differences between it and the first edition, published in 1993, lie in the fact that there has been some updating of text, but more importantly, there has been a better integration of illustrations with text, more use of color illustrations, and more use of contemporary photographs. The volume begins with a classification of languages. This is followed by ten chapters that discuss Indian tribes within a distribution of geographically oriented cultures. For example, there are sections on the "Northeastern Woodlands" and the "Great Basin." Within each of these chapters, entries are arranged alphabetically by name of tribe. Numerous maps assist the reader to orient tribes to locations, and each of the chapters begins with an overview of that particular region. A final chapter briefly discusses the present Native American situation. A short bibliography, a glossary, and several directories conclude the work. Although other reference works provide greater detail, this volume is useful for its brief discussions, its attractive illustrations, and its intelligent introduction, which discusses complexities associated with this subject.

8-204. Thompson, William N. *Native American Issues: A Reference Handbook*. Santa Barbara, CA: ABC-CLIO, 1996. 293 pp. Index. ISBN: 0-874-36828-6.

As is the case with others in the Contemporary World Issues series, this work intends to present the reader with basic information arranged in a standard format. Here, the introductory chapter describes such issues as sovereignty, gambling, and political jurisdiction, as well as developments in Canada along with those in the United States. This chapter is followed by chapters providing a chronology and biographies. The latter one profiles Native Americans and a handful of European Americans. The next two chapters provide information on court cases, legislation, statistics, and points of view from both ethnic groups. The final chapters present a directory and an annotated bibliography of print and nonprint resources. The chapter on legal issues and statistics includes summaries from both U.S. and Canadian venues. There are no illustrations. Like other volumes in this series, this publication is suitable for both high-school and undergraduate audiences requiring an overview of significant contemporary Native Americans issues. 🖳

8-205. Pritzker, Barry M. *Native Americans: An Encyclopedia of History, Culture, and Peoples*. 2 vols. Santa Barbara, CA: ABC-CLIO, 1998. 868 pp. Index. ISBN: 0-874-36836-7.

Pritzker takes a somewhat different approach than most reference works in dealing with Native Americans. In his two-volume set, he provides ten chapters, each describing the native inhabitants of a particular region of Canada or the United States. Each chapter includes an introductory essay describing the regional culture; this is followed by entries for the individual tribes. Although detailed discussion of prehistory and mythology has been omitted, information on tribes discusses both historical and contemporary topics. Brief information is provided on many aspects of society, culture, and customs. Occasional photographs accompany the text. The second volume includes a glossary and a bibliography, the latter of which includes general and regional books rather than items dealing with specific tribes. There are no bibliographies with individual entries. The writing style is suitable for high-school and college students alike. Although the information on individual tribes will be of value to student researchers, this work is perhaps of greatest use for its regional approach to Native Americans. 🖳

8-206. Reddy, Marlita A., ed. *Statistical Record of Native North Americans*. 2nd ed. Detroit: Gale Research, 1995. 1272 pp. Index. ISBN: 0-810-36421-2.

Statistical information regarding Native Americans can, of course, be found in several government publications, but this work attempts to present statistics in a single volume for easy reference. Statistics are broadly divided into categories such as history, demographics, education, culture and tradition, and government relations. In most cases, statistical tables are simply reprinted from the original source, with a reference to that source. Some tables are highly specific in nature. The index is more useful for locating information by geographic locale or tribal unit than by subject. This work is valuable for statistics for Canadian Native Americans, though these are presented in a separate chapter rather than integrated with U.S. statistics. This volume provides a useful starting point for statistics up to 1993; other sources must be consulted for statistical information after that time.

Nuclear Energy

8-207. Atkins, Stephen E. *Historical Encyclopedia of Atomic Energy.* Westport, CT: Greenwood Press, 2000. 491 pp. Index. ISBN: 0-313-30400-9.

As Atkins himself indicates, the use of atomic energy has gone through a number of phases, ranging from widespread acceptance to great suspicion and resistance. This encyclopedia allows the interested reader easy access to a variety of factual information about the subject. Entries are arranged alphabetically and vary from a paragraph to several pages in length. Categories covered include biographies, programs, agencies, legislation, and specific incidents, either planned or unplanned. There are no cross-references, but each entry concludes with a listing of one or more references for additional readings. Occasional photographs supplement the text, and the back matter includes a detailed chronology and a lengthy bibliography. The writing style is suitable for high-school and college students. Although somewhat spe-

cialized in nature, this reference work can be consulted by those new to the field of atomic energy and by those who want basic information on such well-known incidents as Chernobyl and Three Mile Island. 💻

8-208. Kruschke, Earl R., and Byron M. Jackson. *Nuclear Energy Policy: A Reference Handbook.* Santa Barbara, CA: ABC-CLIO, 1990. 246 pp. Index. ISBN: 0-874-36238-5.

Like other volumes in this series, this work follows a format common to all. The initial chapter provides an introduction to the topic of nuclear energy policy, stressing nuclear power and production, its costs and benefits, and the management of nuclear waste. The second chapter provides a detailed chronology, while a third chapter sets forth brief biographical information on figures involved in the development of nuclear physics and nuclear energy policy. A fourth chapter encompasses excerpts from relevant documents and other background information. Among the documents are speeches, laws, hearings, court cases, and treaties. Statistical information also appears in this chapter. The final chapters include a directory and an extensive set of bibliographies for both print and nonprint materials. As is the case with the rest of the series, this volume is suitable for both high-school and undergraduate researchers.

Religion

8-209. Roof, Wade Clark, ed. *Contemporary American Religion.* 2 vols. New

York: Macmillan Reference USA, 2000. 861 pp. Index. ISBN: 0-028-64928-1.

The value of this work for social science researchers lies in the fact that it examines religious life in the United States at the end of the twentieth century and relates it to contemporary concerns. Thus, it is a work more closely related to the social sciences than to theology. Articles are arranged alphabetically by subject. Some are on issues under discussion in the political arena: "Abortion," "Child Abuse by Clergy," and "Moral Majority." Others deal with religious groups, ranging from Roman Catholics to Branch Davidians to followers of *Star Trek*. Biographies and discussions of religious practices and beliefs make up most of the rest of the entries. Most articles are a column to several pages in length and include cross-references and a bibliography. Numerous photographs supplement the text. Most of the contributors are drawn from either the U.S. academic community or are associated with one or another religious faith. The writing style is suitable for high-school as well as undergraduate students, but this set can be recommended to all other researchers interested in contemporary religion in the United States. 💻

8-210. Anglim, Christopher Thomas. *Religion and the Law: A Dictionary.* Santa Barbara, CA: ABC-CLIO, 1999. 451 pp. Index. ISBN: 1-576-07028-X.

The legal aspects of religion in the United States are a continual topic of discussion. This volume focuses on those parts of the First Amendment that deal with religion and excludes discussion of free speech and free press. Altogether, about 250 articles appear here, arranged alphabetically. Among the general categories of articles are court cases, constitutional theory, historical background, jurisprudence concepts, and articles that discuss the means by which American courts have attempted to balance religious liberty against other important individual and social interests. Entries range in length from several paragraphs to several pages. The volume concludes with tables of cases and statutes and a bibliography of approximately fifty pages in length. There are no bibliographic references with individual articles, however, nor are there illustrations. Compared to the *Encyclopedia of Religion in American Politics* [entry 5-141], this work provides greater detail on some subjects while ignoring others (such as biographies). Most student researchers will wish to consult both.

8-211. Utter, Glenn H. *The Religious Right: A Reference Handbook.* 2nd ed. Santa Barbara, CA: ABC-CLIO, 2001. 382 pp. ISBN: 1-576-07212-6.

This is currently a hot-button topic with the potential to get even warmer over the next couple of years with the rising influence of the Christian right in American politics. This particular work has eight sections, including biographical sketches of prominent people in this movement, quotations, select print sources, periodicals, and a directory of organizations. The directory of organizations chapter has full contact information along with Web sites and a short history of the group. An index links these chapters together. There is also a chronology for the dates 1835–2001, but the overwhelming number of entries is for the last twenty years.

Sexual Harassment

8-212. Jones, Constance. *Sexual Harassment.* New York: Facts on File, 1996. 280 pp. Index. ISBN: 0-816-03273-4.

This volume is divided into three major parts. The first part provides an overview: an introduction to the topic of sexual harassment and its law, a chronology, and relevant biographical information. The second part is a research guide for the reader and provides an annotated bibliography of approximately 100 pages as well as listings for appropriate organizations and agencies. The final portion of the book is a series of appendixes that includes the full text of a number of important federal enactments and court cases. Altogether, the appendixes are about 75 pages in length. The inclusion of these documents is one of the strengths of the volume, for it allows the reader access to a number of texts that would be tedious to find otherwise. There are no illustrations. Nevertheless, this is a fine starting point for both high-school and undergraduate students searching the topic of sexual harassment.

8-213. Eisaguirre, Lynne. *Sexual Harassment: A Reference Handbook.* 2nd ed. Santa Barbara, CA: ABC-CLIO, 1997. 285 pp. Index. ISBN: 0-874-36971-1.

This work follows the usual format of volumes in the Contemporary World Issues series: an introductory chapter is followed by chapters providing a chronology, biographies, factual and statistical information, a directory of organizations, and an annotated bibliography of both print and nonprint resources. One of the values of this work is that the author has attempted to provide viewpoints on both sides of the sexual harassment issue. Thus, there are biographies of both Anita Hill and Clarence Thomas. The chapter on "Facts and Statistics" is over eighty pages long and describes many different aspects of harassment, including differing perceptions of men and women. Also of value is a short introductory statement that tells readers how to read citations for cases and statutes. Finally, a short glossary defines a number of legal terms relevant to the issue. As is the case with others in this series, this work is suitable for both high-school and undergraduate students.

Social Issues

8-214. Kronenwetter, Michael. *Encyclopedia of Modern American Social Issues.* Santa Barbara, CA: ABC-CLIO, 1997. 328 pp. Index. ISBN: 0-874-36779-4.

The author of this volume indicates that his purpose is to provide basic information on controversies facing the United States and to do it in a single source. Obviously, issues cannot be explored in great depth in a work of only a single volume. The entries are arranged alphabetically. Some, such as abortion, child abuse, and gun control, are likely to occur to any student. Others are less standard topics for term papers; "Corporate Responsibility," "Miranda Rights," "Spanking," and "Women and Church" are examples. Most entries range from a page to several pages in length. Some, but not all, include cross-references and brief reading lists. There are no illustrations, and Kronenwetter has chosen not to emphasize statistics due to their tendency to date quickly. Compared to the six-volume *Encyclopedia of Social Issues* [entry 8-215], this work of course provides the user with much less detail but is handy for those high-school students and undergraduates who merely need a capsule summary of a contemporary social issue.

8-215. Roth, John K., ed. *Encyclopedia of Social Issues.* 6 vols. New York: Marshall Cavendish, 1997. 1780 pp. Index. ISBN: 0-761-40568-2.

The "Publisher's Note" in the first volume explains that this set is intended to fill the gap between accounts of social issues that appear in ephemeral news sources on the one hand and comprehensive books and encyclopedias on the other. This reference work attempts to occupy the middle ground by providing students with an overview that includes historical background, reasonably contemporary occurrences, and a description of the issues at stake. Altogether, the encyclopedia includes about 1,500 entries arranged alphabetically. Of these, thirty-four are major articles approximately 3,500 words in length. These include such subjects as aging, civil rights,

crime, poverty, and sexuality. The remaining articles range in length from a paragraph up to 1,500 words. Many longer articles include an annotated list of suggested readings. Articles are signed, and contributors, with their affiliation, are listed at the front of the first volume; some are listed only as "independent scholar." Each volume has its own table of contents, and a comprehensive index appears in the final volume. Cross-references appear in uppercase. The text is enlivened by numerous black-and-white photographs. This set should appeal to high-school students and undergraduates, but will be of less use to more advanced researchers.

8-216. Becker, Patricia C. *A Statistical Portrait of the United States: Social Conditions and Trends.* 2nd ed. Lanham, MD: Bernan Press, 2002. 322 pp. ISBN: 0-890-59584-4.

Working from the premise that there is no official federal government publication that provides social indicators, this volume attempts to fill that gap, "depicting societal change over the past several decades" (Becker 2002, introduction) in the process. The volume is divided into two halves. The first is arranged into twelve chapters, each on a specific subject, such as living arrangements, health, housing, and environment. The chapters use a combination of text and graphic displays to demonstrate the issue under discussion. Graphic displays are attributed to their source, and there are numerous footnotes as well as listings of additional publications and Web sites for those readers seeking more information. The second half of the volume is an extended appendix that provides detailed statistical tables that support the main text. Thus, readers have to consult both halves of this work to get a complete picture of the subject at hand. Close attention is also required when consulting the text and graphic displays; the two support one another so closely that the reader usually needs to peruse the text rather than just glancing through the graphic displays. There is no index, but the table of contents is quite thorough for both halves of this volume.

Transportation

8-217. Richter, William L. *ABC-CLIO Companion to Transportation in America*. Santa Barbara, CA: ABC-CLIO, 1995. 653 pp. Index. ISBN: 0-874-36789-1.

Finding basic information on transportation can be frustrating; so all-pervasive is the topic that it sometimes appears to be neglected or taken for granted in reference sources. This single-volume encyclopedia helps to fill that gap. Entries are arranged alphabetically and range in length from a brief paragraph to up to ten pages. There are entries for individual airlines, railroads, canals, and trails. Major pieces of legislation are also covered, and there are articles on specific types of transportation such as trucking. Well-known figures in the field receive short biographies. Each entry concludes with cross-references and a listing of bibliographic references. A detailed chronology concludes the main text, and biblio-

graphic references are repeated in a comprehensive listing that precedes the general index. The major orientation of this volume is historical, but enough coverage of contemporary happenings is included to make it a handy introduction for those students seeking an overview of American transportation topics.

8-218. Wilson, Rosalyn A. *Transportation in America: Statistical Analysis of Transportation in the United States*. Annual. Washington, DC: Eno Transportation Foundation, 1983–2000. ISBN: N/A.

Information appearing in this resource is gathered from a number of federal government agencies, trade associations, and private organizations. The basic arrangement is twofold. The first half of the annual volume includes brief text accompanied by graphic displays illustrating particular topics such as intercity passenger miles, freight carrier revenue, petroleum consumption, and the like. The second half is devoted to statistical tables that buttress the text and graphs appearing in the earlier part of the volume. The table of contents shows paging for both the initial section (labeled "Analysis Trends") and the statistical tables. For that reason, it is a simple matter for the reader to go from one section to the other. In some cases, statistics are shown as far back as the 1940s; in other instances, only a few recent years of data are provided. However, there is always information that allows for comparison from the most recent statistics to at least some earlier years. Sources and explanations are provided for the statistical tables. All levels of researchers interested in transportation industry statistics will benefit from consulting this volume if your interests correspond to the years published.

Urban and Rural

8-219. Pillsbury, Richard, and John Florin. *Atlas of American Agriculture: The American Cornucopia.* New York: Macmillan Library Reference USA, 1996. 278 pp. Indexes. ISBN: 0-028-97333-X.

This is one of those atlases where the text is as important as, if not more important than, the maps. The emphasis of the authors is on changes in American agriculture. In most cases, recent data from 1992 or 1994 are accompanied by text, graphs, tables, or maps that indicate the state of the data from past decades. Hence, the reader can easily ascertain where there have been increases or decreases in crop production on a state-by-state basis, as most of the maps show boundaries at the state level. There are sections for each agricultural region as well as listings for individual products ranging from catfish to oats to lettuce, among many others. There is a useful bibliography at the end of the volume; most data probably comes from federal sources, but none of the maps or statistical graphics indicates a source, a definite drawback. There are two indexes, one general in nature, and the other by geographical locale. This latter does include cities and counties as appropriate. This volume is a good starting point for those new to the subject or for those seeking a more user-friendly format than can be found in some of the standard federal sourcebooks.

8-220. Goreham, Gary A., ed. *Encyclopedia of Rural America: The Land and People.* 2 vols. Santa Barbara, CA: ABC-CLIO, 1997. 861 pp. Index. ISBN: 0-874-36842-1.

Rural America might be defined as that portion of the nation that includes communities with a population less than 2,500 or that have a particular type of economy: agriculture, fishing, forestry, mining, or energy based. This reference work provides nearly 300 articles discussing topics and issues relevant to the rural scene. Examples include architecture, barns, housing, media, migration, and wetlands. Articles are arranged alphabetically and generally are three to four pages in length. Each includes a bibliography that lists items from books, journals, and federal publications. A general bibliography can be found in the second volume, although it does not include all items listed in the individual bibliographies. Occasional photographs supplement the text. Each volume includes a complete listing of the entries, and an index in the final volume provides additional access. Most of the contributors are drawn from the academic community or from federal and state agencies dealing with rural issues. The writing style is suitable for undergraduates, and the information provided will be of assistance to graduate students and other advanced researchers as well. Few reference works deal with this subject, so this volume will be of special value in libraries where there is interest in rural America. 🖳

8-221. Shumsky, Neil Larry, ed. *Encyclopedia of Urban America: The Cities and Suburbs.* 2 vols. Santa Barbara, CA: ABC-CLIO, 1998. 974 pp. Index. ISBN: 0-874-36846-4.

Similar in nature to the *Encyclopedia of Rural America* [entry 8-220], this set describes American cities and suburbs both historically and in the present. Rather than descriptions of individual cities, the emphasis instead is upon urban phenomena, individuals, events, and the like. Arrangement of entries is alphabetical; typical entries include "Apartment Buildings," "Attitudes toward Cities," "Buses," and Al Capone. Articles are up to four pages in length and include cross-references and bibliographies. Contributors are scholars with relevant specialties. Occasional photographs are included. In addition to a comprehensive index, the second volume also includes a listing of entries by their subject matter and a "Selected Bibliography." This work will be of use to scholarly researchers, but the writing style is also accessible to high-school students and undergraduates. It is a handy alternative to those reference works that specialize in descriptions of major cities. 🖳

Violence
8-222. Levinson, David. *Aggression and Conflict: A Cross-Cultural Encyclopedia.* Santa Barbara, CA: ABC-CLIO, 1994. 234 pp. Index. ISBN: 0-874-36728-X.

"Aggression" as defined in this volume includes a broad variety of human behaviors intended to inflict harm upon others, whether by physical, verbal, or nonverbal means. Also included are individual and collective behaviors. Examples are drawn from approximately 100 cultures worldwide. For that reason, the reader will encounter some aggressive behaviors that are familiar: crime, rape, war, and wife beating. Others are more esoteric, at least in American society: cannibalism, headhunting, and "Raiding for Slaves." Entries are arranged alphabetically and range up to six pages in length. Each includes cross-references and a bibliography. Bibliographic references are repeated in a general bibliography at the back of the volume. Occasional illustrations accompany the text, and there is a section of maps at the center of the volume that allows the reader to locate the various societies described in the entries. Reading level is suitable for both high-school and undergraduate students dealing with the topic of violence.

8-223. McCue, Margi Laird. *Domestic Violence: A Reference Handbook.* Santa Barbara, CA: ABC-CLIO, 1995. 273 pp. Index. ISBN: 0-874-36762-X.

As defined in this volume, domestic violence is considered to be "spousal abuse and, more particularly, the abuse of men against women with whom they have or have had an intimate relationship" (McCue 1995, preface). Abuse of the elderly is not considered. The format is similar to that of other works in the Contemporary World Issues series. An introductory chapter describes the basic issues. This is followed by a chronology of some length, biographies, a chapter on statistical information and legal issues, a directory of organizations, and an annotated bibliography of print and nonprint resources. Compared to other volumes in the series, this one has fewer statistics and documents, concentrating instead on legal ramifications. The reading level is suitable for both high-school and college students.

8-224. Utter, Glenn H. *Encyclopedia of Gun Control and Gun Rights.* Phoenix: Oryx Press, 2000. 376 pp. Index. ISBN: 1-573-56172-X.

As the title indicates, this reference work attempts to discuss the issue of gun control with reference to all sides of the debate. Altogether, there are approximately 300 entries arranged alphabetically. Some of the subject areas covered include court cases, government agencies, and groups for and against gun control, issues, events, legislation, and biographies of significant individuals. Most entries are a page or a couple of pages in length and conclude with cross-references and listings for additional reading; the latter sometimes include Web sites. A lengthy introduction provides statistics and an overview of the subject, while an entry for the Second Amendment itself summarizes the points of view. A number of illustrations accompany the text. A series of appendixes provide text of state statutory and constitutional provisions pertaining to gun rights, organizations, and a chronology.

Among the final entries in the chronology is one for the high-school shootings in Littleton, Colorado, which also has an article under "Littleton, Colorado, School Shooting." This topic continues to attract wide student attention as a topic of interest.

8-225. Kurtz, Lester, ed. *Encyclopedia of Violence, Peace, and Conflict.* 3 vols. San Diego: Academic Press, 1999. 2672 pp. Index. ISBN: 0-122-27010-X.

This encyclopedia attempts a broad approach to its subject matter, dealing with issues of violence at the national, social, tribal, and individual levels. Articles are arranged alphabetically and include such topics as "Arms Control," "Child Abuse," "Hate Crimes," "Popular Music," and "Women and War." Articles average about ten pages in length, with some nearly twice as long. Cross-references and bibliographies appear at the end of each. The articles also begin with the outline of the contents and a glossary of potentially unfamiliar terms. Each of the three volumes includes a contents listing for all three in the set, as well as an arrangement of article titles by subject matter. Other than graphic displays, there are no illustrations. Most of the contributors are American academicians, but there is also representation from other nations as well. Thanks to its eclectic approach, the length of the entries, and the serious but readable tone, this set recommends itself to researchers at the college or university level, including both undergraduates and faculty members. 💻

8-226. Kinnear, Karen L. *Gangs: A Reference Handbook.* Santa Barbara, CA: ABC-CLIO, 1996. 237 pp. Index. ISBN: 0-874-36821-9.

Those student researchers seeking basic information on gangs can begin with this work. The introductory chapter describes the issue in brief. This is followed by a long chronology, biographies, statistical information, text of federal and state laws and documents, and a short section of quotations from experts and gang members alike. The volume concludes with a directory of organizations and an extended annotated bibliography that includes both print and nonprint resources, among them Internet sites. The individuals for whom biographies are provided are almost all academic researchers, not actual gang members. As is the case with other volumes in the Contemporary World Issues series, this book is suitable for both high-school and college students who require beginning information and a listing of sources for additional research. 🖳

8-227. Newton, David E. *Violence and the Media: A Reference Handbook.* Santa Barbara, CA: ABC-CLIO, 1996. 254 pp. Index. ISBN: 0-874-36843-X.

The role of violence in the media, and its effects on individual human beings, is a controversy that continues to vex the United States. This work first provides an overview of the subject, discussing motion pictures, cartoons, television, and music briefly. Ensuing chapters provide a chronology, biographies, and summaries and text of relevant documents.

The biographies include individuals representing both sides of the issue. The chapter dealing with documents encompasses laws, regulations, legal cases, policy statements, and research reports. The final chapters provide directory information and an extensive annotated bibliography including print and nonprint sources. As is in the case with other volumes in this series, this work provides a basic introduction to the subject suitable for both high-school and undergraduate students; the chapter on documentary sources is one of the more valuable parts of the work. 🖳

8-228. Gottesman, Ronald, ed. *Violence in America: An Encyclopedia.* 3 vols. New York: Charles Scribner's Sons, 1999. Index. ISBN: 0-684-80487-5.

This encyclopedia defines violence quite broadly, construing it to "include injury, or threat of injury, inflicted by one or more people on human beings, other species, the natural environment, or property" (Gottesman 1999, preface). Violence at the hands of government entities, in the form of war and capital punishment, also is described. Altogether, this set includes 595 entries arranged alphabetically. About 30 of these are thematic essays ranging in length from 5,000 to 12,000 words. Another 200 entries discuss their topics in a format of 1,000 to 5,000 words, while the remaining articles are fewer than 1,000 words. Typical entries include "Black Panthers," "Cold War," "Letter Bombs," "Serial Killers," and "Workplace." Entries include bibliographies and cross-references, and illustrations add immediacy to the text. The final volume includes appendixes that serve as directories to organizations, relevant publications, and Web sites. In general, the contributors are drawn from the ranks of U.S. academicians, but the writing style will be suitable for undergraduates and even high-school students. This set may be especially useful for its discussion of notorious individuals and episodes.

Welfare
8-229. Greve, Bent. *Historical Dictionary of the Welfare State.* Lanham, MD: Scarecrow, 1998. 159 pp. ISBN: 0-810-83332-8.

Greve, a Dane, presents a cross-cultural approach to the welfare state in this reference work. The volume begins with a chronology and a basic introduction to the topic. Entries are then arranged alphabetically, and include subjects such as "Benefits in Cash" and "Fiscal Policy." In addition, there are entries for individual nations, providing capsule descriptions of the development of the welfare state in each. Most, of course, are in economically advanced countries. The entries are short, ranging from a paragraph to about a page in length. Cross-references are indicated through the use of the abbreviation "q.v.," which may baffle student users. A bibliography of twenty pages can be found at the back of the volume. The major value of this work is the fact that it compiles information in regard to basic concepts of the welfare state and the varieties of welfare systems seen from nation to nation. More ad-

vanced students and scholars will be its main beneficiaries.

8-230. Hombs, Mary Ellen. *Welfare Reform: A Reference Handbook.* Santa Barbara, CA: ABC-CLIO, 1996. 165 pp. Index. ISBN: 0-874-36844-8.

Each of the volumes in the Contemporary World Issues series concentrates upon a particular issue; thus, the topic of this work is welfare reform. The format is the same as others in the series. An overview chapter provides the reader with a short discussion of key issues in regard to welfare reform. This is followed by chapters providing a chronology, biographies, facts and statistics, and documentary sources. The latter includes documents from the Bill Clinton administration, viewpoints of conservatives, a couple of documents from interested organizations and individuals, and viewpoints from earlier presidential administrations. The next chapter discusses legislation and pertinent litigation. The final three chapters provide a directory and annotated bibliographies of print and nonprint sources, including Web sites. A glossary and an index finish up the volume. Those high-school and undergraduate students requiring basic introductory information for term papers on welfare reform can turn to this volume for assistance. 💻

Women
8-231. Frost-Knappman, Elizabeth. *ABC-CLIO Companion to Women's Progress in America.* Santa Barbara, CA:

ABC-CLIO, 1994. 389 pp. Index. ISBN: 0-874-36667-4.

While researching a book on the history of women's suffrage in America, Frost-Knappman became persuaded that information on the struggle of women for equal rights was far more abundant for the nineteenth and twentieth centuries than it was for earlier times. This work aims to correct that oversight by presenting the general reader with brief information pertaining to all of American history. Some entries are brief biographies of noteworthy women, while others discuss court cases, laws, organizations, and topics such as "Contraception," "Corset," and *"Lowell Offering"* (a periodical of the 1840s). Entries range in length from a few sentences to about a page. Cross-references are indicated for more substantive entries. Occasional illustrations supplement the text, and a chronology and a bibliography round out the volume.

8-232. Andermahr, Sonya, Terry Lovell, and Carol Wolkowitz. *A Concise Glossary of Feminist Theory.* New York: Arnold, 1997. 287 pp. ISBN: 0-340-59663-5.

In their introduction, the authors, who are British academicians, state that their work reflects a move in feminist theory from sociology and history to philosophy and cultural and literary studies. Therefore, this dictionary will be of greater interest to women educated in women's studies programs than to those more engaged with everyday feminist situations. Emphasis is upon such 1990s concerns as postcolonialism, queer theory, struc-

turalism, and traveling theory. More than simply definitions, the entries also describe theoretical background, often referring the reader to contending viewpoints. Brief references are included in the text; complete references can be found in a bibliography at the back of the volume; this bibliography, numbering over forty pages, is more complete than is usually the case with dictionaries of this sort. Some definitions are no more than a paragraph, but none are more than a couple of pages in length. Although the authors have attempted to reach a reasonably broad audience, this field of study is by nature complex, so this work will be of value to scholars and others with a background in feminist theory more than it will be to beginning inquirers.

8-233. Seager, Joni. *Penguin Atlas of Women in the World.* New York: Penguin Books, 2003. 128 pp. Index. ISBN: 0-142-00241-0. (Title Varies: *State of Women in the World Atlas.*)

As is the case with other "State of . . ." publications by Penguin, this small atlas uses a colorful array of maps, symbols, and statistics to provide the reader with international comparisons in regard to a particular subject, women in this case. Approximately 34 two-page maps acquaint the reader with specific topics, such as abortion, marriage and divorce, contraception, rape, and property, among others. Proper interpretation of the data requires the reader to pay close attention to the combination of colors, symbols, and statistics that accompany each map. On the other hand, international comparisons are made easy by the use of bright colors that display the progress (or lack of progress) of women in each nation. A "World Table" at the back of the volume provides statistical comparisons among the nations of the world in ten different categories. Explanatory notes and a listing of major sources also appear at the end. This work will be of greater interest to general readers and to undergraduates than it will be to scholars, but it does compile a good deal of information that otherwise might be laborious to ferret out. The point of view is definitely feminist.

8-234. Taeuber, Cynthia M., comp. and ed. *Statistical Handbook on Women in America.* 2nd ed. Phoenix: Oryx Press, 1996. 354 pp. Index. ISBN: 1-573-56005-7.

As is the case with other statistical compilations, this work provides the reader with a generous number of statistical tables gathered from a large number of sources, primarily the federal government and its agencies. The statistical tables presented here are arranged into four major categories: "Demographic Events and Characteristics," "Employment and Economic Status," "Health Characteristics," and "Social Characteristics." The last category includes topics such as marriage, divorce, education, voting, crime, victimization, and criminal offenders. Reference to the original source is provided with each table or graph. A glossary explains terminology.

Further interpretation is provided in text that precedes each of the four major categories. This is a useful source for students or other beginning researchers needing statistical data on American women; more advanced researchers and those seeking up-to-date figures will turn to other sources.

8-235. Stromquist, Nelly P., ed. *Women in the Third World: An Encyclopedia of Contemporary Issues.* New York: Garland, 1998. 683 pp. Index. ISBN: 0-815-30150-2.

One of the goals of this reference work is to provide a single, reasonably comprehensive source for information regarding women in the third world. The arrangement is topical, not alphabetical. Major categories include "Conceptual and Theoretical Issues," "Political and Legal Contexts," "Sex-Role Ideologies," "Demographics and Health," "Marriage and the Family," "Women and Production," "Women and the Environment," "Enabling Conditions for Change," "Movements for Change," and "Geographical Entries." Each of these major sections includes three or more separate articles written by individual contributors. As much as possible, contributors were women chosen from third world societies. The editor admits that the result is a variety of approaches to the subject; balancing this is the fact that viewpoints can be found here that might not have been included otherwise. Each article includes a listing of references, and there is also an annotated bibliography at the back. Several appendixes reproduce the texts of relevant documents. In general, the contributors are scholars and specialists, and this volume is directed at a scholarly audience, including more advanced undergraduates.

8-236. Kinnear, Karen L. *Women in the Third World: A Reference Handbook.* Santa Barbara, CA: ABC-CLIO, 1997. 348 pp. Index. ISBN: 0-874-36922-3.

Like other volumes in the Contemporary World Issues series, this work provides the reader with basic background followed by a lengthy annotated bibliography. An introductory chapter describes the general situation of women in the third world, with brief discussion of subjects such as gender roles, health, violence, work, and human rights. This is followed by a detailed chronology, biographies of significant individuals, some general statistics, and reproductions of texts of relevant international agreements affecting women. The bibliography encompasses print and nonprint resources, including a number of Internet sites. Also included is a listing of organizations with descriptions and addresses. This work will be of use to both high-school students and undergraduates requiring beginning information on this subject.

8-237. McFadden, Margaret, ed. *Women's Issues.* 3 vols. Pasadena, CA: Salem Press, 1997. 1041 pp. Indexes. ISBN: 0-893-56765-5.

Almost 700 entries are included in this set; the length of entries ranges from 100 to 4,000 words. The entries discuss terms, individuals, organizations, historical events, and contemporary issues. Among the latter are articles that deal with such subjects as Supreme Court cases, education, employment, health, and the arts. Articles over 1,500 words in length include a bibliography, while those over 2,500 words are accorded an annotated bibliography. Arrangement is alphabetical, and cross-references lead the reader from one relevant article to another. A number of illustrations and graphic displays supplement the text. Each volume includes its own table of contents as well as listings of entries for the entire set arranged both alphabetically and by category. The final volume includes a number of appendixes, among them listings of women's studies programs, historical sites, museums and archives, organizations, a listing of Supreme Court decisions affecting women, and a chronology. Also included in this final volume are a comprehensive bibliography and a filmography. Contributors are drawn from the U.S. academic community for the most part, and emphasis is on women's issues in the United States and Canada. This set is suitable for both high-school and undergraduate students.

8-238. Tierney, Helen, ed. *Women's Studies Encyclopedia.* rev. and exp. ed. 3 vols. Westport, CT: Greenwood Press, 1999. 1607 pp. Index. ISBN: 0-313-29620-0.

This is one of the more useful reference works in the crowded field of women's studies. The articles attempt to cover women's concerns in a comprehensive fashion, including such subjects as "Battered Women," "Dance," "Rape," and "Victims of Crime." Articles are up to several pages in length. References appear at the end of most entries, although the number of items listed varies a good deal. Cross-references are few in number. The contributors, who sign their articles, are mostly U.S. academicians. Nevertheless, there are a good number of articles pertaining to feminist concerns in other major nations and regions of the world, as well as entries pertaining to women's history, particularly in literature. A short "Selected Bibliography" appears at the end of the third volume, along with a comprehensive index. There are no illustrations. Tierney died as this set was nearing completion, so that may account for some weaknesses in cross-referencing and inconsistency in the provision of bibliographies. Still, this set will provide undergraduates with beginning information on many topics associated with the women's movement. 💻

8-239. United Nations. *World's Women, 2000: Trends and Statistics.* 3rd ed. New York: United Nations, 2000. 180 pp. ISBN: 9-211-61428-7.

A number of United Nations agencies collaborated in the compilation of this publication that appears to come out around every five years. Its goal is to demonstrate the contributions of women worldwide to the economy, politics, and the family in the hope that policy makers will be persuaded to change circumstances unfair to the gender. Tables and graphic displays are grouped into six chapters covering subjects such as population, households and families, population growth, health, education, employment, and "Power and Influence." The tables and graphic displays are accompanied by text that enhances and interprets the data. Sidebars provide additional information. References to sources are provided as well. Technical notes are also included; as usual, the reader must take into consideration variations among the nations of the world in terms of interpretation and reporting of data, and variances in timeliness. One weakness of this volume is the fact that there is no index, so the reader must work from the table of contents to find the desired information. However, this is a useful starting point for those wanting comparative information on the status of women around the world.

Web Sites: U.S.
Domestic Policy Issues
Although Web sites oriented toward political science, politics, and governmental affairs are plentiful, relatively few are of research value. Too many fail to integrate the convenience of a graphic interface with provision of substantive full-text information. Those sites that overwhelm the user with advertising or that confront researchers with a multiplicity of confusing links have been excluded. Those remaining in the array generally provide a reasonably uncluttered interface with links to a range of full-text sources that ideally mix factual information with opinion pieces. Think tanks predominate in the group. At one

time, such organizations might have been thought of as nonideological agents examining policy issues in a fairly nonpartisan and neutral way. However, many think tanks now are unabashedly advocacy groups promoting a particular point of view. Regardless whether the researcher agrees with a particular viewpoint, it is useful to find such views clearly articulated on a number of controversial issues. The annotations indicate when a particular group is conservative, liberal, or elsewhere along the political spectrum.

8-240. American Enterprise Institute for Public Policy Research. http://www .aei.org. E-mail contact: info@aei.org.

Perhaps the best known among conservative think tanks, the American Enterprise Institute (AEI) is influential with conservative presidential administrations and legislators. Its Web site states that it is "dedicated to preserving and strengthening the foundations of freedom—limited government, private enterprise, vital cultural and political institutions, and a strong foreign policy and national defense." As of April 2005, the Web site included information on the war on Iraq, partisanship in American politics, health policy, and a number of other topics. 💻

8-241. The Brookings Institution. http:// www.brook.edu. E-mail contact: webmaster@brookings.edu.

The Brookings Institution has been extant since approximately 1916. Its Web site states that it is an "independent, nonpartisan organization devoted to research, analysis, education, and publication focused on public policy issues in the areas of economics, foreign policy, and governance." In-depth research is possible on the topics of current interest to the institution. For example, in April 2003, the Web site included several types of texts pertaining to welfare reform: congressional testimony, policy briefs, analysis, and commentary, as well as links to upcoming events. 💻

8-242. The Cato Institute. http://www .cato.org. E-mail contact: webmaster@ cato.org.

The Web site states that the Cato Institute "seeks to broaden the parameters of public policy debate to allow consideration of the traditional American principles of limited government, individual liberty, free markets and peace." The Web site provides links to commentary and news on a variety of domestic and foreign policy issues. There is a definite streak of libertarianism running through a number of this think tank's members. Domestic issues of interest in April 2003 included social security, Amtrak, and federal court nominations. Links to archival topics are also provided. 💻

8-243. Center for Economic and Policy Research. http://www.cepr.net. E-mail contact: cepr@cepr.net.

The Center for Economic and Policy Research was founded in 1999 by Dean Baker and Mark Weisbrot, both of whom were still directors in April 2003. It has as its mission "to promote democratic debate on the most important economic and social issues that affect people's lives." Topics are both domestic and international in scope. Examples of domestic issues include college-graduate debt, drug costs for the elderly, dividend taxes, and housing affordability. Entries represent newspaper columns and papers by the directors and their staff; the general outlook is liberal. 🖥

8-244. Center for Policy Alternatives. http://www.cfpa.org. E-mail contact: info@cfpa.org.

The Center for Policy Alternatives, founded in 1976, calls itself "the nation's leading nonpartisan progressive public policy and leadership development center serving state legislators, state policy organizations, and state grassroots leaders." As this statement indicates, the center deals with state issues. Its Web site includes an array of information on state issues such as child care, the death penalty, domestic violence, the environment, and many others. Other links lead users to topical demographic data at the state level. Also of value are links to the individual state legislatures. 🖥

8-245. Center for Responsive Politics (Opensecrets.org). http://www.open secrets.org. E-mail contact: info@crp.org.

The "Open Secrets" Web site is an extraordinarily useful resource for those seeking information regarding political campaign funding and spending. The site is operated by the Center for Responsive Politics, which states that it is a "non-partisan, non-profit research group based in Washington, DC that tracks

money in politics, and its effect on elections and public policy." The site allows users to search for spending information for their own representatives, comparisons in the most recent election, listings of donors by both name and topical area, and reports on relevant items in the news. In May 2003, these reports included campaign finance reform, medical malpractice reform, prescription drugs, and others. This site can be highly recommended to any researcher investigating campaign finance issues. 🖥

8-246. Center for Study of Responsive Law. http://www.csrl.org. E-mail contact: csrl@CSRL.org.

This rather idiosyncratic site is an effort by the Ralph Nader organization "to encourage the political, economic and social institutions of this country to be more aware of the needs of the citizen-consumer." As such, it reflects the interests of Nader and his group. The initial page has information about projects of the organization, but the greatest interest lies in a series of links entitled "Essential Information," "Public Citizen," "Citizen Works," "Public Interest Research Groups," and "The Nader Page." Each leads to full-text resources on issues of interest to that particular component of the Nader organization. Typical topics include prescription drugs, automobile safety, and taxes. Although this site focuses somewhat on consumer issues, it is of value to student researchers following up on the topics that have made Ralph Nader well known over the years. 🖥

8-247. The Century Foundation. http://www.tcf.org. E-mail contact: info@tcf.org.

Formerly known as the Twentieth Century Fund, The Century Foundation is generally regarded as one of the more liberal think tanks. Its Web site states: "as a nonpartisan, but not neutral, organization, our underlying philosophy regards government as an instrument, not an enemy, of the people." Its Web site features recent opinion pieces by its staff and links to topics of current interest. Among such topics in May 2003 were "economic inequality," "the aging of America," "media and society," "American foreign policy," "US politics and policy," and "the economy." Unfortunately, the site features relatively little full text. Ordinarily, the user is given a brief overview and then linked to sites elsewhere. 💻

8-248. Common Cause. http://www.commoncause.org. E-mail contact: grassroots@commoncause.org.

Common Cause describes itself as a "nonprofit, nonpartisan citizen's lobbying organization promoting open, honest and accountable government." The Web site features a "Press Library" that archives press releases of the organization; a "Soft Money Laundromat" that allows for searches by donor name, geographical location, and industry; and "States," which links to issues of interest within each of the states that have to do with campaign finance, open government, and similar issues. Most of the text on the site focuses upon issues of immediate interest to the organization. 💻

8-249. Economic Policy Institute. http://www.epinet.org. E-mail contact: epi@epinet.org.

The Economic Policy Institute states on its Web site that it is a "nonprofit, nonpartisan think tank that seeks to broaden the public debate about strategies to achieve a prosperous and fair economy." The site includes press releases, opinion pieces, and policy briefs on topics pertaining to the economy. There are separate components for "Living Standards and Labor Markets," "Government and the Economy," "Trade and Globalization," "Education," and "Sustainable Economy." Some files are in PDF format and include statistical tables and charts. Also of value is an online calculator that indicates the basic budget required by size of family and urban locale. Altogether, this is a site that will appeal to researchers seeking a liberal viewpoint on the American economy. 💻

8-250. Heritage Foundation. http://www.heritage.org. E-mail contact: info@heritage.org.

The Heritage Foundation is one of the better-known conservative think tanks. Its mission is to "formulate and promote conservative public policies based on the principles of free enterprise, limited government, individual freedom, traditional American values, and a strong national defense." Its Web site provides opinion pieces reflecting that point of view. A featured item on the Web site in May

2003 was that advocating a reduction of taxes on capital gains and dividends. Other opinion pieces at the same time included "The Myth of a Child Care Crisis" and "Increased Abstinence Causes a Large Drop in Teen Pregnancy." Compared to other think tank sites, the full-text offerings here are relatively slender, but they do provide viewpoints that illuminate conservative thinking on issues both domestic and foreign. 🖳

8-251. *The Hill.* http://www.hillnews .com. E-mail contact: None.

The Hill states that it is a "nonpartisan, non-ideological weekly newspaper that describes the inner workings of Congress, the pressures confronting policy makers, and the many ways—often unpredictable—in which decisions are made." This Web site provides nonsubscribers with a portion of the text otherwise available to subscribers. Included are feature articles, opinion pieces, and columnists, with pollsters and pundits featured prominently. The focus is on the current happenings on Capitol Hill. The value of this source for casual researchers and students is its examination of issues agitating the political elite. 🖳

8-252. Louisiana State University Libraries. "LSU Libraries Federal Agencies Directory." http://origin.lib.lsu.edu/gov/ fedgov.htm. E-mail contact: docslib@ lsu.edu.

One of the better online directories, this site allows users to search for federal government agencies through a number of

approaches. One link directs the researcher to a hierarchical listing of federal government agencies, while another is an alphabetical listing. One can also search by "Boards, Commissions and Committees," "Executive," "Independent," "Judicial," "Legislative," and "Quasi-Official." Finally, the user can also conduct inquiries through a search box. The site is a partnership of Louisiana State University and the Federal Depository Library Program and therefore has a reasonably official provenance. 🖳

8-253. Moving Ideas Network. http:// www.movingideas.org. E-mail contact: manager@movingideas.org.

Formerly known as the Electronic Policy Network, this site is a project of the *American Prospect* magazine and hence features resources from a liberal point of view. The Web site is rather busy, but it does feature a great number of full-text articles and opinion pieces gathered from a number of venues. Both domestic and foreign policy issues are covered. The mission statement indicates that "MIN posts the best ideas and resources from leading progressive research and advocacy institutions." Apparently, there are 100 member organizations, so this site serves as something of an aggregator for progressive ideas. 🖳

8-254. National Association of Counties. http://www.naco.org. E-mail contact: None.

For the most part, this site is aimed at professionals in the field of county government, but it does include some extremely useful information for researchers and laypeople. Particularly helpful is the link to "About Counties." Here, the researcher finds a wealth of statistical and demographic information about counties and their governments, including individual counties nationwide. Other links lead the user to government at state and municipal levels. The interface allows for a number of topical approaches. In all, this site provides one of the most complete and cleanest directories to local government information found on the Web. ▪

8-255. National Center for Policy Analysis. http://www.ncpa.org. E-mail contact: ncpa@ncpa.org.

The Center for Policy Analysis states that its mission is "to seek innovative private-sector solutions to public policy problems." As such, the center has a conservative approach to policy issues. The Web site includes opinion pieces on recent topics of interest as well as links to policy issues such as "Crime," "Environment," "Health," "Social Security," and "Unions," among others. Another set of links, "Both Sides," provides pro-and-con arguments on topics such as those listed above and garnered from news sources. The main caveat for this site is the fact that some of the topic areas appear not to be updated as frequently as might be desirable. ▪

8-256. National Priorities Project. http://www.nationalpriorities.org. E-mail contact: info@nationalpriorities.org.

The National Priorities Project has as its mission to offer "citizen and community groups tools and resources to shape federal budget and policy priorities which promote social and economic justice." It therefore provides a liberal point of view in regard to the subjects it takes as its areas of interest. These topics concentrate on federal spending and tax policies, with particular emphasis upon defense spending versus spending for social issues. Among the subjects under discussion in May 2003 were "The Cost of Invading Iraq," "Alternative Economic Stimulus Plans," and "A Safer America." Also available are statistical analyses for the various states in terms of spending on social programs and the tax burden on lower-income citizens. ▪

8-257. New America Foundation. http://www.newamerica.net. E-mail contact: webmaster@newamerica.net.

Billing itself as neither left nor right in ideology, the New America Foundation proposes to "bring exceptionally promising new voices and new ideas to the fore of our nation's public discourse." The feature that will have the most appeal to users is a collection of full-text articles garnered from magazines and newspapers generally regarded as liberal in approach; the articles evidently are written by individuals associated with the foundation. Access to the articles can also be obtained through clicking on a link for "Issues." These issues are arrayed into eight subject areas; among them are "Education," "Democracy," and "Environment." ▪

8-258. Project Vote Smart. http://www .vote-smart.org. E-mail contact: comments@vote-smart.org.

Founded in 1992 by Jimmy Carter, Gerald Ford, Barry Goldwater, and George McGovern, among others, Project Vote Smart takes as its mission a dedication "to serving all Americans with accurate and unbiased information for electoral decision-making." At this Web site, the user can find contact information for his or her elected officials, as well as biographies and information on issue positions, campaign finances, interest groups, and voting records. Information varies and sometimes depends on cooperation from the elected official. Also available are key votes in Congress. Researchers who don't know their elected officials can enter a nine-digit zip code (or a home address if the nine-digit zip is not known) to find a list of links to names of elected executive and legislative officials at both the national and state levels. Candidates for office are also listed. This handy Web site has many uses, but is perhaps most valuable for identifying elected officials and providing their contact information. 💻

8-259. Public Agenda Online. http://www .publicagenda.org. E-mail contact: None.

Founded in 1975 by Daniel Yankelovich and Cyrus Vance, Public Agenda has a twofold mission: on the one hand, it assists leadership to understand the "public's point of view on major policy issues," while on the other hand, it attempts to "help citizens better understand critical policy issues so they can make their own more informed and thoughtful decisions." The initial screen has links to policy issues currently in the news as well as a listing of, with links to, twenty-two areas of policy concerns. Some examples include "Abortion," "Child Care," "Gay Rights," and "Medical Research." Within each of these issues, there are a number of links to full-text resources that describe the issues from various points of view, providing possible solutions (again from varying ideological perspectives) and facts and statistics to bolster the opinions. The one limitation of this site is the fact that questions beyond the basic issues will go unanswered. For example, the policy links relating to "The Environment" do not touch upon issues regarding public lands. Otherwise, this is an excellent site for student researchers looking for pro-and-con arguments on a number of societal concerns. 💻

8-260. Stateline.Org. http://www .stateline.org. E-mail contact: editor@ stateline.org.

Operated by the Pew Center on the States, this Web site assists journalists, policy makers, and other researchers to become "better informed about innovative public policies." The site has various resources of interest. Under "Issues," the researcher finds about a dozen major categories with links to basic information. Among the topics are "Campaign Finance," "Education," and "Taxes/Budget." "States" has links to each of the states, guiding the user to information on the legislature, the governor, and the state home page itself. "State News Roundup" provides links to current news stories of importance, arranged by state. To a certain extent, this site has a greater appeal to journalists and policy makers than it does to student researchers; nevertheless, it can be recommended to the latter group for topics of interest at the state level. 🖥

9

Biographical Reference Sources
for Political Figures

9-1. Colamery, Stephen N., comp. *African Leaders: A Bibliography with Indexes.* Commack, NY: Nova Science Publishers, 1999. 249 pp. Index. ISBN: 1-560-72721-7.

This bibliography covers twenty-eight major African political leaders, excluding those in the Muslim northern tier of countries. It is arranged alphabetically by leader's name. Under each individual's entry, there are citations of books, book chapters, government publications, and journal articles relevant to this person's political activities and life. Each person receives up to ten pages of bibliographic references. Generally, the longer a leader's hold on power endured, the more is written about that person. Foreign-language materials are included in the citations. Typical entries are for Steve Biko, Jomo Kenyatta, Robert Mugabe, and Julius Nyerere. Only the very elite of African political leaders are written up for this bibliography. Inexplicably, only one leader has all his citations annotated, and in great detail. The index adds nothing overall to the book.

9-2. *American Leaders, 1789–1994: A Biographical Summary.* rev. ed. Washington, DC: Congressional Quarterly, 2000. 546 pp. ISBN: 0-871-87841-0.

The biographical information found here is extremely brief, generally amounting to a listing of significant dates: birth, political milestones, and death. The volume is divided into six categories of offices, including president, vice president, cabinet members, Supreme Court justices, members of Congress, and governors. A short introductory statement precedes each category and provides a collective political and demographic profile of the members of that group. Much of the information here can be found in other Congressional Quarterly publications, but this is a handy quick source for those researchers who may desire a single-volume compilation regarding these offices.

9-3. O'Brien, Steven G. *American Political Leaders: From Colonial Times to the Present.* Santa Barbara, CA: ABC-CLIO, 1991. 473 pp. ISBN: 0-874-36570-8.

Short biographies of approximately 400 American men and women appear in this volume. Most are those who have been elected or appointed to national offices. Among those included are presidents, vice presidents, unsuccessful presidential candidates, secretaries of state, chief justices of the Supreme Court, Speakers of the House, and influential diplomats, senators, and other appointees. The biographies range in length from a half page to as many as four pages and concentrate upon the individual's political career. At least one bibliographic reference concludes the biography; significant individuals receive several bibliographical entries. Many of the profiles include a portrait of the individual, and there are cross-references to other biographies in the volume. A time line at the back of the work allows the reader to identify contemporaries and their political positions. The writing style is suitable for both high-school and undergraduate students who require only brief information on a political figure or who desire a group of such biographies.

9-4. Utter, Glenn H., ed. *American Political Scientists: A Dictionary.* 2nd ed. Westport, CT: Greenwood Press, 2002. 516 pp. ISBN: 0-313-31957-X.

This book focuses on the theoretical contributions of roughly 200 eminent political scientists. Those listed are scholars who were selected because they lived in the United States or accomplished much of their professional work there. Excluded are those scholars who were noted primarily for being economists, sociologists, or other social scientists. The arrangement is alphabetical, and each entry is about one-and-one-half pages in length. There is a short section on "Selected Works," which highlights the contributions of those listed here, and there is even short space given to works on them. The entries give the defining areas of importance for each political scientist listed by giving their career highlights and the core of their research interests. Many of the political scientists included were born prior to 1970, but this second edition made a decided effort to include more women and minorities. Typical entries include John Merriman Gaus, Richard E. Neustadt, and James N. Rosenau. Each entry has been signed. Appendix 1 is a list of political scientists by degree-granting institution, while Appendix 2 lists them by subfields of interest within the discipline. 💻

9-5. Miller, Randall M., and Paul A. Cimbala, eds. *American Reform and Reformers: A Biographical Dictionary.* Westport, CT: Greenwood Press, 1996. 559 pp. Index. ISBN: 0-313-28839-9.

Although the individuals whose biographies appear in this volume were more concerned with social reform than with civic reform, their careers collectively display trends among social movements in the United States from the abolition era to the late twentieth century. Their efforts impacted government policy significantly and therefore are of interest to political scientists. Altogether, there are biographies of thirty-eight reformers, and each biography is written by a historian or other academician familiar with that individual and his or her achievements. The biographies range in length from ten to twenty pages. Each concludes with endnotes and a bibliography of important secondary sources. Reformers from recent decades include Betty Friedan, Martin Luther King Jr, Russell Means, and Ralph Nader, among others. A lengthy chronology traces reform history from 1775 through 1994. The index assists the reader to trace common themes across the biographies. The writing style is scholarly in tone, but nevertheless accessible to general readers and to undergraduates.

9-6. Whitman, Alden, ed. *American Reformers: An H. W. Wilson Biographical Dictionary.* New York: H. W. Wilson, 1985. 930 pp. ISBN: 0-824-20705-X.

The United States has long provided a home for the reform-minded. This volume provides brief biographies of 504 men and women known as reformers. Those selected for inclusion in this work had to be of national significance, and the biographies emphasize their work in reform movements as opposed to general biographical information. The biographies range from about one page to several pages and usually include a portrait of the biographee. Bibliographies are provided with each entry. An alphabetical listing of all reformers appears at the front of the volume, while a listing by

category appears at the back. This work is of importance for historical figures but excludes those reformers active after about 1960. For example, among those biographees active in women's rights are Susan B. Anthony, Margaret Fuller, and Julia Ward Howe, but no names familiar from recent decades. The writing style is suitable for both high-school and undergraduate students. See *American Social Leaders* [entry 9-7] for a comparison of these two works.

9-7. McGuire, William, and Leslie Wheeler. *American Social Leaders.* Santa Barbara, CA: ABC-CLIO, 1993. 500 pp. ISBN: 0-874-36633-X.

Approximately 350 biographies of American men and women appear in this volume. Four major categories of individuals were included: those who might be described as reformers; those termed "public intellectuals"; journalists; and inventors, industrialists, and philanthropists. The biographies are arranged alphabetically and usually are one or two pages long. Some include a portrait of the individual in question. Cross-references are provided to related biographies, and one or two bibliographic references are included as well. A listing of all those included in the volume appears at the front. Unlike *American Reformers* [entry 9-6], this volume emphasizes contemporary reformers as well as those from the past. For example, some of the familiar names appearing here include Jesse Jackson, Ralph Nader, and Gloria Steinem. *American Reformers*, on the other hand, provides biographies of some lesser known figures that do not appear here, so the two works complement one another. The writing style is suitable for both high-school and undergraduate students.

9-8. Hardy, Gayle J. *American Women Civil Rights Activists: Biobibliographies of Sixty-Eight Leaders, 1825–1992.* Jefferson, NC: McFarland, 1993. 479 pp. ISBN: 0-899-50773-5.

The reader should be advised that "civil rights" is defined in its widest possible context. For the purposes of this handbook, it could apply to Native Americans or other indigenous peoples, African Americans, Hispanics, children's advocates, lesbians and gays, the aged, and more. As the title indicates, sixty-eight women have been chosen for their activism in these or related areas. The criteria for selecting any of these women are lacking. Alphabetically arranged entries provide the highlights of each person's life. Information is taken from print and online sources, and from personal contact. Entry formats reflect an organized pattern from entry to entry. Every entry begins with a chronology, biographical information, and then a bibliographic portion that provides a wide assortment of secondary- and primary-source materials pertaining to works both on and by the individual. Typical entries include Aileen Clarke Hernandez, Constance Baker Motley, Coretta Scott King, and Sarah Winnemucca. Appendixes give birth places, ethnicity, fields of activity, geographic location, and religious affiliation

of the biographees through the use of comparative data tables.

9-9. Lentz, Harris M. *Assassinations and Executions: An Encyclopedia of Political Violence, 1900 through 2000.* rev. ed. Jefferson, NC: McFarland, 2002. 291 pp. ISBN: 0-786-41388-3.

The purpose of this encyclopedia is to introduce to people the various world leaders who have been murdered, especially if done so via political assassination or execution. The span of coverage ranges over 100 years from 1900 to the near millennial marker of 2000. Listed are heads of state or government, ambassadors, leading national personages, and military officers. The book is arranged chronologically. The prologue contains a narrative listing of world leaders killed prior to 1865. Entries can vary in length from one sentence to two pages, with most being on the shorter side. Entries give dates, names, context, and results of assassination as well as other data. Included are many of Stalin's victims, the German military officers executed for the failed attempt on Hitler's life, and many more. The first edition covers 1865 through 1986, so both editions may be wanted for expanded coverage.

9-10. Bartke, Wolfgang. *Biographical Dictionary and Analysis of China's Party Leadership 1922–1988.* New York: K. G. Saur, 1990. 482 pp. ISBN: 3-598-10876-1.

This work is organized into two major parts and provides fairly brief biographical information on China's main political leaders over a sixty-six-year period. Part 1 lists Chinese Communist Party people who were members of the Central Committee. It includes all Central Committee members and alternates for the second through thirteenth Central Committees. Approximately 75 percent of the biographies have photographs; many have several different photos taken over time for comparative purposes. Part 2 is divided into twenty-five chapters, with the first eight dealing with the Politburo and the next seventeen with the various Central Committees. Tabular information as well as pictures of members of various Politburos is given.

9-11. Eccleshall, Robert, ed. *Biographical Dictionary of British Prime Ministers.* New York: Routledge, 1998. 428 pp. Index. ISBN: 0-415-10830-6.

Mostly British scholars contribute to this reference work on Great Britain's prime ministers. Arrangement is chronological beginning with Robert Walpole and concluding with Anthony Blair. The period covered is from the eighteenth century to date. Entries are roughly ten pages in length and attempt to evoke the historical context of the times. Entries are scholarly in tone, with student reading lists attached to each entry. Contributors cite many other scholars in the field and quote them directly. The clear emphasis is the prime minister's life while in office and his/her relationship with the political parties and other politicians, political convictions, policies, and so forth. The volume contains a very good index. Each article is signed. 💻

9-12. Mahoney, M. H. *Biographical Dictionary of Espionage.* San Francisco: Austin and Winfield, 1998. 622 pp. ISBN: 1-572-92065-3.

Entries were chosen based on how well each agent illustrated a particular characteristic of espionage or operational technique in the field. Many of the spies selected for inclusion are American or European and were active during the cold war era. There are indeed historical spies listed, such as Rahab (The Harlot) and Paul Revere, but they appear to be of secondary importance. Arrangement is strictly alphabetical by biographee, and each entry offers several pages on these people's spying techniques, rings, who they spied for, arrest records, and so forth. Each entry ends with a "Points of Interest" section that provides some unusual stories, coincidences, and aspects of their private or work lives that readers of this work may find illuminating. Also given are aliases and probable birth/death dates. Some of the entries, such as the one on Julius and Ethel Rosenberg, are surprisingly poignant. Understanding the operative's particular motivation for taking on the role of a spy also makes good reading.

9-13. Bell, David S. *Biographical Dictionary of French Political Leaders since 1870.* New York: Simon and Schuster, 1990. 463 pp. ISBN: 0-130-84690-2.

This is a biographical dictionary aimed clearly at high-school and undergraduate students as well as the general public. There are over 400 major French political figures from 1870 through 1989 listed. Each entry is about one page in length but packs a lot of information into that listing. Most of the page is taken up appropriately with the person's political life. It gives the individual's role in government, within political parties, public offices held and when, and the like. There is a very short listing of readings at the conclusion of each entry. All articles are signed, with most contributors based in the United States, the United Kingdom, or France. They are almost all academics. Appendixes include the French presidents and their respective dates of office, the prime ministers and their dates, and the entire Fifth Republic Party leadership. Readers looking for the private lives of these political leaders should look elsewhere.

9-14. Alexander, Robert J., ed. *Biographical Dictionary of Latin American and Caribbean Political Leaders.* New York: Greenwood Press, 1988. 509 pp. Index. ISBN: 0-313-24353-0.

This reference work was written as a complement to *Political Parties of the Americas* (1982) [F. Holler, 4th edition, entry 2107]. This 1988 work is similar in coverage and scope except that Canada is now omitted. Many of the same contributors from the earlier work have written the more than 450 biographical sketches for this updated work. Entries include the biographies of the key political figures over the nineteenth and twentieth centuries in Latin America and the Caribbean region. The twentieth-century people greatly outnumber the nineteenth-century political figures examined. Information pro-

vided includes the person's career, family background, education, and certain non-political activities. Arrangement is strictly alphabetical, with one-page entries that are signed. Short bibliographies are attached to every person's entry. Appendix A is a chronology from 1804 through 1985, while Appendix B has the biographees clustered by country. The larger countries, such as Chile and Argentina, tend to receive disproportionately better coverage. This volume contains a good index.

9-15. Gorman, Robert A. *Biographical Dictionary of Marxism.* Westport, CT: Greenwood Press, 1986. 388 pp. ISBN: 0-313-24851-6.

There are roughly 210 Marxist philosophers and activists from fifty nations included in this biographical reference work. The focus is on more traditional or orthodox Marxists. The coverage of third world Marxist figures is particularly strong. The book has in its introduction a very good short essay on the meaning of philosophical materialism, the foundations of Marxism. This book was published in conjunction with a companion work, *Biographical Dictionary of Neo-Marxism* [see entry 9-18, also by Gorman]. Each entry averages one-to-four pages in length and offers a wealth of biographical information basics, such as birth and death dates; education; the individual's role regarding Marxism; whether or not he or she was an activist, scholar, or party leader; and brand of Marxism. Entries conclude with a selective list of primary and secondary works related to the individual. The main body of the book is strictly alphabetical. Contributors are primarily international scholars. There is an appendix of biographees by nationality.

9-16. Baylen, Joseph, ed. *Biographical Dictionary of Modern British Radicals.* 3 vols. Atlantic Highland, NJ: Humanities, 1988. ISBN: 0-710-81319-8.

The term "radical" here defines an individual whose life purpose and work involved more than a mere moderate change of policy or revision in the operation of political, social, and/or economic institutions. Radicals generally desired to alter the traditional order of the landed aristocracy and Church of England by changing the fundamental social and economic pillars of society through governmental action and social welfare legislation in order to create a more equitable distribution of wealth. The contributors are international scholars. Each of the alphabetically ordered entries is several pages long and provides background on the individual's private and public lives. An attempt is made to place individuals within both their proper historical and British radicalism contexts. Entries conclude with a list of writings by the biographee and books about him or her; some of these lists are quite lengthy.

9-17. Nicholls, David. *Biographical Dictionary of Modern European Radicals and Socialists,* Vol. 1, *1780–1815.* New York: St. Martin's Press, 1988. 291 pp. Index. ISBN: 0-312-01968-8.

For the purpose of this biographical work, the editors define radicals as those individuals who wished to alter the existing economic, social, and political structures by either political action or theoretical writings. Volume 1 explores over 187 radicals, of whom most are either French or German. Only six women are included here. Given the narrow dates of this work, the French Revolution obviously furnished a long roster of the names included in Volume 1. The format of each entry is similar. It contains such information as an account of the individual's life, contributions to radicalism, assessment of type of radicalism displayed, and additional readings on the person. An entry can be up to five pages long. Each person receives an ample amount of information without going overboard. This volume is a great ready-reference source for names, dates, events, and the like. The index is sparse and will offer minimal assistance.

9-18. Gorman, Robert A., ed. *Biographical Dictionary of Neo-Marxism.* Westport, CT: Greenwood Press, 1985. 463 pp. Index. ISBN: 0-313-23513-9.

This work serves as the companion volume to *Biographical Dictionary of Marxism* [see entry 9-15, also by Gorman] and lists only "nonmaterialist" Marxists. There are a total of 205 entries, 10 of which are more topical in nature, such as "Prague Spring" or "Liberation Theology." All the entries average about two-and-one-half pages and are well written, finishing with a bibliography consisting of primary works and secondary materials.

The opening essay, "Introduction: The Mosaic of Marxism," is a wonderful primer on this arcane topic. Males make up the overwhelming number of entries. There is an appendix by nationality along with a general subject index.

9-19. Wigfall, Patricia Moss. *Biographical Dictionary of Public Administration.* Westport, CT: Greenwood Press, 2001. 166 pp. ISBN: 0-313-30203-0.

This book contains several page-long entries on the luminaries in the field of public administration in order to present the student with a clear understanding of the fundamental issues and thinking that helped shape the field into what it is today. It includes the pioneers and the more contemporary names associated with public administration. The lives and work of public administration's major personalities are compiled here in relatively short pieces that follow a standard format. This format includes a short personal history, followed by the person's primary contributions to the field. Then, space is allotted for a bibliography of books both by and on the person. Sample entries include Amitai Etzioni, Robert A. Dahl, and John Kenneth Galbraith. Many of the biographees are considered major figures in other fields such as sociology, political science, and the like. This book is intended to serve students as an adjunct to primary public administration textbooks. See chapter 8 for other reference sources on public administration and for nonbiographical materials.

9-20. Johnpoll, Bernard K., and Harvey Klehr, eds. *Biographical Dictionary of the American Left.* New York: Greenwood Press, 1986. 493 pp. Index. ISBN: 0-313-24200-3.

Along with Communists, Socialists, anarchists, and syndicalists, this biographical dictionary also encompasses radical movements of the agrarian nineteenth-century United States, such as communalism. Those profiled must have had "some substantial importance to the history of American radicalism or some other noteworthy accomplishment" (Johnpoll and Klehr 1986, introduction). Radical intellectuals and many members of the New Left of the 1960s were also excluded. Some of those profiled, such as Eugene Debs and Emma Goldman, are well known, but there are many otherwise obscure individuals as well. Biographies range in length from a single page to almost ten, depending upon the significance of the individual and the information available. Cross-references and bibliographic sources are indicated. There are several appendixes; these provide a chronology and collective information about the biographees. The contributors are drawn from the U.S. academic community, but the writing style is accessible to undergraduates as well as more advanced researchers.

9-21. Lazitch, Branko. *Biographical Dictionary of the Comintern.* rev. ed. Stanford, CA: Hoover Institution Press, 1986. 532 pp. ISBN: 0-817-98401-1.

In order to qualify for a listing in this biographical dictionary of 753 people, one must have served in the Comintern's overall directorate, such as its Executive Committee, Executive Committee Presidium, Executive Committee Secretariat, or its Control Commission. Also, anyone who spoke at a Comintern Congress between 1919 and 1935 or was a delegate to the enlarged plenary meetings of the Executive Committee from 1922 through 1933 is included. Individuals who played an especially vital role in the Comintern or in any of the Communist movements also were listed as well as members of the Comintern apparatus, leaders of various international organizations, and heads of the Communist Youth International. There is a standardized format for each entry, which includes basic biographical data and a political biography of the individual within the Comintern and/or the Communist Party. Entries are highly factual and succinct, of approximately one-half a page.

9-22. Rees, Philip. *Biographical Dictionary of the Extreme Right since 1890.* New York: Simon and Schuster, 1990. 418 pp. ISBN: 0-130-89301-3.

This book contains biographies of politicians, philosophers, novelists, poets, and others who were Fascists, Vichy supporters, National Socialists, virulent anti-Semites, or drawn to extreme nationalist movements. The author of this work has an admitted proclivity to include those people who moved from leftist to the extreme Right over the course of their lives. Each entry ends with a very short bibliography of sources. Most people listed in this biographical work are Europeans. It is an excellent source of information for some relatively lesser known right-wing figures in modern history.

9-23. Katz, Bernard S., and C. Daniel Vencill, eds. *Biographical Dictionary of the United States Secretaries of the Treasury, 1789–1995.* Westport, CT: Greenwood Press, 1996. 403 pp. ISBN: 0-313-28012-6.

The Department of the Treasury now plays an important role in the U.S. economy, and its secretary is a key official in the formulation of economic policy. This volume provides biographies of all the secretaries through 1995. The arrangement is alphabetical, with each secretary receiving a biography of at least two pages and the more significant ones receiving close to ten; recent incumbents tend to claim greater attention than those from the early years. Biographies end with a bibliography of relevant books and articles. The volume begins with a chronology and an introductory discussion that helps to provide context. Most of the contributors are American economics professors. While this work obviously will be of interest to specialists, the biographies are also accessible to undergraduate readers.

9-24. Rahr, Alexander, comp. *A Biographical Directory of One-Hundred Leading Soviet Officials.* Boulder, CO: Westview Press, 1990. 210 pp. ISBN: 0-813-38015-4.

This directory serves as a guide to most prominent members of the Soviet leadership. The data composing the main body of this work are taken largely from official Soviet sources. That data have been supplemented by other sources, such as letters from people included as entrants. Each biography conforms to a standardized format, and this includes career, political life, speeches and publications, travels abroad, and awards and honors. About 50 percent of the entries have photographs included, and most are about two pages in length. The arrangement is strictly alphabetical by name.

9-25. Robbins, Keith, ed. *Blackwell Biographical Dictionary of British Political Life in the Twentieth Century.* Cambridge, MA: Blackwell Reference, 1990. 449 pp. ISBN: 0-631-15768-9.

This is a biographical work intended to highlight leading British political figures. The author attempts to define the relative stature and importance of these people. Prime ministers, chancellors of the Exchequer, foreign secretaries, and home secretaries receive the lengthiest entries, while the more selective inclusion of journalists, union leaders, civil servants, military people, and the like get somewhat less substantive treatment. The organization of the main body is alphabetical by name in a standard format that always provides birth/death dates, place of birth, parents, education, events involved in, political party affiliations, offices held, negotiations attended, and so forth. There are occasional photographs

and a few further readings. Using a succinct writing style, this work is very good for more general readers, high-school students, and undergraduates.

9-26. *Bowker-Saur Who's Who of Women in World Politics.* New York: Bowker-Saur, 1991. 311 pp. Index. ISBN: 0-862-91627-5.

This biographical resource directory highlights prominent women in politics around the countries of the world. Part 1 gives 1,500 biographies of international women in alphabetical arrangement. Entries are standard directory type and include position, birth, education, political career, interests, address, and the like. A survey done for this work determined that these women's expertise falls into several areas: education, social welfare, peace, and environmental issues. To be included, the individuals must be either a head of state, member of the government, national legislator, political party or trade-union leader, or a regional figure of some importance. Part 2 gives some statistics on the number of women holding various positions such as head of state. Part 3 is an index to individuals arranged by country.

9-27. Ransley, John, ed. *Chambers Dictionary of Political Biography.* New York: Chambers Kingfisher Graham, 1991. 436 pp. ISBN: 0-550-17251-3.

Entries on approximately 1,100 men and women who helped define the contemporary political landscape make up this book's contents. Each biographee has made a "significant contribution" to their country's political history. Entries are usually limited to one long paragraph of information that concentrates on the political lives of the individuals. Some entries provide the titles of works written by the individual covered, and many have cross-references to other people. Individuals selected for inclusion span the era from antiquity and classical Rome up to more contemporary times. While the political biographies of people who lived in developing countries are not lacking, names drawn from Europe and the United States clearly predominate in number. There is a fifty-page glossary of political terminology, including both English and non-English-language phrases. There is also a modest collection of political quotations, which are cited if the source is indeed known. There is no index available.

9-28. *China Directory in Pinyin and Chinese [Zhongguo zu zhi bier en ming bu].* Annual. Tokyo: Radio Press, 1984–.

This appears to be an annual publication, and it may have ceased publication. The text is in English, Chinese, and Japanese. There is a directory of all People's Republic of China Communist Party officials by function, State Council officials, military organization heads, mass organization heads, heads of various social and economic organizations, and the like. Each person's status in relation to the Thirteenth Central Committee of the Communist Party of China is given. There are surprisingly no addresses or telephone numbers. There are death dates and the dates the various

offices were assumed by the individual biographee. This is a sketchy work. (Note: The last edition examined was for 1991.)

9-29. Frankel, Benjamin, ed. *The Cold War, 1945–1991.* Vols. 1–2, *Leaders and Other Important Figures in the United States and Western Europe.* Vol. 3, *Resources: Chronology, History, Concepts, Events, Organizations, Bibliography, Archives.* Detroit: Gale Group, 1992. ISBN: 0-810-38927-4.

This three-volume set attempts to illuminate the cold war period by providing biographical information about key people on both the U.S. and Soviet side of the divide. Volume 1 contains biographical entries for roughly 150 political and military leaders from the Western side. These individual biographee entries examine a bit more of the whole person rather than just the individual in his/her role as a cold warrior. These entries are somewhat longer, and the suggested reading lists are longer than those found in *Encyclopedia of the Cold War* [entry 6-126]. It is also more heavily illustrated. In Volume 2, about 125 Soviet bloc and second and third world leaders who were actors in the cold war are listed. Not all third world individuals included in this chapter were necessarily aligned with the Soviet bloc. Examples of these are Chiang Kai-shek and Vaclav Havel. Arrangement is strictly alphabetical. Volume 3 is in some regards the most interesting. It highlights various cold war topics, terms, events, treaties, and the like. A chronology of events from 1939 through 1991 is also included here.

The forty-page history of the cold war era is concise and excellent for high-school and/or undergraduate students. There is also a good, basic bibliography of relevant works and archival sources. See Chapter 6 for other works on the topic of the cold war.

9-30. Economist Books. *The Columbia Dictionary of Political Biography.* New York: Columbia University Press, 1991. 335 pp. Index. ISBN: 0-231-07586-3.

Providing succinct individual portraits of the movers and shakers who influence politics today, such as heads of state, members of government, political party leaders, leading parliamentarians, prominent regional or state governors, leading trade unionists, heads of dissident groups, Euro-politicians, and the like, is the primary goal of this work. Everyone who was still alive on the cut-off date of December 31, 1990, is included as entries. All the entries (more than 2,000) are arranged alphabetically and must be considered very concise. British spelling predominates. Visually, one entry tends to run into another, imparting a cluttered look to the pages. The entries, however, are quite well done, and the contributors mince few words. Entries are about twelve-to-eighteen lines long and contain boldfaced cross-references. An index by country along with all biographees listed finishes up this work.

9-31. *Current World Leaders: Almanac.* Santa Barbara, CA: Current World Leaders, 1957–. ISSN: 0192-6802. http://www.cwik.org.

The June 2002 issue examined contained information on 193 countries, 31 colonies and dependent territories, and 39 international organizations and alliances. The arrangement is straightforward, with the chapters on national governments, colonies, and international organizations all in alphabetical order. Each country has similar directory-type entries. Typical categories for these entries are for natural resources, land use, ethnic composition, gross domestic product, major government officeholders, and the minister. The entries average out at about one-and-one-half to two pages per country. (Note: The Web-based version of this work is known as *Current World Information Knowledgebase* and is updated monthly.) 💻.

9-32. Alexrod, Alan. *Dictators and Tyrants: Absolute Rulers and Would-Be Rulers in World History.* New York: Facts on File, 1995. 340 pp. ISBN: 0-816-02866-4.

This work examines over 600 people who were leaders and had power corrupt them in some way or another. The criteria for inclusion is wide ranging and is generally defined as individuals who have crossed the lines that gave their sovereignty authority in the first place, whether to God or to the people. These individuals often seized power or ruled in an illegitimate manner. Biographees are listed alphabetically. Whether or not all people listed here fully meet the author's stated criteria is debatable to some extent. Leonid Brezhnev, Trajan, and Chou En-lai are three such examples.

The work is written in a popular, easy-to-read style. There are some pictures included, and there is often a book or two attached to the main entry that is intended for additional reading. This volume is best for public libraries and lower-division undergraduate or high-school students.

9-33. Barrows, Floyd D. *A Dictionary of Obituaries of Modern British Radicals.* New York: Harvester Wheatsheaf, 1989. 490 pp. ISBN: 0-710-81013-X.

Modern British radicals are seen as beginning with John Wyclif and the Lollards in the latter part of the 1300s. The British radical movement has been especially strong since around the mid-1700s. An introduction offers a good treatise on the history of British radicalism, and it notes the fundamental changes in radicalism occurring in Britain over the last two centuries. While British radicals were originally more interested in government reform and growing concessions to the burgeoning middle class, they have turned their attention over time to economics and matters of world peace. The British radicals listed in this particular work correspond pretty much with those who were published in *Biographical Dictionary of Modern British Radicals* [entry 9-16], edited by Joseph Baylen. The 360 obituaries are arranged in standard A-to-Z order. The great majority of the obituaries are a couple of pages long. Obituaries are complete and the source of the obituary is always given.

9-34. *A Dictionary of Political Biography.* New York: Oxford University Press, 1998. 523 pp. ISBN: 0-192-80035-3.

These 1,000 entries in alphabetical sequence describe people who have had an impact on political events around the globe during the twentieth century. Each entry blends description with analysis and specifically provides background, career, and achievements of the individual biographee. Biographies are included for people who have been active since the year 1900. Included in this work are all major officeholders in the United States, the United Kingdom, the Soviet Union, and Germany at the national levels. Emphasis is on elected officials, not appointees. The contributors are mostly European academics. There are a good number of cross-references within entries, but no index. This work is best for high-school and undergraduate students.

9-35. Lentz, Harris M. *Encyclopedia of Heads of States and Governments, 1900 through 1945.* Jefferson, NC: McFarland, 1999. 508 pp. ISBN: 0-786-40500-7.

This is a companion volume to the same author's 1994 book, *Heads of States and Governments: A Worldwide Encyclopedia of Over 2,300 Leaders, 1945 through 1992.* The more recent volume includes all countries with independent governments during the period from 1900 through 1945. Some semiautonomous political units such as Vietnam and Egypt are also covered. Countries are listed in A-to-Z dictionary fashion by their standard English-language name. The arrangement of the entries begins with the name of the country, followed by a geographical and historical overview and biographical listings by heads of state in chronological order. These entries are then followed by a similar arrangement for the respective heads of government. The paragraph format used here makes the information somewhat difficult to scan quickly, but a wealth of information is contained here on the family lives of individuals, their travels, major policy initiatives, education, death dates, and more. Ninety of the countries included in this work are now defunct or incorporated into other nation-states. Samples of those include the Orange Free State, Montenegro, Saxony, and Czechoslovakia.

9-36. Hamilton, Neil A. *Founders of Modern Nations: A Biographical Dictionary.* Santa Barbara, CA: ABC-CLIO, 1995. 505 pp. ISBN: 0-874-36750-6.

This biographical work defines a "modern" nation-state as one that existed when the work was published. It excludes all mythical or legendary founders from consideration. It also omits all nations that are now defunct, such as the Soviet Union. There is no attempt made to be exhaustive, and this is especially true for the United States. The book is divided into two parts. The first part, forming roughly 80 percent of the entire work, is an alphabetical listing by country with all the founders of the nation given in that entry. Each entry averages approximately two pages. About half the entries in this section have accompanying pictures of the individuals. The second part offers simple one-paragraph snippets about

each nation-state included and adds minimal value for information that is easily found in other standard reference sources. This work is best suited for the general public, high-school students, and lower-division undergraduates.

9-37. Del Testa, David W., ed. *Government Leaders, Military Rulers, and Political Activists.* Westport, CT: Oryx Press, 2001. 245 pp. Index. ISBN: 1-573-56153-3.

The editor has selected the 200 "greatest" leaders throughout all of history for inclusion in this work. Each biography is descriptive of the person's life, and then their long-term legacy is analyzed. The major criterion for being written up in this encyclopedia is a government leader's ability to transform their society or even the course of human history. Each entry is accompanied by a concurrent chronology of world events and the individual's life achievements. Every article is signed and exactly one page long no matter how monumental the figure may have been in history. There are black-and-white pictures or drawings of individuals that are of varying quality. Entries appear to be quite idiosyncratic in their selection status. How else would one describe a work that gives equal print to Betty Friedan, Charlemagne, and Boris Yeltsin? Approximately 10 percent of the people listed here were still alive at publication time. A modest bibliography of monographs is included along with an index. ⌨

9-38. Blumberg, Arnold, ed. *Great Leaders, Great Tyrants? Contemporary*

Views of World Rulers Who Made History. Westport, CT: Greenwood Press, 1995. 354 pp. Index. ISBN: 0-313-28751-1.

This work offers a unique perspective of a coterie of political leaders from around the world and their respective strong and weak points, good and bad public policy choices, and the like. A total of fifty-two individuals are covered, but the author flounders in the explanation of the selection criteria's contours. Hitler and others of his ilk are excluded due to the "excesses of their tyranny." Stalin is included, however, because of his contributions to history. Vespasian and Trajan are given space, but Caesar Augustus is not. Entries are arranged alphabetically and begin with a short introduction. They are several pages long and contain a suggested-reading list. A number of leaders omitted from serving as main entries in this book are, however, sometimes found in the index section in a comparative context to other leaders. The writing style leans toward the more popular vein. 🖳

9-39. *The Hutchinson Encyclopedia of Modern Political Biography.* Boulder, CO: Westview Press, 1999. 527 pp. ISBN: 0-813-33741-0.

The scope of the concepts of political space and actors has broadened significantly in the current world setting. This work reflects the growing trend of this process. The biographical encyclopedia includes only men and women who represented the leading individuals in the world at the year 2000 AD for the previ-

ous 100 years. The author deserves some credit for making a conscious effort to include a number of third world people and also other less standard ones such as Bella Abzug, Frank Zappa, and Ralph D. Abernathy. The entries concentrate on people's public life or political career events. Frequently, the exact political leanings of the individual are articulated. For example, it is stated that Bob Hawke, an Australian Labor politician and prime minister for almost a decade, was "on the right wing of the party." The average entry is about one-quarter page long. A few black-and-white pictures are scattered throughout the pages. Appendixes are for heads of state by country, chronology by birth year, and a listing by country of origin. Despite the original intentions for inclusion, U.S. and U.K. names predominate by far. 🖳

9-40. Truhart, Peter. *International Directory of Foreign Ministers, 1589–1989 [Internationales Verzeichnis der Aussenminister, 1589–1989].* New York: K. G. Saur, 1989. 475 pp. ISBN: 3-598-10823-0.

The year of this book's publication date marks the 400-year anniversary of the first minister in 1589 by Henry III. This work explicitly draws quite substantially on *Regents of Nations,* a three-volume set published in 1984 through 1988, but it updates entries and goes well beyond the time frame of that multivolume work. The work opens with a nicely written essay on the history of the foreign minister as it pertains to a country's foreign affairs, policies, and administration. The main body of this historical directory is arranged by region of the globe, followed by listings of individual countries. Entries are solely a roster, arranged by date of service, of foreign ministers who held office. No biographical or other information is provided on the individual ministers. (Note: There is a 292-page supplement [Ergaenzungsband] for 1945 through 1995, which was published in 1996 by K. G. Saur.)

9-41. DeLeon, David, ed. *Leaders from the 1960s: A Biographical Sourcebook of American Activism.* Westport, CT: Greenwood Press, 1994. 601 pp. Index. ISBN: 0-313-27414-2.

This volume presents biographies of approximately eighty individuals who were radicals or activists during the 1960s. The arrangement is topical rather than alphabetical, with biographies apportioned into six areas. These are "Racial Democracy," "Peace and Freedom," "Sexuality and Gender: Liberation from Stereotypes," "For a Safe Environment," "Radical Culture," and "Visions of Alternative Societies." Some biographies are relatively brief, but the more significant individuals receive entries as many as eight pages long. Especially useful is the fact that the biographies attempt to indicate the significance of the individual's work and what has happened to them since. Photographs of the biographees are included. Each entry includes a bibliography, and each of the six major categories is provided with introductory text that also includes a bibliographic listing. The contributors are mostly members of the U.S. academic community. For those

readers who came of age in the 1960s, the names will be familiar: Eldridge Cleaver, Philip Berrigan, Bella Abzug, Paul Ehrlich, Joan Baez, Angela Davis, and many others. Contemporary students, however, may not have heard of a good many of these figures, so this work provides a useful introduction to the era and its reformers.

9-42. McCauley, Martin, ed. *Longman Biographical Directory of Decision-Makers in Russia and the Successor States.* Harlow, Essex, UK: Longman Current Affairs; Detroit: Gale Group, 1993. 726 pp. ISBN: 0-582-20999-4.

This work attempts to serve as a kind of Who's Who of the post-Soviet-world elites rising up out of the ashes of the USSR and the other successor states at the dawn of a new era in that region of the globe. The directory focuses most of its attention on Russia, the Ukraine, and Belarus. The elites are drawn from all aspects of politics, government, economics, military, media, or religious life. There is a strong degree of admitted subjectivity in selecting people chosen for listing during this transitional and turbulent period. Some individuals are claimed to be lacking only because there was little reliable or balanced information available on them. The elites that did find their way into this biographical directory were divided into three groups: old Communist elite, new Communist elite, and new elite. Entries placed under these categories are alphabetical by person's name and average about one page of space. Each entry contains such information as place and date of birth, education, military service, political service, and the like.

9-43. *Mexican Political Biographies, 1884–1935.* Austin: University of Texas Press, 1991. 458 pp. ISBN: 0-292-75119-2.

See entry 9-44.

9-44. Camp, Roderic Ai. *Mexican Political Biographies, 1935–1993.* 3rd ed. Austin: University of Texas Press, 1995. 743 pp. ISBN: 0-292-71174-3. 🖥

These two companion works provide succinct yet informative biographies of prominent Mexican political figures. Included are presidents, cabinet secretaries, assistant secretaries, officials, mayors, senators, supreme court justices, party leaders, ambassadors, military commanders, and governors. Both works are alphabetically arranged by individual name. Standard entries average one-half page and give birth/death dates, education, family ties, government positions, military experience, political party positions, and sometimes trace noted family clans. A number of appendixes list supreme court justices, senators, and the like by date or by date and state where appropriate.

9-45. Sonderling, Nelly E., ed. *New Dictionary of South African Biography.* 2 vols. Pretoria: Vista University, 1995–1999. Index. ISBN: 1-868-28134-5.

This biographical dictionary serves as a successor to a five-volume set published from 1968 through 1987 and entitled *Dictionary of South African Biography.* While the updated work contains biographical information for 129 individuals, the older set contained approximately 900 biographical entries per physical volume. Each entry in the newer work includes a black-and-white photograph, and the people selected for inclusion have largely moved away from white, male-dominated political leaders and toward those who were extraparliamentary leaders who pushed for a wide array of various political and social reforms. An attempt was made to include more women as well. Entries in general tend to focus less on the private lives of the individuals and much more on what made those people worthy of mention in the political and/or social arenas. Format is strictly alphabetical, and entries run about one to two pages. Everyone mentioned appears to be deceased. Some typical names included are Diederik J. Opperman, Charlotte Makgomo Maxeke, and Shadrack Fuba Zibi. There is a combined index that includes both the newer and older works.

9-46. Nolan, Cathal, ed. *Notable U.S. Ambassadors since 1775: A Bibliographical Dictionary.* Westport, CT: Greenwood Press, 1997. 430 pp. Index. ISBN: 0-313-29195-0.

This is an extremely selective work of U.S. ambassadors who led distinguished careers primarily while serving in Europe or Asia. U.S. ambassadors to other developing countries are not excluded, but are clearly given second-tier consideration.

Some people have been included simply because they may have been associated with some particular milestone in the history of the U.S. Foreign Service itself. There are only fifty-five entries in this work, and they average about three to six pages in length. The biographic profiles include standard basic information and facts, along with highlights of an ambassador's career or political perspective. There is also a brief bibliographic section of works by and works about that person. All entries are signed, and there is an index to the work. 🖳

9-47. Adi, Hakim. *Pan-African History: Political Figures from Africa and the Diaspora since 1787.* London: Routledge, 2003. 203 pp. ISBN: 0-415-17352-3.

This fairly recent work on the history of Pan-African biography includes men and women of African lineage whose very lives have been forever intertwined with the social and/or political emancipation of African peoples and those residing in the African diaspora around the globe. Those who struggled against the twin evils of racism and slavery were also included. Pan-Africanists were regarded as interested in strengthening the overall unity of all those of African descent in order to solve the "colour line" issue and to "secure civil and political rights for Africans and their descendents" (Adi 2003, preface). The Caribbean area became a focal point for Pan-Africanists, and the influence of the international Communist movement on the Pan-Africanists is also noted.

9-48. Wiseman, John A. *Political Leaders in Black Africa: A Biographical Dictionary of the Major Politicians since Independence.* Brookfield, VT: E. Elgar, 1991. 248 pp. ISBN: 1-852-78047-9.

Over 485 political leaders from Africa are listed alphabetically. These are individuals at the very top level of the political elite, and very few women's names appeared when this work was compiled over a decade ago. Each individual's entry is about several paragraphs long. More eminent and longer-serving leaders, such as Jomo Kenyatta, receive several pages of print information. Entries do little more than trace the political life and activities of the leader, providing dates, offices held, political party affiliations, and so forth. A chronology of major events in Africa from 1960 through 1990 is included.

9-49. Stachura, Peter D. *Political Leaders in Weimar Germany: A Biographical Study.* New York: Simon and Schuster, Academic Reference Division, 1993. 230 pp. ISBN: 0-130-20330-0.

The 135 individuals included in this biographical work are limited to Reich chancellors, distinguished ministers, political party leaders, noted parliamentarians, chairmen of major government agencies, and some provisional politicians. A sprinkling of civil servants has been tossed into this group as well. The author purports this work to be the first English-language biographical study of the Weimar Republic's most significant political leaders. The individual entries provide basic background and career information, and a "critical" assessment of that person in significance and overall value to the politics of the Weimar Republic. A total of five women are included here in these 400- to 1,000-word entries. There is a decent bibliography at the end of the book's main section containing a number of German-language materials. A chronology of the Weimar Republic rounds out the features of this work.

9-50. Glickman, Harvey, ed. *Political Leaders of Contemporary Africa South of the Sahara: A Biographical Dictionary.* New York: Greenwood Press, 1992. 361 pp. ISBN: 0-313-26781-2.

The primary purpose of this dictionary is to present its readers with biographical profiles of the major sub-Saharan political leaders who have made substantive contributions since 1945. The contributors to this work are international in scope, and the four- to six-page entries themselves are alphabetically arranged, with each concluding with a short bibliography on the individual. These main entry topics could include overall importance of the person, political offices held, major political actions, and/or political hurdles faced. The focus of all the entries is the political lives of the individuals being covered, not their personal lives. All entries are signed. Entries include both white and black individuals from the area. This particular work is especially notable for providing solid historical context to current political issues.

9-51. Wilsford, David, ed. *Political Leaders of Contemporary Western Europe: A Biographical Dictionary.* Westport, CT: Greenwood Press, 1995. 514 pp. ISBN: 0-313-28623-X.

The seventy-one biographical entries composing the main body of this book vary in length from one to seven pages. The criteria for inclusion into this alphabetically arranged work are quite unclear, and the final result is a most subjective assortment of individuals who made the roster at the expense of those who did not. Erich Honecker is listed, but his predecessor, Walter Ulbrecht is not. On the other hand, political leaders such as Santiago Carrillo who, while influential, may not have headed a government are included. Several Western European political leaders have been excluded from coverage, and they are from Iceland, Luxembourg, Monaco, Switzerland, and several other relatively smaller political entities. Contributors are international in scope and are academics drawn mainly from political science departments.

9-52. *Political Leaders of Modern China: A Biographical Dictionary.* Westport, CT: Greenwood Press, 2002. 278 pp. Index. ISBN: 0-313-30216-2.

This is a roster of China's political elite from the period of the first Opium War (1839–1842) to the beginning of the twenty-first century. There also is a chronology and an essay on the very nature of China's modern political leadership. The work was put together with the assistance of thirty international scholars. The main body of the book has 100 Chinese leaders written up in several-page-long articles. These entries present primarily the individual's political life, actions, and offices, with only scant personal details. Cross-references are built in, and each entry has been duly signed. An index appears at the end.

9-53. Reich, Bernard. *Political Leaders of the Contemporary Middle East and North Africa: A Bibliographic Dictionary.* New York: Greenwood Press, 1990. 557 pp. ISBN: 0-313-26213-6.

This highly selective biographical dictionary features seventy highly political leaders of Middle Eastern or North African countries. These individuals have been active mostly during the post–World War II era. Each entry has basic information on birth and death dates and career. Much of each entry concentrates on examining the political career of these leaders. The well-written entries by mainly American and Middle Eastern scholars provide ample information on individual personalities, political strategies, international roles, and even political psychology. There is a brief bibliography including works by and about the subject at the conclusion of each entry. Most of these works are in the English language.

9-54. Justice, Keith L., comp. *Presidents, Vice-Presidents, Cabinet Members, Supreme Court Justices, 1789–2003: Vital and Official Data.* Jefferson,

NC: McFarland, 2003. 297 pp. ISBN: 0-786-41044-2.

This is a complete roster of names of all the men and women who have served in any of the positions listed in the title of this book. It is in fact an update of a 1985 publication, *Public Office Index.* The work begins with the U.S. presidents and their respective cabinet officers. Overall, listings of names are either alphabetical or in chronological order. The information provided for each person is in fairly standardized format and usually includes dates of birth and death, residence, date of appointment, date left office, and a few other categories that can vary slightly from person to person.

9-55. Day, Alan J., ed. *Profiles of Worldwide Government Leaders.* Annual. Bethesda, MD: Worldwide Government Directories, 1995–. Index. ISSN: 1080-7063.

This annual is designed to list every current minister, head of government, and head of state for every one of the 195 countries listed. Even many of the relatively tiny island nations of the world, such as Saint Kitts and Nevis, are included, while others, such as Barbuda, are not. There is a highly standardized format for each country. The biographical details are quite basic. There is an index of people, but no others. (Note: The last annual edition seen was for 1998.)

9-56. Button, John. *Radicalism Handbook: Radical Activists, Groups, and Movements of the Twentieth Century.*

Santa Barbara, CA: ABC-CLIO, 1995. 460 pp. Index. ISBN: 0-874-36838-3.

John Button describes himself as a radical, and he provides the reader with an overview of the subject that to a certain extent reflects his own viewpoint. A lengthy essay on the subject of twentieth-century radicalism is followed by two biographical sections and a concluding section on "Groups and Movements." In the front matter, Button describes the criteria for inclusion of biographees. Those in certain areas, such as civil rights, gay rights, the peace movement, and radical economics, are among those included. Also included are those preferring nonviolent means, those with an international reputation, those with a broad view of radicalism, and those who have inspired others. An effort was also made to make the biographical choices international in the sense that many biographees were chosen from cultures other than those of Western Europe and the United States. The section on groups and movements, about one-fourth of the text, includes entries for the "Clamshell Alliance," the "Cuban Revolution," "Earth Day," and the "New Left," among others. Biographees and groups and movements alike receive about a page of text, including a short list of references. The somewhat complicated arrangement of the volume makes it imperative for the user to consult the index.

9-57. Scanlon, Jennifer. *Significant Contemporary American Feminists: A Biographical Sourcebook.* Westport, CT:

Greenwood Press, 1999. 361 pp. Index. ISBN: 0-313-30125-5.

Altogether, fifty feminists are portrayed in this volume. A few were noteworthy political figures (Bella Abzug, Shirley Chisholm, and Patricia Schroeder), but most were active in other fields, including art, literature, the judiciary, and the feminist movement itself. The biographies average about seven pages in length and include a biographical overview, a discussion of the individual's accomplishments, and a bibliography. The bibliography includes works by and about that individual. A more general bibliography appears at the end of the volume. There are no illustrations. Most of the contributors are drawn from the U.S. academic community. The fifty individuals chosen for inclusion were selected by an editorial board; the editor admits that some readers might quibble about well-known names that were excluded. Still, this is a fine starting point for those researchers searching for a particular biography or who wish to become acquainted with significant individuals in the feminist movement. 💻

9-58. Parrish, Michael. *Soviet Security and Intelligence Organizations, 1917–1990: A Biographical Dictionary and Review of Literature in English.* New York: Greenwood Press, 1992. 669 pp. ISBN: 0-313-28305-2.

This work presents itself as a biobibliographic guide to the security and intelligence organizations of the former Soviet Union. Part 1 is a biographical dictionary containing entries on approximately 4,000 mid-level and senior officials who served in any of these security bodies: the People's Commissariat of Internal Affairs (NKVD), the State Political Administration (GPU), the United State Political Administration (OGPU), the Ministry of Internal Affairs (MVD), the Committee for State Security (KGB), the militia, the border troops, and other similar security agencies. An editorial decision was made to exclude well-known spies, such as Kim Philby, or Soviet defectors, such as V. Krivitskii. Part 2 is a survey of books in English that pertain to Soviet security and intelligence organizations published during this period. Of the total volume, 75 percent of the text is biographical information, and the remaining 25 percent is bibliographic entries. The bibliography component is arranged alphabetically by individual author and contains no journal articles. Each entry is annotated, often with up to one paragraph of explanatory notes.

9-59. Minnick, Wendell L. *Spies and Provocateurs: A Worldwide Encyclopedia of Persons Conducting Espionage and Covert Action, 1946–1991.* Jefferson, NC: McFarland, 1992. 310 pp. ISBN: 0-899-50746-8.

Over 700 agents, mostly Western intelligence agents rather than their Eastern/Soviet counterparts, involved in espionage and covert activities are listed here in alphabetical format. The individual entries deal almost exclusively with the agent's life within the working con-

fines of their respective intelligence communities. Many of the entries are quite short, perhaps just one paragraph. At the end of each agent's entry, there are several citations on these people. They are drawn overwhelmingly from either the *New York Times* or *Facts on File*. There is a short glossary of spook terms and a chronology of events from 1946 through 1991. There is a good introductory reading list on espionage agents published in books since the end of World War II.

9-60. Volkman, Ernest. *Spies: The Secret Agents Who Changed the Course of History.* New York: John Wiley, 1994. 288 pp. ISBN: 0-471-55714-5.

Not seen. 💻.

9-61. *Statesmen Who Changed the World: A Bio-Bibliographical Dictionary of Diplomacy.* Westport, CT: Greenwood Press, 1993. 669 pp. ISBN: 0-313-27380-4.

Just over sixty statesmen of the "modern Western world" have had their respective biobibliographies chosen for this highly selective work. There were two purposes for publishing this work. The first was to learn about the individual's life and career, and the second was to write up bibliographic essays that describe the general availability of archival materials both by and on the individual statesman and his or her impact within the sphere of international affairs. There is a bibliography at the end of each entry. Only several women's names appear throughout this work. Main entries average nine to ten pages long, with some bibliographies consuming several of those pages. A number of appendixes are at the back of the book, including those on historical personages who did not make the cut for this book. Others are lists of diplomatic, political, and military events, while others are conferences and treaties or glossaries of terms used for international organizations or international affairs.

9-62. Purcell, L. Edward, ed. *The Vice Presidents: Bibliographical Dictionary.* updated ed. New York: Checkmark Books, 2001. 490 pp. Index. ISBN: 0-816-03109-6.

Vice presidents from John Adams through Al Gore receive their due in this reference book. Each is accorded an article of about nine pages in length and a portrait. Articles conclude with a list of references, mostly to secondary sources, and a listing of the credentials of the contributor. The latter is a welcome change from the usual reference-book format, which exiles contributor credentials to a separate listing at the front or back of the volume. Although the intent of this volume is to emphasize the contributions of these men to the office of vice president and to politics, much of the biographical information is somewhat anecdotal, a sign, perhaps, that the vice president generally seems to play a peripheral role in the administration to which he belongs. This work concludes with a short listing of "General References" and appendixes, including a lengthy chronology. This volume will be especially useful

for students but can be consulted by advanced researchers as well.

9-63. Rake, Alan. *Who's Who in Africa: Leaders for the 1990s.* Metuchen, NJ: Scarecrow Press, 1992. 448 pp. Index. ISBN: 0-810-82557-0.

This biographical directory contains entries for most of the prominent political people living in Africa south of the Sahara. The work concentrates on those people who are currently in power. Entries concern the individual's entire life from date of birth up to the publication date of this book. Special attention is given to these individuals' political deeds. The main body is arranged by country in alphabetical order. Each entry contains a brief assessment of the character and career of the person being discussed, followed by an entire life history. Primary attention is given to the major population groups or larger nation-states, such as Nigeria, Kenya, South Africa, Ghana, Tanzania, Uganda, and Cote d'Ivoire. Country background information contains brief background on population, heads of state, government, political parties, and the like. The individual political figures each receive approximately one- or two-page entries. People listed are political luminaries of the African continent along with their close inner circle. Information is uniformly cursory throughout. There is an index.

9-64. Theis, Paul A., ed. *Who's Who in American Politics.* Biennial. 2 vols. New York: Bowker, 1967/1968–. 2524 pp. Index. ISSN: 0000-0205.

The biographical listings in this directory are arranged by state and include politicians active at both the state and national levels. The preface states that those included must have made "significant contributions to political dialogue" and be active currently or in the recent past. Judges and other court officials are also included. The sixteenth edition, published in 1997, included nearly 30,000 listings for the fifty states, the District of Columbia, and U.S. dependencies. Information is similar to that of most Who's Who books and usually includes address and phone number. The front matter has listings for the cabinet, Supreme Court justices, state delegations to Congress, state Governors, and state chairmen, among others. An index in the second volume gives an alphabetical index to the biographees.

9-65. *Who's Who in Asian and Australasian Politics.* New York: Bowker-Saur, 1991–. 475 pp. ISBN: 0-862-91593-7.

This work intends to fulfill two purposes. The first is to serve as a biographical directory with contact information for all the top political leaders, major political party activists, and trade-union leaders. There are over 3,000 of these biographical entries arranged alphabetically, and they cover the main portions of each individual's personal and political life highlights, especially the latter. The second purpose is fulfilled by the second part of the book, which is a country-by-country survey and political directory that covers all of the executives of the regional and national government, as well as members of the leadership of the various political parties. (Note: Only the 1991 volume was examined.)

9-66. Editorial Board of Who's Who in China, comp. *Who's Who in China: Current Leaders.* Beijing: Foreign Languages Press, 1989. 1126 pp. ISBN: 0-835-12352-9.

This biographical dictionary contains 2,185 entries for officials in the Chinese government, party, and military. The text, contents, and appendixes are all in both English and Chinese. Entries are quite succinct and provide very little of the Chinese official's private life. The entries contain information on the organizations with which the individual was affiliated and indicate whether or not he or she was an officer, along with dates of affiliation. Many of the entries have black-and-white pictures, generally of mediocre quality. One appendix is a "Table of Major Organizations and Their Leading Officials." A 1994 revised edition is also available but housed in fewer libraries in the United States.

9-67. Lipset, Seymour Martin, ed. *Who's Who in Democracy.* Washington, DC: Congressional Quarterly, 1997. 247 pp. ISBN: 1-568-02121-6.

This is a biographical encyclopedia that highlights the lives of 156 individuals who have made a major impact on democracy or democratic theory or practice. The selective list of people chosen spans 2,000 years, and biographees are philosophers, scholars, and heads of state or various national, religious, women's, and human rights leaders, among others. The contributors are all scholars from the United States, Canada, the United Kingdom, and several South American countries. A significant number of this work's entries have been taken from Congressional Quarterly's *Encyclopedia of Democracy* [entry 4-19]. Only thirty-six entries are new to this work. Entries average approximately one to two pages in length and have short bibliographies added at the end. Each entry discusses the individual's unique contribution toward democracy and very little else. There is virtually no personal data. A black-and-white picture or illustration accompanies every entry. Most individuals are male and lived within the last century. 💻

9-68. *Who's Who in European Politics.* 3rd ed. New Providence, NJ: Bowker-Saur/Reed Reference Publishing, 1997. 873 pp. ISBN: 1-857-39163-2.

Over 8,000 individuals who meet at least one of the following criteria have been chosen for this biographical reference work. A person must have been either a head of state, member of the government, member of the national legislature, political party or trade-union federation leader, or otherwise played an important role and be regarded as a mover and shaker. Short, standard, Who's Who–type entries are the rule. At the end of the bi-ographical directory section is a "Political Directory" arranged by country that provides heads of state, government leaders, legislators, and others. Entries appear in both the native language and an English

translation. Both parts include Western and Eastern European nations. This third edition has opted to include the Russian Federation as well.

9-69. *Who's Who in International Affairs.* 3rd ed. London: Europa Publications, 2002. 690 pp. Indexes. ISBN: 1-857-43156-1.

This biographical directory lists approximately 7,000 notable people who are generally well known and active in economic, international affairs, and political circles. Included are individuals who are either diplomats, leading politicians, heads of state; who appear regularly at intergovernmental-organization sessions; who are journalists or writers; or who are regarded as experts in the field of international affairs or have some impact on international policies and events. A standard entry in this directory would include very concise information about the entrant's life, affiliations, title, education, career, address, telephone number, and publications. Third world people are quite well represented here. There are two indexes: one by organization and another by nationality.

9-70. *Who's Who in Latin America: Government, Politics, Banking and Industry.* 4th ed. 2 vols. New York: Norman Ross Publishing, 1997. Indexes. ISBN: 0-883-54225-0.

This biographical work lists over 2,000 people determined to be prominent who resided in any of the thirty-six nations in South America, Central America, and the Caribbean. The individual's overall stature must be recognized at the regional or national level in order to be listed. The order of the entries is alphabetical within country. Entries vary widely in length. Some are listed with simply an address, telephone number, and occupation, while other entries are significantly longer and offer the reader a glimpse into the person's accomplishments and career history. There are two indexes, each for one of the two physical volumes only, a bit of an inconvenience if a person's country of origin is unknown. The criteria for inclusion remain unclear and unstated. Fidel Castro, for instance, is not listed under Cuba.

9-71. Greenfield, Stanley R., ed. *Who's Who in the United Nations and Related Agencies.* 2nd ed. Detroit: Omnigraphics, 1992. 850 pp. Indexes. ISBN: 1-558-88762-8.

This is a specialized handbook that provides relatively short biographical entries of any person who has headed the United Nations (UN) Secretariat, its specialized agencies, or its related organizations during the year 1991. It also includes the ambassadors to the United Nations and the various agencies located in New York, Geneva, and Vienna. The entries are of standard biographical directory type and length. There are several appendixes. One gives each UN member state's official language and date of UN membership. Addresses and telephone numbers of each state's permanent mission to the UN in New York City are given. One index is by organization and another by nationality of the individual.

9-72. Palmer, Alan. *Who's Who in World Politics: From 1860 to the Present Day.* New York: Routledge, 1996. 363 pp. ISBN: 0-415-13161-8.

This biographical dictionary provides encyclopedia-like, one-half-page entries of men and women who have helped to shape the orderly process of government or to define its theoretical limits over the last century and a half. The definition of politics is construed in its broadest possible context. This work lists rulers, chief administrators, insurgent leaders, soldiers, and strategists on a highly selective basis. It also contains a number of political theorists, such as Karl Marx, as well as those who have taken on the responsibility for leading the women's movement. The work is arranged strictly in alphabetical order by individual's name, with the great majority of entries coming from Japan, the United States, and the United Kingdom. There are cross-references integrated into each entry. All of the entries in this biographical work center on the public lives of the individuals rather than their private ones. This work is surprisingly light on Chinese politicians and leaders. It is not arranged in the standard directory format of many common Who's Who–type publications.

9-73. Law, Cheryl. *Women: A Modern Political Dictionary.* New York: I. B. Tauris, 2000. 276 pp. ISBN: 1-860-64502-X.

This biographical handbook about women involved heavily in the women's movement over the last 100 years is divided into two separate historical periods. Phase one covers the years 1914 through 1967 and includes women who were relatively well known during that period or those women who contributed significantly to women's emancipation but have been forgotten by history. Phase two spans the years 1968 through the early 1980s and lists women who were either living or active at the date of publication. These women have been in any group that has attempted to alter the overall position of women in society, change outmoded ideas about women, or change women's sociopolitical status in their relationship with men. Some typical entries drawn from this book are Betty Friedan, Andrea Dworkin, Germaine Greer, and Sheila Rowbotham. Most women listed are from the United Kingdom or the Commonwealth countries, but Americans have been included. A list of organizations has been compiled, along with a modest bibliography of reading materials and a glossary of acronyms.

9-74. Opfell, Olga S. *Women Prime Ministers and Presidents.* Jefferson, NC: McFarland, 1993. 237 pp. ISBN: 0-899-50790-5.

Twenty-one women presidents and prime ministers of various countries are listed in chronological order from 1960 to around 1992. Articles are five to fifteen pages long and are decidedly non-scholarly in content and style. The women chosen are drawn mostly from the top ranks of the well known. They include such people as Golda Meir and Indira Gandhi. Lesser personages, however, such as Elizabeth Domitien and Kazimiera Prunskiene, also receive coverage but perhaps with somewhat less print space. Entries concentrate almost exclusively on the political life of the individual. Political party affiliation, deeds of political activism, and previous election campaign information are all informational pieces usually found here. A rudimentary bibliography for most of the twenty-one biographees is provided.

9-75. Zarate's Political Collections (ZPC). http://www.terra.es/personal2/monolith.

The political leaders of the world and selective international organizations are either listed here or linked to the Research Teaching, Documentation and Dissemination Center for International Relations and Development (CIDOB) biographical Web site. The country listing provides the heads of government and dates in power, as well as their political affiliation and a small picture. Another section divided into the heads of European governments receives similar treatment. Active European leaders get linked to the CIDOB Web site. Women world leaders form another major category. The section devoted to Spanish government is especially strong. The largest section is probably the one on "Rulers of All Countries," but all the biographical information, and it is quite extensive as well as current, is in Spanish back in the CIDOB Web site. Finally, there is a political obituary for the years 1990 to date. ⌨

Author Index

Abrams, Irwin, 281
Aby, Stephen H., 113
Adi, Hakim, 526
Alcock, Peter, 346
Alexander, Robert J., 157, 514
Ali, Sheikh Rustum, 246, 278, 311
Alkin, Marvin C., 43
Allcock, John B., 299
Allen, Larry, 459
Allen, Louis, 358
Allin, Craig W., 448, 452
Allison, Robert J., 78–79
Altbach, Philip G., 46
Altschiller, Donald, 386
American Anthropological Association, 17
American Chamber of Commerce Research Association, 24
American Council of Learned Societies, 97–98
American Enterprise Institute for Public Policy Research, 501
American Historical Association, 71
American Library Association, 3–4, 163
American Political Science Association, 128, 140
American Psychological Association, 102–103

American Sociological Association, 116, 123
Ameringer, Charles D., 357
Amnesty International, 284
Andermahr, Sonya, 497
Anderson, Ewan W., 264, 303, 361
Anderson, Lorin W., 46
Andor, Lydia Eve, 272
Andrews, Alice C., 47
Anglin, Christopher Thomas, 488
Anzovin, Steven, 58
Aplin, Richard, 383
Appiah, Kwame Anthony, 7
Appleton, Andrew M., 249
Archer, J. Clark, 181
Arlinghaus, Sandra Lach, 60
Arms, Thomas S., 296
Arnold, Guy, 288, 359, 366
Art, Henry W., 51–52
Asante, Molefi K., 418
Ashford, Nigel, 149
Assendelft, Laura van, 219
Aster, Sidney, 271
Atkins, G. Pope, 326
Atkins, Stephen E., 153, 275, 308, 487
Atwood, Thomas C., 407
Auerbach, Susan, 480
Austin, Erik W., 220
Aversa, Elizabeth, 4
Awe, Susan C., 2
Axelrod, Alan, 83, 520

Axelrod-Contrada, Joan, 133

Bacon, Donald C., 174
Baer, George W., 312
Bahamonde, Ramon, 254
Bahmueller, Charles F., 302
Bailey, William G., 160, 437
Bainbridge, Timothy, 320
Baker, Colin, 444
Bakers, Daniel B., 142
Balay, Robert, 3
Baltes, Paul B., 13
Bankston, Carl L., 427, 482
Baratta, Joseph Preston, 321
Barberis, Peter, 391
Barbour, Philippe, 318
Barfield, Thomas, 17
Barker, Graeme, 73
Barker, Robert L., 118
Barnaby, Frank, 283
Barnard, Alan, 20
Barnes, Patricia G., 193
Barnouw, Erik, 474
Barone, Michael, 238
Barrows, Floyd D., 521
Bartke, Wolfgang, 512
Baughman, Judith S., 78
Baumohl, Jim, 465
Baxter, Pam M., 101
Baylen, Joseph, 515
Beach, William W., 181
Bealey, Frank, 130
Becher, Anne, 446
Becker, Patricia C., 490

Subject Index

Title Index

Primary discussions of a work are identified by **bold page numbers**.

Web Site Index

About the Editors

Stephen W. Green has most recently served at the University of North Carolina at Charlotte as both Research/Special Project Librarian and as Head of Reference. He has had managerial positions at Colorado State University's Morgan Library; the Hillman Library at the University of Pittsburgh; the Auraria Library, which serves several Denver academic institutions; and the Research Libraries of the New York Public Library. Steve obtained a BA and MA in Political Science from New York University, and an MLS from Pratt Institute. He has served as liaison to several Political Science Departments, which included collection development and instructional duties. A number of his book reviews have appeared in *Library Journal, Choice, ARBA,* and *Colorado Libraries,* and he published several chapters in previous editions of the standard reference publication *Magazines for Libraries.*

Douglas J. Ernest has been a member of the library profession since 1970, generally in reference capacities. He has been employed at Colorado State University Libraries since 1981 and presently holds the position of Government Publications Librarian. He is the author of a number of articles as well as "Agricultural Frontier to Electronic Frontier," a book-length history of the Colorado State University Libraries.